IN TWILIGHT AND IN DAWN

McGILL-QUEEN'S NATIVE AND NORTHERN SERIES

(In memory of Bruce G. Trigger)

Sarah Carter and Arthur J. Ray, Editors

IN TWILIGHT
AND IN DAWN

A Biography of Diamond Jenness

BARNETT RICHLING

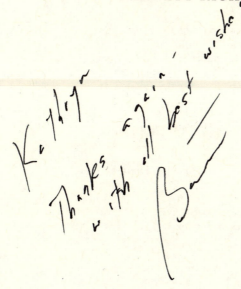

McGill-Queen's University Press
Montreal & Kingston · London · Ithaca

Legal deposit third quarter 2012
Bibliothèque nationale du Québec

Printed in Canada on acid-free paper that is 100% ancient
forest free (100% post-consumer recycled), processed chlorine
free

This book has been published with the help of a grant from
the Canadian Federation for the Humanities and Social
Sciences, through the Aid to Scholarly Publications Program,
using funds provided by the Social Sciences and Humanities
Research Council of Canada.

McGill-Queen's University Press acknowledges the support of
the Canada Council for the Arts for our publishing program.
We also acknowledge the financial support of the Government
of Canada through the Canada Book Fund for our publishing
activities.

Library and Archives Canada Cataloguing in Publication

Richling, Barnett
In twilight and in dawn : a biography of Diamond Jenness /
Barnett Richling.

(McGill-Queen's native and northern series ; 67)
Includes bibliographical references and index.
ISBN 978-0-7735-3981-5

1. Jenness, Diamond, 1886–1969.   2. Anthropologists –
Canada – Biography.   3. National Museum of Canada –
Officials and employees – Biography.   I. Title.   II. Series:
McGill-Queen's native and northern series ; 67

GN21.J45R52 2012   301.092   C2012-902117-2

Set in 9.8/12.4 Baskerville 10 Pro with Bodoni BE
Book design & typesetting by Garet Markvoort, zijn digital

To JoAnn

Contents

Illustrations

Preface

On returning to his native New Zealand from year-long research in British (Papua) New Guinea, Diamond Jenness entertained high hopes of parlaying that experience, along with his newly minted Oxford diploma in anthropology, into a scholarly career at home. It was Christmas 1912, two months shy of his twenty-seventh birthday. Weeks later, seemingly on a whim, he set that aspiration aside – permanently, as things turned out – and accepted an out-of-the-blue invitation to spend the next three years with the Canadian Arctic Expedition, an exploring mission dedicated to expanding the horizons of scientific knowledge of the Dominion's polar seas and sprawling hinterlands to the north and west of Hudson Bay. The rest, as the old saying goes, is history, his painstakingly detailed descriptions of early contact-period Inuit life in the vicinity of Coronation Gulf, combined, a decade later, with seminal archaeological discoveries of the ancient Dorset and Old Bering Sea cultures, firmly fixing Jenness's place beside the likes of Franz Boas, Knud Rasmussen, and Vilhjalmur Stefansson as a founding father of arctic anthropology.

Having survived the Arctic and then the trenches of wartime Europe, Jenness's still-uncertain job prospects suddenly brightened in 1920 with his appointment to the Anthropological Division of the Geological Survey of Canada, forerunner of today's Museum of Civilization and until mid-century employer of nearly all of the country's minuscule cohort of professional anthropologists. Settling in Ottawa, he would stay on at the museum for twenty-plus years. In keeping with the division's legislated mandate to document indigenous cultures and languages in every corner of the country, by the thirties his investigations had grown to include foundational studies of seven First Nations whose reserves dotted the landscape from Ontario's Georgian Bay to the coasts and interior ranges of British Columbia. Along with research and writing, he reluctantly shouldered a hefty administrative burden, succeeding Edward Sapir as the division's second chief in 1926 and continuing Sapir's campaign to bolster anthropology's flagging post-war fortunes in an institutional setting of bureaucratic indifference and fiscal stringency. In the midst of the Great Depression, moreover, he willingly committed himself to an equally exasperating, if far more urgent, cause, one that engaged him to the very end of his days: fostering social and economic justice for the whole of Canada's Aboriginal population by advocating reforms to hidebound, repressive state policies. Together with participating in some of the prominent theoretical debates within his field, fostering collaborative ties between the museum and other (mostly foreign) institutions and scientists, encouraging the training of anthropologists at home, and contributing to the work of major professional organizations – including serving a term as president of the American Anthropological Association, the only Canadian ever to hold that post – his many and varied accomplishments during the interwar period underscore Diamond Jenness's standing as a notable figure in the discipline's development at home and abroad. Widely regarded as such in his day, his work earned formal recognition in numerous awards, among them five honorary degrees, the Rivers Medal of the Royal Anthropological Institute of Great Britain and Ireland, the Royal Canadian Geographic Society's Massey Medal, a posthumously published Festschrift, and, a year before his death, in 1969, installation as a Companion of the Order of Canada, this country's highest civilian honour.[1]

References to the sizeable product of Jenness's scholarship, especially that portion of it stemming from his Canadian fieldwork, abound in the professional literature, past and present. But scholarly interest in the man himself has largely faded; excluding obituaries, appreciations, and the like, no more than twenty papers dealing with various dimensions of his multi-faceted career have appeared in the four decades since his death. Understandably, the largest share of these focus on his groundbreaking works on arctic ethnography and archaeology, by far the most numerous of his scientific accomplishments, and certainly the best known. The balance take up a hodgepodge of topics, several examining his use of photography in New Guinea, several more his tenure (and travails) as chief of the Anthropological Division, and the rest, his engagement with problems arising from Ottawa's conduct of Aboriginal affairs.[2] Making liberal use of archival and published sources, nearly all these studies present straight-forward narrative accounts of their respective subjects, describing the particulars of what and why, where and when. A few go beyond the merely descriptive by examining select portions of the documentary record in a critical light, dissecting key writings to reveal the theoretical and political assumptions they embody, and assessing the significance of Jenness's contributions for anthropology and, in the case of his policy-related activities, for public life in Canada.

❖

People of the Twilight, Jenness's popular account of the two years he spent with the Canadian Arctic Expedition at Coronation Gulf, introduced me to the Inuit and to the craft that comprises the anthropologist's stock-in-trade: fieldwork. The very same two-dollar paperback copy I read as a college sophomore upwards of forty years ago sits on my bookshelf to this day. Though it would make for a more appealing anecdote, I can't credit that first reading with turning my own occupational aspirations toward anthropology. Nor did it influence my decision, as a graduate student, to conduct fieldwork in an Inuit community on the subarctic shores of Labrador. Nevertheless, those decisions eventually brought me back to that book – actually, to its author, someone whose writings on the Arctic, including a monograph examining the history of Inuit-state relations in Labrador, contributed in no small part to my understanding of the past and present of the peoples of Canada's far north.

While I was familiar with those studies, I knew precious little about the circumstances under which they had been produced, or, for that matter, the person whose work it was. Consequently, when a chance arose in the mid-eighties to satisfy that curiosity, I started in on what eventually became a wide-ranging and sometimes vexing search for pertinent details in a host of libraries and archives, and in the recollections of those of his colleagues and family I had the good fortune to interview. Having been asked the question about myself from time to time, I wanted to know why Jenness chose to become an anthropologist in the first place, especially since he made that decision in an era when aspirants for paying positions far outnumbered openings virtually everywhere and when his Oxford credentials all but assured him a foreign service posting in India or elsewhere in the empire. More important, I hoped to discover those formative influences and experiences assimilated over the fullness of a lifetime – personal and professional, intellectual and institutional, social and political – that impressed themselves in his character, shaped his world view, and found expression in the body and soul of his work.

Although fashionable nowadays, my primary purpose in taking on this project was not to parse Jenness's myriad contributions to anthropology and public life in keeping with current styles of critical analysis that privilege modern-day sensitivities and points-of-view, political and theoretical alike. This is not to imply that I reject outright what many historians refer to as presentism – an approach that seeks to measure what happened yesterday against the yardstick of what's happening today. Rather, it is to say that reading the past this way poses potential complications, not least in running "the risk of distorting it – whether willfully, to suit our own purposes, or unintentionally, by unwarranted assumptions and because of meager information" bearing on crucial matters such as motivation and intention or the context in which decisions were made and events played out.[3] With an eye to avoiding pitfalls that continue to impress me as far more real than apparent, my preference was, and remains, to leave that tricky business to others. Instead, I resolved to discover who Jenness was, how things were in his day for him, for other anthropologists, and for the indigenous peoples among whom they worked, and how these factors together shaped and reshaped his thinking and guided the trajectory of his career. Stated more plainly, my aim from the get-go has been to understand the man as a product of his own times and circumstances and in so doing to appreciate the substance of his anthropological work not in terms of "some present or absolute standards of 'rationality,'" as presentism typically allows, but in terms of its "reasonableness" relative, in the first instance, to prevailing (that is, historical) standards. These standards embrace existing modes of thought and analysis and public opinion germane to the questions and problems – scholarly and otherwise – that engaged him over the years and to which his work comprised responses.[4] For the purposes immediately at hand, this entails situating Jenness in a context partly defined by the day's disciplinary and professional priorities, partly by the conditions of his employment with the National Museum, and partly by the changeable temper of the times and places in which the successive stages of his life and career unfolded. So conceived, the hoped-for result is an impartial portrayal of someone who was certainly conversant with developments in anthropological thought and practice, much as he was with the manifold injustices perpetrated against Aboriginal peoples under Canadian policy, but whose engagement in these and yet other spheres must be understood in relation to the possibilities and constraints inherent in the oft-contradictory roles he played as scholar-scientist, civil servant, and private citizen. Historicism – in essence, an orientation that privileges understanding the past "for the sake of the past," and does so with "appropriate allowances for prevailing historical conditions" – rather than its presentist counterpart, frames the narrative rendered in these pages.[5]

Presented in more or less chronological fashion, the biography's first fourteen chapters follow Jenness through the full sweep of his eighty-three years – from his comfortable upbringing in the socially progressive milieu of turn-of-the-century New Zealand and his unexpected if enthusiastic embrace of anthropology at Edwardian Oxford and in New Guinea, to service in two world wars and the string of Canadian researches that elevated his professional standing from journeyman to master craftsman, and finally to a productive retirement as independent scholar and vocal critic of government policy. Shifting gears, the epilogue offers a post-mortem of sorts, reflecting on the sundry influences and conflicting pressures that shaped and reshaped the main threads of Jenness's career, and in the light of recent criticisms of his work, sizing up if, and why, his legacy still matters.

Having explained the book's raison d'être and approach, an authorial word or two about the inner character inhabiting the professional persona seem in order.

As biographical subjects go, Diamond Jenness proved less cooperative than I had hoped he would be once my research into his life was underway. He died eighteen years before any thought of writing about him ever popped into my head. Inconvenient, to be sure, but my real problem with him is altogether different. To put it succinctly, the man lacked pretension, personal or professional, despite his numerous and occasionally hard-won accomplishments. I will be the first to admit that an unassuming nature, while comparatively rare, scarcely warrants mention in any serious catalogue of troublesome character flaws. Here's the rub: to the way of thinking of someone who is genuinely modest, as Jenness, by all accounts, truly was, the very idea that anyone might deem the story of his life worthy of being told, or being read, would be risible, if not downright absurd.

Among the sundry implications of this quirk, the one that cast the largest shadow over my efforts to piece together the many facets of his career, was Jenness's evident aversion to preserving much of anything for posterity. This was glaringly so in the case of those sorts of personal documents – private letters to family and friends and associates, for instance, or field journals and notebooks from his wide-ranging investigations across Canada and Alaska – that researchers depend on to lay bare the story behind the story. True, a graduate student, Nansi Swayze, managed to interview him in the late fifties, their few hours' of work together resulting in an exceedingly breezy biographical composite. I suspect the retiree only agreed to the proceedings because the book Swayze was working on was meant for grade school kids in Canada.[6] That episode aside, the reminiscences Jenness penned toward the very end of his days best exemplify the situation, speaking as they do to a stubborn reluctance to put himself in the spotlight. Initially resistant to the idea of writing anything remotely autobiographical, a pastime well-meaning family proposed as advancing age and a failing heart stranded him at home in the countryside near Ottawa, exactly why he acquiesced is a secret taken with him to the grave. In any event, what eventually came of the effort is pure Jenness: a miscellany of recollections – the best part of them little more than travelogue – illuminating some of life's more memorable moments, but starved of the candid revelations and deeper ruminations ordinarily expected of the memoirist. Better still, he capped off his labours by sub-titling the manuscript "Some Memories of a Taugenichts" – German for a neer-do-well, a good-for-nothing. In augmenting and editing the essays for publication some forty years later, his son Stuart substituted "Memoirs of Diamond Jenness" in the place of "Taugenichts," assuming the original was inconsistent with the sort of "serious-minded, scholarly man" his father had been.[7] I suspect the switch would have left the old man feeling slighted.

Stuart Jenness warned me about what to expect along these lines as I was settling into research, pointing out that his father had "left little for biographers to get their teeth into."[8] In most respects, he was right, some of the richest material my searches uncovered having come from the impeccably preserved files of the select few to whom Jenness wrote on personal and professional matters over the years. Predictably, their replies to him are nowhere to be found. His son observed elsewhere that the man was "never one to save things once he considered their usefulness ended." Among documents slated for discard were the marvellously detailed diaries he kept during his stint with the Canadian Arctic Expedition in Alaska and at Coronation Gulf. To his lasting credit, Stuart rescued the three handwritten volumes from oblivion and eventually shepherded them into print. Likewise, he forestalled a similar fate for the seven chapters of memoir, salvaging the typescript from the same clothes closet where their practically minded author had stashed the aforementioned diaries a short while before his death.[9] Practically everything else that has survived owes its continued existence to bureaucratic fiat: as an administrator of the Anthropological Division, Jenness's extensive if largely routine correspondence – nearly twenty years' worth, enough to fill eight reels of microfilm – automatically became part of the institution's official record. Thank goodness for small mercies.

If it were somehow possible to fill in the gaps by arranging an interview with Diamond Jenness, even at this late date, my preference would be to meet him in the Ottawa hospital room where he was sent to recuperate from assorted bumps and bruises sustained in an auto accident shortly before Christmas 1957. With a life-long penchant for self-effacing humour, the septuagenarian revelled in repeating his tale of harrowing misadventure to whomever was in earshot, starting off by reciting the police report particulars – foggy rural road, misjudged corner, forty-foot descent into gravel pit, Volkswagen DOA – then explaining that on discharge, his doctor offered every assurance "that my skull was un-usually thick and that he could find nothing inside it."[10] When my work was in its infancy, Richard Slobodin offered up a version of the story with a different denouement, one whose possibilities intrigued me then, as they do even now. Instead of growing fuzzy-brained in the wreck's aftermath, as might be expected in the circumstances, the patient finds himself blessed with unusual clarity of thought and memory, if only for a day or two. One can scarcely imagine a more opportune moment for a biographer to sit, notebook in hand, primed to inquire into the motivations behind this, or thoughts and feelings about that, the very topics deliberately ignored in the pages of his un-memoir-like memoirs. Unable to arrange such a sit-down, the list of my unanswered questions remains long. Whenever necessary, therefore, I've opted for plausibility to plug holes in the narrative weave.

ACKNOWLEDGMENTS

First, an acknowledgement of regret. Writing this biography lasted much longer than I ever imagined it would. So long, in fact, that it outlasted far too many of those people whose willingness to impart their recol-lections of Diamond Jenness was instrumental in getting my work off the ground in the first place. Some, like Frederica de Laguna, Graham Rowley, and William Taylor, shared his passion for unravelling the mysteries of arctic culture history and looked to him as a mentor and esteemed colleague in their chosen field of endeavour. Others knew him only in retirement when, free of the work-place constraints under which public servants laboured then, as they do now, he turned his attentions to projects of his own choosing. The best known of these was his compara-tive study of "Eskimo Administration" under four flags, a study of his-tory and policy that brought him into the orbit of Slobodin and Walter Rudnicki, staffers at the Department of Northern Affairs and Natural Resources. They, together with Jim Lotz, Diana Rowley, and Gordon Smith, northern specialists all, were candid in their opinions and sup-portive of my plan to write about their friend and associate.

Several people graciously filled me in on the fine points of Jenness family genealogy and lore. Here I owe a sizeable debt of gratitude to Diamond's three sons, John, Robert, and especially Stuart who, like me, is keenly interested in seeing his father's many accomplishments become better known in his adopted country and has been nearly as impatient to see this book through to completion. From a hemisphere away, Dorothy and Robert Ballantyne, Dorothy and Lewis Jenness, and Kelly Jones answered my numerous queries, and, during a research trip I made to their New Zealand homeland in 1991, Lewis and the two Dorothys served up hospitality and a wealth of insight into their late cousin's early years. Other pertinent details were ferreted out in the archives of the Wellington Provincial Historical Committee, Wellington Boys' College, Victoria University of Wellington, and several of the city's libraries, especially the Turnbull. I am also grateful to the university's Stout Research Centre and to its director at the time, Jim Collinge, for offering a temporary work space and for inviting me to speak about the Canadian career of one of the university's earliest graduates.

Over the years, I have benefited greatly from the assistance, advice, and encouragement of numerous librarians, archivists, and fellow anthropologists (and historians) here in Canada, in the United States, England, Australia, and New Zealand. Their number include professors Jennifer Brown, William Fenton, George Fulford, Harry Hawthorn, George Park, Donald Smith, Wayne Suttles, James Urry, and Michael Young, curator Elizabeth Edwards of Oxford's Pitt Rivers Museum, Louise Dallaire and Benoit Thériault at the Canadian Museum of Civilization, Anthony Zito at Catholic University of America, and Library and Archives Canada staff too numerous to mention by name. All deserve a very special vote of thanks. So, too, do Ian Dyck, Jonathan Crago, and a trio of anonymous readers, each of whom provided a well-reasoned evaluation of the book's strengths and weaknesses, and in one case, some much-needed advice that a biographer does not signal the full objective of his writing simply by affixing "a biography of ..." to its title. Finally, I am exceedingly grateful to Joan McGilvray for the great care she took in editing the manuscript, and especially for her insight and diplomacy in sorting through its sundry trouble-spots. Projects such as this one typically depend on funds to defray some of the heavier costs of research, especially travel, as they do on time to transform reams of notes and drafts into a book fit to read. In this respect, special recognition is due to the Social Science and Humanities Research Council of Canada, Mount Saint Vincent University, and the University of Winnipeg for awarding grants in aid of the various phases of my work, and to the two universities for providing teaching-free terms that allowed me to spend long hours writing (and re-writing) at the computer.

More often than not, those who help you most are the ones who are closest to you. Sometimes they say the things you want to hear in the midst of indecision; sometimes it's the things you need to hear, strong medicine to get you through a paralyzing loss of confidence. And sometimes it takes the form of unexpected if well-appreciated assistance, much as Kathryn Arbuckle offered in volunteering to wield the red pen through half a dozen chapters. Ken Dewar has been a staunch friend and ally from start to finish, always ready to commiserate, as he was to offer wise counsel. But of the many debts accumulated along the way, none comes anywhere close to the one I have racked up to JoAnn Richling, my long-time friend and partner in this life. I marvel at her (usually cheerful) willingness to put up with my frequent bouts of procrastination and writing-induced shenanigans over the years. These few words of acknowledgment are but the most meagre of down payments. Thank you.

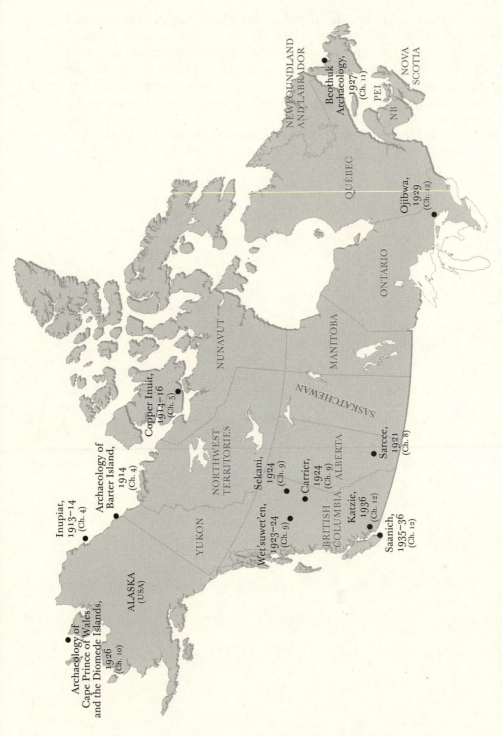

Locations in Canada and Alaska where Diamond Jenness did fieldwork, 1913–36. Map courtesy of Weldon Hiebert.

IN TWILIGHT AND IN DAWN

– let him who writes free of his time's imaginings
cast the first stone –
Clifford Geertz, *Works and Lives*

CHAPTER ONE

Antipodean Arcadia,
1886–1908

RESPECTABLE BEGINNINGS

As the nineteenth century drew to a close, the worst of the troubles that had plagued New Zealand's colonial economy since the 1870s finally subsided. Better times brought improving fortunes to the country's entrepreneurs, shopkeepers, professionals, and farmers, who made up the expanding middle class.[1] Its ranks were the near-exclusive preserve of Pakehas, a term adopted from the language of the indigenous Maoris to describe the Dominion's European (chiefly British) settler majority. Most Pakehas lived in urban areas – Auckland and Wellington on the North Island, Christchurch and Dunedin on the South – though a steadily growing number were also scattered throughout the countryside on small to medium-sized holdings. In the main, these were people for whom rising economic prosperity strengthened faith in individualism and the workings of private enterprise, values tempered by the virtues of respectability, a predominant theme in the evolution of modern New Zealand society.

Respectability implied many things. Outwardly it meant working hard, being honest and sober, remaining faithful to family, community, church, and empire. Inwardly it entailed self-discipline. In many ways, respectability, rooted in part in the familiar conventions and mores of Victorian England, reflected the ethos of the English mother-culture, which was fundamental to the "habits of mind" and the developing identity of white New Zealanders as a whole. The insular environment in which these features developed elevated New Zealand's middle class to a position of greater prominence in the new society than was the lot of their counterparts in the old. If not one of the country's "ruling classes," they were a major source of its "ruling ideas."[2]

At the grassroots level, these ideas were conspicuous in churches and voluntary organizations devoted to high-minded causes such as temperance, public education, and charity work among the poor. Nationwide, they found expression in the social democratic agenda of the governing Liberal Party, first elected in 1891. Over the course of their twenty-one-year tenure, the Liberals crafted a self-styled brand of "state socialism" – the beginnings of the welfare state in New Zealand – implementing significant changes in agricultural and land policies, labour and industrial legislation, public health and education, and taxation, as well as introducing universal suffrage. All were designed to attenuate "the worst excesses of poverty and industrial oppression" created by the country's home-grown landed gentry and small capitalist elite.[3] At century's end, the ruling party also initiated measures aimed at ameliorating conditions among the Maoris. With the appointment of MP James Carroll, a Ngati Kahungunu Maori, as minister of native affairs in 1899 and, two years later, the rise of an activist student movement called Kotahitanga mo Te Aute, later dubbed the Young Maori Party, came important reforms affecting land, economic development, local governance, and health care.[4] State institutions thus assumed wide-ranging responsibility for mitigating society's ills and in the process fostered an ethic of egalitarianism, the "New Zealand dream of 'security in equality.'"[5]

Diamond Jenness was born and came of age in this formative period of progressive liberalism, whose ideals and conceits played no small part in defining the contours of his political and intellectual orientation, and forging the cast of his professional persona. For Pakehas, a consensus in public values and attitudes had begun to surface, moulding, in turn, a distinct national identity built on meritocratic principles and a commitment to social justice. Jenness was unquestionably a product of these heady times, particularly in the unequivocal liberalism of his world view and his Victorian optimism about the prospects for progressive social change. In all, his early experiences were positive, defining the more distinctive traits of his character and outlook but also animating some of the leading aspirations of the long and varied anthropological career he would eventually pursue half a world away in Canada.

While Jenness's own beginnings coincide with the emergence of modern New Zealand, his family's connections to the country extend back to its early development following Great Britain's formal annexation of the territory in 1840. His paternal grandmother, Matilde Minifie, was among the first generation of British immigrants brought out under a New Zealand Company settlement scheme to transform the colony into

In Twilight and in Dawn

an "antipodean Arcadia" of hardworking, reputable settlers.[6] At fifteen, she emigrated from Somerset with her recently widowed mother, Elizabeth, and three older brothers. They sailed from Gravesend in September 1839 aboard *Adelaide*, one of the many ships under the New Zealand Company charter. The voyage, by way of Tenerife and Capetown, took six months. On 7 March 1840 the weary passengers disembarked at Port Nicholson, near the new settlement of Wellington, on the wind-swept and earthquake-prone southern tip of New Zealand's North Island. One month and one day earlier a delegation of Maori chiefs, together with the colony's newly appointed lieutenant-governor, William Hobson, had signed the Treaty of Waitangi. Great Britain would use the treaty to claim sovereignty over all of New Zealand, while the Maoris saw it as the newcomers' recognition of their right to self-determination in their ancient homeland, Aotearoa.[7]

Within a year, Matilde met and married Nathaniel Jenness, a twenty-three-year-old Massachusetts-born carpenter, himself newly arrived in the south Pacific. Family tradition has it that Nathaniel sailed aboard a New England whaler bound for the hunting grounds off New Zealand's eastern shores. Crewmen made a practice of coming ashore at the Bay of Islands and Wellington to find respite from the deadening routines of shipboard life. Perhaps the colony's meagre comforts, more appealing than an ordinary seaman's lot, induced the young sailor to stay behind. During six years of marriage, he and Matilde had five children, including George Lewis Jenness, Diamond's father. Nathaniel succumbed to blood poisoning in 1848, at the age of thirty. His young widow soon remarried. Her new husband, Daniel B. Rash, was a ship's carpenter. They had four children together, two daughters and two sons.

In 1873, George Jenness married Hannah Heayns, a twenty-year-old immigrant from Cornwall. They, too, resided in Wellington, still a small mercantile and warehousing centre, and, beginning in 1865, New Zealand's capital.[8] Over the next two decades, the couple had fourteen children, eight daughters and six sons. Four died in infancy.[9] Diamond, born on 10 February 1886, was the second youngest of the surviving boys. The family home was at the corner of Willis and Mercer streets, a relatively prosperous area of mixed commercial buildings and residences. Land reclamation projects have since put the address a healthy distance from Wellington harbour, but in the 1880s their house backed on the beach.

The senior Jenness supported his family as a watchmaker. Operating a retail store in Wellington from 1869 onward, he combined repair services with the sale of imported timepieces and jewellery. His reputation as an expert artisan and technician earned him public commissions to install turret clocks in city buildings, including the Athenaeum – fore-

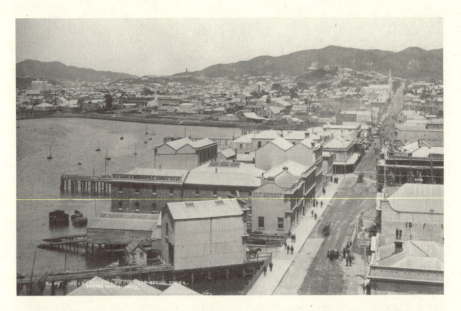

Willis Street, Wellington, New Zealand, ca. 1887. Burton Brothers Collection.
BB 22891/1; Alexander Turnbull Library, Wellington, NZ

runner of Wellington's Public Library – and Government Buildings, original headquarters of the Dominion's ministries of state. The shop provided a comfortable existence, weathering recurrent bouts of economic stagnation that put numerous small businesses into bankruptcy and many workers into the ranks of the unemployed.

The most tangible expression of their good fortune came in 1888 when the family moved to a spacious single-storey house on the western slopes of the Lower Hutt Valley, just north of Wellington. Lower Hutt today is an urban area of some 100,000, but in the late nineteenth century it was a sparsely populated rural precinct, with few amenities. Set back about a quarter mile from Harbourview Road on a sixteen-acre parcel, their home offered a commanding view of the river valley and the mountains ringing Wellington. A stream with a waterfall crossed the property, prompting them to name the place Waihinga, a Maori reference to cascading water. A second storey was added to the house in 1894, providing much-needed space for a family of twelve. While much of the grounds were covered in native bush, the property also included fruit orchards, flower garden and well-manicured lawn, greenhouse, tennis court, and a small workshop fitted out for watch repairing and engraving. The family did not employ household servants but paid workers came weekly to look after domestic and garden chores.

In Twilight and in Dawn

Jenness family at home in Lower Hutt, New Zealand, ca. 1907. Left to right (standing): Violet, Frederick, Grace, Arthur, May; (seated): Amy, Diamond, Hannah, George, William; (on floor): Leonard, Pearl. Photo courtesy of Leonard Jenness family, Stokes Valley, New Zealand

George Jenness died in 1923, his wife, Hannah, a decade later. Diamond's brother William inherited Waihinga and it remained in family hands until after the Second World War. Today, a neighbourhood of middle-class suburban housing occupies the site; one of its tree-lined streets bears the name Jenness Close.

In keeping with the day's ethos of middle-class respectability, Hannah and George, and later two of their sons, were involved in the temperance movement as members of the Rechabite Lodge.[10] George served as a trustee of the local Mechanics Institute, an organization dedicated to adult education for the working classes. The Jennesses also maintained ties to the Methodist Church and May, the family's second-born, became the first missionary sister with the Methodist Overseas Mission. She was sent out to Dobu, the smallest of four islands in the D'Entrecasteaux group, off the southeast coast of British (Papua) New Guinea, where she met Andrew Ballantyne, an Australian of English birth, who had begun his own Methodist missionary career that same year. They married and soon relocated to the mission station on nearby Goodenough Island, where Diamond would join them in 1912, following his studies at Oxford, for his first true taste of anthropological research. Unlike his older sister, he maintained only nominal ties to the church of his youth but, like his staunchly Methodist parents, held firm, life-long beliefs about the inherent dignity of all peoples, and his otherwise secular, pragmatic approach to the world around him reflected the reformist and progressive instincts of the evangelical churches of the period.

Music figured prominently in family life, the children playing instruments – the flute in Diamond's case – and learning musical theory. So, too, did reading, the house at Lower Hutt containing a well-stocked library whose shelves were lined with a mix of contemporary literature and classical Greek and Latin texts. Physical activities and sports were similarly encouraged. Fit, lean, and all of five and a half feet tall when fully grown, Diamond was among the more athletic of his siblings. He was also a proficient outdoorsman and an accomplished sharpshooter, the latter skill honed during visits to a cousin's sheep station where he hunted wild pigs and goats. He turned this early experience of "camplife in the bush" to good effect more than once during arctic fieldwork, earning the approbation of Inuit companions for repeated success in shooting caribou.[11]

A universal system of secular, state-supported primary schooling came into existence in New Zealand in 1877, but access to education beyond that level remained the privilege of those with financial means for some time thereafter. Benefiting from their father's modest prosperity, Diamond and older brothers William and Frederick were the first Jennesses to attend Wellington Boys' College. Open to this day, the school is the city's oldest public secondary institution, dating to the early 1850s. Its pupils acquired a grounding in the sciences and humanities, and socialization in the proprieties of middle-class life. Only Diamond and sister May, who attended Wellington Girls' High School, continued on to university, both at the city's newly opened Victoria College.

As a teenager, Jenness showed considerable academic promise. By this time he was living away from home, staying with relatives in suburban Petone and riding a streetcar across town to his high school in south Wellington. In 1898, at age twelve, he won the first of a succession of awards, the Queen's Scholarship, in a competition for students under fourteen. This paid for two years of secondary education and three years of college. In his final year at Wellington Boys' he won sixth form prizes in mathematics, science, Latin, French, and English, and was named school Dux, the leading student. Siblings who attended the school after him grumbled that his was a tough act to follow.

Post-secondary study at Victoria College came next, beginning in 1904. Founded six years earlier, the college, an affiliate of the University of New Zealand, had an enrolment of about two hundred students.

What it did not have was a campus or buildings. The location of its permanent home remained a hotly contested issue for some while, embroiling college, municipal, and state officials in squabbles over land use, property rights, public funding, and private munificence in support of higher education. In the meantime, students resorted to temporary facilities in Wellington's Boys' and Girls' high schools where classes were held mainly at night, science courses in one location, humanities in the other. On the bright side, the protracted battle over locating the college fostered a strong sense of cohesion and purpose among students and professors alike – "brotherly comradeship ... [compensating] for the absence of a home of our own," as the *Victoria College Review* put it in its inaugural issue in 1902.[12] The quibbling ended with selection of a site in the Kelburne Park area, on the city's west side. Construction of the first building started the same year Jenness began studies. A much-expanded Victoria University of Wellington stands on the same spot today, perched atop a precipice high above the downtown core, its locale affording a picture-postcard panorama of the city, its harbour, and the scenic mountains beyond. Among its buildings is Jenness House, so christened when the university's anthropology faculty moved to new quarters in the eighties.[13]

Jenness earned a BA with first-class honours in languages and literature in 1907. His undergraduate program included courses in mathematics and chemistry, but classics was his first love. In a reminiscence written nearly thirty years later, he recalled an initial meeting with the college's founding professor, J. Rankine Brown, confiding in the noted scholar that his great ambition was to "master" Plato and Aristotle in the original.[14] In his final year, the college offered him scholarships in both Latin and Greek. Permitted to hold only one, he opted for the award in Greek, his favourite subject. He went on to a brief stint of graduate work as a senior scholar under Brown's tutelage, receiving an MA in 1908, again with first-class honours. A short thesis, "Tiberius," won him the Jacob Joseph Scholarship for research and entrance to Oxford's Balliol College, where he planned to pursue his keen interest in the great works of the classical age.

George von Zedlitz, Jenness's most esteemed teacher at Victoria College, deserves considerable credit for nurturing his student's penchant for languages and literature, and for encouraging him to continue studies abroad. German-born (of German and English parents) and Oxford-educated, von Zedlitz had only recently immigrated to New Zealand, taking the professorship of modern languages at Wellington in 1902. The two became acquainted during Jenness's first undergraduate term when he enrolled in French as well as Latin. Their relationship assumed a new and important dimension during the summer months of 1906.

Von Zedlitz lived in Lower Hutt, less than a mile from Waihinga and invited his pupil to join him for weekly readings of Homer's *Odyssey*, a literary work the professor relished "as a tale of travel and adventure" since he himself had travelled widely and experienced "many strange lands and peoples."[15] Jenness came away from these evenings in awe of von Zedlitz's intellect and inspired with a new-found curiosity about life beyond the familiar world of Wellington and its environs. He later admitted that his own immaturity and lack of sophistication at the time prevented him from appreciating the breadth of his tutor's scholarship, personal character, and cosmopolitanism. Jenness counted a well-worn copy of the *Odyssey* among his most prized possessions during arctic fieldwork and then as a soldier near the front lines during the First World War, taking solace in re-reading the original Greek whenever loneliness and fatigue threatened his lapse into despair. Odysseus's words "Courage, my heart, thou hast endured worst things," acquired a mantra-like quality, offering a private bulwark against the unremittingly harsh and perilous conditions he faced on the battlefield.[16]

The importance of his relationship with von Zedlitz, one built on mutual scholarly interests and personal affection, is well attested to in a small collection of letters from student to mentor, penned between 1913 and 1917. Jenness usually described the anthropological work that engaged him, once offering a thumbnail sketch of Iñupiat (North Alaskan Eskimo) grammar that he had worked out after a winter's sojourn on the Beaufort Sea coast. At the same time, he rarely failed to invoke the enthusiasms of his intellectual coming-of-age or to reflect on his indebtedness to von Zedlitz as the "guide and teacher of my younger days."[17] As his career matured following study at Oxford and successful Papuan and arctic fieldwork, their association evolved from its roots in academic patronage to friendship and colleagueship. This is reflected in the changed tone of later correspondence, occasional offers of personal and professional advice, and in the deliberate shift from the deferential "Dear Professor" to the familiar "Dear Von Zedlitz" with which the letters open. They lost touch after the First World War. But during what was to be his final trip to New Zealand in late 1947, just months before von Zedlitz's death, Jenness called on his professor and the two warmly renewed their ties.

A crucial aspect of the von Zedlitz friendship dates to the war years, while Jenness was in Canada's Arctic. With the outbreak of hostilities, New Zealand was awash in pro-British patriotism, an expression of the Dominion's colonial beginnings, its continuing imperial allegiance, and the Anglophile orientation of native-born settler culture and identity. A particularly virulent nationalist strain spread xenophobic propaganda against residents of German origin, many of whom were fired from government jobs, while others faced internment. Though no longer a German citizen, von Zedlitz had not yet obtained British nationality. Under the circumstances, he felt compelled to resign his professorship within days of Britain's declaration of war. In a show of unconditional support for one of their own, the Victoria College Council refused the resignation and von Zedlitz warily resumed his duties.

In the wake of Gallipoli's horrors in the spring of 1915, a debacle that exacted a terrible toll on New Zealanders – Pakeha and Maori alike – anti-German agitation reached a feverish pitch. The public demanded von Zedlitz's immediate removal. In the meantime, he had become something of a cause célèbre, accused of aiding the enemy by operating a clandestine radio station. Opposition members in the House of Representatives, the country's parliament, denounced Prime Minister William Massey's Reform Party for failing to order von Zedlitz's arrest, alleging that the influential family of Alice Fitzherbert, von Zedlitz's New Zealand–born wife, had dissuaded leading government members from doing so. Bowing to mounting pressure for the professor's censure, if not his head, the government enacted the Alien Enemy Teachers Act in October 1915, legislation whose actual (if unstated) intention was to force the College Council's hand on the matter. With the dismissal thus a fait accompli, the council's members showed collective contempt for the act by voting their colleague a year's salary and unequivocally declaring regret over the shoddy way the affair had played out.[18]

Ensconced on the remote arctic shores of Coronation Gulf, word of both his teacher's predicament and the war that precipitated it belatedly reached Jenness in late 1915. His sympathetic reply to the beleaguered professor was as condemnatory of blind nationalistic fervour as it was supportive of his friend. He wrote of feeling betrayed by his compatriots' abandonment of decency and sobriety, and by the ease with which they succumbed to suspicion and hate, as well as his disillusion with their willingness to abandon ideals that he naively believed were inherent in New Zealand's emergent society and a legacy of its British heritage. "I am ashamed of my fellow countrymen," not just because of their enmity toward von Zedlitz himself, but for the irrational futility of indulging in "'patriotism' which takes the form of attacking every individual of the nationality with which one happens to be at war."[19]

MYTH AND NATIONHOOD

If the roots of his youthful embrace of scholarship are evident, those of his eventual turn to anthropology are not. On the surface, a chance acquaintance with two students during his early days at Oxford, Marius Barbeau and Wilson Wallis, both aspiring anthropologists from North America, played the determining hand, the pair's enthusiasm for their studies proving an irresistible lure to their new friend. But according to

Harry Hawthorn, an expatriate New Zealander whose career also took him to Canada, there was another, deeper motivation behind Jenness's decision: an enduring interest in cultural differences first sparked by friendships with Maori schoolmates at Wellington Boys' College.[20]

It is left to the imagination to decide what directions this boyhood inquisitiveness may have taken; perhaps visiting the homes of Maori friends and immersing himself in local life, or making solitary jaunts through the Hutt valley countryside searching for remnants of the indigenous past. The only ray of light Jenness himself shed on the subject comes in a terse, if suggestive, reference to quite a different activity: collecting New Guinean ethnographic objects during his student days at Victoria College.[21] His sister May, then immersed in mission work, was doubtless their source. It is unclear whether she sent them home as souvenirs or if Diamond requested them because of a nascent interest in things anthropological. During his own Papuan sojourn, he added to this private collection.

Even if he had yet to acquire genuine intellectual interests in the so-called savage or primitive peoples and cultures of the world, he must have had at least passing familiarity with the main currents of anthropological thought and practice in New Zealand at the time. After all, this was an era when middle-class Victorians, women and men alike, cultivated recreational and educational interests in various branches of science and natural history, anthropology prominent among them. Visiting museums and zoological parks, holding memberships in the local Mechanics Institute or naturalist society, and collecting botanical specimens or ethnographic curios for display in a household cabinet were more than fashionable activities: people considered them means to self-improvement and respectability. Moreover, such genteel pastimes offered the better-educated and more mobile classes a much-needed diversion from the rough and ready utilitarianism of colonial Pakeha culture, particularly its rural variety.[22]

As with its British and North American counterparts before the First World War, New Zealand anthropology enjoyed a healthy measure of popular appeal, its assets running the gamut from public displays of Pacific ethnographica to an accessible descriptive and interpretive literature aimed at an informed lay readership. No less important, direct involvement in scientific and scholarly activities at the time was not contingent on academic and professional credentials, as it largely is today. In fact, the first, and for some time the lone, paid position in the field, the curatorship Eldson Best held at the Dominion Museum in Wellington, was only established in 1910 and anthropology's recognition as a college discipline did not come for another nine years when Jenness's boyhood chum, H.D. Skinner, joined the faculty of University of Otago in Dunedin.[23] Simple interest was qualification enough, the majority of participants being men of affairs who were open to wide-ranging intellectual pursuits in addition to their ordinary occupations. Gatherings of provincial learned and literary societies, some dating to the 1840s, and of the Dominion's premier scientific body, the New Zealand Institute, founded in 1867, provided settings for lively discussion and debate. Their agendas regularly featured anthropological topics, as did the pages of the Institute's *Transactions* and other publications.[24]

Not surprisingly, diverse aspects of Maori culture, history, and language absorbed anthropology's devotees above all else, yet none as completely as the question of beginnings, the quintessential "whence of the Maoris."[25] As a forum for their specialized interests, a small group of avocational ethnologists and linguists headed by S. Percy Smith organized the Polynesian Society at Wellington in 1892. Their purpose was to encourage preservation of as complete a record of Maori customs and traditions as possible, as they feared that esoteric indigenous learning, the ancient whare wananga, was on the verge of disappearing with the imminent passing of tribal elders. A quarterly *Journal of the Polynesian Society*, under Smith's editorship, quickly became the principal outlet for communication and debate among those at home and abroad – amateur and professional – with serious interests in the Maoris, other Polynesians, and the peoples and cultures of the wider Pacific. Symbolic of their independence of metropolitan influences, the founding members bypassed the customary naming of a British royal as the Society's patron, offering the honour to Queen Lilioukalani of Hawai'i instead.[26]

In an interesting departure from the more usual course of disciplinary history elsewhere, New Zealand anthropology was both known and well received in certain quarters of Maori society, albeit for singular reasons. Many prominent Maori leaders and MPs looked favourably on Pakeha scholars who undertook the urgent work of documenting and preserving ethnographic detail. They saw the collective results of these efforts as making an important contribution to the revival of Maori fortunes – the so-called Maori "renaissance" – after years of precipitous demographic, cultural, and social decline.[27] A few even joined their Pakeha colleagues in the effort, publishing the results of their own original researches from the distinctive perspective of the cultural insider. The Polynesian Society counted Maoris among its officers, members, and contributors from the beginning, some with sufficient political connections to benefit society activities and coffers.[28]

Most turn-of-the-century New Zealanders were more likely to consume anthropological ideas in the arena of civic affairs than in the meeting rooms of learned societies or the exhibition halls of museums. Nowhere was this more evident than in the realm of evolving Maori-Pakeha relations, then, as now, a central issue in the country's social and political life. With an express interest in the Maoris' past and present and an abiding faith in the efficacy of their science, the day's anthropologists were naturally inclined to inform public opinion on what they then conceived, for good or ill, as the "Maori Problem."[29]

❖

In New Zealand, as throughout the colonial world, natives and newcomers understood their relationship in dissimilar, often contradictory ways. Disputed sovereignty and contested rights to land and cultural self-determination were consistently the most vexing points of difference between them. In the face of these differences – some unresolved to this day – Maoris endured great hardship, their future in the emerging Dominion far from certain. Epidemics of sickness, alcohol, and poverty exacted a fearsome toll on their communities in the 1800s, much as they had among indigenous peoples from Australia to Africa, from Asia to the Arctic. Disillusion and despair followed. And for the survivors, nearly all of whom lived in rural, often remote parts of the country, tangible signs of Pakeha liberality were rarely in evidence. A dwindling land base, economic and occupational marginalization, poor standards of housing, sanitation, and health, and de facto segregation from the mainstream of national life made up the all-too-common lot of most Maori. In practice, Maori and Pakeha remained "well insulated" from one another, each people in its own solitude, each in a separate New Zealand.[30]

In sharp contrast, the country's Pakeha majority were disposed to see the new society as racially tolerant and harmonious. The era of bloody inter-tribal and inter-ethnic warfare following British annexation was now well past, and neither reservations nor the legal apparatus of wardship had come in its aftermath. Moreover, Maoris were recognized as British subjects and enjoyed parliamentary representation through four designated seats in the House of Representatives. Special protections and rights – concerning land, for instance, and local governance – were also implemented, all under the administrative auspices of a separate Native Department, later the Department of Maori Affairs.[31] Taken together, such steps had few parallels in the empire, or beyond it. From this perspective at least, the Dominion government had avoided some of the worst excesses of colonial administration employed elsewhere in the period and in the process gained a reputation, at home and abroad, for open-mindedness and fair treatment.[32]

That said, assimilation, not pluralism, was the ultimate goal of New Zealand state policy towards Maoris and had been from the time of the Treaty of Waitangi. To a Victorian mind steeped in the precepts of Social Darwinism, assimilation was both necessary and certain, the "fatal impact" of Maori contact with Europeans, who deemed themselves morally and intellectually superior, having doomed them, like other tribal peoples, to inevitable social and cultural collapse.[33] Without amalgamation of the races, the reasoning went, the prospect of extinction, already evident in steady population decline and social demoralization, was practically inescapable. The "progress" of their race, therefore, had little to do with the realization of political autonomy or the preservation of what James Carroll later termed Maoritanga, the essential values and identity of "Maoriness." Instead, it was contingent upon their release from the encumbrances of primitive ways, notably the communalism of tribal organization and the powerful superstitions surrounding mana and tapu – beliefs about the sacred sources of personal power and authority. Only by such means could they enter and participate in national life on equal terms with Pakehas, terms consistent with British-Pakeha values and institutions, not with a bi-cultural conception of society.[34]

An unusual and inventive dimension of what was otherwise conventional thinking about the course of native-white relations was the assertion of putative racial and historical kinship between Maoris and Europeans. This idea gained a measure of acceptance among Pakehas, so much so, in fact, that it acquired the character of a charter myth of settler culture. As such, it provided ideological justification for advancing the cause of assimilation to breathe new life into the vestiges of a supposedly dying people, and, more importantly, to forge a single (albeit British) nation constituted under the 1840 Treaty of Waitangi. Oddly enough, the notion of common ancestry also appealed to many Maoris, though its value for them was often more as a means to resist assimilation than to embrace it.[35]

Members of the anthropological community gave credibility to this uncommon proposition through their research and writing on the beginnings and transformations of indigenous society. Applying theories of cultural diffusion and comparative philology and mythology then in vogue, a succession of monographs and papers established the heroic ancestry of the Maoris. The epic story of Aotearoa's settlement by seafarers from the northern reaches of Polynesia half a millennium ago – the Great Fleet canon – is the most enduring legacy of this national anthropological tradition.[36] Shorter-lived, but no less important, was a thesis claiming Maori-European kinship, one that proposed that Maori lineage could be traced back generation upon generation to an ancient source in Indo-European (Aryan) civilization. By arguing for Aryan origins, leading figures such as Percy Smith, W.E. Gudgeon, and Edward Tregear sought to diminish, though not entirely eliminate, the racial, intellectual, and moral distance between New Zealand's two peoples.[37] Proclaiming the existence of racial affinities rooted in shared if distant ancestry, they urged complete amalgamation, "reunification of the Aryans," as the new nation's goal.[38]

Regardless of their questionable underpinnings, such theories and analyses played to certain effect in public life. One reason for this was that several of their most persuasive Pakeha proponents were men whose influence extended beyond the confines of New Zealand's scholarly and scientific circles. Percy Smith was the Dominion's surveyor general, Gudgeon a judge at the Native Land Court, and Tregear a high-ranking civil servant in the Department of Labour. And there were others, academics, clergymen, politicians of various persuasions. Indeed, Tregear's "connections with people in high places" probably account for the fact that the government printer issued his monograph *The Aryan Maori* in 1885.[39] The other reason, equally important, was the political message embodied in the work itself, a message pressing for acceptance of the Maoris as full partners in the business of nation building. As Tregear put it, "The ordinary European need not blush to his own brotherhood with ... the heroes of Orakau," a reference to a major battle during the New Zealand Wars of the 1860s.[40] Offering scientific evidence that the indigenous past was only slightly less estimable than that of Europeans, these anthropologists sought to redeem the Maoris as a people, showing them not to be "congenital inferior[s] doomed to extinction, but ... wayward brother[s] who could be saved."[41] It was hoped that such viewpoints would endow the Maoris with an uncommon degree of recognition, something decidedly out of the ordinary in an age when native peoples and cultures routinely endured unrelenting coercion and debasement under colonial and post-colonial regimes. At the same time, these arguments provided justification for the government's increasing activism in the field of native affairs, a role in keeping with the interventionism of Liberal "state socialism."[42]

On the other side of the ledger, the actual consequences of assimilation to this point were harsh, the government's aggressive land acquisition policies, its support of Christian missions, and other measures contributing to a downward spiral of Maori economic, cultural, and political fortunes. Various groups had been mobilizing resistance to the process since British annexation, though perhaps most forcefully (and successfully) in the nativist King Movement (Kingitanga) that coalesced in the 1850s and the Unity Movement (Kotahitanga) three decades later.[43] By the turn of the century, however, a new generation of leaders was on the scene, an articulate elite, educated in state schools and universities, and, unlike their predecessors, fully conversant in both Maori and Pakeha ways. James Carroll was certainly one of them. Yet in many respects the most accomplished and influential of their number was Apirana T. Ngata. Of Ngati Porou tribal descent, Ngata was a Canterbury-trained lawyer, long-serving MP for the Eastern Maori riding, and eventually native minister in the United government that came to power in the 1920s. Arguably also New Zealand's first applied anthropologist, he championed the use of ethnological perspectives in setting policy and administering indigenous affairs at home and abroad in the country's Pacific territories.[44]

Early in his career Ngata helped found the Young Maori Party and became one of its leading activists, campaigning tirelessly for reforms in crucial areas such as public health, defending tribal lands against alienation, and encouraging local economic development. An ardent nationalist, his position was by no means an outright repudiation of all things Pakeha. Instead, he was committed to the idea that Maori interests, and ultimately an effective and just accommodation between the cultures, were best served through Maori-controlled assimilation. Initially articulated in the 1890s and developed further in later years, the strategy he espoused capitalized on then-current anthropological thinking on the question of origins to make a case for preserving, and nurturing, a strong indigenous (read racial) identity, one distinct from that of Pakehas but no less worthy. The roots of this identity, he argued, lay in the cultural product of the Maori genius that Smith and his Polynesian Society colleagues publicized: the ancient language, sacred learning, the epic of the Great Fleet. But he tempered this view with an eminently pragmatic concession: the need to modify, even suppress, certain "antiquated and pernicious customs" before Maoris assumed their rightful place next to Pakehas in society's mainstream. Ngata had in mind especially the communal obligations and rivalries of family and tribe, elements of tradition seen as antithetical to the organization and principles of commercial agriculture and to other forms of modern economic activity essential to the revival of Maori fortunes.[45]

As he later described the situation to his close friend and associate Te Rangihiroa (aka Peter Buck), himself a physician, politician, and later an anthropologist at the Bishop Museum in Honolulu, the end of the nineteenth century marked the dawning of an all new phase of Maori history. Their people now faced the necessity of applying aspects of their cumulative acculturative experience to deal with the new problems of change confronting them. "I rather think that in moments of introspection you and I ... must acknowledge that our hearts are not with [a] policy of imposing culture-forms on our people," Ngata explained. "Our recent activities would indicate a contrary determination to preserve the old culture forms as the foundations on which to reconstruct Maori life and hopes."[46]

Sentiments and theories aside, British-Pakeha values and institutions alone predominated throughout these years, defining the most basic norms of acceptability for New Zealanders generally and pulling Maoris inexorably toward assimilation. Assimilation, in one guise or another, would remain official state policy in the country into the 1950s.[47]

◈

The period from 1890 to 1910 was an era of progressive change in New Zealand, an era of wide-ranging social and economic reforms and of an emergent egalitarianism, particularly among the growing middle classes. As someone whose own coming of age in conditions of modest prosperity and respectability neatly coincided with that of his birthplace, it is a safe bet to assume that neither the spirit nor the accomplishments of these years were lost on Diamond Jenness. Contemporary moral, political, and intellectual enthusiasms impressed him in a decidedly positive way, influencing both his political leanings and his private outlook on the world at large and, no less importantly, tempering the character of the anthropology he formally acquired at Oxford and then practiced over a career spanning more than half a century. Even as a long-time expatriate in Canada, he never wavered in his admiration for the kind of society his contemporaries sought to build for themselves and for generations of New Zealanders to come. Moreover, his faith in the meritocratic principles and ideals of humanitarianism and social justice that guided their efforts proved no less enduring.

The effect of these formative influences is most plainly evident in what surely stands as the overriding concern of Jenness's professional work: bringing fairness and justice to the evolving relationship of indigenous peoples and the modern state. The development of his thought on this problem, a process begun in earnest with his initial experience in British New Guinea and slowly matured through long-term research among Inuit and First Nations in Canada, owes a substantial debt to the brand of democratic, progressive liberalism that pervaded the New Zealand of his youth. Put simply, the course on which his country embarked in this period persuaded him of the greater justice to be achieved in minimizing – both in theory and practice – the social and racial distance presumed to exist between peoples. Central to the public face of state policy on indigenous affairs, and an underlying assumption of Victorian Pakeha anthropology, this position had already found practical expression in the small but growing number of Maoris entering national life on an equal footing with white New Zealanders and, perhaps more significantly, in the grassroots revival of population and culture among the majority of Maoris still living in the countryside. One of Jenness's greatest ambitions in professional life was to persuade Canadian policy makers to steer a similar course. How that went is spelled out in later chapters.

CHAPTER TWO

The Second Horse,
1908–1911

UP FROM BELOW

Diamond Jenness embarked for Oxford in July 1908. He was twenty-two. The steamer voyage, including a fortnight's layover in Italy, lasted seven weeks, lightning-fast compared to the six months his grandmother Minifie had spent at sea seventy years before. Her generation of settlers had bravely ventured off to an uncertain future in what was then a little-known corner of a vast, global empire. Britain remained central to their descendants' world view, continuing to loom large in Pakeha identity and sentiment even though most had never set foot on its soil. Anthony Trollope memorialized the strength of those feelings during his tour of Australia and New Zealand in the early 1870s. "Among John Bulls," the novelist wrote, New Zealanders were unquestionably "the most John Bullish ... more English than any Englishman at home" and devoted to the "supremacy of England to every place in the world." "The great drawback to travelling in New Zealand," he goes on, "comes from the feeling that after crossing the world and journeying over so many thousands of miles, you have not at all succeeded in getting away from England."[1] A "rhetoric of exile" arose early in Pakeha society and persisted for some time. In keeping with this sense of nostalgic belonging, passenger liners, like the one taking Jenness northward, were known as "home boats." Many years later Jenness recalled that "from childhood [I] was taught, like other New Zealanders, to consider [England] home."[2]

His compatriots rarely realized the dream of return. The chief exceptions were "people of talent," artists and writers, intellectuals and academics, for whom New Zealand's "cultural homogeneity" was "dispiriting and dulling." Most often it was the temper of their isolated colonial existence that pushed them away, the absence of opportunities to achieve professional or artistic ambitions proving a source of personal frustration and disappointment, an unhappy situation that only began to improve in New Zealand after the Second World War.[3] Jenness's eventual decision to join the country's expatriate ranks stemmed from the limited prospects for the academically trained and professionally minded anthropologist he had become. On the more immediate matter of his reasons for continuing his studies abroad in the first place – a decision that long preceded any thought of a permanent leave-taking – it is safe to assume at least one motive – his chances for a career at home, or anywhere – stood to gain immeasurably from an English sojourn and, more particularly, from cultivation of an Oxford connection.

Jenness's initial impression of Oxford – beyond the obligatory mention of persistent chill and the "plague of fogs," that is – comes in a terse note to his sister Grace, written part way through his first term. Rather than going on about the grandeur of the ancient university architecture or the pomp of centuries-old Balliol College ritual, he offers up some rather unflattering comment on his fellow students. "I can't say I am much struck with Oxford men so far," he explains. "Many of them are mere boys," used to being "kept pretty well in restraint." But faced with "a bit of liberty" in their new surroundings, they simply "don't know how to use it ... Every now & again the childishness or boyish freakiness breaks out."[4] Recruited largely from Eton and other of the country's leading public schools, these were the young men who comprised the up-and-coming generation of Britain's elite, those who would dominate its government, finance, and commerce. Whatever else their antics meant to him, in a round-about way their patrician pretences and undisciplined ways may well have boosted his confidence about coming to Oxford, especially since those of his classmates born to wealth and position were more likely to dismiss him as an ambitious, unworthy colonial than to accept him at face value, as someone who had actually merited admission on the strength of a solid record of academic achievement.

Still, this was the lot of most outsiders, Oxford and Cambridge both lingering in a "vacuous conservatism" more amenable to the dispositions of inherited privilege than to the self-improving aspirations of ordinary respectable people of modest background.[5] Indeed, little more than half a century had passed since the ancient universities had cracked open their doors to degree candidates from the newly emergent middle classes and the non-conforming churches or made a place for new fields of learning in the natural and physical sciences, or anthropology, in an environment that had traditionally been the near-exclusive preserve of classicists, moral philosophers, and high church theologians. Educational reform came in response to the democratizing and meritocratic trends brought by rising industrial and commercial pros-

In Twilight and in Dawn

perity at home and expanding imperial interests abroad from the 1850s onward. Even so, the structural and curricular changes they gradually encouraged – increasing secularization, professionalization of faculty, vocational training for non-clerical occupations – were not universally welcomed in all corners of academia, a political situation whose consequences included anthropology's much-belated acceptance as a subject of formal instruction.

Jenness said nothing further about any of these issues, either then or in later years. But Edmund Leach's instructive remark about fellow anthropologist Raymond Firth, Auckland-born and twenty-three years old when he arrived in London in 1924, casts light on the circumstances his compatriot had met sixteen years before. While "clearly fascinated by the aesthetic resources of the metropolis," Leach wrote, Firth found the "irrational snobberies of the English upper-middle class ... both alien and bizarre."[6] This would have been especially so for someone who, like Jenness, had been raised in a more egalitarian social and educational milieu than existed in England early in the new century, even given the turbulent pace of social change – in national politics, class and gender relations, public policy – then unfolding throughout much of British life.[7]

Despite its decades-long commitment to implement reforms in curriculum, internal governance, and so on, Oxford's timeworn values and sentiments proved especially resistant to change. Balliol was no exception. While suggesting that the distinguished old college – Oxford's second oldest, founded in 1263 – "always had a good reputation for not preserving social divisions too rigidly," one of its modern historians freely admits that, in the final analysis, its "attitudes and ways of living broadly conformed to the ideas and behaviour of the great [public] schools and of the families who sent their sons to those schools as a matter of course." "Inevitably," the writer continues, "it was part of the education of the Balliol undergraduate who came up from below, socially speaking, to bring himself to take on the ways and manners, and the values, of the sons of the governing classes." All this was occurring in a period when the proportion of students from families of privilege coming to the university as a whole, not just Balliol, was in decline, falling to about ten percent across the colleges in Jenness's day.[8] Nonetheless, a cursory glance through the 1908–09 *Balliol College Register* speaks volumes on the social profile of his classmates, a healthy portion of whom were the scions of British peers and members of the bourgeoisie, many with Balliol credentials of their own. He truly must have felt himself an outsider in their company since their social circles, and the avenues for advancement open to them, were not his own. Fittingly, one of the few college mates with whom he kept in touch after graduation was an Australian named Alexander Leeper, also a Classics student, whose career first led to a temporary posting at the British Museum, then to the Foreign Office and Diplomatic Service.[9]

Jenness's decision to pursue classical studies did not signal aspirations for a life in academia. His sights were set on a more practical goal, something along the lines of a foreign service posting in India or East Africa. By reputation, an Oxford degree in Classics was widely regarded as the epitome of learning, a foundation ideally suited to the successful man of affairs – the "educated amateur," in late-Victorian idiom – because it promoted "general faculties of reason that could be exercised in any situation."[10] The rules governing placement in the prestigious Indian Civil Service had recently been revised, allowing candidates to complete university studies before writing qualifying examinations. Well aware of how the system worked, he confided in his sister that success was not merely a matter of academic merit but of merit and solid connections combined. "There are some awfully good [jobs] going, but only 1st class men & men with a bit of influence behind them get them."[11]

This ambition was doubtless influenced by J.L. Strachan-Davidson, then Balliol's master, a man who took great personal pride in his college's record of preparing candidates for Civil Service appointments at home and in the empire, as well as in its broad commitment to instilling public spiritedness in its students. Strachan-Davidson was of the opinion that those entering posts in the overseas service, particularly in India, ought to "embody the highest standards of intellectual training and Western culture," standards reached through "the mental and moral discipline and the grasp of fundamentals given by the school of *Literae Humaniores*," Oxford's venerable and enduring legacy to classical education and Balliol's scholastic forte. Given the master's de facto standing as "liaison officer" to Civil Service officialdom, a good many of whose members were his former pupils, Jenness needed to look no farther than his own college for that critical "bit of influence."[12]

Jenness found little to disagree with in the routines of college life. Lectures in each of three eight-week terms occurred in the mornings, no more than two per day, and tutorials in the afternoons. Hours in between were usually free, allowing time for athletic and other non-academic pursuits. As his American classmate (and fellow aspiring anthropologist) Wilson Wallis later recalled, serious study was reserved for vacations and breaks between terms, the terms themselves annoyingly "interrupted with lectures, writing papers for tutors, and various social demands."[13] Apart from attending Sunday evening concerts in the Balliol chapel, Jenness used what spare time he had to keep up a daily regimen of physical exercises and to practice shooting, his boyhood skills remaining well honed with twice-weekly sessions. He later substituted boating on the Thames as a pastime, complaining in a letter to his brother Frederick that the costs of buying cartridges and getting to and from the practice range, a short train ride away, had spiralled beyond his means. Family bore the cost of his upkeep, an unavoidable arrangement that dictated frugality throughout the whole of his three years in England and fostered a deep "moral obligation" to pay back every penny his parents had loaned him.[14] Before departing for England, he instructed Victoria College to make payable to his father the proceeds from his Jacob Joseph Scholarship.

◈

As a candidate in the School of Literae Humaniores, better known as Greats, Jenness read Greek and Roman literature, history, and philosophy under a succession of Balliol College tutors: A.W. Pickard-Cambridge, J.A. Smith, and A.D. Lindsay. In 1911, he received a commendable second standing in the Final School examinations. By then he was deeply absorbed in anthropology and just weeks away from a return voyage to the south Pacific. His lone comment on the concluding Greats ordeal, the viva voce, was characteristically understated; he explained to his professor Robert Marett that it had "lasted only 35 min & did not seem very serious." Musing about the standing he had been awarded, he wondered if it were entirely "satisfactory for a man who – as the Master said each handshake – insisted on riding two horses."[15]

When he was in his seventies, Jenness intimated that his decision to ride the second horse, anthropology, owed more to happenstance and impulse than anything else. A chance meeting in 1908 with Charles Marius Barbeau, then a twenty-five-year-old Québécois Rhodes Scholar in residence at Oriel College, Cecil Rhodes's alma mater, set the stage. With Canadian degrees in humanities and law freshly in hand, Barbeau had arrived at Oxford the previous fall after a summer-long detour in France, his self-proclaimed spiritual homeland. In Paris, he took courses at the Sorbonne and l'École d'Anthropologie, meeting Marcel Mauss and other scholars associated with Émile Durkheim and their *Année sociologique* group, named for the pioneering journal of ethnology and comparative sociology they had founded in 1898.[16] The experience whetted his appetite for more. Once settled at Oriel, he entered the Natural Science School as a BSC candidate and, from there, made his way into the fledgling diploma course in anthropology, inaugurated only two years before. In short order Jenness joined him, finding Barbeau's excitement and passion for the subject hard to resist.[17]

The pair, soon fast friends, found a fellow enthusiast in American Wilson D. Wallis, like Barbeau a Rhodes Scholar with a background in classical philosophy and law. Together they made up the second class to earn academic credentials in anthropology at Oxford, completing their diploma examinations in the spring of 1910. All eventually went on to professional careers in the field – a remarkable accomplishment for the time, given the extremely limited job prospects between the world wars. Jenness and Barbeau landed employment with the Anthropological Division of the Geological Survey of Canada and Wallis succeeded in American academia.[18]

Viewed in the light of contemporary practice, the fields of classics and anthropology appear to stand worlds apart, one the quintessence of humanistic learning and the very core of the western tradition of liberal education, the other among the utilitarian social sciences, which are of comparatively recent academic and professional vintage. However, when Jenness opted to supplement Greats with a short course in the nascent science of man, as it was then known, the gap between the two was negligible at best, at least in Britain. Anthropology was just then gaining recognition as an academic discipline in English universities, if only as a minor subject for undergraduate instruction. Advanced studies, and the professional status they promoted, were still years off. Many of the day's senior anthropologists thus began their careers in more established fields like medicine or the classics, as in Marett's case, while others had public-school backgrounds strong in Greek and Latin literature, history, and philosophy, as did Edward B. Tylor, doyen of the country's small anthropological circle. Rather than limiting their interests solely to studying the "dark-skinned, non-European, 'uncivilized' peoples" with whom the field is commonly associated,[19] they also brought to bear the latest developments in ethnology, linguistics, and archaeology in interpreting ancient Mediterranean life and thought. The work of William Ridgeway, holder of Cambridge's Disney chair in classical archaeology and in 1909 president of the Royal Anthropological Institute, is a case in point. At a time when most classicists persisted in the long-held view that "everything connected with Greece and Rome, Egypt and Babylonia [stood] on a completely different plane from every other culture," Ridgeway offered a dissenting opinion, arguing from the tenets of Victorian social evolutionary theory that these civilizations had not developed "sui generis" but through a succession of stages beginning with a formative one "comparable to that of modern savages."[20] The eminent James G. Frazer put the matter slightly differently in the introduction to the 1900 edition of his masterwork, *The Golden Bough*, accounting for the origins of magico-religious belief and practice among the classical ancients within an inclusive ethnological framework. Modern inquiry into the nature of human culture, he wrote, "aims at bringing home to us the faith and the practice, the hopes and the ideals, not of two highly gifted races only, but of all mankind ...

In Twilight and in Dawn

enabling us to follow the long march, the slow and toilsome ascent, of humanity from savagery to civilisation."[21]

Oxford's committee for anthropology sponsored a lecture series on Greek and Roman history and literature in ethnological context in the fall of 1908, Jenness's first term. The six lectures took as their central theme the theoretical and methodological contributions of each discipline to understanding the "domain of human culture" as a whole, not simply its supposed higher "forms," the traditional bailiwick of the humanities, or its lower, up to then the speciality of anthropologists. Delivered by an eclectic group that included European archaeologist Arthur Evans, keeper of the Ashmolean Museum, and Hellenist Gilbert Murray, they demonstrated the relevance of comparative linguistic and ethnographic evidence drawn from non-literate societies to interpretations of Mediterranean antiquity.[22] Apropos of Ridgeway, they also challenged the conventional view in mainstream classical scholarship that ancient Greece was somehow "a magnificent but lonely island," effectively untouched by influences from "the barbarians" and, in essence, unaffected by the universal laws of social evolution that most anthropologists of the late Victorian and Edwardian periods presumed accounted for regularities in human cultural development.[23]

All things considered, there was more to Jenness's decision to take up anthropology than his finding Barbeau's lead "difficult to resist."[24] He had already dabbled around its edges while still in Wellington, as his collection of Papuan ethnographica suggests, and had surely acquired at least passing familiarity with some of the homegrown anthropological theories then in fashion in New Zealand. Once at Oxford, new and unanticipated opportunities opened for incubating whatever embryonic interests he had. It is easily imagined that the most important of these stemmed from attempts by classicists and anthropologists to identify the intellectual affinities and common purposes of their respective fields of inquiry. If nothing else, anthropology showed certain promise in offering a new, comparative perspective on the "stages" of Mediterranean culture's rise and eventual decline, a subject that had intrigued Jenness since his early college days.[25] This being the case, the diploma course was attractive because he considered it a worthwhile complement to the conventional curriculum covered in Greats, not necessarily as an alternative to it.

Intellectual satisfactions aside, acquiring even passing familiarity with the diverse peoples and cultures scattered throughout the empire would serve him well in launching a career in Britain's foreign service. Ranking officials had recently come to recognize the benefit of some anthropological knowledge for candidates aspiring to overseas postings, especially those directly involved in administering indigenous populations. Having been encouraged in this view since the mid-1880s by prominent scientists and scholars who touted the applied value of ethnological intelligence as a way to garner public financial and institutional support of their activities, government's de facto endorsement played an important part in pushing the field toward acceptance as an academic discipline and, after the First World War, toward the full professional status it gradually came to enjoy.[26] In the meantime, students who passed through the diploma program in its formative years were en route to careers in India, Africa, and the Pacific. Most served as colonial officers, a few as missionaries, some with duties that included collection of information about the languages and cultures and physical characteristics of the peoples under their authority.[27] Judging by the foremost attributes of his own career-long service with the Canadian government – a strong preference for empirical and later applied (i.e., policy-related) research – Jenness's professional persona had more in common with those who saw anthropology primarily as a means to serve practical and public ends, not theoretical and academic ones. In this regard at least he was very much a product of Edwardian Balliol and, more generally, of pre-war British anthropology. The lectures he attended and the authors he read during two years of study left Jenness with a taste for pursuing anthropology further, though not necessarily on a professional basis. Excitedly anticipating what was to be the next phase of his initiation, an apprenticeship served on Oxford's behalf as a special research student in New Guinea, he declared himself consumed with "anthro 'mania,'" and expressed a special debt to Marett for providing unflagging encouragement.[28] The unforeseen course these formative experiences eventually induced him to follow, first to Melanesia, then to the Arctic, and finally to a post in Ottawa, came as a complete surprise to some of his friends and associates. Friend and fellow New Zealander Henry Skinner, himself a Cambridge-trained anthropologist, sized up the situation in quaint if curious language, wondering "Who would have thought ... that [someone], whose only vice was his respectability, would prove false to his plighted love, the classics, and would pursue and capture the shy maid anthropology?"[29]

THE HYBRID MONSTER

The state of early twentieth-century British anthropology was much the same as in New Zealand, its ranks comprising a robust mix of amateur enthusiasts and a smattering of scholars and academics, its appeal strongest among ordinary citizens who consumed science for their educational and social improvement. But while ethnologically inclined Pakehas and Maoris entertained relatively parochial interests in Maori culture and greater Polynesia, their British counterparts cultivated horizons spanning the farthest reaches of empire, writing and lecturing on everything from the minutiae of tribal custom and technology to what the redoubtable popularizer of Darwinism, Thomas Huxley, dubbed the "question of questions ... the place which man occupies in nature."[30] On the organizational front, scientific and learned associations, notably the Royal Anthropological Institute and Section H (Anthropology) of the British Association for the Advancement of Science, took the lead in promoting research and communication, much as they did in New Zealand and elsewhere. Natural history museums, except for their collecting and curatorial functions, played a lesser role in these activities, universities a small if growing one through the teens and into the twenties. In fact, despite its intellectual origins as a "hybrid monster," part child of the classics, part of the natural sciences,[31] anthropology was probably as marginal to the main academic currents of Edwardian Oxford (and Cambridge) as Jenness himself was to the social world of the upper-crust young men with whom he shared residence at Balliol.

Beginning in the 1870s, a combination of public funding and private philanthropy spurred anthropology's transition from avocation to occupation in the United States, first by providing work for a small number of ethnologists and archaeologists in government agencies and museums, then, late in the century, by easing its entry into academia as a scientific discipline.[32] By comparison, institutional change unfolded more slowly in Britain, so much so that when Jenness arrived in 1908, the best Oxford, or any of its sister universities, had on offer was a general diploma program. While more comprehensive than what he might otherwise have gotten from attending meetings of the Anthropological Institute or Polynesian Society, this was still a far cry from the level of instruction necessary to produce specialized expertise in this, or any, field. In the United States, Columbia, Harvard, and a few other universities had started training North America's founding generation of professional anthropologists in the early 1890s. (Ironically, the first student to earn a doctorate, Alexander F. Chamberlain, was a Briton raised in Ontario.[33]) Graduate-level anthropology began at English universities only in the 1920s, and a good forty years after that in Canada and New Zealand.

In an era of rising expectations and accompanying institutional reform, the ethos, if not the internal order, of England's two ancient universities remained hardened against change. Nowhere was this more apparent than in the lingering divisions separating the "intellectual aristocracy," Noel Annan's much-quoted catch-phrase for the small yet politically powerful Oxbridge elite, and the growing segment of the university population whose class and religious backgrounds had, until comparatively recently, restricted their presence in the student body and all but barred them from going on to hold academic appointments. At issue between them was the very purpose of education, the conservative old-guard, men like Strachan-Davidson, vigorously defending the classical curriculum and its claims for nurturing the "faculties of reason," against a "reforming intelligentsia" determined to promote practical instruction based on sound "scientific principles."[34]

Both universities established examination schools in the natural sciences during the 1850s but Oxford's defence of its ancient prerogatives remained strong: a "deep-rooted cultural antagonism," felt mainly in the conduct of internal politics, hindered its development of the sciences into the early decades of the twentieth century and contributed to the university's reputation as a place better suited to turning out "educated amateurs" versed in the arts and humanities than vocationally trained, career-oriented "brain workers."[35] The depth of this hostility is palpable in an 1880 letter from Vice-Chancellor Benjamin Jowett, Regius Professor of Latin (and another of Balliol's masters), to a like-minded Charles Dodgson (AKA Lewis Carroll), nearly three decades into the process of curricular change. "[T]hose who ... are entrusted with the care of ancient studies," he warned, "have a hard battle to fight against the physical sciences which ... will certainly lower the character of knowledge if ... not counter-acted."[36] With that level of opposition, anthropology – a "reformer's science" waging its own battle against the "usurpation of intellectual authority by a sacerdotal caste," as Tylor saw things – seemed all but fated to languish on the margins of British academia for many years, its "anti-theological, pro-rational" theories of the human biological and cultural pedigree amounting to an affront to establishment thinking.[37]

Its dubious status as a valid area of study aside, anthropology had been represented at Oxford in one or another form for a good thirty years before Jenness came on the scene. The appeal it held for some classicists has already been mentioned. It was no less in favour among natural scientists, particularly after Darwin's 1859 publication of *On the Origin of Species* and the wide-ranging arguments that followed in its wake. Within a year of that scientific milestone, the evolution controversy reached feverish pitch in an epic debate between Thomas Huxley and Samuel Wilberforce, bishop of Oxford. Staged at the Victorian showplace of Oxford science, the recently opened University Museum, legend has it that "Students jeered, Lady Brewster fainted, and Admiral Robert Fitzroy ... captain of the *Beagle*, waved his Bible and screamed that Darwin was a viper."[38] Whether or not hosting this landmark event "ranged [Oxford] on the side of the apes rather than with the angels," the stature of natural science certainly gained in its aftermath. However, Huxley was surely over-reaching when he proclaimed that the university's instruction in these fields was now without peer.[39]

The swelling tide of public interest in the monumental questions Darwin raised paid anthropology few academic dividends over the next two decades. That began to change in 1884, the year Oxford took the unprecedented step of elevating Edward Tylor to a readership from his former post as keeper of the University Museum, the first academic appointment in the fledgling discipline anywhere in Great Britain. His promotion coincided with another: the British Association's granting of sectional status to anthropology after many years as biology's understudy. He became the section's first president.[40] Parenthetically, its inaugural meeting had consequences for anthropology's future in Canada. Convened in Montreal, the Association's first-ever overseas gathering, delegates organized a special Committee to Investigate the North-western Tribes of the Dominion of Canada in hopes of encouraging systematic research on the Dominion's first peoples and cultures. They also lobbied the federal government in Ottawa for public endowment for this work and for establishment of a national ethnological museum. Their politicking, carried on by various organizations and individuals on both sides of the Atlantic for the next quarter-century, finally paid off in 1910 with the founding of the Anthropological Division of the Geological Survey of Canada, Jenness's employer for virtually the whole of his career.[41]

To take Tylor's promotion as a sign of anthropology's rising fortunes is to misread the circumstances, at least in some measure. The appointment actually came about as a condition attached to Oxford's successful effort to obtain a major museum collection belonging to Augustus H. (Lane Fox) Pitt Rivers. A titled military officer and energetic amateur archaeologist whose main expertise lay, appropriately enough, in the evolution of weaponry, General Pitt Rivers's bequest included establishment of a lectureship to further public appreciation of the 14,000 artifacts he had amassed. The university not only consented to the appointment, remunerated at £200 annually, but made anthropology a special subject in the Final Honours School of Natural Science. Moreover, it invested upwards of £10,000 in building a permanent home for the collection: the Pitt Rivers Museum.[42] Even so, the gatekeepers of Oxford's academic affairs remained unprepared to elevate anthropology beyond special standing for some time, rejecting a bid in 1895 to grant examination status in the Honours School, then holding firm in their opposition until finally approving the diploma program ten years later. Meanwhile, Tylor had little choice but to content himself with lecturing to the occasional student who appeared at the Pitt Rivers, a result, at least in part, of stiff administrative regulations governing entry to his course.

Official intransigence all but assured that the "Father of Anthropology remained without progeny" in the field he had done so much to promote in his own country and elsewhere.[43]

Putting the best possible face on the university's 1895 decision to deny anthropology's place among the natural sciences, Charles Hercules Read, keeper of ethnography at the British Museum and later a founding member of Oxford's committee for anthropology, reckoned that "the times were not yet ripe and the science itself as yet too indeterminate," to warrant full examination status. Looking back on this disagreeable business many years later, Marett saw fit to lay some of the blame at the feet of his senior colleague, arguing that Tylor's lectures rarely attracted more than a handful of students anyway. Alternatively, Tylor discerned the workings of conspiracy among academic hard-liners, at one point complaining to a colleague that "we are face to face with an organized attempt to replace Oxford under the rule of Classics and Philosophy."[44]

When the long-awaited breakthrough was finally at hand in 1905, it may well have been because the times, to paraphrase Hercules Read, were finally "ripe," even though, in the minds of many anthropologists, the field remained no less "indeterminate." Two years earlier, members of the Anthropological Institute had heard President Alfred Cort Haddon describe their discipline as "our Cinderella Science," the problems of delimiting its "legitimate scope" from that of other fields, in his view, threatening its assertion of separate scientific status.[45] It bears noting that in heralding the Oxford Diploma as a "new and very important step," Read overlooked the fact that Cambridge had established a degree-granting board of anthropological studies the year before! A pithy rejoinder from the Cambridge board appeared shortly thereafter in the pages of *Man*. Appended to the letter was an obsequious note of remorse from the editor: the journal never intended to harm the "susceptibilities of the distinguished signatories of the manifesto," he solemnly informed his readers. Anthropological instruction had also begun in 1904 at the London School of Economics, an affiliate of London University.[46]

Whatever initial acceptance the new diploma course enjoyed may have owed a greater debt to practical considerations than to scholarly or scientific ones. A host of luminaries and supporters had been trumpeting the importance of ethnological information for Britain's imperial interests since late in the previous century. Originally intended to coax the state into offering institutional support, this same argument eventually became a justification for the budding discipline's claims to academic and professional legitimacy, both at home and in the empire. James Frazer put the case succinctly, observing that "apart from its value as a subject of general education," anthropology "is of special importance in the training of all those whose duties bring them into contact with native races."[47] This thinking likely explains the presence of an aspiring missionary, A. Hadley, in Oxford's first diploma class in 1907 and was certainly germane to Jenness's decision to enrol a year later. A number of others who entered the program before the First World War were similarly preparing for administrative careers overseas; a few – R.S. Rattray and C.K. Meek probably the best known – also became anthropologists in their own right.[48] Marett attributed steady growth in the numbers of diploma candidates at Oxford, among them officers and probationers in the public service, to explicit encouragement from the Colonial Office, a practice that continued until wartime conditions spawned new priorities and a temporary decline in enrolments.[49] In the twenties, universities in Sydney and Cape Town followed the Oxbridge lead, incorporating anthropological subjects into their training courses for missionaries and colonial officers. However, a proposal to offer similar instruction at a new school of anthropological and Polynesian studies in New Zealand failed to pan out.[50]

Oxford's inaugural anthropology class consisted of two other pupils besides Hadley: Francis H.S. Knowles, a specialist in physical (biological) anthropology who for a brief time was on staff at the Geological Survey of Canada; and Barbara Freire-Marreco, later to become a research fellow at Somerville College. Among its other foibles, Oxford, like Cambridge, did not confer academic degrees on female graduates. Equally indicative of the times, women were permitted to take the same courses as men but many among the virtually all-male faculty balked at teaching altogether when women were in attendance. Apparently Tylor was not one of them. In fact, Anna, his wife, was said to have been the only person to hear all of his lectures! Marett related a "wicked story" that made the rounds at his colleague's expense, suggesting that a nameless passer-by claimed to have overheard the professor summing up a lecture with "And so, my dear Anna."[51]

Anthropologists at Edwardian Oxford continued to face the arrogance of disapproving insiders for some time to come; on Marett's promotion to reader in 1910, for instance, they voiced disbelief that he, a Greats man and fellow of Exeter College, would squander his talents on studying "the habits of backward races."[52] As Tylor knew from long experience, and his juniors were now finding out for themselves, academic politics had as much, maybe more, to do with personal social standing and presumptions of intellectual respectability as with the scholarly and professional merit of new lines of inquiry. To patrician eyes, the middle-class and non-conforming backgrounds from which many anthropologists came – Tylor, for instance, was a Quaker – meant they were not sufficiently gentlemen and their science, in consequence, was unworthy of recognition as a proper discipline. Conditions at Cambridge were scarcely better; there, anthropology's leading advocates, Alfred Haddon and William H.R. Rivers, had arguably accomplished little more on the academic front than their counterparts at Oxford. If anthropology found a nurturing setting anywhere during this period it was at the London School of Economics, an institution whose independence of hidebound social and intellectual conventions was a legacy of its radical Fabian origins. "The greater the successes of LSE anthropology," Edmund Leach wryly observed of the period, "the less likely it became that the conservative Establishment in Oxford and Cambridge would touch the subject with the end of a barge pole."[53]

◈

Oxford's committee for anthropology, established in 1905, assumed responsibility for preparing a new syllabus and then guiding it over the necessary administrative and collegial hurdles. Tylor, by reputation still a "towering figure," served as chair, though with advancing years he had become "wandering and repetitious" and thus less influential than he had once been.[54] In consequence, most of the preliminary organizing and internal politicking fell to two much younger colleagues: committee secretary and "General Whip" John L. Myres, a classical archaeologist, and the energetic Marett, soon to be made reader in social anthropology. The pair also shouldered the onerous task of recruiting students, no mean feat, as Marett observed, since anthropology was still in its "incubation period" and "we could not promise the makings of an income" to even the most promising of candidates.[55] Rounding out the committee were Hercules Read and Marett's two "working partners," Henry Balfour and Arthur Thomson, who joined him in teaching once the diploma course finally got off the ground in 1907. Balfour, curator at the Pitt Rivers since 1891, taught prehistory and material culture, while Thomson, a comparative anatomist in the Department of Human Anatomy, lectured on physical anthropology. Social anthropology, the term Frazer popularized to describe the comparative study of tribal social institutions, was Marett's preserve.[56]

Beyond delivering lectures and organizing seminars, the committee devoted much time to promoting anthropology inside and outside the university. Acting the part of lead "proselytizer," as he described himself, Marett was instrumental in arranging special events, such as the successful 1908 symposium on anthropology and the classics, and, just weeks later, in reviving the long-moribund Oxford Anthropological Society. This last served the purpose especially well, attracting a membership of nearly one hundred before the term was out. Under Balfour's presidency, it quickly established affiliations with the Royal Anthropological Institute and the Folklore Society. (In 1913, Jenness's

In Twilight and in Dawn

Faculty and students, Oxford committee for anthropology, ca. 1910. Left to right (front): Henry Balfour, Arthur Thomson, R.R. Marett; (rear): Wilson Wallis, Diamond Jenness, Marius Barbeau. National Anthropological Archives, Smithsonian Institution, 88-13456

first professional paper appeared in the pages of *Folk-Lore*, the Society's journal of record.[57]) Meetings also provided an open forum for the discussion of topics in every branch of the new discipline, a steady stream of guest lecturers effectively comprising an adjunct faculty for the fledgling school of anthropology. In its inaugural year, speakers included Oxford palaeontologist William Sollas discussing "Heidelberg Man," a fossilized mandible discovered in Germany in 1907 and since associated with archaic *Homo sapiens*; Cambridge research student Alfred R. Brown (later Radcliffe-Brown) recounting his recently completed Andaman islands fieldwork; and Marett and Tylor debating Marett's decade-old theory of a pre-animistic stage in the evolution of religion.[58] Yet it was the participation of Haddon and Rivers from Cambridge as well as LSE's Charles G. Seligman that contributed most to advancing Oxford anthropology and ultimately to edging the discipline in Great Britain away from its amateur roots and toward full professional status.

Unlike the fraternity of armchair anthropologists still holding forth at Oxford, these three were among the first British ethnologists to observe tribal society for themselves, initially as co-leaders of the groundbreaking Cambridge Torres Strait Expedition in 1898–99, then in individual field trips to other parts of the empire over the next decade.[59] In undertaking such work, they fostered a sharp break from earlier ethnologists' more usual practice of acquiring ethnographic information at second-hand from missionaries and other overseas correspondents who collected relevant details using questionnaires, particularly the best known and most frequently used, *Notes and Queries on Anthropology*, first issued in 1874. Comparatively few on-the-spot reporters had the requisite background to approach their subjects with more than an intuitive sense of procedure. The Torres Straits veterans argued that the "mainspring of error" in the resultant data stemmed from the untutored observer's unwitting tendency to read "his own unconscious prejudices and ... outlook into the statements ... [of] those who view life from ... a totally different ... standpoint."[60] To remedy the problem, the discipline needed scientifically trained researchers equally concerned with "how to inquire" as with "what to inquire about." To that end, Rivers devised what came to be known as the "concrete method," a strategy that employed genealogical techniques to elicit and record "bodies of dry fact," reliable and objective sociological data he believed were "incapable of being influenced by bias, conscious or unconscious." This approach, a foundation-stone of modern ethnographic field research, figured prominently in "A General Account of Method," one of Rivers's several contributions to the extensively revised fourth edition of *Notes and Queries* that appeared in 1912.[61]

With Marett's blessings, the three innovators became "extramural ethnographic mentors" to Jenness and other up-and-coming anthropologists planning to undertake empirical investigations of their own. By the twenties doing fieldwork – ordinarily no less than a year of research within a single society – was well on its way to becoming "the central ritual of the [British anthropological] tribe" eventually emerging as the hallmark of individual professional standing into the bargain.[62]

Switching the focus of research from library to tribal village did more than alter a long-standing division of labour within British anthropology. The shift also had major consequences for assumptions long central to disciplinary theory. Formerly a "bundle of interests held together by the evolutionary frame of thought," the threads of that bundle began unravelling as the findings of first-generation field workers showed indigenous societies and cultures to be more complex and varied than originally thought. The wealth of new and, arguably, more trustworthy evidence they brought home further challenged the prevailing conception of a world unfolding in orderly and progressive fashion, a "naive scheme of worldwide unilinear evolution" that rested on high-flown, unsubstantiated speculations about the uniform workings of the human mind.[63] In its place, ethnographic investigation was painting a wholly different picture of "multiplex cultural development," with the past and present of individual peoples and cultures shaped by variable conditions of environment and by the spread of ideas and practices via historical contacts and diffusion, not simply by factors of heredity alone.[64] Not yet prepared to forsake evolution altogether – that was to happen after the First World War though the completely re-worked 1912 edition of *Notes and Queries* was a harbinger of things to come – Britain's anthropologists were nonetheless striking out in a new direction. Their approach, predicated on empirical investigation, now depended on painstaking, first-hand examination of single societies and the inextricable connections among their numerous aspects, cultural and psychological, economic and political, technological and ideational. "This is not to abandon the hope of discovering universal tendencies amid the bewildering variety of man's efforts after culture," wrote Marett in 1910. "It is simply to defer that hope until we are in a better position to appreciate each piece of evidence in relation to that organic context whence most of its significance is derived."[65]

Diploma in hand, Jenness wasted little time preparing to meet "primitive man" at first hand in British New Guinea, a place Rivers regarded as the "greatest storehouse of ungarnered lore which remains for the ethnologist" to explore.[66] Fieldwork was the logical next step in satisfying his self-professed "mania" for knowing more about a world that, to this point, existed largely through theories debated in lectures and disembodied artifacts on view at the Pitt Rivers. Fieldwork was what the discipline now demanded, a demand made all the more pressing by wide-spread fears that many of the world's peoples and cultures were verging on extinction, threatened by colonialism's inexorable advance. Obtaining accurate and complete information thus constituted the young discipline's most compelling need, "the factor of urgency, wholly or almost without importance in other branches of science ... one from which the anthropologist can never escape."[67] A career was in the offing.

CHAPTER THREE

On a Bwaidokan Veranda,
1911–1912

THE PITHECANTHROPUS HIMSELF

Members of the Committee for Anthropology took an active hand in
helping their promising apprentice sort out the details of organizing
and funding his upcoming expedition. In addition to appointing Jenness Oxford's first research student in the discipline, they raised £250 to
subsidize his travel, purchase equipment, and allow him to collect specimens for the Pitt Rivers Museum. Robert Marett oversaw fund-raising,
sending solicitations for "pecuniary assistance" to seventeen Oxford
colleges. Eight, including Balliol, contributed, as did the common university fund, which alone provided a fifth of the total. Henry Balfour
and Arthur Evans were among the private benefactors.[1] Jenness had a
will drawn up naming the committee as beneficiary of his notes, photographs, and equipment should the unexpected happen and was asked
to put up a cash indemnity against the chance that he would fail to
finish a full twelve months of fieldwork. His father, George, agreed to
act as guarantor.[2]

These funds didn't cover all the expedition's costs, forcing Jenness to
borrow an additional £100 from his parents. He was embarrassed by his
dependence on others, at one point apologizing to Marett for "having
to put the screw on you" to meet pressing obligations before sailing.
(Reserving a berth for the voyage to New Zealand was first on the list.)
He later expressed a strong "moral obligation" to repay his family, not
only for their help with the Papuan venture but for his upkeep at university as well. This amounted to a "rather heavy financial burden for one
who depends on his wits alone."[3]

The committee was equally helpful in clearing the way over political
hurdles, ensuring that their student's plans found an ally in a well-placed

Oxford connection: J. Hubert Murray, the recently appointed chief administrative officer of Australia's Papuan territory and brother of classicist Gilbert. When the two met in Port Moresby as Jenness was en route to Goodenough Island, the governor issued a standing invitation to call on his services "if ever I needed his help."[4] Motivated by pragmatic considerations far more than scholarly ones, Murray saw his visitor's fieldwork as a potential source of useful intelligence on the diverse peoples under his jurisdiction. To that end, after the First World War he instituted a formal position of government ethnologist for Papua, a job whose duties included reconciling "native opinion" with British ambitions for the colony's "native development."[5] Given that he would later respond favourably to Marett's recommendation of Jenness for the post, Murray's initial impressions of the young New Zealander were doubtless positive. The two shared similar views on the potentially ameliorative effect that a sympathetic Western presence among non-Western peoples could have and on anthropology's capacity to advance this objective by enlightening the colonizer about the colonized with reliable ethnographic information. Inspired by the positive example of Maori-Pakeha relations in the New Zealand of his youth, Jenness didn't endorse the sentiment, then gaining favour among some anthropologists, that colonized indigenous peoples were best left alone. On the contrary, his opinion came closer to that of Maori politician-anthropologist Apirana Ngata in recognizing selective change as a desirable outcome. The goal of such change, Jenness believed, was neither the outright destruction of traditional culture nor eventual obliteration of native identity: rather, it was to insure that indigenous peoples enjoyed equitable access to the material and political means necessary to participate in the new society emerging around them on their own terms.

The pending expedition intrigued the popular press, the dailies regaling readers with stories of high adventure in exotic locales. "A flood of press-cuttings came in this morning," a skeptical Jenness remarked, "the usual garbled newspaper account half-true half-false."[6] More to his liking was word that England's close-knit anthropological community had received his plans with enthusiasm. Its leading lights were eager to offer advice and encouragement during the hectic months preceding his planned August departure. A late spring visit to Cambridge occasioned interviews with James Frazer, Alfred Haddon, and William Rivers. The latter provided a copy of his recently published paper on the genealogical method, his innovative approach to obtaining "concrete" facts about their societies from local informants.[7] With Haddon, discussion concentrated on physical anthropology, especially the accuracy and usefulness of pigmentation metres and other devices that made up a well-stocked anthropometrist's kit. Famously steadfast in refusing to leave his own study, Frazer nonetheless offered counsel on what he regarded as the most fruitful lines of inquiry, all enumerated in *Questions on the Customs, Beliefs, and Languages of Savages,* his often-revised rival to *Notes and Queries.* Disseminated to foreign correspondents and travellers over the years, the pamphlet's special focus on the evolution of myth, magic, and religion made it a work that "belong[ed] more to the period of the 1880s ... than to the first decade of the twentieth century."[8] Jenness was also introduced to the professor's wife, Elizabeth, the redoubtable Lilly. Apparently more up to date in her interests than was her husband, she gave practical advice on making sound recordings on location in the field. An uncredited news clipping from the time – "The Phonograph for Ethnological Purposes" – notes that Mrs Frazer "has of late years instructed intending travellers in the art of taking phonographic records, and has supplied them with the necessary outfit." She recommended purchase of an Edison Home model, the machine of choice among "all our explorers," along with a gross of blank wax cylinders. How ironic that Mrs Frazer had taken up this specialized calling: by 1910 her hearing had failed entirely.[9]

In London, Charles Seligman happily "opened up the storehouse of his knowledge to me," while back at Oxford, Balfour, an inveterate traveller and experienced field naturalist, gave practical guidance in coping with mundane problems of health, hygiene, and nutrition in the tropics. He undoubtedly also had a point or two to make about collecting artifacts for the Pitt Rivers. Marett, all the while, kept a tolerant eye on the proceedings, receiving periodic updates on specifications and costs of equipment, and serving as a sounding board as his increasingly harried student puzzled through just whose expert counsel to accept on each and every detail.[10]

Jenness planned to travel to Papua by way of New Zealand. Though scheduled to sail from England in mid-August, his departure for Wellington aboard the passenger ship *Ionic* was delayed nearly a month by a tumultuous, nation-wide strike of transport workers. As thousands of soldiers quelled disturbances in the streets and on the piers of London and Liverpool, he waited out the troubles on the tranquil Sussex coast, "reading & idling about" his rented lodgings and trekking over the nearby downs with their "neolithic dewponds & cattleways." Balfour's lectures on technology and prehistory had been the first to whet Jenness's appetite for archaeology, a penchant sharpened further by his "having dug a little in France" during a summer holiday in 1910. This last took place in and around Les Eyzies de Tayac, in the Dordogne, site of the 1868 discovery of 30,000-year-old skeletal remains dubbed Cro-Magnon Man. Over the course of a few weeks, his unauthorized fos-

sicking yielded about eighty stone artifacts from that primal era, all subsequently given into the Pitt Rivers' care.[11] For the moment, however,
the nagging uncertainty of what lay ahead in New Guinea overwhelmed
any pleasure to be had in exploring Sussex's ancient landscape. "My
imagination refuses to soar back to palaeolithic ages," he explained in
a note to Marett, the mix of anxiety and impatience over his delayed departure fuelling a deeply pensive mood.[12] *Ionic* finally embarked from
the London docks on 7 September 1911. Its Wellington-bound passengers would not step ashore again until the closing week of October.

His much-anticipated homecoming after a three-year absence was all-
too-brief. Having arranged to sail for New Guinea by way of Sydney,
Australia, on 10 November, Jenness found himself with merely a fortnight for reunion with family and friends. Regaling Marett with a jovial account of their reception, he described how they "have been to a
mild degree killing the fatted calf – you know it is always the prodigal
son so feasted." His homecoming, and the pending adventure in Papua,
caused a stir outside Wahinga as well, parents and siblings "[showing]
me around as though I were the pithecanthropus himself, till sometimes
I feel like a new Tartarin going forth to do battle with the monsters of a
dark & dangerous continent."[13]

In the midst of this hectic schedule, he found time to meet with Augustus Hamilton, an amateur archaeologist and, since 1903, keeper of
the city's Dominion Museum. This was more than a courtesy call, since
making Hamilton's acquaintance was a politically wise step for a young
man in need of well-placed contacts to realize his ambition of landing an
appropriate position at home once fieldwork was over.[14] It isn't known
whether he also managed to see Elsdon Best, the museum's curator of
ethnology. If the two met, however, it's unlikely Best would have been
encouraging. According to his biographer, the man was so vexed by his
own working conditions, especially the government's reluctance to allocate funds for publishing research findings, that he contemplated destroying his papers rather than bequeathing them to the public trust.[15]
More optimist than realist at this stage of his life, Jenness's hope of
gaining a foothold on the local scene was slow to fade. Just months after
sailing for the Arctic in 1913, a letter to George von Zedlitz inquired
whether Victoria College might be cajoled into establishing a chair in
the discipline. None existed at any of the country's universities to that
point. "If they do," he urged his mentor, "put in an application for me –
you can supply all the necessary references."[16]

Reaching Sydney in good time, Jenness boarded the steamer *Matunga* on 17 November for the outward passage, arriving in the Milne Bay town of Samarai, the port of embarkation for Goodenough Island, fourteen days later. But strike-bound English ports held up the departure of his baggage for Australia just long enough to miss trans-shipment. A six-week delay was anticipated. Having had the foresight to carry a few essentials with him – camera and photographic plates, notebooks, anthropometry kit – at least he didn't have to spend the interim idly.[17] The ship made two brief calls en route to Samarai, first at Port Moresby, Papua's capital since Britain had declared its protectorate over the southern portions of New Guinea in 1884, and then nearby Yule Island, in the Gulf of Papua. Jenness's main business in Port Moresby was introducing himself to Governor Murray. At the second stop, headquarters of the Catholic Missionaries of the Sacred Heart, he met resident priests who treated him to a short course on local customs and mores, their knowledge derived from years of first-hand experience.[18] Missionaries of various affiliations had been making wide-ranging ethnological inquiries in Papua for over half a century, some publishing their findings in leading British journals.[19]

A week's layover in Samarai presented an unexpected opportunity to ply his untested skills with callipers and tapes, courtesy of the district medical officer. Jenness's unwitting subjects were inmates of the local hospital, thirty men in total. Data on stature and cephalic indices were supplemented with photographs and a brief descriptive note on name, age, and home community. Previously, the novice anthropologist had come no closer to a living, breathing specimen than the model Arthur Thomson had employed during a final examination exercise in 1910: "Here you have before you a native," Thomson explained to his unsuspecting pupils, introducing a stark naked man who had just entered the room; "show us the measurements you would take in the allotted five minutes."[20] The Samarai experience made painfully obvious that hours of practice in the laboratory were poor preparation for the real thing. Many of the patients suffered from syphilis and other ailments that dissuaded Jenness from making any but the most superficial measurements and he appealed to his supervisor's discretion in reporting on the episode to Thomson; "Tell [him] not to be too critical over my measurements," he implored Marett; "The long frizzy hair makes it difficult to be correct within a millimetre or so & one is sometimes puzzled how much to allow for the hair."[21]

A pearl trader named Veribeli ferried Jenness over the journey's last leg to Goodenough Island, departing Samarai on 8 December. Rounding

On a Bwaidokan veranda, Goodenough Island, New Guinea, 1912. Left to right: Grace and Diamond Jenness, May (with Diamond Allan), and Rev. Andrew Ballantyne. Photo courtesy of R.R. Ballantyne family, Dunedin, New Zealand

East Cape, the skipper steered his cutter northward into Goodenough Bay, the body of water that separates Papua's southeastern mainland from the mountainous islands of the D'Entrecasteaux archipelago, the first of several island clusters mariners meet on sailing outward into the southern reaches of the Solomon Sea. Named for the French navigator who recorded their position in 1793,[22] the group consists of three large islands, Fergusson, Goodenough, and Normanby, and numerous smaller ones, the main being Dobu and Sanaroa. Although volcanic in origin, none has an active volcano. Sulphurous hot springs and geysers are common, doubtless reminding Jenness of Rotorua and its environs, an area of thermal activity south of Auckland that Maori have long regarded as sacred. The most northerly island of the chain, Goodenough features spectacular topography, its steep, cloud-enshrouded central ranges towering 8,000 feet above the grass and forest-covered plains and mangrove swamps of the coastal zone. Lesser peaks on its southern and northwestern shores present a similarly dramatic aspect, rising directly from the sea and leading the gold prospectors, labour recruiters, itinerant traders, and other Europeans who arrived after British administrator William MacGregor initiated regular contacts in 1888 to limit their activities to the more accessible (and populous) low-lying areas.

The interior remained unknown to all but a few outsiders, its rugged terrain providing an effective barrier against periodic police patrols and other incursions of colonial authority.[23]

Safely navigating the treacherous reefs and currents off southeastern Goodenough, Veribeli landed his passenger at the hamlet of Wailagi on 11 December. Its Methodist mission, founded in 1898, was the island's only permanent European establishment and for the past five years had been home to Jenness's sister May and her husband, Andrew Ballantyne. The occasion marked the first meeting of the brothers-in-law, as Andrew's lone visit to New Zealand had occurred while Diamond was at Oxford. They lodged their guest in the manse, a modest, wooden building, with obligatory veranda. Although a far cry from the fabled solitude of the ethnographer's tent, its location in the heart of the populous Bwaidoka district afforded a close-up view of the passing scene. The arrangement of native dwellings achieved much the same purpose, a small cluster of houses fronting on a stone tuvaka, or platform, from which residents kept close watch on their neighbours' comings and goings.[24] No less importantly, the mission's few European amenities offered Jenness respite from the physical and cultural strangeness of the world he had entered. Thus ensconced, his initiation into the anthropological tribe was to begin at long last. He was two months shy of his twenty-sixth birthday.

AN OXFORD SKEPTIC

Jenness's Goodenough research was a product of its time, reflecting the state of British anthropology itself, deftly balanced between the twilight of speculative evolutionism and the dawning of a more empirically grounded discipline. This is apparent in his research plan prepared some months before.[25] Step one was to survey the D'Entrecasteaux group, charting the geographic distribution of its peoples and identifying their distinguishing racial, linguistic, and cultural features. This type of survey was an early form of fieldwork whose purpose was to establish boundaries between so-called culture areas and assess the supposed degree of evolutionary advance of their inhabitants. Haddon and Charles Seligman had conducted such an investigation in parts of British New Guinea, a region that included the Trobriands, D'Entrecasteaux, and other Solomon Sea archipelagos. They concluded that these islanders, together with peoples of the adjacent mainland shores, shared enough traits in common to warrant grouping them together into a single cultural province of fishers and farmers which they named the Massim.[26] Reasoning along similar lines, Jenness found that the inhabitants of Goodenough and portions of nearby Fergusson Island, some twenty miles across Moresby Strait, constituted a subdivision of the Massim, the Northern D'Entrecasteaux. Linguistic and cultural features distinguished them from the Dobuans of the archipelago's southern reaches.[27]

By the turn of the century, this type of areal reconnaissance had begun giving way to a different form of investigation, one Haddon dubbed the "intensive study of limited areas." The new strategy called for studying social and cultural life in far greater depth than surveys allowed, "'coax[ing] out of the native by patient sympathy' the deeper meaning of the material collected."[28] Heeding this example, Jenness's second step was to make what he called a "special study" of Goodenough and north Fergusson, learning the language and using it to compile a detailed record of local customs and traditions.[29] But while honouring the spirit of Haddon's message, in practice, his first attempt to apply it fell short. Like virtually every novice ethnographer, regardless of time period, he had to feel his way through what invariably turns out to be physically, emotionally, and intellectually demanding work for which seminars, reading, and the coaching of ethnographic mentors are insufficient preparation. Compounding the problem, anthropologists tend to become their own harshest critics. Jenness was no exception. He chided himself over the slowness with which he learned to speak Bwaidokan, over the myriad details of everyday life that went unrecorded or, worse, may have gone unnoticed altogether, and he demeaned the finished product of his labours, however factually "correct," as paltry, little more than a "mere skeleton." "Often I think of it as a dismal failure," he confessed to Marett; but "I was young and inexperienced, willing enough to do all I could find to do, but not knowing what to do." A dozen years after Oxford published *The Northern D'Entrecasteaux,* an account of Goodenough's society and culture, Berkeley anthropologist Alfred Kroeber wrote to its author with high praise, describing the book's treatment of Goodenough society as "compact, pregnant and well rounded ... easily one of the best pieces ... extant on Melanesia." By then immersed in North American research, a modest Jenness replied that he had all but forgotten the book's very existence.[30]

At the start of the twentieth century, Goodenough islanders, like most Massim peoples, were horticulturalists, cultivating staples such as yams, bananas, coconuts, and taro. Pig husbandry, reef fishing, and hunting for birds, wild pigs, and kangaroos supplemented the diet. Small hamlets, each home to a few extended families, were dispersed around the landscape, not just in fertile areas along the shores but in the forested

Fauia village, Goodenough Island, New Guinea, 1912. D. Jenness; © Pitt
Rivers Museum, University of Oxford, 810206

hills and rugged mountainous terrain up to several thousand feet above
sea level. Jenness estimated that half the population resided in the up-
lands at the time of his stay, some making gardens on the slopes to
the effective limit of cultivation, around 4,000 feet. Bound by common
culture and language, the people nevertheless ascribed important differences among themselves on the basis of locality, the sharpest distinction being drawn between those living on the coastal plains and those
at higher elevations. Much as Margaret Mead would later describe in
her accounts of the Manus islanders, these differences found expression
in pejorative, stereotyped attitudes and beliefs that influenced social
relations. To coast dwellers, mountain people feared the sea and were
ignorant of fishing, preferring to hunt animals, including the snake, a
creature toward which there is "not so much a taboo ... as an instinctive
horror and loathing." Mountain dwellers ridiculed their lowland neighbours' dread of snakes and of the high country itself. Each expected the
worst of the other and so refrained from entering unknown territory
to avoid misfortune, or even death, at the hands of the "fierce cannibal
tribes" allegedly resident there.[31] Jenness figured that the location of
many hamlets on remote slopes afforded a measure of protection from

In Twilight and in Dawn

hostile neighbours as well as from the occasional depredations of sea-borne marauders from North Fergusson or the Dobuan territory beyond.[32]

If he entertained romantic illusions beforehand that he had entered a tropical paradise, its inhabitants Rousseauian noble savages feasting on nature's bounty and living free of civilization's constraints, the anthropologist's first days in the field disabused him of such fantasy. On arrival, the islanders were in the throes of drought-induced famine. Dry spells occur periodically in the Massim, but only rarely lead to widespread hunger from crop failure.[33] This time, conditions in low-lying districts, including the Bwaidokan area, were severe enough to produce "great dislocations in the ordinary mode of life."[34] With higher population densities, poorer soils, and less abundant game than existed at higher elevations, "many of the natives have been sorely pressed, & some of the children & old folks would certainly have died had we not fed them" from mission stores.[35] Research got off to a slow start in consequence as the people were more concerned with filling their bellies than helping to fill the anthropologist's notebooks. Jenness joined Ballantyne in relieving the most destitute cases with rations of rice and biscuits. The obligation to feed students attending the Wesleyan school added to the strain on mission stocks, necessitating trading and foraging expeditions to outlying areas in hopes of obtaining garden produce and fresh meat for consumption back in Wailagi. These forays rarely succeeded: "For several days on end we scoured the villages far & near and some days we managed to buy scarcely enough for a single meal. In our own stores flour, butter, dripping etc were exhausted. When the [mission] schooner arrived [in early May] we had 3 small tins of meat & 6 biscuits to go on with – and then for some days the gun had eked out the supplies."[36] Even the returning rains did little to ease the situation, at least in the short run, as people turned from scrounging food to nurturing their slowly rebounding gardens with great diligence. "Whether this will tide the natives over till the next yam harvest seems uncertain," Jenness reported in late July; "at present they are gardening every spare moment of their time ... Why did I not come here a year earlier? – it would have made anthropologizing much easier."[37]

However understandable, this complaint was misplaced since, as Australian anthropologist Michael Young discovered on Goodenough in the late 1960s, a veritable "food and hunger fixation" lay at the core of local ethos.[38] Young traced the origins of food-related beliefs and practices to enduring anxieties about a "fickle environment," describing customs such as competitive yam exchanges as "institutionalized preparedness for drought and famine." Finding that islanders saw famine as the outcome of human (ill)-will brought to bear through magic – the "sorcery of scourge," in his alliterative phrasing – he concluded that dietary staples loomed large in the dynamics of social control, serving as "political resources" affecting both individual behaviour and inter-community relations. Appropriately, the wamo, or yam, symbolized Goodenough society itself.[39]

Jenness did notice that people "are especially sensitive on all questions relating to food," but he missed the wider significance of their preoccupation, here and there describing some of its manifestations while failing to grasp the bigger picture. This is illustrated in anecdotes about feeding pupils at the Wailagi mission, anecdotes he regarded as more humorous (or peculiar) than revealing of deeper meaning. In one he writes of students asking Ballantyne "to reduce their daily ration of food, for 'if we eat a great deal now ... our stomachs will become distended; then when a famine comes how shall we fill them?'"[40] In another, a child, arriving late at mealtime, finds his share consumed by other students. But "Instead of approaching the missionary and asking for more, the boy would go off to his hamlet ... and stay there for several weeks."[41] Put bluntly, being without food was a cause of personal shame, calling attention to another's hunger, a form of insult. At the community level, famine signalled doom, the very "shedding of sociality and culture" itself.[42] The distress Jenness witnessed at Bwaidoka and elsewhere was real enough. What he did not comprehend were the lengths to which individuals would go to deny their own hunger, since failing to do so threatened their autonomy and opened them to the coercive influence of others. Worse still, he imagined they might ultimately become food themselves, Goodenough's people having an "evil reputation" as "amongst the worst cannibals in Papua."[43]

Beyond intermittent food shortages and the political tensions they fostered, the population was also beset by health problems. Most common were yaws and related skin disorders, infections that, without penicillin, often result in debilitating limb deformities. The mission served as the island's clinic where regular "hospital work" ranged from treating accident and burn victims to nursing patients suffering with malaria and other maladies.[44] The ravages of European-introduced diseases, many like syphilis already endemic along Papua's mainland coast, were only beginning to be felt in the northern D'Entrecasteaux. Since relatively few whites had set foot on the islands up to this point, such illnesses were mainly imported by returning migrant labourers. All too often, these boys and young men came back from the colony's mines and plantations bringing pathogens along with metal knives, tobacco, and other "treasures of our civilization."[45]

On top of tending to others' ailments, Jenness had to contend with several of his own. Daily temperatures averaging in the mid-eighties,

In Twilight and in Dawn

and unrelenting high humidity, meant that the simplest cuts and scrapes festered and ulcerated unless treated immediately with antiseptic. Even then, infections were nearly unavoidable. He suffered repeatedly from sores, rashes, and other "natural plagues of this country," and during one five-week stretch was laid up with skin ulcers and boils acquired while trekking along rough mountain trails through spear grass and over razor-sharp lava outcroppings. Compounding these problems, he contracted malaria soon after arrival. Endemic throughout the Massim, malaria was a more serious affliction for Papua's small European population than among its native inhabitants.[46] The two eldest of the Ballantynes' four children, Wanini Pearl and Edmund Lancelot, had already succumbed to the scourge. Their father eventually did so as well, in 1915, at the age of thirty-nine.[47] It was the hope of preventing a similar destiny for their young son Diamond Allan that prompted his mother's New Zealand furlough in early 1912, the couple wisely electing to leave the baby in the care of family at Waihinga. Before her departure, May was similarly concerned for her brother's welfare, keeping him under wraps in the manse for days at a time whenever he suffered bouts of ague.[48]

Combined with the stress of first-time fieldwork, these ailments exacted a toll on Jenness's psychological state. Skirting the issue in reports to Marett, a single letter to Marius Barbeau is less guarded. Written four months into the research, it reveals an underlying loneliness and sense of isolation. Beyond the familiar company at Wailagi, he told his Oxford chum, the nearest whites, another missionary couple, were forty miles away on Normanby Island. "Probably a trader's boat is hovering about the coast," he added, "but we know of none." Continuing in a similar vein, he lamented the long intervals between mails, sometimes three months from one to the next, and the haphazard route precious letters from home took in reaching Goodenough, carried by itinerant traders plying the sea lanes connecting Samarai with the islands beyond. These fixations are classic signs of culture shock, an unrecognized phenomenon at the time, yet a common side-effect of immersion in unfamiliar surroundings. Admitting that the experience so far "is not altogether roses & honey," Jenness forced himself to put the best face on an obviously trying situation: "malgré tout," he closed on an ingenuous note, "I am having a great time. The natives are interesting, fauna & flora are fascinating, there is always plenty to do."[49]

Andrew Ballantyne probably knew more about the place and its people than any other European, having spent a great deal of time visiting even the most remote mountain villages while pursuing his pastoral duties. As valuable as his knowledge of geography and customs surely was, his familiarity with the widely used Bwaidokan dialect was an even greater asset. If born of practical considerations, his interests also had a scholarly side, his off-duty hours given to formal studies of grammar and philology. By teaching a few parishioners to write their language using "a plain phonetic script," a system assigning "continental value" to each consonant and English equivalents to vowels, he encouraged the more skilled of them to transcribe myths, songs, and other oral traditions. A young lad, "our native boy" Pita Ludeba, demonstrated an exceptional talent for quick and accurate transcription, a qualification that earned him de facto status as research assistant to both Ballantyne and Jenness.[50] The missionary translated a good many of these texts into English, a project May Ballantyne would complete following her husband's unexpected death.

Jenness's own progress with Bwaidokan speech was painfully slow, the process of learning an unwritten language striking him as altogether different from learning French or Greek. By the end of his sojourn he had mastered enough of the dialect to engage in simple conversation. Yet the long months devoted to the effort were dogged by frustration and self-doubts, doubts worsened by his cognizance of the recent Cambridge dictum, spelled out that very year in the newest edition of *Notes and Queries*. In Rivers's words, anthropologists with facility in local speech can, in concert with due attention to method, produce "work of enormously higher value than anything which the world has yet seen." "Do you find the study of the language very difficult?" Jenness meekly inquired of Barbeau, who was then in the midst of research among the Iroquoian-speaking Wyandot Indians for the Geological Survey of Canada.[51]

Initially agreeing to act as interpreter, it wasn't long before Ballantyne became more involved in his brother-in-law's research, helping him conduct interviews and translating the texts of stories and songs recorded with the Edison phonograph. "I hope you & Mr Balfour & the rest of the Committee will have no objection," Jenness wrote to Marett early in the proceedings, "but as a large part of my information & results will be derived through [Ballantyne] indirectly if not directly, it was only fair to him that he should share the credit of them – if any there be ... He seems fairly critical in his methods & is broad-minded enough," he added, mindful of the crucial connection between the scientific value of ethnographic data and the means employed to collect them.[52] Two major works eventually appeared under the in-laws' joint authorship, posthumously in Ballantyne's case. Whereas *The Northern D'Entrecasteaux* was largely the product of Jenness's investigations, *Language, Mythology and*

Songs of Bwaidoga was a true collaboration, the anthropologist contributing a grammar, lexicon, and a hundred manuscript pages of songs and stories transcribed in the "Bwaidogan tongue," the missionary providing textual translations. Initially serialized in the *Journal of the Polynesian Society*, the latter work was subsequently reissued in book form.[53]

Beyond the expediency of their partnership, Jenness believed that he owed the measure of acceptance he enjoyed at Bwaidoka and elsewhere to his personal relationship with Ballantyne and the mission. In his estimation, the islanders regarded clerics more favourably than other newcomers, namely traders who doubled as labour recruiters – so-called "blackbirders" – and colonial officials, especially the police officers whose visits sometimes ended tragically for members of the local population.[54] "I am not very prejudiced for or against missions," Jenness observed of the situation, "but it is a plain fact that here on Goodenough and Ferguson the name 'missionali' serves as a passport everywhere. In many villages at the least suspicion of your being a government officer or a trader ... the natives will all run away."[55] Travelling companions frequently introduced him around as the minister's kinsman, an introduction, Jenness claimed, that insured a friendly reception, even in places where whites were regarded with misgiving and fear.[56]

The Oxford committee voiced no opposition to the collaboration, but such arrangements were not without their critics. For decades past – a period of "epistolary ethnography," in George Stocking's words – armchair anthropologists had regularly enlisted the aid of missionaries in obtaining information on peoples in remote corners of the globe.[57] But by the mid- to late teens, the rising generation of professionally minded British ethnographers had begun distancing themselves from their former partners, a slow but steady parting of the ways pushed along by their insistence that only academically trained researchers were properly qualified to produce the reliable facts their modernizing discipline now demanded. The once-esteemed work by missionaries was increasingly dismissed as amateurish and biased. Making a bad situation worse, the impetus behind their ethnography also fell into question, their motivations no longer seen to lie with advancing knowledge or even with encouraging their compatriots to view tribal peoples in a sympathetic light. Baser purposes were suspected, with both cleric and colonial official held to be turning to the "crushing machinery of European law and moral regulations" to subvert native polity, and ultimately to eradicate indigenous culture altogether, all in the name of inculcating Christian civilization.[58]

While expedient, the decision to collaborate with Ballantyne eventually caught up with Jenness, garnering "some rather caustic remarks" in the pages of Bronislaw Malinowski's classic study of Trobriand society,

Argonauts of the Western Pacific.[59] In a long footnote, the author cites two illustrative passages in *The Northern D'Entrecasteaux* – one dismissive of the efficacy of traditional death rituals, the other making light of magical means for controlling weather and crops – to make his case that Jenness had all but abandoned empiricism for the missionary's narrow mindset. This, Malinowski contended, led Jenness to treat Goodenough belief and practice with contempt and thus to disregard the discipline's modern-day objective of getting at the native point of view. "It is strange to find a trained ethnologist, confessing that old, time-honoured rites have no meaning," Malinowski wrote in sharp rebuke; "And one might feel tempted to ask: for *whom* it is that these customs have no meaning, for the natives or for the writers ... ?" Effectively chastising a fellow anthropologist for having dismissed tribal beliefs on the basis of Western prejudice, the charge was nothing less than "tampering" with the "one authority that now binds the natives ... their own tribal tradition."[60]

The stridency of his public views aside, Malinowski was not averse to consulting missionaries on ethnographic matters himself, at least not during the mid-teens when he was immersed in his own Massim fieldwork. His relationship with New Zealander M.K. Gilmour, the so-called "Grand Inquisitor of the Methodist Mission," whose long career began in 1901 on the main Trobriand island of Kiriwina, warrants particular mention. Meeting him for the first time in 1915, Malinowski was impressed with the man's knowledge of Trobriand language and his deep if "unsympathetic" understanding of local customs, describing him as "Intelligent, energetic, keen, with a mentally broad outlook and a certain amount of culture ... [and] a really good understanding of the native mind (limited by Missionarism)." He also made very good use of what was to be Gilmour's only substantive contribution to the anthropological literature, the first published account of one of the region's most distinctive social institutions: the complex overseas trade network linking various of the northern Massim archipelagos. Employing the article, issued as part of the colony's *Annual Report for 1904*, as a guide in his own investigations, Malinowski regarded the work as "substantially correct, and on the whole formulated with precision" when considered in the light of evidence he himself had gathered. With the appearance of his pioneering *Argonauts*, this ritualized system of exchange, known as *kula*, gained central importance in modern anthropological theory and, in the process, a kind of immortality in disciplinary history.[61]

Gilmour played a role in Jenness's research as well. The two met in early 1912 when Jenness accompanied Ballantyne to the Methodist regional headquarters on Normanby Island. Gilmour had been in charge of the station there for several years and his familiarity with southern D'Entrecasteaux society rivalled his knowledge of the Trobrianders. He offered his young compatriot a good deal of ethnographic background on the whole of the region, information Jenness eventually used in setting his growing stock of observations on Bwaidokan political authority, totemism, and other subjects into a broader, comparative perspective. Indeed, he was so swayed by the missionary's competence, and the thoroughness of his understanding of Kiriwinian society in particular, that he came to suspect some of Seligman's earlier conclusions about the northern Massim, now in print, might well be wrong. Not wanting to press the issue too far, Jenness asked Marett to keep his opinion on the matter out of general circulation.[62]

Once May and baby Diamond had departed for home, the brothers-in-law settled into a regular routine of interviewing those "who best know the customs," sometimes consulting two or three men – apparently always men – at once. Jenness found Frazer's *Questions* "immensely useful" in organizing the work, if only in providing "broad lines of enquiry."[63] He also experimented with Rivers's genealogical method, compiling charts outlining family relationships and totemic affiliations, key elements of social organization, but came to feel that it was ineffective as a means to dig deep into Bwaidokan social history as people seemed capable only of "vague recollection" of their grandparents' generation, and literally nothing beyond that.[64] He ventured no explanation of why this might be so, although the facile dismissal suggests a compelling Eurocentric bias toward the fundamental nature of history itself. More classicist than anthropologist at this early point in his career, he doubtless expected, but ultimately failed to discover, some equivalent, however archaic in form, to the traditional western canon, with its authoritative roots in the written word. Oddly enough, Rivers's claim for the pioneering technique, in fact its "greatest merit," lay with its presumed capacity to probe the past in order to lay bare the character of indigenous institutions and values. The need to do this, he argued in the original 1910 paper, stemmed from the near-impossibility of finding tribal peoples whose cultures had not already been affected by western ideas and practices.[65] With sustained European contact dating back no more than a dozen years, however, indigenous ways were still very much in evidence on Goodenough Island, even among those living closest to the Wailagi mission.

Six months into the fieldwork, Jenness announced that he was ready to "operate farther afield," as he and Ballantyne were satisfied that they had "broken the back of investigations into native Bwaidogan life."[66] As a result, he took to "tramping far and near" through the districts beyond the mission compound, sometimes returning to places the two men had visited together previously, sometimes seeking out spots as yet unknown to him. Having picked up enough Bwaidokan to get along reasonably well on his own, he even attempted to take notes on totems and other complex topics, though not without his brother-in-law "taking pains to check" afterwards.[67] These jaunts also allowed him to indulge a new-found interest in string figures, more popularly known as cat's cradles. He recorded nearly fifty variations during his travels, employing a notational system invented by Rivers and Haddon during their investigations in the Torres Straits. The Cambridge colleagues attributed theoretical significance to such figures, believing they showed that "some aspects of 'savage' culture were both clever and intricate," a hard-won supposition in an intellectual context still steeped in racist evolutionary thought.[68] Beyond whatever intellectual fascination the game held for him, Jenness's knowledge of cat's cradles was a boon to fieldwork, serving to break the ice with young and old wherever he travelled. As Kathleen Haddon remarked of her father, for whom string figures became a "pet obsession," "who could suspect of guile a man who sits among children playing with a piece of string?"[69]

As winter approached, opportunity arose to join a party of Wagifans, "the most progressive of all the Goodenough folk," in sailing around the island in their newly built canoes. The two-week trip took them to numerous villages, some previously unseen by any European. A native constable named Matagewana – "rather a friend of mine, possessing more individuality & initiative than any native I know" – handled his introduction to the voyagers. "Living & sleeping with them the barriers appeared to be broken down," Jenness recounted delightedly, his companions, no less those they met along the way "[speaking] quite freely of their customs – in fact [taking] pains to point them out ... Even in new villages the natives – especially the old men – give me a good reception." "I think this proves [they] have confidence in me & regard me more as one of themselves," he concluded, obviously proud of his singular accomplishment.[70] These two weeks yielded the most personally rewarding results of the entire year's research, and arguably the most significant as well, providing the aspiring ethnographer with a taste, however fleeting, of what would soon gain widespread recognition as the ultimate goal of modern fieldwork: in Malinowski's words, "to grasp the native's point of view, his relation to life, to realise *his* vision of *his* world."[71] "I seemed to get right down into native life," Jenness enthused. "It was weird to sit in the circle round the fire – with 20 or 30 natives about me swaying their heads and bodies to the tune of some mournful chant."[72] A similar scene unfolded shortly thereafter, this time among travellers from the Faiyavi district, who had ventured across

Moresby Strait to Fergusson Island in search of betel nut, a widely used intoxicant. Camped on a desolate beach one evening, the anthropologist found himself, along with other bachelors, being instructed in the "'art of love' – the magic rites and incantations for winning a maiden's heart," life lessons proffered by their married companions. The fireside proceedings lasted into the wee hours.[73] Once back at the mission, he engaged the services of an old man willing to perform courting songs for the phonograph: "had to turn all the women & girls out" in consequence, "& then he sang so low that it was almost inaudible."[74]

In prefatory remarks to *The Northern D'Entrecasteaux,* Marett lauded his pupil's resourcefulness in the field, pronouncing "Touring ... the ideal method of anthropological research."[75] What Marett, a home-bound scholar, failed to appreciate was that the method afforded a greater advantage than simply broadening the field for harvesting dry sociological facts. More importantly, it opened the door to experiencing first-hand the sights and sounds and smells of daily existence, to participation in both ordinary and extraordinary activities, to putting "flesh and blood" on the "skeleton" of "tribal constitution."[76] This was hardly possible from the confines of a mission-house veranda. Ethnographers before the First World War rarely employed what is now called participant-observation as a deliberate research strategy, though like Jenness, there were those who were led to it by circumstances. However intriguing these glimpses of what Malinowski ponderously dubbed "the imponderabilia of actual life," Jenness was ambivalent about them at the time, seemingly unconvinced of the connection between these experiences and the scientific work at hand. Cautiously broaching the subject, he confided to his tutor that "Sometimes I fear I have not got into the real native life – it all seems too open & straight-forward ... I can't think 'native' tho' as I suppose one ought to, much as I try. Oxford scepticism is too much for me."[77] A year later in the Arctic, these doubts would begin to vanish.

September brought the most arduous of his Goodenough tours, an excursion to hamlets in the sparsely populated interior ranges of Mounts Tukekela and Madawana. Few of their residents had ever met Europeans face to face, which had prompted the trip. The journey began at the coastal village of Belebele where two young men, Matakoi and Sali, were engaged as guides and porters. The party met with peaceful receptions along the route, yet the sight of a white man bewildered shy villagers. At Naila, a hamlet perched some 2,000 feet above the sea, Jenness's "two boys" were barraged with questions about their companion:

how he "came to speak their language and where had [he] learned their games." Within a short while, some skilfully performed cat's cradles proved Kathleen Haddon's assertion: "a laughing crowd [surrounded] me, thronging so close that I felt like the robber baron when the rats invaded his castle."[78] The following morning, he accompanied hunters into Mt Madawana's upper reaches in search of kangaroos, a day-long climb beyond the mountain's forested zone to the grassy and rock-strewn summit, 5,000 feet above the hamlet. A parting offer to reciprocate his hosts' hospitality in Bwaidoka went untaken; "Later I found out the reason: [the hamlet chief and his son] were afraid that they might be killed and eaten in the hostile villages that lay between them and the coast."[79]

Not long after his mountain-climbing adventure, a serious relapse of malaria confined Jenness to the manse for a second time. Planned trips to the nearby Trobriands and Amphletts were now out of the question, as was more strenuous trekking to other out-of-the-way districts on Goodenough. Instead, the weeks leading up to his December departure were spent sorting through notes, fending off plagues of mosquitoes, and, most importantly, regaining strength for the voyage home to New Zealand.

CHAPTER FOUR

Chance and Necessity,
1913–1914

FOR CANADA AND FOR SCIENCE

When he reached New Zealand in the waning days of 1912, Jenness learned that it had been a tumultuous year at home, marked by bloody labour disputes and the defeat of the long-serving Liberal government. For the time being, his malarial attacks were behind him, evident in the energy with which he turned to drafting his report to Oxford. In two months he had written 140 manuscript pages of the "ordinary sociological treatise" and organized material into appendices on genealogical relationships and hamlet totems. But not everything went smoothly: in early March Wellington newspapers announced that the ss *Turakina* had burned and gone aground near Rio de Janeiro. It was carrying nearly the whole of his year's collections back to England: ethnographic artifacts for the Pitt Rivers Museum, the sound recordings he had been at great pains to make, some seven hundred butterflies obtained on behalf of an Oxford naturalist, and the field equipment that the committee for anthropology had furnished. By good fortune, all but the natural history specimens survived the disaster, although many months of uncertainty were to pass before word of the shipment's salvage finally reached him.[1]

Around this same time, another equally unexpected development occurred: he received a telegram from Edward Sapir, chief of the Anthropological Division of the Geological Survey of Canada. Its terse message read: "Will you join Stefansson Arctic Expedition and study Eskimos for three years? Reply collect." This was quickly followed by a second: "All expenses paid from New Zealand, $500 per year in field, salary when work up results. If accept, cable, sail Victoria, B.C. Send instructions general delivery. Sapir."[2]

The sender's name was vaguely familiar, but Jenness knew nothing of Vihljalmur Stefansson or of his plans to lead an expedition into the Arctic. Only later did he learn that his friend Marius Barbeau had recommended him for the job, prompted by inquiries from Robert Marett and Wilson Wallis about the prospects of finding him employment somewhere in Canada.[3] In the meantime, he hadn't the slightest idea of how his name had come to the attention of anthropologists and explorers half a world away, let alone what his response to them should be. What qualifications, or interest, did he have for northern fieldwork, particularly now that his time in the D'Entrecasxteaux had whetted his appetite for more of the same? Having lived the better part of his life in temperate climates and having experienced snow exactly once,[4] an opportunity to live and work in the remotest part of Canada must have struck him as daunting, if not preposterous. All things considered, Diamond Jenness was anything but a natural for arctic exploration.

Yet odder things happen, especially to someone whose professional aspirations stood little hope of being realized in a country where anthropology remained firmly in the hands of the Percy Smiths and Edward Tregears of the tightly knit Polynesian Society circle. Within a week he cabled acceptance. Borrowing the cost of a one-way passage from his father – by now an irksome habit, it would seem – he sailed from Auckland on 18 April, reaching Canada twelve days later.[5] Barely two months had elapsed between the time Sapir's initial message was received and its recipient stepped off the ship in Victoria, British Columbia, the expedition's port of embarkation.

The long ocean crossing was a time for second guessing, for brooding over the decision's short and long term implications: the wisdom of throwing in his lot with Stefansson – little more than a name at this point – in a part of the world both brutal and unforgiving; the consequences of setting aside Pacific ethnology, at least for the time being; the uncertainties over where all of this might ultimately lead. He worried that a prolonged absence in the Arctic would delay his final report on Papuan society and language. Worse still, he worried that such a delay amounted to failing Oxford and those, above all his parents, who had scrambled to fund his fieldwork in the first place. And what of his own ambitions and hopes? If there really were a chance to build a career around fresh researches in New Guinea, publishing on the D'Entrecasteaux was a crucial first step in that direction, one that would establish his credentials and thereby improve the odds of securing a coveted appointment at Victoria College, or at one of New Zealand's other universities, should a position materialize.

In other respects, he was cautiously optimistic that what lay ahead might be a ticket to bigger and better things in Canada, perhaps a permanent posting at the Geological Survey once the expedition was over. Sapir hadn't encouraged, or even hinted at, such a possibility, offering only a modest annual salary, plus living expenses in the field and a small stipend afterwards for writing up the results at survey headquarters in Ottawa. But at a time when his best shot at gainful employment in New Zealand was finding an ordinary schoolteacher's position, the chance that one thing might lead to another abroad made the risk worth taking.[6] The die was cast. And while he had no way of knowing it at the time, the decision would lead him on an arduous passage into professional anthropology, and into a new career, and life, far from the familiar surroundings of home. The first of his compatriots to acquire university training in the young discipline, Jenness was to become the first of New Zealand's many expatriate anthropologists as well.

Among circumpolar nations, Canada proved slow to embark on scientific exploration of its vast Arctic territories. Britain's Royal Navy, obsessed for generations with finding a polar sea route to Asia, laid much of the groundwork. By the mid-nineteenth century, however, Americans, Germans, and Norwegians had emerged as major players in virtually every branch of northern science and continued as such for the next fifty years. Anthropology was no exception. Franz Boas's formative field experience, the year (1883–84) he spent with Baffin Island Inuit around Cumberland Sound, is the best-known case in point. A landmark in disciplinary history, as in the man's long and highly influential career, several scientific institutions in his native Germany had sponsored his pioneering research, while a German geophysical expedition, sailing under the banner of the inaugural International Polar Year (in which Canada did not participate), had ferried him northward.[7] Afterward, and despite his best efforts, Boas was unable to convince Ottawa to provide even modest support to further his path-breaking investigations. Having designed an ambitious follow-up project to ascertain Inuit-Indian affinities across the continent's northern tier, he approached the Geological Survey for funding in 1886 but came away with nothing more than an offer of help in reaching Hudson Bay.[8] Replying to Boas's inquiry, Robert Bell, the survey's assistant director, captured the spirit of the moment: "Everything done by members of our Govt. (or equally if done by their Departments) is tinged with our home politics. Politicians in Canada don't care for science enough to do anything purely for its own sake," the climate of opinion among them favouring investments beneficial to commercial and industrial development alone.[9] More than two decades were to pass before anything resembling systematic anthropological research among Canadian Inuit began in earnest. Even then, as Jenness learned soon enough, the government's commitment to its organization and funding was neither generous, nor reliable.

Northern anthropology was not singled out for special treatment. In fact, the country's sitting parliamentarians and ranking bureaucrats showed little inclination to promote scientific research on any of the country's Aboriginal populations. From 1884 to 1909 they ignored repeated calls from learned societies, both domestic and foreign, to establish a publically endowed bureau to mount a systematic, Dominion-wide anthropological survey.[10] What little organized activity occurred in the interim was largely due to special committees operating under British Association auspices and to the occasional Geological Survey field worker permitted to study the natives as a sideline. This work, none of it in the Arctic, was perennially underfunded and understaffed, and, with the exception of Boas's involvement, was the bailiwick of avocational ethnologists and archaeologists. In the meantime, museums in the United States and Europe lavished money on Canadian projects, carting off a wealth of artifacts in the process. Ottawa's only concession, initiated in 1890, was an annual vote of $500 to purchase ethnographic specimens for the Geological Survey's natural history collection. After five years, even that was rescinded, ostensibly for reasons of economy.[11]

Anthropology's situation eventually improved, but not because politicians had a change of heart about the field or intended to use ethnographic knowledge to inform the conduct of native affairs, something advocates had hoped would happen when they began campaigning for public support.[12] Rather, its fortunes rose on a rising tide of nationalism in the early 1900s. Prime Minister Sir Wilfrid Laurier's Liberal government engendered this mood with policies aimed at expanding Canadian economic and territorial interests westward and northward, and shoring up state sovereignty. The venerable Geological Survey played a leading part, its activities increasingly devoted to the work of "rolling back [the country's] frontiers," mapping wilderness lands and waters, exploring for resources, and showing the flag where territorial claims were in dispute, as they were in the Arctic. Interior Minister Clifford Sifton reinforced these priorities by reorganizing the survey in 1907: once a quasi-independent agency, it became a branch of the newly created Department of Mines. Almost as an afterthought, the legislation that set up the new department included anthropology among its responsibilities, as well as palaeontology, botany, and zoology.[13]

Changes to the Geological Survey's mandate were meant to contribute to obtaining a "complete and exact knowledge" of the country's natural history. The Victoria Memorial Museum, forerunner of what became the National Museum of Canada in 1927 but still on the drawing board at the time, was to serve as repository of that knowledge and the showplace of Canadian progress.[14] Named survey director in 1907, geologist Reginald W. Brock recommended that an anthropological branch be established and an academically trained anthropologist put in charge to initiate research and to build a representative ethnological collection. Appealing to his superiors' nationalist sensibilities, he pointed to the fact that foreign museums had long been the principle beneficiaries of artifact collecting on Canadian soil, leaving the country poorer.[15] On a different plane, he referred to the urgency then motivating anthropological work among peoples whose traditional cultures were rapidly disappearing. Investigations "must be undertaken at once or it will be too late," he argued, knowledge would be "lost forever ... [with] future generations of Canadians ... unable to obtain reliable data concerning the native races of their country."[16] Armed with supporting resolutions from the Canadian branch of the Archaeological Society of America, the British Association for the Advancement of Science, and the Royal Society of Canada, all offered as unequivocal evidence that "public opinion is awakening to the urgency, importance, and value of this work," Brock succeeded in rescuing anthropology from its former "spasmodic and secondary" state.[17]

The Anthropological Division's founding in 1910 gave cause for optimism as Ottawa committed money to implement systematic and comprehensive research, hire qualified staff, and elevate the science to professional standing. By the time Jenness came on the scene, its research program was in high gear, its work organized into separate sections for ethnology and linguistics, archaeology, and physical anthropology, its six permanent and six temporary employees deployed from the Maritime provinces to Vancouver Island. The coming expedition represented welcome expansion in an important new direction.

At the age of thirty-four, Manitoba-born Vilhjalmur Stafansson was already a veteran explorer and anthropologist, having recently returned from a four-year expedition to the western Arctic in 1912 with Rudolph Anderson, a young biologist and classmate from their days at the University of Iowa. Among his objectives was the search for elusive Inuit tribes he believed had never been contacted by Europeans. The search took him east of the Mackenzie River to Canada's Coronation Gulf region, territory of the people he called Copper Eskimos, so named for their use of the metal in various implements.[18] His published reports to the Geological Survey contain some of the earliest ethnographic descriptions of this little-known population. Stefansson's work also had a controversial side, very much in keeping with his penchant for self-promotion: the purported discovery of "Blond Eskimos," allegedly the mixed-race descendants of Greenlandic Scandinavian colonists.[19] Stefansson was a shameless promoter of pet theories, perhaps none as consequential as his conviction that southerners would find the Arctic a "friendly" place, if only they learned to live there as the Inuit did.

The coming expedition – billed at first as the Second Stefansson-Anderson Expedition – was the most ambitious of Stefansson's polar ventures and would prove productive of both scientific results and headlines. The American Museum of Natural History and the National Geographic Society were the original backers, pledging $45,000 to the cause. However political considerations in Ottawa transformed the undertaking overnight. Hoping for additional funding, the well-connected Stefansson lobbied Prime Minister Robert Borden directly. Pitching the case in patriotic terms, he urged the government's support for a project whose main objective was to be discovering new lands and sources of natural wealth within the Dominion's remote northern boundaries. To his delight, he came away from the meeting with more than he had bargained for: Borden's commitment to finance and organize the entire operation in the name of the national interest. The prospect of mapping unknown areas, and discovering exploitable mineral wealth, had political and economic allure, especially since the country was just beginning to assert sovereignty in the high Arctic and knew little about what potentials the region held. Any technical and scientific information gleaned in the process, though less urgent, would be icing for the cake.[20] Thus was born the Canadian Arctic Expedition, which became a wide-ranging voyage of geographic and scientific discovery and, by later reputation, a high-profile boondoggle that had cost many lives and as much as a half-million dollars of government money by the time the last of its men and ships returned home in 1918.

The expedition's organization bore all the familiar hallmarks of government involvement: it was complex, cumbersome, bureaucratic, and expensive. Ministries of customs, fisheries, mines, and interior all had a stake. As commander, Stefansson was solely responsible to G.J. Desbarats, deputy minister of Naval Services, the branch under whose jurisdiction the undertaking ultimately fell. He was given general authority over some seventy men – including fifteen scientists recruited in several countries and scores of sailors – as well as discretion in recruiting personnel and using public funds to buy vessels – six in all by the expedition's end – equipment, provisions, and other necessities. Parliament made annual appropriations to foot most of the bills, usually without question. Audited statements of public expenditure appeared under the official title, "Cruise of the Northern Waters."

In Twilight and in Dawn

Members of the expedition, Esquimalt, BC, June 1913. Left to right (standing): Henri Beuchat, Bjarn Mamen, Diamond Jenness, Burt McConnell, John Cox, J.J. O'Neill, Fritz Johansen; (seated): William McKinlay George Wilkins, Kenneth Chipman, Robert Bartlett, Vilhjalmur Stefansson, Rudolph Anderson, James Murray. Missing from photo: Alister Forbes, George Malloch. Library and Archives Canada/Credit: George Hubert Wilkins/ Department of Marine fonds/PA074066

The expedition was divided into two sections, one devoted to geographic exploration, the other to scientific research. The Northern Party, with Stefansson at its head, had as its primary objective searching for new lands along the northeastern bounds of the Beaufort Sea and laying claim to any discoveries for Canada. Anderson assumed charge of the Southern Party, a multi-disciplinary team whose job was to carry out scientific investigations around Coronation Gulf and Victoria Island. The Geological Survey oversaw the work of the expedition, hired and paid its personnel, and set the standards and procedures for the conduct of research. Four of the expedition's members, and its only Canadians, were seconded from the survey's permanent staff; the remainder were recruited abroad. There were two anthropologists, Jenness and a Parisian named Henri Beuchat. Both were made temporary survey employees and paid $500 per year, the minimum salary for civil servants of the day. This distinguished them as the lowest-paid of the expedition's scientists, a distinction about which they – and others – were rightly aggrieved. Marett wrote to Sapir about just how appalling he found the situation, particularly for "a man of Jenness's experience and worth." "No one can realize better than myself how thoroughly inadequate Mr Jenness' salary ... is," the sympathetic response from Ottawa began; "In fact, I have long believed that anthropologists and other scientists are very foolish to put themselves to so many financial sacrifices in order to gain opportunities to do the work they are interested in."[21]

Two other anthropologists expressed interest in accompanying the expedition: American William H. Mechling and William Thalbitzer, a Dane. Mechling's was a familiar face in Ottawa, as he had researched Micmac (Mi'kmaq) and Malecite folklore for the survey's Anthropological Division in 1911. Still a graduate student, the press of other responsibilities soon convinced him to drop the idea of starting a new area of interest. "Besides," he confessed to Sapir, "my family object seriously to my going with [Stefansson] for three years."[22] Thalbitzer, on the other hand, was a serious prospect, and Sapir hoped he would sign on, given his expertise in Inuit language. Stefansson paid his way from Copenhagen to London in March 1913 so that the two could discuss the upcoming voyage. On Thalbitzer's account, his host treated him with indifference, brusquely dismissing his request to join the expedition at a later date so that he might complete a project already in progress. Afterward, Stefansson erroneously claimed that Thalbitzer had turned down the opportunity owing to his wife's failing health.[23]

This incident did little to improve Sapir's already low opinion of the explorer, an opinion based on doubts about his commitment to serious fieldwork. Sapir's misgivings surfaced for the first time in 1911 in a letter to Boas where he remarked that "The trouble with Stefansson's work ... is that it is not bad enough to ignore, yet not good enough to call forth an enthusiastic support"; his collection of Copper Inuit texts, for instance, stories taken down in the original, were "only middling in merit." Stefansson's insatiable desire to popularize science was mainly to blame, as anything that garnered good press struck him as more important than producing sound scholarship. Sapir and Boas regarded his priorities as misplaced, judging him ill-equipped to advance anthropology's slowly awakening interest in the Arctic. "To tell the truth," Sapir confessed, "I am not very enthusiastic about the whole thing and would prefer to recommend some thoroughly reliable man [such] as Thalbitzer."[24]

Stefansson didn't look to the coming expedition as an opportunity to pursue anthropological topics: rather, he saw it as a chance to break new ground with what he heralded as the "fourth stage" of polar exploration, a strategy for living and working in the Arctic predicated on adopting indigenous diet, dress, shelter, and transport. Later dubbed "living by forage," its purpose was to reduce dependence on the costly and unwieldy arrangements that had hindered so many exploring parties in the past. Yet he knew that "fourth stage" principles simply did not accord well enough with real life conditions to be trusted in every facet of an expedition's organization, at least not one of any scale or one that valued its members' safety and well being. Given this, the Canadian Arctic Expedition, like earlier ventures, carried an enormous cargo of food and supplies and made elaborate arrangements for moving men and freight around the landscape. Like many of their predecessors, however, its members grappled, sometimes unsuccessfully, with innumerable problems, often resorting to "living by forage" out of sheer necessity, not because they were being steadfastly true to a philosophical principle.

Stefansson's thoughts about recruiting personnel similarly favoured friendly Arctic doctrine. In the last analysis, he observed, "the right temperament is more important than health or strength," and certainly more important than scientific interests, in assessing the qualifications of those who would accompany him. Judged by this idiosyncratic measure, Jenness may have been a natural arctic explorer after all. Having received Sapir's matter-of-fact summation of the New Zealander's qualifications – Oxford-educated, experienced field worker, physically suited to living in rugged conditions, does not wear eyeglasses – Stefansson counselled: "Offer [him] what you suggest if you consider him best man in Physique temperament training."[25] As subsequent events would show, Jenness's fortunes clearly owed more to his physical endurance and even-tempered nature, and to survival skills learned in youth, than to his academic preparation. But attention to such abilities was not apparent in the recruitment of many of the other scientists. This became cruelly apparent in the case of Henri Beuchat, one of eleven men who perished in the wake of the expedition's most infamous episode: the loss of its flagship *Karluk* in January 1914.

Rudolph Anderson, eventually Stefansson's staunchest and most persistent critic, came to consider his partner's lax standards in selecting candidates palpable evidence of administrative incompetence, perhaps even criminal negligence. He later remarked of Beuchat that, despite an "agreeable personality and great ambition," the poor man was simply ill-prepared to handle the rigours of camp and trail. Worse still, he was "unskilled in caring for himself under difficult circumstances," such as those he ultimately faced, with the direst of consequences, after *Karluk*'s destruction in the ice-blocked Chukchi Sea. Stefansson's indifference probably sealed oceanographer James Murray's fate as well. Anderson believed that Murray, a veteran of Ernest Shackleton's 1909 expedition to Antarctica, was simply too old to endure the harsh conditions he met only a short distance from Wrangell Island, the site from which the wreck's survivors were finally rescued the following September.[26] Over its six-year span, the Canadian Arctic Expedition claimed the lives of sixteen sailors and scientists, eleven in connection with the *Karluk* disaster. In 1926, the government erected a monument to their memory in Ottawa's Dominion Archive building; it bore the inscription "For Canada and for Science."[27] How coldly ironic that the commemorative plaque itself went missing some forty years later, lost in the shuffle when the archives were moved to their present quarters on Wellington Street.

In a day still captivated by the romance and high adventure of polar exploration, Stefansson stood apart as a media darling, a larger-than-life personality very much in demand on the public stage. Yet his image-conscious style played differently among those engaged to accompany him northward, men, some with no arctic experience whatsoever, whose safety and security would rest in his hands for the foreseeable future. Rumours began circulating before *Karluk* sailed, fuelled by doubts and fears over the expedition's organizational and administrative soundness, its logistical arrangements, and their commander's seeming inattention to crucial details. Worries about the ice-worthiness of the aging, wooden-hulled flagship ranked high among their concerns, as did the adequacy and quality of food supplies. Subsequent events would show these to be far from idle fears.

One of the survivors of *Karluk*'s loss, William McKinlay, later described the "strange disease" he and his mates suffered in the weeks following the wreck, attributing it to the pemmican Stefansson procured. Denying responsibility for the problem, as was his style, Stefansson nevertheless harboured his own suspicions, speculating that the rations' high protein content might have caused kidney dysfunction among those who managed to reach shelter on Wrangell Island. Anderson was less clinical in his diagnosis, accusing his partner of ignoring such potential dangers in his rush to tie up loose ends in the weeks preceding their departure. He later remembered Stefansson being so frantic that he refused to allow analysis of the provisions to insure quality: "Damn purity tests – don't let anybody work you into suicidal delays," is how he recalled his associate's reaction. "Protein poisoning" was suspected in two deaths among the Wrangell Island castaways.[28]

The litany of charges and counter-charges over this and other matters, large and small, all liberally bathed in the taint of scandal and misdoing, continued to make good reading long after the last of the expedition's members returned home. For his part, Stefansson never relented on any of the big issues, condemning the mutinous actions of subordinates who defied his orders and insisting that exploration, not science, was the voyage's ultimate purpose and the raison d'être for Ottawa's involvement. He and Anderson never saw eye to eye on any of these questions, an embittered Anderson convinced that his partner had used him, and the entire undertaking, to advance his reputation and private interests.[29] In later years, Jenness deemed tragic his colleagues' failure to reconcile their many differences, though it was Anderson alone who refused to let go of the troubles between them. In keeping with his own more genial character, Jenness professed a personal liking for Stefansson from their first meeting, a sentiment that later blossomed into a life-long friendship kept up in correspondence and occasional reunions. But during his years in the Arctic, and for a time afterward, he, like many expedition colleagues, groused about the commander's executive abilities and judgment. While en route to Alaska, he aired apprehensions about the voyage's management and preparedness for what lay ahead, certain that Stefansson "has no idea of the magnitude of the task he is undertaking, being consumed instead with 'airy notions of living in the country like Eskimos.'" He also complained about small-minded restrictions on keeping private journals and sending out-going mail through Ottawa, presumably "to prevent leakage of news" promised to selected media outlets.[30] One wonders whether he would have boarded the steamer from Wellington had he known in advance about Stefansson's quirks, and about the uncountable ways they would affect his life and work in an Arctic that, to the first-time traveller at least, seemed anything but friendly.

Some background reading aside, Jenness's real preparation for the work ahead began in earnest once Henri Beuchat reached Victoria in mid-June. At thirty-five years of age, the Frenchman had already gained recognition at home for his library-bound studies of New World indigenous peoples, publishing on South American languages and archaeology, and on arctic ethnology and mythology. Of working-class origins and largely self-educated, his intellectual interests went well beyond anthropology, ranging from astronomy and chemistry to cuneiform and hieroglyphics. In 1902, he became a student in the École des hautes études at the Sorbonne. His scholarly interests soon brought him into the *Année sociologique* group, the flourishing school of comparative sociology identified, first and foremost, with Émile Durkheim and Marcel Mauss. This connection, in turn, led to the principal distinction that qualified Beuchat for a place on Stefansson's expedition: collaboration with Mauss, albeit as junior partner, on the ground-breaking "Essai sur les variations saisonnières des sociétés eskimo." Drawing on a wealth of published sources, the piece examined Mauss's notion of dual social morphology: patterned fluctuations in social organization and in the rhythms of daily life and their relationship to economic and material conditions in winter and summer. Arguably the first systematic ecological analysis of social life, their study stands as a classic of arctic scholarship and constitutes one of the very few attempts to build anthropological theory from the data of Inuit ethnology.[31]

Beuchat's invitation to go north was "the first great joy of his life," an opportunity for someone who, as Barbeau would later write, "despaired of ever getting away from libraries, museums, and the exacting trivialities of his Parisian environment." In short, the voyage represented "a unique chance of emancipation," destined to revive the spirit and broaden the mind and in the process earn the bookish fellow status as one of the first French ethnologists to take up fieldwork in the tribal world.[32] His excitement proved infectious. Although Jenness visited Paris in the summer of 1910 and heard Mauss speak, his introduction to Beuchat came only once the two reached Victoria. Hitting it off from the start, Jenness welcomed his associate's coaching on the intricacies of phonetic transcription, his confidence not yet restored after muddling through the unfamiliar sounds of Bwaidokan speech. Finding a copy of Thalbitzer's analysis of Greenlandic phonetics in the expedition's well-stocked library was nearly as helpful.[33] More generally, Beuchat initiated his junior into the wider realms of Eskimology, expounding on pet theories and critiquing the ideas of others whose writings he often reviewed in the pages of *L'Anthropologie*. After several weeks together at sea, Jenness was brimming over with praise for his new-found friend and colleague, pronouncing him a "rare acquisition to our party" and a most-welcome partner in the great project awaiting them in Copper Inuit country.[34] Their unforeseen separation just weeks later, Beuchat aboard the doomed *Karluk*, Jenness safely ashore, left their plans in tatters.

MAROONED

Karluk sailed from Esquimalt Harbour on 17 June 1913. Captain Robert Bartlett, a veteran of arctic navigation, charted a northward course along British Columbia's famed inside passage toward the small Alaskan port of Wrangell, then steered northwest through the Aleutians and on to Nome. It was here that an initial muster of personnel and two other vessels – the motor schooners *Alaska* and *Mary Sachs* – was to take place, followed by a second at Herschel Island, near the Canada-Alaska boundary. From there, the expedition's two sections would part company, Anderson's party heading eastward to Coronation Gulf aboard *Alaska*, Stefansson's, aboard *Karluk,* northward to the Parry Islands and beyond. *Mary Sachs* was to serve as the expedition's auxiliary transport, shuttling passengers and supplies between the parties as need arose.

The voyage's first leg was far from a relaxing summer cruise. Nearly everyone aboard had something to say about Stefansson, their gripes ranging from expedition logistics to questions about the man's competence to lead them into the Arctic. Then there was the weather, *Karluk* making its way through fog-enshrouded waters and frequent storms, hardly conditions conducive to allaying anxieties, or calming the stomach. Finally, the long days at sea gave all hands a close-up look at the expedition's suspect flagship, its cramped quarters and decks piled high with sacks of coal and miscellaneous supplies for which proper storage had not, or could not, be found below. A brigantine-style steamer of 1880s vintage, the vessel was originally a whaler, but by the time ownership passed to Stefansson's hands, it had been tied up for years, idled by the flagging fortunes of the north Pacific whalebone industry. Captain Bartlett was particularly dismayed by the ship's slowness and poor manoeuvrability, and, despite its metal-reinforced bow, he was unconvinced the vessel could withstand much of a beating from the pack ice that lay ahead. "If she gets frozen in," Jenness presciently wrote to Henry Balfour, "the chances are she will be crushed." Only Stefansson remained unconcerned, cavalierly advising the minister of naval services, J.D. Hazen, that "no great fears for our safety need be entertained. We may of course, all be gone; but the chances are that we shall all or most of us be safe."[35] His companions, already deeply skeptical, must have taken the coldest of comfort in their commander's incautious views for their personal welfare.

Like the weather en route, the stopover in Nome was stormy; the qualms first raised in Victoria receiving a second airing, while Stefansson remained steadfastly indifferent to his companions' misgivings. Making matters worse, his orders assigning men and cargo to the various ships unexpectedly put Jenness and Beuchat back aboard *Karluk,* not *Alaska,* the Southern Party's transport. He later claimed the switch was intentional, a plan to get the two to Herschel Island as quickly as possible so they could make an early start on research among the Mackenzie River Inuit, who regularly frequented the place. Jenness remembered events differently, recalling that Stefansson had "attached me temporarily" to the northern party for the simple reason that *Karluk* could carry more passengers.[36] Oblivious to the possibility that one or more of the vessels might not make the rendezvous, Stefansson simply preferred to "sort things out at Herschel Island."[37] When the voyage

Karluk caught in pack ice off Camden Bay [Alaska], August 1913. Library and Archives Canada/Credit: George Hubert Wilkins/Department of Marine fonds/ PA074047

finally resumed, the old whaler's passengers included nine scientists, thirteen sailors, and seven Iñupiat men and women recruited from Point Hope and Barrow to handle everything from hunting to sewing parkas and boots. Also aboard was an extraordinary load of cargo, piled above decks and below, making *Karluk* ride dangerously low in the water. On top of it all were twenty-eight sled dogs and a cat that had been smuggled on at Esquimalt; McKinlay recalled how the dogs' "yowling, yapping and scrapping [added] to the general confusion. If anyone could now tell what we had on board, or where it was, well ..."[38]

On 12 August, six days after rounding Point Barrow, Alaska's northernmost extremity, and heading eastward toward Herschel Island, Bartlett met the sea ice that, by day's end, would take control of *Karluk*'s movements, and her destiny. They were within hailing distance of Camden Bay. Collinson Point lay a short distance beyond. At the bay's eastern edge, winter's rapid advance had already forced *Mary Sachs* and *Alaska* to make land, their passengers unaware of the flagship's situation. Unable to break free of the ice, *Karluk* began a slow, months-long westward drift through the Arctic Ocean.

A fortnight after the floes had trapped *Karluk*, halting its eastward progress, and with little hope of relief from their grip, Stefansson made plans to dispatch a shore party to meet up with the other two vessels, or at least to get word of their predicament to Anderson. Because they were the only scientists whose work required them to be on land, the others busying themselves with soundings, meteorological observations, and the like, Beuchat and Jenness were conscripted for the mission. Kataktovik, a man hired just weeks earlier at Barrow, was to accompany them. They were fitted out with two sleds, fourteen dogs, a large skin boat, a month's worth of provisions, scientific and camping gear, some outgoing mail, and nearly $1,000 in cash and cheques to defray travel costs and to hire anyone whose assistance they required en route. Not to miss a chance for publicity, Stefansson also instructed Jenness to telegraph any newsworthy bits to the *New York Times*, the expedition's North American paper of record. The trio's objective was to join the Southern Party, presumed by now to have reached Herschel Island. Should circumstances prevent them from doing so, however, the anthropologists were authorized to carry on with their investigations independently.

Delayed for days by turbulent weather and frigid temperatures, the party got away at last on 29 August, heading for Flaxman Island, just ten miles distant. Hours later they were back aboard *Karluk*, the thin, snow-covered ice and their unwieldy cargo making the going simply too dangerous to continue. They had covered two miles at best. Things worsened during their retreat when Beuchat fell through the ice and had to be conveyed to the ship propped up inside the skin boat, itself badly damaged in the attempt.[39] For the Frenchman, the accident offered a cruel foretaste of worse to come.

Three weeks later, the ship now out of sight of land, a second shore party was organized. Unlike the first, its purpose was to replenish *Karluk*'s stores with caribou meat. Mere days before the steamer began what was to be her final, portentous drift, Stefansson led six men shoreward. Jenness was a last-minute addition to their number; Beuchat remained aboard.[40] As before, they were equipped with dogs, sleds, and tents and carried food enough to last two weeks. But their outing had a dramatic and, for them, providential result, *Karluk*'s disappearance preventing their return and throwing the expedition into disarray.

By 20 September, the shore party's first day out, *Karluk* had been becalmed for a week, the winds remaining light, heavy ice jammed solidly against the mainland shore. On day three, easterly gales began pushing it westward, leaving large stretches of open water between the moving floe and the now-receding coastline. Stefansson speculated that it had broken free, found an open lead, and was under way for Herschel Island. In reality, it remained frozen in, the drifting pack ice slowly carrying the whaler, and the twenty-five people still aboard, north-westward, toward their miserable fates in the ice-choked Chukchi Sea.[41]

Marooned on the north Alaskan coast with five companions, Jenness found himself separated from his colleague Beuchat and still hundreds of miles shy of the Southern Party's destination in the western Canadian Arctic. His camera, anthropometric instruments, books, and papers all remained on board. What few possessions he carried were stowed in a small rucksack. The early pages of his diary were also missing, which explains why the extant journal's opening entry is dated 20 September instead of 17 June, the day the expedition set sail from Esquimalt. After leaving *Karluk* he suffered several bouts of malarial fever, six over a span of thirteen days. The attacks sapped much-needed strength for the demanding travel ahead and eventually, overwhelmed by weakness, he abandoned the usual practice of running alongside the dog sleds and climbed aboard with the baggage. Lacking warm clothing – heavy gear also left behind – the bitingly cold air of early autumn worked its own brand of hardship.[42] Then there were nagging fears for the safety of *Karluk*'s passengers, no less for those aboard the other vessels, last seen on the stormy Bering Strait weeks before. At the time, Jenness summed up his own situation in matter-of-fact terms, yet it is not hard to imagine that even an intrepid arctic traveller might have found such circumstances unsettling, if not immobilizing.

On reaching the sparsely populated mainland near the mouth of the Colville River, the hunting party headed westward toward Cape Smythe, 150 miles away. This was the nearest place to restock their dwindling provisions – living by forage having proved less than successful to this point – and to obtain whatever news they could of their vanished seaborne comrades. (Herschel Island, the only other reliable point of supply in the western Arctic, was twice as far in the opposite direction.) Blessed with good weather, the trek over the nearshore ice took twelve days. Iñupiat camps along the way offered welcome hospitality and a chance for Jenness to meet some of the people with whom he would later pass the winter. Upon arrival, they learned that *Mary Sachs* and *Alaska* were icebound at Collinson Point, some 300 miles to the east, and that Anderson and company were quartered safely for the duration. Nothing was known of *Karluk*. The expedition now needed a radically revised plan of action.

Regrouping at Collinson Point became Stefansson's first order of business and he hoped to reach there before the light-starved days of winter made travel precarious and delayed him even further. His plans for Jenness were less definite, one day having him join those heading for a rendezvous with Anderson, the next, leaving him in Barrow to begin research in that quarter. Finding the idea of wintering in the village attractive, Jenness felt no reason to argue with his leader's considered opinion that anthropological work was more urgent here than it was at the Mackenzie Delta, several hundred more miles beyond Camden Bay. Besides, he confided in his diary, Cape Smythe "will be much more comfortable."[43] Given the uncertain state of his health, the convenience of a well-stocked trade store and the steady company of a few friendly and gracious Europeans were more than comforting. The local white population numbered four: Messrs Brower and Hansen, rival merchants, both married to Aboriginal women, and Mr and Mrs Cram, a missionary couple from Seattle who doubled as public functionaries, she as schoolteacher, he as postmaster.

Ever mercurial, Stefansson finally settled on a third alternative: dispatching the anthropologist to winter with an Iñupiat family at Harrison Bay, one of their stopping places after leaving *Karluk*. This would provide opportunity for a crash course in the local language, valuable preparation for the coming fieldwork at Coronation Gulf. It would also be a chance to acquire a feel for the people and the land. That finally resolved, Stefansson engaged Kaiyutak, a fifteen-year-old bilingual "half-caste" from Cape Smythe, to travel with Jenness as interpreter. The teenager was offered a $15 monthly wage and permission to moonlight by trapping furs. A fine-quality white fox pelt at the time bought $15 to $20 worth of trade goods, a handsome return.[44]

GREAT MOMENTS IN THE HISTORY OF ETHNOGRAPHIC FIELDWORK

The Northern Arctic 1913

Marooned on the winter ice, Diamond Jenness discovers the Eskimo have twenty different terms for an anthropologist

Drawing courtesy of James Urry.

Jenness welcomed the chance to begin proper research at long last, feeling he had so far done little: taking a few anthropometric measurements when *Karluk* called at Point Hope; helping Beuchat compile a word list from the various dialects spoken by their native Alaskan shipmates; collecting cat's cradles – as in Papua, part scientific work, part pastime. With returning good health, his spirits improved, as he had worried that persistent spells of fever and chills might necessitate staying behind until he had recovered completely. He suffered with ague once after arriving at Cape Smythe, but merchant Charles Brower found a stock of quinine tablets that soon relieved the symptoms. "Don't let my people know" about this illness, he implored von Zedlitz, solicitous of his parents' peace of mind.[45] Happily, the attacks became less frequent, and less severe, in the weeks ahead, and all but disappeared after the New Year.

❖

The indigenous Iñupiat have inhabited the Alaskan coastline from the vicinity of Point Barrow southwest to Cape Prince of Wales for centuries. They are whale hunters of great renown and share a common language with Inuit living to the east as far as Greenland. Starting in the 1880s, their world began to change dramatically as commercial whaling vessels arrived along their shores. Most whalers hailed from New

In Twilight and in Dawn

England, their crews a hodgepodge of races and nationalities – Americans, Polynesians, Africans, Canadians – whose sole purpose was to obtain whalebone, used in manufacturing stays for the women's undergarments in vogue at the time. Merchants like Brower appeared next, bringing an array of imported goods that fostered division of the native economy into subsistence and exchange sectors. The first signs of state authority materialized: Christian missions and schools. On top of it all came a demographic catastrophe: scourges of measles, influenza, and other infectious diseases that exacted a terrible toll, reducing the population by half, maybe more. In its aftermath, people from other parts of the Alaskan coast, and from the interior, migrated into Iñupiat territory, most coming to trap furs and trade with resident merchants. Similar circumstances were not long in opening the door to Iñupiat expansion eastward into the Mackenzie Delta. Here, even more devastating virgin-soil epidemics followed establishment of Herschel Island as a winter base for the American whaling fleet. In short order, the Aboriginal population of Canada's far western Arctic had been brought perilously near extinction.[46]

After a generation of turmoil and change, the Iñupiat were certainly not the pristine primitives most of the day's anthropologists regarded as ideal subjects of investigation. This attitude was born out of the great project of salvage ethnology, a project aimed at documenting traditional (i.e., pre-contact) cultures across the globe before they were irretrievably lost in the spread of European ideas, technology, and microbes.[47] Jenness's initial impression of Barrow's people, conveyed in a letter to Marett, confirms this: "The Eskimos about here are losing most of their old customs," he wrote; "The tattooing of women is not continued among the younger generation. Mr Brower tells me that they even come to him to have sleds & umiaks made by his workmen." He anticipated finding a more fertile ethnographic field at Harrison Bay, where the family with whom he was to winter – inlanders, or Nunamiut, from the Colville River area – were reputed to have been "very little in contact with the whites." As he soon discovered, even they did not measure up to expectations, the weakening of "ancient customs" signalling their exposure to Euro-American ways.[48]

Professed disappointment aside, Jenness observed closely the numerous manifestations of change wherever his travels took him. Among the more interesting passages in the Alaskan portions of his diary are detailed, frequently droll descriptions of cultural loans running the gamut from newly acquired habits of personal hygiene – practices Stefansson likened to religious sacraments because missionaries had introduced them – to inventive cookery, blending imported and country foods. He also took note of the variability of physical characteristics among the natives he encountered, indicative, he believed, of the decline of the "'pure' Eskimo" in a region that had become a crossroads of peoples from across the planet.[49] Impressed by what he had seen, he drafted a paper describing the impact of Western influence on north Alaskans while still in the thick of fieldwork at Coronation Gulf. This, and a second piece examining the same process among Copper Inuit, anticipated culture-contact (i.e., acculturation) studies in anthropology by nearly two decades.[50] Some forty years later, the unfolding of social and cultural change became the central thread running through his popular account of wintering at Harrison Bay, a motif captured in the book's title: *Dawn in Arctic Alaska*. An earlier memoir, *People of the Twilight*, describes an ancient way of life at Coronation Gulf poised on the brink of a similarly momentous transformation.[51]

Faced with the mildly disillusioning social reality that was early twentieth-century Alaska, Jenness remained hopeful of eventually coming face to face with a people whose way of life was as yet little affected by foreign influences, roughly akin to the situation he had happened upon in Goodenough Island's more isolated mountain villages. Stefansson did nothing to dissuade him from this sort of thinking, convinced as he was that heretofore unknown tribes occupying remote island ranges northeastward from the Mackenzie still awaited first contacts with the outside world.[52] Needless to say, the explorer's protegé delighted in the possibilities of what lay ahead, openly enthusing about his chances of "meeting the *real stone age Eskimos*" once the Southern Party reached Coronation Gulf.[53]

◆

With Kaiyutak and a second man, Asecaq, from Point Hope, as company, Jenness departed Brower's establishment in late October 1913 for Harrison Bay, some eighty miles distant. The shoreline they traversed was dotted with winter encampments, each sheltering two or three Iñupiat families. In times past, this long, bleak season had been spent hunting seals and fishing at inland lakes, but in recent years trapping fox furs had relegated traditional subsistence activities to secondary importance. This made for a relatively sedentary existence, well-suited to an anthropologist aiming to study language and collect folk tales. The travellers' final destination was the camp of a family Jenness had met while in transit to Cape Smythe, which was situated on the bay's southwestern shore. Aksiatak and Otoyuk, with young daughters Kukpuk and Siliuna, and a toddler son, Katairoaq, had recently abandoned their summer skin tent for winter quarters, a wood-frame and sod cabin. They were sharing their twelve-by-fifteen-foot dwelling with four others:

Aksiatak's sister Qapqana, her husband, Aluk, their infant son, Suiva-liaq, and a young girl, Pungasuk. Once the newcomers appeared, the household swelled to twelve, a crowd even by Iñupiat standards. Out of sheer necessity, the brothers-in-law added on a second room of roughly similar dimensions in an attempt to accommodate everyone a bit more comfortably. Jenness dubbed this house Iglu I. Around the New Year he helped build Iglu II, a smaller cabin at Cape Halkett, handy to the trapping grounds that encompassed portions of the neighbouring coast and some of its near-shore islands.

Given all the changes occurring in northern Alaska, the presence of a white man in their midst did little to upset day-to-day life around Harrison Bay. Even Aksiatak was familiar with many of the things, practical and frivolous, introduced from the outside but now commonplace at Barrow and other villages. He had an inkling about anthropologists as well, having previously billeted Stefansson and endured his endless questions. Apart from firearms and metal implements of various description, many Iñupiat owned kerosene-fired primus stoves, sewing machines, crockery and eating utensils, clocks, wristwatches, and calendars. Aksiatak's furnishings featured a prized gramophone and "some execrable records, fortunately little used," as a grateful Jenness was relieved to learn.[54] Others fashioned homemade equivalents, turning discarded items such as fuel tins into cooking pots and wood stoves. Flour, sugar, tea, and other foods were dietary staples, the variously prepared mukpaurat, or bannock, eaten at virtually every meal.[55] Unlike his later experience with the Copper Inuit, Jenness – or Jennie, as he came to be known along the shore east of Barrow – was not the constant object of his hosts' curiosity. Nor did they vie for his favours as a trading partner, alternately courting and harassing him to supply exotic goods. The 300 pounds of provisions their guest brought with him from Cape Smythe were certainly a welcome supplement to the household larder, particularly specialty items such as rice and chocolate, but it was the white man's generous line of expedition-backed credit at Brower's store, not the supplies themselves, that made him a tolerable addition to their little community.[56]

Clocks and watches were ubiquitous all along the coast, but the rigid conventions of European timekeeping were less accepted. Much like the Iñupiat, the vicissitudes of weather, and the anthropologist's own moods, determined how he spent each day. Sometimes he wrote up notes and transcribed story and song texts to the near-exclusion of all else, sometimes he sat quietly on a sleeping platform, taking in the scene, or joined in whatever activities others were presently engaged. Adroit with a rifle, Jenness skied into the countryside to shoot ptarmigan; less often, he tagged along when someone ventured out to inspect a trap line or to hunt for big game. He also pitched in with domestic chores, cutting up whatever firewood could be found and lending a hand with building Iglu II, the winter's major project. He thought of these activities as compensation for his hosts' unstinting hospitality. "You generally contribute something in the way of food so that your hosts lose nothing by their hospitality, for they really are glad to see you," always eager for news and appreciative of the company.[57]

The children in Aksiatak's house, ranging in age from about twelve to less than a year, absorbed much of Jenness's attention. He relished playing cat's cradle or other games with them but also found them helpful sources of information in their own right, discovering expressions of values and attitudes in their ordinary activities. This was especially so for the youngest ones who, like himself, were in the early phases of socialization, learning the basics of language and feeling their way around the limits of behavioural norms and expectations. Local speech was "frightfully difficult" to learn, its sounds unfamiliar, its grammatical rules hard to discern, and even harder to systematize. Only on discovering that Stefansson had struggled for months on end to acquire minimal proficiency did he begin to feel better about his own modest success.[58]

Assisted by Kaiyutak's interpreting and prompting, by the time he left Harrison Bay he had mastered enough Inuktitut to carry on simple conversations. In between, frequent games of cat's cradle, a favourite pastime of hosts and guest alike, provided congenial occasions for learning and practicing the language, particularly when his playmates were children. A blind woman, referred to as Mrs Añopqana, took special interest in his progress, "invariably [asking] me if I can talk Eskimo yet" whenever he visited her at Cape Halkett. She took pains to correct mispronunciations and grammatical slips in a good-natured way, treatment much preferable to those confidence-demolishing moments when a newcomer's halting speech or incorrect usage provoked laughter or, worse, derision. Whether he managed to avoid such embarrassment, or simply refused to own up to it, he was certainly wary of the pitfalls and vulnerabilities such errors threatened, even for seasoned field workers. Hearing that Stefansson had once mistaken a popular contemporary song for an ancient hunting charm, a blunder that appealed to the Iñupiat sense of humour, Jenness confided in his diary that "such is the fate ... of many an ethnologist – more often than is supposed."[59]

Jenness felt Henri Beuchat's absence acutely at Harrison Bay, not just his good company but his "genius for language."[60] Without a published grammar at hand for reference, the tasks of analyzing grammatical structure and describing phonology proceeded slowly. His correspondence with Sapir, one of the continent's premier linguists, shied away from any but the most superficial comment on his progress.[61] Not so with von Zedlitz. In one rambling letter, he neatly summarized his results to date, describing several of the language's main grammatical and phonological features and spelling out, in light-hearted fashion, some of the problems they posed for speakers of European languages. "If you were an Eskimo scholar," he explained at one point, "you will find a multitude of alternate endings, long interminable suffixes, or you will pile up infix after infix in a single word until it reminds you of the pictures you sometimes see of John Bull – there is a head somewhere at one end and feet at the other, but they are swallowed up in the enormous body."[62]

Transcribing speech sounds was more troubling. With a standardized phonetic alphabet still on the drawing board, Jenness found it necessary to make frequent modifications and additions to the method Beuchat had taught him aboard *Karluk*. "We unearthed a new sound yesterday, for which we invented a new symbol," his diary reads. "It is half n half y, we write it ñ & seems to be very common. It appears in the word for man ... which we write iñuk." Hardly an elegant solution in a field demanding precision and consistency, he trusted that "someone who knows" would eventually straighten out the tangles in his makeshift system, once the expedition was over. Meanwhile, evidence of this tinkering and experimentation appears throughout the diary, perhaps most noticeably in the variety of renderings of personal names. "You know what an ignoramus I am about everything relating to [phonology]," he told von Zedlitz. Overstating the case for effect: "I have to record [speech] where scarcely a single sound coincides with any known to Europeans or to the rest of the world."[63] Even so, on reaching Coronation Gulf, he was sufficiently confident in his facility with the language to act as interpreter for his colleagues and, in time, to spend a long period alone with the unilingual Copper Inuit.

In watching children's interactions with adults, he was reminded of Stefansson's observations about parental tolerance toward misbehaving children, a level of permissiveness the explorer deemed to be well beyond that of the average European. Stefansson attributed this attitude to ancient religious beliefs, notably the idea that an ancestral soul inhabits a newborn child, becoming its guardian spirit, and thus commanding respect.[64] In the main, the children under Aksiatak's roof received liberal treatment, their "whims & caprices ... humoured," their curiosity about the innards of watches and the sharpness of scissors patiently endured. As with most things, though, there were limits; on witnessing an episode of hair-pulling, Jenness gleefully noted that Stefansson's theory "received its death blow today as far as these families are concerned," Aksiatak having dealt a "sharp knock" that sent the offending youngster "screaming to his mother."[65]

Strained relations between the household's two sisters-in-law, Otoyuk and Qapqana, exposed a darker side of family life. After some reflection, their guest concluded that the barely submerged hostilities between them stemmed from several factors, the most obvious being personality differences and a niggling rivalry over foolish issues such as who was the more skilled in preparing European foods. But a deeper, more serious issue loomed over their relationship: Otoyuk's blatant indifference toward her eldest daughter, Kukpuk, a posture stemming from Aksiatak's interference when she had tried to abandon the child at birth. The woman's neglectful treatment of the twelve-year-old rarely passed unnoticed, even provoking neighbours' disapproving gossip.[66] Rather than sparking open reproof, or worse, such potentially disruptive behaviour was usually greeted with disarming reserve. As with parental indulgence of children, Jenness wondered if this, too, had its limits, speculating about the families' chances of "endur[ing] each other's company without a major eruption."[67] Given the intensity of domestic life in winter – a season of prolonged darkness, perishing cold, periodic food shortages, and few safe outlets for volatile emotions – his concern was far from idle.

Even while keeping above the fray, the anthropologist harboured a few grievances of his own, taking care to vent them only in the pages of his diary. For instance, where Qapqana proved a willing teacher, volunteering stories and songs and other tidbits of ethnographic interest, neither Aksiatak nor Otoyuk would impart any but the most meagre details of their knowledge and experience. This reluctance was especially bothersome since the couple were virtual novices in Euro-American ways and so were a potential goldmine of information on Nunamuit customs and traditions, largely uncharted ethnological territory at the time.[68] Equally irksome was Otoyuk's alleged stinginess at mealtimes. In generous moments, Jenness conceded that inland roots accounted for her "mathematical housewifery," a prudent strategy for staving off hunger even when provisions were adequate, as they were at present. At other times, frustration overtook him, his patience worn thin with the measly portions of bannock she dished up at meals. An entry for January reads: "this has become so chronic now that I am beginning to wonder what it is like not to be hungry."[69]

Recounting myths and legends made for a long winter evening's entertainment in the cramped cabin at Harrison Bay. The loquacious Qapqana stood out above the others as an accomplished raconteur. Now and then Jenness contributed a story of his own – the Greek legend of

Atalanta, the Arabian Nights, Tom Sawyer – courtesy of young Kai-yutak's interpreting. Like playing cat's cradles, storytelling combined pleasure and work and he took down stories verbatim for translation and analysis. In keeping with the style of ethnography then in fashion among a rising generation of American anthropologists, most of them Boas's students, Sapir counselled that "the very best sort of ethnological material you can get would be texts obtained from dictation."[70] Not yet certain enough to employ the method himself, Jenness conscripted Kai-yutak to the task, promising a "fine bandolier" in exchange for a note-book filled with stories. The teenager was definitely not the equal of his Bwaidokan counterpart Pita Ludeba, his struggles with the complex-ities of transcription, and limited knowledge of Inupiaq and English grammar, resulting in only a handful of texts after weeks of work. Dis-gruntled by the added responsibilities with which he had been saddled, Kaiyutak resigned as interpreter when he and Jenness returned to Cape Smythe in February.[71] Unable to find a replacement, thereafter Jen-ness did his own transcribing and, as his fluency improved, gradually worked through the translations on his own. The fruits of this labour appeared in a published collection of nearly one hundred myths and legends, half from Alaska and the Mackenzie delta, the remainder from Coronation Gulf. Just five originated with the Colville River people at Harrison Bay, presumably the sum of Kaiyutak's efforts. At the exped-ition's temporary quarters on Camden Bay, employees Jennie Thomsen and Fred Ailuat contributed numerous Iñupiat tales; unlike the rest, they were rendered in "quaint 'pigeon' English."[72]

❖

Having been given only the vaguest of official instructions the previous fall, Jenness decided to return to Cape Smythe in mid-winter and await new orders. The move was timely, coming at a point when household provisions were diminishing and the long silence from both Stefans-son and Anderson was becoming worrisome. The westward trek took a week, ending on 10 February, his twenty-eighth birthday. Comfortably housed and fed thanks to Charles Browers's hospitality, over the next fortnight he busied himself with linguistics, catching up on reading, writing letters home and to the families of the missing Beuchat and Wil-liam McKinlay, and employing a church harmonium to revise melodies of songs taken down "by ear."[73] And he anxiously awaited long-overdue news of the expedition.

That troublesome silence finally ended with the arrival of Burt McCon-nell, Stefansson's personal secretary. McConnell had come to collect the anthropologist and accompany him back to Camden Bay. Setting off on the last day of February, it took them the best part of a month to cover the distance, the trip marred by patches of rough weather and by testiness between the companions. At its conclusion, a trail-weary Jenness marked the occasion thus: "The journey from Barrow is over, & I am heartily glad for McConnell & I have not got on well together at all."[74]

A trapper's cabin served as the Southern Party's winter quarters at Camden Bay. Its larders were well stocked, a decided relief after the short rations and sameness of fare on offer at Chez Otoyuk. "There is no possibility of being ever hungry," a satisfied Jenness announced after two days in camp.[75] Nor was there much chance of boredom, new faces appearing daily as a steady stream of natives and newcomers passed through en route to spring hunting grounds or came calling from ice-bound whaling and trading ships scattered up and down the coast. The lengthening days and comparatively warmer temperatures of arctic spring similarly lifted the mood, occasional jaunts in search of fresh meat or to visit neighbours now more pleasurable than outings had been in the dead of winter. Four more months were to pass before the return of open water permitted the expedition to resume its eastward course.

It was during this period that one of the expedition's most notorious misadventures occurred – the March 1914 mutiny at Collinson Point, Alaska. *Karluk*'s disappearance some months before was its trigger, the ice-bound vessel having drifted out of sight carrying not only twenty-five passengers but most of the Northern Party's cargo and crew as well. Desperate to avoid abandoning his high-profile plan to lead an exploring party across the frozen Beaufort Sea in search of new land, Stefansson announced his intention to commandeer equipment and supplies earmarked for the Southern Party, as well as some of its scientists. Anderson resisted, refusing to sacrifice either men or supplies and with them the chance of succeeding in the work awaiting them at Coronation Gulf. Jenness was not present at Collinson Point when the blow-up occurred but in the expedition's contentious aftermath used the pages of the well-respected journal *Science* to refute Stefansson's charges of insubordination, asserting that Anderson, as the Southern Party's executive officer, justifiably acted on behalf of the Geological Survey in keeping its scientific mission intact. In the end, Stefansson yielded and Anderson's full company, and cargo, reached their intended destination.[76]

Jenness was soon to receive new instructions from Stefansson, but in the interim, aided immeasurably by the loan of Anderson's typewriter, he set about catching up on organizing the backlog of notes accumulated since first stepping ashore months earlier. Discovering a well-worn copy of Samuel Kleinschmidt's grammar of the Labrador and Greenlandic dialects among some of Beuchat's misplaced baggage, was pure serendipity, the book providing useful comparative data for analyzing key features of Iñupiaq speech.[77] So, too, was meeting the bilingual Billy Natkusiak, one of the three men who had accompanied Stefansson to Coronation Gulf back in 1910. Natkusiak offered tantalizing snippets of information about the resident Copper Inuit, a population whose very existence had been open to conjecture among Europeans for years. Now bound for their home turf himself, Jenness took careful note of Natkusiak's impressions of the Kagmalit – the "new Eskimos" – as they were known to their Mackenzie Delta neighbours to the west.[78]

Jenness's next project was to be the excavation of house ruins on Barter Island, some fifty miles to the east. The work there was not slated to begin until June, to allow for a bit of thawing. He devoted the preceding weeks to surveying the shoreline for traces of past activity while accompanying a freighting party hauling fuel to the Mackenzie. The highlight of the excursion turned out to be ethnological, not archaeological, the result of camping with the over-wintering sailors of *Belvedere*, a trading vessel stranded near the international boundary. The ship's multinational and inter-racial crew – Cape Verde islanders, a Russian-Eskimo "half breed," a Nova Scotian "blue nose," and, to the anthropologist's special delight, seven Siberian Eskimos – were a garrulous lot, some of whom were pleased to contribute their favourite cat's cradles to his burgeoning collection. By the time the Southern Party finally set sail for Coronation Gulf in late July, the number of string figures he had recorded, many with accompanying chants, stood at over one hundred, their origins spanning the Arctic from Siberia to the Mackenzie. "[These] should prove valuable ethnologically in working out the migrations of the Eskimos" between regions and continents, he enthusiastically informed Marett.[79]

Last-minute details demanded attention in the days leading up to his departure for Barter Island. Most important was hiring an Iñupiaq trapper named Aiyakuk as his field assistant. The man's stepson Ipanna was also engaged, the pair accepting $300 in return for two months' work. A veritable bargain, the arrangement entitled Jenness to lodge in Aiyakuk's tent, travel in his skin boat, and receive domestic services – cooking and sewing – courtesy of Aiyakuk's wife, Tuglumunna.[80] Assembling an excavation toolkit was less convenient, the implements furnished by the Geological Survey, like so much else, having remained aboard *Karluk*. With a bit of ingenuity, Jenness and his mates fashioned crude tools from odds and ends scavenged around camp: a bit of iron from a schooner's bow was fashioned into two spades, files turned into scrapers. Most serviceable of the lot were an axe, pick, and shovel appropriated from one of Stefansson's many caches. A Kodak 3A camera, standard survey issue, rounded out his equipment. In the end, the last was barely used, Jenness taking only seventeen photographs at the excavations, a small fraction of the hundreds he made during his time with the Copper Inuit.[81]

◆

With the shore ice still suitable for sled travel, Jenness and company needed two days to cover the distance to Barter Island, arriving on 28 May. They planned to remain until the Southern Party's ships were again able to sail, probably some time in July. Finding two families camped on a sandspit at the island's northwest tip, they pitched their own tents alongside. One neighbour, Teriglu, was something of an entrepreneur, digging around archaeological sites for curios to sell to outsiders. His fossicking turned up the season's most valuable discovery, a "perfect mine of treasures" consisting of two complete human skeletons, "apparently a man & his wife, & all their property." Peeved at his competitor's "annoyingly [and repeated] good luck," Jenness bought the most interesting of his finds and then put him on the payroll for good measure.[82] By chance, Oyaraq, head of the other family in camp, volunteered equally valuable help. Not only did his "careful scratching among the ruins" demonstrate his "perfect genius for discovering good things," he was a veritable treasure trove of ethnographic information, shedding light on the people who had lived and died here in the past.[83]

Archaeology in the Arctic, and elsewhere, was in its infancy around the time of the First World War, its practitioners largely self-trained, its objectives a mix of antiquarianism and speculative reconstruction of prehistoric cultures. The development of radiocarbon dating and of modern techniques of excavation and analysis were still decades off, with the process of compiling and systematizing comparative data on the spatial and temporal distribution of artifact types and other evidence only just begun. That being the case, it is understandable why, half a century after the fact and after half a century of theoretical and methodological advance in both archaeology and prehistory, Jenness chose to portray himself as a mere "scrounger in the earth" in Alaska, literally rummaging for scraps like the first robins of spring.[84] In keeping with his penchant for self-effacement, the remark belies the methodical way he approached the work at hand. Danish archaeologist Therkel Mathiassen is ordinarily credited with making the first systematic excavations in the Arctic in the early twenties, work that identified the cultural remains of a people called Thule, the immediate ancestors of modern Inuit. There is, however, reason to think that Jenness holds a rightful claim to that distinction.[85]

In Twilight and in Dawn

"Having no archaeological experience," Jenness explained at length to Marett, himself a dabbler in prehistory, "I had to make my own system" for uncovering and documenting structures and artifacts buried in the permafrost or scattered about on the surface.[86] He proceeded in roughly the way modern-day archaeologists would, though without benefit of specialized excavation tools or any more precise means of measurement than pacing off distances. He began by mapping out the spatial distribution and determining the physical dimensions of houses, graves, and other structures in three village sites, assigning each one an identifying number. The general condition and ground plan of the ruins were then noted, as were positions of sleeping areas, blubber lamps, and other features. Finally, he plotted locations of the principal artifacts and skeletal remains found in each structure and catalogued them using numbers corresponding to the structures from which they had come.[87] So far, so good. Where difficulty arose was in coping with the conditions under which the excavations themselves took place, conditions demanding an openness to experimentation and considerable forbearance.

Aiyakuk set up camp near some ruins on the island's western shore, but their work was split between this and a second, more promising site: a sandspit some three miles to the east, where the modern North Slope Borough of Kaktovik now stands.[88] Unable to use boat or sled, precious time was lost each day in trekking back and forth across the tundra. Thawing at the eastern locality appeared sufficiently advanced to allow immediate excavation but, once their digging began, shovels hit frost just below the surface, a problem Jenness tried to remedy with fires built atop the ruins. To his horror, the method did more than warm the ground; it destroyed stone artifacts, causing them to crack apart.[89] This meant waiting for the milder days and prolonged sunlight of early summer to achieve the desired result. Predictably, the weather failed to cooperate, daily temperatures hovering around the freezing mark. The overburden at the sites, in places as much as eighteen inches of soil and decomposed wood covered by loose turf, thus remained partly frozen throughout their stay on the island. As a result, excavation required "a great deal of hard work, some four to five hours each day with shovel & scraper," much more than the novice archaeologist had anticipated.[90] In some cases, up to four days were required to expose one house-floor, the near-solid ground yielding no more than a few inches before an interval of another day or two was needed to allow additional thawing. "It is a labourious process very trying to one's patience, especially when, after spending a great deal of time clearing out a large house, you get nothing or next to nothing for your pains."[91] With limited time at his disposal and many sites to be dug, necessity dictated working several structures at once, the crew often keeping at it into the wee hours under Alaska's midnight sun.

His Iñupiat companions contributed as much to interpreting what was being unearthed as they did to the digging itself. And they offered helpful comparative detail as well, pointing out similarities and differences between material culture or customary practices to the west and east of Barrow. Virtually everyone took an interest in the proceedings, each day's findings talked over once family members settled in for the evening. Now and then, a daily update produced unexpected consequences, as happened with Tuglumunna, Aiyakuk's wife. On discovering that the white man had brought an exhumed human skull into their camp, she immediately became distraught, frantically explaining that "she heard the tent shake & rattle ... for no visible cause, then the neighbouring tent in which she was sitting ... shook as though it would fall." The agitation, both Tuglumunna's and the tent's, stopped once the suspect remains were crated up, a measure her husband wisely urged be carried out with all haste.[92]

"The two months were like a nightmare," Jenness later told Barbeau.[93] Even so, the end product is impressive: sixty-nine winter houses – most of driftwood and sod construction – partially or completely dug, another ten identified but left unexcavated, and six graves examined. Teriglu dug a further five houses on his own. The resulting yield of specimens was equally substantial, a varied collection of upwards of 3,000 artifacts and skeletal remains, human and animal, eventually being registered in Victoria Memorial's accession lists.[94] Taking into account such obvious factors as the state of organic preservation and the presence of some European-derived material, Jenness speculated that most of the ruins were probably no more than 150 years old. More recent comparisons of this material and artifacts from firmly dated sites elsewhere in Alaska suggest occupation as early as 550 years ago, well within the horizon of pre-contact times.[95]

How odd that a man soon to gain international standing as a preeminent arctic archaeologist and culture historian never published his pioneering Barter Island research nor, for that matter, analyzed the evidence. The detailed notes he compiled were simply filed away, left to collect dust over the remainder of a long and varied career.[96] The collection eventually did see the light of day, incorporated into a report Edwin S. Hall, Jr. prepared for Alaska's North Slope Borough in 1987. Jenness knew of the American archaeologist's interest in the work years in advance, helping him track down the long-forgotten material in National Museum files just two years before his death.[97]

❖

In Twilight and in Dawn

His whaleboat stacked to the gunwales with packing crates – twenty were needed for the haul of artifacts – Aiyakuk ferried Jenness back to Camden Bay and the expedition ships, now riding at anchor. Their timing was impeccable as *Alaska* and *Mary Sachs* were both fully loaded and ready to set sail.

On rejoining his Southern Party mates, Jenness was disheartened to learn that there was still no news of the *Karluk*. Nearly a year would elapse before they received definitive word of its shocking end: on 11 January 1914 it had been crushed in the frozen polar sea, the "icy grave-yard of many a whaling ship." As the long-awaited shout "She's going" was heard, the captain's final act had been to crank up the ship's Victrola in order to play Chopin's "Funeral March."[98] News of the disaster had been nearly as slow in filtering down to Ottawa, Sapir mistakenly apprising Jenness in June 1914 that, while no lives had been lost, Beuchat and three companions, as yet unaccounted for, were presumed safe somewhere on the Siberian shore. His spirits buoyed, an optimistic Jenness had penned a hasty note to his missing comrade, offering hearty congratulations on his "safe emergence from the Arctic wastes."[99] It was to be several more months before the truth became known at Coronation Gulf with the story of Robert Bartlett's heroic rescue of the dozen survivors, many malnourished and in ill health, and of the wretched ordeal Beuchat and three companions had faced as they struggled to make land on Wrangel Island.[100]

In a sad postscript to this tragic affair, Sapir approached his deputy minister, R.G. McConnell, about securing a government pension for Beuchat's widowed mother, Elisabeth. For years the woman's sole support, her son, on joining the expedition, had arranged for her to receive the whole of his meagre salary. Henri's death, coupled with the added hardships brought by the outbreak of war in Europe, plunged her into dire straights. Humanitarian considerations aside, Sapir reckoned a $500 annual pension amounted to justifiable, if minimal, compensation for a foreign scientist who died while engaged in service to Canada, adding further that "neglect on our part of his surviving mother would not be calculated to put us in very enviable light in the eyes of our French allies." In the end, no one in the Department of Mines hierarchy was swayed, not even on moral grounds. Making matters worse, a bureaucrat in finance ordered the last of Beuchat's regular paycheques withheld. In what was to be his last letter to Sapir, in which, as in earlier ones, he protested the injustice he and Jenness felt over their paltry salaries, the Frenchman had eerily predicted "the future will pay us for this mean treatment."[101]

◆

On the afternoon of 25 July, one day after Jenness's return from Barter Island, the Southern Party departed Camden Bay for Herschel Island, a year overdue. The voyage put him in a cheerless frame of mind, his letters written at the time full of uncertainty, if not regret. One to Marett is indicative, brimming with gripes about the pitfalls of doing fieldwork under stressful, even chaotic, conditions. "Please don't think that we complain. I don't expect any of us expected an easy time," he explained. "I merely want to impress upon you that, on this expedition at least, considerations of toil or discomfort are not allowed to weigh against research." Impressed with the determination shown by his fellow scientists, he was quick to add, on a lighter note, "your humble correspondent … cannot for very shame refuse to try & follow their example."[102] His tone is little different with von Zedlitz, as he second-guesses his accomplishments on the all-important linguistic front. "I wish I could have you here for a few days," he writes, desperate for guidance with the syntactic complexities and unfamiliar sounds of local speech. "It troubles me rather sorely as there are another two years ahead."[103] Yet for all his worry, he had accomplished quite a bit, picking up a working knowledge of the Barrow dialect, sorting out its basic grammar, and compiling a thousand-word lexicon.[104]

One bright spot shone through all of this self-doubt: the value of immersing himself in day-to-day life at Harrison Bay and Barter Island. The experience convinced him that doing so was sounder, and more productive, than interviewing natives in the shadow of the Ballantynes' veranda. Anticipating Malinowski's now-famous dictum by a good eight years, he recognized the special worth of documenting the imponderabilia of everyday existence unfolding before him, making a habit of recording observations of people and places and things, interspersed with reminders of his own impressions. The very thought of what had gone unnoticed, and unregistered, on Goodenough – thousands of things, big and small, the flesh and bones of ordinary Bwaidokan life – left him "profoundly dissatisfied" with what he had accomplished there, an effort hardly worthy of the "brilliant success" he believed was Oxford's due.[105]

CHAPTER FIVE

Kiss of the White Man, 1914–1916

THE PEOPLE ARE FRIENDLY

Ten days' sailing brought *Alaska* and *Mary Sachs* to Herschel Island, their way through ice-clogged seas made all the more perilous by fog and shifting winds. Lying just inside Canadian territorial waters off Yukon's coast, the island had had quite a reputation in the late 1800s, throngs of rowdy sailors and whalers making it "the world's last jumping-off place, where no law existed and no writs ran."[1] Conditions now much tamer, the stopover allowed time to regroup in the aftermath of *Karluk*'s disappearance. With Vilhjalmur Stefansson off exploring on the frozen Beaufort since March, it fell to Rudolph Anderson to sort out the parties' competing needs for what remained of the expedition's personnel and supplies. Against the backdrop of the alleged Collinson Point mutiny, late word from Ottawa ordering that scientific work at Coronation Gulf "not be weakened for the purpose of organizing another northern party" arrived at an opportune moment.[2] The Southern Party thus remained intact, Anderson instructing its members to prepare *Alaska* and the newly purchased *North Star* for the voyage's final leg. He dispatched the others – those originally assigned to the Northern Party – to head north aboard *Mary Sachs* for a rendezvous with Stefansson at Banks Island; they sailed on 11 August 1914. Mere hours before Anderson and company were to embark, however, trouble struck again, fierce gales driving *North Star* aground and flooding its engine with sea water. Spent, drenched, and chilled to the bone from a night-long struggle to secure the schooner's moorings, Jenness chalked up the experience to the expedition's string of "fearfully bad luck."[3] *Alaska* finally departed on 17 August, most of the party and freight on board. Readying the refloated *North Star* took longer but, with Jenness and two companions as crew, the vessel cast off the following afternoon.

North Star's passage to Coronation Gulf was physically and mentally draining, one crewman minding its temperamental engine, his shipmates taking turns steering and keeping watch as they picked their course through icy, fog-bound waters. The morning of 27 August found them stuck fast within hailing distance of Bernard Harbour, the spot Anderson had chosen to set up headquarters. The way in was blocked by heavy floes as well as by pea-soup fog. An anxious Jenness longed for relief from the sleepless nights on deck, perhaps more for the simple pleasure of undressing. After departing Herschel Island, he had managed to remove boots and socks exactly once and hadn't changed clothes since quitting Barter Island.[4] One last trial remained: pushing and prodding their small craft through a narrow, ice-infested channel to her berth alongside *Alaska*. Exertion making them oblivious of time, the three coaxed *North Star* safely into "our winter harbour" mid-morning on the 28th, an exhausting finale to a northward voyage begun at Esquimalt fourteen long and tempestuous months before.

Bernard Harbour lies near the western entrance to Coronation Gulf, on the mainland side of Dolphin and Union Strait. Victoria Island, after Baffin the largest in Canada's immense arctic archipelago, sits opposite, its nearest point some thirty miles distant across the strait. Like Herschel Island, it, too, was destined to become an outpost of western civilization, defined as such by the ubiquitous Canadian triumvirate of Mounties, missionaries, and merchants. But when the Southern Party came ashore they found little more than a rocky beach. With the first hint of polar winter already in the air, making preparations for the unforgiving season ahead was their first order of business. Within a fortnight, their main project was finished: a twelve-by-sixteen-foot one-room cabin built of locally cut sods and lumber freighted north for the purpose. The party's six scientists would call it home, while the sailors and native assistants made do with separate, less elaborate quarters. Despite Jenness's unflattering description of it as a "rude hut encased in earth," the main residence was fairly substantial, its walls well insulated, its interior illuminated with oil lamps and, later, by a "carbide gasometer," a primitive Coleman lantern.[5] The shelter also boasted a sizeable library, its shelves brimming with works on northern science, including books on Inuit language and ethnology, a complete set of the 1911 edition of *Encyclopaedia Britannica*, and an eclectic sampling of literature. Apart from his precious Homer, Jenness's literary tastes at the time ran to eighteenth- and nineteenth-century German writers, a parcel from home bringing him titles by Goethe, Heine, and Schiller.[6] More satisfying still were regular Saturday night bridge games, an institution begun during the layover at Camden Bay. Once their comfortable if cramped quarters were completed, the tenants celebrated with post-prandial cigars "all around."[7]

Canada's Arctic comprises an enormous expanse of tundra and ocean bounded by mountainous Baffin Island to the east, the Beaufort Sea to the west, and the treeless continental interior to the south. Today, nearly all this region lies within the territorial borders of Nunavut and the North West Territories, their Inuit populations scattered in villages and towns. Before the 1950s, most still lived a nomadic existence on the land, with caribou, fish, and seals comprising their dietary mainstays. The people of the Coronation Gulf–Victoria Island region, the Copper Inuit, were no exception. Stefansson depicted them as "hitherto undiscovered people" when he first visited their country in 1910, a people he believed were all but untouched by influences from the outside world. His characterization, overstated though it was, convinced many anthropologists that early twentieth-century Copper Inuit represented a rarity among the world's peoples, a society of pristine hunters.[8] It also puts Jenness's remark about "real stone-age Eskimos" in context, Stefansson's early reports to the Geological Survey having left a strong impression that the gulf's inhabitants were still living much the same primal existence as their forebears had in times long past.[9]

It was true that the people here had had less experience of whites and white ways than Inuit at the Mackenzie delta or along the eastern shores of Baffin Island, regions whose waters teemed with whales and thus with commercial whalers drawn northward from different parts of the globe. The absence of whales in the many straits and gulfs surrounding their home ground accounted for a good measure of that insularity. When the Southern Party arrived, a Prince Edward Islander named Joseph Bernard was one of the few other whites alive who knew of Coronation Gulf, having passed the winter of 1910 in the harbour that now bears his name and pioneered trade with its inhabitants.[10] Others had preceded him into the area, lured by the hope of discovering the Northwest Passage, the fabled sea route to Asia across the top of the world. A cherished prize of European navigators and monarchs since the 1500s, the so-called "perfect craze" produced a wealth of geographic and scientific information on the Arctic, including some untutored descriptions of its native denizens.[11] The price of this intelligence came high, however, the search consuming fortunes, reputations, and lives. The last is epitomized in the exploits of Samuel Hearne, reputedly the first, and for many years the last, white man to set foot on the shores of Coronation Gulf. Trekking overland from Hudson Bay, he descended the Coppermine River to its mouth in the summer of 1771. Triumph soon turned to disaster when his Indian companions, Chipewyan Dene, attacked and killed several Inuit families encamped a short distance upstream, an act attributed to ancient enmity between the two peoples.[12] Subsequently

Diamond Jenness with Copper Inuit at Bernard Harbour, Nunavut, 1914.
Canadian Museum of Civilization, Fritz Johansen, 1914, 42232

christened Bloody Falls, the site of this tragedy, as well as its name, were to acquire personal significance for Jenness in 1915. Camped here on his twenty-ninth birthday, he was attacked by a wolf who took a mouthful of flesh from his arm before succumbing to a bullet from Anderson's rifle.[13]

After a half-century's lull, the years from 1819 to 1855 witnessed a veritable who's-who of Anglo-American explorers traversing the cental arctic littoral, many in search of Sir John Franklin's ill-fated third expedition, which had gone missing in 1845–46 while hunting for the elusive passage.[14] These expeditions led to occasional contacts with Copper Inuit but, unlike those to the west and east, did not open the way to commercial ventures. Even so, these transitory experiences did not leave Copper Inuit life untouched. Their fortuitous discovery of the British vessel *Investigator,* abandoned at the northern tip of Banks Island around 1853, offers an intriguing case in point. A veritable treasure-trove, the ship contained a wealth of metal and soft woods whose salvage over the coming decades fostered incipient technological change, most notably in the use of iron and copper – hence the group's name in the anthropological literature – in the manufacture of items traditionally fashioned from bone and antler.[15]

Jenness pronounced the Copper Inuit "remarkably healthy" in 1914, seemingly free of the tuberculosis, gonorrhea, syphilis, and other contact-era scourges that had devastated indigenous communities elsewhere. He suspected they had not escaped entirely, foreign microbes doubtless having entered the country with exploring parties or, more likely, with native traders arriving from bordering regions where exposure to infectious diseases was common. Even so, there was no evidence that contagions had caused depopulation or widespread social disruption. Rather, outbreaks that did occur were localized and, like periodic shortages of game or sledding accidents, a cause of "small-scale disasters," not wholesale ones.[16] The story would be far different after 1920, the "kiss of the white man," in Jenness's eerie phrasing, turning out to be the deadly price of an inescapable seduction.[17]

Anyone who has seen Robert Flaherty's 1922 documentary *Nanook of the North* remembers his depiction of the title character's first brush with the arcane side of European technology. Appearing baffled if delighted by the sounds emanating from a wind-up gramophone, an inquisitive Nanook removes the wax record from the machine, examines it closely, then bites the disc, determined to release the animating spirits he's certain reside within.[18] The few Inuit who first called at Bernard Harbour in the autumn of 1914 approached the novelty they found there with equally unabashed wonder, their exuberant, sometimes jovial investigations of the encampment and the qallunaat – white men – who lived there producing scenes reminiscent of Flaherty's classic. The main house attracted much of their curiosity, especially its glass windows, which, word quickly spread, were not made from ice after all. In the spirit of the moment, Jenness described the plight of two men peering through one of the iceless windows at the crowd gathered within, kept from joining their companions because they couldn't locate the door. Quick to make light of the situation, Qamiñgoq, "something of a humourist," shouted instructions, imploring the pair to climb onto the roof and slide down the stovepipe. The next day Qamiñgoq again held stage, this time on seeing his reflection in a mirror. "Who is this? What is his name," he repeated to everyone's glee, his audience reduced "to a perpetual state of laughter." "They are all extremely curious & have no hesitation in asking for anything & everything that takes their fancy," Jenness noted in his diary, adding that none seemed especially perturbed when refused.[19]

Most of their callers already had some experience with the likes of Bernard and Stefansson. Even so, there was little to suggest that these incipient (and quite recent) contacts had affected them in any appreciable way, leaving them much as Jenness imagined the Iñupiat had been before the deluge of outsiders arrived in their midst. He was particularly fascinated by details rarely if ever seen in Alaska even then, such as clothing styles, the tattooing on women's hands and faces, and men's tonsorial preferences – hair closely cropped at the crown, side whiskers shaved off. He was also interested in Inuit character, although his view was doubtless influenced by a theory, long since discredited, that "primitives," their lives strictly governed by custom, lack individuality. He read the people's readiness to affect "our manners" as an expression of "undeveloped personality," "their pliant wills yielding submissively to the aggressiveness of the outsider." "Compared with the Eskimos of Alaska," he concluded, "these natives were astonishingly primitive."[20]

His modest competence with the language earned Jenness the job of Southern Party interpreter, protocol officer, medic, and chief trader. The others deferred to his judgment on most issues, inquiring "what I think best to be done" about feeding their visitors, inviting them into quarters, and so forth. If grateful for their confidence, he still wrestled with misgivings about the limits of his colleagues' tolerance for the near-pandemonium the Inuit occasionally stirred up in camp. "[They] go out of their way to help me & put up with a great deal of annoyance & inconvenience," he noted, the remark tinged with guilt since it was his own research that stood to gain from having the people around. Yet he was not above complaining of a welcome wearing thin, here and there making disparaging remarks about "parasitic guests" whose persistent demands "threaten to eat us out of house [and] home."[21] The appearance of solid winter ice, and with it the chance to leave Bernard Harbour behind, could not come soon enough.

That long-awaited and much-anticipated opportunity finally arrived in mid-November. His plan for the moment was simple: to pass the winter at Ukullik, a sealing camp situated out in the strait, near the Liston and Sutton islands. The start of fieldwork in Copper Inuit country was finally at hand.

Despite its theoretical innovation, Marcel Mauss's treatise on dual social morphology was a product of armchair scholarship, its arguments drawing on ethnographic evidence largely derived from the writings of explorers and missionaries.[22] For Henri Beuchat, the chance to study the Copper Inuit at first hand had thus been ideally suited to refining the work, doubly so since they were unrepresented in the copious literature he and Mauss had combed through preparatory to publication. Aboard *Karluk*, Jenness had agreed to concentrate on anthropometry and material culture at the gulf, which would have allowed his senior colleague to focus on substantiating Mauss's leading contention: namely, that the form and scale of social life varied in concert with the seasons, growing denser, more intense, and communal in the harshness of winter, more diffuse and private in the all-too-brief summers.[23] With their partnership now impossible, Jenness had little choice but to tackle the research in all its dimensions. The measure of the success he achieved is well attested to by the resulting product of two years' labour, a product encyclopaedic in scope and impressive in scale, arguably one of the most comprehensive studies of an arctic people ever made.[24]

Beuchat's project did not die with him. Having discovered a copy of Mauss's seminal paper among his colleague's belongings at Camden Bay, Jenness became familiar with its general perspective and, over the ensuing months, kept track of instances where his own findings confirmed or disputed the author's. His travels permitted him to observe the rhythms of everyday life as the people moved across the landscape with the seasons. He took note of relations among house forms, community and domestic organization, religious belief and practice, and the material conditions of subsistence – natural and technological – at different times of the year. In the end, the cumulative experience of his stay at Coronation Gulf failed to convince him beyond a doubt that native social and intellectual life were "radically different at the two seasons," differences Mauss had depicted as winter's intense communalism and "strong religious and moral unity of mind" and summer's social fragmentation and "religious and moral impoverishment."[25] There was no question that variable material conditions affected the annual round of hunting and fishing and, by extension, the movement, size, and composition of local groups, the types of houses families occupied, and even the numbers who witnessed a shaman's conjuring. Yet aside from such adjustments as "nature compels," Jenness concluded, "there is really no fundamental change in their lives at the two seasons, but merely an external difference occasioned by, and directly reflecting, the difference in their climatic and economic environment." This was equally the case in matters of religion as in the dynamics of social life, his observations seemingly at odds with Mauss's sweeping assertion that all but the most private of rituals – namely birth and death customs and the observance of taboos – withered away as the people took up their highly dispersed, inland summer migrations. "Their religion is not dropped ... with the winter," he argued in reply; even shamans' performances "may be given ... at any season ... and in any place," not just inside the kashim or dance house, a ubiquitous feature of winter camps. Moreover, "nothing in their social organization or their religious beliefs" kept the people from adopting new patterns in either season, should changing economic or material conditions warrant. Indeed, this had already occurred among the Iñupiat when commercial trapping transformed their ancient winter existence. Similar change was soon to take root in Copper Inuit country, its first signs appearing before the Southern Party returned home in the summer of 1916.[26]

Some three years after *Life of the Copper Eskimos* appeared in print, Jenness penned an intriguing note to Mauss in which he reflected on his few conclusions about the dual social morphology thesis. Adopting an apologetic tone, he expressed relief on learning, via Barbeau, that "you did not take my ebulition [sic] against your theory too seriously." "I still think the case overdrawn," he continued, yet the main assumptions framing *Seasonal Variations* "opened my eyes to many things that I would otherwise have overlooked. Beuchat, had he lived, would not have made the mistakes I have made, and would have seen more deeply into Eskimo culture." Hidden in a Parisian archive for decades, this letter speaks equally to its author's hallmark modesty, his enduring respect for Beuchat and Mauss, and, most importantly, his growing self-awareness that direct, prolonged experience of a people does not by itself guarantee privileged understanding of their ways of life. "If I could rewrite my book on the Copper Eskimos there are many things about which I would be less positive, and many things which would require considerable revision." Of all its limitations, however, the one he regarded as least excusable was his blanket insinuation that the insights of "an armchair philosopher" hardly measure up to those of "the man who is on the spot."[27]

Great excitement marked the early weeks of winter as the Inuit hurriedly prepared for the transition from their nomadic existence on the land to the more settled life of seal hunting camps atop the ice-bound sea. Families from both sides of Dolphin and Union Strait descended on Ukullik, the population of their snow-house settlement eventually reaching some seventy-five. Jenness remained with them for the better part of December and January. Unlike his reception at Harrison Bay, his presence here and elsewhere caused a great sensation, people coming forward to shake hands – an affectation apparently acquired from Joseph Bernard – exchange names, and raise a "perfect babel ... We are friendly ... the people are friendly ... the people are glad."[28] But as had happened earlier at Bernard Harbour, he soon tired of their unbridled attentions, men and women alike examining his possessions, vying for admittance to his lodgings, pressing demands for barter, and occasionally pilfering an item or two when opportunity arose. Diary entries reveal the resultant volatility of his mood, passages peppered with caustic comments about the persistence and mendacity of this or that person and with meditations on peace and quiet, the Inuit seeming to have "no conception apparently of a man's wishing to be silent."[29] In his estimation the Puivlirmiut, summer inhabitants of southwestern Victoria Island, were the worst offenders, the beleaguered anthropologist unashamedly confessing to have stayed "with [them] as long as I did only because I was securing ethnological material – but I could not stand it much longer." "They were rather getting on my nerves ... I believe only the fear that I should refuse to buy anything at Ukullik later – prevented any extensive stealing."[30]

Complain as he might, these annoyances underscored the considerable sway he held among the Inuit, influence derived from his capacity to cut them off from trade whenever circumstances warranted. Compounding the people's anxieties was their wide-spread belief that Jenness had the ability to "magicize" them in revenge for alleged wrongdoings. Indeed, they took for granted that all qallunaat possessed such powers, an endowment that, as with their own great shamans, included the capacity to cure illness or visit misfortune, even death, on others. This foreboding spilled over in dramatic fashion when the anthropologist found himself threatened by a man who had seized his steel knife when a proposed trade for the prized item was refused. A bystander intervened before any harm was done, persuading his belligerent compatriot to relinquish the weapon and thus bring the standoff to a bloodless end. "Things looked very awkward at one moment," Jenness wrote at the time, adding only some equally terse thanks to the brave fellow who stepped in on his behalf. But in print, the story acquired a more heroic denouement, the author describing the "magical" effect his sternly spoken warnings in English had had on opponent and onlookers alike. "The natives ... thought them a curse that would bring some dire calamity upon their heads," he imagined, assuming that their uncertainty was focused on his putative mastery of powerful familiars such as the spirits of animals or the shades of dead qallunaat.[31]

Although in private Jenness was inclined to make light of their fears, in public the people's belief that he was possessed of extraordinary powers was something he was at pains to ignore. This became clear some time later when he stood accused of causing the death of a man at Ukullik. Local opinion held that the unlucky victim had been "bewitched," allegedly in retaliation for stealing from the newcomers. Uloqsaq, a renowned shaman, put the matter to trial by divination, the proceedings conducted partly in "white man's talk" to allow for communication with qallunaaq spirits. Blame lay elsewhere, he announced, likely with white men beyond Copper Inuit country. He was simply "too shrewd not to know where [the people's] interests lay," Jenness cynically remarked of the outcome, that, and the likelihood that Uloqsaq was too "intimidated by my presence" to have found otherwise.[32]

Given that alternative arrangements were simply impractical, Jenness made a practice of lodging with one or another family wherever he travelled, sometimes bunking down alone in an unoccupied corner, other times finding a place among the householders huddled together on the sleeping platform under caribou skin robes. Coming down from the mission-house veranda and entering the native's hut brought the routines and intimacies of family life into sharp focus. It also evoked strong feelings of ambivalence and vulnerability on those occasions when the flow of events led him to unfamiliar moral ground. This happened during his stay with Haviuyaq and Itoqunna, a couple whose professed dislike of "English food" was recommendation enough to settle in with them. "There was an interesting insight into the customs of the Eskimos last night," begins the entry for 11 December, just days after he had taken up residence under the couple's roof. He then candidly described his reaction to the custom of spouse exchange, having discovered, quite by surprise, that his host's bedmate that evening had been Niq, his cousin Aksiatak's wife; Itoqunna, in turn, spent the night in Niq's place. With the women returned to their husbands the next morning, a mischievous Haviuyaq poked fun at his boarder's innocence, inquiring good-naturedly, and to the delight of everyone in earshot, "'Where is Itoqunna' – alluding to my question of the night before," and then, to Jenness's further embarrassment, asking if "I still wanted to sleep alone."[33] Similar offers were repeatedly rebuffed, as were occasional marriage proposals. Kaullu, a twenty-something "merry widow," was his most persistent suitor. He indignantly accused the Inuit of failing to "understand a man not wishing that sort of thing," all the while being oblivious to the gesture as a form of hospitality and to their views on celibacy.[34] Committed as he was to grasping the native point of view – the lessons of Goodenough and Alaska still fresh in mind – here was one area where the participant part of participant-observation had its limits.

"The custom [of spouse exchange] is of course well known among savages from books," he had to concede. Yet "strangely enough," encountering it so unexpectedly and at first hand, "shook my nerves more than anything else I have seen in the arctic – even more, I think, than [sailor] Andre Norem's suicide" at Camden Bay the previous winter. His equanimity disturbed, even broaching the subject as a point of detached anthropological curiosity seemed grossly inappropriate. "I feel rather ashamed of my weakness in this respect as an ethnologist," he confided, noting that he was tempted to ask his hosts a few clarifying questions but was unable to bring himself to do even that.[35] As his inhibitions gradually eased in the days ahead, he learned that the exchanges between Haviuyaq and Aksiatak marked their close friendship and kinship and not, as he had initially thought, à la Mauss, the transition from summer to winter. It is easy to imagine how a man of prim and proper upbringing might struggle with either explanation, each seeming to imply a degree of moral license inimical to domestic order, even among "primitives." As he soon learned, the practice disrupted neither communal harmony nor marital relations, "incidents [being] so usual as to pass unnoticed." Unnoticed by everyone but him, that is.[36]

◆

A fair portion of time and energy was devoted to obtaining ethnographic specimens for the Victoria Memorial Museum. Blessed with a clientele eager for trade, it was not long before he had a sizeable collection of clothing, domestic and hunting implements, and other items. But if obtaining specimens was comparatively easy, carting them around the countryside was not, especially in the warmer months when travel was chiefly on foot. There were problems to grapple with in winter, too, items being lost or damaged when sleds, piled high with baggage, tipped or met any of a dozen other hazards. A good deal of collecting thus occurred in and around Bernard Harbour, a process made simpler as people from the far corners of the region began calling at the station once word reached them that white men were on the strait. Things that could not be collected, like snow houses and fishing weirs, he either sketched or photographed, and he also employed the survey-issued Kodak 3A to produce an invaluable record of ordinary articles in everyday use. A conscientious record-keeper, Jenness logged in nearly everything he bartered for, making note of when each piece was acquired and whether matches, ammunition, or other high-demand imports were given in exchange. Supplemented by his colleague's occasional acquisitions, some 2,500 artifacts were eventually accessioned in Ottawa, a timely collection documenting a native technology sliding toward extinction.[37]

Karluk's disappearance, with calipers and other instruments aboard, offered a temporary reprieve from the awkward job of collecting anthropometric data from the Iñupiat. When a new set reached the gulf from Ottawa, however, Jenness set about taking measurements in a more or less systematic fashion, eventually recording the particulars of 124 adults – two-thirds of whom were men – from twelve different local groups. Following guidelines prepared by English physician F.C. Shrubsall for the 1912 edition of *Notes and Queries in Anthropology*, he took a battery of eleven separate measurements: three of the head, seven of the face, nose, and jaws, and one of overall stature. In addition to estimating each person's age, he described other distinguishing features: body weight, colour and texture of head and facial hair, eye colour and shape, shape of lips. And with the cooperation of Anderson and expedition photographer Hubert Wilkins, he produced a representative portfolio of photographic portraits, including both front and profile views of numerous individuals.[38]

While nothing like the disquieting experience he had met with earlier in New Guinea, doing anthropometry at the gulf presented its own brand of difficulties, difficulties best handled, as was often the case, with equal measures of ingenuity, patience, and good humour. Winter camps such as Ukullik were well suited to conducting this sort of investigation, their fairly large populations comprising a mix of people from different localities, the season permitting as close to a sedentary existence as arctic hunters might expect to enjoy. Yet finding sufficient space indoors, not just to contain the crowds that regularly gathered to witness the proceedings but to work without constant interruption, was no simple matter. By default, the main dwelling at Bernard Harbour was pressed into service when need arose, though its interior, already chock-full of furniture, scientific gear, and specimens, to say nothing of its usual inmates, offered less than spacious accommodation. Away from headquarters, the local kashim worked reasonably well as a makeshift laboratory. The Copper Inuit version of the dance house was not a stand-alone structure, as occurred elsewhere. Rather, it was the high-domed forecourt of a multi-family dwelling: in effect, two or more snow houses joined together.[39] Although barely comfortable, a combination of seal oil lamps and body heat generally kept temperatures in the kashim tolerable. Their major drawback was lack of sufficient light for reading instruments, sooty train-oil lamps not quite equal to the task and ambient light from outdoors ranging from little to none. On the plus side, the dance-house roof, unlike an ordinary igloo, was usually high enough for a grown person to walk around without stooping. This allowed sufficient clearance to use a fully extended anthropometer.[40]

By good fortune, the least of his worries was finding subjects willing to be measured. In most cases, payment of a fishhook or two for men, some matches or a steel needle for women, was sufficient inducement to all but the most timid. There were even a few who volunteered to undergo the procedure a second time, their first experience dating to Stefansson's 1910 visit. Rather than being an unwelcome ordeal, measuring sessions frequently took on a festive air, attendees "always ready to tender advice and assistance" and to keep the mood light with "jesting remarks" about every phase of the anthropologist's work.[41] We can only imagine what the Inuit – or the Papuans, for that matter – really thought of this poking and prodding, surely one of the more eccentric, and inscrutable, of the white man's rituals.

While sufficiently conversant in Inuktitut to measure heads and barter for stone lamps, Jenness fretted that a still-imperfect command of the language limited his investigation of cultural intangibles such as religion and morality, and even the collection of texts, which Edward Sapir had urged. Silas Palaiyak, his native assistant, offered little help, the youth's abilities as an interpreter hampered in part by his halting English, in part by crucial differences between his own Mackenzie River dialect and the dialect spoken at Coronation Gulf.[42] The situation improved immeasurably the following winter when Patsy Klengenberg joined the expedition. Fifteen at the time, the bilingual "half-caste" proved a competent interpreter and a worthy student, learning to read and write under the anthropologist's tutelage. Time benefited Jenness's language skills, too, the experience of accompanying the Puivlirmuit in their months-long travels on Victoria Island without benefit of an interpreter serving the purpose admirably. For the interim, circumstances left him feeling "greatly handicapped," his realization that children "grasp what I am trying to say quicker than the older people" doing nothing to boost confidence in the ethnographic data he was collecting, or to allay worries over what he was missing.[43]

Early February brought the sun's long-awaited return and with it a chance to venture beyond the confines of Dolphin and Union Strait. Travelling with two companions, his itinerary took him up the valley of the Coppermine River, to his date with the ravenous wolf, then back through the westernmost precincts of Coronation Gulf, a journey of four-weeks' duration. Near the ice-bound islands of the Duke of York archipelago, they came upon a sealing camp whose population comprised a "mixed crowd" that hailed from various localities. The visitors were welcomed with a friendly if restrained reception, one Jenness attributed to their "growing used to white men" in their midst. Signs of contact were evident everywhere, "many [having] guns ... some spy glasses ... & pots & kettles etc abound."[44] As he learned from Uloqsaq, the local luminary who later ascertained his innocence in the alleged death-by-sorcery affair, Joseph Bernard and other itinerant merchants were not the sole source of imported wares: they also arrived overland from as far south as Great Bear Lake. Stefansson claimed to have encouraged communication with this distant quarter back in 1910, linking whites with Inuit through Dene intermediaries. "I did not desire to bring my unspoiled

Coronation Gulf people into contact with civilization," the explorer later recalled, "but it seemed the thing could not be staved off for more than a year or two, anyway."[45] True enough. Consider Uloqsaq's desire "to impress [Jenness] with his wealth & importance": after showing off his prized possessions and the separate-but-equal apartments in which his two wives lived, he unabashedly flaunted nouveau-qallunaat tastes by treating his guest to afternoon tea served in cups and saucers.[46]

Only later did Jenness learn that some of the items he saw in the settlement – a cassock, religious texts in Latin and French – were in fact evidence of the darker side of the future Stefansson foresaw. The sad story began unfolding the following autumn when officers of the Royal North West Mounted Police were dispatched to the gulf to investigate the disappearance of Jean-Baptiste Rouvière and Guillaume Le Roux, Oblate priests en route to Copper Inuit territory in 1913. The police eventually determined that the pair had met a violent end near the infamous Bloody Falls. Two men, Sinnisiaq and (a different) Uloqsaq, were eventually charged with murder and sent to Edmonton for trial in 1918. To them belongs the lamentable distinction of being the first Inuit to face charges under British law. Only by dint of good luck did they avoid a yet more grievous status, that of being the first of their compatriots to face the gallows. Moved by political considerations more than clemency, the government permitted their return home from confinement after serving two years of what were to be life sentences. The gesture was calculated to "exert a salutary influence on their tribe."[47]

LIKE THE HEROES OF HOMER

By mid-March, the depths of winter had passed, the hours of daylight growing longer, the air noticeably milder. For the Inuit, these early harbingers of spring signalled the approach of the inland phase of their yearly round, one that would have them living a nomadic, solitary existence until autumn. With the early days of May, family groups departed the thinning sea ice for interior hunting ranges where they fished in lakes and streams, and hunted caribou on the tundra. In 1915, Jenness joined one such group on its journey across the land, something few if any qallunaat had done, then or since. Pleasant temperatures and round-the-clock sunlight aside, the privations and gruelling hardships they endured made winter seem "almost a holiday" by comparison.[48] By experiencing them, the anthropologist came ever closer to the Malinowskian ideal, and perhaps closer to it than Bronislaw Malinowski himself was to realize in his own Trobriand researches: comprehending the native's inner perspective on life, "*his* vision of *his* world."[49]

A middle-aged Puivlirmiut couple, Ikpukkuaq and Higilaq, headed the party Jenness accompanied through the Victoria Island interior. It

In Twilight and in Dawn

Ikpukkuaq near Lake Ammalurtuq, Nunavut.
Canadian Museum of Civilization, Diamond
Jenness, 1915, 36965

was Ikpukkuaq who had defused the knife episode some months before, a gesture that had led to friendship between the two and then to the agreement that found them travelling together as putative father and son. In a sense, their arrangement was "more in the nature of a business proposition" than anything else, the anthropologist pledging to compensate his companions with a Winchester .44, powder, cartridges and other items, and to contribute a dog team and assorted equipment toward the season's outfit.[50] Still, the time they spent in one another's company nurtured genuine warmth between them, as it did between Jenness and others of the little cluster of families over which Ikpukkuaq presided. But his favourite was Qanajuk, Higilaq's daughter from a pre-

Higilaq at Bernard Harbour, Nunavut. Canadian Museum of Civilization, Rudolph Martin Anderson, 1916, 39058

vious marriage. The affection was mutual, the teenager soon acquiring the nickname Jennie because of the special connection she felt toward her qallunaaq brother.

With his own baggage assembled for the journey ahead, Injuqoaq – "old man," as Jenness was known, a name befitting someone with long whiskers – departed Bernard Harbour on 13 April. He and his companions were bound for a temporary camp on the strait's opposite shore, staging area for the group's landward migration. That was the last time he would see his expedition mates or hear the English language for the next six and a half months.

The return to solid ground unfolded slowly. Still, the leisurely pace of their preparations did little to mask the people's eagerness for a change of scene and diet. Within a month, half a dozen families, nineteen men, women, and children, would reach Okauyarvik creek, their custom-

In Twilight and in Dawn

ary gateway into the island's southwestern interior. Without the usual clamour for trade, Jenness found their company refreshingly congenial, nothing like his previous encounters with them at Ukullik. "They are treating me very well – as suits their own interests of course," he admitted. "I really am much more comfortable among these Eskimos than I have ever been before."[51] As for the affable Ikpukkuaq and Higilaq, his adoptive parents, "I wish I could talk freely to them ... they are very communicative & would teach me many of their customs." [52] All things considered, he added, they make good company "despite many 'peculiarities' rather repugnant to a European but natural to them." Accustomed to a great many Inuit ways at this point, Jenness had yet to appreciate their taste for well-rotted meat and fat, a supply of which he and Ikpukkuaq had recently retrieved. The sheer misery of freighting the cargo homeward in the warm spring air did nothing to improve his opinion of native gustatory preferences. "It weighted not only the sled," he wryly recalled the scene, "but the surrounding atmosphere." Prudently, "I kept to the windward of it ... but distance seemed to make no appreciable difference."[53]

The territory through which they travelled – Wollaston Land on European maps of the day – was bounded in the south by Dolphin and Union Strait and in the north by Prince Albert Sound. Its "backbone," the Colville Hills, ran across the treeless terrain from east to west "in wavy ridges," their elevations no greater than 800 feet. Scattered among these hills lay countless lakes, which teemed with trout and freshwater char. These were the mainstays of Puivlirmiut subsistence through the height of summer, much as venison was during the caribou's southward migration in fall.[54] The firearms father and son carried gave them a decided advantage in killing game; their companions relied on the more familiar bows and arrows. Still thinking like a white man, Jenness grumbled over the "prospect of their depending on me for hunting," ancient custom dictating that a man's good fortune be shared all around. Even so, he quickly added, "I am obtaining some good ethnological notes, & the more there are to travel with the better the opportunity there is of seeing native life."[55]

A fortnight elapsed en route to Prince Albert Sound, the way slowed by hard sledding over hills and tundra now thinly covered with the last of the season's slushy snow. This is where the Puivlirmiut expected to find Tormiat – or Kanghirjuarmiut – the name by which they knew their distant neighbours on the sound. Stefansson had earlier reported seeing blond-haired, blue-eyed, and fair-complexioned individuals among them, an astounding claim Jenness hoped to verify. Higilaq further piqued his anthropological curiosity about this remote group by recounting a tale of long-ago starvation, a dreadful time that forced the survivors among them into "chopping [the dead] up with axes like caribou" to stay alive. The mere thought of such things, she assured her son, unnerved her own people.[56]

Anxiety reigned for a week until the Tormiat finally materialized. Until then, opinion was split over whether to search for them or simply move on. "It is better ethnologically to spend a summer with the band I am with, & watch their summer life, than to run around the country" in what might well be a fruitless effort, was how Jenness saw things. Besides, as far as he knew, no white person, not even Stefansson, had ever "spent a summer living the life of the Eskimos ... so I have a unique opportunity & still have a chance of seeing the 'blonds.'"[57] Meanwhile, Higilaq sought to allay everyone's uncertainty by performing a divination, consulting her qallunaaq son's potent familiars. "It was the most palpable fraud imaginable," Jenness remarked of the proceedings, roughly akin to head-lifting, the conjurer explaining that if the bundle of his shirts she held in her hands felt heavy when a question was put to it, the reply was yes, if light, then no. "The answers were supposed to emanate from me, or rather from the spirit that dwells in me," he noted, hardly surprised when each inquiry produced the expected results: the Tormiat were indeed coming, their arrival imminent. "If this proves untrue, it is my spirit that lied, not the medium of [the diviner] ... It is very convenient for the medium to be able to refer failures to the spirit."[58]

The late spring gathering lasted four days, the Inuit chatting, dancing, and feasting in "high revel." For the Tormiat, who had little experience of qallunaat, it was the anthropologist who held their attention. "They are all amazed that I should know anything at all about their land and movements," no less speak their language. Unfortunately, their astonishment translated into reticence, and even feigned ignorance, whenever he asked about their customs. In any event, their mere presence answered the biggest question of all: there were "no signs of 'blondness' that do not [also] appear in the more southern Eskimos."[59] The get-together came to a hasty conclusion when a Tormiat women, Nateksina, flirted with Ikpukkuaq as Higilaq looked on. Nateksina "suddenly leaned forward and pressed her face against [his]," was how Jenness described the indiscretion, a gesture that left its recipient "more offended than flattered." His wife's anger forced the Puivlirmuit to decamp the next morning.[60] Feelings of marital insecurity resurfaced months later in a private moment between mother and son when Higilaq mentioned this and a second incident involving her adopted daughter, Kullaq. She asked Jenness to let her know if he "saw any woman 'kiss' [Ikpukkuaq]" again. "What did it matter anyhow?" he asked her, his embarrassing discovery of spouse exchange the previous winter still fresh in mind. "He's such a fine looking man," came the answer. "Apparently even an Eskimo woman can be jealous," the anthropologist naively confessed to his diary, what little he had seen of the intimacies between husbands and wives having previously persuaded him that this could never be so.[61]

This was not to be the last of Higilaq's marital worries. In October, she and Kullaq traded "real Billingsgate" – foul-mouthed invective – over some trivial matter or other. The intensity of their row, culminating in Ikpukkuaq driving a frightened and stark-naked Higilaq into the frigid night air, added credence to lingering rumours of a second flirtation, this one very close to home.[62] If that weren't trouble enough, Kitiksiq, Ikpukkuaq's former wife, paid the couple a surprise visit the following spring. The reunion was a disaster, she desiring to reclaim her ex, he "cling[ing] fondly to Higilaq." An awkward domestic arrangement soon emerged that found the spurned Kitiksiq settling in next door and a hapless Ikpukkuaq furnishing her with food and other necessities. Jenness noted that "the two women disregard each other as far as possible, and Ikpuk evidently feels the burden."[63]

"I am growing Eskimo in my ways," Jenness boasted, "care less about dirty pots or dirty person – drink more cold water – tend to have my mouth agape when travelling. It requires an effort to keep 'white.'"[64] That was in early June. By month's end, he was singing a different tune. What had begun as a prosperous season quickly became spare, the fishing unreliable, wet weather hampering efforts to supplement stocks of dried trout and venison already inadequate to feed hungry people and hungrier dogs. The group responded by splitting up, each family heading off on its own until the gathering caribou herds of late summer would permit them to reunite. Now faced with a steady diet of raw trout, frequent rain making it nearly impossible to find fuel dry enough to use for cooking, the once-robust anthropologist realized he was not "Eskimo" in every respect. The mere thought of consuming anything uncooked was nauseating, as was the sight of his companions doing so. "They never clean [fish], but eat the black ordure with great relish ... [their] hands and face... smeared all over with it." Certain that going hungry was preferable to such "indigestible" fare, he took solace in daydreaming about the "dainties" that awaited his return to the well-provisioned Bernard Harbour.[65] "I ought to be in first-rate condition from the outdoor tramping, but short rations have reduced my strength," he lamented, the penetrating dampness of early arctic summer doing nothing to lift the spirits. "It's a pity I can't adopt an Eskimo's digestion as well as his clothes," the Inuit themselves, no strangers to real privation, seeming to be "all fat and content" at the time.[66]

Despite looming ill-health, Jenness struggled to carry on much as usual, joining the others at fishing places, searching the hillsides for stray caribou, shouldering a share of the baggage in moving from one camping spot to the next. Then, in mid-July, an unquenchable thirst and bouts of acute intestinal pain and diarrhoea left him listless and irritable, his discomfort aggravated further by swarms of bloodthirsty mosquitoes as ferocious as their Papuan cousins. Unsure of her medicine's efficacy when the patient was white, Higilaq thought it wise to attempt a cure anyway, consulting her son's shirt to divine the illness' cause, then exorcising the offending agent. Ignoring the patient's self-diagnosis of "insidious dysentery" brought on by too much raw meat and too much water, she settled on a malevolent spirit dispatched from a distant quarter. "Personally," Jenness quipped, "I place more faith in the laxative I took this morning & the two pills of iron & arsenic tonight."[67] "It is simply a matter of making them understand ... my point of view," he wrote another day, his tolerance of Higilaq's conjuring eroded by deepening frustration and worry over the situation. "They fancy my sickness is due to magic & that diet has nothing to do with it."[68]

Whatever their views on its cause, the family went to great lengths to see him through the illness. Recovery came slowly, his stamina lingering at low ebb, symptoms continuing to flare up despite a more agreeable diet and several days spent curled up in a sleeping bag, "hardly able to move." Worn down and stressed out, his disposition suffered too, his usual even-temperedness broken by fits of unrepentant complaining and crankiness and, on one occasion, a violent outburst that left one of his dogs – "a great nuisance all along," he insisted – dead of a gunshot wound. Even a meal of freshly killed goose offered no comfort, its meat "very palatable under other conditions, but here ... insipid and indigestible." "I am heartily sick of Eskimo life with its filth & squalor" he fumed in disgust, "& long for decent food & rest & quiet."[69] If he entertained thoughts of dying, he dared not write them down. As for the Inuit, the implications of his lingering illness were an obvious source of concern. "The Eskimos are speculating as to whether I am going to die" he noted, their fears understandably focused on whether "the folks at the station will be angry and hostile to them if I do."[70]

The first days of August brought signs that the crisis might be passing, his strength restored sufficiently to allow him back on his feet. The recovery was well timed, as preparations for following the caribou were now in full swing. The weeks ahead would prove the most gruelling of the group's inland migration, their pace, ten or fifteen miles a day over mosquito-infested and waterlogged terrain, amounting to a forced march compared to their almost leisurely travels since spring. Added to that were endless hours spent pursuing their quarry, sometimes subsisting on scraps of dried venison and back fat, sometimes gorging themselves "like the heroes of Homer."[71] Considering the lingering tentativeness of his health, it is remarkable that Jenness managed to keep up. Feeling closer to sixty than thirty at times, he marvelled at his companions' endurance, adults and children pushing themselves for days on end, sometimes on short rations, usually under the crushing weight of packs laden with green caribou skins, often without benefit of sleep. He welcomed even the slightest breaks from the grinding routine, but these offered no relief from the mental exhaustion that accompanied it. Recurrent fantasies of being rescued enticed him into musings about family and friends and home. "Strange how one visions every stage of the journey – the boat voyage – the meeting etc," he wrote, momentarily oblivious to everything but his own wistful longings for the sights and sounds and smells of a more familiar world. "Is it mere home-sickness," he wondered, "or a weakening of the intellect?"[72]

By early September, winter was again bearing down on Victoria Island, the ground already snow-covered for weeks, inland lakes and coastal waters starting to freeze over. Before long, great herds of caribou, their rutting season at an end, would begin massing along the island's southern shore, the most risky stage of their southward migration – traversing the strait – about to commence. However much Jenness might have yearned to follow their track to the mainland, and then on to Bernard Harbour, that would simply have to wait since human beings, unlike caribou, lack any "special 'ice instinct'" for negotiating so perilous a route as this time of year presented.[73] The remainder of their Wollaston Land sojourn passed uneventfully, scattered families assembling once again near the coast, their attentions now turned to the impending return of winter. As he had done the previous autumn, Jenness kept a watchful eye on the progress of freezing in the strait, his fitfulness peaking on those few days when atmospheric conditions allowed the Liston and Sutton Islands – stepping-stones on the well-travelled route to the mainland – to loom into sight on the southern horizon. On 7 November, with the ice finally suitable for travel, he and Ikpukkuaq, their sled piled high with goods, departed before sun-up for the mainland. They made Bernard Harbour the following evening, the way speeded by fine, windless weather.

◆

Stacks of mail and bundles of newspapers awaited his return to headquarters. It is hard to imagine anything hitting with more effect than the ill-tidings of world war, now, incredibly, into its second year. Some news from William McKinlay, late of the doomed *Karluk,* was also on hand. McKinlay's letter, written from his native Scotland, recounted the rescue mission at Wrangel Island the previous September and confirmed the miserable fates of Beuchat and ten others in the aftermath of the *Karluk's* loss. There were local developments to catch up on, too, none as momentous as the arrival of an Anglican deacon, Herbert Girling, and a corporal in the Royal North West Mounted Police, Wyndham Valentine Bruce. Girling had come to introduce the Copper Inuit to Christianity, Bruce to inquire after the missing Oblate fathers Rouvière and Le Roux. Within the year they were joined by W.G. Phillips of the Hudson's Bay Company, the veritable third pillar of Canada's nascent northern administration, and soon thereafter by others bringing alien diseases and alien ideas about race, power, and privilege. The prospect of what lay ahead for the Inuit weighed on Jenness's mind, particularly on Victoria Island as he observed Ikpukkuaq and the others in their everyday lives or struggling to comprehend the odd ways of their foreign companion. "One wonders how much alcohol they would consume if it were procurable & how long the race would last in consequence," he mused at one point, prompted by the sight of them drinking nothing more corrupting than melted snow. Whenever conversation turned to the refusal of expedition members to sleep with local women, he first tried to explain the great harm that "less scrupulous" whites had already visited on their western neighbours, then insinuated that their own fortunes would doubtless be the same. Glumly, he concluded, "It is sad to see the ravages our diseases make among the native in all parts of the world, but it seems inevitable."[74]

Despite this grave prognosis, Jenness held to the faint hope that the scale of imminent peril might be lessened if the Dominion government were persuaded to take swift and decisive action. However long the odds, he resolved to put background information on the urgency of the situation in Copper Inuit country into the hands of the Mounted Police, trusting that they, in turn, would pass details up the line. "My chief reason in sending a statement," he reasoned in his diary, "is to urge that precautions be taken against the indiscriminate influx of white men and western Eskimos saturated with diseases." Addressed to Commissioner Aylesworth B. Perry, the communiqué recommended a quarantine, banning outsiders from entering the territory without first obtaining a certificate of good health from the medical officer stationed on the Mackenzie.[75] With its priorities focused elsewhere, Canada's wartime government never contemplated such a measure. Yet, even if it had, the issue had already been rendered academic, Jenness's letter reaching Perry in Regina just as the invasion's advance guard began filtering into Coronation Gulf and environs. Along with rifles and steel traps they brought tuberculosis, measles, and venereal disease, a potent mix that was not long in transforming the Copper Inuit into "economic slaves in the service of European civilization" and threatening a demographic catastrophe to rival the one that had decimated their north Alaskan and Mackenzie river compatriots.[76]

Having spent the preceding months shuttling back and forth between Bernard Harbour and Ukullik, once February 1916 rolled around Jenness trained his sights eastward, on the distant reaches of Coronation Gulf. If conditions allowed, he intended to travel as far as the Kent Peninsula, the outer limits of Copper Inuit territory. This quarter reportedly had a sizeable population, some of whom had yet to have direct contact with whites. Accompanied by his interpreter Patsy, Higilaq's adult son Avrunna, and Girling – the missionary seeking some on-the-job training, a baptism by ice and snow, as it were – he left on the morning of the fifteenth, the thermometer registering thirty below. Had he had even an inkling of what was to come, he might have elected to stay put, awaiting spring's return and with it, preparations for the Southern Party's departure. Only weeks before he admitted to wearying of the grinding routines; "I think we are all tired of the Arctic, even Dr. Anderson," he allowed in a letter home; "I certainly have no wish to see it again."[77]

Ready or not, his last wintertime expedition proved to be an arctic experience par excellence. Lasting a month, the trip across the storm-swept gulf took them as far as the Jamieson Islands, northwest of Bathurst Inlet, the full excursion, out and back, covering some three hundred miles. Cooperative at first, the weather became a formidable obstacle midway through the journey, the blizzards and bitter cold that had prevailed for the better part of January suddenly returning in full fury. Sometimes lasting for days on end, these storms made travel a punishing ordeal, the frigid gales, by a stroke of terrible luck, blowing in their faces regardless of the direction they headed. Apart from struggling to ward off frostbite, Jenness also contended with a rebellious stomach, attacks of diarrhoea as severe as those he had suffered the previous summer troubling him on and off for weeks. If there were a bright side to all of this, it was in their decision to travel close by the mainland shore, making it possible to find driftwood and the occasional caribou or hare. This allowed a measure of comfort indoors, even if there was none to be found outside.[78]

The journey's trials paled next to the privations the winter of 1916 visited on the area's inhabitants. Jenness had witnessed mild symptoms of this early in the new year at Ukullik, where storms that prevented hunting had reduced many families to eating scraps of seal skin and allegedly resulted in several cases of infanticide.[79] Conditions were little different out in the gulf: "signs of starvation still confronted us on every side."[80] As ever, the anthropologist was impressed by the patient good humour and unflagging optimism with which the Inuit faced adversity, their hardships taken as no reason to dispense with customary generosity toward visitors. This was made painfully evident at the Jamieson Islands, the most remote, and perhaps the hardest-hit, of the settlements they visited. Several of its inhabitants appeared "more distressed by their apparent inhospitality at being unable to offer us the usual presents of meat," than by the fact of their own "pinched faces and empty cooking-pots."[81]

The journey's final week may have been the toughest of all, the westward trek slowed by savage headwinds, howling blizzards, and numbing cold. Three days were lost to travel when blinding snow cut visibility to mere feet. Already anxious to reach home, their rapidly depleting stores added to everyone's impatience, the dogs being put on starvation rations, people making do on two spartan meals a day.[82] Awaking to an early morning lull on 16 March, they wasted little time in resuming their homeward course. Two days' sledding brought them to Cape Krusenstern, at the strait's entrance, another two to the station. All arrived spent, frostbitten and in dire need of a decent meal.

By late June, Bernard Harbour was free of ice, *Alaska* now riding at anchor. All hands were busy preparing for departure, specimens, supplies, and personal belongings crated and loaded aboard, the ship treated to minor repairs and a fresh coat of paint for the long voyage ahead. The main house was left standing, a gift to the Anglican mission that was soon to be up and running. There were long-standing promises to be fulfilled, too, Jenness making ample provision for Girling to issue ammunition and other essentials to Ikpukkuaq and family as need arose. "It was melancholy to reflect, during these last days, how little I had done, how little I could do, to ensure the welfare of my family during the years to follow," he later recalled, fully aware of the sweeping changes, and dangers, they and their compatriots would soon face. Sadder still was the memory of a seance Higilaq had held that spring, whose purpose "was to induce my spirit to come to their help whenever they are in distress, after I have gone away." "Hearken to our call," she and Ikpukkuaq implored. "Sometimes ... I should not be able to hear," he cautioned in response, deeply moved by "their simple faith and trust in me." "Yes" Higilaq said, "sometimes one can do nothing."[83]

CHAPTER SIX

In the Trenches,
1916–1919

BELEAGUERED HOME FRONT

In stark contrast to their ordeal three years before, the Southern Party's homeward voyage was uneventful, *Alaska's* passage to Nome taking a month, to Seattle, aboard the steamer *Northwestern,* an additional two weeks. Completing the journey by rail, the passengers disembarked at Ottawa's newly opened Union Station in early October. They arrived without fanfare, the public's interest in the venture, as it had been from the start, drawn not to scientific discovery but to Vilhjalmur Stefansson's celebrity and the tragedies and controversies that swirled around him. Absent the limelight, perhaps thankfully so, the expedition's rank and file were left to step quietly off the train and into the maelstrom of a country consumed by war.

Jenness's first weeks in the city were fraught with anxiety and doubts about what the future might bring and what lay immediately before him. Feeding his gloom was the feel of daily life in the capital and the atmosphere on the streets, indeed across the Dominion, which was charged with a feeling of crisis whipped up by a trio of divisive political issues: mandatory conscription, imposition of an income tax, and prohibition. Further darkening the national mood were the equally profound troubles of a war-weary populace, ordinary citizens struggling with inflation and shortages, and with inescapable fears for the safety of fathers, brothers, and husbands in uniform overseas. Against this public backdrop came the personally dispiriting news that the Geological Survey was unable, more likely unwilling, to sweeten the terms of its original offer of post-expedition employment, concessions Edward Sapir had tried, but failed, to wring from his superiors. Jenness's travails on Canada's behalf were reason enough to expect a longer-term commitment and to resent the survey's evident intransigence in the matter. Of course, the $140 monthly wage that accompanied the temporary appointment on offer was hardly negligible; indeed, it must have seemed like a small fortune, worth more per year than his pay for the preceding three years combined. Believing himself "perfectly free to follow my own interests," what remained was to find a way of reconciling two competing priorities: on the one hand, his sense of professional obligation to anthropology, and on the other, an equally felt responsibility to serve the empire in its time of crisis.[1]

Word of the outside world penetrated Canada's remote western Arctic slowly, which had left the Southern Party with limited and imperfect knowledge of the perilous course on which the European powers had embarked. In fact, just one mail packet, delivered in November 1915, had found its way to Coronation Gulf during their entire stay. Personal letters, the first they had received in eighteen months, brought shocking details of the conflict and of family and friends – including Diamond's brother Frederick – now off fighting or enduring war-related trials at home.[2] "I expect it will all be ended before we reach civilization again," Jenness wrote to his much-troubled friend and mentor George von Zedlitz, "but if it should not be, and volunteers are required, I shall offer my services." "Not that I want to fight," he continued, "the very idea of shooting at men with whom you have no quarrel is horrible – but it would be a clear case of duty, as far as I can discern."[3] Unanimity in support of the Allied cause reigned at Bernard Harbour, yet only Jenness and John Cox, a survey topographer, would eventually follow through, enlisting together in the Canadian forces. Expedition photographer George Wilkins served too, taking an officer's commission in the Flying Corps of his native Australia.

Having brooded over his plan for nearly a year, Jenness was surprised at the unenthusiastic reception his enlistment plans received from associates at the Anthropological Division. Marius Barbeau, said to be deeply disturbed by the grave dangers facing his beloved France, remained more indifferent than opposed, unwilling to allow wartime conditions to interfere with his own work and assuming that Jenness would prefer to do the same. Unlike his wife, Marie Larocque, he was also disinterested in Prime Minister Borden's plan to bring in compulsory military service, a move resisted in most quarters of French Canada where the fate of the British Empire was anything but a compelling issue. "I daren't mention the word 'conscription' in a letter to you," Jenness wrote his friend months later, "lest [Mrs. Barbeau] should excommunicate me altogether."[4] In Sapir's opinion, the war itself could not be ignored. As a naturalized American of Polish ancestry, however, he shared none of the New Zealander's deeply felt attachment to Britain

In Twilight and in Dawn

and, given his pacifist predilections, saw nothing heroic or patriotic in battlefield sacrifice. Instead, opposition to the "hellishly evil" conflict reflected his deeply rooted pessimism about the turn world events had taken, a turn that threatened to subvert the spirit of reason and learning in which he, like many of the day's intellectuals, placed great faith.[5]

Hoping to dissuade Jenness from enlisting if for no other reason then to improve his immediate career prospects, Sapir appealed once more to survey management, imploring director William McInness to put a better deal on the table. Pulling out all the stops, he framed the case on professional and ethical grounds, pointing out that his young colleague's work in the Arctic not only rivalled the very highest standards in the field but was accomplished under extremely harsh, even life-threatening conditions, when he fell ill on Victoria Island. "Facts such as these ... show clearly our moral indebtedness to Mr. Jenness." Anything short of a permanent appointment now, Sapir's reasoning continued, only increased the odds that, with the conflict finally over, he would opt to return to the Pacific – that is, to the proffered post of Government Ethnologist in British New Guinea – for "both financial and sentimental reasons." By failing to provide tangible incentives for him to stay on, "we are to all intents and purposes throwing away all the good that, as far as anthropology is concerned, has come out of the Canadian Arctic Expedition."[6] Strong words. They fell on deaf ears.

The war was ostensibly to blame for the inattention with which Sapir's lobbying was received, the continuing financial emergency it fostered leading to cutbacks in practically every branch of Geological Survey work that did not contribute directly to military preparedness or national strategic planning. At the same time, and ultimately of longer-lasting consequence for the still-fledgling Anthropological Division, many of the bureaucrats who controlled the survey's purse strings, and thereby determined its priorities, held anthropology in low regard, insisting that it was science done for its own sake, not a practical field, like geology, able to contribute directly to the country's current and future material well being. The opinions of R.G. McConnell, deputy minister of mines, were typical. In a letter to M.F. Gallagher, his private secretary, the deputy candidly reviewed the particulars of Jenness's case. There was no question of the anthropologist's qualifications, instead it was the intrinsic value of the type of work he did that was in doubt: could the department justify paying such men salaries that were "away in advance of what we are able to offer technical men engaged in important economic work?" As the deputy saw things, Jenness would not come cheaply, perhaps misreading Sapir's intervention to mean that the New Zealander's true game was to force the Geological Survey to match the $2,500 annual salary that went with the New Guinea post or else risk his early resignation. "The Anthropological Division," McConnell went on, "*a purely scientific one*, is already costing the Department over $17,000 a year in salaries and a further amount, which I am endeavouring to make as small as possible, for field expenses … a further increase in the permanent salary list would not be justified even if conditions were normal."[7]

Disheartened that something more palatable was not in the cards, Jenness grew uneasy with his own motives, embarrassed by allowing "mere money … to guide me" in matters of such import. Unable to find a sympathetic ear among his small circle of Canadian acquaintances, he turned to Robert Marett for counsel. "Am I doing right?" he inquired of his former teacher; "I want to fight, & don't want to throw away 3 years field-work, but I must do one or the other. I wish you would advise me candidly."[8] With Oxford transformed by events across the English Channel, many of its students under arms and much of its ordinary work disrupted for the duration, a patriotic Marett proved supportive in response. Along with advice on which military branches would make the best match for his knowledge and experience, he offered assistance in landing his protégé a commission in the British forces, something worthy of a Balliol man. After months of stressful indecision, a few reassuring words from abroad brought some respite. Jenness determined to stay on at the Geological Survey until May 1917, concentrating on Copper Inuit material that "cannot be obtained by any later observer (since the natives are rapidly changing)," and leaving the remainder – notes on language, technology, archaeology – for others to work through.[9] Evenings would be reserved for the long-neglected D'Entrecasteaux manuscript, a chore he returned to soon after settling into temporary lodgings on Osgoode Street. Then, assuming the war dragged on, he would resign from his survey job and enlist in Canada's army, expecting to see action by summer's end. "In this way I shall have done my duty to Oxford and to the government here – without failing in what is due the empire," he explained to Marett, clearly relieved to be done with the matter at long last. "Perhaps peace will come before I am ready. I hope it will, for it will save much misery, but if it does I shall feel almost too ashamed to come to England when I have done nothing to help her in her need."[10]

Even if Sapir's lobbying had paid off, factors beyond the squabbling over employment terms played into Jenness's thinking about joining the Anthropological Division on a permanent basis. The stale air of bureaucratic intransigence coursing through the survey's corridors gave him greatest pause, officials and political higher-ups – figures such as Mc-Connell and McInnes, the latter "both incompetent and useless," in his estimation – demonstrating an aversion to accepting guidance on scientific or administrative matters from subalterns, regardless of their qualifications.[11] With rare exception, these were men, nearly all geologists, who had little understanding of the methods of contemporary anthropology or appreciation of its claims to scientific and professional authority. Wielding the ultimate leverage of budgetary oversight, they alone determined who would be hired, what projects funded, which reports published, and when the persistent "clamor for ... popularization" would take precedence over scholarly priorities in the division's research agenda.[12] Nor were they above interfering in scientific work or questioning disciplinary standards, on occasion going so far as to order the "doctoring" of field reports when they deemed their contents to be objectionable.[13] At a moment when the first generation of university-trained anthropologists was striving to assert an increasing measure of autonomy over their emerging field, a goal then being realized in American academia, the discipline's arranged marriage with Canada's civil service made for a less than heavenly match, prospects for keeping pace with intellectual and professional developments elsewhere being tied to prevailing official attitudes about how, if at all, anthropologists might serve the public interest. Little surprise that Jenness would find these conditions "anything but satisfactory" and that, in weighing the alternatives, he might reasonably prefer to return to the South Pacific and the post of government anthropologist for Papua that Marett had brokered for him with Papua's colonial administration over staying on in Ottawa for any longer than was strictly necessary.[14]

Timing, of course, is everything. Had he come on the scene before the war, rather than two years into it, his assessment of the situation doubtless would have been different. The Anthropological Division's future was very bright in its earliest days, rapid growth of staff and operating budgets coming as signals that Canada intended its new research agency – the first of its kind in the empire – not merely to emulate Washington's Bureau of American Ethnology in purpose but to rival it in stature. This good fortune owed much to the astute politicking of survey director Reginald W. Brock, a mining geologist and former Queen's University professor, who was anthropology's strongest, and quite possibly its only, advocate inside government at the time.[15] Well regarded on both sides of Ottawa's political divide, he assumed the directorship in 1908 while the Liberals were in power, then received promotion to deputy minister of mines under the Conservatives six years later. By all indications, his recommendations carried weight: in fact, the decision to create a permanent archaeological and ethnological survey under Geological

Survey auspices, and to place it in the hands of an academically qualified specialist, followed directly on his move into the director's office. Launching a campaign to upgrade employment standards throughout the Geological Survey – past practice long favouring patronage appointments – his preference for hiring a "scientific, trained ethnologist" as the new division's chief was nothing if not consistent.[16] Not even the most reputable of the country's old-guard anthropologists, amateurs all, could meet these qualifications. Nor could their contributions to research bear scrutiny in the light of recent disciplinary developments, their work still rooted in the questionable assumptions and methods of Victorian-era ethnology, with its emphasis on racial classification and universal evolutionary schemes.[17] "Much to my regret," Franz Boas counselled Brock when asked for an opinion, "I cannot think of any Canadian whose experience and knowledge would justify recommendation." In his estimation, the modern field taking shape in the United States – or at least that branch of it under his considerable and growing influence – demanded a degree of methodological rigour best achieved through academic preparation. Moreover, he insisted, it was necessary to find someone able "to handle every line of attack of anthropological problems" – ethnological and linguistic, archaeological and biological. To the dismay of those who, in the spirit of ardent nationalist and former survey director George M. Dawson, believed that "birthright [conferred] automatic entitlement" to the prestigious new post, Brock hired "the most brilliant" of Boas's students, Edward Sapir.[18] The job, Brock explained in his offer of employment, "is pretty much what the man makes of it," including sufficient autonomy "to build up a strong department and to carry on successfully the scientific studies which should be undertaken in this attractive field."[19] Sapir would hold the chief ethnologist's position until 1925, when he departed for a professorship at the University of Chicago.

Unlike his predecessors Dawson and A.P. Low, both of whom had done ethnographic work in the course of their duties as survey field geologists, Brock had little, if any, such experience. Nonetheless, he displayed a solid understanding of what modern anthropology was about, particularly the priority accorded to original data obtained through sustained fieldwork, and was sympathetic to the urgent need for salvage ethnography: documenting rapidly changing indigenous cultures before reliable knowledge of them was beyond retrieval.[20] His backing paid the fledgling division handsome dividends in relatively short order, most notably in the accelerated development of a qualified scientific staff. Just months after Sapir's appointment, the archaeologist Harlan Smith, late of New York's American Museum of Natural History and a member of that institution's ground-breaking, Boas-led Jesup

In Twilight and in Dawn

North Pacific Expedition, joined him in Ottawa. Following them were Ontarians Frederick Waugh and William Wintemberg, accomplished amateurs hired as museum assistants in ethnology and archaeology respectively. The last permanent appointee was physical anthropologist Francis Knowles, Arthur Thomson's Oxford protégé. Eleven others, most graduate students or newly minted PhDs trained in the United States, worked on short-term contracts, of which there were never fewer than six a year. Among them were Jenness and Barbeau's classmate Wilson Wallis and Boas's students Alexander Goldenweiser and Paul Radin. Finally, Scottish-born amateur James Teit, another Jesup Expedition veteran, was retained on outside service, an arrangement under which he conducted research from his home base in British Columbia's southern interior.

Along with personnel came money, funding for fieldwork and collecting museum specimens growing from less than four percent of the survey's research budget in 1911 to twice that level three years later.[21] Brock also gave his blessing to an anthropological series under the survey imprint, an initiative that saw twenty monographs and papers published by 1915.[22] With an eye to the future, moreover, he encouraged his division chief's efforts to promote anthropology as an academic discipline at one or more Canadian universities, agreeing with Sapir that the profession's development at home would benefit from a corps of specialists trained at home. To that end, in 1914 Sapir sought to establish an affiliation with either McGill or Toronto, each within reasonable commuting distance of the nation's capital. Neither school was prepared to make the commitment to the new field. Not so the University of British Columbia where, two years later, Charles Hill-Tout, the doyen of west coast avocational ethnologists, was nominated to be founding professor of what would have become the country's first department. Asked for his opinion of the choice, Sapir was adamantly opposed, following Boas's lead in asserting that academic preparation was the sine qua non for positions so clearly central to advancing the field's professional growth. In the end, the university put its proposal in abeyance, not to be revived until mid-century.[23] Hill-Tout, needless to say, was deeply aggrieved.

A break-through of sorts came just after the First World War when Toronto's St Michael's College named polymath Sir Bertram Windle to a professorship in anthropology, a position that entailed little more than offering the occasional lecture. In 1925, however, the year Sapir decamped for Chicago, the university's administration took a more hopeful step, appointing Canadian-born and Cambridge-educated Thomas F. McIlwraith as lecturer and assistant curator at the affiliated Royal Ontario Museum. Even then, the discipline's stock was very slow to rise, a full decade passing before departmental status was finally granted and additional academic staff hired. In consequence, anthropology at Toronto contributed comparatively little to the division's fortunes, or to boosting the profession's lowly standing elsewhere in Canada, for that matter, in the years preceding the Second World War.[24]

Apart from opening the door to professionalization, Sapir's appointment "revolutionized and continentalized" anthropology in Canada by enshrining what Barbeau ironically described as "the American point of view" – that is, the tenets of historical ethnology – as the foundation of the division's nationwide research agenda. The essentials of this view, sometimes characterized as historical particularism, originated with Boas in the 1880s and derive not from American but from German intellectual roots, resting on a crucial distinction between natural science – the deduction of laws from observable phenomena – and historical science – inductive understanding of phenomena in and of themselves. Disposed toward a study of humankind whose first order of business was adopting means and ends consistent with the second of these, Boas set about laying the groundwork for an alternative to the day's anthropology along lines defined by his systematic critique of the evolutionists' natural science assumptions and methods.[25] The result, at once empirical, descriptive, and inductive in style and historical and relativist in substance, was to dominate the discipline on this side of the Atlantic into the mid-twentieth century.

Setting aside as largely unfounded the evolutionary principle that cultures progress through a succession of uniform stages driven mainly by increasing powers of rational calculation, Boas articulated an approach, distilled in good part from German romanticism, that depicted cultures as unique entities, each the outcome of its own history, each needing to be understood on its own terms. Accordingly, he saw a people's way of life, as well as their ethos and character, as developing over time as the cumulative product of varied and complex factors, some internal to their society, such as innovative responses to ambient conditions, others external, the result of contacts with other peoples, usually those nearby but occasionally further away. Cultural growth itself, he argued, is largely fortuitous, subject first and foremost to the chance workings of diffusion, a process in which borrowed cultural elements are integrated, often after modification in accordance with what he loosely identified as the affective spirit, or "genius," of the adopting group. The history of any culture is thereby "dependent partly upon the peculiar inner development of [each] social group, and partly upon the foreign influences to which it has been subjected."[26]

Contrary to the deductive and speculative typological schemes that had engaged Victorian scholars, the anthropology of the so-called Boasians examined culture inductively, through a relativist lens, the task directly before it being the historical reconstruction of individual cultures on the basis of empirical evidence. "If anthropology desires to establish the laws governing the growth of culture," a goal Boas himself was initially loath to abandon, "it must not confine itself to comparing the results of the growth alone, but ... the processes of growth" as well. To that end, "the history of human [i.e., cultural] evolution must be derived from a comparison of individual historical developments."[27]

Research in Canada held great promise for unravelling some key problems pertaining to the historical development of indigenous North American civilization, the focal point of the Boasian research agenda. Spelling them out in a paper first presented in Quebec to the International Congress of Americanists in 1906, Boas observed that, unlike the "peculiar uniformity of culture" evident among the peoples spread throughout the continent's vast heartland, a uniformity presumably resulting from widespread diffusion, those inhabiting marginal regions, notably the Dominion's remote subarctic and arctic hinterlands, possessed "ethnic characteristics of their own." At issue was whether or not these traits were typical of an earlier form of culture, one little affected by the tide of change "that swept over the middle parts of the continent and left their impress everywhere."[28] This, he believed, was a preeminent question facing Canadian anthropology and resolving it by means of in-depth field investigations was critical to the larger enterprise of piecing together the numerous strands of hemispheric culture history.

Sapir adopted his teacher's programmatic paper as the de facto scientific charter of the new agency under his direction, writing confidently at the time that "the reconstruction of the social and psychic history of man is not as readily accomplished as the Spencers, Frazers, and Westermarcks might have us believe." Rather, he continued, "we can put reliance only in such historical reconstruction as follows from a close study of the complex ethnographic data of a given time and place."[29] With that, he and his associates inaugurated an ambitious project whose objective was a "thorough and scientific investigation of the native races of Canada, their distribution, languages, cultures, etc."[30] As was typical of the period, they approached the task with a sense of urgency; "the increasingly rapid disappearance and, more than this, cultural absorption of the Indians," Sapir wrote at the time, "makes it imperative that research work among the various tribes be instituted 'hammer and tongs.'" "No shortsighted policy of economy should be allowed to interfere with the thorough and rapid prosecution of the anthropological problems of the dominion. What is lost now will never be recovered again."[31]

These were impassioned words, penned in furtherance of a goal deemed to be of great historical and scientific moment. But the high note on which this timely endeavour was launched soon faded, the government's commitment to its newly created research bureau turning out to be conditional on the vagaries of in-house politics, the quirks of individual bureaucrats, and, in the final analysis, the acid test of public accountability rather than sympathy for the aims of anthropological science and its salvage ethnography project. The reality of this became all too clear in August 1914 when Britain declared war on Germany and Brock resigned to take a deanship at the University of British Columbia. Without its only well-placed friend, and with Ottawa failing to assign special war-related duties to the anthropologists on its payroll, the division's robust program soon withered, its allocations slashed to pay for Geological Survey activities geared almost exclusively to the war effort.[32] No permanent jobs were lost but contract positions were severely curtailed. So, too, were allocations for research and collecting, which dropped from $8,000 in 1914 to a mere $650 four years later. Publication was similarly affected, the printing of annual reports stopped for the years 1916–18.[33] As anthropology lapsed into near-dormancy, geology flourished, appropriations for personnel and field investigations rising more than twenty percent before war's end. While qualified geologists were in great demand, the supply was grossly inadequate, military enlistments siphoning off some men, jobs in private industry claiming others. The resultant braindrain left a hefty portion of the survey's yearly wartime budget unspent. Meanwhile, anthropology struggled to maintain a mere semblance of its original self in the face of severe cutbacks.[34]

Brock's departure probably had a greater bearing on anthropology's post-war prospects than on its fortunes during the war. Had he remained deputy minister, it is likely that he would have breathed new life into the battered and bruised Anthropological Division once government-mandated stringencies were lifted. In spite of a reputation for "subordinat[ing] the academic to the economic," his past record of support suggested better things to come, far better than what actually occurred during the tenure of the next deputy, R.G. McConnell, the author of Jenness's dilemma, and a man Sapir reckoned to be not "in the slightest degree interested in anthropology."[35] McConnell, also a geologist, was wedded to a far different view of government science than was his predecessor, asserting that the "energies and the funds entrusted to [the Department of Mines] must necessarily be largely expended in assisting ... in the economic development of the country."[36] In practical terms, this meant that all the "purely scientific" fields operating under its umbrella – anthropology, biology, palaeontology – would remain relegated to the lowest rungs of survey priority, a situation that continued even after their transfer to the National Museum of Canada

National Museum, Ottawa, 1912. Canadian Museum of Civilization, 18806

when it was formally created in 1927. Inadequate budgets, persistent personnel shortages, and ceaseless bureaucratic meddling were to be anthropology's lot under federal auspices for decades to come.

As if the big picture weren't grim enough, wartime working conditions inside the Victoria Memorial Museum were corrosive, exacting a heavy toll on staff morale. The Dominion's much-heralded repository of scientific knowledge, located on Metcalfe Street, first opened its doors to the public in 1912, the same year as the city's venerable Chateau Laurier hotel. All of the Geological Survey's scientific divisions and collections were housed here, moved from the cramped quarters on Sussex Street that had been its home since it had come to Ottawa from Montreal in 1881. The National Gallery of Canada occupied a portion of its east wing, a "temporary" arrangement that continued for fifty years. When a calamitous fire destroyed the House of Common's Centre Block on the night of 3 February 1916 – a disaster that claimed seven lives and was widely attributed to "Hun treachery" – the government immediately appropriated a sizeable portion of the museum's space for the country's lawmakers. At the time, both houses were in session and the relocation happened so quickly that MPs held their first cross-town sitting the next afternoon! This awkward arrangement continued until restoration of the Parliament Building was completed four years later.[37] In the meantime, the museum's regular tenants were dispersed to makeshift quarters here and there. Anthropological Division offices were switched to one site, research collections, now in storage, to a second, while the survey library, photographic labs, and drafting facilities stayed put. Two second floor exhibition halls – one devoted to arctic and northwest coast ethnology, the other to eastern and central regions – remained intact, although public access was drastically scaled back.[38]

Apart from the constant upset he and his colleagues faced at work, Jenness's brief stay in Ottawa did little to improve his initial impression of the city, or the country. Days before leaving for military service overseas, he told von Zedlitz of his growing disenchantment with the place, writing with an earnestness seemingly meant to dispel any lingering self-doubts about choosing enlistment over an uncertain future with the survey. "Canada is in the throes of a political struggle just now which seems likely to develop into a racial struggle," he explained, referring to the deepening domestic crisis in French-English relations over francophone education rights and Quebec's opposition to the government's proposed conscription legislation. "There have been signs of rioting already ... and I should not be surprised if it did not become serious before very long ... Ottawa, lying as it does on the border of Québec and Ontario, is the very centre of the strife."[39] On a broader front, he also despaired of the Dominion's abilities to convert its vast natural wealth into real economic growth for the good of its people, lamenting that all manner of resources had been, and continued to be, "shamelessly squandered." He attributed this to a single overriding cause: the failings of national leadership. "Political morality is at a very low ebb, lower than the average Englishman or Australasian can conceive of. New Zealand may have its faults, but as a country to live in it is infinitely preferable to Canada."[40] Hardly the sentiments of a contented expatriate.

All things considered, the deck seemed stacked against a future in Canada, Jenness relishing the prospect of heading home once the war was over. "I have always longed to return to the South Seas and Papua is a glorious field for work," he enthused in a letter to Marett in January.[41] By April, the odds had shifted, courtesy of a timely intervention on the part of George Foster, an MP from New Brunswick, the sitting minister of trade and commerce and, perhaps most important, an Oxford graduate willing to help out a fellow alumnus. The politician made clear that the young man's status as a civil servant, however temporary at present, nonetheless entitled him to a federally mandated paid leave of absence for the duration of his military service. This, in turn, was solely conditional on his giving three years to the Geological Survey upon returning to civilian life.[42] Jenness had every reason to be pleased with the arrangement, doubly so, in fact, since the preceding months had given rise to an unspoken but more compelling incentive to make his way back to Ottawa after the war: a workplace romance with Eileen Bleakney, Sapir's secretary. Moving quickly from friendship to courtship, the couple planned to marry once Diamond's duty to king and country was done.

His resumé replete with educational and professional achievements, Jenness expected to be offered a commission in the Canadian army and a non-combat assignment overseas. A posting far from the battle lines in France was preferable, perhaps one in the Balkans, Mesopotamia, or Africa, where the work would be interesting and he could avoid being "swallowed up in the mass."[43] But being qualified for a commission was one thing, getting it something else again. Having politely declined Marett's offer to help secure one in England, what remained was "unattractive service" with the 10th Canadian Siege Battery, recently organized as a special draft at McGill University.[44] He enlisted in May, as did John Cox. Just weeks later they were in transit overseas, boarding a troop ship in Halifax on 22 June and disembarking at Otterpool Camp, near Shorncliffe on the English coast, a fortnight later.

Those first days in uniform were vexed by rumours that his unit was about to be converted from artillery to infantry duty, a not uncommon practice at this stage of the war. With little taste for an ordinary foot soldier's lot, he launched an eleventh-hour scramble for reprieve from the trenches. As before, Marett instructed him to call on well-placed Balliol men for help in finding shelter in the intelligence branch or the Colonial Office, places where his ethnological and linguistic expertise might be put to good use. Nothing turned up. Neither did the rumoured switch to infantry duty. Instead, the would-be intelligence operative spent an English summer training on 18-pounder guns and a French autumn and winter in the thick of action. The armistice was still fourteen months away.

Private Jenness was relieved to see France at long last, finding actual war a welcome change from "fooling away one's time in endless parades & button-polishing," as well as from the rough treatment meted out to ordinary recruits-in-training.[45] Yet what passed as front line duty in those first days – driving horses and tending mules – was not what he expected, either. The wrangler's life received tongue-in-cheek treatment in homeward correspondence: "I & another man – as ignorant of the brutes as myself – were attached to a pair of mules – one a hard-mouthed ill-tempered brute that nearly sent me back to Canada with a broken sternum ... I am hoping however than [sic] my attachment to them will not be of very long duration."[46] Unsettled by the thought of shovelling manure and mending harnesses for the duration, he wasn't long in reviving hopes of transfer to more agreeable employment or, better still,

In the Trenches, 1916–1918   123

Portrait of Diamond Jenness. Canadian Museum of
Civilization, Rudolph Martin Anderson, 1917, 67220

miraculous redemption from combat altogether. Rescue of a sort came
in November with reassignment to an artillery battalion operating in
a "rather quiet" part of the front, close to German lines. Quickly promoted from gunner to spotter, he remained with the unit until a secondment sent him to the Canadian Corps Survey Section for the war's final
weeks. Meantime, the day-to-day grind of battle grew routine, so much
so that after three months he was describing the experience almost off-
handedly: "I can now dive for cover as well as anyone when shrapnel or
High Explosive shells come sailing through the air – and grab for my
mask at the first notice of gas."[47]

There were precious few distractions from war's ceaseless din and
physical discomforts. Even the simple pleasure of reading was a near-
impossibility, at times just leafing through his prized copy of Homer's
Odyssey having to suffice. Serious writing was out of the question, though

In Twilight and in Dawn

he managed letters to family and friends and fiancée, always datelined with the obligatory "Somewhere in France." Correspondence received in Ottawa attests to his close friendship with Barbeau, ties that later were to come undone, the victim of office politics at the Geological Survey. Disclaiming even rudimentary knowledge of money, Jenness implicitly trusted his classmate to look after his financial affairs, such as they were, a responsibility that required keeping an eye on bank deposits and buying the occasional war bond. Letters to Barbeau were also filled with personal confidences about Eilleen Bleakney, and with expressions of gratitude for the many kindnesses he had shown her in his absence. The romance, it seems, blossomed under the discreet chaperonage of the Barbeaus, the foursome enjoying a springtime outing now affectionately remembered as "a milestone in my history." "You may find in our engagement the clue to my desire to remain in Ottawa" following the war, Jenness coyly remarked in a long and newsy letter, that and "[my] desire to enjoy your society more than I have been able to in the past."[48]

By chance, several of the men with whom he served were scientists, including John Cox, now stationed nearby with another siege battery. As conditions allowed, they "gave seminars" to one another on their respective fields of expertise, as much for amusement as for mutual edification. Jenness relished these sessions, later crediting them with improving his facility with botany and zoology. On occasion, the group found wider audiences for their knowledge. With characteristic wryness, he explained to Barbeau that after sitting through a longish talk he gave at the YMCA on the Arctic Expedition, most of the soldiers in attendance were happily "resting behind the lines."[49]

Jenness saw action in most of the major Canadian campaigns of the Great War's concluding months, including the critical battle at Amiens in August 1918, and was at Mons, in Belgium, site of the Canadian forces' easternmost advance, when the fighting stopped for good. Within days of the armistice, his unit shifted onto German soil, now under the banner of the Army of Occupation. Stationed in the countryside between Cologne and Bonn, there was little for the troops to do apart from "killing time with physical exercises ... and odd 'fatigues'" while awaiting demobilization and eventual repatriation to Canada.[50] In a bid to make more productive use of the time, he sought and received permission to visit Cologne's ethnological museum. When the city was suddenly declared off-limits owing to the misconduct of Canadian troops, he settled for a bit of rest and relaxation in Rome and Florence instead. "Half the enjoyment of a holiday is lost through being in uniform," he complained of the excursion; even so, he was grateful to be back in the Mediterranean, still fascinated with the world of his youthful imagination.[51]

With an eye to more practical pursuits, he also applied for leave to travel to Oxford, hoping for a chance to consult Marett and Henry Balfour about the long-overdue D'Entrecasteaux report before demobilization and his much-anticipated reunion with Eilleen Bleakney. On leaving Ottawa in 1917, he had entrusted the partially complete manuscript to Barbeau's care; in turn, his friend had agreed to proofread its 260 typescript pages and then, once the German threat to trans-Atlantic shipping had ended, forward them to the university.[52] Doubtful that the military would deem the cause of scholarship a worthy one, Jenness was pleasantly surprised when official notice arrived that the request had been granted. Crossing the channel in mid-February 1919, he wasted none of the precious time allotted to him, consulting former professors and finishing the work set aside for the sake of military service twenty months before. Within a year, Oxford's Clarendon Press had issued *The Northern D'Entrecasteaux*, Jenness's first substantial contribution to the anthropological literature and the fulfilment of a deeply felt obligation to his parents, to Marett, and to others who had made his inaugural fieldwork possible, especially his late brother-in-law Andrew Ballantyne.

By great good fortune, his unit was among the first ordered home from Europe, reaching Ottawa on 21 April. Formal discharge followed six days later. A short while before departing Europe, Jenness had written to Stefansson about the experience and the reasons for his decision to volunteer rather than stay safely behind at the Geological Survey. "I am glad that I was able to take an active part," he explained, "I felt when I enlisted ... many men were shirking their duty and bringing dishonour on their country and an unnecessary increase of hardship on other people." To "stand aside, and let others fight the battle of civilization," he believed, would have been both dishonourable and unthinkable.[53] Happy to have survived with body, mind, and spirit intact, he was no less happy to have done the right and proper thing in what seemed a right and proper cause. All the same, he rarely spoke of the war again.

CHAPTER SEVEN

An Unloved Stepchild, 1919–1931

PUBLIC SERVANT

With a fiancée anxiously awaiting his return to Ottawa, the city seemed a far different place in 1919 than it had at the close of the Arctic Expedition. Diamond and Francis Eilleen Bleakney had met at the Geological Survey not long after she became Edward Sapir's secretary and had had a whirlwind romance. Born and raised in Ottawa, Eilleen was now twenty-six, he six years and one day older. Despite attempts at subterfuge, their engagement was a poorly kept confidence around the office. "I have to laugh whenever I think of how very careful Miss B & I were to keep our secret from everyone, & yet even Dr. Sapir seems to have been aware of it. But for heaven's sake – or for Miss B's sake," he implored Marius Barbeau in a letter from wartime France, "don't let it be known outside."[1] Coyness aside, the request was aimed at sparing Eilleen needless worry over the security of her $500 a year job – civil service regulations at the time required female employees to resign when they married. On the last day of April 1919, the couple took their vows in a downtown Baptist church in front of a few dozen friends and relatives. Two days later, they boarded a west-bound train for Vancouver, and from there embarked on a three-month wedding trip in New Zealand.[2]

Despite the employment-related uncertainty of their earliest days together in post-war Ottawa, the newlyweds wasted little time in setting up a home and starting a family. They purchased a run-down duplex – Diamond called it a "funny little shack" – in the city's Glebe district, a neighbourhood of shops and residences, and devoted evenings and weekends to do-it-yourself renovations.[3] Two of their three children were born while they lived there, John Lewis in 1921, and Stuart Edward (after Sapir) four years later. By the time the third, Robert Allan, came along in 1930, the Jennesses had moved to more spacious surroundings in Eilleen's childhood home on Broadway Avenue. They remained there until the late fifties, when the couple left the city behind for a winterized cottage near the village of Wakefield, in the Gatineau Valley countryside. As for their sons, all went on to advanced studies, John in geography, Stuart in geology, and Robert in economics. All eventually resettled in their natal city, taking positions in different departments of the federal government. In that regard, at least, they followed in their father's footsteps.

On returning from his wedding trip, Jenness went back to his temporary job at the survey and the mass of arctic material awaiting his attention. In his absence, Sapir had rekindled his lobbying, hoping to arrange more favourable terms of employment for his colleague before the honeymooners reached the city. In pressing the case with William Foran of the Civil Service Commission, he again raised the prospect of losing Jenness's considerable expertise to the Papuan colonial service. To forestall such an eventuality, he urged Foran to recommend an appointment of no fewer than three years' duration, at a starting monthly salary of $175. Still below scale for someone with Jenness's credentials and professional experience, Sapir thought that the extra money might be incentive enough to keep his newly married colleague in Canada, particularly since a war-induced inflationary spiral had yet to subside.[4] Months of silence ensued.

At long last, a glimmer of hope appeared in the spring of 1920 when the commission announced an opening for an associate ethnologist on the Anthropological Division's staff, its first new hire since the war began. The job description called for a virtual factotum, a position with responsibilities spanning research into the ethnology, languages, and physical anthropology of Aboriginal peoples, as well as the folk traditions of the Dominion's English and French populations. Applicants were also required to have special knowledge of Inuit culture, Sapir's way of insuring the competition's outcome.[5] With Oxonian Francis Knowles having been forced to resign by ill-health in 1919 and Geological Survey management having refused to renew James Teit's outside contract that same year, augmenting their permanent complement – currently standing at five – was crucial if the division's pre-war agenda was to get back on track. The news of the position thus sparked cautious optimism that conditions were changing for the better, funding for research and collecting already showing signs of rebounding from the low point reached in 1918, a mere $652, to a more respectable (if hardly adequate) $6,000 plus by the 1920–21 fiscal year.[6]

By sheer bad luck, political wrangling between Treasury Board and the Civil Service Commission delayed the hiring process until fall.[7] In

In Twilight and in Dawn

the meantime, Jenness was left to weigh his options once again. He knew that the odds were long for landing a job in New Zealand, this despite recent editorializing in the local scientific press about the urgent need for institutional supports and new blood to update the country's once-vibrant (but still amateur-dominated) anthropological community.[8] The better bet lay with securing an academic appointment somewhere else, preferably one that afforded "ample opportunities for field-work."[9] But with the discipline still years way from gaining any standing, even at the undergraduate level, in Canadian universities, this would necessitate relocating to the United States, or possibly to Great Britain. As it happened, that summer he received an offer to join the faculty at Seattle's University of Washington for considerably more than his current pay.[10] While tempting, the still-flickering hope of a permanent posting with the survey, coupled with Eilleen's deep attachment to Ottawa, persuaded him to decline. The gamble paid off, the commission finally confirming his appointment in October 1920 at a starting salary of $2,580. "It has been a long fight," a relieved Jenness happily reported to Barbeau.[11] Four years long. For better or worse, he would remain a public servant for another twenty-seven. Indicative of the rocky road ahead, he and Douglas Leechman, hired as a museum assistant in 1924, were the last additions to the Anthropological Division's permanent staff until the Second World War had been fought and won.

On the arrangement made before his 1917 enlistment, Jenness's official duties on returning to civilian life were supposed to be restricted to writing up his Arctic Expedition material, a full-time job in itself. Sapir had other plans, however, plans he first broached while the matter of his associate's continuing employment still lingered in bureaucratic limbo. With the public purse strings finally beginning to loosen, he seized the opportunity to restart his nearly moribund ethnological survey by proposing that his junior colleague move into two new lines of research: collecting English-Canadian folklore in rural Ontario and, more important, taking up ethnographic work among Athapaskan speakers – Dene, in contemporary parlance – in the country's sprawling western Subarctic. While unopposed in principle, Jenness was troubled by the timing, thinking it sensible to refrain from accepting new assignments while his employment situation remained undecided but worried that refusing might undermine his chances of securing the appointment he believed was his rightful due. "It's no use my drifting away from my Eskimo reports if I am not going to be made permanent," he wrote to Barbeau, fishing for a bit of friendly advice on how best to proceed.

Within weeks the thorny matter was settled, Sapir agreeing to postpone western fieldwork for the time being and putting Frederick Waugh in Jenness's place to delve into folklore. "Don't you honestly think my viewpoint is correct[?]," he inquired of Barbeau. "Remember that you and Sapir have both established reputations for yourself, while I have nothing yet to show for all my years of fieldwork."[12]

As if ploughing through the mountain of material he had gathered during three years in the Arctic weren't job enough, Vilhjalmur Stefansson unexpectedly foisted an equally daunting task on him midway through 1920: editing the Northern Party's ethnological findings, work the explorer claimed he was too busy to attend to himself. At least the information "would be of value for my own report," Jenness had to concede.[13] By the time he was ready to begin his first Athapaskan research as a regular member of the division in summer 1921, he had churned out an impressive body of writing, the product of a prolific period following his and Eileen's return from the south Pacific. Besides completing the manuscripts of *Life of the Copper Eskimos* and a monograph on cat's cradles, some seven hundred typescript pages in total, he was close to finishing a collection of myths and folklore, and had made considerable headway on three other reports earmarked for publication in the expedition series: a comparative grammar and vocabulary, data on physical anthropology, and a compilation of music, the last, a collaboration with American musicologist Helen Roberts.[14] Except for the work on language, all were in print by 1925. There were several important papers, too, including his formal refutation of Stefansson's "Blond Eskimo" claims and a discussion of the early stages of culture change in Coronation Gulf, a companion piece to the article on Alaska drafted during his Wollaston Land stay with Ikpukkuaq and company.[15] As things turned out, Sapir could scarcely begrudge agreeing to a temporary delay in launching his colleague in a new direction. He would have his sorely needed Athapaskanist soon enough. In the meantime, the Anthropological Division acquired a first-rank arctic specialist and Jenness, the makings of the respectable reputation he had laboured long and hard to build.

While he was busy at the typewriter, a storm began brewing that would eventually embroil him, and several of his reports, in a very public controversy. Its source was Rudolph Anderson's seemingly insatiable desire to see his one-time partner and friend, Vilhjalmur Stefansson, held accountable for alleged wrongs committed during the Canadian Arctic Expedition. The dispute, which lasted upwards of five years (1919–23)

and reached as far as the prime minister's office, ultimately produced no clear winner or loser, though it certainly contributed to Stefansson's slow but steady fall from favour among Ottawa's political elite.[16] In the meantime, plenty of ink was spilled, plenty of passions roused, and plenty of questions asked about the prerogative of scientists – even those on the government payroll – to keep the results of their work safe from meddling politicians and bureaucrats.

Jenness was more spectator than combatant during the quarrel's early stages, although his continuing association (and friendship) with Anderson – now chief of the survey's Biological Division – swayed his sympathies. Even so, his relationship with Stefansson was undeniably cordial, the two meeting now and then when the explorer visited Ottawa and exchanging congenial letters in between. As befitting his outsized character, Stefansson saw himself as mentor rather than colleague, already attempting to pull strings to win Jenness's early release from military service in 1919, then advising the cash-strapped newlywed on the most lucrative outlets for popular publication a year later.[17] As a fellow anthropologist, he also took a keen interest in the progress of his associate's scientific writing, happily agreeing to read draft chapters of *Life of the Copper Eskimo,* offering clarifications of certain ethnographic details, and suggesting stylistic changes to strengthen the text overall. Jenness welcomed the "frank criticisms" and promised to make more of his material available for perusal.[18] All innocent enough, or so it seemed at the time.

The tenor of the dispute, and Jenness's role in it, took a dramatic turn in the closing days of 1921 when the Macmillan Company released *The Friendly Arctic,* the explorer's 700-page narrative account of the expedition. Mixed in with the expected retelling of his numerous exploits and accomplishments were passages meant to set the record straight on a host of charges that his Southern Party critics had been levelling against him for years: allegations that his actions had forced what he referred to as mutiny at Collinson Point, his presumed mishandling of logistical arrangements, even the veracity of claims regarding "living by forage" and other aspects of the so-called "fourth stage" of polar exploration. Long apprehensive that his now-estranged partner intended to appropriate the full story as his own in just this way, Anderson had hoped to secure a modicum of balance by insisting that each party be allowed to produce an official record of its activities, the two to be issued together as the initial volume in the planned series of reports on the expedition's scientific results. This never happened. By turning to a private outlet instead, Stefansson assured himself considerable license to say what he believed needed saying – something the scrutiny of the Department of Naval Service's arctic publication committee would not have permitted – and, in the process, defend his carefully cultivated reputation from the attacks of his Geological Survey antagonists, many of whom were portrayed in "less than rosy colours" in the book. Adding insult to injury, the lengthy memoir managed to take on the weight of publically endorsed legitimacy by featuring some flattering introductory remarks from the pen of Sir Robert Borden, Canada's prime minister, and one of Stefansson's staunchest supporters.[19] Little wonder that *The Friendly Arctic* met with a less-than-friendly reception at Geological Survey headquarters; Jenness, like Anderson, was left red-faced by its insinuations and spoiling for a fight. At stake, both believed, were their own good names and the integrity of their scientific accomplishments in the north, honest, hard-won accomplishments made possible by funds from state coffers.

Unable to rouse much support among their superiors for pursuing the matter through internal channels, Anderson and Jenness resolved to initiate their own defence and, ultimately, a defence of the public's sizeable investment in the expedition. They talked to the press. In mid-January 1922, several big-city newspapers ran Canadian Press stories questioning Stefansson's self-serving motives and, on a far more serious note, accusing him of administrative incompetence and fiscal wastefulness – "foraging ... on the people who pay the taxes."[20] Damning stuff, and certainly sufficient grounds for the government to launch a formal inquiry, at least in the minds of the two aggrieved scientists. Given the day's political alignment, much of it arrayed against them, an inquiry was not in the cards, even though an ever-confident Stefansson was himself unopposed to the idea. Instead, this first round of publicity produced little more than a stern warning from high up in the Department of Mines hierarchy against further interviews. Obviously, the prospect of survey personnel escalating a quarrel that had the potential to pit different government ministries against one another was a quarrel best avoided. As an alternative, Deputy Minister Charles Camsell proposed enlisting the assistance of an outsider to rebut Stefansson by reviewing his book for a respected scholarly journal. His nominee for the task was Southern Party geologist John O'Neill, late of the Geological Survey and now a faculty member at McGill University. Despite his evident sympathies, O'Neill declined.[21] By default, then, the matter was again in Anderson and Jenness's hands, and they were not long in resuming a fight that soon found Jenness going head to head with his erstwhile commander.

A great deal of frustration and ill-feeling might have been saved had they immediately pressed the deputy for permission to write the review that O'Neill had been unwilling to write. Only months later did they get around to doing just that, with Jenness volunteering to take on the job. The result was a long and craftily worded response, less a review than a statement of counter-claim in which the author cited relevant details and quoted at length from official documents and correspondence to refute Stefansson's most contentious allegations, point by point. It also took critical aim at an earlier review of *The Friendly Arctic* in which "extravagant claims" were made for the strategy of living by forage, heralding it as "a new and strictly scientific method" destined to revolutionize arctic exploration. Jenness's piece appeared, with Camsell's blessing, in a July number of the American journal-of-record, *Science*.[22] However, what he and Anderson really wanted was an official inquest, convinced that this was the surest way to obtain an authoritative reading of the disputed facts and thereby lay to rest the wrongful allegations levied against members of the Southern Party.

Already rebuffed in their attempt to marshal public opinion to the cause, the two colleagues' next step was a direct appeal to Charles Stewart, the minister of mines. Toward the end of February 1922 they, together with O'Neill and survey topographer Kenneth Chipman, also late of the Southern Party, sent the minister a formal petition requesting establishment of a commission to look into all aspects of the Canadian Arctic Expedition and to "determine the truth or falsity" of Stefansson's charges against them. Lodged as the charges were in the pages of a book "which, to the uninitiated, seems to be an official publication" – remember the prime ministerial introduction – the complainants believed his allegations were nothing if not slanderous, defaming them personally and, by association, impugning the reputation of the Geological Survey.[23] However justified their grievances, the minister was no more inclined to risk an inter-departmental feud now than he had been weeks earlier, any credible inquiry necessarily having to delve into the roles played by the Naval Services and mines ministries in organizing and funding the expedition. Learning that the matter was again making headlines only hardened Stewart's opinion, leading him to reissue his earlier edict against contacts with the media and to remind Anderson, Chipman, and Jenness of their proper work.[24] Denied a full hearing of their complaints under government auspices, the pages of *Science* became their only recourse.

As things turned out, it was this sober, if trenchant, article, and not the barrage of accusatory interviews in the *Toronto Sun* and other dailies that had preceded it, that finally brought Jenness into direct conflict with Stefansson. Before the *Science* piece appeared, Stefansson had continued as if nothing had changed between them, professing that whatever inquiry might eventuate would be political, not personal, in nature and thus leave "our private relations" undisturbed. Besides, he confessed, referring to the highly polarized views in the popular press, the controversy itself was generating just the sort of publicity destined to boost book sales. "This pleases me well, not only from the point of view of income, but more especially [in] getting a wide audience for the message I am trying to convey." Jenness was ambivalent, the letter that prompted Stefansson's remarks, its characteristically polite phrasing aside, suggesting that *The Friendly Arctic* had indeed stirred up strong feelings. Ironically, his purpose in writing in the first place had been to decline Stefansson's offer of an autographed copy of that very book, something "I cannot honourably accept ... and at the same time preserve my own liberty of thought and speech ... It gives me much regret to have to write you this," he continued, evidently torn between loyalty to Anderson and commitment to rapprochement with Stefansson, "but I am sure you will respect my scruples."[25] At the time, Jenness told Sapir that he had declined the presentation copy for fear that Stefansson "might very well taunt me with accepting it" later on. "Do you think me over-sensitive? But you know the man we are dealing with."[26]

The exercise of that liberty appeared to change everything, at least in Stefansson's mind, since his next communication with Jenness came in the form of an attorney's letter warning of possible legal action against him. (None was ever taken.) As the lawyer's letter has not been found – its existence and Jenness's apparent decision to ignore its warning are known only indirectly through references to the matter in the private correspondence of Anderson's wife, Mae Belle – Stefansson's intentions are open to speculation on the basis of circumstantial evidence only.[27] Among the more salient of such evidence is that no similar threats were made against other Southern Party members, a telling point since the rebuttal-cum-review printed over Jenness's name was obviously the product of close collaboration among them all. Given that, the warning could not have been meant to blunt further criticism of Stefansson's executive abilities and motivations, at least not entirely. After all, the scandal-hungry press had treated the affair in a far more sensational (and potentially libellous) way than the rather staid approach taken in *Science*, yet those other columns seem not to have provoked a similar response. Stefansson was not without his admirers and supporters, including some who used the pages of scholarly journals to praise the explorer's worthy accomplishments while simultaneously taking Jenness to task for publishing unfounded criticisms.[28] The most interesting of these rejoinders – and undeniably the most damning – was a long contribution from Stefansson's Northern Party associates Harold Noice and Burt McConnell. It, too, was published in *Science*, appearing some eight months after the original review signed by Jenness. In it, the authors offered substantial evidence to the effect that the justifications Jenness put forward on behalf of his "faction" had been built on "adroit misquotations" from the existing documentary record, including a convenient misrepresentation of a set of instructions from G.J. Desbarats, deputy minister of naval services, on the crucial issue of ultimate command of the expedition. To seal their argument against what they saw as the most egregious of Southern Party claims – the denial that there had been a mutiny at Collinson Point – the authors appended the full text of a recently penned letter from Desbarats attesting to the fact that Jenness's selective treatment of his official instructions had indeed given "*a different impression to that which [was] intended.*"[29]

All this aside, there is good reason to assume that what actually troubled Stefansson was his belief that Jenness was scheming to use reports in the expedition series to continue taking pot-shots at him with a view to detracting not from his standing as an explorer but rather as an authority on arctic anthropology, the only branch of science in which he could rightly claim expertise. His suspicion undoubtedly stemmed from perusing the manuscript of *Life of the Copper Eskimos* back in 1920, portions of which drew attention to some apparent inconsistencies in his own ethnographic observations or which "disagree more than [they] should with my experience."[30] Appearance of Jenness's "The 'Blond' Eskimos" in the *American Anthropologist* shortly thereafter only exacerbated the situation, as its concluding remarks offer a reasoned repudiation of one of the explorer's most cherished, if contentious, assertions. (Before sending it to the journal, Jenness had wisely asked Franz Boas to review the manuscript, allowing that neither he nor Sapir were sufficiently skilled in the analysis of anthropometric data to risk submission without benefit of expert comment beforehand. Except for a few minor points, Boas's general opinion was favourable, noting in particular his personal satisfaction that Jenness had "disposed so effectively of the sensational report of Mr Stefansson."[31]) In Stefansson's estimation, however, there was worse yet to come: the results of Jenness's anthropometric studies of the Copper Inuit, including more data on the supposed "Blonds," were nearing publication under government auspices just as the debate in the pages of *Science* was heating up.

Overtly professing fears for the integrity of the expedition's scientific accomplishments while tacitly hoping to stave off harm to his personal reputation as an anthropologist, Stefansson began drawing on his considerable political capital around Ottawa to insure that nothing of an allegedly controversial nature passed the final edit. An earlier attempt to get Desbarats to order "suppression or emasculation" of passages in *Life of the Copper Eskimos* on the grounds that they "disagreed with the view of the commander" had failed. Now he was prevailing on other officials, including Charles Camsell, to treat *Physical Characteristics of the Copper Eskimos* in this way. The smell of renewed public controversy was so strong that Desbarats even considered pulling the plug on the publication program altogether.[32] Happily, this, too, came to naught, with a formerly dismissive Camsell suddenly emerging as a strong ally on behalf of his harried but still-determined staff anthropologist. Clearing the way for the second manuscript to be issued in unexpurgated form, he assured Edward Prince, head of the publications committee at Naval Services and someone who thought eliminating "offending passages" was a good idea, that "Mr Jenness is activated by no personal animus in any of the statements made ... I am as anxious as anyone to avoid any controversy on this subject," he continued, "but from recent experience I am inclined to think that Mr Stefansson is not inclined in the same way."[33] Though entering the fray late in the game, Camsell also defended Anderson et al. against the charge of mutiny at Collinson Point. Having the last word in *Science*, he wrote that "To designate this incident as a mutiny is using too strong a term, for it was a decision on the part of the so-called mutineers to adhere to instructions originally given them by the Geological Survey." He then concluded that "if there were sufficient grounds for such a charge steps would have been taken long before this by the government to punish the offenders."[34]

By the time this dissension finally ran its course, Jenness was fully absorbed in new work, having begun the Athapaskan research he had postponed nearly two years before. It would be some while yet before he and Stefansson again corresponded, but when they did, in 1926, it was without any trace of their old disagreements.

For Jenness, four productive years of fieldwork and publication were suddenly interrupted in 1925 by Edward Sapir's resignation. Deeply troubled by his wife's protracted illness and untimely death the preceding year, and long discontented with having to sacrifice research to meet endless administrative demands, Sapir announced his intention to leave the Geological Survey for an associate professorship at the University of Chicago.[35] The departure left the division with three potential candidates – its only scientific officers – to replace him as chief: Barbeau, Harlan Smith, and Jenness. With Sapir on "retiring leave" and the others off in the field, Jenness became acting chief by default.[36] Warily shouldering the responsibility for the interim, he, like Smith, professed no interest in assuming the post on a permanent basis. Not so Barbeau, who went so far as to call on Rodolphe Lemieux, then speaker of the House of Commons and a personal acquaintance, to lobby for the appointment on his behalf.[37] Therefore when Museum Director L.L. Bolton named Jenness, a choice ostensibly made on the understanding that none of the three had actually "press[ed] a claim" for the position, strong feelings were stirred up: embarrassment on Jenness's part, resentment on Barbeau's.[38] The ensuing brouhaha claimed their seventeen-year friendship as a casualty.

By all indications, Jenness had no idea that he was about to get the nod as the Anthropological Division's second chief. Writing to Barbeau about Sapir's resignation, he declared himself out of the matter altogether, feeling only pity for whomever the job fell to because of its loathsome administrative duties. Only a short time before, in fact, he had decided against applying to head up the American Section of the University Museum in Philadelphia, preferring to remain in Ottawa precisely because he relished the "freedom and little administrative work" his present job entailed.[39] His predicament became palpable three weeks later when he confessed that if seniority were not to be taken into account, as apparently it was not going to be, Sapir intended to recommend him as the new chief. "I told Sapir, quite frankly, that I could not take the position over ... you and Smith," he again wrote Barbeau, explaining further that he had also urged Bolton "not [to] consider me in the running ... unless both you and Smith turned it down."[40]

Making matters worse, management fully expected that he would assume the post full time at the beginning of the year, reading his cooperation in assuming acting duties as proof of his willingness to take that next step. Genuinely upset by the course of events unfolding while his two senior colleagues were away from Ottawa, Jenness observed, partly out of embarrassment and partly out of regret over decisions to which none of them had been party, that "if I took the position over your heads I should feel that I had stabbed two of my best friends in the back. I don't think any of us cares for the position very much ... I certainly do not ... if either you or Smith accepts it I shall be immensely relieved."[41] Compromised by a situation seemingly beyond his control, he could do little more than offer assurances that he would make no decisions as acting chief that would later tie the hands of the person eventually promoted to the division's top spot. Still uneasy over the affair, the very next day he wrote to Barbeau again, telling him that he earnestly wished for the business to be settled amicably. "Whatever happens, I shall try to do nothing unworthy of our friendship, and shall consider your interests before my own."[42]

Sapir actually preferred Smith, not Jenness, for the job, having broached the matter with the fifty-six-year-old Michigan-born archaeologist in private letters sent several weeks before news of his imminent departure became public. Assuming all along that he was "in line" for the job should circumstances warrant, a flattered Smith was doubtful nonetheless, unsure of his willingness, and ability, to "steer between the rules [and] red tape" of survey and museum bureaucracy while simultaneously promoting the interests of his colleagues. "I would rather quit than have friction," he explained in reply.[43] Though he and Sapir were friends both inside the office and out, Sapir's tentative inquiries still came as something of a surprise, Smith apparently unaware that his colleague thought well enough of him professionally to recommend that charge of the division be put in his hands. His perception likely stemmed from past disagreements between them on matters of scientific and professional standards, differences of opinion that, by some accounts, arose from Smith's lack of academic training in anthropology and allegedly caused him to feel discriminated against at work.[44] While never flatly turning down Sapir's endorsement, his sentiments, particularly qualms about whether management higher-ups (and perhaps some of his own co-workers, too) considered him suitable for the task, achieved the same effect. "I hate to change bosses," he told Sapir, seeming to dismiss the matter altogether; "I prefer my old boss to uncertainties."[45]

Why Sapir recommended Jenness over Barbeau, and why, given his protests to the contrary, Jenness then consented, are questions whose answers are far from obvious. What is certain is that by 1925 Barbeau had become something of an odd man out. In particular, his growing involvement over the previous decade in nurturing the study of French (and Anglo-) Canadian folk culture – a spin-off of early fieldwork among the Iroquoian Wyandot in Quebec – did not sit well with Bolton and other survey and museum officials whose narrow conception of the Anthropological Division's mandate effectively precluded anything other than research on the country's First Peoples. Management's position left Sapir with a predicament: having to justify allocating staff and money, always in short supply, to a field of inquiry that was arguably less urgent than salvage ethnology in Aboriginal communities. Ever mindful of the power wielded by those in control of the purse strings, he leaned toward acquiescence, now and then reminding his feisty and self-assured associate that, without "any desire to minimize the value of the folk-lore to which you have chiefly devoted yourself of late ... our proper work is, as you must admit, the study of the aborigines of the Dominion."[46] Of the bigger picture, "We must be careful not to spread our resources too thin," he wrote to Boas, a long-time supporter of Barbeau's seemingly tireless efforts in Quebec and, it must be added, the person who had urged the division to initiate this line of research in the first place; "I regret, on the whole, that we have taken up so much time with French folklore, as it is."[47]

Quite apart from the administrative pressures he was under, Sapir's professional relationship with Barbeau was uneasy, his ambivalence toward the man very much a factor in weighing options for his replacement. On the one hand, he clearly, if perhaps a bit grudgingly, admired Barbeau's impressive accomplishment in compiling and analyzing enormous numbers of folk songs, tales, and other material, going so far as to praise it as "the most thorough-going and systematically carried out investigation of European folk-lore that I am acquainted with." The fact that the two collaborated on a collection of traditional French Canadian songs testifies to Sapir's approval, at least on intellectual grounds. On the other hand, he found facets of Barbeau's personality difficult to abide. "Carrying on a conversation with him is often as painful as an ordeal," he confided to Berkeley anthropologist Robert Lowie; "How he delights in the use of platitudes and how childishly his self-esteem paces, all out of step!"[48] This last proved especially troubling, the independently minded Barbeau inclined to see himself as above the bureaucratic rules and conventions that lamentably, if inevitably, dogged everyone's work at the museum. A reputation for being a "chronic over-spender" did nothing to ameliorate his standing. Intermittent flare-ups in the division's already rocky relationship with unsupportive directors and penny-pinching accountants were the unavoidable result, memoranda flying to and fro, noses put out of joint, Sapir repeatedly caught in between. His biographer claims that Barbeau took offense, bothered by what he perceived as Sapir's needless capitulation to authority and perhaps resentful still that, by dint of timing alone, "a foreigner and outsider," not he, a native-born Canadian, had become chief of the Anthropological Division.[49] It's hard to imagine such deeply held feelings going unreciprocated, at least in some measure. Nonetheless, Sapir's decision not to endorse Barbeau as his successor might be better read as prudent than spiteful.

In the circumstances, Jenness became chief by a simple process of elimination, Bolton judging him less objectionable than Barbeau. That said, he came to the promotion well recommended and Sapir found in him a conscientious and "untemperamental colleague" and eventually a sympathetic (and life-long) friend.[50] For his part, Jenness counted Sapir as a mentor. Deprived of academia's intellectual stimulus throughout his tenure in Ottawa, Sapir made do by organizing informal discussions of disciplinary issues whenever the opportunity presented itself.[51] The contract researchers who came and went in those days – many fresh from graduate studies at Columbia and elsewhere in the United States – figured prominently in these seminars-on-the-fly. Jenness was among the regulars, profiting in particular from Sapir's expertise in linguistic method and theory. The importance of this tutoring became evident soon after his friend's departure for Chicago: writing about the state of on-going research on Sarcee (Tsuu T'ina) and other Athapaskan languages he admitted "Now that you have gone, I don't think I will have the courage to tackle those spluttering tongues any more. The Eskimo's is bad enough." As for progress on an Inuktitut dictionary, "thanks to your training, I think it will not be without value. If it proves rotten, I am to blame; if it is good, you are."[52]

However favourably Sapir viewed Jenness's scholarly accomplishments, his own experience over the previous decade and a half had disabused him of any notion that such a promotion was fitting reward for success in research. In fact, the situation was just the opposite, the countless administrative and in-house political demands that fell on the incumbent inevitably being met at the expense of time that could otherwise have been devoted to proper scientific work. This may explain why his first choice as a replacement was Smith, someone who was seventeen years Jenness's senior and, understandably, beginning to slow down his pace of field activities. If it had to be Jenness, as it apparently did, the one feature of his work that made him well suited to take charge of the division, at least to Sapir's mind, was his commitment to a broadly based conception of anthropological practice. Still widely regarded as a cornerstone of the discipline in North America today, the so-called four-field approach rests on an integrated, holistic perspective on the human condition that draws on evidence from archaeology, ethnology, linguistics, and physical anthropology. Having imported this Boasian "four-square structure" into the national anthropological agenda when he arrived at Ottawa, Sapir immediately set about implementing it by recruiting personnel with specialties in each area.[53] While some worked in more than one branch – Barbeau and Sapir in ethnology and linguistics, Smith in ethnology and archaeology – only Jenness covered all the bases, starting with his stint in the Arctic and continuing for years thereafter. As expected, on becoming chief he endeavoured to hold firm to the course his predecessor had steered.[54] To his considerable disappointment, however, the poisonous chemistry of politics and bureaucracy that permeated the museum in the period stymied his best efforts to rejuvenate the Anthropological Division into anything like its robust, pre-war state.

After spending a restive autumn as acting chief, Jenness's appointment to the permanent position became effective in January 1926, just weeks shy of his fortieth birthday. The job carried all the same responsibilities that Sapir had had except one: charge of the exhibitions, which Smith inherited. It also meant a bit more money. Already bumped to the rank of ethnologist in April 1925, a reclassification paying $3,300 per year to start, the subsequent promotion just nine months later added about

$200 more to his pay packet.[55] True to form, he was outwardly stoical about what lay ahead, shouldering the chores that went with the office as a matter of public duty. "Your recommendation concerning the succession was carried out, somewhat to my dismay," he told Sapir, one month into the job, "but I will do the best I can." Privately, the affair remained disconcerting. Only half in jest, he told Knowles, now back in his former Oxford surroundings: "You should not have congratulated me on succeeding to [the chief's] position, but rather have extended your sympathy."[56] Like Sapir before him, Jenness never fancied himself an administrator. Experience in the job did nothing to change his attitude.

As he knew it would, the amount of time given over to office routine – everything from preparing estimates and supervising field projects to answering an endless stream of public inquiries on every conceivable topic – quickly grew, as that for research and writing diminished. Though grumbling on occasion that "gadding about in the field every summer is beginning to get on my nerves," his only real complaint in this respect was that he regularly accumulated research material in such quantity that there were simply too few hours in the day to work it up properly once back behind his desk.[57] In fact, he had lost little of his youthful enthusiasm for fieldwork, his acceptance of the administrative post having more to do with a well-honed sense of responsibility than with seeking respite from the innumerable stresses and strains of trooping off to far-flung corners of the Dominion practically every year. This was patently obvious in the ambitious agenda he set for himself while still serving as acting chief, proposing to make four research trips over the next five years. Except for a return to the British Columbia interior to finish Athapaskan work begun in 1923, the remainder would take him into new territory: northwestern Alaska and Newfoundland for archaeological surveys, far-northern British Columbia to continue James Teit's war-time ethnographic work with the Tahltan and Kaska, the upper Mackenzie Valley for an ethnological survey of Dene groups in that quarter, and finally Hudson Strait and the east coast of Hudson Bay to initiate ethnographic and archaeological investigations.[58] Besides, the difficulties plaguing the division since the mid-teens, including the erosion of full and part-time staff, weighed against contemplating an early exit from fieldwork.

While these problems were predictable, his promotion "over the heads" of two senior colleagues exacted a more perturbing, and unforeseen, price: Barbeau's friendship. What had been a companionable personal and professional relationship since their Oxford days suddenly became formal and cool. Chummy and frequent letters filled with mutual encouragement and confidences all but ended, replaced by terse if polite reminders of business needing attention. And while an air of cordiality prevailed at the office, ties outside were severed. To Eilleen Jenness's mind, Barbeau stood alone as villain in the piece, to the extent that she even denied that it was he who had opened the door to her husband's career by recommending him for a spot with the Canadian Arctic Expedition. Colleagues who knew him in retirement recalled that Jenness rarely spoke of his oldest Canadian friend, an expression not of lingering contempt, they believed, but of profound sadness and regret.[59] That the subject wasn't even broached in his memoirs, a project taken up solely for therapeutic purposes, is especially telling, the burden of unresolved feelings over a long-ago contretemps tangible to the very end of Jenness's days.

This unfortunate turn of events was undoubtedly triggered by more than hard feelings over a missed promotion. If there were some other, more troubling problem bubbling below the surface, it was probably the same one that had precipitated the rift between Sapir and Barbeau: the issues surrounding research on French Canadian folklore. In relating the tale to an interviewer some forty years later, Barbeau recalled writing to Jenness from rural Quebec in the early autumn of 1925, assuring him that he had no difficulty with his being put in charge of the division.[60] Even so, the first clouds began to gather a short while later when he wrote again, this time to enlist the acting chief's assistance in securing an extra $600 needed to wrap up the season's fieldwork. In reply, Jenness explained that the request, eventually acceded to, had provoked trouble at the office, museum director Bolton grousing about Barbeau having exceeded the $1,750 allocation originally allotted for his research and making it clear that this type of work did not belong within the division's sphere of activity in any case. Bolton also wrote directly to Barbeau, his letter shockingly blunt in its criticism of the anthropologist's contemptuous attitude toward internal accounting practice.[61] "You can read between the lines as well as I," Jenness cautioned his friend in the light of what had transpired, then added, on a personal note, that "I am not finding this business of Acting-Chief any pleasure, and the sooner you get back and take my place, or Smith, the happier I shall be."[62]

Not long after this exchange, the die was cast. Barbeau returned to Ottawa to the news that Jenness was soon to receive the promotion he had supposedly forsworn and to reproving lectures from management about his spending habits and the inappropriateness of work in French Canada. As had happened to Sapir, it was now Jenness's turn to be drawn into the fray. On Barbeau's account, some time near the end of 1925 the two met and, on allegedly being "ordered to confine his work to Indians," he delivered his well-practiced defence of folklore research and then walked out of his friend's office and out of his life. Already disgruntled with what he took to be Sapir's readiness to acquiesce, he was now flabbergasted at the prospect that Jenness was similarly unwilling to stand up for him.

Following in his predecessor's footsteps, Jenness subscribed to the view that the division's raison d'être lay with studying "the fast-disappearing Indian and Eskimo tribes," and therefore held firm in the view that, given "our limited resources we should concentrate mainly on them." Ten years later his thinking remained unchanged. Convinced that the federal government needed to establish a separate museum to preserve national folk traditions and history, he maintained that it was nonetheless "unwise for the Division of Anthropology to expand in this direction, when it is not able to carry out the real task for which it was created, viz. a complete ethnological survey of the Indians before they are entirely absorbed in the surrounding civilization." In truth, the argument is a bit overstated considering that when he joined the division in 1920, his job description included studying the culture, folklore, and traditions of the "inhabitants of Canada," either "of aboriginal or European extraction."[63] Moreover, other members of staff had been contributing to the museum's growing collections of Euro-Canadian folklore since the teens, among them Frederick Waugh, William Wintemberg, James Teit, and Montrealer E.Z. Massicotte, who was hired on contracts for that purpose in the early twenties. Even Eilleen Bleakney had a hand in this work, collecting songs and other traditions in and around Ottawa during the war.[64]

In the face of all the criticism, Barbeau's personal resolve never wavered, his workload alternating between field research on the Pacific coast and (occasionally self-financed) collecting in the Quebec countryside for years to come. In turn, the museum offered modest support for folklore studies, perhaps fearful of an embarrassing backlash from French Canada should he be fired or should this branch of his activity be formally censured.

DAWN BEYOND THE HILLS

It wasn't long before the job he didn't want became the job he wished he'd never accepted. Beyond personal misgivings about being promoted over the heads of senior colleagues and the "horrible bore" of tending to day-to-day office routine, there was an in-house political dynamic that, since the mid-teens, had treated the Anthropological Division as the Geological Survey's "unloved step-child," left to "feed on [whatever] crumbs were thrown its way."[65] When he took over as chief, Jenness's ambitions were modest, hoping to preserve as much of Sapir's original program as was possible. Yet despite his best efforts to arrest it, the slide begun during his predecessor's watch continued under his own, driven by a narrow institutional conception of science in the public interest and by a "completely anomalous" administrative structure that denied the museum any real measure of independence from the wider Department of Mines bureaucracy.[66] Compounding the problem was management's reluctance to cede to division chiefs any but the most limited discretionary authority to set priorities or maintain professional standards. The mix was a recipe for conflict, one that left the Anthropological Division with a depleted and demoralized staff, and a badly compromised research agenda. Without a well-placed ally – another Reginald Brock – Jenness finally tired of the uphill struggle after five frustrating years, tendering his resignation as chief and returning full-time to what few scientific duties Depression-era conditions would allow.

William H. Collins loomed large as the principal architect of anthropology's lingering post-war malaise, and as such, became the focus of Jenness's growing discontent. Epitomizing the institution's peculiar organization, Collins held two key positions at once, becoming survey head in 1920, then taking Bolton's place as museum director five years later. Despite claims that he was serving in this extra capacity "without emolument" and on an acting basis only, he hung on to both jobs for more than a decade.[67] In his dual capacity he exerted considerable power, shaping policies and setting priorities that affected everything from the size of research budgets to the allocation of exhibition and laboratory space, from the merit of proposed field projects to the language of published reports. The extent of his purview was in itself nothing new, Brock and William McInnes having wielded similar authority in years past. Unlike them, however, Collins was inclined toward an autocratic and highly conservative style of management, the result of an "over-conscientious nature that led him to interfere unduly in the affairs of his subordinates, his lack of interest and skill in political relationships, and his narrow, unimaginative concept" of the Geological Survey's role in general. More given to professional interests in Precambrian geology than to the task of promoting the multi-faceted museum to his political masters or the Canadian public, his main accomplishment in sixteen years in office was running an economically efficient ship; but, as one critic put the case, his approach did little to keep government science "relevant to changing times."[68]

Not surprisingly, Jenness and Collins rarely saw eye to eye on anything to do with the Anthropological Division, or the National Museum, for that matter. While the anthropologist put the onus for the disheartening circumstances he and his colleagues faced on their lack of administrative and professional independence, the senior geologist

In Twilight and in Dawn

was of a different mind, seeing the alleged victims as authors of their own troubles. Giving public (and official) voice to his appraisal of the situation in the department's annual report for 1926, Collins cuttingly observed that, "besides having little need for scientific intercourse with the main body of geologists, mineralogists, and others," staff anthropologists and biologists also "had little or no knowledge of the traditions and customs of the Geological Survey." This was a state of affairs, his criticism continued, that engendered both pride and a "spirit of exclusiveness" among them, a sure-fire formula for internal dissension.[69]

The upshot of Collins's thinking was a discordant rivalry between the two solitudes under his charge, a rivalry that, given the prominence of survey officials in the museum hierarchy, all but assured that the interests of anthropology (and biology) would come second to those of geology. Collins's 1928 directive reassigning space inside the perpetually cramped Victoria Memorial building was typical, his decision "practically destroy[ing] all further activities on the part of the archaeological section" by causing a substantial portion of its collections to be relocated to an unheated, poorly lit (and allegedly rat-infested) warehouse situated some distance away. In proposing an alternative for preserving anthropology's minimal requirements, and with the director's recent pronouncement about "traditions" firmly in mind, Jenness explained that his suggestions were "not actuated by any feeling of hostility towards the Geological Survey. On the contrary I have the highest appreciation of its work. But I have an equally high appreciation of the work of the *National Museum* and see no reason why the two institutions should not advance together ... *helping and not crushing* each other."[70]

Inequities in the distribution of institutional supports worked their own brand of hardship. By 1930, the shortage of stenographers and clerks had become so acute that Jenness was forced to cart home two or three hours of routine paperwork each evening just to keep his head above water.[71] More importantly, he harboured genuine fears for the viability of some of the division's long-standing projects, worrying in particular that without clerical help Smith would be unable to keep up with the perpetually expanding archaeological files he was compiling, as would Barbeau with his energetic researches in Quebec and British Columbia. Desperate for some tangible improvement in working conditions, he pressed the case with Collins in the bluntest of terms, arguing that "Once [Smith and Barbeau] have drifted away from their regular duties it will be almost impossible to bring them back, and the Museum, while still paying for their services, will have largely lost them."[72] More harmful to anthropology's long-term prospects was the steady erosion of scientific staff, beginning with the loss of Knowles and Teit in 1919, then Waugh's mysterious disappearance and presumed death in 1924, and finally Sapir's departure just months later.[73] None was replaced, though not for want of active recruiting on either chief's part. The indifference of their superiors to rebuilding was problem enough but further complicating matters were 1918 amendments to the Civil Service Act that limited employment to British subjects, preferably Canadian residents, a step that played havoc with the long-standing practice of drawing contract field workers from the ranks of American academia.[74] The new requirements made Cambridge graduate Thomas McIlwraith the division's top job prospect in the early twenties. Sapir tried to insure the young Ontarian's future with the survey by sending him to British Columbia to gain field experience, an arrangement that resulted in highly productive research with the Bella Coola (Nuxalk), beginning in 1922. Once that work was done, the opening both men had assumed was imminent failed to materialize. A disappointed McIlwraith thus set his sights elsewhere, landing a temporary position at Yale before accepting a lectureship at the University of Toronto in 1925, the first Canadian academic appointment of an academically trained anthropologist. Another seven years passed before he was joined on faculty by Australian C.W.M. Hart, four more before the university granted the discipline departmental status. Writing to Jenness with news of Hart's 1932 appointment, McIlwraith quipped sardonically that "If Toronto anthropology has been increased 100%, you may say that there has been an increase of 33% in the professional ethnologists of the Dominion."[75] Such was the field's lowly state at the time.

Optimistic that McIlwraith's appointment at Toronto augured well for advancing the cause of professionalizing anthropology at home, Jenness encouraged his colleague to recruit promising students, offering to send them to the field as student assistants, a Civil Service Commission classification used to determine a candidate's suitability for regular employment. While a plausible plan, practice proved otherwise. For one thing, the museum was more favourably disposed to paying temporary researchers the going daily rate of $2.85 than it was in assuming the costlier obligations that came with augmenting the division's permanent workforce. For another, McIlwraith struggled to establish the discipline's footings in a setting dominated by senior academics and administrators "who ought to know (but don't) what anthropology is."[76] Meeting greater success in adding to the Royal Ontario Museum's collections than in churning out budding anthropologists, by the outbreak of the Second World War his efforts had garnered just two recruits, F.P. Cosgrove in 1927 and John MacPherson three years later. The division sent MacPherson to Lake Abitibi, on the Quebec-Ontario border, for a brief stint of ethnographic fieldwork with northern Ojibwa, but Cosgrove, scheduled to spend a season doing such work among the Beaver

(Dunne-za) in northeastern British Columbia, had a last-minute change of heart. Not wanting to waste the opportunity, or the allocated funds, Sapir suggested that Fang Kuei Li, one of his linguistics students at Chicago, take Cosgrove's place. Jenness readily agreed to pursue the matter but doubted the recommendation would pass muster with management, convinced of "objections being raised … on account of [Li's] nationality." As feared, Collins deemed the Chinese national unsuitable, though he took pains to dampen objections on purely racial grounds by insisting that the Department of Mines had no funds to support research on Aboriginal languages. The funding finally went to Cornelius Osgood, also studying at Chicago, who began dissertation research at Great Bear Lake the following winter.[77] As for Li, Sapir arranged a grant from a source in the United States that got him to the western Subarctic in 1927 to begin work on Athapaskan dialects. Even then he encountered trouble, Jenness successfully intervening when Canadian officials at the international border questioned the student's entitlement to re-enter the United States on completing his investigations.[78]

The nearest Jenness came to filling one of the division's vacancies occurred in 1930 when C. Daryll Forde's name came to his attention. Born in England and trained at University College London, Forde was then finishing a two-year Commonwealth Foundation fellowship at Berkeley. His credentials fit the bill admirably. Nationality aside, Forde was a generalist, having acquired archaeological experience in Europe under the eminent V. Gordon Childe, then doing ethnographic fieldwork among Hopi and Yuma in the American southwest. For once, management appeared ready to act, a determined Bolton explaining to the Civil Service Commission that "it is impracticable to secure recruits for the Division of Anthropology from the student assistant class owing to the fact that the subject is not taught in Canadian universities. Dr Forde is the only man in … a period of six years who might be a possible candidate for a position as Ethnologist."[79] Before they could issue a six-month contract to "test" the man's suitability for permanent service, Forde wrote to say that he was heading home to become chair of geography and anthropology at the University College of Wales, in Aberystwyth.[80] Jenness received the news with predictable dismay. Still, his gaze remained fixed on achieving the main prize, finding "a comparatively young graduate … willing to accept a permanent appointment … I have no one in sight in Canada," he told Forde, but in the circumstances, he clearly preferred a British to an American candidate "since a Britisher would retain his nationality in Canada and be more likely to devote his whole career to us."[81] He sent out feelers to Robert Marett, Henry Balfour, and A.C. Haddon, thinking that a suitable prospect or two might yet emerge from that quarter. None did.

Alone among the division's sections, physical anthropology had undergone a revival of sorts in the aftermath of Francis Knowles' untimely resignation in 1919. Sapir had hired Knowles before the war to initiate an anthropometric survey of the Dominion's Aboriginal population, a project whose expected yield of comparative data – like that from the detailed study of languages – was considered vital to realizing the Boasian goal of reconstructing cultural histories across the continent. Frail health cut short Knowles' career after a single field season, a misfortune that halted systematic investigations indefinitely. Before departing for academia, Sapir had tried to recruit L.H. Dudley Buxton, another Oxonian, to fill the vacancy. No luck. Jenness, however, fared better, eventually wringing funds from management to revive the stalled project by engaging the needed expertise on a part-time basis. With Collins's blessing, in 1927 John C. Boileau Grant received the first of several contracts to carry out summertime surveys among groups living in some of the country's remoter precincts. A physician and professor of anatomy at the University of Manitoba, later at the University of Toronto, Grant's knowledge of, and interest in, anthropometry stemmed from previous experience working for the Indian Affairs Branch as a medical officer attached to northern treaty parties.[82] Thrilled by the chance to get this line of investigation back on track, Jenness scrambled to organize Grant's first field season, arranging to send him north of Manitoba's Lake Winnipeg to collect cranial, facial, and body measurements and blood type data from resident Swampy Cree and northern Ojibwa (Saulteaux) populations. Similar work continued over the next two years, first with Chipewyan and Western Woods Cree in the Lake Athabasca region of northwestern Saskatchewan, then with Beaver in the Peace River country of northeastern British Columbia.[83]

Had the Dirty Thirties not brought the return of fiscal stringency, Grant was prepared to undertake at least two more field trips, one into the west among the Kutenai (Ktunaxa) and neighbouring prairie groups, the other to Athapaskan speakers of the Yukon basin and the lower Mackenzie. He was set to accompany a 1932 expedition to Hudson Bay and Baffin Island until an unexpected problem with accommodation aboard the government's Arctic Patrol vessel forced its last-minute cancellation. "I shall be very disappointed if the anthropometric survey cannot be continued," Jenness wrote to his associate at the time, "for, although I no longer have any responsibility in the matter [having resigned as chief just months earlier], I am more proud of initiating this work than anything else I was able to carry out while I was Chief of the Division."[84] Fearing a long wait before the museum would again make funds available for fieldwork, he urged Grant to seek backing elsewhere. Encouraging words from two prominent physical anthropologists in the United States, Ernest Hooton and Harry Shapiro, helped secure a small grant from the National Research Council in 1933. Hooton was especially supportive of the initiative, having contributed to the project since its inception by answering the division's periodic calls for technical assistance with data analysis. Unable to offer tangible compensation, an appreciative Jenness settled on a symbolic gesture instead, dubbing the Harvard professor (and former Rhodes Scholar) "our titular advisor" on all things anthropometric.[85] As events transpired, the council's $500 research award went unspent. Grant returned to the field for the museum one last time, in 1937, not to the northern territories as originally proposed but to the Stoney people of southern Alberta.

All things considered, the administrative decision to revive physical anthropology, even on a provisional basis, is surprising. After all, Grant's work hardly advanced the nation's economic wellbeing, the preferred yardstick for measuring the worthiness of research since the days of wartime retrenchment. Equally remarkable, the museum authorized speedy publication of nearly all his results, separate monographs on the Manitoba and Saskatchewan surveys appearing within a year of the fieldwork's completion; a third, issued in 1936, reporting Beaver, Carrier, and Sekani data, the latter two sets collected separately by Jenness in 1923–24.[86] By contrast, most ethnographic and archaeological reports, some dating back a decade or more, reached the government printers at a snail's pace, while others, out of sheer necessity, found outlets with scholarly presses in the United States. A possible explanation for this uncharacteristic treatment may have its roots in the realm of federal native policy, not with some eleventh hour rethinking of the intrinsic value of this, or any other, branch of anthropological research. With ideas about the racially determined foundation of intellectual and moral advance slow to fade from public consciousness in Canada or, for that matter, in settler societies elsewhere, some policymakers likely regarded comparative studies such as these as scientifically reliable gauges of Aboriginal assimilation into the nation's mainstream.[87] Along with page after page of tables and calculations, the reports also examine select somatic traits that purportedly distinguished allegedly "pure" from "part-breed" populations, the latter supposedly indicative of the progressive shift toward "Europeanization," the ultimate goal of state policy. Given the temper of the times, it is hardly remarkable that when University of London scientist R. Ruggles Gates requested government license to visit the Northwest Territories in 1928 in order to undertake research on the inheritance of physical traits in "mixed" populations, his proposal received a warm reception.[88]

This small victory aside, conditions at the museum remained difficult, the depths of the Depression all but foreclosing on fieldwork, and the years thereafter witnessing further withering of staff as Smith retired in 1936, followed by Wintemberg in 1940. At Jenness's own leave-taking soon after the Second World War, only Douglas Leechman and an undoubtedly apathetic Barbeau remained to wish him adieu. As for the Anthropological Division's once-ambitious research program, a quarter century after its inception only fifteen of some fifty Aboriginal groups originally slated for investigation had been studied in depth, the lion's share during the days of comparative peace and plenty presided over by Brock.[89] Meantime, American institutions had taken up the slack, numerous museums and universities sponsoring wide-ranging ethnographic and archaeological investigations clear across the Dominion.

❖

As frustrating as these sorts of difficulties were, they were benign compared to bureaucratic interference with disciplinary standards and practices. Nowhere was this meddling felt more acutely, or with more insidious effect, than in the all-important business of publishing division-supported research. Budgetary considerations often figured in decisions about what to issue, as happened in 1925 when Collins ordered Leonard Bloomfield's 1,800 pages of Saskatchewan Cree stories drastically pared down to save money, or on other occasions when works were released for publication elsewhere or left to gather dust in museum files.[90] Actions of this sort, while annoying, are hardly out of the ordinary, particularly in state-supported institutions. However, now and then it was content, not page-length, that was questioned. In the early days, Brock was more concerned with building a credible national research program than he was with scrutinizing manuscripts for the references to sexuality or bodily functions that occasionally cropped up in ethnographic accounts. Not so his successors. They took a more cautious tack, one predicated on the view that nothing issued by the government printer should prove in any way offensive to the norms of public propriety.

A single publication galvanized the censorious mood that descended on the war-time survey: William H. Mechling's *Malecite Tales*. Published without trouble in 1914, two years passed before the compilation, which included a story entitled "The Talking Vagina," came to the notice of Deputy Minister R.G. McConnell, at a time when the museum building was home to parliamentarians displaced by the Centre Block fire. A mortified McConnell demanded strict review of all future submissions on anthropological topics and ordered the outright excision of any passages deemed objectionable. Sapir responded with a sharply worded defence of professional standards, rebuking his superior for authorizing subaltern geologist-bureaucrats to arbitrarily censor material.[91] His protests were ignored, as was his proposal to rely on an established scholarly convention: substituting Latin phrases to mask questionable content. The issue abated for the duration of the war, the result of a complete ban on all publication, including annual reports. It surfaced again in the mid-twenties, however, re-ignited by two works on northwest coast culture whose forewarned authors, Harlan Smith and Thomas McIlwraith, had already taken precautions, including judicious use of Latin, in preparing their texts. Putting a brave face on an increasingly untenable situation for which he, as chief, was made to bear responsibility, Jenness told McIlwraith that "The general feeling around the building seems to be that anthropology is half pornology [sic], and what isn't spicy is so dull and uninteresting that no one will read it anyway." Smith's piece on customary medical practices made its way into print in 1929 despite the indignation its indelicate topics allegedly provoked among some of the survey's rank-and-file geologists.[92] McIlwraith was not so fortunate. His manuscript inched its way through a torturous five-year ordeal that ended in 1930 when the museum suddenly declared itself unable to publish owing to severe budgetary restraint. In the meantime, Jenness found himself uncomfortably caught between an academic colleague who considered "censorship of scientific material as preposterous" and an equally determined deputy minister given to declaring that the Dominion "could publish nothing which might offend a 12-year-old schoolgirl."[93]

Years later McIlwraith figured that fewer than 20 of the 1,713 manuscript pages he had produced contained questionable text.[94] Still, those few pages proved of immense consequence, enough to do more than merely scuttle publication of what Jenness believed to be "the finest work ever offered us." They were equally felt in the measure of scrutiny to which later submissions, and the division's activities in general, were subject. Chastened by the experience, Jenness felt obliged to recommend informal self-censorship to associates in order to stave off renewed friction with management. At a point when tensions over McIlwraith's work were nearing the boiling point, he advised Cornelius Osgood to avoid "unpleasant" matters in writing reports and to take special care to omit anything "you would hesitate to show to your sister or to any lady of your acquaintance."[95] Shortly thereafter, field instructions issued to I.A. Lopatin, a student from the University of British Columbia bound for work with the Kitimat (Haisla), warned that "We have experienced the greatest difficulty with other reports in the past, because they either contained folk tales with unpleasant passages in them about sexual matters or else they dealt with sexual customs." Such details might well be "rigorously deleted, even at the expense of the loss of scientific information ... I would advise you ... only to collect those tales and traditions which have a direct bearing on the social organization and social life."[96] Though hardly an ideal solution, the Great Depression did bring respite from the need to compromise professional standards by suspending practically all research and publication for the foreseeable future.

◆

Given the unfavourable climate that settled on the museum following Brock's departure, it is no wonder that Jenness, and before him Sapir, despaired of seeing any real improvement in anthropology's fortunes without a fundamental change in administrative structure and practice. "I cannot carry on under the present organization – with responsibility but no authority, the goat whenever anything is wrong without the power to decide policies or any control over the work of the Division," he agonized in a letter to McIlwraith. "There must be a complete revolution in the place if I am to continue. Things are getting worse and worse all the time."[97] By late 1930, resignation from the chief's office was a virtual certainty unless someone higher up the chain of command, someone like Deputy Minister Charles Camsell, were to loosen the survey's stranglehold on the National Museum. Sadly, that was not to happen until Frederick J. Alcock came on the scene as chief curator in 1947, his fresh approach soon breaking the "iron confines" of the ancien régime by making available new positions, new money, and a measure of professional autonomy not seen since the early teens.[98] 1947 was the year Jenness took formal retirement from the public service.

On what turned out to be the eve of his resignation, Jenness, clearly in a fighting mood, laid the case for de facto independence before Camsell in uncharacteristically blunt terms, asserting that "the National Museum of Canada, or at least the Division of Anthropology, can make no headway as long as it is subordinated to the Geological Survey. This very subordination prevents it from seeking or obtaining the support of the public and of the government." Days earlier, he had expressed the same concerns to Collins, then concluded by declaring that an impasse had been reached over a "fundamental difference in our views of responsibility, a difference that has probably been the source of all the difficulties and disagreements between us in the past ... [these] seem inevitable as long as our views remain so incompatible," he continued, "and neither my health, nor yours, can hold out under the strain."[99]

Camsell professed reluctance to accept his chief's resignation, seemingly convinced, as was Collins, that there was "plenty of ground for agreement." Jenness disagreed, hearing little to persuade him that even the smallest change was in the offing, let alone the wholesale revamping of museum administration – perhaps along the lines adopted at the Royal Ontario where authority was vested in a "disinterested and public-spirited Board" – that he (and McIlwraith) advocated. With nothing new on the table, he resigned and returned to his former duties, any thought of moving on from the museum itself rendered meaningless by the deepening economic crisis at home and abroad. In the end, the demands Jenness made of management were modest: that he would report exclusively to the director, and have discretionary authority in spending division funds and in issuing instructions to field workers. Whatever else they were, such demands were hardly a manifesto for revolution.

Barbeau was again passed over as chief. Instead, Camsell did something no less awkward: he named Collins to the position. Six years later, Jenness resumed the office, stepping back in on Collins's death. Now fifty, and with the last of his fieldwork for the museum behind him, he stayed on in a more or less nominal capacity through the war. Remarkably, the bumps and bruises experienced along the way did little to diminish his faith that the Anthropological Division was verging on a "new lease on life"; as an optimist at heart, "one always hopes for a dawn beyond the hills."[100]

CHAPTER EIGHT

Peoples of Memory,
1921

HORSE AND BUGGY ETHNOGRAPHER

On its founding in 1910, the Geological Survey's Anthropological Division became the institutional analogue of Washington's Bureau of American Ethnology, much as E.B. Tylor and other backers had intended when they began their lobby of Canadian lawmakers back in 1884. Both agencies operated in conjunction with a national museum and received public subsidy to preserve and disseminate the results of first-hand studies of indigenous peoples and cultures. Both employed permanent staff. Both found common justification for their scientific pursuits in the moral imperative of ethnographic salvage, the timeworn if compelling theme of the rapidly "vanishing savage" that lingered on as a call to action well into the twentieth century.[1] Nonetheless, the work started under Edward Sapir's leadership and continued by Diamond Jenness actually had more in common with projects underway elsewhere, institutions where Franz Boas's unflagging efforts as organizer, fund-raiser, and teacher paid off in a new generation of anthropological surveys carried out along the lines of historical ethnology rather than the older evolutionary approach still informing Bureau investigations. New York's American Museum of Natural History was home to the first of these surveys: the renowned Jesup North Pacific Expedition (1897–1902). It was followed two years later by Vanishing Tribes of North America, a longer-term project whose primary focus was the Great Plains. A third was based in Berkeley where, in 1903, Alfred Kroeber began the Ethnological and Archaeological Survey of California within the University of California's recently established Department of Anthropology. All four adopted diffusionist methods to study how cultures develop, an approach premised on the notion that similar beliefs and practices identified through close comparisons of peoples inhabiting the same geographic region, or even widely separated ones, are "more likely to be due to dissemination than to independent origin." In little more than a decade, the seemingly indefatigable Boas had realized a pivotal objective of his ambitious plan to build a "well-organized school of anthropology" on this side of the Atlantic, helping to launch major research programs whose field workers, a loosely coordinated corps, most of them academically trained professionals, gradually compiled an enormous body of information for the purpose of reconstructing the history of American culture, group by group, region by region.[2]

Numerous factors influenced how this work was carried out. Above all stood the conviction that precious little time remained to document what anthropologists of the Boasian stripe took to be authentic (i.e., pre-contact) culture: customs, traditions, and artifacts as yet untouched by the rising tide of change engulfing the continent's First Peoples. Their single-mindedness on this score found form in the priority they accorded ethnographic and linguistic investigation. Archaeological material, effectively ethnological evidence acquired with a trowel, was deemed safe enough to remain unearthed until the more urgent business of recording whatever information still remained in the here and now was accomplished.[3] Judging by the cumulative product of forty years' effort on both sides of the border, more had survived the deluge than was initially suspected. Even so, some ethnographers, particularly those who were given to interpreting externalities – the wearing of store-bought clothing, for instance, or attendance at church – as indicative of extensive cultural loss and thus of the passing of authenticity from daily life, feared it was already too late. Consider the words of J. Alden Mason, a Berkeley graduate hired on contract by the Anthropological Division in 1913 to begin ethnological investigations in Canada's remote western subarctic. On discovering that the Athapaskans resident around Fort Smith used horse-drawn wagons and lived in log cabins, he informed Sapir that "This was the place where you said I might find it profitable to spend all my time, but the degree of civilization attained by all these northern tribes is, to an anthropologist, disappointing." Another Berkeley man, linguist Pliny Goddard, reported much the same thing when he visited another Athapaskan people, the Beaver, in an equally out-of-the-way corner of northern Alberta in 1913 for the American Museum. As he explained in the introduction to his published report, "Not much of ethnological interest is directly observable at Vermillion since the outward aspects of life have yielded to the long continued influence of the fur traders."[4]

The more usual reading of the situation rested on the premise that erosion of a culture's outer features did not necessarily spell erosion of its inner domain – its defining modes of thinking and feeling about self, society, and the cosmos. Robert Lowie, one of Boas's earliest students and a veteran of fieldwork in both countries, put the case succinctly: "Naturally it would be better if we could observe Indians as they were in 1492, but when dozens of individuals retain a firm faith in the visions they recount and are willing to pay exorbitant fees to get themselves into the Tobacco society, their culture is not yet 'decayed' even if they begin cutting their hair, wear trousers, and buy the white man's axes." So conceived, the ethnographic approach was not limited to what might be "directly observed" on the ground; it also entailed investigating qualities of mind and emotion, attributes "never directly observed [but which] can be inferred only from ... oral self-revelations."[5] To Boas and a good many who followed his lead, it was the second of these objectives that comprised the fieldworker's most important task and purportedly produced ethnology's most valuable, and authentic, data: probing the "inner-most thoughts," the "mental life" of a people in order to capture the essence of their understanding of their own culture – "the culture as it appears to the Indian himself." "For this reason I have spared no trouble to collect descriptions of customs and beliefs in the language of the Indian," Boas remarked of his early work with the Jesup Expedition, "because in these the points that seem important to him are emphasized, and the almost unavoidable distortion contained in the descriptions given by the casual visitor and student is eliminated."[6]

While open to participant-observation where circumstances allowed, the Boasians' preferred field technique, indeed the hallmark of their ethnographic style, was the collection of such descriptions in the form of texts: verbatim transcriptions of dictated myths and legends and accounts of personal and collective experience. By itself, recording oral traditions was not new to anthropology but conceiving of such narratives as reflections of mind was, with each seen as an expression of underlying principles of cultural logic – what Sapir described as systems of "native classification" – uniquely articulated through the words and syntactic features of the narrator's native tongue. So, too, was imbuing them with the authority of the written record, making them into historical ethnology's equivalent of the textual sources of western classical scholarship.[7] Texts gave voice to what Boas (and German ethnologists before him) interpreted as the spirit or "genius" of a people, the interior (psychological) dynamic at play in shaping and re-shaping a culture's distinctive style and substance, and thus, they believed, the key to unravelling its history. As the raw material of ethnological and linguistic analysis, bodies of phonetically transcribed texts, usually with accompanying literal translations (but rarely with interpretive annotations), were routinely published. Routinely outside of Ottawa, that is.

There, Leonard Bloomfield's *Sacred Stories of the Sweet Grass Cree* was the first and last work to appear under Geological Survey or National Museum imprint, and then only after a rancorous exchange between Jenness and his superiors over the scientific value of including the original Cree versions. With an eye to the added costs of typesetting phonetic characters, museum director Collins was initially prepared to issue the stories only in English, as the survey had done with other compilations in years past. An enormous manuscript to begin with, permission to publish Bloomfield's texts in the desired form was finally granted subject to the excision of a substantial portion of the original material. The Linguistics Society of America agreed "without hesitation" to print the remainder.[8]

As a modus operandi, collecting texts was particularly well suited to the conditions researchers most often met in the field at the time, in which they were less likely to glean desired ethnographic details from observing a group's contemporary reality than from the tales its oldest members told. This certainly was Jenness's experience with the Iñupiat in 1913–14, the extent to which myriad trappings of western civilization had already eclipsed "ancient customs" along the Beaufort Sea coast leaving the collection of texts the "only alternative method" for studying those customs. Long convinced that the practice yielded "the best sort of ethnological material," Sapir encouraged him in its use in the Arctic, did so again on sending his junior colleague off to tackle his first Athapaskan research in the summer of 1921, and yet again, eight years later, with reference to Cornelius Osgood's pending research among certain Dene groups whose traditional cultures were "badly disintegrated." "I doubt whether direct questioning on ethnological matters leads to much," he counselled at the time, but a researcher "might still be able to obtain something if one followed up the hints given in personal narratives of various kinds." Yet Jenness was hardly alone in discovering that taking down a passable text required at least a modicum of proficiency in the local language, and considerably more in order to ask an intelligent question or to probe more deeply into a given topic.[9] Time had been on his side in the north, his crash course in Iñupiaq at Harrison Bay serving as invaluable preparation for the coming two years among the Copper Inuit. Circumstances were quite different in his subsequent work: a succession of relatively brief investigations, the longest of them six months in duration, undertaken among five different Indian First Peoples, speakers of five different languages.

Short stints of fieldwork were the norm during these years, the consequence of limited funds and, for those with academic appointments, the scheduling of university teaching terms. Compounding the problem, especially for the majority who were based at institutions in the east, were the long and arduous journeys needed to reach reserves and settlements scattered across the continent's western and northern hinterlands, distances necessarily traversed in slow stages via rail, river craft, horseback, and, occasionally, on foot. Theirs was the generation of "horse and buggy ethnographers," as Lowie famously remarked. In memorializing his contemporaries, however, he had more in mind than their experiences as inveterate travellers. More importantly, he was referring to the unavoidable methodological concessions they had to make because only rarely did any of their number have the luxury of a prolonged stay in the field, with enough time to gain a solid grasp of the local speech or, for those prepared to rough it, to accompany a hunting party into the bush in order to observe aspects of life no longer observable in the settlement. "Most of us, then, not from choice but from necessity, shall have to compromise and do the next best thing: learn what [language] we can and 'use' it; record as many texts as we can" and rely on interpreters "not because we like to, but because we have no other choice."[10] Such was Jenness's experience, in a nutshell.

Boas's method for identifying processes of cultural growth was predicated on detailed examination of "customs in their relation to the total culture of the tribe practicing them, [and] in connection with an investigation of their geographic distribution among neighbouring tribes." This type of comparative approach, he argued, provides a means to sort out the relative effects of external environmental conditions, internal psychological factors, and inter-group contacts on the development of cultures and their component elements. On the assumption that proximity increased the probability of like traits having arisen from like historical causes, the requisite starting-point for such research was always to be "a well-defined, small geographic territory." "Only when definite results have been obtained in regard to this area is it permissible to extend the horizon beyond its limits," Boas continued, making explicit that the ethnologist "must always demand continuity of distribution as one of the essential conditions for proving historical connection."[11] Linking historical process with the distribution of traits across space gave form to the idea of "culture area," a geographic region whose resident populations tend to resemble one another in subsistence strategies – generally the result of occupying similar habitats and exploiting similar resources – and in many aspects of social and intellectual life, presumably the products of diffusion. Edward Sapir used the concept to organize the nation-wide investigations in his charge, recruiting scientific staff as specialists in one, sometimes two of the sizeable areas into which an-

In Twilight and in Dawn

thropologists ordinarily divided Canadian territory at the time: namely the Eastern Woodlands, Plains, Plateau-Mackenzie, Pacific Coast, and Arctic.[12] On succeeding Sapir as chief, Jenness became the lone exception to this pattern of areal specialization, eventually working in all five in an effort to reduce the backlog created by the perennial shortfalls of money and personnel that plagued the Anthropological Division from the mid-teens onward.

❖

When Sapir took over directorship of the Anthropological Division in 1910, knowledge about the peoples and cultures of these regions varied markedly. Certain Pacific coast dwellers, for instance, and the Iroquoian nations of the east were already reasonably well represented in the anthropological literature. For a good many groups, however, particularly those dispersed across the immensity of Canada's subarctic interior, relatively little had been done by way of reliable description, with some imperfectly known through the sketchy writings of explorers and fur traders, others practically invisible. Researching these cases to the prescribed Boasian standard of thoroughness, and doing so in a timely fashion, would have stretched division resources far beyond their limits. Moreover, they comprised only a portion of the division's agenda. No less urgent were a range of ethnological and linguistic problems pertaining to some of the better-reported nations, which had been the source of the comparative evidence that served as the basis of the extant culture area scheme itself. Two areas in particular stood out in this regard: the Plateau-Mackenzie and the Eastern Woodlands, both groups subsequently redefined on the basis of fundamental environmental and cultural factors. Jenness adopted a partially revised version of the area scheme in his synoptic coverage of some forty different groups in *The Indians of Canada*, sorting Plateau-Mackenzie peoples into one of two newly named regions according to whether their lands fell within the Pacific (Cordillera) or Mackenzie-Yukon drainage systems. He also separated Woodlands populations into two broad divisions, one comprised of Iroquoian farmers, the other of Algonkian hunters.[13]

With so much to do and so few people to do it, Sapir elected to start the Anthropological Division's nationwide survey by putting the greatest share of available resources into investigating what was then one of historical ethnology's bigger problems: the seemingly "anomalous position" of the politically complex Iroquoians in a culture area primarily populated by "loosely organized tribes" of Algonkians. At issue was determining whether the village-based farming way of life of the Iroquoians had developed in situ – as is now widely thought to be the case –

or had been imported into the eastern Great Lakes region by migrants from the south.[14] Ten men eventually contributed to one or another aspect of this multi-dimensional undertaking between 1911 and 1915. Of their number Marius Barbeau, Francis Knowles, Frederick Waugh, and Boas's student Alexander Goldenweiser concentrated on Iroquoian subjects, their work taking them to reserves in Quebec, Ontario, upstate New York, and in Barbeau's case, as far afield as the Wyandot reservation in Oklahoma. Three others did fieldwork with Algonkians: Cyrus MacMillan and William Mechling in the Maritime provinces, and Paul Radin, another of Boas's proteges, in southeastern Ontario. Finally, Sapir, Harlan Smith, and William Wintemberg conducted research in both sectors, the former surveying Iroquoian and Algonkian languages and his colleagues investigating archaeological sites.[15] MacMillan, an English instructor at McGill, was the lone member of this team without anthropological credentials. In the circumstances, Sapir thought it wise to complement his work on Nova Scotia and Prince Edward Island Micmac (Mi'kmaq) oral traditions by recruiting Wilson Wallis to continue studies of that same group in New Brunswick, a project begun the year before under University of Pennsylvania Museum sponsorship. The usually compliant Reginald Brock rejected the plan, claiming that it amounted to needless redundancy.

It warrants mention that Sapir also tried, again without success, to initiate investigations in the eastern Subarctic, then deemed part of the expansive Woodlands but long since re-designated as a separate area. This remote precinct was home to mobile bands of northern Algonkians, Cree, and Montagnais-Naskapi (Innu) hunters whose territories encompassed the vast sweep of boreal forest lying between Ungava and James bays, and the lower St Lawrence. Owing to their location and way of life, mounting an expedition in that direction was certain to be a costly proposition, one requiring a considerable investment of time in order to achieve anything more than superficial results. Sapir dismissed Boas's suggestion that the division initiate a cooperative venture with the Bureau of American Ethnology, convinced that such arrangements were prone to counter-productive misunderstandings. That aside, there was the matter of finding the right person for the job, someone equipped for the rigours of camp and trail, and capable of handling the favoured linguistic approach to ethnography.[16] Several names were bandied about, including Radin and the bureau's Truman Michelson. The plan was soon shelved, however, not to be revived until the early twenties when Waugh made two trips to Quebec-Labrador, the second of which ended in his disappearance and presumed death en route home from fieldwork with Montagnais on the lower St Lawrence.

Despite the attention and resources devoted to the Iroquoian anomaly, the Athapaskan project to which Jenness was drafted after the First World War was, to Sapir's mind, "probably the greatest single need of ethnological research in Canada."[17] As many as twenty different groups, speakers of closely related languages belonging to the northern branch of the Athapaskan family, occupied lands scattered throughout the Plateau-Mackenzie culture area, most in the lowlands west of Hudson Bay, the remainder in the mountainous interior of Yukon and northern British Columbia. Together, they were said to be the least known ethnographically of all Aboriginal peoples within the country's borders. Moreover, Sapir was of the opinion that it was among populations in such geographically remote regions – including Algonkians in the eastern subarctic – that "we may expect to find the simplest and most fundamental forms of Aboriginal American culture," assuming, as Boas's "marginal theory" proposed, "that there is such a thing as a fundamental culture substratum." The task of distilling a definitive set of "typical" Athapaskan traits other than language, however, appeared complicated by their penchant for modifying, sometimes transforming, their cultures by borrowing ideas and practices from beyond their own borders.[18] "I do not think that this adaptability should be considered as a characteristic racial trait," Boas asserted in his 1910 programmatic paper on Canadian research problems. Rather, it "seems much more an effect of the lack of intensity [i.e., of psychological integration] of the old Athapascan culture" that, when coupled with their small, highly dispersed populations, left "these tribes susceptible to foreign influences."[19] Later generations of ethnologists would interpret this tendency differently, seeing it not as weakness but as a purposeful strategy aiding their capacity to thrive in various natural and social settings, not just in the Subarctic but on Canada's great plains and even in Oregon, California, and the semi-arid expanses of the American southwest, home to the Apache and Navajo nations.[20]

As with its remote eastern counterpart, mounting investigations in Canada's western Subarctic presented a good many logistical problems, among them the inevitable difficulties of hinterland travel and, of greater consequence, locating field situations conducive to the sort of study then deemed of greatest ethnological value. More often than not, this last required working away from settlements and passing the long winter in the north. Lowie knew this all too well after his one and only excursion into Canadian Athapaskan territory for the American Museum in 1908, having invested a full month travelling to the southern shore of Lake Athabasca from New York in return for a few, relatively unproductive weeks at Fort Chipewyan. By his own admission, the customs born of the area's fur trade piqued his interest more than what little he was able to observe of indigenous customs around the post. Five years later, Mason discovered something similar when he began surveying various populations along the upper reaches of the Mackenzie for the Anthropological Division. "The difficulties of work in the north are very great," he reported at season's end, going on to describe the district's two "classes" of Indians: those permanently attached to the posts and the nomadic "bush Indians ... the interesting ones ethnologically, but the least approachable" for research purposes, particularly during their infrequent visits to the settlements. Only James Teit seems to have met with more amenable conditions when Sapir engaged him in 1912 to work with two Stikine River peoples, the Kaska and Talhtan, in northwestern British Columbia. He reported that the people there were generally open to his many questions during their late spring to early fall musters at the region's main centre, Telegraph Creek.[21]

With all the limitations inherent in this approach Sapir still found satisfaction in having gotten this project off the ground in the first place, trusting it would eventually yield a worthwhile body of ethnographic and linguistic detail and, in the process provide an equally valuable corrective to the frequently questionable accounts of missionaries and other early observers. Indeed, he was so convinced of success that even before Mason's first contract was signed, he crowed about the progress to come in a letter to Teit, confident that "Between the two of you, we should soon be able to break the back of Athabascan ethnology."[22] Alas, what started well soon faltered. In 1914, plans to send Mason back to the Mackenzie for six months were scrapped when the division's entire research budget for the year was halved. Teit fared slightly better, undertaking one more excursion to the Stikine in 1915 before wartime retrenchment cut off funding and, with it, his hopes for expanding research across the border into Yukon.[23] Starting in 1921, then, it fell to Jenness to pick up where his predecessors left off. Instead of retracing their northward steps, however, his initiation took place in an altogether different natural and cultural setting: Alberta's southern plains, home ground of the Sarcee.

A WONDERFUL EAR FOR PHONETICS

The segment of Canada's ethnological map that depicted the country's mid-section, the great steppe-land sprawling across a broad swathe of its three prairie provinces, was no more complete in the early 1900s than were the segments portraying its remote subarctic interior. In Sapir's considered opinion, much of the area was an ethnological terra incognita, some resident groups "hardly more than mere names." Nevertheless, the plains culture area, of the five, figured least in the division's original research program. In fact, before Jenness was dispatched in that direction, only one other ethnographer, Wilson Wallis, had visited the region under the division's auspices, working among the Siouan-speaking Dakota in southern Manitoba on the eve of the First World War.[24] A matter of practicality, not neglect, channelling resources elsewhere reflected the priority that Clark Wissler, Boas's successor as curator of ethnology at the American Museum, was giving to the entirety of this vast region, whose southern limits nearly touched the Gulf of Mexico. In the summer preceding Wallis's trip, Wissler sent Alanson Skinner to Manitoba and Saskatchewan to investigate Plains Ojibwa and Plains Cree customs. Six years earlier, his apprentice, Lowie, had undertaken a "reconnoitering tour of the High Plains" whose itinerary, through portions of southern Alberta, included short stopovers with the Northern Blackfoot at Gleichen and Plains Cree at Hobbema and seven intensive weeks of fieldwork among the Stoney Assiniboine near Morley. Shortly thereafter, it was Pliny Goddard's turn; visiting the Sarcee twice before the outbreak of war, the Athapaskan language specialist concentrated on recording texts, much as he had done during his first stay on their reserve back in 1905 when he was an assistant professor at Berkeley.[25] With research funds still in short supply, sending Jenness to the same community was done, at least in part, for reasons of economy since travel to their reserve, on the outskirts of Calgary, was quicker, and less expensive, than to any other of the Dominion's far-flung Athapaskan enclaves. Sapir planned to make the trip too, intending to concentrate on Sarcee speech – part of his decades-long researches into the family of Athapaskan languages – while his colleague investigated social organization and collected artifacts. To their mutual regret, worry over his wife's failing health unavoidably delayed Sapir's western trip until the following summer. Jenness went on alone, left to his own devices in grappling with an unfamiliar setting and an unfamiliar language, which his more linguistically adroit associate colourfully characterized as one of "the son-of-a-bitchiest ... to actually know."[26]

The Sarcee were to be the first of seven First Nations with whom Jenness would do fieldwork over the next fifteen years. His time with them was also his first exposure to the deplorable conditions then prevailing across nearly the whole of Canada's far-reaching network of reserves and to the incalculable forms of native resistance to federal policies dedicated to their complete assimilation into society's mainstream. These experiences affected him profoundly, engendering abiding personal concern for the people and for their struggles against heavy odds. As a civil servant, however, he was obliged to refrain from offering any but the most anodyne comment on the day-to-day realities of reserve life or from examining sensitive issues that risked putting Ottawa's conduct of native affairs in an unfavourable light. Government seldom directed its anthropologists to look into policy-related problems, preferring the predictable advice of Indian Affairs bureaucrats and missionaries over that of more sympathetic, critical, and reform-minded outsiders of whom, as later pages will show, Jenness was certainly one.

◆

By all accounts, the Sarcee are relative newcomers to the Canadian high plains, their initial arrival dating to the colonial period, perhaps as recently as the early 1700s. Oral tradition suggests they are an offshoot of the Beaver, nomadic hunters in the forested Peace River country to the northwest. Split off from their compatriots owing to some pivotal event, likely an internal conflict, the new group's founding population gradually drifted onto the open plains beyond the North Saskatchewan River. Here, livelihood was centred on bison, a mode of subsistence steadily transformed when horses and firearms reached the region toward century's end. While retaining their ancestral language, the Sarcee remade aspects of their social organization and beliefs by grafting on a suite of traits – many common to other plains-dwelling peoples of the period – derived principally from their Algonkian-speaking Siksika Blackfoot neighbours. The most conspicuous of these were pan-tribal men's associations, each with its own rites and social functions, and the communal ceremonial complex known as the Sun Dance. Intermarriage fostered cultural borrowing. So, too, did incorporation of the Sarcee into the Blackfoot Confederacy, a military alliance of the Siksika and the closely related Peigan (Piikani) and Blood (Kainai) tribes born of the expanding fur trade and the episodic warfare and raiding it sparked on both sides of what today is the international boundary.[27]

The confederates entered into a peace and land cession treaty – Treaty Seven – with the Crown, in 1877. Strongly opposed to relinquishing their independence as nomadic hunters, members of the Sarcee's five extant bands reluctantly settled at a place called Blackfoot Crossing, a reserve set aside for them and their allies near Gleichen, to the east of the newly established Fort Calgary. Within six years, Bull Head, the nation's leading chief (and treaty signatory), waged a determined campaign for fairer treatment from Ottawa that resulted in his people's relocation to Fish Creek, a tract situated in the foothills of the Rockies, close to the nascent city's southwestern edge. Despite the move, "confinement" took a terrible toll on their health, morale, and culture, as it did among indigenous peoples throughout the continent. Between 1880 and 1920, the ravages of tuberculosis, influenza, and other infectious diseases reduced their population from roughly 450 to 160. As numbers diminished, so did their former economy, the decimation of the once-countless bison forcing them to resort to farming and stock ranching under the coercive tutelage of Indian Affairs. Political autonomy and religious freedom – including the right to hold Sun Dances – were suppressed under the legislated authority of the omnibus Indian Act.[28] To Jenness's mind, this onslaught had left the Sarcee a materially impoverished and culturally dispirited people, their circumstances rendered all the more harsh in suffering the racist scorn of white neighbours.[29] Years later, he would write that they appeared to have "lost all desire to recuperate, all desire to stand on their feet." Worse, such conditions seemed likely to spell their demise as an ethnically distinct people, perhaps by the twenty-first century.[30] In truth, Jenness held out little hope for the long-term cultural survival of Athapaskan communities across the northwest, concerned that they "lacked stamina and self-confidence in the presence of unforeseen difficulties" arising from the state's relentless drive to strip them of every last vestige of their aboriginality.[31] Though hardly unscathed by the experience, the modern Tsuu T'ina First Nation, as they are now known, some 2,000 strong, have proven his gloomy forecast wrong, its members demonstrating more resilience than circumstances in the opening decades of the twentieth century suggested was likely, or even possible.

Reaching the reserve on the last day of June, Jenness turned to Indian Agent Thomas Murray for help in locating lodgings for the two months he planned to stay. Anxious to avoid the "inconvenience of camping out," Sapir had written ahead from Ottawa in hopes of securing rooms for both of them in the Anglican-run residential school. That became impossible when a sudden spike in tubercular cases, the scourge of Aboriginal populations across the Dominion, prompted Murray, also a physician, to commandeer the place as a makeshift sanatorium.[32] As an alternative, he referred the newcomer to the Whitneys, a "half-breed" couple who offered to house and feed him for two dollars per day. A "very reliable and willing" fellow, John Whitney, fluent in Sarcee, not only agreed to assist with his tenant's research by acting as both interpreter and consultant but also performed many of the seventy-four songs Jenness recorded on wax cylinders using a phonograph borrowed from his landlord's neighbour. The lone drawback in their otherwise convenient arrangement was the ten bumpy miles separating Whitney's home from the reserve's main settlement, a distance traversed on horseback and which, at least on the anthropologist's maiden ride, left him "a wreck – sore knees & sore elsewhere."[33]

His arrival coincided with a recent addition to the Sarcee calendar: their annual excursion to the Calgary Stampede, inaugurated by the

Old Knife and his wife inside their tipi, Sarcee Indian Reserve, Calgary.
Canadian Museum of Civilization, Diamond Jenness, 1921, 53314

city a dozen years earlier. Instead of hindering a quick start to fieldwork, the timing played to Jenness's advantage, as a steady stream of
cash-strapped fair-goers brought him their "old heirlooms" in hopes of
making enough money to cover the cost of a week's stay in town. As
with all other aspects of research, what was required by way of ethnographic specimens were "genuine" pieces, those supposedly unaffected
by the accretion of white influences. Merely identifying such items often
proved a tall order. Sapir had spoken to the problem in advising Waugh
on how to proceed in collecting examples of Iroquoian manufactures
in 1911. On explaining that the "aboriginal element should always be
peeled out," he went on to admit that "this is not always an easy task,
and ... in many cases even the older Indians are not quite clear in their
minds as to what is merely comparatively old and what is thoroughly
aboriginal."[34] Already an experienced collector, Jenness still found this
side of the job more involved than he was used to, particularly given
how different conditions were among the Sarcee and the Copper Inuit,
or the Bwaidokans, for that matter. But at least he was reasonably well
financed for the purpose, having left Ottawa with $300 earmarked for
buying artifacts and receiving $400 more on persuading museum man-
agement that time was running short to obtain pieces that hadn't been
produced for the tourist trade at Banff and elsewhere.[35]

Before his fieldwork, the museum's collections contained 4 artifacts
attributed to the Sarcee. Afterwards, they held 130, plus a few speci-

mens of Cree, Siksika, and Stoney provenience. "On the whole I think it is a good collection," he informed Sapir, "obtained very cheaply, considering the prices ... [Pliny] Goddard seems to have paid" when he last visited the reserve in 1914 on behalf of his deep-pocketed New York employer. Included in the lot were a sacred medicine bundle and associated paraphernalia, arguably the most ethnographically significant of his acquisitions and, at $170, its costliest. The seller related some of the lore surrounding the bundle's history and customary use, and offered to organize a performance of the ceremonial dance in which the items figured had the anthropologist been willing to foot the bill for feeding participants and onlookers.[36] Equally valuable was Jenness's discovery, seemingly by accident, that the Sarcee had made and used pottery in the recent past, a practice all but abandoned once white traders introduced more durable (and serviceable) ironware. Sapir confirmed his colleague's finding during his own visit to the reserve a year later. Into the bargain, he obtained two replicas from an elder who, though not a potter herself, was able to fashion facsimiles on the basis of childhood memories. These modern-day renderings of an otherwise lost craft, together with about 200 additional artifacts, nearly doubled again the museum's once-paltry Sarcee accessions.[37]

By the turn of the twentieth century, the Sarcee had earned a reputation for resisting state-sponsored assimilation, showing themselves to be "more tenacious of their customs and superstitions than other Indians," at least in the opinion of one government official who knew the situation at first hand.[38] Still, twenty years later, much of the way of life Jenness intended to document now existed more in the memory of elders, and in oral traditions inherited from generations past, than in everyday existence on the reserve. About a dozen elders, all men, most of considerable age, agreed to be interviewed, each receiving three dollars daily for his time and trouble. The anthropologist's questioning ranged across numerous subjects, most of the resulting evidence supplementing what scanty information was already in print, the remainder filling in glaring gaps in Goddard's "incomplete and rather confused account" of the Sun Dance. The narratives Jenness recorded provided detail enough for him to sketch out what remains to this day the standard ethnographic source on the Sarcee, describing the main features of their social, political, and economic organization and corresponding norms and values, and with them, the individual life course, female and male, from birth to death. Arguably of greater import, at least in terms of the Boasian project, were the elders' reflections on the realm of belief and ritual, the dreams, visionary experiences, and quests for sacred knowledge in an incorporeal dimension alive with sentient animal spirits and the power of that knowledge to promote individual and collective well being. The origins and qualities of important medicine bundles figured prominently in these accounts, as did personal recollections of Sun Dances held in the days before its suppression by government fiat. Jenness would return to this mode of inquiry in subsequent fieldwork, the resulting corpus of carefully transcribed narrative accounts and legends offering a valuable window onto subjective thought-worlds unlike any familiar to the western mind and yet no less real and compelling.

The sizeable product of some six weeks' worth of interviewing was taken down principally in English, with only a handful of narratives in the vernacular, as text method purists preferred. "The task is much simplified through having an excellent interpreter," Jenness explained to Sapir after a month on the job; "If I can attune my ears to the sounds with some approach to accuracy and speed, it won't be so hard to take down a passable text that you can use" for analytical purposes. With limited time at his disposal, the novice Athapaskanist was hard-pressed to acquire any but the basics of spoken Sarcee and to teach Whitney a standardized form of phonetic notation with which to transcribe the elders' words in the original. Sapir was hoping his colleague might be able to produce reliable data on the language's phonetic properties, especially tone – modulations of pitch affecting meaning – a trait he had already identified in several of its sister speech forms. "Am trying to feel the language," Jenness shyly confessed of his first humbling encounters; "I am sure there is tone – a high certainly, but I am not sure about a middle." Interestingly enough, the feature completely eluded Goddard's more practiced ear, but Sapir was able to verify its presence soon after reaching the reserve in 1922. On receiving word that the issue was finally settled, Jenness responded with typical good humour: "I have a wonderful ear for phonetics! I spent two months among the Sarcees and did not know whether there was tone or not; and you discover it in one day! ... Don't you think you had better take up Athabascan exclusively now instead of myself?"[39]

The discovery of tone in Sarcee convinced Sapir (mistakenly) that it was a definitive characteristic of Na-Dene, his preferred name for the new linguistic stock he proposed, one that included the known Athapaskan languages, along with three others he suspected were distant kin: Eyak, Haida, and Tlingit, all spoken in the Pacific northwest. He was equally certain that the grouping represented "the most un-American" of all New World languages, claiming that their closest living relatives were likely tonal languages spoken in China and elsewhere in Asia.[40] "If the morphological and lexical accord which I find on every hand between Nadene [sic] and Indo-Chinese is 'accidental,'" he enthused in a letter to Kroeber, "then every analogy on God's earth is an accident."[41] Contrary to Boas's theorizing about an ancient "cultural substratum," moreover, the Na-Dene hypothesis implied that Athapaskan peoples were descended from a more recent wave of Old World migrants than the original waves generally thought to have given rise to all Amerindian populations, a view still current today. Equally current is the claim for direct linguistic affinity with an Asiatic source, although recent studies now point to a putative connection to the Yeniseian family, the last survivor of which is spoken by the Ket people of north-central Siberia. The finding has encouraged some linguists to propose the name Dene-Yeniseian for the long-mooted, continent-spanning stock. Proponents seem confident that among its New World members, Eyak and Tlingit are in, but Haida is out.[42]

◆

His first fieldwork since Coronation Gulf now behind him, Jenness returned to Ottawa, where stacks of half-finished Arctic Expedition manuscripts and the concluding acts of the *Friendly Arctic* imbroglio would relegate everything Sarcee to the back burner for the immediate future. As things turned out, his ethnographic report on the season's investigations, though completed not long thereafter, did not see the light of day until 1938, one of many victims of museum policy. For want of a musicologist to transcribe the music, moreover, the body of songs Whitney had helped him collect went unpublished altogether.[43] Meanwhile, the evident success of his associate's initial foray into the Athapaskan field prompted Sapir to begin organizing its follow-up: an expedition to the Hazelton area in British Columbia's western interior, home of the Bulkley River Carriers (Wet'suwet'en). A year earlier, Barbeau had made the first of several trips to this same locale, investigating the neighbouring Gitksan, Tsimshian-speakers whose abutting territory lay along the middle course of the Skeena. "I am interested to learn that you are close to the Carriers," Sapir wrote to Barbeau at the time, thinking he might turn the situation to double advantage by encouraging him to "carry on some investigations" among the other group as well, particularly into the linguistic sujet du jour – tone. An agreeable Barbeau did what he could. However, in a setting where a "partly unspoiled" population, as he described it, was managing to preserve many of their old ways, the job of thoroughly studying Carrier culture and language really called for a second set of eyes and ears.[44]

With a wife and small child to consider, Jenness was less than enthusiastic about his next assignment. Troubled by the prospect of a prolonged absence from home, he proposed an alternative that would allow Eilleen and son John to accompany him, thereby side-stepping familial squabbles. He had the Bella Bella in mind, a little-known, non-

Athapaskan people who lived on the temperate mainland coast. "I hate like the mischief to spend the winter after next at Hazelton," he confided to Barbeau, but "Sapir is kicking against my going to the west coast." On the bright side, he had to admit, Hazelton was probably the only town in northern Athapaskan country where his wife and toddler could winter in reasonable comfort, much as Barbeau's own family had done in 1920. "We shall see," he told his friend, the trip, scheduled for autumn 1923, still a year away; "many things may happen between now and then."[45]

They did. Combing through published and archival sources – chiefly the narratives of explorers and fur traders, and the scholarly contributions of Oblate missionaries Emile Petitot and Adrian-Gabriel Morice – soon led Jenness to see the coming expedition, and the larger Athapaskan project, in a far more favourable light.[46] In fact, halfway through his time on the Bulkley he requested, and received, permission to remain in the field for an additional three months, sufficient time to visit remote Sekani communities in the Rocky Mountain Trench, an immense valley dominating the landscape of the province's northeastern interior. What most intrigued him were evident parallels between certain Athapaskan customs, folklore, and spiritual beliefs and practices which he had read about in the literature and traits he knew at first hand among Inuit to the north, beyond the tree line. "One does not feel that the Eskimos are so peculiar after all – despite the kayak and the harpoon," he told Sapir, speculating, as had Boas before him, that correspondences of this sort might well be crucial to unravelling yet another facet of the origins puzzle: the relationship of Inuit to indigenous populations elsewhere in the hemisphere.[47]

CHAPTER NINE

Jostling Tribes,
1923–1924

CULTURAL CROSSROAD

British Columbia's interior is part of an immense physiographic province, an expanse of mountains, rivers, and boreal forest that stretches from the western slopes of the Rockies into Yukon and the trackless Alaskan interior beyond. It is home to some half dozen Athapaskan-speaking peoples, among them a cluster of geographically dispersed groups – Jenness referred to them as "sub-tribes" – commonly known in the anthropological literature as Carrier. Celebrated explorer Alexander Mackenzie is credited with popularizing the name, said to derive from a mourning custom in which a chief's widow carries his cremated remains until a public feast is held to mark his death. Today, many Carriers prefer to be called Dakelh, "people who go upon water." The branch living along the Bulkley River, a major tributary of the Skeena, are known by a different name: Wet'suwet'en, "people of the lower drainage." Their lands lie in the shadow of the Coast Ranges, at the western flanks of Carrier country, some two hundred miles inland from Prince Rupert.[1]

Oral tradition holds that, from earliest times, the Wet'suwet'en, with the Gitksan and Sekani, dwelled at a village called Dizkle, situated upriver from Hazelton. The three peoples lived there for generations until an omen, which appeared in the form of a pair of fearless squirrels, foretold of impending catastrophe "at the hands of the sky-god Utakke." Fearing for their lives, the Sekani fled northward, the Gitksan downriver to Gitanmaax (Hazelton), and the Wet'suwet'en to different places in the valley of the Bulkley, locales each group inhabits to this day.[2] Jenness toured Mosquito Flat, the spot where Dizkle is reported to have stood, searching for visible traces of its long-ago existence. None was found. Afterward, he told Marius Barbeau that he hoped to return to the area some time soon to make a proper excavation, a job requiring a full summer season since the village's remains were said to lie several feet below ground. "There are probably dozens of sites that would repay investigation in the Carrier country alone .... I heard of a cave in a mountain that has been inhabited for generations, the debris of one generation being piled on top of another."[3] As with so many other worthwhile projects, this one, too, was left unrealized.[4]

Contemporary anthropological opinion generally favours an account of Wet'suwet'en history that is at odds with local tradition in one crucial respect: the assertion that their forebears resettled in this area after leaving a proto-Athapaskan homeland somewhere farther north. Comparative linguistic analysis, in conjunction with archaeological findings, points to a probable place of origin in Yukon or the eastern Alaskan interior.[5] Jenness, working at a time when there was little such evidence to corroborate their stories, thought it might well be impossible to reconstruct the Wet'suwet'en past, or the past of any Aboriginal group, for that matter, beyond the limits of living memory. The many legends he collected, though essential as ethnographic sources – what contemporary usage might consider to be ethnohistoric sources – seemed to him less valuable for purposes of historical inquiry, at least by western standards, because they typically conveyed idiosyncratic, rather than "correct," constructions of notable events and figures, and blurred the line between the prosaic and fantastical.[6] Skepticism notwithstanding, the business at hand, as in Alberta two summers before, was at once historical and descriptive: documenting the local way of life as the outgrowth of internal and external factors operating over time. To that end, Jenness sketched a picture of development on the Bulkley that began with migration from one of two possible directions: either from the north, via the Liard and Stikine Rivers, or from the Mackenzie lowlands, to the northeast, by way of the Peace River and its tributaries. Over "countless centuries," he elaborated, various peoples had converged on the British Columbian cordillera, turning it into a virtual "melting pot" where "tribes ... jostled against one another, mingled, and changed." Among them were Athapaskans, nomadic foragers whose societies consisted of relatively small, politically autonomous bands. Migrating from east of the Rockies, those called Sekani remained in the arctic drainage system and thus retained many facets of their original, family-based mode of living. Chilcotin (Tsilhqot'in) and Carriers, by contrast, pushed into the Pacific Basin, a habitat whose salmon-rich rivers were capable of supporting growth of larger, village-dwelling populations and, with them, more complex polities.[7]

In penetrating the interior's westernmost limits, the ancestors of the two northernmost Carrier groups, Babine (Nat'oot'en) and Wet'suwet'en, also found themselves in what, for them, was a novel human environment, one under the sway of influences stemming from the Pacific coast. Over time, the newcomers accommodated to these surroundings in ways that left them more like one another and, by degrees, less like Carriers elsewhere. The dialects they speak make this plainly evident, many linguists now classifying them as variants of Babine-Witsuwit'en, a separate language closely related to, but nevertheless distinct from, that spoken by the Dakelh. Their forms of social structure are similarly distinctive, resembling and, it is widely thought, principally derived from, non-Athapaskans living up and down the Skeena and adjacent Nass rivers. Specialists disagree whether these structural changes occurred during the contact era, or before it, as Jenness assumed. What is agreed is that adopting a compatible system of clans, hereditary titles, and heraldic crests enabled the Wet'suwet'en to strengthen alliances with the Gitksan and other regional trading partners by anchoring them in an idiom of shared kinship. Combined with the assimilation of new spiritual beliefs and of public feasting – the potlatch or denii ne'aas, "people coming together" – as a multi-purpose forum of governance, the overall effect, in Jenness's judgment, was nothing short of revolutionary. Later he would temper this view, pointing out that the Wet'suwet'en were far from slavish imitators or mere clones of their near neighbours. Rather, he characterized their culture as "extremely fluid ... so full of vitality and life that it was capable of absorbing numerous elements from abroad without impairing its essential vigour."[8] As with his account of early migration and diffusion, this observation carries the imprint of Boasian historical ethnology, alluding as it does to the inner spirit, or genius, of the Wet'suwet'en.

European contact ushered in a second, ultimately more fateful wave of change. Beginning on the Pacific Coast in the eighteenth century, it gradually intensified in the nineteenth as fur traders built posts throughout the inland district that famed Nor'wester Simon Fraser christened New Caledonia.[9] Settlers and fortune-seekers followed, bringing disease and encroaching on tribal lands customarily held as corporate property by matrilineally extended family groupings called houses, which were sub-divisions of clans. After mid-century, the coming of Roman Catholic missionaries and the apparatus of Canadian Indian administration dealt what was arguably the era's biggest blow, their policies and practices disturbing, though not eradicating, as was their intent, the indigenous social and moral order. Only the Beaver, in the Peace River lowlands, came under the terms of a post-confederation federal treaty, Treaty Eight, ratified in 1899. Elsewhere, a provincial Indian Reserve Commission began parcelling out reserves in 1876, doing so without negotiation or recognition of land rights stemming from their original possession of the country. Worsening an already contentious issue, the parcels assigned, allotted on the basis of roughly ten acres per household, were negligible compared to the practice elsewhere in the Dominion.[10] There may have been as many as 2,000 Wet'suwet'en at the start of the tumultuous period of colonial expansion. At the time of his visit, Jenness pegged the group's numbers at roughly 300 individuals.[11]

◈

Barbeau did what he could to allay his friend's concerns about wintering on the Bulkley. Having already spent two seasons at Hazelton, most recently that very summer, he was well placed to provide practical intelligence and personal insight about the town, its nearby reserves, and a good many people on both sides of its gaping racial divide. "I have not found a single man yet whose face did not light up when I mentioned your name," Jenness wrote not long after he, Eilleen, and baby John arrived in mid-October. "Your stay here has smoothed my path immensely, and everyone welcomes me because I am a friend of Mr Barbeau."[12] As often happens in fieldwork, wherever and whenever it is done, the path was not entirely free of bumps. Finding appropriate lodgings headed his list of worries, the idea of settling for "an isolated place in the woods where [Eilleen] would be dreaming of bears all the time" striking him as a sure-fire recipe for marital discord. Barbeau appeared to have saved the day on that score by informing him of a vacancy, the property of Father Joseph Allard, conveniently located in Hagwilget and costing just thirty dollars a month. The recommendation seemed ideal until Jenness inspected the wood-frame house for himself. It turned out to be ill-equipped, poorly heated, and on the shabby side, scarcely an improvement on passing the subarctic winter huddled in a tent. Crisis was averted by the timely discovery of more suitable quarters in Hazelton. The price of domestic peace came high: forty dollars a month rent for lodging, another ten for an office in the otherwise spacious front room of the priest's Hagwilget shack, and thirty more for a horse to cover the four miles separating town and reserve.[13]

With the cold season closing in, many of Hagwilget's people were away from the community until Christmas-time, hunting or cutting timber for the railway. This complicated the crucial search for an interpreter since the Wet'suwet'en who remained behind were mainly young fellows "who know nothing, or women[!]." There were two prospects, both elders. One was Donald Grey, a prosperous, "somewhat sophisticated" man who spoke English quite well but was ambivalent about committing to the job. Felix George, a long-time mission interpreter and hereditary chief of Thin House, a division of the Frog-Raven clan, was the other. Initially reluctant to engage George because of his halting English, Jenness's doubts soon vanished once the pair got down to business. George turned out to be "a veritable mine of information. He is patient, too, and will sit with me for five or six hours a day without a murmur."[14] Their first weeks together bore fruit on all fronts but one – language, the anthropologist's ear no better attuned to the sounds of Witsuwit'en than to those of its cousin Sarcee. "Don't laugh too much over my phonetics," he implored Edward Sapir, on submitting a few preliminary observations, including tentative identification of high and low tones, after only a week in the field. "I am having plenty of trouble ... but feel a little more at home than when I went to Calgary. It may be a false confidence, though." A month later, the story was little better: "Don't expect much in the way of tones; they baffle me utterly, although I am sure of a high and low." Unfortunately, his attempts to pick up the basics received more hindrance than help from George since the elder was given to shifting repeatedly (if unconsciously) between his native François Lake sub-dialect and the variant typically spoken at Hagwilget. Worse still, "if I get anywhere at all approximating the sounds he says they are right & you know what that means – nine times out of ten they are wrong."[15] At one point, a sympathetic Sapir suggested using a phonograph to record the language, "chiefly sets of words that resemble each other in all respects but tone." This wasn't done, probably for want of a machine. Jenness's travails did yield one minor victory, however: a complete text, painstakingly transcribed in phonetic notation, checked over by a fluent speaker, and then sent on to his colleague to "disentangle the essentials" for his own purposes. Meantime, he kept plugging away at the language, even while imagining Sapir sitting behind his desk in Ottawa, "holding up [his] hands in holy horror" at the pathetic results trickling in from the west.[16]

George's limitations as a language teacher were amply compensated for by the breadth of his knowledge of local customs and traditions. Aided by the man's capable interpreting during interviews with other elders, Jenness was not long in compiling a body of descriptive detail "as extensive as anything published by Morice."[17] Most of the information then available in print on the Wet'suwet'en, on Carriers more generally, and on other British Columbian Athapaskans came from the pen of the intellectually ambitious, French-born cleric, Adrien-Gabriel Morice. A talented linguist, Morice had acquired a working knowledge of Dakelh speech over the span of a twenty-year residence (1885–1904) at Fort St James, on Stuart Lake, producing seminal papers on the language that found favour even with the usually critical Sapir.[18] Equally prolific as an ethnologist, his descriptions of traditional subsistence activities and material culture are regarded to this day as thorough and reliable. Jenness therefore opted to concentrate on aspects of Wet'suwet'en life whose treatment was wanting, or absent, in Morice's work: social organization and religion.[19] The results of Jenness's comparative investigations in Hagwilget, and later on Fraser Lake and Stony Creek, Carrier reserves lying to the southeast of Morice's long-time home base, lend credence to the contemporary view that coastal influences diffused to groups in the central interior at a relatively late date, borne eastward along contact-era trade networks. For one thing, features such as clan organization and potlatching appeared more fully developed, and far more integral to the fabric of everyday Wet'suwet'en life, than was the case elsewhere. For another, the overall feel of religious doctrine impressed him as being less Athapaskan, as was evident, for instance, in the accretion of ideas about the spiritual sources of chiefs' authority or the causes and treatment of "medicine-dream sickness," illnesses attributed to spirit possession.[20]

As with sacred beliefs and practices borrowed from non-Athapaskan neighbours, early Wet'suwet'en experience of Christianity did not subvert the "supernatural world of their forefathers, but merely added a second one." The first "borrowed" beliefs were expressed in the syncretic and revivalistic Prophet Dance movement that had reached their territory decades before the coming of Catholic missionaries. Once priests were on the scene, they initiated a long and relentless campaign to win the people's "undivided allegiance" to a faith, no less an entire way of life, that was purged of all nativist elements, old and new.[21] Feasting, the iconic potlatch, was their main target, symbolizing for Morice and his fellow missionaries, and for Ottawa lawmakers who legislated its prohibition in 1884, the very antithesis of Christian morality. Many people on the Bulkley, as elsewhere, defied the ban, but around 1913 the Hagwilget community yielded to the unrelenting pressure and burned the ceremonial masks and other heraldic paraphernalia they had used to demonstrate hereditary titles and associated prerogatives. Although feasting continued after this, if in a diminished form, it seemed to devolve into "mere entertainment divorced from its old social significance."[22] Amplified by the effects of demographic decline, church-run schools, and economic change, the ramifications of the mission's project, in Jenness's judgment, were both culturally and socially de-stabilizing, values and customs "that held sway for countless centuries ... ruthlessly flung aside under the new regime brought in by the white man." Of its many consequences, however, he thought none would prove as detrimental over the long term as generational alienation, elders struggling to "reconcile their traditional ideas and beliefs with the new ones so suddenly thrust upon them from without," while mandatory schooling cut off their children, and grandchildren, from that tradition without providing much of value in its place.[23] While the inadequacies of state-sponsored education would later become a recurrent theme in his efforts to inform, and reform, Canada's approach to native affairs, it was the internal conflict experienced by his Hagwilget consultants that most shaped his appreciation of the cultural dilemma they faced. Many of their stories, especially first-hand accounts of Bini, the most illustrious of the nineteenth-century prophets, served to ground Wet'suwet'en resistance to the forces of assimilation in historical context. However, witnessing for himself a medicine ritual conducted covertly to evade the disapproving gaze of officialdom brought the palpable tensions between two very different world views into much sharper focus.

Practically all the ethnographic material Jenness obtained came from interviews, not by way of direct observation. To his understandable disappointment, the year's main potlatch, at Hagwilget, was to occur in August, months after his intended departure, and the smaller one around Christmastime, which he had hoped to attend, wasn't held at all. His bad luck turned to good in late February, however, the result of someone else's misfortune: an elderly woman, suddenly fallen ill with kyan, a malady attributed to possession by "the dreaded mountain spirit."

Understood in terms of beliefs and practices partly derived from the Pacific coast by way of the Gitksan, partly from older Athapaskan roots, kyan was a form of medicine-dream illness – at one point, Jenness (unhelpfully) described it as a "state of dreamy phthisis" – whose delusional victims are prone to violent behaviour and may, if untreated, lapse into insanity. Only those who themselves have recovered from this or similar afflictions are thought capable of withstanding, even controlling, the indwelling spirit's power and of driving it from the patient's body.[24] With the onset of symptoms, members of this highly specialized medicine society gathered at the home of Old Sam, husband of the stricken woman, to begin the prescribed treatment. When their drumming and singing caught the attention of a passerby, an intolerant white schoolteacher, he demanded they "cease their humbug" and then stormed off to complain of the alleged deviltry to Hagwilget's Indian agent and police constable. More worrisome to the participants than stirring up trouble on that front was their fear that a priest, or worse, Dr H.C. Wrinch, director of Hazelton hospital, might become involved. In the past, such interventions had typically ended badly, some patients dying because they were prevented from receiving traditional medicine, others being committed to Essendale Mental Hospital, the provincial asylum near Vancouver, following diagnosis as incurably insane. Anxious to avert a similar fate for Mrs Old Sam, her attendants took evasive action, shifting the closely guarded proceedings to Felix George's house, in a secluded part of the reserve. As a reflection of their considerable trust in

Jenness, they asked him to join them, assuming that the presence of a white man – a sympathetic one at that – would enable him to speak authoritatively in their defence should further complaints of "improper or harmful" conduct eventuate. (Happily, none did.) The single evening during which the ritual took place, a mere two hours from start to finish, turned out to be the most ethnographically insightful experience of his five months with the Wet'suwet'en.

Jenness's account of what transpired in George's house provides a fair indication of his progress in overcoming the self-professed Oxford skepticism that permeated his Bwaidogan and Inuit researches. Nothing about the patient's behaviour, or that of her attendants, he explained, seemed "fictitious [or] consciously self-induced," convincing him that kyan sickness was quite real and that Wet'suwet'en medicine, however unlike its western counterpart, was ultimately efficacious. When considered within a context of cultural knowledge that posited a world "full of supernatural beings who are constantly interfering in human affairs," it stands to reason that some individuals might well be susceptible to hallucinatory hysteria, as well as to the "beating of the drum, the rhythm of the music" to "bring the patient under ... control." In 1929, four years before Jenness published on the illness and its treatment, a chance encounter with Frederick Banting at a meeting of the Royal Society precipitated a brief exchange of letters between them on the subject. While admitting that the descriptive details were themselves inherently interesting, Jenness protested that his interpretation – what he later termed the "rational explanation" – was plainly amateurish. The eminent medical researcher, and recent Nobel laureate, disagreed, suggesting that the work stood to make a valuable contribution to mental health theory and practice and urging its submission to a Canadian medical journal to gain maximum exposure. "An Indian Method of Treating Hysteria" eventually appeared in the pages of *Primitive Man,* a publication, strangely enough, of the Catholic University of America. The choice of a fairly conventional outlet speaks to its author's modesty, no less to his conviction that the phenomenon amounted to little more than an ethnological curiosity. Still, in a lone sentence, he allowed that Wet'suwet'en medicine just might have something of value to offer its western analogue in the still-developing treatment of psychosomatic disorders, the very point of Banting's original suggestion.[25]

The Victoria Memorial Museum was well furnished with Gitksan and Wet'suwet'en artifacts courtesy of Barbeau, who had been "bitten by the collecting bug" since his first trip to the region in 1915. Besides, there was "practically nothing" worth buying, most of the traditional items Jenness saw in and around Hagwilget striking him as indistinguishable from those in evidence in Hazelton. The lone exceptions were several old (and presumably rare) ornamental stone labrets, customarily inserted in the lower lip as markers of high social rank. The practice is said to have inspired early French observers to refer to all the western Carrier groups by the same name, Babines, "pendulous lips."[26] Purchasing the labrets presented no difficulties, but the story was far different when Sapir commissioned him to secure one, possibly two, totem poles to supplement three others already in the museum's collections. The search, which dragged on throughout the better part of the winter, eventually came up dry. However, in the process Jenness repeatedly traversed the same politically sensitive terrain that surrounds appropriation of indigenous cultural patrimony today.[27]

Preliminary enquiries around town suggested that there were poles available at reasonable prices. A Gitksan specimen in the village of Kispiox had recently sold in the $150 range, although its buyer, the American Museum of Natural History, also faced an outlay of two to three times that amount to cover shipping charges to New York.[28] Encouraged, Jenness recommended to Sapir that $300 (exclusive of freight) be set aside, a figure he assumed would purchase two interesting poles. The green light came within weeks. Meanwhile, he turned to Barbeau for guidance, deferring to his colleague's previous experience and knowledge in these matters. Should he try for one at Hagwilget, he wondered, having been told that every Wet'suwet'en-owned pole was actually the work of Gitksan artisans? "Just tell me which ones to buy and I'll try and make arrangements."[29]

Return mail contained the first of several suggestions: a fallen pole at Kitsegukla. The same letter also brought word of a grander scheme, one that added new wrinkles to what was beginning to shape up to be a delicate business: a proposed federal investment in the restoration and preservation of the region's inventory of totem poles. A measure of local public support for the initiative was then emerging, partly spurred by allegations of unscrupulous foreign buyers hunting for prize specimens on Vancouver Island, partly by the plain fact that neglect, and the elements, were causing poles to rot away. Compared to other parts of British Columbia, the upper Skeena River still boasted a sizeable number. This was reason enough for Barbeau, in league with some of Hazelton's leading citizens, to lobby for creation of a regional park where revitalized poles might stand in the very ground in which they had first been raised. With state policy since confederation dedicated to eradicating native traditions and identity, conserving cultural heritage in this way was an unusual – and unexpected – step, to say the least. It is likely that the prospect of economic spinoffs provided the real motivation, public and private interests seeking to capitalize on the area's tourism potential by using the poles to lure visitors travelling westward aboard Canadian National trains. With the plan officially adopted midway through 1924, the railway agreed to contribute logistical and technical assistance, with Ottawa providing the funding and on-the-ground expertise in the persons of Barbeau and Harlan Smith. Duncan Campbell Scott, long-serving Deputy Superintendent-General of Indian Affairs, chaired a special committee to supervise the work. Barbeau and Sapir were named sitting members.[30]

Rumours of what was in the offing flew around Gitksan-Wet'suwet'en country, fostering resolve against parting with any pole, including derelict ones, at any price. Wary of government intentions, some Gitksan even opposed restoration of their own property. Others foresaw windfalls, Jenness reporting that the anticipated $100 benchmark might turn out to be well below current asking prices for moderately-sized specimens of twenty to twenty-five feet in length. Riding a rising tide of expectation, the few who were willing to sell set their sights high, beginning in the $250 to $300 range, and one fellow at Skeena Crossing, whom Barbeau recommended, wanted $500. None of this sat well with museum management, Director William McInness opining that $250 was "plenty" for even the finest pole and that the one at Skeena Crossing, for which Jenness had begun negotiating, ought to fetch less. "Possibly the best method would be not to insist too much ... on your desire to get one or two poles," Sapir cautioned; instead, "hint at it now and then and wait until they suggest purchase to you themselves. This, as you know, is often the best way in which to bring them to terms." No such luck. Feeling duty-bound by McInness's dictum, Jenness's "long palaver" with the pole's owner came to naught, a mere $25 separating them in the end.[31]

Before conceding defeat, one last lead warranted investigation: a reportedly fine specimen at the former Gitksan village of Old Kuldo. Located some eighty miles above Hazelton on the Skeena, the place had been a point of trade with neighbouring Nisga'a until a murderous dispute between them in the mid-1800s resulted in its abandonment. Jenness relished the idea of trekking to the site, enticed by the adventure of traversing back-country in the midst of subarctic winter. With "old timer" Angus Beaton as guide, the way out and back, a full week's journey on horseback and snowshoes, followed the route of the Yukon telegraph line. Beaton knew the terrain intimately, having long experience there as a trapper, gold prospector, and telegrapher.[32]

The companions reached their destination on the third day out. Precious little of Old Kudlo remained standing, the ruins of houses and

Remains of a totem pole at Old Kudlo, British Columbia.
Canadian Museum of Civilization, Diamond Jenness, 1924, 60624

totem poles barely visible under a heavy blanket of snow. Some judicious digging revealed the prize that had brought them this long way.
Measuring thirty-seven feet from end to end and some two and a half
feet in diameter, the pole, associated with the Wild Rice house of the
Wolf clan, was truly a "remarkable" specimen and, according to Barbeau, was among the oldest along the upper Skeena. Given the circumstances, moreover, it was in surprisingly sound condition. Jenness was
especially impressed by the fineness of the carving, far more detailed

than most seen elsewhere on his travels. Whoever had undertaken the work had clearly gone to considerable lengths, not least in obtaining the cedar from which it was fashioned. The nearest stand of comparably sized trees, Beaton said, was a fair distance away.[33]

Getting this singular specimen to the railway for shipment to Ottawa was bound to pose a logistical challenge, its remote situation requiring floating the pole down the Skeena in summer or dragging it over the frozen river in winter. "If handled rightly," Jenness confidently assured Sapir, the pole could probably be obtained for $75, thus off-setting the heavy expense of transport. None of this was to be. From Angus Beaton's discreet inquiries, he learned that the pole's owners were trapping in the bush and would not be back before his departure for Vancouver in a few weeks' time. Rather than letting the matter go, he suggested that Barbeau make a bid for it when he was next in the area. Alternatively, the Anthropological Division could retain Beaton for the purpose.[34] Days later, the situation changed again, this time on news that two elders at Kispiox were the rightful owners. Dashing off to see them in high hopes of concluding a deal, Jenness met firm resistance instead, hearing from one "that he would rather sell his own child" than part with the property. The American Museum's recent purchase probably helped galvanize widespread opposition, no one daring to share the "bad odour" now clinging to those of their compatriots who gave, or sold away, valuable pieces of Gitksan heritage. Resigned to the public mood, Jenness apprised Sapir "that in another ten years ... when most of the old men have died off, it will be easier to purchase poles."[35]

Originally scheduled to return to Ottawa in March, Jenness approached Sapir about staying on into summer in order to broaden the geographic range of his researches. Ruling out an expedition down the Mackenzie, the region J. Alden Mason had visited before the First World War, he proposed heading deeper into the Cordilleran interior instead. An extra three months, he thought, would be sufficient to reach Sekani territory, several hundred miles to the north and east of the Bulkley, a mountainous, heavily forested area drained by the Finlay, Parsnip, and upper Peace Rivers. Sapir consented, and quickly came up with an extra $2,500 to cover expenses. There was one condition, however: getting home in time to attend the meetings of the British Association for the Advancement of Science, slated for August in Toronto.[36] "I expect to have the trip of my life" Jenness enthused, imagining himself heroically navigating wilderness rivers by canoe en route to this remote quarter of the province. By retracing "the old route of Mackenzie and the

Hudson Bay people ... I might quite likely strike some isolated bands ... who retain more of their old culture," he mused, evoking his exhilaration at the prospect of encountering "Stone Age Eskimos" in the Arctic, ten years before.[37] If he were to cover the same ground today, he would scarcely recognize the country, portions of the Parsnip and Finlay – twin sources of the Peace – having been engineered into Williston Lake, an immense reservoir feeding water to the W.A.C. Bennett hydroelectric dam. Back in 1924, though, the landscape was little different than when the fabled Alexander MacKenzie had seen it during his search for an outlet to the Pacific, 130 years before.

The Jennesses journeyed uneventfully from Hazelton to Vancouver via steamer from Prince Rupert, reaching the city in early March. Unlike her husband, Eilleen was happy to see the last of the interior, her winter beset by illness and pangs of loneliness. At months end, she and young John headed home. Meantime, a local Geological Survey man introduced Jenness to several helpful contacts in town, among them a veteran Hudson's Bay Company inspector well versed in the particulars of travel to out-of-the-way northern localities. This timely contact persuaded the ambitious adventurer-anthropologist to abandon negotiating the tricky springtime waters of the Parsnip and Finlay on his own, doubtless to his wife's considerable relief. As a safer bet, he accepted an offer of passage aboard a company vessel that plied the route to Forts McLeod and Grahame, the principal Sekani settlements. "The HB people will look after me all along the line," he dutifully notified headquarters; they have also promised "to see that I get every facility and the best Indians [as interpreters and consultants] available, at the least possible expense."[38]

Never one to knowingly pass up a chance to obtain fresh linguistic material, Sapir advised his colleague that he knew of several Athapaskan speakers from the north residing in the city, at least one of whom might well be receptive to being interviewed. Jenness succeeded in finding one of them, Mrs Arnot, a "half-breed" Kaska from Dease Lake, in the Stikine River area where Teit worked before the war. They agreed on a convenient schedule of afternoon sessions at the survey's downtown offices. To Jenness's disappointment, the elder professed ignorance of her people's customs and traditions, thus foiling his plan to inquire specifically into the distribution of hunting grounds bordering on Carrier and Sekani territories. She was fluent in Kaska, however, one of several dialects closely related to dialects spoken in Tahltan and Tagish communities in northwestern British Columbia and southern Yukon. As with every one of his previous forays into Athapaskan, Jenness met the usual difficulties in distinguishing one sound from another, a problem compounded by his consultant's tendency to talk just above a whisper.

In the end, their sessions allowed him to record a set of correspondences for his Wet'suwet'en word list and, in the process to "dig up some linguistics" for Sapir.[39]

Seeing his family off for home on 31 March, Jenness also took leave of Vancouver, catching a ferry to Seattle, where he planned to continue linguistic work on the more familiar forms of Iñupiaq. Having contemplated the possibility of doing so for some time past, "much tedious correspondence" eventually paid off when he learned that a group of youths from various villages on the Alaskan coast were in town, receiving training under Bureau of Education auspices. Armed with lexicons he had compiled during the Arctic Expedition, his aim was to verify and augment what was already a valuable body of comparative data on Barrow, Mackenzie, and Coronation Gulf speech. "If the Eskimos prove exceptionally good informants, I may possibly spend a fortnight" in Seattle, he advised Sapir, before crossing the border into the States; "for it is easier to return to Carrier country than to get to Alaska."[40] A hectic week ensued, one spent putting in seven-hour days with his young consultants aboard the moored schooner that served as their quarters, then returning to his hotel in the evening to write up results. The effort left him exhausted but "really enthusiastic" about what he had accomplished in so short a time. His main success was verifying the whole of his original Barrow vocabulary, ably assisted in the task by a fellow from Wainwright "whose dialect was practically identical with that of the neighbouring Barrow natives." He also made headway with a new dialect, the one spoken around Cape Prince of Wales on Bering Strait. "This last would have delighted your heart from the changes it registered in its phonetics," he enthused in a letter to Sapir that also acknowledged the invaluable "training" his colleague had provided him in identifying all-important sound shifts in language; "I shouldn't be surprised if this dialect wouldn't be a key dialect to many of the more southern ones," he added, a surmise that, on the strength of his subsequent investigations in Alaska, turned out to be on the right track.[41]

Jenness booked return passage to Prince Rupert on 7 April, the first leg of an expedition worthy of the day's most intrepid horse-and-buggy ethnographer. From there, his itinerary would take him eastward to the emerging town of Prince George, site of a long-time fur trade post near the confluence of the Fraser and Nechako Rivers, and finally northward to Sekani territory aboard a river freighter. With the Parsnip unnavigable much before May, he had several weeks free to devote to fieldwork with Carrier living near Fort Fraser, a short distance west of Prince

George. Boarding at a local railway hotel, he made daily visits to two nearby reserves, spending ten days at Fraser Lake (now Stellat'en), another five at Stony Creek (Sai Kuz). To his surprise, the area's Indian agent, Mr McAllen, was a fellow New Zealander, a happy coincidence that paid returns in assistance with the usually trying business of settling in and enlisting consultants. At Fraser Lake, he hired a fellow named Chief Thomas to interpret for him. The man spoke practically no English, but he did have a reasonable command of the pidgin French that Métis employees had introduced to trade posts in these parts in the previous century. "We did all our talking in French and got along pretty well," Jenness told Barbeau of the experience; "but it would have been amusing to a person who knew real French to watch us jabbering and gesticulating in two horrible jargons."[42]

West coast cultural influences were less evident in this quarter than in Wet'suwet'en territory, he reported to Sapir; "There never were any big houses," referring to the spacious dwellings used by extended families, "and the crests, which are the same as at Hagwilget, belong to the clan and not to any house in the clan." Moreover the potlatch, adopted here in the last century, has long since fallen "out of date." On the other hand, religious beliefs and folklore impressed him as "more Athapascan" than coastal in flavour, particularly young men's ritual pursuit of the animal spirit guardians that provide them with medicine powers associated with the hunt and, on rare occasions, with the knowledge of divination and healing ascribed to shamans alone. The phenomenon of spirit possession, and its associated curing practices were apparently all but unknown. Finding "very little to gather in the way of sociology," he focused his attentions elsewhere, recording several dozen legends as a complement to the substantial Bulkley River collection, purchased a smattering of artifacts, about fifty in total, and with "a lot of palaver & peaceful persuasion," took anthropometric measurements from seventy-three people, all but eight "pure Carrier, as far as is known."[43] This last was an altogether different experience than the one he had had among the Wet'suwet'en, both women and men proving reluctant to suffer the indignity of the procedure's poking and prodding. Even offering to pay fifty cents per person, a decent price considering the daily three dollar wage for a consultant, resulted in few takers, just twenty-one adults agreeing to be measured, nine of whom were hospital patients in Hazelton under Dr Wrinch's care. John Grant, the physician hired to undertake anthropometric surveys for the division beginning in 1927, subsequently analyzed and published these and additional data obtained from the Carrier and from twenty-five Sekanis at Fort McLeod. "As a people they are much more tractable than the Carriers," Jenness observed of what was to be his final go-round with the ever-ticklish business; "With the latter I had to use considerable diplomacy to get them measured & with the Sekani it is much easier."[44]

Taking up anthropometry in British Columbia actually occurred as an after-thought, the division's official instructions for this and his previous Sarcee fieldwork having bypassed it entirely in favour of concentrating on ethnological and linguistic investigation. The respite from calipers and tapes must have been especially welcome at a time when the sting of the Stefansson brouhaha was still quite noticeable. However, some effusive praise for the recently released report on physical characteristics of the Copper Inuit revived his flagging interest sufficiently to warrant sending to Ottawa for a set of instruments. The supportive words came from Louis Sullivan, an anatomist and physical anthropologist who "pulled me over the coals" when the *American Anthropologist* published Jenness's contrarian assessment of Stefansson's cherished "Blond Eskimo" claim, in 1921. Reading the more comprehensive version in the Arctic Expedition series changed his mind, its sound analysis, and reasoned conclusions prompting Sullivan to urge fresh, comparative studies among other Aboriginal populations. "Do you mind if I take some measurements among the Hazelton people?" Jenness queried Barbeau, ever mindful of his friend's prior claim to everything Gitksan; "I may, provided you have no objections to my poaching on your field."[45]

The Bay's freighter wasn't able to depart the Prince George docks until mid-May. The delay provided time to pick up supplies, above all mosquito netting, indispensable for camping out in the boreal springtime in a modicum of comfort and sanity. By previous arrangement, he was also on hand to meet the westbound train carrying an "overseas friend," Frederick Salter, now a lecturer in English literature at the University of Alberta. The two had met during the war's final months, both serving as lowly artillery spotters with the same 58th field battery. As fully enamoured of wilderness adventure as his former comrade-in-arms, the New Brunswick–born Salter jumped at Jenness's invitation to share the experience, even more at doing so as field assistant-cum-camp cook. In return for boiling the coffee and frying the bacon, the Geological Survey paid him a weekly wage of twenty-one dollars.[46]

Once under way, travel along their river route was painfully slow, the honourable company's scow needing three days to reach Summit Lake from Prince George, another three to make its first port-of-call, Fort McLeod, on the swollen Parsnip. Disembarking here, Jenness and Salter arranged for a motor launch to pick them up in about three weeks to ferry them the last ninety miles to Fort Grahame. From there, the companions would be on their own, a canoe being placed at their disposal to complete what would be the expedition's penultimate, and most memorable, stage: a month-long excursion down the Peace to the railhead at

Dunvegan, Alberta, a distance of several hundred miles. An unequivocal comment on the state of hinterland travel in those years, Jenness explained to a sceptical Sapir that their chosen route was actually the cheapest and quickest way home from this quarter and, barring mishap, would find him back in good time for the Toronto conference.[47]

NO REFUGE

Alexander Mackenzie opened the contact era in British Columbia's transmontane interior when his 1793 navigation of the upper Peace River brought him upon a people he called Rocky Mountain Indians. That was just one of a handful of names early white adventurers used for the Sekani, a group then divided into four regional bands whose hunting ranges comprised an expanse stretching north-westward from the Rockies to the watershed of the Liard. A dozen years after McKenzie's landmark expedition, the North West Company opened Fort McLeod, on the Parsnip, home turf of the southernmost of the bands: Tsekani (Tsek'ehne), "people of the rocks." Their name, in anglicized form, later came to be applied to the entire tribe through the writings of Daniel Harmon, a company man stationed in Carrier territory for a decade, beginning in 1809.[48] By some estimates, Sekani population may have been as high as two to three thousand at that time but, as happened with terrible regularity across Aboriginal America, disease, conflict, and social disruption eventually exacted an unimaginable toll of human life. A 1923 Department of Indian Affairs census enumerated just sixty women, men, and children resident at Fort McLeod, one hundred more upriver at Fort Grahame.[49] Neither place was then a reserve, official designation coming in later years. A full century was to pass before the Fort McLeod Sekani – the Tesk'ehne First Nation – finally gained long-promised status under an adhesion to Treaty Eight, the only one of the so-called numbered treaties of the post-confederation period to include lands in British Columbia.

Given the strong cultural and linguistic similarities between Sekani and Beaver, Athapaskan specialists assume – as did Harmon before them – that, like Beaver and Sarcee, the two were once affiliated, perhaps forming a single tribe. Just when Sekani established themselves in this part of British Columbia is uncertain. A common view holds that what began as a seasonal occupation for hunting large game became permanent sometime in the early to mid-1700s when Cree, supplied with firearms by fur traders in the east, started penetrating the region lying between the southern shores of Lake Athabaska and the Peace River country. The ensuing turmoil led some of the area's original inhabitants to ally with the newcomers and to adopt elements of their Algonkian culture. Others retreated westward to the slopes of the Rockies or, in the case of those since identified as Sekani, to the north-central highlands beyond.[50] Two of their founding bands – Sasuchan and Tseloni – staked out territories above Findlay Forks, a region whose western limits abutted lands of the Babine and Gitksan and, in the far north, of Kaska and Tahltan. Subsequent contacts resulted in exchanges of goods and marriage partners, and in transmission of new ideas and practices, many emanating from the distant Pacific coast. In the case of Tsekani and Yutuwichan, bands situated below the forks, cross-border exchanges flowed in two directions: one linking them genealogically and culturally with Carriers, the other, particularly for the Tsekani, with the Beaver, an attachment sufficiently strong to leave Jenness at sea over how to distinguish one people from the other, except perhaps on arbitrary grounds. In a letter written soon after arriving at Fort McLeod, he frankly admitted that what information was already to hand "leaves me hopelessly confused about the Beavers. I have the names of at least 4 distinct tribes [bands] in the area around Dunvegan & Fort St. John. One I know is Cree, the others I cannot make head or tail of." A stop at one of their communities, Hudson Hope, en route back to Ottawa, did little to clarify the situation. There, he observed, the people "who are usually classed as Beavers, might be included with almost equal justice among the Sekani."[51]

Despite its geographic remoteness, Sekani country offered scant refuge, the rugged valleys and mountainous terrain incapable of shielding its inhabitants from history's flow and thereby preserving them in a pristine state, as the anthropologist's imagination had induced him to hope might be the case. Instead, evidence to the contrary – especially evidence of a steadily expanding white presence – was everywhere, creating the impression in Jenness's mind that, aside from still drawing their livelihood from the land, the people around Fort McLeod "had gone to pieces" as a tribe. Signs of this were most conspicuous in the outer dimensions of everyday life, the same sorts of things that had earlier convinced J. Alden Mason and Pliny Goddard that little of ethnographic value remained for study among the Athapaskan groups they had visited before the First World War. For instance, Sekani families, professing Catholics all, now lived in riverside settlements year round, largely in response to relentless pressures on land and game sparked by the 1861 Omineca gold rush and its aftermath. As well, a preference for passing the long winters in European-style wood cabins was slowly but surely pushing customary bark and hide lodges and tents into obsolescence. Imported clothing, utensils, and other items of everyday use were so ubiquitous on the Parsnip that Jenness felt certain there would be "absolutely nothing in the way of specimens" to purchase. "Most of

Sekani women and children in front of a house, Fort Grahame, British Columbia. Canadian Museum of Civilization, Diamond Jenness, 1924, 60707

the women don't even know how to make a crude birch-bark basket. The same is true of the Fort Grahame Sikani [sic], I believe," a forecast largely borne out during his abbreviated stay upriver at the end of June. Nevertheless, interviews with elders yielded information on the production and use of indigenous manufactures, as well as a sampling of illustrative pieces, some one hundred items altogether, which he acquired for the museum.[52] More importantly, they also brought to light a rich vein of ethnographic material about a people whose traditional social and religious lives were more "typically Mackenzie or N[orthern] Athabascan" in character than were those he had documented elsewhere over the preceding months.

Subsequent reports of his findings, along with two letters dispatched to Ottawa – both written at Fort McLeod, the first and newsier of them posted by a trapper heading down river to Prince George – are all silent as to the particulars of the individuals he interviewed and the conditions under which they worked. Judging from the published result of his investigations, however, two things appear certain. First, he found reliable interpreters to assist with the job of recording what eventually amounted to nearly a hundred typescript pages of personal accounts and oral traditions, in itself a notable accomplishment for a period of fieldwork lasting only a month. Second, and more noteworthy still, the detail of this material stands as testament to the well-honed skills and patience Jenness brought to the task and, in the opinion of a later-day researcher, to his reception as a "trusted and sympathetic friend" among those who imparted their stories.[53] By the end of the first week at Fort McLeod, he had worked with four elders, "not one of whom," he complained, "is much good for language." Even so, they were good enough to guide him toward verification of two tones, similar to those in Wets'uwet'en speech, and to allow compilation of a small word list for comparison with sample vocabularies collected elsewhere.[54] Clearly at ease with the novelty of a white man who lived in a tent and was eager to learn from them, his consultants showed themselves to be more garrulous and open than had their counterparts on the Bulkley. Jenness was treated to a taste of this early on when he broached the seemingly innocuous matter of the nature and scope of connections between local Sekani and Carriers in the vicinity of Stuart Lake. While one in three adults in the settlement claimed full or partial ancestry from that quarter, he was astonished to discover that nearly all were passionately contemptuous of their Carrier kin, deriding them as "ugly and greasy fish-eaters" for wrongly encroaching on Tsekani and Yutuwichan lands in the past.[55]

Relations with their near-neighbours were conducive to more than marriages, feuds, and fomenting a pervasive sense of victimization. They also provided fertile ground for experimenting with new customs, customs introduced by Carriers who, in turn, had adopted them from Gitksan, Babine, and Wet'suwet'en sources. Autonomous, egalitarian bands constituted the original foundation of Sekani social life, much as they did among all northern Athapaskans, both west and east of the Rockies. Each embodied a few bilaterally extended families – Jenness described their present constitution as "somewhat amorphous but with a distinct tendency towards the patrilinear" – whose material support derived from the resources of a shared territory and whose leadership, albeit informal, was entrusted to respected members.[56] A process akin to the one that had so markedly transformed society on the Bulkley generations beforehand had begun to unfold in the vicinity of Fort McLeod in the early 1800s. As a way to solidify ties with Carrier trading partners, local families reorganized themselves into matrilineal clans corresponding in name and number to the five clans already in place at Stuart Lake and vested authority over them in chiefs. This new polity was short-lived, however, being allowed to lapse, in Jenness's opinion, because the attempt at social engineering afforded no particular advantage "under the new conditions of life" – that is, the region's rapidly expanding fur trade. Rather, it "merely provoked the scorn of Europeans." To the south, their neighbours also lost much of the clan system, presumably to the same causes, though a few of its vestiges, as

In Twilight and in Dawn

Jenness discovered among the Carrier west of Prince George, survived the turbulent second half of the nineteenth century. In sharp contrast, the effects of the experiment at Fort McLeod were probably never more than ephemeral, virtually every trace disintegrating so thoroughly as to erase any but the faintest inkling of them from living memory.[57]

◆

"I fancy the Fort Grahame Indians hardly differ from the Sekani here," he wrote in late June. "If that is the case I shall probably spend little more than a week or 10 days with them."[58] Feeling increasingly pressed for time, the companions barely lasted a week before pulling up stakes and paddling off on their highly anticipated voyage down the Peace. Along with excitement, their pending leave-taking was tinged with a measure of ambivalence, not least because the situation Jenness came upon upriver turned out to be different, and more engrossing, than initially anticipated. The population, since the 1890s a mix of Sasuchan and Tseloni Sekani – peoples of the "black bear" and "end of the rocks," respectively – was caught up in a revival of sorts, "deliberately dissolving their old social structure and developing a new one with matrilinear descent and phratric [i.e. clan] exogamy." As had happened to the south, an earlier generation of Sasuchan had been through this once before. Yet unlike the state of things at Fort McLeod, vivid memories of key events linking past and present had continued to be preserved in local oral tradition, beginning with the intensification of Sasuchan-Gitksan contacts after Fort Connolly was built on Bear Lake, adjacent to the upper Skeena, around 1825. Plagued by stormy relations for decades, a potlatch staged to foster peace between them took place at mid-century. According to the elders Jenness interviewed, the feast spurred their forebears to adopt clan organization, "each man assigning himself to the phratry of a friend or relative among the Gitksan and Carriers [Babines]." Amity, unlike clans, proved harder to instil, lingering troubles finally inducing the Hudson's Bay Company to relocate its post to safer confines on the Finlay, where Fort Grahame now stands. Cut off from their usual trade outlet, all but a few of the Sasuchan followed suit. Contacts among the three peoples declined in consequence, dissipating Sekani interest in clan affiliations in the process. The trend was quickly reversed in 1919 when the absence of the requisite "phratric organization" prevented a visitor from Lake Babine from hosting a potlatch in the settlement. Reminiscent of the way popular interest was stirred up by the Prophet Dance when it reached Sekani country in the 1830s, the incident sparked a determined effort to remake themselves yet again. The community not only reinstituted clans with chiefs at their heads but even flirted with incipient social rank as individuals acquired titles through sponsorship of feasts.[59]

The rise and fall and rise again of clans was not the only consequence of contacts with their western neighbours. There was also the formation of a new band out of the remnant of those who had chosen not to withdraw eastward after Fort Connolly closed – mainly Sasuchan married into Gitksan families. Known to their Finley River compatriots as T'lotona, they established themselves to the north of Bear Lake in a steppe-like habitat – the so-called Groundhog country, hence the band's English name, Long Grass Sekani – only recently abandoned by a Tahltan clan decimated by illness.[60] Oddly enough, it was a tip from a Hazelton police interpreter, Constance Cox, the previous fall that allowed Jenness to learn of their existence from an elderly Gitksan widow who was living nearby. Initially informed that the woman, Luskayok, had been sold to the Tahltan as a very young child, he made arrangements to meet her in hopes of eliciting a few details useful for revising and editing James Teit's unfinished report on the peoples of that district. Her personal story turned out to be other than first advertised, though ultimately, no less informative. Through Mrs Cox, the elder revealed that she had spent the better part of her seventy-some years with the T'lotona Sekani, thirty of them as wife of a chief whose lineage included kin from Kispiox, her own natal village. Her life in the north had come to pass in the wake of a quarrel that erupted near Bear Lake around 1865, leaving several dead on each side, including a Sekani man killed by her maternal uncle. Without a son to offer in compensation, Luskayok's family proffered their daughter instead. Barely in her teens at the time, she would not see home again until 1907, following her husband's death.[61]

Having worked with her over a span of two weeks in January, Jenness deemed the results of Luskayok's interviews mildly disappointing. An exceedingly taciturn nature made her "not much of an informant," the elder offering little more than spotty recollections of the band's contacts with their Tahltan and Kaska neighbours. Even so, "I got a few notes from her which will help in editing Teit's MSS," he told Sapir. "Poor old Teit did very fine work, and it would be nice for the division to show its recognition by bringing out his last work as soon as possible." Sapir agreed. Another in a long list of worthy projects to fall through the cracks, this one eventually came to fruition when June Helm MacNeish, then at the start of her Athapaskanist career, resurrected the material from museum files and prepared it for publication in the mid-fifties.[62]

Decades after spawning their T'lotona offshoot, the Sasuchan settled down at Fort Grahame, joined there by the Tseloni Sekani. The ensuing merger between the two gave rise to another social experiment, this one suggestive of Louis Riel's Métis nationalist philosophy. It took the form of a break-away faction called Otzane, a band whose members, about forty adults and children in 1924, were managing to preserve a migratory existence in what was once traditional Tseloni territory, beyond the headwaters of the Finlay. Old Davie, their founder and leader, was the son of a Sasuchan mother and French-Canadian father, and husband of a Tseloni woman, the last providing the foundation for the group's claim to their home grounds. On first glance, Otzane autonomy appeared to be about resisting the many discontents and perils of settlement life. However, their composition revealed an additional factor in play: Davie's efforts to cultivate "a new band of breeds" by selecting men of diverse parentage as husbands for his four daughters and permitting other mixed-blood families to join them. Sometimes trading on the Finlay, other times on the Liard, by sheer good fortune the band visited Fort Grahame during Jenness's too-brief stopover. Far from a rag-tag crew, their number were well dressed and, more tellingly, looked both hale and hearty. And at their head stood Davie, by now nearing seventy, but still "wield[ing] the authority of a Hebrew patriarch," protecting them from frivolous distractions by ordering that camp be struck on the shore opposite the village.[63]

While successful to date, the future of Otzane independence was far from certain. Equally uncertain was the future of Fort Grahame's re-adoption of clan organization. Seen against the backdrop of recent Cordilleran history, and especially the rapidity with which far-reaching changes were unfolding, Jenness figured the odds against both were long. With the influx of whites in pursuit of their own brand of independence unlikely to abate any time soon, moreover, those odds were certain to grow even longer.

Their homeward journey from Sekani country turned out to be even more thrilling than Jenness and Frederick Salter had bargained for, or so Jenness recalled many years later in an interview. Trouble struck while they were still at Fort Grahame: the canoe and local guide they had been promised were nowhere to be found. Short on options but still game, they commandeered a long-neglected punt to carry them through the mountains and into the western Alberta plains. In the early going, powerful currents and log jams on the river, still swollen by spring run-off, made for a harrowing ride. Harrowing quickly turned to hazardous when they reached the Finlay's junction with the Peace, a turbulent stretch whose cataracts, if attempted, might well have brought their adventure, or the adventurers themselves, to an untimely end. By a stroke of good fortune, rescue came in the person of a local teenaged boy who chanced upon them as they contemplated their next move from the safety of dry land. Leaving the pair to pick their way along the bank, he confidently navigated the boat through the rapids and landed it, no worse for wear, in a calm stretch below. Apparently as laconic as he was skilled, or simply fearless, the youngster greeted their arrival with an understated "There's your boat!"[64] Having already had thrills enough to last a lifetime, the companions could hardly feel upset by the smooth sailing they met over the remainder of their route to the railway station at Dunvegan.

In Twilight and in Dawn

CHAPTER TEN

Ancestors and Cradles, 1926

A GOOD STUNT

After nearly a decade of stagnation, the Anthropological Division's financial picture finally began to brighten in the mid-twenties, though barely enough to support more than one or two researchers in the field at a time. With a longish stay in the northwest now behind him, Jenness's next shot at fieldwork was at least a year off, possibly more. Meantime, he already had his sights set in two directions, one old, one new. First, he planned to return to British Columbia, this time to the territories of the southern Carriers and their Chilcotin neighbours. Then it was to be down the Mackenzie to restart the work J. Alden Mason had initiated among Chipewyan and other Dene groups south of Great Slave Lake in the summer of 1913.[1] Given all this, certainly the last place he imagined going, at least in the foreseeable future, was a place he had once professed to have no desire to see again: the Arctic. However, when the next chance to strike out from Ottawa was finally at hand nearly two years after his return from the cordillera, that's precisely where he headed: to Alaska's Bering Sea coast, in search of answers to the question of Inuit origins.

A new era in arctic anthropology dawned in the fall of 1921 when the Fifth Thule Expedition arrived in Canada's far north to begin wide-ranging investigations into the region's natural and human landscapes.[2] Greenland-born explorer Knud Rasmussen headed the party of fourteen men and women, Danes and Polar Inuit (Inughuit). Over the course of three years they compiled a massive body of information, later reported in ten official volumes and scores of papers, and collected some 20,000 artifacts and specimens. Rasmussen gathered a substantial portion of this material during a remarkable sled journey that began at the outer reaches of Hudson Bay and ended, eighteen months and thousands of miles later, at Siberia's East Cape. On attaining the Alaskan coast, he fired off a telegram to Copenhagen with the following message: "Have established indisputable connection Eskimos Greenland to the Pacific and intermediate points. Greenland tongue readily understood from Magnetic North Pole to Bering Strait."[3] As newsworthy and inspiring as his accomplishment was, it was the lesser-known but ground-breaking contributions of the explorer's colleagues, Kaj Birket-Smith and Therkel Mathiassen, that figured most prominently in Jenness's turn toward the intriguing problems of arctic culture history.

As the luckless Henri Beuchat had done before them, Birket-Smith and Mathiassen had joined the expedition in hopes of testing a mentor's theories, in their case those of geographer Hans Pedr Steensby of the University of Copenhagen. Like those of Beuchat's collaborator Marcel Mauss, Steensby's theories rested on the premise that natural environment influenced various dimensions of everyday Inuit existence. It was not social morphology that interested him, however: in a take on German historical ethnology, his aim was to lay bare the origins and subsequent development of their "economic culture" – in essence, the material bases of the singular Eskimoan way of life. To do this, he began with the proposition, à la Boas, that economic culture was the cumulative product of both localized innovations and traits borrowed from other peoples. By mapping the spatial distribution of specific traits linked to the occupation of both inland and coastal zones, he deduced that inland features, notably caribou hunting and dwelling in skin tents, were more widespread and hence represented an older cultural stage than did coastal ones, with their emphasis on ice hunting and snow houses. This led him to the conclusion – one that would endure, albeit wrongly, for years to come – that the "Pre-Eskimo" primal stock was "more 'Indian' than 'Eskimo,'" probably originating in interior ranges "between the Barren Grounds and the northern part of the [Canadian] prairie." Over time, he argued, some of their number had migrated to the arctic littoral, perhaps lured northward by great herds of caribou and musk oxen on the open tundra, or driven seaward by the hostility of neighbours. In any case, "The essential impulse to the development of Eskimo culture ... [came once they] ... accustomed themselves to stay at or on the sea ice in winter and hunt seals." Their summer existence, as before, remained oriented to the land. From a postulated home ground between Coronation Gulf and Melville Peninsula, Steensby's so-called "Palæeskimos" spread outward, some reaching

Greenland, others the Bering Sea. The westward drift, in turn, spawned a second "Neoeskimo" stage as new "foreign influences" were absorbed, most likely, the theory held, from Japanese and Pacific Indian sources. The result was an amalgam, combining elements of the ancient land adaptation with a new maritime focus based on open-sea hunting for whales and other sea mammals. Like their forebears, these Neoeskimos also dispersed, an eastward stream retracing "the old Palæeskimo paths of distribution" where they "improve[d] and enrich[ed] the older cultural form wherever it was met."[4]

Only Birket-Smith came away from the field reasonably certain of having found evidence supporting his professor's theory, evidence embodied in the people he dubbed Caribou Eskimos. In the expedition's early days, Inuit in northern Baffin Island told Rasmussen of a "remarkable tribe who spoke the same tongue as themselves, but who lived their lives in quite another fashion ... in the interior of the country [where] they had no connection with the sea or the hunting of aquatic animals." Seeing these people for himself during an extended stay in the low-lying tundra south of Baker Lake convinced Birket-Smith that theirs was indeed "the most primitive Eskimo culture known, perhaps a survival of a Proto-Eskimo culture from the time when the transition to coastal life had not yet taken place." Theory and fact failed to accord in one crucial respect, however: the unimportance (or complete absence, in some cases) of open-sea hunting among neighbouring groups such as the Igloolik, Netsilik, and Copper Inuit, all of whom dwelled along central arctic coasts for part of each year. Nowadays, this is attributed to their occupation of regions whose adjacent marine environments are ill-suited as habitats for whales and other migratory sea mammals, while no such limitations occur from the Mackenzie delta westward, or east of Baffin Island, precincts where this type of hunting flourished. Birket-Smith, however, proposed a way around the problem by grafting a fourth and final "Eschato-Eskimo" phase onto Steensby's original scheme, attributing the otherwise glaring inconsistency to "a fresh advance of comparatively recent date ... from the interior [that] largely obliterated the Neo-Eskimo character of the coast culture."[5]

While his co-worker was busy on the Barren Grounds, Mathiassen searched for traces of the long-ago past in the ruins of seaside settlements. The most extensive (and celebrated) of his several excavations took place at Naujan, near modern-day Repulse Bay, where he unearthed remnants of a pre-contact culture "differing sharply from the culture of the recent tribes" of the central Arctic.[6] The evidence suggested that it had been a place where people once hunted whales and walrus, and lived in substantial sod and whalebone winter houses, year after year. Its location on ancient raised beaches situated far above the present shoreline implied considerable antiquity, dating back perhaps a thousand years before the present. Certain implements from the site bore sharp resemblance to artifacts recovered in Greenland's remote northwestern Thule district during one of Rasmussen's earlier expeditions. Accordingly, Mathiassen christened his ancient Naujan sea hunters Thule Eskimos.[7]

Thule culture certainly had the look and feel of Steensby's Neo-Eskimos. Its source, moreover, appeared to be a western one, probably the Alaskan and Siberian coasts north of Bering Strait, "the regions to which we have time after time had to turn in order to find parallels to types from the Central Eskimo finds."[8] Where mentor and student parted company, and where Mathiassen and Birket-Smith were also at odds, was with respect to an underlying issue – what of the so-called Palæeskimo? Excavations at ten different sites, Mathiassen reported, turned up no trace of them. In fact, "everywhere we find at the bottom of the refuse heaps and in the earliest ruins a typical Thule culture, bearing ... a stronger stamp of marine hunting the deeper we go." Not yet prepared to reject the Barren Grounds people as "a remnant of the Primordial Eskimos," an alternative theory demanded consideration. By reversing the inland-coastal sequence, an idea originally proposed by another Danish scholar, ethnologist Gudmund Hatt, some years before, Mathiassen argued that Caribou Inuit culture might well be "residual," not "primitive," their inland adaptation resulting from coast-dwellers being "enticed into the country ... by the great herds of caribou." Should this ultimately prove to be so, he reasoned, then Thule represented the first occupation of the central Arctic. Moreover, the sought-after "cradle of the Eskimo culture" itself had to lie somewhere in the west, not in the continent's subarctic heartland as Steensby originally proposed.[9]

Encouraged by snippets of news in the Ottawa press about the Danes' progress, Jenness decided the time was right for the Anthropological Division to revive its involvement in Canada's Arctic. Committed as he then was to Athapaskan work, he devised a stopgap measure to augment the museum's archaeological collections by enlisting the aid of government personnel already stationed in the north. His idea was simple: offer volunteers a crash course in field archaeology, providing training sufficient for them to undertake systematic digs on their own. Such a scheme, he believed, would yield twin benefits: helping to preserve the scientific value of whatever material was unearthed and discouraging Inuit from unwittingly destroying sites in their desire to sell their pot-hunting discoveries. His plan found favour among the upper echelons of RCMP bureaucracy and was quick to bear fruit, the first shipment of specimens – from police posts on Baffin and Ellesmere islands – reaching the division's offices in 1923. "It was a good stunt of mine to memorialize the [police]," a delighted Jenness wrote Edward Sapir from Wet'suwet'en country. "If we boost them a little – perhaps with a note in the newspaper – we might get them to do more digging in Ponds [sic] Inlet and Chesterfield," areas Mathiassen's investigations pinpointed as likely to hold ruins dating back half a millennium or more. Besides, "I'm sure [Harlan] Smith would rather have the police dig them out than go himself!!!"[10]

The "stunt" soon paid an extraordinary dividend: awaiting Jenness's return from British Columbia midway through 1924 were packing crates forwarded from the eastern Arctic courtesy of L.T. Burwash, an official with the interior department's newly organized Northwest Territories Branch. Inside were about 2,000 artifacts from two localities that were separated by fewer than a hundred miles as the crow flies. The smaller collection, the yield of casual rummaging in long-abandoned encampments on Coats Island, at the mouth of Hudson Bay, arrived without any documentation, Burwash having simply purchased it from the island's resident shopkeeper. The other lot, from Baffin Island's Cape Dorset, was a different story. In keeping with the division's instructions, he had obtained it by more or less systematic investigation, supervising a crew of diggers and recording details of site elevations and features, ground disturbance, and so forth. However, the novice archaeologist breached a cardinal rule of practice by neglecting to keep separate those items retrieved from different layers, and different locations, within the site itself. Jenness summarized the problem this way: "They jumbled everything together into bags, not caring whether they mingled modern harpoon heads of their own manufacture or the discarded weapons of a forgotten past." In the circumstances, making sense of the artifacts, mainly domestic and hunting implements, meant classifying them solely on the basis of how they looked and how they were made.[11]

Once laid out in the lab, the best part of the material turned out to be a hodgepodge of items of modern and Thule derivation, the latter identified through comparisons with artifact types described in a preliminary account of Thule Expedition findings issued in 1924.[12] As for the remainder of the artifacts, objects for which there were no evident counterparts, Jenness had little to go on beyond the occasional published description of arctic specimens with indeterminate cultural provenience. The museum's own holdings included four such pieces, bone harpoon heads with an accompanying note tracing them to the northernmost extremity of Hudson Bay. "Isolated, these harpoon heads remained a mystery;" a statement no longer true once they were set among

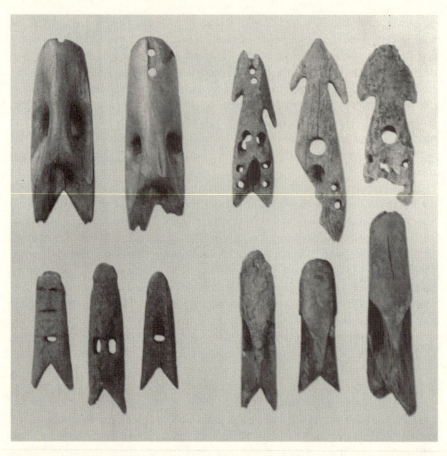

Harpoon heads from Cape Dorset, Baffin Island, Nunavut. Canadian Museum of Civilization, Diamond Jenness, 1925, 62245

the several hundred Cape Dorset articles that fit neither the Thule, nor historic Inuit, mould.[13]

Unmistakable similarities in design features and styles of manufacture set the anomalous objects apart from the rest of Burwash's collection. Compared to the rounded or semi-cylindrical shape of shaft sockets on Thule harpoon heads, for instance, these had "peculiar sockets," narrow and rectilinear in form. Equally distinctive were unusually small, triangular-shaped chipped – not polished, as were Mathiassen's Thule specimens – stone projectile points, the business end of lances and other hunting weapons. Most were fashioned with concave bases, a trait not found in artifacts from better-known cultural horizons. Yet another oddity was the complete absence of drilled holes, a conspicuous departure from other Eskimoan tool kits, including the Thule, in which

In Twilight and in Dawn

bow-drills figured prominently in manufacture. Instead, lashing holes had been gouged out, certain indication of what Jenness took to be a simpler and, he imagined, older technology. As telling as these dissimilarities were, he attached even more significance to marked differences in patination, discolouration of bone and ivory implements caused by organic decomposition and by prolonged exposure to the elements. The collection's unidentified objects were typically darker than the others, suggesting greater age. Burwash's note that many of the artifacts came from a raised beach situated twenty to thirty feet above sea level corroborated this opinion. With all that came a potential complication: a significant portion of the artifacts had been recovered from house ruins similar in size and construction to those at Naujan. Elsewhere, Jenness observed, dwellings of this type "seem to have yielded objects of the Thule culture only." While conceding that only a fragment of the picture was now revealed, the Cape Dorset finds did seem to imply that "Mathiassen's Thule tribes, wandering to the south of Baffin Island, [must have] found another people [already] in possession of the coast." These Dorset Eskimos, as Jenness named them, belonged to a cultural horizon ostensibly older, and more primitive, than Thule, "but certainly not the culture of the first Eskimos who settled on the coast and gained their livelihood by hunting sea mammals," Steensby's hypothesized Palæeskimo. "Of that earliest culture," he wrote, "we have yet to find the remains."[14]

This wasn't Jenness's first foray into the little-explored terrain of arctic culture history. That had come in "The Copper Eskimo and Their Early Home," a paper read at the 1922 meeting of the American Anthropological Association. In a fuller (and differently titled) version published a year later, he advanced two central arguments germane to the question of origins. First, that the Coronation Gulf–Victoria Island region had formerly been home to a population whose material culture contained elements indicative of western roots, elements still in evidence in the Mackenzie Delta and Alaska but absent among the Copper Inuit. Remains of this previous occupation were scattered across the landscape. On Victoria Island and the mainland opposite, for instance, he had come across the ruins of sod and driftwood winter houses, and Northern Party members had found a long-abandoned village of some thirty dwellings, partly constructed of whale bone, on Banks Island's southwestern shore. Equally intriguing were the western-style harpoon heads and other implements recovered from these sites, bits of plain earthenware pottery, middens containing whale bones, and above all, the virtual absence, as in the west, of copper artifacts.[15] Though Mathiassen had yet to christen this ancestral culture, these were undoubtedly traces of his Thule maritime hunters.

The question was not whether Copper Inuit country had been set-tled by migrants from the Mackenzie, or beyond, at some point in the long-ago past: it clearly had been. Rather, the problem was determin-ing what had happened to that earlier population. Had poor whaling in the waters of Coronation Gulf, and in Dolphin and Union Strait, induced them to abandon the region, leaving it open to a wave of new-comers utilizing a different economic strategy? Or, as Mathiassen later wondered, had they "slowly altered their mode of life and [become] the ancestors of the Copper Eskimos of the present day"? If the latter, as subsequent research eventually confirmed, such a process would have entailed a switch in subsistence activities from hunting on the open sea to ice hunting through breathing holes, adoption of the snow house, and loss of key elements of technology, notably sea-going umiaks – large, open skin boats – and kayaks. In Jenness's judgment, available evidence pointed to the greater likelihood of the first scenario, its al-ternative implying that the culture of the bands around the Gulf would have retained a more discernible measure of "western character" than appeared to be the case.[16] What, then, of these newcomers? Their cul-ture, his second argument advanced, found its "nearest affiliations ... not with the Eskimos of the west but with those of the east and south-east." This assertion rested on more than similarities of material cul-ture, such as the conspicuous absence of the specialized gear associated with full-blown marine hunting. There were striking parallels of "lan-guage, traditions, and customs" as well, "all point[ing] to the Copper Eskimos," and with them, to the Netsilik, as "being merely a subgroup of the Eskimos of Hudson Bay." Finally, their general mode of exist-ence – Steensby's economic culture – appeared to be more akin to an inland-adapted way of life than a maritime one, "the sea useful to them only when it is frozen solid like the land." Anticipating Birket-Smith's conception of an Eschato-Eskimo stage by several years, Jenness con-cluded that ancestors of the Copper Inuit, and of the neighbouring Net-silik, "migrated to the coast from inland only a few centuries before the appearance of the Copper Eskimos in Coronation Gulf." Elsewhere, he suggested that the interior Dubawnt and Yathkyed Lakes region, west of Rankin Inlet, was their probable starting point. This migration had been part of "a general movement from inland about seven or eight cen-turies ago, both to the northern coast line and to the western shores of Hudson Bay," and was doubtless driven by the northward expansion of subarctic Athapaskans into the Barren Grounds. These same Dene, Jenness believed, were also the probable source of Inuit knowledge of copper for making weapons and other items of everyday use. As for the specifics of the inlanders' Eskimoan (or Indian?) lineage, however, he offered no opinion, though by implication they must have been des-cended from stock with deep roots in this part of Canada.[17]

Of the two problems before him – the relationship of Thule to modern-day Inuit and to prehistoric Dorset – it was Dorset's status that commanded the greater share of Jenness's time and energy through the twenties, and his continuing interest for a good many years to come. This wasn't because he deemed the idea of a comparatively late movement of inland peoples to the arctic coast to be beyond dispute. In fact, just months before his initial interpretation of Copper Inuit origins appeared, he wrote to Birket-Smith in hopes of learning if the latter's researches among the Caribou Inuit had turned up any solid evidence that "will support or militate against my theory."[18] Rather, working out the details of the Dorset-Thule connection promised to lead down a trail that would ultimately reach back in time to the mainspring of "the Eskimos and their peculiar civilization." Achieving a "permanent solution" to this long-debated problem, he observed in 1923, "can hardly be satisfactorily attempted until more excavation has been done among the ancient ruins of Canada and Alaska."[19]

Needless to say, Dorset's proposed status as separate from, and possibly older than, Thule, sparked a great deal of interest in Copenhagen. The claim instantly fostered a sense of common purpose as well, Jenness and his Danish counterparts agreeing to cooperate in tracing the entire family tree back to its oldest root. A flurry of letters exchanged ideas as well as data gleaned from past and ongoing research, broadening the picture of what was already known and speculating about what remained to be discovered. Although his groundbreaking *Archaeology of the Central Eskimos* (1927) was still several years from publication, Mathiassen had already analyzed a large portion of the geographically diverse Thule Expedition material, material which (unwittingly, it seems) threw new light on the mysterious Dorset, its spatial distribution, and perhaps even its parentage. Excepting the Naujan site, nearly all the other localities excavated in 1922–23 yielded samples of the unusual implement types Jenness had assigned to the new culture, and a site on Bylot Island, near Pond Inlet, contained "nearly pure C. Dorset Culture." Similar artifacts, notably harpoon heads with distinctive socket design and small stone projectile points with concave bases, had shown up farther afield, too, the latter on the Atlantic coast of Labrador, the former in Greenland's Cape York district, on King William Island in Netsilik country, and in a collection Rasmussen had obtained during his stopover at East Cape, Siberia. New material shipped to Ottawa from arctic police posts added yet more pinpoints to the expanding Dorset map, Jenness finding tell-tale evidence from southeastern Ellesmere Island, Baffin Island, and the east coast of Hudson Bay. Whatever it was they were dealing with, Mathiassen wrote, could "hardly be regarded as a total Hudson Bay phenomenon." His more cautious Canadian collaborator was dubious about pushing the boundaries as far west as the

Siberian shore, explaining that he had seen nothing similar among the tens of thousands of western Arctic specimens at his own museum and at several others in the United States. Even so, he was quick to add, "I would not dogmatize," and especially not before any systematic digging had been done in the region.[20]

Unlike his new Canadian colleague, Mathiassen was not shy about staking out a firm position on Dorset's status. While allowing that the apparent absence of bow drills might well indicate a more primitive, and hence older, culture, there was always the chance that the tool had been abandoned in certain localities, perhaps owing to the lack of suitable raw materials for fashioning drill bits.[21] The reliability of patination as a marker of age was even less certain. His reasoning here was straightforward: discolouration and other signs of decay tend to be most evident in artifacts resting at or near the surface, where they are most susceptible to the weathering effects of freezing and thawing. Those embedded in sub-surface layers, on the other hand, "are often very new looking, on account of the better chances for preservation" in the permafrost. To his mind, the only solid piece of evidence bearing on the critical question of age came from Burwash's Cape Dorset sites, their recorded elevations corresponding nicely with the time horizon proposed for Thule. "Judging from my own material," Mathiassen concluded in the scant two pages ultimately devoted to the subject in his seminal 1927 report, "I am inclined to regard the C. Dorset culture as a peculiar, very locally stamped phase of the Thule." Even if that were the case, came Jenness's public rejoinder, "it must be a particularly ancient variation," a plausible theory given the broad sweep of territory to the north and south of Hudson Bay, no less to the east and west, through which these distinctive artifacts had diffused. With greater age came one other possibility, proposed by Mathiassen: "that [Dorset] sprang from an earlier Eskimo source still unknown," one he imagined had "failed to survive in conflict with the more advanced cultures of Thule and post-Thule times."[22] Discoveries in the decades to come eventually showed this last to be the case, the weight of evidence pointing to the Dorset as direct descendants of Paleo-Eskimo pioneers, bearers of a Siberian-derived culture, the Arctic Small Tool Tradition, whose eastward spread had brought them into Canada's far-northern hinterlands upwards of three thousand years before the Thule – a well-armed, war-like, seafaring people – were to make their fateful debut.

Aside from exchanging information and airing pet theories, the three men used the mails to sound one another out on a joint expedition to

Alaska, all agreeing that this region, a virtual terra incognita in archaeological terms, probably held the key to unravelling the puzzle of Eskimoan ancestry. Jenness broached the idea first, prepared to postpone scheduled Athapaskan research in favour of a collaborative project to take place as early as 1926. The proposal, though appealing, came to naught, his potential partners lacking time and money to invest in such a venture much before decade's end, if then. All the same, Birket-Smith, Mathiassen, and Rasmussen were thinking along similar, if loftier, lines, discussing a more ambitious undertaking, one to rival Boas's Jesup Expedition. Their idea involved teams of Danish and Canadian researchers working on both shores of the Bering Sea, "with diggings in Alaska, near East Cape, and Kamchatka" and possibly "in the Tlingit Archipelago and the interior of British Columbia."[23] This grand scheme never came to fruition either, frustrated, at least in part, by growing concerns over encroaching on scientific turf to which institutions in the United States were beginning to lay claim. Nor was Jenness successful in recruiting either man to take up new Canadian fieldwork under National Museum auspices, even with the lure of permanent employment afterward. Instead, he settled for a solo expedition to Bering Strait in 1926, the Anthropological Division's first arctic fieldwork since the First World War, and its last for nearly a decade to come.

If finding Dorset in the jumble of Burwash's collection was a stroke of remarkable luck, convincing his bosses in the Department of Mines hierarchy to authorize research in Alaska rates as a minor miracle.[24] As had frequently been the case since the wartime emergency, financial constraints loomed large. Following Jenness's return from Coronation Gulf, just one other division member had set foot anywhere in Inuit territory, and then quite unintentionally, by dint of poor planning. That had happened in 1921–22 when Frederick Waugh went to Labrador's Voisey's Bay region in hopes of wintering with a band of elusive Naskapi hunters. Unable to make any but fleeting contacts with them, he had retreated to the nearby coastal village of Nain, where he busied himself with ethnographic inquiries among local Inuit.[25] By the day's standards, Waugh's expedition carried a heavy price tag, costing in excess of $2,500, which, however, paid for eighteen months in a remote area and for the full-time services of a field assistant. Jenness, on the other hand, was now proposing an expenditure of nearly $5,000 to allow him and William Wintemberg to devote four months to archaeological investigations on both sides of the Bering Strait, an outlay equalling two-thirds of the division's entire research budget for the year. Subsequent negotiations with management resulted in the request being scaled back by half, museum director William Collins agreeing to send only Jenness and allotting $3,200 for the purpose.[26]

Beyond perennial troubles with wresting funding from government coffers, division staff had to contend with policies limiting research and collecting to Canadian (or in the case of Newfoundland and Labrador, British) soil. Defensible for a publically supported national museum, application of this policy, usually strictly enforced, was nonetheless an irritant to anthropologists investigating peoples and problems whose geographic dimensions occasionally failed to square with the Dominion's otherwise ample borders. Sapir spoke to the issue as early as 1911, citing examples of groups such as the Inuit and Mohawks whose homelands spanned international boundaries, or the Wyandot, a branch of whom had migrated from Quebec to Oklahoma in the nineteenth century. In cases such as these, he argued, scientific "'trespassing' is logically necessary" in order to carry out the formal mandate for which the division held responsibility.[27] With a supportive director in Reginald Brock, Sapir had had some leeway in the matter, sending Waugh to New York to study Iroquoian material culture and Barbeau to Oklahoma for work with the descendants of Wyandot émigrés. With Brock's resignation and the onset of war in Europe, however, that latitude was reigned in. Given these circumstances, it was probably the Bering Strait project's extraordinary potential, rather than any special pleas on Jenness's part, that led to the policy's waiver. After all, here was an opportunity for the country's premier scientific institution to bask in the limelight of a high-profile pursuit: searching for remains of some of the continent's earliest inhabitants. With Washington's Smithsonian Institution poised to launch its own Alaskan expedition with an identical objective, moreover, the timing could scarcely be more opportune. "There must surely be something lurking under the soil" up there, Jenness kidded Sapir, just weeks before heading out west; "traces of your Sinitic-Athabascans, perhaps."[28]

Hardly an equal to the Danes' grand collaboration, the coming expedition was ambitious nonetheless. Actually, it might better be described as overly optimistic, or just plain unrealistic, since Jenness was no novice when it came to the countless difficulties met in travelling and working in northern latitudes. Allocating one month for getting to and from the field and three for digging on the Strait's Alaskan and Siberian shores was challenge enough. Into the bargain, he also intended to do linguistic work, adding to files of comparative data on western Eskimoan dialects. Impractical perhaps, yet the plan was understandable since the chances of a similar opportunity appearing anytime soon were slim to none. "I wish you could come with me and divide the work," he wrote to Mathiassen; "It will probably be my last trip to Eskimo territory for many years," newly acquired duties as division chief now claiming priority on his to-do list.[29] "If I could divide myself into two persons," he confessed some years later, "one of them would give his whole time to Eskimo archaeology and ethnology. As it is, I have been forced ... to devote all my efforts to ... our Indians tribes [while] my archaeological collections from the Bering Sea and from ... Barrow and Barter Island remain untouched."[30]

Disappointment at Mathiassen's inability to join him was tempered by news that the Smithsonian was sending Aleš Hrdlička to the Bering Sea coast that very summer. Along with gathering intelligence for a full-blown archaeological expedition to the region set for the following year, Hrdlička's aim was to search for skeletal and related evidence substantiating the theory that the hemisphere's indigenous populations were ultimately of north Asian origin. Hrdlička was a proponent of this and a companion theory that envisioned their ancestors having reached the New World by way of Bering Strait 10,000 or more years ago.[31] Situated a mere fifty miles across the strait from Siberia's East Cape – the shortest distance between the continents – the area encompassing Cape Prince of Wales and the Diomede Islands, some twenty miles offshore, made a natural starting point for hunting down hard evidence of long-ago migrations. "I trust you will save everything in this latter line," he urged Jenness, referring to any human bones that might turn up in the course of the Canadian's own investigations on this same stretch of coastline; "for such remains more than anything else may be hoped to shed true light on the past."[32]

Assuming that he and Hrdlička would be aboard the same passenger steamer from Seattle to Nome, Jenness suggested putting idle shipboard time to good purpose by working out an informal, cooperative arrangement of benefit to their respective institutions and projects. "We might visit Cape Prince of Wales and the Diomede Islands together and pool resources," he proposed for starters. Should time and weather allow, moreover, there were long-abandoned village sites at nearby Nome that could be examined more profitably if they were to divide the work between them. As luck would have it, a last minute itinerary change routed Hrdlička through Juneau instead of Nome, all but eliminating the chance to coordinate efforts in advance. Their paths eventually crossed in late July, if only briefly, when they travelled together from the mainland to Little Diomede. There they spent a single day scouring the heights behind the village for skeletal remains before Hrdlička took leave of the island to continue his tour of the shoreline as far north as Barrow. Otherwise, what little cooperation there was between them came once they reached home again in early autumn, the two exchanging ideas about the long road ahead. "I am naturally thinking a great deal about next year and perhaps the years after," Hrdlička wrote, "and will be very grateful if you will have confidence enough in me to keep me in touch with your plans with a view to a possible closer cooperation."[33]

STEPPING-STONES ACROSS TIME

Embarking on the first leg of his transcontinental journey in late May, Jenness rode the rails for a full week to reach Seattle. From there he met the steamship *Victoria* for passage to Nome. A comfortable ten-day voyage, the experience was surely a far cry from the misery he and his expedition-mates had endured as the *Karluk* plied the same route thirteen years before. What hadn't changed was the Bering Sea's notorious summer gales and fogs, conditions that soon wreaked havoc with his carefully drawn plans. Things started off smoothly enough, the schooner *Silver Wave* conveying him around Seward Peninsula's outer shores from Nome and on 20 June depositing him at the village of Wales. Thereafter, however, problems ensued, beginning with rough seas that kept him for a fortnight longer than intended at Wales, and then for nearly as long on Little Diomede. Where nature left off, Soviet red tape took over. Before leaving Ottawa, he had received permission to work in Siberian territory: on Ostrov Ratmanova – Big Diomede Island – just two miles across the international boundary (and dateline) from its smaller American sister, and on the Chukotka Peninsula at Uelen, near Mys Dezhneva – East Cape. In return, Russian officials expected that any recovered artifacts would remain in the country and that a copy of his field report would be forwarded to the commissariat of education in Moscow. Reasonable enough. However, when the American government vessel that eventually rescued him from storm-bound Wales called ashore, on board were the official papers needed to enter Siberia. It was only at that point that Jenness learned that he was required to report to authorities in the city of Petropavlorsk, 1,000 miles south of East Cape, before proceeding with his research. Coming at a time when Soviet-Canadian relations were strained over what was arguably the most misguided of Vilhjalmur Stefansson's many arctic schemes – the infamous Wrangel Island affair of 1921–24, the explorer's brazen attempt to claim Canadian sovereignty over the remote island in the Chukchi Sea – he knew better than to take Moscow's onerous (and entirely unexpected) condition as a personal affront.[34] Besides, having already lost so many days to the elements, he was now hard pressed simply to attend to business on the American side. Siberia would simply have to wait.

Situated on Cape Prince of Wales, at the westernmost edge of the Seward Peninsula, the two Iñupiat hamlets that make up the village of Wales afford access to one of the best marine hunting grounds in the north, several species of sea mammals, including walrus and the behemoth bowhead whale, frequenting the adjacent waters of Bering Strait. This accounts for the village's history of comparatively dense settlement, its nineteenth-century population of about 500 making it one of Aboriginal Alaska's largest. Nevertheless, its people had not escaped the disease and social upheaval that were the lot of native communities up and down the coast after decades of contact with European and American whalers, traders, missionaries, and sourdoughs. When the Southern Party called here briefly on their homeward voyage in 1916, Wales was by no means desolate – it had a Congregationalist church, and a school operated under the authority of the United States Bureau of Education. The government had introduced reindeer herding two decades earlier as a strategy to bolster an age-old hunting economy disrupted by the intrusion of foreign technology, institutions, and ideas. In the winter of 1917–18, however, disaster struck, with Spanish influenza – the pandemic that killed millions worldwide in the aftermath of the First World War – claiming a third of its 600 residents.[35]

The first person Jenness encountered on landing at Wales was Clark Garber, an Ohioan doing double duty as schoolteacher and jack-of-all trades for the Department of Interior. Doubtless glad of the unexpected company of a visitor from afar, Garber and his wife arranged for room and board, the former in the school house, the latter "beans and rice as a steady diet," or so Jenness later claimed. Garber also helped with the project at hand, recruiting "an old man and half a dozen boy scouts" to assist with the digging. As was their summertime custom, practically all of the village's adult men were elsewhere, some tending reindeer herds on outlying ranges, others finding jobs at the distant Tin City mine.[36] Together with his squad of schoolboy helpers, Jenness dug three sites, one within the confines of Wales, the others close by. Most of their energies were devoted to a low mound situated immediately behind the village. It contained numerous features, of which they excavated eight: five dwellings and three kitchens. Unearthing the ruins was tedious and time-consuming, shovels striking permafrost just six inches below the tundra's soggy surface while the floors of the structures they sought to expose were, on average, three feet down. Having learned the hard way on Barter Island what comes of using bonfires to speed the warming of frozen ground, there was no better option than letting the soil defrost on its own, a process yielding some two inches of thawing per day in the cool, damp summer air. Being delayed at Wales by stormy seas thus turned out to be a small blessing, buying the crew sufficient time to excavate a dozen wood and whalebone structures at the three sites, and with them some 1,800 archaeological specimens.[37] In slack moments,

Jenness donned his linguist's hat, recording a thousand words of local speech to supplement the data he had collected on Seattle's waterfront two years before.[38]

Given the possibility of finding himself stranded indefinitely on Cape Prince of Wales, the long-overdue arrival of the United States Coast Guard vessel *Bear* on 25 July came as a welcome relief. Even so, a certain irony attended the occasion, its impatient passenger anxious to embark for a place – Little Diomede, a two square mile rock in the middle of storm-plagued Bering Strait – where his chances of being marooned by disagreeable weather, perhaps for the coming winter, were higher still. The ship's accommodating Captain Cochrane offered to ferry him across and collect him again in twelve days' time. The outbound trip went smoothly. Not so the return. Twice Cochrane was forced to turn away, a pounding surf making it too dangerous to approach Little Diomede's lone landing place, a narrow, rock-strewn beach directly below the village. "The Arctic breeds fatalism rather than gloom," Jenness would later write, clearly putting a positive spin on what was obviously a trying personal situation. "I felt no special anxiety as the days flowed peacefully by," a claim all but ignoring the intestinal indisposition he had been suffering for some days past, "the result, doubtless of my diet, for the survival rate from my cooking has always been low."[39]

Rescue came at last on 18 August when a small motor launch manoeuvred ashore despite the heavy sea, fog, and wind that had twice forced Cochrane away. By remarkable coincidence, his rescuers were brothers Alf and Robert Porsild, Danish-Canadian biologists on a fact-finding mission for Ottawa to investigate the potentials, and pitfalls, of introducing Alaska-style reindeer herding among Inuit in the Mackenzie Delta. After a two-day respite, the party, now including the self-poisoned anthropologist, shoved off again. With Robert Porsild at the helm, the launch rocked and rolled its way to the mainland through conditions every bit as treacherous as they had been for weeks past. Wobbly of knees and stomach, a grateful Jenness disembarked at Teller where the services of "a foolish doctor ... did me no good." Nine days later he was in Nome and by 20 September – several weeks ahead of schedule – back home in Ottawa where his health was restored after a stint in hospital where, recalling Victoria Island, the official diagnosis was intolerance for "unusual diet." Updating Alf Porsild on the outcome of his troubles, he explained, tongue in cheek, that "if I stick to ordinary civilized food with plenty of vegetables and fresh fruit, I should live to 150 years or less."[40]

"I am delighted to learn from one of the newspapers of your safe return," Hrdlička wrote from Washington in early autumn, having himself been a passenger aboard the *Bear* on both occasions when it tried,

In Twilight and in Dawn

but failed, to reach Little Diomede. "We made all efforts ... to get you off the island and once you must have seen us, but the weather was so stormy that we could not land." "We had a wild trip from the Diomedes to Teller," began the reply; "we expected several times that the boat would break in two." How different this experience had been from the picture he would later draw of the seeming ease with which native Alaskans and Siberians regularly traversed the fifty-mile wide Bering Strait. "Each summer a party of Siberian Eskimo, or of Chukchee, choosing a favourable north wind, puts out to sea in a small skin boat, and in one day crosses to the Diomedes. There it camps and in one day more crosses to Wales."[41]

Leaving Little Diomede as Jenness was arriving, Charles Menedelook, the island's government teacher, was every bit as hospitable as Garber had been at Wales, offering him use of the schoolhouse for lodgings and suggesting who best to hire for the work ahead. The resident missionaries, a Norwegian couple, were an altogether different story. New to the place themselves, they seemed almost oblivious to their surroundings, virtually ignoring the hubbub stirred up when the ship appeared and acting in a "strangely aloof and uncommunicative" manner when the visitor from Canada paid them a courtesy call later that day. What little conversation ensued didn't even make mention of their religious affiliation, leaving Jenness to speculate that they may have been Pentecostals, latecomers to the soul-saving business in coastal Alaska. Local gossip added nothing to their story beyond the fact that neither husband nor wife spoke even rudimentary Iñupiaq. Reflecting on their meeting a long while after the fact, Jenness admitted feeling a certain admiration for them, choosing as they had "this desolate and lonely island for their mission."[42]

Even blessed with good health, fine weather, and a leisurely schedule, an archaeologist might well have found Ingalik, as Little Diomede was known in Iñupiaq, a tough nut to crack. Essentially a steep-sided, flat-topped crag rising 1,300 feet above the sea, habitable space is at a premium. Indeed, were it not for the abundant sea mammals in the surrounding waters, the island might never have become anything more than a temporary stopping place for wayfarers crossing between the continents. Naturally enough, topography accounts for its limited population size, perhaps no more than 160 during the era of Russian exploration in the 1700s, only 80 according to an 1880 American census, and 94 at the time of Jenness's visit. To deal with their cramped surroundings, the Ingaliqmuit had little choice but to build stone houses directly atop the remains of derelict dwellings from earlier periods. Complicating the picture, "enormous rocks ... are continuously sliding down the mountainside conceal[ing] all traces of the more ancient ruins" and, one read-

"Main St.," Little Diomede Island, Bering Strait, Alaska. Canadian Museum of Civilization, Diamond Jenness, 1926, 67782

ily imagines, crushing a hapless resident from time to time. Into the bargain, residents were in the habit of picking through the ubiquitous midden heaps in search of fossilized ivory to sell, a counter-productive activity since repeated disturbance compromised the deposits' archaeological value.[43] On the bright side, dealing with permafrost – here only four inches below the surface – was practically child's play.

Ingaliqmuit, like their compatriots at Wales, generally left their homes in summer for economic opportunities elsewhere, mainly in the bustling commercial port of Nome, where they were renowned as carvers of ivory. Adult men who stayed behind were thus glad of the chance to land a few weeks of paid employment in the archaeologist's crew, even if it meant tackling a job better suited to explosives and hydraulic machinery than mere elbow grease. With so many obstacles to contend with, not least the omnipresent wind and fog and cool temperatures, only three of the five dwelling sites Jenness examined were eventually excavated, each containing a house nearest the surface and a second directly underneath. Whether or not there were yet older houses farther down was difficult to ascertain, a definitive reading requiring a large-scale quarrying operation to get beyond the accumulation of boulders at lower levels. Despite the overburden of stone, many of the bone and ivory artifacts they recovered were badly decomposed, some to the point of turning to dust when handled, the result of water trick-

In Twilight and in Dawn

ling down through the rock over time. Objects found in middens, on the other hand, were usually in a fine state of preservation because the permafrost made all but the uppermost few inches of the heaps virtually impermeable to seepage. An attempt to dig one midden was a partial success, the slow rate of thawing preventing excavators from getting any deeper than three feet, only the last six inches of which were undisturbed by fossickers. Still, the effort was hardly futile, the exposed pit turning out to be "prolific in specimens of all kinds."[44]

Their labours on Ingalik were interspersed with two brief outings to neighbouring Big Diomede, looming through the fog to the east. The narrows they traversed by umiak spanned what would soon become one of the twentieth century's most pivotal geo-political divides, their starting point lying in what had been American territory since its purchase from Russia – satirized at the time as Seward's Folly – in 1867, their destination, Ostrov Ratmanova in Russian, the most easterly outpost of the newly emerging Soviet Union. According to a 1926 census, the larger of the pair of Diomedes was home to a mere twenty-seven Iñupiaq, all living in the village of Imaqliq, on the island's western shore. A second settlement, Kunga, is thought to have been abandoned in the previous century. Life here, as was the case for indigenous peoples of the adjacent continent, was as yet little affected by state policies governing the so-called small peoples of the north.[45]

With the Soviet navy patrolling the surrounding waters in the gunboat *Krasnyy Oktyabr*, perhaps wary of "another invasion by aggressive imperialists" along the lines of Stefansson's absurd provocation on Wrangel Island, a clandestine visit to Big Diomede was scarcely a risk-free proposition. Still, Jenness reckoned the odds of sparking an international incident – and winding up in a dank Siberian cell – were slight, what little risk existed well-worth taking when weighed against the benefits to be derived from scouting out the island's archaeological potential.[46] By way of precaution, their reconnaissance was limited to an uninhabited strip of rugged shoreline, well away from Imaqliq. While just as mountainous as its eastern companion, at four times its size, its settlement pattern was less crowded, thus eliminating people's need to stack houses one atop the next. Rock falls obstructed access to several old sites in the area, and scavengers, searching for bits of ivory, had so disturbed a number of trash piles as to render them all but worthless for archaeological purposes. Even so, Jenness and company dug two houses and a midden in just forty-eight hours, an accomplishment possible largely owing to the relative ease of excavating here despite the chance of being hauled up on charges of espionage. Working conditions were so much better, in fact, that another crossing had been in the offing until several days of contrary winds scuppered the plan.[47]

Among the objectives of that unrealized third outing was examination of a pair of stone dwellings perched one hundred feet above sea level on Big Diomede's eastward-facing slope. These structures had the look of ramparts, built "at this inconvenient level," Jenness theorized, to defend against marauders coming from the American mainland shore. This was just one of many pieces of physical evidence corroborating traditional lore about intermittent conflict in both pre- and early post-contact times. Equally indicative were remnants of body armour – breastplates fashioned from strips of ivory or antler – that turned up in layer upon layer of occupation at Wales and on the Diomedes. Adding to this picture of a strife-ridden strait were the remains of a rock barrier constructed on the eastern side of Cape Mountain, the 2,000-foot slope towering above Wales village; its purpose was certainly defensive, "shield[ing] the warriors from the arrows of their enemies." Finally, discovery of an "extraordinary number of tools and utensils" in the ruins of two dwellings, again at Wales, gave material dimension to oral traditions about "forefathers, harassed by raids from Siberia, [having] abandoned Wales and fled to Barrow."[48]

Over the long centuries, recurrent outbreaks of belligerence were an inevitable byproduct of economic and social relations linking communities on both sides of Bering Strait. In the words of one on-the-spot European observer in the late 1700s, "where there is trade – there is plunder," maritime Chukchi raiders seeking valuable marten and other Alaskan furs for resale to Russian merchants on advantageous (if sometimes bloody) terms. A different take on the polarities behind these hostilities emerges from the pioneering ethnographic work of Edward William Nelson, an American weather observer stationed in nearby Norton Sound, from 1877–81. Citing local legends, he noted that from time to time Diomede islanders were allies, not victims, of Siberian raiders, joining them in attacks on mainland Iñupiat villages along the stretch of coastline from Kotzebue Sound to Port Clarence. And on at least one occasion, he suggested, the two Diomedes seem to have taken opposing sides in a short-lived struggle, dwellers on the smaller island allying with confederates from Cape Prince of Wales in what ultimately proved a losing cause.[49]

Apart from the obvious, Jenness was certain that the ramparts, armour, and oral traditions also illuminated, if only obliquely, the two-pronged problem in historical ethnology that had brought him to Alaska in the first place: determining on which side of Bering Strait Eskimoan culture originated and whether it had spread outward from its cradle via diffusion or with the movement of peoples from one continent to the next.[50] Clearly not incontrovertible proof that "any actual migrations of tribes from Asia to America" (or vice versa) had occurred at some indeterminate time in the past, what evidence he did recover nonetheless convinced him that "migrations [were] not only feasible, but highly probable." "If Bering strait ... [were] not a constant barrier to either warfare or trade," he concluded, "still less could it have been a barrier to the migrations of small bands from one continent to the other."[51] Firmer in his convictions than his Canadian colleague, Hrdlička described the entire region as a "veritable amphitheater of migration, of comings from the less hospitable Asia to America," and the Strait itself as a "sea-lake – scene of one of the main migrational episodes of mankind."[52] The theory that New World Indians descended from Asians who had travelled this same route was already widely held in scholarly circles. More controversial was the precise timeframe of their initial arrival, although nowadays few dispute the dating of this event to late Pleistocene times, somewhere between the final three to fifteen millennia of the great ice age that ended some 10,000 years ago. An even broader consensus now exists on a related issue: for the earliest migrants, the way across was not via the Bering Strait per se but over an intercontinental land bridge – Beringia, at times upwards of 1,000 miles wide – that opened whenever episodes of glacial advance caused a drop in sea levels sufficient to expose the Strait's shallow floor. Back in 1926, land bridges and the like were still matters for speculation, studies of the region's Pleistocene geology, climate, biology, and anthropology all still in their infancy.[53] As for identifying the individual strands of arctic history, and tracing each one back through time and space to its source, what little archaeological research had been done up to then had barely scratched the surface.

Once back in Ottawa, Jenness pronounced the field season at once interesting and discouraging, his findings "not as complete or far-reaching as I wanted." In part, it had been simple bad luck to meet so many delays and petty annoyances, with summertime conditions on the Bering Strait proving nearly as formidable as those in winter, the intractable (and season-less) Soviet bureaucracy equally so. On top of stormy weather and stormy politics, of course, were the health problems that eventually forced his early departure for home. But his real disappointment stemmed from having failed to unearth even the barest shred of hard evidence that would establish whether "Eskimo culture arose in Alaska or elsewhere."[54] That said, the expedition was certainly no write-off. His excavations yielded more than 3,000 artifacts, including 1,400 from the challenging Diomede ruins. The bulk of this material appeared to belong to two periods. Only the more recent could be dated with any certainty, probably to sometime after the mid-seventeenth century when the first Cossack venturers opened a trading post on the Anadyr River in Siberia's far east. This was indicated by the presence of small amounts of iron, glass, and the like, items of Russian origin that reached Iñupiat hands by way of intermediaries across the Strait.[55] Absent such tell-tale material at deeper levels, what lay below was obviously older, some probably by several centuries, although he could do no better than put this portion of the collection into rough chronological order. This was accomplished by analyzing stylistic changes in sealing harpoons, the one indigenous artifact type of the many recovered that "underwent changes of style at different periods." On this basis – a technique known in archaeology as seriation – he determined that the temporal sequences exposed at all three localities were essentially analogous. Equally important, most of the Bering Strait collection demonstrated direct parallels with the tools and implements Mathiassen identified as Thule culture in Canada; in fact, "the remains from the two regions are so remarkably homogeneous that they plainly represent a single culture."[56] Later researchers adopted the designation Western Thule to distinguish the culture's Alaskan branch from its slightly younger Canadian-Greenlandic offshoot.[57]

What turned out to be the summer's most noteworthy finds came to hand by happenstance. Spending an idle moment watching a meat cache being dug on Little Diomede, Jenness noticed an odd-looking ivory harpoon point lying at a depth of about eight feet. Importantly, the soil surrounding it showed no sign of disturbance. Virtually everything about the heavily discoloured object seemed unusual, at least by the standards of the Dorset, Thule, and contemporary Inuit and Iñupiat material culture with which he was familiar. To begin with, its overall design was more complex, its features including "three terminal barbs arranged symmetrically, one on each side of the base and one in the middle, an open socket with rectangular slots for the lashings, and two deep slots in the forward part to hold small blades of stone." More surprising was the decorative motif skilfully incised in the ivory: "a strange type of curvilinear art" was how he described it to Sapir, "half Melanesian and half [Northwest coast] Indian in its suggestions" and unquestionably "unlike any Eskimo art I had ever seen before." In the days following the discovery, he purchased several similarly engraved specimens from local villagers, souvenirs they had taken from other caches or perhaps the spoils of ivory hunting in middens. One additional piece, a fragment of harpoon shaft, was found lying exposed atop a trash heap, adjacent to the schoolhouse. Rounding out this small collection were several more specimens he later obtained at Teller, once again, all "peculiar types ... profusely decorated with etched circles and lines."[58]

In Twilight and in Dawn

In a repeat of his Dorset experience, Jenness soon learned that other examples of this "curiously engraved" material had come to light previously, though none by means of systematic excavation. In fact, when the two were together en route to Little Diomede, Hrdlička showed him one of a handful he had acquired on St Lawrence Island, south of the strait, during a stopover there in July. Another, an amulet from Nome that was "practically identical" to one in Jenness's small collection, had been reported in a 1916 paper by George B. Gordon, curator of the University of Pennsylvania Museum.[59] On learning of his Canadian colleague's findings, Mathiassen promptly arranged to send photographs of a few others, again from Bering Strait. However, the Dane also knew of yet more from an unanticipated quarter, near the mouth of Siberia's Kolyma River. Reputed to be "the westernmost known Eskimo specimens," they had been collected some years earlier by Norwegian explorer Harold Sverdrup; all were presently on loan to the National Museum in Copenhagen.[60]

Ordinarily so small a body of evidence, and particularly one for which precious few contextual details were available, would scarcely warrant drawing even the most tentative of conclusions. Yet these were no ordinary artifacts, the harpoon heads standing distinctly apart from known types in their design and manufacture, each characterized by "fine scroll work quite unlike the usual Eskimo carving, or indeed any carving known in America." "I found what I believe to be a new Eskimo culture," Jenness boldly told Sapir soon after returning from the field, a culture that appears to be "quite old, although I should hesitate to put its date beyond the Christian era, perhaps not nearly as old as that."[61] Less confident in print, he shied away from making any but the most general claims of age in summary statements that appeared over the next two years, asserting only that the people who produced these singular implements and surprisingly sophisticated artwork must have occupied Alaska's Bering Sea shoreline before the rise of Thule.[62] However, he did add two further observations, neither more than a surmise at the time, although they were eventually confirmed by other archaeologists. The first was that, its resemblance to northwest coast Indian styles notwithstanding, the source of the curvilinear art – and perhaps of the entire culture – lay somewhere in the Old World, most likely in northeastern Asia. Second and more importantly, he theorized that this culture's influence had not been confined to its "true [Alaskan] centre" along the seacoast but over time had diffused, or been carried northward, as far as Barrow. This, in turn, made it a likely precursor of later cultural developments. He christened the find the Bering Sea Culture. Henry Collins, the Smithsonian archaeologist who continued searching for its remains into the thirties, renamed it Old Bering Sea, recognizing the culture as the probable ancestral source for the maritime-adapted Neo-Eskimo tradition of which Thule was the latest and most widespread phase.[63] Professions of disappointment aside, for the second time in two years, Jenness had succeeded in identifying a new piece of the complex puzzle that was the story of Inuit ancestry.

◈

Ambivalence was nowhere in evidence when it came to work on Eskimoan language, fortuitous circumstances resulting in collection of fresh data to supplement the comparative vocabulary of western dialects begun under Beuchat's tutelage in 1913. The largest share of this new material doubled what was already a fairly sizeable Wales lexicon, local volunteers having contributed an additional 1,000 word stems to those Jenness had obtained previously on the docks of Seattle. However, three shorter word lists of several hundred items each were arguably the more valuable of the season's results, each in a dialect little known to the day's linguists and together sufficient, Jenness hoped, "to ... work out the principal phonetical rules" of the language, an Eskimoan Grimm's Law of sound shifts.[64]

On two occasions, first at Wales and then on Little Diomede, chance meetings with East Cape Eskimos resulted in opportunities to record some of the speech of that precinct. Jenness chose not to follow suit with the dialect of Diomede itself, judging it to be "intermediate between that of Wales and East cape." He also observed that forms spoken in northern Alaska – at Barrow and Point Hope, for instance – seem to "change but little," while the one at Wales contained "pronounced" differences that "take on some of the features of the East Cape dialect, which is hardly intelligible to the Barrow natives."[65] In hindsight, these observations proved to be perceptive, coming at a time when the process of mapping and classifying the various divisions and subdivisions of the Eskimo-Aleut language family had barely begun. The present-day product of that work demonstrates that certain of the speech forms he characterized as dialects of a single language – so-called "typical Eskimo" – in fact belonged to separate languages split off from a Proto-Eskimoan stock sometime in the first millennium AD. Accordingly, linguists now assign the speech of Wales and the Diomedes (and Barrow) on the one hand, and of East Cape on the other, to two different sub-branches of the family's Eskimoan branch: Inuit-Inupiaq and Yupik, respectively. Of these, the former comprises a single, widespread language whose cognate dialects and sub-dialects are heard in communities from Alaska's Bering Sea coast across the Arctic to Quebec-Labrador and eastern Greenland. Yupik, by contrast, consists of five languages, two found solely in Alaska south of the Strait, two more – Naukanski, the language of East Cape, and Sirenikski, now extinct – exclusively in Siberia, and the fifth, Central Siberian, in both. Regardless of the linguistic and social gulf this classification seems to imply, some specialists now consider the boundary separating Naukanski and Inupiaq to be less well defined than the one separating Inupiaq from any other Yupik language, including its geographically nearest neighbour, Central Alaskan Yu'pik. Against a historical backdrop marked by centuries of trade and travel and cultural borrowing across the Strait, much of it passing through the Diomedes, it comes as no surprise that lexical similarities between them are stronger than phonological ones. Jenness's characterization of the islands as intercontinental "stepping-stones" thus found its linguistic counterpart in his description of their shared speech form as standing midway between those spoken on the American and Asian shores.[66]

Another lucky encounter, this one with a "well-educated native" from the Norton Bay community of Inglestat (probably modern-day Inglutalik), in the northeastern corner of Norton Sound, served to broaden the emerging linguistic (and historical) picture. Jenness's brief collaboration with the fellow paid the anthropologist a double dividend: small (300–400 word) vocabularies from communities on either side of the Eskimoan linguistic divide, Malimuit and Nunivak. In the former, the speech of his consultant's natal village, Jenness detected a much stronger resemblance to the Barrow vernacular – both are now classified as subdivisions of North Alaskan Iñupiaq – than to any of the Seward Peninsula Inupiaq sub-dialects in places like Nome, Teller, Wales, or the Diomedes. Moving deeper into Norton Sound (and then southward, toward the Yukon Delta and beyond), the degree of linguistic difference becomes greater still. Here, the people of villages such as St Michael, speakers of the Unaliq (or Norton Sound) dialect of Central Alaskan Yu'pik, were able to "understand only with great difficulty" the speech of Inglestat's residents. This conspicuous anomaly led him to infer that "Arctic Eskimos" had intentionally resettled in this sub-arctic district sometime in the past, with Inglestat probably the "final outpost" of their southward spread. Recent research attests to this migration, the area's burgeoning trade inducing the so-called Malimiut emigrés to leave Kotzebue Sound, north of Seward Peninsula, in the early to mid-1800s.[67]

The second word list obtained at Inglestat was in the Nunivak Island dialect, one of four comprising Central Alaskan Yu'pik. His consultant claimed to have lived on this low-lying island, northwest of the Kuskokwim delta, for many years. "Whether he spoke [the dialect] ... with phonetic accuracy, however, is less certain, for there was no opportunity to check his speech against that of a native-born Nunivak Islander."[68] A few dozen words eventually found their way into his *Comparative Vocabulary of the Western Eskimo Dialects* (1928). Jenness's initial hesitancy over phonological considerations was well-founded, however, the sounds of Nunivak, like those of East Cape speech, striking him as "deviat[ing] considerably from the typical Eskimo like the Wales dialect," whose own sounds – as with those heard at Barrow, on the Mackenzie, and in Coronation Gulf – were more familiar to his ear. Some contemporary linguists attribute these differences to the conservative nature of the five Yupik languages: that is, to their general tendency to "preserve[ ] a lot of Proto-Eskimo features that have disappeared from most Inuit [i.e. Inuit-Inupiaq] dialects" over the centuries.[69] At the time, Jenness toyed with quite a different idea, one that viewed the "phonetic peculiarities" evident in Nunivak and East Cape as outgrowths of linguistic borrowing from non-Eskimoan sources. Allowing himself a modest opportunity to theorize in print on the problem, he suggested that all the groups bordering the Bering Sea once spoke "a single dialect, slightly varied in different places but from a larger standpoint forming a unit contrasted with the dialects to the north and east." These variations, he reasoned, "resulted partly from local developments, and partly from the influence of neighbouring Indian [Athapaskan] and Chukchee tribes."[70] Prevailing thought nowadays has all but ruled out foreign loans and is split on whether the five Yupik languages were ever largely undifferentiated.[71] These speculations aside, Jenness was on solid ground in concluding that the "dialects of the Siberian coast and of the Yukon and Kuskokwim deltas diverged more widely from those spoken north of Norton Sound [and indeed from one another] than [did] the latter from the dialects of far-distant Greenland and Labrador." His early identification of Norton Sound as the geographic "dividing point" between what are now generally regarded as the two branches of Eskimoan, together with his appreciation of the extent to which they differed from one another, stand as lasting contributions to the field of Eskimo-Aleut linguistics.[72]

Plainly aware that his findings on language had "important bearing on the early story of the Eskimos," Jenness was nonetheless reluctant to take a position on the problem in its fullest dimension. Instead, he maintained that more detailed studies of the Alaskan and Siberian dialects – and of archaeology and physical anthropology, for that matter – were needed before a definitive statement might be put forward. Even so, he ventured some tentative conclusions from the limited evidence already on hand, setting them out in a 1933 assessment of the state of research – somatic, linguistic, and ethnological – into the question of Eskimoan origins. Arguing from a "commonly agreed" assumption "that the greatest diversity of dialects usually (though not always) occurs in or near the region of a language's birth," the coastlines fronting the Bering Sea

In Twilight and in Dawn

clearly comprised "the original centre of dispersion of the language."[73] A second assertion focused on the historical relationship of the modern-day Iñupiaq dialects spoken north of Norton Sound and their close cognates east of the Alaskan boundary. The former, he observed, "appear to preserve a more Archaic tinge" than the latter, notably in their retention of certain "peculiar" phonological characteristics "that have been modified to the eastward." In brief, these details pointed to a language whose history was one of "more or less progressive change from north Alaska to Greenland, as though what was originally a single dialect had been carried eastward and undergone increasing modification with isolation and distance." "If such a movement did take place," he added, "it can hardly have been exceedingly ancient, for otherwise the ... modifications would have been greater than they actually are."[74] Cautious tone aside, this was plainly the language of Mathiassen's Thule Eskimos, which had spread eastward from Alaska, along with the maritime-adapted Neo-Eskimo way of life, beginning sometime around 1,000 AD and still spoken to the present day by their Inuit descendants in Canada and Greenland. Here, then, was evidence Jenness had hoped for but failed to recover from the ruins at Wales and the Diomedes, evidence that would help resolve the question of whether the cradle of Eskimo culture lay in the western or central Arctic.

CHAPTER ELEVEN

A Sisyphean Puzzle,
1927–1935

INSULAR THINKING

Therkel Mathiassen greeted Jenness with unexpected tidings on his return to Ottawa: a Danish organization promoting cooperation with foreign scientists was offering a rare opportunity for them to conduct fieldwork together in Alaska. "Personally I should like nothing better than
to join you in an archaeological expedition," began the reply. However,
a newly interested party needed to be taken into consideration before
planning could proceed. The party in question, the anthropological
wing of the National Research Council in Washington, had recently resolved to foster international collaboration in investigating prehistoric
migration from the Old World to the New. There was little question of
the need for coordination, Jenness conceded, possibly a committee or
conference mandated to "outline the problems to be undertaken and
perhaps apportion the work among several organizations." The idea
also made good political sense, particularly now that "the United States
seems to be waking up to the importance of [Alaskan] field-work." At
the very least, he counselled Mathiassen, "a foreign organization going
to Alaska should move cautiously, and work as far as possible in cooperation with the Smithsonian Institute and other U.S. organizations, to
avoid overlap and rivalry."[1]

The task of carrying forward the council's commitment was delegated
to American archaeologist Alfred V. Kidder, president of its Division
of Anthropology and Psychology. Kidder assumed that Aleš Hrdlička's
report to the upcoming gathering of the American Anthropological
Association would kindle wider interest in the historical development
of Aboriginal cultures in Alaska. Even so, reaching a "definite understanding as to methods, zones of work, financing, etc." would neces-

sitate a separate meeting later, one that would bring together the small circle of researchers involved in the field. In the meantime, Kidder was contacting specialists at foreign institutions to sound them out on the merits of collaboration, perhaps under the umbrella of what Franz Boas envisioned as an international committee on circumpolar problems. "What will come of this I do not ... know," Kidder admitted to Jenness. Still, he must have had a sense of where things were heading, particularly since Hrdlička, the catalyst behind these inquiries, favoured as low-key an approach as possible. "While by no means averse to the cooperation of others," Hrdlička told his associate in Ottawa, "I would rather see our own work, that is yours and ours, proceed independently ... unhampered and uncomplicated."[2]

Jenness was like-minded, preferring "a strictly limited and clearly defined" arrangement that would facilitate the exchange of information and avoid costly duplication of effort while respecting the priority of different institutions to conduct fieldwork in their respective arctic regions. This last proviso "cannot be construed too rigidly," he observed further, the broad geographic scope of the problems under study, coupled with the limited number of archaeologists available to investigate them, demanding a fair measure of flexibility. Nonetheless, "the rule should never be infringed without good reason," a step meant to "avoid international misunderstanding and ill-will," as well as the personal "jealousy and suspicion" that tend to arise when one partner "thinks that the other is getting most of the glory or an undue share of the specimens." In the circumstances, the wisest course to follow was one that respected the prerogative of each country's anthropological establishment to assume the role of gatekeeper in its own backyard. "Had I known of any U.S. organization which was undertaking similar work to my own in Alaska," he modestly confessed to Kidder, "I should not have felt justified in making the trip" in the first place.[3]

Public talk of cooperation aside, Jenness knew that his interest in returning to the Bering Sea might be undermined by awakening ambition south of the border. "My private impression," he wrote in candour to Kaj Birket-Smith, is that "the Americans are just beginning to realize the importance of archaeological work in Alaska now that their attention has been called to it by outsiders and they wish to have a finger or perhaps their whole hand in the pie." If the two flattering articles appearing in *The New York Times* that autumn are any indication, perception of the situation south of the border spoke to that very ambition, the first of the pieces unequivocally proclaiming "Hrdlička Says Early Asiatics Migrated Here."[4] For the record, Jenness, too, received notice in the *Times*, but only after an aggrieved, if hardly disinterested, Stefansson intervened with the editors on his behalf. Publication of the first piece "annoyed me very much," he informed Jenness, "Hrdlička ... making it appear that he had been doing a great deal in Alaska archaeologically, that it was real pioneer work, and that no one else had been doing anything at all." While better than nothing, what the paper printed under the headline "Eskimo Relics Lay Basis for History: Ottawa Museum Official Back from Alaska with Data on Ruins of Early Race," was all but lifeless, based in large part on a Victoria Memorial press release that epitomized lacklustre formality. It goes without saying that the media-savvy Stefansson had something else in mind, drafting copy whose opening line declared "What may be an epoch-making series of discoveries in the pre-history of America has been made ... by Diamond Jenness." Leaving nothing to chance, that same sentence went on to lay claim to the discoveries' veracity by noting that the man who made them had cut his teeth in polar research as "anthropologist of the Stefansson Arctic Expedition."[5]

Anxious to avoid misunderstanding, or a dust-up in the public press, Jenness thought it judicious to forego another Alaskan expedition unless the Smithsonian, or some other American institution, invited him there. In cautioning his Danish colleagues to do likewise, he was equally adamant that the door to Canada's far north remained open to them. "I should regret to see Danish or American scientists going into the Arctic and doing work which we should do ourselves." Given the scale of research problems still to be sorted out, and the scarcity of human and financial resources to devote to the purpose, however, "I should regret equally as much if outside scientists refrained from working in Canadian territory, because they are afraid of arousing jealousy or ill-will."[6]

Quite unexpectedly, an invitation from the United States crossed Jenness's desk just months later. It came from Kidder, offering him the chance to lead an expedition to Alaska during the coming summer. Encouraged by the previous season's results, officers of the Smithsonian and the National Geographic Society had struck a partnership to initiate long-term research into Bering Sea culture history, the Smithsonian assuming responsibility for scientific staff, the society for funding. But there was a hitch: finding a qualified specialist to head up the project. Naturally, an American was preferred. As Kidder openly acknowledged, however, "there is no man available here." In fact, there were then few such people anywhere. Banking on his employer's willingness to provide Jenness with leave, the American partners proposed covering his salary, travel, and field expenses for half a year, sufficient time to see the program through its initial stages. As an added incentive, his participation "would help to bring about ... the greatly ... desired cooperation between the various nations interested in Arctic work," cooperation that might pave the way to future collaboration.[7]

Kidder had his answer within days. Jenness agreed to "loan" his services for the project's initial phase, conditional on a single provision: that his role be limited to an instructional one, "train[ing] one of your own men in Eskimo problems and archaeological methods in the Arctic, so that he can continue the work in Alaska in future years unaided." The Smithsonian already had an apprentice in mind, Henry B. Collins, a junior staff archaeologist. On Hrdlička's advice, a site for the project's inaugural season had been selected, too: St Lawrence Island, well south of the Diomedes, in the Bering Sea. Norton Sound seemed a better place to start, Jenness thought, convinced that the mainland would pose fewer logistical problems than the outlying islands.[8] Having situated the linguistic divide between Yupik and Iñupiaq speech forms in the Sound, moreover, his instincts told him that the region was likely to yield important new evidence bearing on Eskimoan origins and development. Two decades later, American archaeologist J. Louis Giddings would prove him right; his discovery of remnants of a 4,000-year-old tool-making industry – the Denbigh Flint Complex, named for Cape Denbigh, east of Nome – is now generally regarded as the foundation of New World Eskimoan culture. Its source was the Siberian Arctic Small Tool Tradition, so called for its characteristic inventory of unusually small-sized, chipped-stone projectile points and other implements.[9]

As unforeseen as the invitation from Washington had been, word that the project had "gone on the rocks" was even more so. Just three weeks after offering him the job, an incredulous Kidder informed Jenness that a frivolous matter had brought planning to an impasse: the president of the National Geographic Society was insisting that the expedition operate under his organization's name alone and not, as the Smithsonian logically assumed, the names of both sponsors. Kidder's discrete inquiries revealed "certain underlying frictions" between the two, unspecified irritants apparently grave enough to foil a plan whose ostensibly more contentious details – finance, personnel, rights to disseminate results – had been settled quickly, and amicably. With the society's officers "quite immovable" on the issue, resisting his attempts to salvage the deal, an embarrassed Kidder was left to extend sincere apologies and a firm assurance that nothing in the proceedings had even hinted at the "possibility of our plans miscarrying."[10]

Jenness responded to the tidings with equal measures of regret and relief, regret at the loss of a rare opportunity, relief that previous work and family commitments hastily set aside for the sake of the coming expedition could now be resumed. In truth, he had been unsure about participating all along, and not just because of the still-uncertain state of his health following the trials of Little Diomede. Before learning that the plan had been scrubbed, he told Sapir that the offer "seemed impossible to turn down ... if only for the prestige of the Division." But the personal stresses and strains of trooping off to the field season after season were beginning to take their toll, a complaint made worse by the mountain of research material still awaiting attention and the added responsibilities associated with being division chief.[11] Little wonder he preferred making a previously arranged trip to Newfoundland, followed by a seaside holiday with Eilleen and children in Nova Scotia, to facing the unpredictability of another Bering Sea summer. Meanwhile, the Smithsonian salvaged what it could from the situation by mounting a scaled-back expedition, sending Henry Collins and physical anthropologist T. Dale Stewart to survey the southern coastline from Bristol Bay to the Yukon delta. For Collins, this was to be the first of many Alaskan field trips to come, his investigations eventually taking him as far north as Point Hope. His most important work, however, and surely the most satisfying for Jenness, who followed its progress closely, began in 1928 on St Lawrence and the nearby Punuk islands. "I found some unusually interesting conditions at [the village of] Gambel on the northwestern end of the island," Collins wrote of his 1930 field season, "five old sites ... which had been abandoned successively one after the other. The oldest of these," he continued, "turned out to be that much needed thing, a pure site of Old Bering Sea Culture," above it an occupation dubbed Punuk, and finally, recent material nearest the surface. The resultant chronology thus laid the framework for an Eskimoan cultural lineage linking the Siberian-derived Old Bering Sea with Thule, a sequence whose earliest stages have since been dated to the beginning of the Common Era and possibly earlier.[12]

The Anthropological Division's primary interest in Newfoundland was in unravelling the enigma of the Beothuks, by then extinct for a full century. At issue were familiar problems of origins and affinities, and, in particular, whether they comprised an outlier of the subarctic Algonkian stock that Boas's 1906 Canadian research agenda had identified as one of the continent's oldest, and "least affected types of northern marginal culture." With rare exception, scholars of the day regarded the Beothuk as a people effectively frozen in time, a people who, until their ultimate demise, were "the last true representatives" of a pre-Algonkian cultural tradition – familiarly called Red Paint culture, technically the Maritime Archaic – long since vanished elsewhere.[13] But for Jenness, it was a relatively minor matter touched on in James P. Howley's compendious 1915 monograph on Beothuk history and lore that framed a second line of inquiry in the region, one that quickly acquired a life of its own.

While assuming that Newfoundland had been Indian territory more or less exclusively in pre-contact times, Howley conceded a "strong suspicion" that some bone and ivory artifacts found near Port aux Choix, on the west coast, might actually be remnants of an Eskimoan occupation.[14] Jenness was interested in illustrations of these pieces in Howley's book, particularly a handful of sealing harpoons that resembled previously identified Dorset types. He didn't share Howley's view of their possible origin, at least not initially. Instead, he proposed a more complex scenario of diffusion resulting from Beothuk "contact with the old Eskimos of Hudson Bay." Whether this contact had occurred in Newfoundland or, as seemed more plausible at the time, in Labrador remained to be determined. In either case, he was certain that the implements themselves, while of Beothuk manufacture, traced back to a Dorset source.[15]

Apart from shedding new light on the geographic range of Dorset, the prospect of uncovering an ancient relationship between Eskimos and Beothuks raised the further possibility of Indian loans in Dorset culture, or, as subsequent theories would (mistakenly) contend, that Dorset itself ultimately derived from Indian roots buried somewhere in the continent's subarctic forests. Jenness had already toyed with the likelihood of some such connection, the idea initially surfacing as he mulled over the status of certain artifacts in the L.T. Burwash collection from Cape Dorset that lacked evident parallels in the Thule toolkit. Of special interest were triangular, chipped-stone projectile points with concave bases. Nearly all the samples he was aware of had come from eastern Hudson Bay, a region whose southern margins abutted Algonkian territory. Given the setting, he ventured in a letter to Mathiassen, "I strongly suspect Indian influence" in material from this quarter, "influence that extended probably all over Eastern Canada and dates back several centuries at least."[16] His opinion was received with interest in Copenhagen, particularly by Birket-Smith, who was similarly speculating about the origin of concave-edged stone scrapers recovered in Greenland, items again without apparent Thule analog. Repeating his position on the bigger question of Dorset's relationship to Thule, Mathiassen suggested that these scrapers represented a local variant of an otherwise widespread implement type. A contrary-minded Birket-Smith told Jenness that the pieces actually bore "a very strong resemblance to [pre-Algonkian?] New York forms, precisely as your Cape Dorset arrowheads with concave bases," and thus might well derive from an original archaic Indian source in the northeast. At least the Danes were able to agree on one score: corroborating evidence of an Indian-Eskimo link, if one ever existed, was likely to be found on the Quebec-Labrador and adjacent Ungava peninsulas, regions where the two peoples' territorial ranges intersected. Jenness's initial take on the pieces in Howley's illustrations convinced him that northern Newfoundland and the lower north shore of the Gulf of St Lawrence deserved equal attention.[17] Should time allow during the coming expedition, he resolved to begin searching for that evidence along the northernmost fringes of the island's Great Northern Peninsula, mere miles from Labrador, across the turbulent Strait of Belle Isle. Later seasons, he hoped, would see the geographic focus of investigations broadened in the direction of Hudson Strait.

Reaching St John's in early June, his first stop was the old port city's Geological Museum for a first-hand look at the Eskimo-like artifacts that had initially piqued his curiosity. Beyond these pieces, what he found on display was a veritable monument to the industry and dedication of native-born James Howley, the museum's erstwhile curator and putative founder of Newfoundland anthropology. Repeating a familiar Victorian-era story, Howley's fascination with the Beothuk stemmed from long service with the island dominion's Geological and Topographical Survey, of which he became director in 1898. From the late 1860s until 1909, nine years before his death, he made numerous treks through inland and coastal regions, exploring the landscape and mapping its natural resources. He also gathered sundry information about the Red Indians, so named because of their liberal use of red ochre in personal adornment, burials, and other customary practices. The product of this effort was substantial, his collections of Beothuk artifacts and skeletal remains supplementing an even greater wealth of historical documentation and oral evidence. Among the latter were folk traditions obtained from Micmac guides who frequently accompanied him on his travels, and from descendants of some of the colony's early European settlers.[18] With the trail through Beothuk country thus broken, Jenness elected to follow two of its better-known branches, first into the central interior, then seaward to the southern and western precincts of Notre Dame Bay.

Perhaps no more than a thousand strong at the dawn of the contact era, Beothuks were thinly spread over a territory that originally encompassed nearly all of insular Newfoundland. Rather than being the isolated remnant of archaic Red Paint culture, as was once believed, their way of life is now thought to trace to a late pre-contact culture called Little Passage, which flourished at the beginning of the second millennium BC. These people lived a semi-nomadic existence built on hunting caribou at interior rivers and lakes in fall and early winter and seals, fish, and birds at coastal habitats during the remainder of the year. By the mid- to late 1700s, the spread of European settlement around the coasts eventually choked off their access to salt water, all but confining them deep in the interior, primarily along the upper course of the Exploits River and in the vicinity of Red Indian Lake. Assailed by disease and conflict, their number steadily withered over the following decades, as they were increasingly hard pressed to eke out a living with fewer and fewer able-bodied hunters, insufficient game to sustain them year round, and virtually no reliable ties to white traders or other sources of supply short of pilferage.[19] Beothuk extinction is generally considered to have come in June 1829 with the death from tuberculosis of Shanawdithit, the last survivor of a party of three women captured by white settlers in Notre Dame Bay six years before.[20]

The forested inland quarter, the last vestige of Beothuk home ground, is where Jenness began his survey, although by then more than its former inhabitants had disappeared. The woodland caribou were also gone, Newfoundlanders having hunted the island's once-sizeable herds to the brink of extinction after the trans-island railway opened up the interior in 1898. On the eve of the First World War, University of Pennsylvania ethnologist Frank Speck had found abundant traces of previous native occupation in these areas, much of it in a fair state of preservation. Easiest to locate were the ruins of mamateeks, dwellings fashioned of poles and birch bark set in shallow pits, and of caribou fences, long lines of felled trees, still attached to their stumps, used by hunters to marshal migrating herds into lakes and rivers where they were dispatched more efficiently than on dry land.[21] A decade later, Jenness entered a transformed human and natural landscape, old encampments surrounding Red Indian Lake now inundated by a massive river diversion created to power pulp and paper production at Grand Falls, downstream on the Exploits. The year of his visit also saw the start of lead and zinc mining at Buchans, near the lake's northern shore. Hard on the heels of these developments came new settlements and an influx of new inhabitants who, in Jenness's words, "either know nothing of the people who preceded them, or speak of them as of a half-mythical race belonging to an age long past." Left largely to his own devices, his week's effort returned scanty results, just a handful of artifacts from three dwelling sites at Red Indian Lake and a fourth near Badger, west of Grand Falls, hastily dug with the assistance of local youngsters.[22] The work might have been more profitable had he followed Howley and Speck's lead in hiring Micmac guides, who, with roots in the region at least a century deep, knew the territory well, including the whereabouts of long-abandoned Beothuk settlements from which they occasionally scavenged useful items.[23]

Until their final retreat to the interior, the Beothuk had depended largely on marine resources, small bands spending the better part of each year in the sheltered coves and bays and islands dotting New-

Gleed Island with launch in foreground, Newfoundland. Canadian Museum of Civilization, Diamond Jenness, 1927, 69163

foundland's complex seaboard. The coastline fronting Notre Dame Bay was among the more heavily used areas, its waters rich in game, its hinterland, to the south, easily accessible via the Bay of Exploits and the river draining at its head. "[M]emory lingers a little more deeply" here than in the interior, Jenness observed, the bay's residents steeped in lore about the Red Indians who were still very much in evidence when the first English settlers arrived in the eighteenth century.[24] Many of their fishing villages occupied ground where Beothuk settlements once stood, the newcomers, like their predecessors, favouring places offering fresh water, serviceable beaches, and shelter from wind and weather. Householders were reminded of the now-vanished native world every time their kitchen gardens offered up a few stone tools along with a crop of potatoes, or whenever they happened upon old graves in the surrounding countryside. The practical consequence of this proximity was less beneficial to archaeology than Jenness·initially hoped, ransacked sites and discarded artifacts resulting in a good deal of information being lost to systematic investigation. So discouraging a situation convinced him that plain luck alone would govern the success of future archaeologists in unearthing new material.[25] (Reality has since proven altogether different.)

Hiring two retired fishermen as assistants and a launch to ferry them around, Jenness embarked from Lewisporte on the first leg of his seaborne exploration, a circuit through the Bay of Exploits, Notre Dame Bay's southern extremity. Their searches turned up two Beothuk sites previously unrecorded by Howley. One, on a hilly section of mainland

In Twilight and in Dawn

known as Winter Tickle, contained the ruins of a water-side dwelling and a smattering of stone tools and iron fragments.[26] The other was an undisturbed burial of two adults and a child, discovered on a secluded stretch of shoreline on Long Island. As was Beothuk custom, overhanging cliffs sheltered the seaward-facing burials, their human remains blanketed in birch bark.[27] Reminiscent of the back-breaking work on Little Diomede, the trio laboured to clear away boulders that had fallen atop the Long Island site, crushing some of its contents. Metalware mixed in with funerary goods, including carved bone ornaments sprinkled with red ochre, indicated contact-era dating. More interesting, the grave was enclosed in what appeared to be remains of a "miniature wigwam" constructed of poles and birch bark, "a feature of Indian burial not recorded before." If not for its size, he conjectured, one might think the site was not a grave at all, but "the last resting place of a family that had perished from disease or starvation." In fact, such structures – canopies and burial huts alike – were known from Beothuk Newfoundland, as well as from some of their mainland Algonkian neighbours.[28]

Leaving the Bay of Exploits, the tour's second stage took them northwest across open sea toward Green Bay, then down the coast as far as Fleur de Lys, and finally back to Lewisporte via Triton Island and Seal Bay districts. Albert Bayly, a knowledgeable contact in St John's and Howley's former assistant, urged that particular attention be paid to the Green Bay area, advising that four local fishing villages – Burlington, the intriguingly named Rogue and Nipper's Harbours, and the more prosaic Indian Burying Place – "used to be celebrated as the Home of the Red Man."[29] While true to its reputation, investigations here, as on the full circuit through western Notre Dame Bay, produced more in the way of Beothuk-related folklore and plundered sites than fresh material evidence. The lone exception was a previously unrecorded cave burial situated on another Long Island, this one well to the west of the first. Containing little more than a handful of bone ornaments, whatever human remains it once held had doubtless been lost to looters or scavenging animals.

Something altogether different awaited at Fleur de Lys, the final stop on their outward journey. Perched at the end of the Baie Verte Peninsula, where Notre Dame and White bays meet, the small outport boasts a long European history, established as a French fishing harbour in the 1500s, then becoming an English settlement several centuries later. Native peoples knew the place, too, its main attraction found not in the adjacent seas but ashore, in an outcrop of soapstone. More than an exposed deposit, the quarry bore unmistakable evidence of the human hands that had worked it over time, its heavily scarred stone face marked here and there by the forms of unfinished lamps and cooking pots still attached to the surface. Howley claimed that the few pieces of stoneware illustrated in his book were Beothuk handiwork. Jenness was unsure, their conspicuous similarity to arctic soapstone implements pointing to Eskimoan attribution. Of course, there remained the possibility that, like the Port aux Choix collection, they indicated Beothuk borrowing from the Dorset, a possibility he then thought quite likely.[30]

Their cruise through western Notre Dame Bay at an end, the companions parted company on reaching Lewisporte once more. With what little time and money remained, Jenness immediately embarked for the Great Northern Peninsula's remote eastern shore, hoping to further substantiate his emerging Beothuk-Dorset hypothesis. A coastal steamer landed him at Englee, another former French fishing harbour, at the entrance to Canada Bay, some fifty miles due north of Fleur de Lys and fifty miles south of the Strait of Belle Isle. Residents here were also used to finding relics of the native past buried in their gardens. Jenness's own hasty search of a seaside potato patch turned up a crop lying near the surface: a dozen or so small stone and ivory implements bearing the hallmarks of Dorset design, including harpoon heads with rectilinear sockets and gouged lashing holes. That is all he found, the garden's thin soil containing none of the more usual Beothuk items he recovered in Notre Dame Bay, artifacts later described as "closely resembl[ing] specimens from Algonkian sites in eastern Canada and the United States." Nor was there material of European origin.[31] A later generation of archaeologists would express incredulity that he left Newfoundland convinced these finds represented Eskimoan loans to the Indian toolkit, rather than remnants of a pre-contact Eskimo occupation of the island's northern coasts.[32] Jenness suggested at the time that the Englee artifacts, though few in number, "prove conclusively that the Red Indians were in close contact with that extinct Eskimo tribe ... which centred, as far as we know, around Hudson Strait, something like a thousand years ago." Their contacts, presumably occurring somewhere in Labrador, resulted in important exchanges, "the Beothuks borrow[ing] interalia the Eskimo harpoon head and the Eskimos borrow[ing] the Beothuk type of flint or quartz arrow head." Direct relations between the two peoples ended, he surmised further, when archaic Beothuk "were driven into Newfoundland, very likely by an advancing wave of [more culturally advanced] Mountaineer [Montagnais] Indians" sometime before Europeans came on the scene in the early sixteenth century.[33]

Soon after settling back at the museum, Jenness received a letter from Fritz Johansen, late of the Southern Party. Recently stationed at Wakeham Bay with Canada's Hudson Strait Expedition, Johansen, a biolo-

In Twilight and in Dawn

gist, described how he had come across the ruins of long-abandoned winter houses attributed in local oral tradition to "Tuniks [sic]," a people who predated arrival of the first Inuit. Known to ethnologists as quasi-mythical beings described in the lore of groups east of Alaska, Mathiassen's work at Naujan had led him to equate Tunit with Thule Eskimos. Jenness thought otherwise, explaining to Cambridge's A.C. Haddon the preceding year that Dorset "probably represents the legendary 'Tunnit' of modern Eskimo traditions."[34] "I have had my eyes on that region for a long time," he wrote back to Johansen, confident that "some of the old stone houses that you visited ... [might well] contain curious harpoon heads, arrow and knife blades, and other specimens quite different from those in ordinary Eskimo house ruins ... I am very anxious to have this Eskimo culture elucidated in detail and discover how far it extended along the Labrador coast," he added, his still-unsubstantiated claims for Dorset-Beothuk exchanges clearly in mind; "If it reaches no farther out than ... Nain, it will mean that the Beothuks not many centuries ago resided in the Labrador peninsula."[35]

New evidence bearing on this hypothesis was soon at hand. Its source was William Duncan Strong, of Chicago's Field Museum. He was the lone anthropologist with the Second Rawson-MacMillan Subarctic Expedition, headquartered near Nain on Labrador's northeastern coast in 1927–28. Primarily interested in the present rather than the past, Strong's winter-long fieldwork resulted in a detailed account of the same Naskapi band, the Mushuau Innu, whom Frederick Waugh had met with little success six years earlier.[36] On learning of the pending American expedition, however, Jenness succeeded in persuading the American to devote what time he could to the region's archaeology, especially the "very baffling" question of Indian-Eskimo relations and the resultant influences that seem to have "penetrated quite deeply" into the culture of each group.[37] Six months later Strong's preliminary findings were posted to Ottawa from the field. Explorations in the interior reaches of Jack Lane's Bay, he reported, turned up stone artifacts that "appear to be Eskimoan yet ... are very unlike the more modern Eskimo implements ... One cannot help thinking that we may have here an old Indian-like culture anterior to the later bone-ivory cultures" in use among Inuit of more recent times, an inference reiterated the following summer on the strength of additional material uncovered at other coastal localities. "That this culture bears a definite relation to the N[ewfoundland], Maritime and Maine cultures [i.e., the archaic Red Paint tradition] seems quite possible," he observed, an opinion that subsequent research into the ancient Indian past in Labrador, and adjacent regions, would corroborate. But he was eventually proved wrong in proposing a more controversial role for Old Stone Culture, as he called the finds: that it might constitute "a rather simple unspecialized" source from which the two extinct cultures – that is, Archaic Indian and Dorset Eskimo – derived, at least in the northeast. "If this coincidence occurred in the central Eskimo region, or Hudson's Bay," Strong told Jenness, "one would be rather strongly impressed ... that it might be the parent of the Eskimo and perhaps the Algonkian culture, but along the eastern seaboard this seems more questionable."[38] Should it prove to be ancestral to Eskimo culture, moreover, chances are that its beginnings lay somewhere in the interior, as more than a few theorists on both sides of the Atlantic had already proposed. In any event, fresh investigations, particularly on Hudson Strait – the crossroads linking the outer reaches of Hudson Bay with Indian territory on the eastern subarctic mainland – were needed to sort out what was gradually turning into a puzzle of ever greater complexity.

Following up his Newfoundland survey with a stint in the east Arctic thus became the logical next step, a step Jenness hoped to take in 1928. As he was verging on departing for St John's, however, Director Collins effectively quashed that plan by commissioning him to prepare two publications on the country's Aboriginal peoples: one, a summary slated for inclusion in the *Cambridge History of the British Empire*, the other a general textbook for issue under the imprint of the newly renamed National Museum of Canada. A standard reference for decades to come, and arguably his best-known work, at the time Jenness griped that what eventually appeared in 1932 as *The Indians of Canada* was "causing me all kinds of trouble," confessing to Birket-Smith that "I am not qualified to write it, nor I think is anybody else. The worst of it is [the manuscript is] supposed to be finished inside of sixteen or eighteen months and the task really requires about ten years."[39] Short of recruiting someone to carry the Dorset project forward in his place, it looked as if the Anthropological Division's return to arctic research would again be relegated to the back burner.

To stave off that eventuality, Jenness turned to his Danish associates once more, offering to arrange support for one of them to undertake a year's fieldwork. Both expressed interest, but only Mathiassen was in a position to give the proposal serious consideration at that moment. "I hardly think it is possibly [sic] to settle the question without an excavation in Hudson Strait and the east coast of Hudson Bay," he stated, signalling willingness to put claims for Dorset's age and independence of Thule to the test. Optimistic that an arrangement to that end was near, Jenness responded with an added inducement: a full-time posting with the Anthropological Division. "Personally, I feel quite certain that you would be appointed permanently, for we are understaffed at the present time and there is a vacancy that has never been filled." A

In Twilight and in Dawn

position within six months of returning from the Arctic seemed reasonable, he explained, his certainty leading him to ignore the bureaucratic difficulties that generally dogged attempts to place "a non-Britisher" on staff. "With the [government's Arctic Patrol] ship going north every year to supply the police posts," moreover, "you would be able to do all the Eskimo work you wanted."[40] Mathiassen went so far as to inquire about immigration procedures and the museum's pay scale, but in the end he politely begged off, announcing that long-awaited funding for fieldwork in Greenland had finally come through. Disheartened, Jenness wondered "where shall I find a competent man to take up Arctic work?" In typical, self-deprecating fashion, he added that "I am growing old and decrepit myself, and in any case am a mere dilettante compared with you and Birket-Smith."[41]

Unable to tackle the problem in the north, he conscripted William Wintemberg to delve into it more extensively in the south, starting with a 1928 survey of the outer limits of the Gulf of St Lawrence to its mouth at the Strait of Belle Isle. Wintemberg had spent the previous summer reconnoitring the great river's upper course between Trois-Rivières and Tadoussac, work whose primary purpose had been to ascertain the eastward extent of Iroquoian occupation. At Tadoussac, he also looked into Frank Speck's recent claim of a pre-contact Eskimo settlement, finding instead artifacts similar to ones associated with the Red Paint culture discovered years earlier in Maine. "I did not really expect Eskimo there," Jenness told his colleague, "but was hoping for a pre-Algonkian site that might be affiliated with Beothuk remains."[42] Now committed to the project, Wintemberg postponed planned fieldwork in what, for him, were the more familiar surroundings of Ontario's Huron country in favour of a second expedition through the outermost precincts of the lower North Shore. An arduous assignment for someone of delicate constitution, as he was, it was also quite productive, his searches uncovering evidence of a Beothuk presence along the stretch of southern Labrador coastline between Blanc Sablon and Bradore.[43] His most important contribution was to come the following summer, when he travelled to northwestern Newfoundland to pick up the trail where Jenness had left it two years before. Traversing the shores from Bonne Bay to Port aux Choix, he failed to find even one Indian site. Instead, the effort turned up abundant remains of pure Dorset culture: bone, ivory, and stone implements, including harpoon heads with the tell-tale rectangular socket design, and no trace whatever of later Inuit, or European, material. Summarizing the Anthropological Division's fieldwork for the year, Jenness conceded that Wintemberg's recent collections, and by extension his own from Englee and Fleur de Lys, "so closely resemble specimens of the peculiar Eskimo culture found a few years ago ... in Hudson Bay, that they must have been made by an offshoot of the same people" and not by Beothuks, as he had stubbornly claimed at first. Writing privately to a still-skeptical Mathiassen, he extrapolated further from the season's results, concluding that its wide geographic dispersal, coupled with the apparent extent of its influence on archaic Indian neighbours in the northeast, pointed to Dorset longevity as an independent Eskimo culture before it became "fused with and obliterated by the Thule and Modern cultures" in the not-too-distant past.[44]

After spending part of the 1930 field season in a fruitless search for evidence of archaic Indians on the Magdalen islands, Wintemberg prepared to return to Labrador the following summer to survey the complex coastline northward from the Strait of Belle Isle as far as Hamilton Inlet. Regrettably, whatever evidence that region held was to remain undiscovered for the foreseeable future, a casualty of government retrenchment in the face of a deepening depression. Much as they had done during the First World War, the Department of Mines hierarchy wielded a heavy hand in dealing with the emergency. Money for fieldwork, publication, travel to scholarly conferences – anything deemed lacking in "immediate economic value" – dried up practically overnight, effectively stranding scientific staff behind their desks into the mid-thirties. Pay was reduced by ten percent. At least job cuts were avoided, a stroke of great good luck considering that in early 1931 600 civil servants in Ottawa were dismissed and more reductions were threatened. "No one knows where the axe is going to fall next," Jenness wrote to Carl Guthe, an American associate, the public crisis serving to exacerbate the personal one that had convinced him to resign as chief only months earlier. "The Museum is down and out for the time being but I am hoping it is just the darkness before the dawn."[45]

THAT MUCH NEEDED THING

A rare bright spot during this otherwise gloomy period was Jenness's involvement in the Fifth Pacific Science Congress, a month-long affair held in Vancouver and Victoria in 1933 under National Research Council auspices. Drafted as chair of the anthropological and ethnological section, he was also asked to oversee publication of a volume on the "Origin and Antiquity of the American Aborigines," the theme of a special symposium. Despite meeting numerous difficulties in marshalling contributions from some of the field's leading specialists – "Getting the men lined up for this book is almost like a battle," he grumbled at one point – the final product offered a collection of essays whose purpose was to survey the present state of knowledge and identify directions for future research.[46]

Reserving the book's concluding chapter for himself, Jenness used its pages to review the development of arctic culture in the light of evidence from physical anthropology, linguistics, and, most importantly, archaeology, "probably our greatest hope in elucidating the early history of the Eskimo." The meat of the essay lay with treatment of Dorset, his first published statement on the subject since announcing its discovery back in 1925. Effectively a rejoinder to Mathiassen, he conceded that, at first glance, the extent of overlap in the spatial distribution of sites yielding remnants of both Thule and Dorset did seem to cast doubt on claims for the latter's cultural independence of the former. Wintemberg's Newfoundland results – described here only in brief, his colleague's full report not appearing until 1939 – stood out as the crucial exception, Thule being "conspicuously absent" on the island, as it then appeared to be along the full length of the Labrador coastline as well.[47] When weighed against these facts, Matthiassen's theory lacked credibility. Was it reasonable to assume, Jenness asked, that Thule culture and its "peculiar twelfth to fifteenth century phase" (i.e., Dorset) could "preserve their separate characteristics alongside one another" for the duration of their presumed contemporaneity? Was the proposed timeframe for Dorset sufficient to account for the full sweep of its geographic spread, in virtually the same form, from north to south, or for the extent of Indian-Dorset parallels in material culture, presumably the result of prolonged contacts with neighbouring groups in the northeast? And what of the idea that, for a certain period in their history, Thule people had intentionally substituted a relatively "inferior" technology for a more sophisticated one, thereby relinquishing their capacity to hunt large whales, arguably the defining trait of their culture? Finding the theory dubious on each count, he concluded that Dorset must have arisen earlier than, and independently of, Thule, though in certain districts the two probably overlapped for a time before the older culture finally disappeared from the archaeological record. Three years later Mathiassen conceded the point in print. Even then, he remained unconvinced by the second of his colleague's main assertions: that Dorset ancestry traced to an inland source in the eastern Arctic – namely the Caribou Inuit.[48]

Like Birket-Smith, Jenness favoured the idea that the present-day inhabitants of the barrens west of Hudson Bay were living remnants of the earliest stage in Eskimo development and not, as in Mathiassen's opinion, the "degenerate descendants" of Thule Eskimos drawn landward "through a predilection for caribou-hunting." This primal stage, first proposed by Steensby, was built on the harvesting of inland game and fish, similar to the adaptations of Indians bordering them on the south but quite unlike the largely maritime orientation of the Alaskan-derived Thule. Dorset, by comparison, appeared to be transitional between the two, its weaponry and other remains indicating an existence more dependent on land than sea. These were surely credentials of the elusive Paleo-Eskimos, Jenness concluded, the first known people to settle Canada's Arctic. By all indications, however, they were not the forebears of their Neo-Eskimo Thule successors, evidence accumulated to date suggesting a Dorset radiation toward the north and south only, not westward to the Bering Sea, as Birket-Smith had previously theorized.[49]

Mathiassen's objection to these findings rested on two points, the first being that the Caribou Inuit – like the Beothuk – were neither holdovers of a primitive cultural stage, as indeed they were not, nor the descendants of Dorset's progenitors. With the second, he took the debate in an entirely new direction, proposing that the Dorset lineage itself stemmed from Indian and not Eskimo forebears, its obvious Eskimoan cast stemming from contacts with Thule people around Hudson Bay. This was a curious retreat for someone who had long interpreted the culture as a variant of Thule and once claimed a Siberian prototype for its distinctive harpoon head. Mathiassen's American protégé, Frederica de Laguna, later intimated that he had put forward this unlikely position to "salvage" Thule's unique founder status in arctic culture history."[50]

Speculations about the Caribou Inuit aside, Jenness's more general claim of Dorset's Eskimo ancestry has weathered the test of time. In closing his 1933 review, he concluded that the ancient inland dwellers who gave rise to Dorset were themselves "the eastern wing of a far-flung Eskimo stock" whose western branch, "invigorated by foreign [probably northwest coast Indian and Siberian] contacts," eventually spawned Old Bering Sea and then Thule. This line of thinking carries the impress of Henry Collins's influence, the two exchanging letters in 1931 about Collins's unearthing of Alaskan artifacts he considered reminiscent of Dorset types from the oldest strata of his Gambel excavations. Given the possible existence of even older Bering Sea sites demonstrating a more "pronounced Dorset aspect yet," Collins remarked, Dorset itself might actually comprise the "remnants of what was presumable [sic] the original Eskimo culture drift eastward, an earlier parallel to the drift that later carried Thule culture eastward from a Bering Strait beginning."[51] However roughly stated, these ideas on arctic culture history anticipated by some twenty years the discoveries that effectively turned Jenness's "far-flung Eskimo stock" into a late phase of Paleo-Eskimo culture: the caribou and musk-ox hunters of the Arctic Small Tool Tradition who traversed the northern tundras, from west to east, upwards of 4,000 years ago.

◆

The economic doldrums that idled Anthropological Division fieldwork for four long years beginning in 1931 did little to dampen Jenness's enthusiasm for sorting out the intricate threads of the Eskimoan past. Nor did it deter him from trying to promote a larger Canadian commitment to the rapidly developing field of arctic archaeology, particularly in organizing new investigations across the country's northern latitudes. What had flagged was his enthusiasm for doing the shovel work himself. With his fiftieth birthday looming and youthful taste for adventure understandably dulled, the job of searching for fresh evidence bearing on the still-uncertain Thule-Dorset relationship seemed better entrusted to new blood, preferably someone with professional and personal qualities suited to the task and a willingness to stay with the work over the long term. Having tried and repeatedly failed to recruit from the outside, even on a temporary basis, he looked inside instead, to Douglas Leechman, the division's senior museum assistant. Largely limited to curatorial and technical responsibilities since joining the staff in 1924, Leechman was "more than eager" to take on research duties outside Ottawa, much as Waugh and Wintemberg had done previously. His chance, an audition of sorts, came in 1934; the assignment: scouting for habitation sites in the eastern Arctic "with a view to their future examination." Travelling aboard the Hudson's Bay Company supply ship *Nascopie* at Department of Interior expense, the cost of the division's first fieldwork since 1930 was negligible. Not so its returns.[52]

Nascopie took the fledgling archaeologist on a grand tour through eastern arctic waters, the steamer's three-month itinerary including sixteen calls, most at mainland ports from Labrador to the outer reaches of James Bay, the remainder across Hudson Strait on Baffin and Ellesmere islands. Even with an erratic schedule that sometimes allowed days ashore, sometimes mere hours, Leechman managed to gather much valuable information, pinpointing sites all along the ship's route and identifying those few that were most likely to repay future investigation. The chance to put this intelligence to practical use wasn't long in coming: with funding again trickling into the division's long-starved research budget for 1935, he was back in the field that summer, and the next. Both seasons were chiefly spent digging in Arctic Quebec, on the southern margins of the strait, the area Jenness had previously singled out as the ideal starting-point for tracing the full temporal and spatial dimensions of Dorset culture. Neither man was disappointed with the outcome. Excavations in 1935 turned up Dorset artifacts lying below mixed assemblages of Thule and recent material in house ruins at an ancient winter encampment called Nunaingok, on Killiniq Island, off the tip of mainland Labrador.[53] Importantly, their stratigraphic context provided the first uncontested evidence that Dorset predated appearance of Thule, at least in this quarter. Equally noteworthy results followed the next summer on the Nuvuk Islands, near Cape Wolstenholme, several hundred miles west of Killiniq. Here, a settlement of some fifteen ruins was found to contain remains associated exclusively with Dorset.[54] As Wintemberg's earlier work in Newfoundland had done, these two discoveries boosted Jenness's claims for the culture's relative age and independence of the technologically more sophisticated Thule. Oddly enough, what they failed to do was turn Leechman into the Anthropological Division's next arctic specialist, his work after the late thirties largely following in Wintemberg's footsteps through the archaeological landscape of the southern Woodlands region.[55]

Beyond Leechman's contributions, American and British institutions were responsible for what little archaeology took place in Canada's north through the final half decade of the interwar years. Together, four scientific expeditions to the eastern Arctic were mounted, only two of them entailing excavation: Graham Rowley's on Foxe Basin for Cambridge and Robert Bentham's on Ellesmere Island for Manchester. Pittsburgh's Carnegie Museum sponsored the third, to Hudson Bay, quickly followed by George Quimby's visit to the Belcher Islands on behalf of the universities of Michigan and Chicago. Although Carnegie's objectives were chiefly zoological, a stop in the Belchers resulted in purchase of a thousand artifacts – a hodgepodge of undocumented specimens, gleaned through Inuit rummaging – from the local storekeeper. Quimby's collection was also the product of fossicking, but "reasonably specific provenience" obtained through interviews, he suggested, "lend [it] some scientific value."[56]

Feeling that they were, in general, an improvement over the old standby of delegating digging duties to ranking Mounties and government officials, Jenness unfailingly supported these projects, offering guidance on scientific and logistical matters, granting access to museum collections for comparative analysis, trying (without success) to find a qualified archaeologist to accompany the well-financed Carnegie expedition – he had Henry Collins in mind, while Collins recommended his junior associate James Ford – and, as was his habit, taking special interest in the personal welfare of those who were undertaking the work. He also had administrative oversight of their activities, ensuring compliance with provisions set out in the "Eskimo Ruins Ordinance" of 1930. Modelled on a League of Nations convention and similar to measures already in place in Alaska, Greenland, and the Soviet Arctic, the ordinance established a permit system governing excavation in the Northwest Territories and export of "any objects of archaeological or ethnological importance or interest." As virtually the only person in the country with the requisite expertise, Jenness was commissioned by officials of the interior department's Northwest Territories and Yukon Branch to draft the ordinance's accompanying regulations, vet permit applications, and, under a critical 1938 revision, determine which "specimens are required to complete the collections of the National Museum of Canada and are to become the property of that institution."[57] The practice of seeking his counsel had actually begun some years before when excavation permits were issued under the broad authority of a separate 1926 ordinance licensing scientists and explorers. In thanking the anthropologist for his assistance, branch director O.S. Finnie voiced concern over the very real threat Inuit and white pothunters posed to ruins scattered across an immense and thinly policed region. "There is also the possibility of foreign expeditions applying for permits to excavate," an eventuality, he suggested, that "in some cases, we might find it embarrassing to refuse. Might I suggest," the letter continues, its author revealing a degree of ignorance as extensive as the territory under his charge, "that your Division send an archaeologist to thoroughly cover the ground before most of the scientific value is destroyed or before the honour of investigating is asked for by some foreign country[!]"[58]

Excepting the relatively recent specimens geologist Bentham had unearthed on Ellesmere Island, none of it seemingly earlier than the seventeenth century, the other American and British expeditions contributed valuable pieces to the great puzzle of arctic culture history. Typical of many sites across the region, both Belcher Island collections included material associated with that "mysterious" culture, as its ever-unassuming discoverer was given to calling Dorset. Quimby, however, went out on a limb in claiming that his was not a simple jumble of items from various time periods but evidence of a cultural hybrid, dubbed Manitunik, a sixteenth-century Thule occupation bearing marks of Dorset influence.[59] However tantalizing the possibilities this raised, it was the Cambridge-trained Rowley's investigations as a member of the British Canadian Arctic Expedition of 1935–39, that most advanced understanding of each population's place in northern history. Near the end of his long stay at Foxe Basin, he dug a site called Abverdjar, near Igloolik, off Melville Peninsula's northeastern coast. For the third time, starting with Wintemberg's good fortune in western Newfoundland, the work yielded "that much needed thing," a "pure" Dorset assemblage, one missing drills, kayaks, and dog sleds, all typical Thule features. "His material confirms everything we have believed about the Dorset culture except one point," Jenness enthused in a note to Henry Collins, "the art is much more advanced." On the strength of what was previously known about their carving, Collins took the cautious view that Dorset and Old Bering Sea artistic styles were similar, implying a possible connection between the two cultures. Rowley begged to differ, publically siding with Jenness on the critical questions of independence and age.[60]

While the straitened conditions of the thirties limited progress in unravelling problems of indigenous culture history across Canada's Arctic, a mix of New Deal spending and philanthropic endowments underwrote significant advancements on the Alaskan front.[61] Henry Collins, for one, continued investigations for the Smithsonian into the mid-thirties, work culminating in his landmark interpretation of Old Bering Sea and of other antecedents of Neo-Eskimo culture. Similarly fruitful was the development of a research program based at the territory's Agricultural College and School of Mines, forerunner of the University of Alaska. At a time when Jenness could do no better than scrounge free passage for Leechman aboard *Nascopie*, the Works Project Administration awarded $41,000 to the college's Otto Geist, a naturalist and self-taught archaeologist, to undertake excavations on St Lawrence Island, where he had begun digging back in the twenties. Equivalent to nearly three times the annual salaries of the division's entire full time staff in the mid-thirties, fully one fifth of the grant was earmarked for covering the costs of photographic work and publication.[62] Shortly thereafter, the American Museum of Natural History revived an interest that had flagged since the days of Stefansson's early explorations, organizing a collaboration between Geist and Froelich Rainey, a recent Yale graduate and newcomer to arctic research. In turn, Rainey, along with Louis Giddings and Mathiassen's protégé Helge Larsen, added a startling new chapter to the story of the Eskimoan past with their spectacular finds at Point Hope, on the northwestern coast. The site literally teemed with ruins – upwards of 600 dwellings and scores of burial features – and contained an array of artifacts unlike any uncovered to date. Christened Ipiutak, Rainey told Jenness that it was the "strangest kind of half-Eskimo culture ... something pretty rare and pretty ancient which may be a kind of formative Eskimo culture" since it appeared to be lacking evidence of a whaling component, pottery, polished slate, sled runners, lamps, and other definitive Neo-Eskimo elements. After a second season in 1940, he was envisioning Ipiutak as Asian-derived and ancestral to later Eskimoan cultures, "but certainly not primitive. I am rapidly coming to the conclusion that we need no longer look for a primitive proto-Eskimo culture in the Arctic." Rather, he suggested, "people first entered ... with a well-developed Asiatic neolithic culture."[63] Within a decade, Gidding's discoveries at Cape Denbigh would prove him wrong. Since then, Ipiutak's early first millennium dating has fixed its place in the chronological sequence of New World Arctic cultures, although its precise relationship to those cultures that came before and after it remains uncertain. Unlike the Dorset puzzle, Ipiutak remains something of an enigma.[64]

The period witnessed still other projects, most notably, research in southwestern Alaska, territory associated with the so-called Pacific Eskimos: Hrdlička's on Kodiak Island and Frederica de Laguna's around Cook Inlet and Prince William Sound, supported by the University of Pennsylvania Museum. Copenhagen's Nationalmuseet also had a hand in de Laguna's work, sponsoring a joint undertaking in which she and Birket-Smith spent the 1931 field season in archaeological and ethnographic investigations among two little-known peoples: Chugach Eskimos and their Athapaskan-speaking Eyak neighbours. Compared to its Canadian counterpart, the Danish museum was a veritable hub of activity in the mid-thirties, undergoing physical expansion of its facilities and mounting anthropological expeditions to various parts of the globe, including Greenland, Central America, and Iran. "When I contrast the progressiveness and activity of your museum, and of the University of Toronto Museum ... with the deadness of our own institution in Ottawa, I sometimes feel depressed," a dispirited Jenness remarked in a letter to Birket-Smith. "We have no parties in the field, no money to buy specimens, no facilities for publication ... [but then] I should be grateful that I can keep my family in comfort, and give my children a little education."[65] Academic anthropology's chronically anaemic state in Canada proved no less trying, the discipline still barely recognized in the country's universities and without a sufficiency of practitioners, lacking the institutional supports of even one home-grown professional association. "I envy you the stimulus you must receive from colleagues who are close students of the Eskimo," he admitted to Danish scholar William Thalbitzer. "Here in Canada we have persons interested in administration but no one except myself who pays the least attention to their ethnography." And to Alfred Kroeber, at Berkeley: "We live in such solitude up here that I am deeply grateful to all my kind friends below the line."[66]

With the outbreak of hostilities in Europe, secondment to war-related duties effectively ended Jenness's work for the division. Still, his interest in the rapidly expanding field of arctic anthropology, one he had done so much to build, scarcely waned, even in retirement.[67] His last scholarly contribution on the subject came on the eve of Germany's invasion of Poland: a state-of-the-art assessment read in 1938 to delegates attending the inaugural meeting of the International Congress of Anthropological and Ethnological Sciences, in Copenhagen, and then reprised as his presidential address to the American Anthropological Association, in Chicago a year later. Bearing the jazzy title "Prehistoric Culture Waves from Asia to America," the published version combined a synopsis of the decade's main findings in each of the discipline's branches, with its author's take on what the new evidence added to knowledge of Aboriginal origins, migrations, and affinities.

Several hotly debated issues now seemed settled, he began, first and foremost that "Bering Strait ... was the only route of ingress into this hemisphere," the ancestors of "every known division of Indians" arriving over a span of thousands of years that probably ended no later than the last millennium BC, with the appearance of the Athapaskans. Forebears of the Eskimos were the last to cross, certainly by the beginning of the Common Era and quite plausibly before. On the more specific problem of sources giving rise to the three known precursors of contemporary New World Arctic culture – Dorset, Old Bering Sea, and Thule – the jury was still out. Not so with reference to where Dorset fit in the overall developmental sequence. Finally rejecting the idea that it had originated as an "Eskimoized" Indian culture, Jenness declared that it was indeed "genuinely Eskimo," suggesting further that while it "stemmed from the same parent trunk as the ancient cultures of western Alaska," it had branched off earlier than did Old Bering Sea. "This would date their entry into Canada not later than the first millennium BC, and possibly even in the second." The odds, he felt certain, favoured the latter if, as he thought likely, an "invasion of Athapaskan tribes" expanding eastward across the subarctic "pushed the Dorset people out to the coast of the eastern Arctic" from their former inland ranges. Canadian archaeologist William Taylor would pronounce these conclusions "thoroughly radical" some thirty years later, pointing to a timeframe that "now basks in a warm glow of radiocarbon affirmation."[68] A reporter for the *New York Times* who heard his talk in Chicago read something more contemporary, and political, into Jenness's rather staid interpretation of the indigenous past. Headed "'Lebensraum' Wars Old American Tale," Sidney Shalett offered the public an interpretation of his own, fashioning the Athapaskans as a people made "aggressive and virile" by their "long trek" from Asia, their encounter with "peaceful Eskimos and Algonkian Indians" in a land "not rich enough to give them all a living" spawning "the first North American struggle for 'Lebensraum.'"[69] The temper of the times ...

CHAPTER TWELVE

Turning the Page, 1929–1936

DIGGING INTO PEOPLE'S INSIDES

Jenness continued to hope to be able to return to Athapaskan research, even in the mid-twenties at the height of excitement generated by the Dorset and Old Bering Sea discoveries. Since leaving the British Columbia interior, his chief priority had been a second research trip to the region, to southern Carrier and Chilcotin country. Months before heading off to the Alaskan coast, he had corresponded with ethnologist John M. Cooper about whether such a trip might dovetail with the American's own plan to follow up a brief visit to Stuart Lake the previous summer with a full season of fieldwork in that same quarter. Calling attention to the shortcomings of Father Morice's treatment of social organization and religion, Jenness urged Cooper – himself a priest, a northern Algonkian specialist, and a faculty member at Washington's Catholic University – to revisit the missionary's ethnography of Carriers at Stuart Lake and Prince George, as well as of the neighbouring Babine. "So if we can collaborate to clean up the Carrier," he observed, "practically all the Athapaskan tribes in British Columbia will have been studied."[1] None of this was to be, Cooper's attentions being diverted elsewhere while the ill-fated Smithsonian invitation and its aftermath put Jenness's proposed western trip on indefinite hold.[2]

In the meantime, in 1928 an opportunity to revive research in that "badly neglected ethnographical province," the Mackenzie valley, presented itself. On Edward Sapir's recommendation, Jenness hired Cornelius Osgood, a twenty-three-year-old graduate student at the University of Chicago, to study the Hare, hunters in the boreal forests bordering the western margins of Great Bear Lake. "We'd be taking about the same kind of chance with him as I took with McIlwraith – both well read in anthropology, both young and enthusiastic," Sapir advised, sensitive to his colleague's uncertainty over sending a novice to winter alone in a remote corner of the Northwest Territories. With museum officials holding him personally accountable for Osgood's welfare, Jenness, as yet untested in this sort of supervisory role, took special care to warn him against jeopardizing his own health and safety, "something one is too often prone to do in northern settings ... This reads as though I were preaching you a sermon," he acknowledged, sounding more paternal than clerical, "but I know that life can be hard and risks great in the North."[3] Osgood survived the experience. Though unimpressed with his resulting report, both Jenness and Sapir conceded that its shortcomings were understandable in the circumstances: an aspiring ethnographer wrestling not just with a culture heavily influenced by western ideas and practices but, by Osgood's own admission, with his conscience, seeing the deplorable state of native health and their failing economy as "special hindrances" to the progress of his investigations. "The immediate rewards for anthropology were negligible," the rookie conceded in retrospect, but "they were great for me" professionally, his hard-won apprenticeship eventually landing him a post at Yale and new opportunities for fresh fieldwork among Han, Kutchin, and other northern Athapaskans.[4] The first of a new generation of anthropologists to take up research in the western subarctic, he was the last to do so under National Museum auspices until the dawning of a new era in the 1950s.

Though slightly smaller than in the early to mid-twenties, the Anthropological Division's research budgets enjoyed a modicum of stability through 1930, the span of Jenness's initial tenure as chief. As well as supporting Osgood and J.C.B. Grant's anthropometric survey, the situation allowed him to allocate sufficient resources to the ongoing field investigations of permanent staff, the lion's share of which, it bears mention, went to his erstwhile friend Marius Barbeau for three trips to the Nass and Skeena rivers. With progress on the text of what was to become *The Indians of Canada* well advanced and the coming 1929 fiscal year shaping up to be one of the best-funded of the decade, conditions seemed right for his own return to the field. Having ruled out an expedition to Hudson Strait, he settled on a more modest plan, one meant to complete a project left unfinished by Frederick Waugh's untimely death: readying for publication the wealth of ethnographic material his late colleague had collected from Ojibwa in northwestern Ontario between 1916 and 1920.

◆

Appointing an ethnologist to concentrate on the multitude of Ojibwayan-speaking groups spread across the temperate and boreal forests and the plains of central Canada had ranked high among the division's original requirements in 1911 in assembling a full-time research staff. Sapir's favoured candidate for appointment had been friend and fellow Columbia graduate Paul Radin, recently out of a job at the Bureau of American Ethnology owing, Radin believed, to resentment of his close ties to the increasingly influential Boasian school on the part of the bureau's new head, F.W. Hodge. Faced with uncertainty over the spending priorities of the in-coming federal Conservative government, newly elected in 1911, the survey's director, Reginald Brock, had been reluctant to add a second assistant ethnologist position on top of the one just created for Barbeau[5] and Radin was offered temporary employment instead, an arrangement renewed yearly until wartime restraint finally squelched the last lingering hope of filling the need on a permanent basis. By that point he had completed three stints of fieldwork for the division, visiting about a dozen reserves in southeastern Ontario and a few more in Michigan and Wisconsin, two of four northern mid-western states with sizeable populations of Chippewa, as Ojibwa are known on the American side of the border. His Canadian travels took him to communities near the industrial towns of Peterborough, east of Toronto, and Sarnia, a short distance from Detroit, studying language, collecting myths, and recording personal accounts of social and religious customs.[6] In expectation of being engaged for a fourth field season in 1915, he had proposed shifting to the province's more remote and less developed hinterlands, the north and west of Lake Superior. This was territory of the Saulteaux, a branch of Ojibwa whose lands lay within the Lake Winnipeg watershed. Unlike their southern congeners, now largely farmers and wageworkers, hunting and fishing remained the foundation of Saulteaux livelihood. From the perspective of the day's ethnological priorities, however, it was the presence among them of traditionalists who still practised old customs that attracted special interest. In this respect, the Lac Seul reserve, north of Sioux Lookout, stood out, having gained a reputation as a haven for a dwindling coterie determined to maintain the spiritual foundations of a way of life besieged for decades by both missionaries and their Native converts.[7]

Among the early casualties of the Geological Survey's mobilization for war, plans for expanding fieldwork in this direction were delayed until 1916 when Frederick Waugh, not Radin, had been dispatched on an abbreviated reconnaissance of the Lake Nipigon area, northeast of what today is the city of Thunder Bay. Two longer trips to Lac Seul followed, five months in 1919, four more a year later. On reading through the fifty notebooks Waugh had filled during those trips, Jenness was astonished to learn that, in addition to all manner of descriptive detail, they contained the author's first-hand account of one of the more significant of Ojibwa religious institutions: Midewiwin, the Grand Medicine Society, a tradition Radin had hoped to observe for himself during his proposed 1915 expedition. Once widespread around the Great Lakes, the secretive society's curing practices and underlying body of belief, like so much else of indigenous culture, were then rapidly passing from the scene, sidelined in community after community by the spread of Christian teachings and other Euro-Canadian influences. This was certainly the case on the Lake Nipigon reserves Waugh had visited during his first outing. But he delighted in reporting to Sapir that Midewiwin, and other sacred practices, "are in 'full swing'" deeper in the interior at Lac Seul, having been recently revived, after a period of decline, in the absence of a resident missionary.[8] "I think that before [the material] could be worked up into a proper memoir," Jenness told Cooper of his discovery, "it would be necessary for someone to visit the region to get a good grip of Ojibwa customs and thought and to fill in the gaps." To that end, he raised the possibility of a joint venture in the coming summer of 1929 at Lake of the Woods, in the province's Kenora district. Cooper warmed to the idea, having just returned from a "flying visit" to the area that had convinced him of the potential for fuller investigation among Saulteaux there and in adjacent parts of Manitoba.[9]

And then, almost like clock-work, for the fourth consecutive year an unforeseen development interfered with Jenness's plans, this one materializing at the last possible moment: instructions to represent the National Museum at the upcoming Pacific Science Congress in Java, Netherlands East Indies. The unexpected commission was plainly an honour, not least because there was to be only one other member in Canada's official delegation, zoologist C. McLean Fraser, representative of the Pacific Science Council. Even so, its timing – mere days before the departure of the ship on which delegates' passage had been booked – suggests that his name had popped up as a last-minute stand-in, probably for Henry M. Tory, sitting president of the National Research Council. With "barely time to pack my trunks for an immediate get-away," Jenness dashed off for Vancouver and the journey that would take him to the colonial capital Batavia (now Jakarta), by way of Yokohama, Shanghai, Hong Kong, and Singapore, an enjoyable voyage of nearly three-week's duration. After an equally pleasurable month attending the congress and participating in various excursions, he arrived back home in mid-summer, too late to retrace Waugh's steps into northwestern Ontario. By coincidence, Cooper wasn't able to make the trip either, detained in Washington by a family emergency.[10]

Scrambling to salvage what remained of the fleeting season, while also avoiding another long absence from Eilleen and his two young sons, Jenness hastily organized Plan B: a camping trip to Ontario's celebrated cottage country on the southeastern shores of Georgian Bay. An easy day's travel from Ottawa, the region was also home to a large Aboriginal population, one that had attracted only cursory attention from anthropologists to this point. The family pitched their tents on Parry Island, now Wasauksing First Nation, a scant two miles from the modern-day resort town of Parry Sound. Here, as on reserves elsewhere in the province's southern precincts, the community of 250 residents comprised an amalgam of three closely related Algonkian groups, nearly two-thirds describing themselves as Ojibwa, a few as Odawa, and the remainder, about one hundred altogether, as Potawatomi.[11] More recently, they and their compatriots in Ontario and parts of Manitoba have adopted the more inclusive name Anishinabe, "human beings," an expression of long-preserved oral traditions asserting their origins as a single nation. Tradition also speaks of an ancestral homeland somewhere farther to the east and of migrations that first brought them to the Great Lakes and then to the separate territories each occupied at the dawn of the contact era in the seventeenth century: the Odawa on Manitoulin Island and adjacent shores of Georgian Bay, including Parry Island; Ojibwa to the north and west as far as the eastern limits of Lake Superior; and Potawatomi on Michigan's lower peninsula.[12]

The course of history in this area following the arrival of Europeans was an especially tumultuous one, the years after 1650 marked by recurrent epidemics of disease and inter-tribal war, shifting political and economic alliances, and wholesale dispersals into new territories to the south and west as an expanding fur trade pushed the colonial frontier ever deeper into the continental heartland. Nearly two centuries later, Ojibwa still comprised a major presence on what had become British soil, many now occupying more southerly reaches of Ontario, including Georgian Bay, others spreading westward onto the prairies or into the broad belt of boreal forest stretching from James Bay to the hinterlands north of Lake Manitoba. Odawa formed a smaller share of the remnant population, although their numbers had been augmented by émigrés from Michigan seeking to reclaim former turf on Manitoulin Island. Finally, a separate stream of Potawatomi migrants – upwards of 2,000 people – had left several mid-western states in the late 1830s and 1840s for what was then Upper Canada. Many eventually settled at Kettle Point and neighbouring reserves around Sarnia, places Radin had visited before the First World War. Others continued northward, into Georgian Bay. A few of their number, forebears of the contingent at

Parry Island, had opted to relocate there from Christian Island, arriving, en masse, around 1865. Occurring at a time when contested land rights and other thorny issues dominated relations between local bands and colonial authorities, their desire to settle here, and elsewhere, in territories long claimed by peoples of Ojibwa and Odawa descent sparked political tensions that exacerbated an already charged situation. Sixty-five years after the fact, Jenness found that the issue continued to hang over the Parry islanders, bitter memories of that difficult time still capable of stirring up ill feelings.[13]

Before contact, their comparatively temperate surroundings had allowed the Odawa to combine hunting and gathering with the cultivation of crops, a practice borrowed from Iroquoian-speaking Huron near-neighbours to the south. Keeping gardens became widespread around Georgian Bay after the mid-1800s, however, necessitated in large part by loss of traditional hunting grounds to white settlers and to resource-based industries. The thin soils and too-short growing season that limited farming in these parts were a factor in deterring an influx of homesteaders on a scale comparable to the one that flooded the fertile southern portions of Upper Canada between the 1760s and 1830s. Still, the region's other potentials did not escape notice, its bountiful fisheries and forests, and the prospect of mineral wealth, leading the colonial government to negotiate land surrenders that opened the door to economic development across a vast sweep of territory backing on the shores of Lake Huron and its eastern arm, Georgian Bay, and into the Lake Superior hinterland beyond.[14] Parry Island became a reserve under the 1850 Robinson Huron Treaty, the first of three land surrenders implemented during late pre-confederation times and the model for the so-called Numbered Treaties that followed between 1871 and 1921. Within fifteen years of its signing, logging and transport businesses were founded at Parry Sound and by century's end the island's people were living directly in the shadow of Depot Harbour, a commercial port and railway terminus built on expropriated reserve land in 1898. Now a ghost town, at its peak in the late twenties, upwards of 1,500, mostly white residents lived there, outnumbering their Aboriginal neighbours by six to one.[15]

Given this recent history, it is entirely understandable that Jenness planned to stay only a short while before shifting to the more populous, and presumably less bustling, reserves on Manitoulin Island, assuming that their experiences over the previous three decades had left the Parry islanders "too sophisticated and civilized to know much about their old life." He was mistaken. As expected, outward signs of change were everywhere, the local economy now largely dependent on seasonal wage work, store-bought food comprising the staple diet, traditional

In Twilight and in Dawn

dwellings and material culture all but disappeared, the Midewiwin long abandoned. Nevertheless, he soon discovered that "a little scratching of the surface revealed an amazing wealth of old customs, superstitions, and religious beliefs," a vein more than sufficient to sustain seven productive weeks of research.[16]

Months before the Jennesses arrived at Parry Island, Frederick Johnson, a college student and a protégé of ethnologist Frank Speck, briefly visited the reserve to purchase specimens for New York's Museum of the American Indian. He obtained about seventy, but his efforts to gather background information pertaining to traditional customs and beliefs were mostly rebuffed. Afterward, Johnson admitted that certain of his questions had "evoked ... much hostility," presumably, he thought, because Ottawa's relentless campaign to root out all vestiges of native identity had rendered such subjects too sensitive to discuss openly, especially with outsiders. In any case, he took it for granted, as Jenness was mistakenly to do a short while later, that much customary knowledge had long since disappeared, lost to the rapidly changing cultural landscape of Georgian Bay.[17] As things turned out, Jenness managed to bring to light a substantial amount of what, for good reason, had seemed to be beyond recovery. Included in the material was a first-hand narrative account of Midewiwin provided by Jonas King, a "frank pagan" of Potawatomi descent; he and his younger brother Tom were reported to be Parry Island's sole surviving Grand Medicine Society initiates.[18] The fieldwork's success wasn't due solely to Jenness's expertise and patience as an ethnographer, however. It rightly owes a major debt to Francis Pegahmagabow, his interpreter and principal consultant that summer. If, as some anthropologists believe, the ideal field consultant is someone whose inquisitiveness and perspicacity approximate their own, Pegahmagabow was just such a person, an ethnographer in all but name. Jenness described him as possessed of a "profoundly meditative temperament" and a philosophical outlook shaped in part by considerable familiarity with ancient Ojibwa ways, unusual for a man in his early forties, in part by varied experiences of the outside world, notably the meritorious wartime service that had earned him distinction as one of Canada's most decorated soldiers.[19] Close to one another in age, theirs was a collaboration unlike any Jenness had known to this point, a working relationship based on shared intellectual interests and on a personal connection reflecting the ready comradery of battlefield veterans.

"I think it was the best field work I have ever done," he wrote Sapir soon after his arrival back in Ottawa; "I got some intensely interesting notes on the psychology of the Indians and their interpretation of the phenomena around them. It seemed to me to be absolutely new."[20] In fact, psychologically oriented ethnographic investigation – soon to be known in the North American discipline as the culture and personality school – was only in its infancy in the twenties, its pioneers, nearly all trained in the Boasian tradition, concentrating on problems pertaining to culture's impress on personality and to the patterning of individual (and collective) thought and behaviour.[21] Jenness's Georgian Bay material stands as an early contribution to this effort. No less importantly, his work anticipated by several years the better-known researches of A. Irving Hallowell, Ruth Landes, and a dozen other American anthropologists who made a small industry of "psychologizing" the Ojibwa, beginning in the mid-thirties.[22]

❖

The first indication of Jenness's interest in psychological problems is found in a paper he presented to Section H of the British Association for the Advancement of Science immediately upon returning from Sekani country in 1924. Drafted in the field, "The Ancient Education of a Carrier Indian" considers changes in the sacred and secular precepts guiding everyday life that followed from the transformation of Wet'suwet'en society under the influence of their Gitksan neighbours and the means for inculcating them in successive generations.[23] In essence, the paper is a discussion of what nowadays is described as enculturation, anthropology's term for the conscious and unconscious learning that equips individuals to think, feel, and behave in ways recognized as appropriate by those with whom they share a culture. Apart from remarking on the declining relevance of customary teachings and the consequent weakening of community bonds under the forceful sway of Euro-Canadian ideas and institutions, he drew no further inferences from the case material. As other anthropologists would soon argue, this same process is crucial to personality development, instilling in individuals a tendency to behave in ways that are generally consistent with the underlying pattern (configuration) of core values, attitudes, and assumptions characteristic of their society. Accordingly, differences in psychological make-up are not the inborn manifestations of race that Victorian theorists contended they were but the variable imprints of what Ruth Benedict, echoing her mentor Franz Boas, attributed to the mediating influence of culture on a highly malleable, pan-human mental endowment. As she put the matter in the concluding pages of her influential *Patterns of Culture*, people everywhere "are plastic to the moulding force of society into which they are born."[24] Informed by this perspective and others selectively gleaned from psychological theory, principally (neo-)Freudian, a growing number of researchers were to turn their attention to describing and interpreting the general traits of mind and temperament that distinguish one group of people from the next and the specific processes, in particular child-rearing practices, that shape them.

Sapir was at the forefront of the discipline's embrace of psychological anthropology. As well as influencing the thought of two of the school's earliest and brightest stars, Benedict and Margaret Mead, he broke new theoretical ground in his own writings, most famously with his acute insight into the effect of language on cognition. While the bulk of his contributions were not to come until the thirties, after he had left the University of Chicago for Yale, Sapir's ideas about the relationship of language, culture, and personality, and his special interest in the individuality of cultural experience, began taking form during his years in Ottawa. Carl Jung's *Psychological Types*, published in 1923, apparently intrigued him immensely, as it did a small circle of like-minded American colleagues, and with "Jung ... in the air" at the Toronto gathering of the British Association's Section H the following year, he and Alexander Goldenweiser acted as the "ringleaders of a conspiracy to categorize their fellow anthropologists" as introverts or extroverts.[25] Given their close personal and professional ties, it seems a safe bet that this and other occasions, especially his regular chat-cum-seminar sessions with Sapir at the museum, provided Jenness with entree to the emerging field and its possibilities, much as they had done earlier in introducing him to the methodological preferences of American historical ethnology. It is equally certain that his decision to focus on the "psychology of the Indians" at Parry Island was a direct outcome of this guidance.

Two years before that fieldwork, Sapir had responded to his friend's request for pointed comment on the manuscript of *People of the Twilight*, then more or less ready for the publishers. "I found it exceedingly interesting and well told," his remarks began; "all I would note ... is this, that you seem to be a little afraid of digging into your people's insides ... Could you ... give a ... sense of the Eskimos as differentiated people, also the more serious aspects of the personalities of your companions?"[26] The advice was heeded, but not only for the refinement of the Coronation Gulf memoir. It is evident in the substance of Jenness's Ojibwa research, too, an exploration of the lived experience of the six men and one woman with whom he worked and the influence of traditional knowledge on their individual perceptions and understandings of the things of everyday existence. The style of the resulting monograph also bears its mark. As was his usual practice in field reports, its chapters, weighted heavily toward examination of religious beliefs and customs, are filled with illustrative (some quite lengthy) quotes from his consultants' own statements. However, it is the only one of the reports he wrote during his tenure at the museum in which each excerpt is attributed to its speaker by name, and the only to include mini-biographies of the dramatis personae. In all respects save its lack of an explicit theoretical frame, the study was consistent with the emerging disciplinary trend away from cultural reconstruction and toward psychological problems centred on what Boas initially took to be the genius of a people but would later refashion as the "inner development" of integrated cultural patterns.[27]

◆

"It is impossible to comprehend the daily life of the Eastern Indians of Canada without some knowledge of their religious beliefs, and their religious beliefs are unintelligible without an understanding of their interpretation of what they saw around them." So begins "The Indian's Interpretation of Man and Nature," Jenness's preliminary take on elemental tenets of faith among the Parry islanders, which he read to the Royal Society eight months after leaving the field and which would later become the starting point for the more detailed examination of their traditional ideas published as a museum monograph in 1935.[28] Both works are principally descriptive, depicting what, to the Ojibwyan mind, is a unified natural world fully alive with human and other-than-human beings, each possessing a sentient, sensate soul that endows it with intelligence, emotion, and agency. But, here and there, he also raises some psychological implications of this core conception, particularly its effect on individual cognitive and emotional orientation, and on the patterning of behavioural responses to all manner of social situations. Although not represented as such, the result is portrayal of a mental construct commonly construed in the ethnological literature as world view: in broad terms, a people's convictions and sentiments pertaining to the cosmic order, to the qualities of every thing that exists within it, and to causation – most importantly, their explanations of the fortunes and misfortunes, big and small, that inevitably occur in life. In essence, world view encompasses a constellation of values and attitudes that informs a person's sense of self in relation to all else. As such, psychologically minded anthropologists consider it to be an important factor in personality formation and, on a larger scale, in setting a society's prevalent tone.[29]

The psychological profile that emerged from Jenness's work with Pegahmagabow and company is of a people who lived, and for many of their number were continuing to live, in a culturally constituted universe that, however ultimately inscrutable, is perceived as anything but indifferent. It is a place where actions have moral consequences and where the causes of happenings are inherently personal. For them, the distinction between so-called natural and supernatural planes of existence is effectively a meaningless one. They experience each plane, one during waking life, the other in dreams, as being equally real, although what they come to know in dreams invariably matters most to each person's sense of who they are as an individual.[30] Parry islanders learn from an early age that theirs is a world "full of mystery, of unknown forces working in unknown ways for unknown ends," both benign and malevolent. While it is understood that anyone may receive gifts of magical knowledge and power from spirit benefactors, they are also aware that, because different benefactors command different types and amounts of power, human beneficiaries acquire dissimilar gifts.[31] Finally, and of singular consequence in moulding disposition and corresponding behaviour, is the certainty that no one ever truly knows what powers someone else possesses until those powers are put to use. Similarly at a loss to determine which of their own actions – however seemingly trivial or innocuous – might provoke a malignant reaction, even the most mundane of social interactions tend to be suffused with anxieties centred on the ever-present threat that sorcerers in their midst pose to an individual's well-being.[32]

"It is pathetic to observe how universal is this fear of witchcraft among the present inhabitants of Parry Island," Jenness remarks at one point, seemingly incredulous that, in spite of a good deal of change, not least the near-universal adoption of Christianity, an archaism of this type had survived at all. To the contrary, a good many people firmly believed that the threat had actually grown in relatively recent times, a consequence of the church-induced disappearance of shamans, individuals whose medicine powers were capable of countering the sorcerer's deleterious designs. "Every man suspects his neighbour of practising the nefarious art to avenge some fancied grievance, and the older and more conservative the Indian, the more he is held in suspicion." Indeed, it was widely thought that none of the community's adults had entirely escaped the accusations of others, nor escaped harm attributed to magical causes. By default, then, deliberate circumspection was the sine qua non of day-to-day existence, adults habitually concealing their emotions, suppressing aggressive urges, and speaking with measured words in all but the most trusted of settings. Even sharing food seemed to serve an ulterior purpose: helping to dodge the possibility of falling victim to misfortune. "He sets food before chance visitors ... whatever the hour of day or night," Jenness writes, "lest they resent any semblance of inhospitality and later cast a spell on him and his household."[33]

Though sketchier and barely analyzed, Jenness's characterization coincides with the findings Hallowell and Landes would later report from their more extensive researches in other parts of Ojibwa country. Moreover, it bears a striking resemblance to the composite Hallowell pieced together from missionary accounts dating to the early contact period in Canada's northeast. Among the more perceptive of these observations, and very much to the point, is one credited to Father Paul Le Jeune, a leading Jesuit in what was then called New France. Writing of the Montagnais with whom he lived in the late 1630s, the cleric comments that "It is strange to see how well these people agree outwardly, and how they hate each other within. They do not often get angry and fight with one another, but in the depths of their hearts they intend a great deal of harm." That harm, he remarks further, invariably results from sorcery, noting that "I hardly ever see any of them die who does not think he has been bewitched."[34] The consistency of these reports, and other anecdotal evidence from the period, are suggestive of a conservative cultural tendency among northern Algonkians, including the Ojibwa, a bent whose principal psychological manifestation has been the long-term persistence of behavioural and emotional traits linked to sorcery-related anxieties. The statements of seventeenth-century missionaries and twentieth-century anthropologists attest to this propensity, the public face of everyday interactions, at once amiable and equanimous to a fault, disguising the presence of suspicions and tensions bubbling just beneath the surface. "A visitor or outsider looking at the villagers would not guess this," Landes recalled of her own experiences of Ojibwa at Rainy River and elsewhere; "Their calm and/or merry masks are so notorious ... [that the] Potawatomi, for example, consider such expressions as the surest indicators of Ojibwa sorcery."[35]

While their descriptions largely agree, the few inferences to be drawn from Jenness's material favour an interpretation of the configuration that is closer to Hallowell's than to the one Landes offers.[36] All three read it as indicative of a highly individuated personality, one whose formation is fostered in a culture emphasizing self-reliance over interdependency. As such, it contributes to a society that is weakly integrated beyond the confines of family. In Landes' estimation, however, the orientation derives, first and foremost, from the conditions of social isolation under which livelihood is obtained during the long winter season, a time when game is scarce and when subsistence is pursued most effectively by relatively small and highly mobile family groupings. Theirs is a personality type "excellently adapted to the winter life," she notes, "but it finds itself in constant difficulties when custom thrusts a number of families into close proximity," as happens when they converge on villages during the warmer months.[37] For Jenness, on the other hand, religion serves as the chief catalyst, most importantly in the central belief that those faculties and strengths most crucial to securing a person's fortunes in every dimension of life are received as blessings from spirit-beings encountered in dreams. Like most of the

In Twilight and in Dawn

continent's indigenous peoples, the Parry islanders "paid great attention to dreams" and as youngsters nearing puberty were encouraged (and expected) by parents to seek them in accordance with prescribed practice. "The intense vision of childhood brought about by fasting and mental concentration was an experience ... seldom duplicated," Jenness explains, a formative experience "that forced itself on his memory nearly every day of his life." So momentous were these foundational dream experiences to development of the self that revealing their content to anyone risked loss of the blessings they bestowed. This was as much the case for the powers to restore health by retrieving lost souls as for those to induce illness, even death, by drawing souls away through sorcery – that most potent of gifts "which so obsessed their minds in pre-European times [and] still holds them in bondage today." Citing Jenness, Hallowell would later conclude that it is the pervasiveness of this fixation that accounts for the "atomism" of Ojibwa society, making it all but impossible "for people to get together when their outlook is colored by the possibility of malevolence." Given these propensities and the persistent fears motivating them, it is little wonder that community members were more inclined to trust in spirit guardians than in one another in order to preserve "life in the fullest sense, life in the sense of longevity, health and freedom from misfortune."[38]

◆

While his psychological observations fit neatly with those of later researchers, Jenness's conclusions on another aspect of Parry Island life put him squarely at odds with an interpretation that had gone uncontested since the mid-teens. At issue was a historical question, albeit one with theoretical significance for anthropology and policy implications for Canada's administration of Aboriginal affairs: namely, whether a form of private property in land – the so-called family hunting territory – existed in Algonkian society before the arrival of Europeans, the majority view, or arose at some point afterward, as Jenness became the first anthropologist to argue.

Ethnologist Frank Speck, trained at Columbia under Boas, is generally credited with bringing the matter to light, describing similar forms among nine different northeastern groups with whom he did fieldwork between 1908 and 1913 and inferring even wider occurrence on the basis of sundry published reports. What he found was a system whereby individual families held "actual ownership" of sizeable, well-demarcated tracts of land, inherited in the male line "from time immemorial." Each family hunting band, as he conceived of the property-holding group, exercised rights to hunt, fish, and prevent trespass in its territory, and employed selective harvesting practices to conserve the wildlife resources, especially non-migratory species, on which they depended for survival. "The idea has always prevailed," Speck observed in prefacing his synoptic account of the findings, "that, in harmony with other primitive phenomena, the American Indians had little or no interest in the matter of claims and boundaries to the land which they inhabited. This notion has ... been generally presupposed for all native tribes who have followed a hunting life," he explains further, the result of a "common impression that a hunter has to range far, and wherever he may, to find game enough to support his family." Here, then, was authoritative proof to the contrary, a discovery that refuted evolutionist theories linking private forms of property to emergence of allegedly higher stages of culture and challenged prevailing public opinion in both Canada and the United States of Aboriginal peoples as improvident wanderers.[39] Other investigators working elsewhere in Algonkian country in the twenties and thirties, among them Father Cooper and two of Speck's students, Hallowell and D.S. Davidson, reported similar results and drew similar conclusions about the institution's pre-contact beginnings. Therefore when Jenness, pursuing the same line of inquiry, presented evidence to the contrary in 1932, he sparked a decades-long debate over the timing of its development, its distribution, and a raft of subsidiary issues, some still current today.[40]

Interested in the general problem since joining the Anthropological Division, Jenness had investigated land-use practices during his Athapaskan fieldwork in British Columbia before taking them up again in the Algonkian context. He also instructed Osgood to do the same on the Mackenzie, particularly regarding family hunting territories per se.[41] In each case, what his own researches revealed was that the rights Speck claimed were held by individual families were, by ancient custom, vested in a more inclusive grouping: the band in Parry Island and Sekani society, and the clan among the Wet'suwet'en. Sekani families were alone in having freedom to stake out hunting and fishing grounds within their band's territory for the annual round of subsistence activities. On the Bulkley, clan chiefs controlled common fishing berths and divided hunting grounds among members. Finally, on Parry Island, he learned that hunters gathered in the fall every year to settle among themselves where each family would spend the long winter months; places for warmer-weather occupations – fishing, tapping sugar maples, and gathering wild rice – were open to all.[42]

"Dr Speck ... has recorded family hunting territories among all the Algonkian tribes of eastern Canada," Jenness observed, "even among the Ojibwa" in the forested interior east of Georgian Bay, where the American worked during the summer of 1913. "[B]ut this appears to have been a development of the last two or three hundred years, since the advent of the fur trade," its emergence attributed to a confluence of factors ranging from steady demand for beaver and other fur-bearers, and with it, growth of "special interest in the districts with which [families] were most familiar," to a steadily shrinking territorial base owing to the encroachment of white settlers and to land surrender treaties.[43] Even then, despite centuries-long pressure on the region's peoples and resources, conditions "have progressed half, and only half, the distance towards individual ownership," a fact attested to by the adamant assertions of local elders that the band itself had never relinquished communal control of its territory, or what remained of it. However, in more recent times, the band has taken to granting what amount to usufructuary rights in certain tracts to those of its members who continue to rely on hunting and trapping, an arrangement effectively akin to a "permanent lease." Maple groves, by contrast, have remained an open resource, prompting Jenness to remark that the Ojibwa here have been "more tenacious of some of their old communistic practices than their kinsmen elsewhere, although the reason remains obscure."[44]

Apart from his ethnographic reports, Jenness contributed nothing further in print to the ensuing debate, although his findings bolstered those few scholars who were beginning to challenge Speck's main contentions on the basis of their own researches. Arguments and counterarguments of decidedly theoretical stripe featured in the proceedings, as did contested readings of often-ambiguous seventeenth-century documents bearing on Algonkian practices.[45] The problem of when the family hunting territory system (and its various analogues) developed was finally, and decisively, laid to rest in the mid-fifties thanks to Eleanor Leacock, one of a rising generation of anthropologists who were highly critical of the brand of anti-evolutionary and anti-materialist thought that had dominated the discipline for the past half-century and had featured prominently in Speck's work. Her cogent analysis of the extant historical record, coupled with first-hand ethnographic evidence gathered in the course of dissertation fieldwork with Montagnais at Natashquan, in southern Labrador, made a convincing case that hunting territories were in fact a post-contact development, emerging as a response to the fur trade and its effects on wildlife resources, much as Jenness argued two decades earlier.[46]

THE SCHEME THAT WENT WRONG

Practical matters, not scholarly ones, were on Frank Speck's mind when he first wrote about hunting territories and conservation practices back in the teens, putting his findings on the record in defence of what was then a fairly controversial proposition: that Algonkians – indeed, Aboriginal peoples generally – were, and remained, highly capable stewards of their lands and resources and therefore should be allowed to continue managing them without government interference. He came away from pre-war fieldwork convinced that provincial game regulations, coupled with white encroachment on traditional hunting and trapping grounds, particularly in more southerly precincts, were steadily undermining the integrity of this age-old system. Unchecked, its erosion was destined to work ever-greater hardships on community health and welfare, while depleting government coffers through needless expenditures on relief and other subsidies. The groups he visited "have quite definite claims to their habitat," Speck wrote, claims that might "prove to have some value in the field of Indian administration." Nonetheless, he sidestepped the politically sensitive question of whether individualized ownership of hunting territories constituted a form of property under Canadian law. Instead, during the teens, his attentions were directed toward less contentious aspects of the problem as he involved himself in a successful petition aimed at easing certain provincial restrictions on trapping in the Lac St Jean region of Quebec, and in providing assistance to the Temagami Ojibwa band in their long-stymied demands for inclusion under the same 1850 treaty that had created the Parry Island reserve.[47] Starting in the mid-twenties, however, Speck and Father Cooper joined forces in an attempt to press for changes touching on the complex matter of property rights, urging Ottawa's official recognition of the hunting territory system "by some form of leasing or land patent or by some form of recognition similar to that given for mining claims." A guarantee of this type, Cooper observed, "would lead in a relatively short time to restocking of the land and to the return of the Indians as a body ... to economic independence and self-support."[48]

By the time their lobbying began, a substantial amount of ethnographic evidence had been compiled on Algonkians from Labrador to Ontario, including maps showing the boundaries of individual hunting ranges. That was the easy part. Convincing the government to adopt the proposed changes, on the other hand, was no mean feat, since the Indian Affairs establishment, and its largely indifferent political masters, were loathe to countenance deviations from a path whose endpoint – complete assimilation – had been enshrined in law and policy since Confederation. Sapir had learned this before the First World War when he marshalled the support of leading northwest coast specialists in protesting the federal prohibition of potlatching. The ban, on the books since 1884, had been imposed as a means to stamp out "reactionary elements" and "stubborn paganism" and had been the focus of grassroots resistance from the beginning. Five years elapsed before amendments

In Twilight and in Dawn

to the law were made, but they resulted in a pyrrhic victory for those calling for outright repeal: potlatch activities were changed from indictable to summary offenses, a move that empowered local Indian agents to act as both prosecutor and judge, and to mete out sentences at their own discretion.[49]

In its way, the issue of hunting territories was equally charged, although the reluctance of the Department of Indian Affairs to move on Speck and Cooper's recommendations not only revealed sharp contradictions between policy and practice but visited a cruel irony on the people those policies were supposed to help. Obsessed with making Native people economically self-sufficient in order to reduce its own expenditures, the department went to considerable lengths to turn hunters into farmers or, better still, into wage-earning (and tax paying) members of society's mainstream. Consistent with this ambition, it demanded compliance with provincial hunting regulations and even argued that those regulations superseded the rights to hunt and fish guaranteed by treaty. In the 1920s, however, Duncan Campbell Scott, the ranking Indian Affairs bureaucrat, publically acknowledged the necessity of granting "special hunting privileges for Indians in the outlying districts where other sufficient employment is not available" in order to curb the expense of relieving destitute cases.[50] This, of course, was precisely the situation to be found across a wide swathe of northern Algonkian country and precisely the aim of the anthropologists' proposals, yet no action was taken. Scott had a well-deserved reputation for tight-fisted management of his department, tunnel vision when it came to making and administering virtually every aspect of policy, and an aversion to taking counsel from people outside his circle, including the country's anthropologists. As he made patently evident in 1927, "There is no intention of changing the well-established policy of dealing with Indians and Indian affairs in this country."[51]

From its inception, the Anthropological Division's relationship with Indian Affairs had been an awkward one, the inevitable outcome of the quite different interests each had in Aboriginal peoples and their cultures. Owing to the sort of work they did, and where it was done, anthropologists could hardly miss noticing the outward effects of the government's controlling hand in the day-to-day life of local communities. Nor could they fail to notice the social and emotional effects of these policies on individuals, especially in areas where Ottawa's all-out assault on their customs and traditions was still in its early stages. As topics of research, however, such matters were deemed out of bounds, the government holding that the role of the anthropologists in its employ should be restricted to salvaging the remnants of cultures whose final eradication was the ultimate goal of state policy. That said, in rare circumstances, Indian Affairs sought the division's assistance in dealing with specific policy-related issues. One such occasion involved Scott's informal request that Barbeau look into the still-simmering potlatch problem while he was on the Skeena River in 1920. Worried that compliance might fuel local suspicions ruinous to his colleague's work in the region, and aware that some of Barbeau's observations on the institution had already featured in House of Commons debate, Sapir counselled him against reporting to Scott unless specifically directed to do so by Geological Survey management. "I hate to have to make this rule so explicit," he explained, "but I am afraid that if we do not follow it very literally we will find ourselves drifting into the position of genteel spies for the Department of Indian Affairs. We cannot afford to be misunderstood by any Indians in Canada."[52]

For the record, Scott's department also had no tolerance for independent researchers interested in policy-related issues, a position made clear when Speck's associate, D.S. Davidson, was reported to have "fomented trouble among the Indians" during 1926 fieldwork in northern Québec. "While I am always pleased to lend any assistance ... in the advancement of scientific investigations," he wrote of the alleged incident to Jenness, "I feel that I am justified in expecting those who are working among the Indians to refrain from any interference in affairs pertaining solely to Department administration." To forestall the possibility of future trouble, Jenness made a practice of advising foreign researchers to seek approval from Indian Affairs before visiting reserves and to steer well clear of "anything relating to the administration of the Indians."[53]

Along with restrictions on what they could investigate, division personnel, as civil servants, were expected to refrain from offering public comment critical of state policies and to avoid outright even the slightest taint of political partisanship connected with their duties. Though it went against the grain, much as survey censorship of field reports did, rules regarding what could and could not be said were safely managed by a mix of self-censorship and judicious tip-toeing around potentially fraught issues. This is evident in the pages of Jenness's professional publications, practically all of which required official sanction before submission, including pieces destined for scholarly and popular presses. It cropped up in his correspondence, too. When *The Indians of Canada* was nearing publication, for instance, a question about present conditions in the Athapaskan subarctic from Russian ethnographer Julia Averkieva prompted his recommendation that she consult the book's chapter on Indian-white relations. But, he quickly added, keep in mind "that this book will be a Government publication, and that as a Government official I cannot express my opinion on the policy adopted by the department which administers all Indian Affairs." Tellingly, the volume's 400-

plus pages contain no mention of treaties, the Indian Act, or residential schools, even in the chapter he recommended to Averkieva. Similar inquiries typically garnered equally circumspect replies, though from time to time he offered a frank opinion, but always off the record.[54]

By contrast, the injunction against partisan involvement represented a stickier problem, usually because the line between professional interests and responsibilities and personal beliefs was easily blurred. Though hardly unique to anthropologists, the fieldwork experience was, and remains, conducive to conflating the three, depending as it does on gaining people's trust, and sometimes their friendship, by respecting them as individuals and empathizing with their personal and collective struggles. Jenness's defence of Wet'suwet'en medicine can be seen in this light, as can Speck's of hunting territories and Sapir's of potlatching. Given the very public nature of the last, however, it is hardly surprising that Sapir wondered if his involvement might be perceived as politically partisan. "I do not think being Gov. employees will matter," advised James Teit, then on the division payroll and similarly committed to the protest. "We are not mixing in politics or taking sides openly with any political party. The potlatch as whether it should or should not be is altogether a non-political question." Strictly speaking, this may have been so. Still, their actions were hardly shorn of political ramifications since they were mustering moral and scientific support for Aboriginal politicians whose own tactics included appealing directly to Parliament.[55]

Scott retired in 1932, ending a long career with Indian Affairs that included twenty years as its deputy superintendent general. Banking on a new style of leadership as the best chance to overhaul what had become a hidebound, myopic system, a reform-minded Jenness, with strong encouragement from Cooper, agreed to put his name forward as a candidate for the vacancy. His letter of application, half a page long, was sent directly to R.B. Bennett, Canada's prime minister.[56]

For someone who tended to find more misery than satisfaction in administrative tasks, even entertaining this type of career move seems oddly out of character. In reality, it reflected his emerging interest in anthropology as an applied social science, a specialization that began taking shape in Britain and the United States during the twenties and would blossom during the Depression years under the munificent patronage of publically spirited philanthropies such as the Laura Spellman Rockefeller Foundation. Cambridge-trained A.R. Radcliffe-Brown, whom Jenness first met when he spoke at one of Robert Marett's Oxford Anthropological Society gatherings, was in the vanguard of this development, having pioneered a systematic method for analyzing social interaction that he promoted as a valuable tool for addressing contemporary social problems.[57] By chance, the two crossed paths some twenty year later at the Pacific Science Congress in Java, a leisurely setting in which to discuss the Englishman's views on putting anthropological expertise to practical advantage, particularly in the field of native administration. While there, Jenness also made the acquaintance of Robert E. Park, a University of Chicago sociologist best known for adopting an ecological model to study processes of urbanization and immigrant adjustment in the United States.[58] The experience clearly registered with him. So much so, in fact, that when the Depression ushered in severe cutbacks affecting ordinary activities in 1931, he took it as an opportunity to move into policy-oriented research. Jenness may well have been thinking about undertaking a scaled-down version of the study that produced the Meriam Report, a wide-ranging, government-sponsored investigation into conditions among Indians in the United States. Something similar was desperately needed in Canada, but persistent sensitivities ruled that out until the very first national survey was finally commissioned in the sixties.[59] Though less pertinent to his main areas of expertise, and a far cry from the division's usual fare, he was given permission to take up a project that was equally timely: a study of demography, immigration, and the future prospects for Canada's economic development. The subject, he soon realized, was "horribly complex," something "only a first-rate economist ought to tackle." Persevering despite not knowing "one blessed thing about economics," two papers were in print by 1933, one on national population potentials, the other on fisheries. Ever wary of the pitfall of straying into matters of public policy, however, he harboured doubts about receiving authorization to publish at all. "Since [the first piece] touches on some very delicate topics," he told the director of the National Development Bureau, "the Minister might chop my head off."[60]

Enthusiasm for applied work aside, Jenness's decision to pursue Scott's old job came during what was an unusually stressful patch in his professional life, the residue of protracted squabbles with museum director William Collins that eventuated in his resignation as division chief in the waning days of 1930. A spate of letters to colleagues attest to his uncharacteristically gloomy mood, bitterly complaining to one that "there is very little sympathy for Anthropologists in our Department," to another that "things are so unsatisfactory that I may seek another position elsewhere." As appealing as a change of scene may have been, the idea of risking the relative security of a government pay cheque at the very moment the country was in the powerful grip of its economic emergency, seemed foolhardy at best. "It will not be easy to find a post which

In Twilight and in Dawn

will offer an equivalent salary," he told Thomas McIlwraith, grateful that his colleague had inquired into a teaching appointment for him at Toronto, yet doubtful that any such position would materialize there, or elsewhere, in Canada. He had also been mulling over the idea of moving back to New Zealand, but even that left him conflicted, confessing to McIlwraith that faced with the choice, "I shall hate to leave this institution for I think I have now a moderate knowledge of anthropological work [here] and [the Pacific] will mean breaking into a new field."[61] In the circumstances, the Indian Affairs job must have looked very promising indeed, affording security and, more importantly, a real chance to put his knowledge to good use in improving the lot of a population systematically ill-served by government policy-makers and administrators for generations. In the bargain, it had possibilities for broadening the scope of federally funded anthropology to encompass applied areas of research, finding appropriate solutions to the sorts of problems Scott had effectively prevented the division from investigating for two decades.

A month after submitting his application, Scott's successor was announced. The successful candidate was Harold W. McGill, a physician from Calgary whose resumé included two stints with Indian Affairs as medical officer on the nearby Sarcee reserve. Given the way high-level political appointments tend to work, however, McGill's principal qualification for the job was his 1930 election as a Conservative member of Alberta's Legislative Assembly, representing a riding in his hometown. By odd coincidence, Prime Minister Bennett was a Conservative, and a Calgarian, too. "I am not worrying over the scheme that went wrong," Jenness informed Cooper, replying to his colleague's evident disappointment with the outcome; but "I would have liked to have entered a wider field and tried to do something for the Indians."[62] Within months, a small army of anthropologists in the United States were given a chance to do that very thing when President Franklin D. Roosevelt named John Collier to be the country's new Commissioner of Indian Affairs. Collier called on their considerable expertise to good purpose in helping to implement the sweeping reforms of what came to be called the Indian New Deal, a program guided in large part by the findings of the Meriam Report. Many found employment in the Applied Anthropology Unit set up within the Bureau of Indian Affairs.[63]

The following year, Jenness accepted an invitation from one of Collier's associates to attend a conference in Pittsburgh where the commissioner spoke of the road ahead, and especially of the central importance of Native involvement in achieving fundamental change in every aspect of their lives. Favourably impressed by what he had learned, on returning to Ottawa he briefed McGill on the proceedings and then provided him with copies of two documents pertaining to the recently enacted Indian Reorganization Act. The centrepiece of America's new approach, the act's central aim was ending the nation's long-standing assimilation project and restoring tribal autonomy over their lands, governing arrangements, and social and cultural affairs. When he forwarded the material, Jenness's accompanying cover letter concluded with an apology: "Probably you do not wish to be troubled." Its author had good reason to suspect that in selecting McGill, the prime minister had opted for the status quo at Indian Affairs. He was correct.[64] There was to be no new deal for Aboriginal peoples in Canada, at least not for the foreseeable future.

◈

After four years of near-dormancy and lingering uncertainties among staff over its very survival, the National Museum began to revive in the mid-thirties as funds to support research activities were included once more in federal appropriations. Apart from the temporary reprieve that had allowed him to participate in the Pacific Science Congress in Vancouver, Jenness, like his colleagues, had sat out the depths of the Depression in Ottawa, attending to office work. In his case, this meant a fairly steady diet of writing, an effort that yielded the first edition of *The Indians of Canada*, monographs on the Wet'suwet'en, Sekani, and Parry Island Ojibwa, a grammar of western Eskimoan dialects, and the edited volume of Congress papers, *The American Aborigines*, before 1933 was out. In the midst of all this, he also began charting a new line of ethnographic investigation for himself, one he hoped to take up just as soon as conditions allowed. That long-anticipated opportunity finally arrived in September 1935 when he embarked for British Columbia to begin six months of fieldwork with the Coast Salish, a people "sadly neglected" by anthropologists for well over thirty years.[65]

Rather than accompany him, as her husband originally intended, Eileen Jenness took their three sons overseas for an extended stay in Germany instead, remaining there through the following spring. In retrospect, the choice of destination seems curious, to say the least. One thing is certain: neither parent was motivated by approval of the direction events had taken following Hitler's rise to power in 1933. Appreciation of German high culture, on the other hand, loomed large in the formative experiences of both, she cultivating a lasting fondness for its architecture and fine arts while touring the Continent as a teenager in the company of a well-to-do aunt and he, thanks in no small part to George von Zedlitz's guidance, well-acquainted with the works of Goethe, Heine, Schiller, and other luminaries of letters and philosophy. Now hoping to encourage a similar appreciation in their children, John, the eldest at thirteen, was enrolled at a progressive, co-educational secondary school in Marquartstein, a small provincial town in the Bavarian countryside, for what amounted to a year of immersion in the German language. Meanwhile, his mother and younger brothers took up residence in nearby Munich, renting rooms in a local pension. At five, Robert was too young to gain much from the experience, but ten-year-old Stuart thrived, taking piano lessons and happily making the rounds of the city's museums and concert halls with his equally enthusiastic mother. At the height of winter, the three travelled to Seefeld, a village in the Austrian Tyrol, for a month's respite in the sunshine and fresh mountain air and took side trips to Salzburg and Vienna. Relaying family news to Ethel Kenny, his secretary at the museum, Jenness expressed deep satisfaction at the apparent success of "our experiment," proudly explaining that his middle son "almost cried when Mrs Jenness would not take him to a 5 hour performance of Wagner's Lohengrin!" "I'll be quite broke before they return," he added; "However, it will be well worth while."[66]

With his family safely settled in Europe, Jenness began winter-long fieldwork an ocean and a continent away in the temperate surroundings of southeastern Vancouver Island's Georgia Strait shoreline. Lands abutting the strait here and on the mainland opposite encompass the territory of a mosaic of separately named peoples whose several languages and numerous dialects, combined with those spoken around Washington's Puget Sound, make up the Coast Salish branch of the Salishan language family. Living to the east of them in the rugged country of British Columbia's south-central interior and in adjacent portions of Washington, Idaho, and Montana are the Interior Salish, a grouping of nations characterized by similar linguistic diversity. Where and when the original stock arose and subsequently separated are anthropological problems of some longevity. Drawing on his own findings and those of Jesup Expedition colleagues Harlan Smith and James Teit, Boas proposed inland origins and a comparatively recent expansion toward salt water. Once established in the resource-rich coastal zone, he envisioned the migrants' interior-adapted, and less complex, proto-Salishan way of life undergoing major changes, primarily a consequence of absorbing northwest coast cultural influences, especially the potlatch and hierarchical social order, from Kwakiutl and other neighbouring peoples. After holding for more than half a century, in the 1970s this widely accepted interpretation of regional culture history started to unravel, challenged by new archaeological evidence pointing to a developmental sequence with deep roots in the area of Georgia Strait that had spread into the interior with retreating glaciers, perhaps as many as ten thousand years ago. According to this view, the form of Coast Salish culture in existence at the outset of the contact era in the late eighteenth century probably emerged sometime around 500 AD. As Boas initially suggested, some of its more conspicuous features were similar to those found among peoples resident elsewhere on the Pacific coast: autonomous villages composed of extended families – or "houses," in Jenness's phrasing, likening them to the houses of European nobility – whose members shared winter quarters and claimed hereditary rights in fishing places, ancestral names, and various types of esoteric knowledge; society's division into nobles, commoners, and slaves; reliance on fish, above all numerous species of salmon, as the mainstay of existence; and, of course, the integral institution of potlatching. There were differences, too, including the absence of hereditary chiefs, clans, and totem poles, and a custom of reckoning descent through both male and female lines rather than through one or the other alone.[67]

Other than Boas's summary accounts, the principal source on the Coast Salish in British Columbia into the thirties had been the writings of Charles Hill-Tout, a British ex-patriot schoolteacher, and amateur ethnologist whose turn-of-the-century researches into language and culture concentrated on several mainland and Vancouver Island groups. Even so, a decade later Sapir listed the Coast Salish among a half-dozen Northwest Coast peoples about whom "we are relatively uninformed," at least by the standards set in his mentor's "exhaustive series of studies" of the Kwakiutl and, to a lesser degree, in the work of John Swanton on Haida and Tlingit.[68] With a view to filling in the gaps, Sapir had launched his own Canadian career with fieldwork among the Nootka, at Port Alberni, in the summer of 1910, the first of several trips he would make to that quarter before the outbreak of the First World War and the very first investigation conducted under Anthropological Division auspices. Four years later, Barbeau travelled to Prince Rupert to begin what turned into a decades-long involvement with Tsimshian speakers on the coast and landward in the valleys of the Skeena and Nass. After the war, Sapir shifted attention to the Coast Salish and to their geographically isolated linguistic kin, the Bella Coola. Smith was delegated to begin fieldwork on the latter in 1921, eventually making five trips to their territory for studies of material culture and archaeology. Thomas McIlwraith followed Smith a year later, the novice ethnologist meticulously documenting Bella Coola social organization and ceremonial life over a span of three seasons. 1921 was also the year Sapir planned to make a start on the Coast Salish proper, asking his friend Paul Radin, now in California and once again between jobs, to take on the project. Given his tenuous finances, the mercurial Radin was willing. Just weeks later, however, he learned that survey management would not authorize a contract, ostensibly, a discouraged Sapir explained, because the proposed work was purely scientific in nature and thus of no tangible benefit to the country's post-war economic recovery. "The policy which dominates the Survey at present completely disgusts me," he griped, clearly frustrated with the failure of peacetime's long-awaited return to improve the division's flagging fortunes.[69] For the second time since 1929, it fell to Jenness to take on research unavoidably postponed for want of resources, this time after a hiatus of fourteen years.

Two thousand Coast Salish, divided into a dozen or so separate named groups, were resident on Vancouver Island in the 1930s. Their twenty-six reserves, postage stamp–sized parcels, in keeping with provincial practice, lay along the scenic sweep of coastline from Sooke to Comox, at the head of Cowichan Bay, near the town of Duncan and inland on Cowichan Lake. By the end of December, Jenness had visited several of the more northern of these places to gather comparative material, commuting from one to the next in a truck provided courtesy of the Geological Survey. (So much for his days as a horse-and-buggy ethnographer, at least in the literal sense of Robert Lowie's colourful term.) However, the majority of his first three months in the field was spent with the Saanich, a people "everybody appears to have skipped" in previous researches across the island's southern precincts.[70] Numbering just under three hundred, their population was unevenly distributed among four reserves on the eponymous Saanich peninsula. Tsawout, the most populous of them at 106 inhabitants, stood on the peninsula's eastern shore, the others – Pauquachen, Tsartlip, and Tsekum – faced Saanich Inlet, on the west. All were within a short drive from Sidney, the port town where Jenness opted to lodge at a local hotel, a practice he would repeat throughout the duration of his fieldwork.[71] Fewer than ten miles to the south was the provincial capital of Victoria, a city that had grown up on the site selected by Hudson's Bay Company chief factor James Douglas, later governor of the Vancouver Island colony, for a new regional headquarters, Fort Victoria, back in 1843. The city was also home to the province's archives, whose holdings Jenness periodically scoured for pertinent historical documents, and to William Newcombe, a friend, anthropological enthusiast, and semi-official collaborator whose familiarity with many of the Coast Salish communities provided him with practical intelligence that eased the oft-trying task of finding knowledgeable consultants and interpreters. William's interest in native cultures was something of a family affair: Charles, his physician father, built a successful second career collecting ethnographic artifacts for major museums in the United States and elsewhere.

Among the various elders he interviewed that autumn, the time Jenness spent working with one, a man called Old David, proved especially informative, and productive, more than likely a function of his (unverifiable) claim to be 105 years of age.[72] If true, that would have made him a young adult when the Saanich surrendered their ancestral lands to the Crown under one of the fourteen treaties Governor Douglas signed with groups in southern and central Vancouver Island between 1850 and 1854. Moreover, he probably would have known the mix of fear and bravado sparked by the appearance of hostile raiding parties, mostly Kwakiutl, who descended on Salish villages to avenge grievances and take captives, as slaves, a practice that finally petered out in the 1860s. In any case, he, like other elders who allowed the anthropologist to take down their stories, was certainly old enough to have passed many winters with his extended family inside a shed-roofed, post-and-beam house, immense structures of red cedar, some upwards of sixty feet in length by forty wide, long since replaced by dwellings of far humbler dimension and design. He would have participated in potlatches, before Ottawa enacted measures to suppress them, and anticipated the return of whaling canoes from the waters of Georgia Strait, an activity reserved for Saanich and neighbouring Songhees hunters whose high rank and specialized knowledge equipped them to wield the harpoon with lethal effect.[73] "My Indians are coming across nicely with information," Jenness reported after just a month in the field; "I already have enough material to write a fair-sized report, but of course it has to be checked with other Indians." Over the following weeks, that checking led him north from Sidney to several Cowichan communities in the vicinity of Duncan and finally into Nanaimo territory, farther down the island's eastern shore. What came of the effort was indeed substantial, a collection of ethnographic evidence detailing traditional Saanich material culture and the annual subsistence round, family and village organization, the life course and associated rites of passage, social and economic functions of the potlatch, and beliefs about the natural world and humankind's place within it.[74]

After tying up some loose ends on the island in mid-January, Jenness redirected his attention to the profusion of Salishan communities scattered throughout the province's lower (i.e., southwestern) mainland. Apart from a few on the outskirts of Vancouver, most of their reserves lay along a stretch of the lower Fraser River from its mouth on Georgia Strait to the entrance to the precipitous Fraser Canyon, a distance of some one hundred miles. Groups whose ancient homelands encompass this broad, fertile portion of the valley describe themselves as Sto:lo, people of the river. Halq'eméylem, a close relative of Hul'qumi'num, is their lingua franca, spoken among nearly all Vancouver Island Salish. The exceptions are groups in the vicinity of Victoria, traditional territory of the Saanich, Sooke, and Songhees, who speak dialects of a language called Northern Straits.[75] Despite the ample possibilities, his initial weeks in the area were mostly discouraging. The first of several disappointments occurred at Musqueam, inside Vancouver's city limits, where he learned that practically all "the old men" were away from home, not to return for days, possibly longer. Soon thereafter, near Port Hammond, a small town less than an hour's drive up the valley, he ran into a different sort of problem: the wife of an elder, who was himself "willing enough" to answer his visitor's questions, let it be known that she was strictly opposed to his doing so. By month's end, the situation started to brighten when he motored even farther upriver to a reserve close to Chilliwack, where he passed a week with an agreeable fellow called Old Cyrus. However, it was on his return to the Port Hammond area in the early days of February that things finally, and decisively, changed for the better. Much, much better. "I struck a splendid informant" at a tiny place called Katzie, a septuagenarian and renowned "medicine-man" named Peter Pierre. As he explained to Newcombe, the elder's knowledge of religious belief and ritual far exceeded that of anyone "I encountered ... on the island, or at Chilliwack." Years later, Jenness recalled Old Pierre's memory as seemingly "inexhaustible ... I think he must have lain awake every night during the five weeks our association lasted, preparing, like a conscientious professor, the lesson he would give his pupil the next morning."[76] With Pierre's son Simon agreeably taking on the role of interpreter, what eventuated from their collaboration – a monograph entitled *The Faith of a Coast Salish Indian* – was an ethnographic account unlike any to emerge from Jenness's previous fieldwork and remains a singular interpretation of Salishan thought and practice.

The subject matters that engaged the two through weeks of regular morning sessions were, in and of themselves, fairly standard fare: the order of the cosmos; souls and other intrinsic qualities of animate life, both human and non-human; guardian spirits and the derivation of sacred knowledge and the powers of medicine; observances fostering individual and collective well being; rituals marking passage from one stage of life to the next. The differences lay in Old Pierre's studied mastery of traditional, often recondite knowledge, invariably recounted in perceptively observed detail, and his ability to organize and integrate various strands of belief into a coherent expression of world view. Central to his exegesis was a lengthy mythic cycle depicting the story of creation and the sources of moral precepts and customary laws governing all of existence. While a good many of the conceptual themes and events featuring in his portrayal were common to the cosmogonic traditions of other Coast Salish peoples, its conception of an anthropomorphic supreme deity, depicted as the "creator of all things," set Old Pierre's version noticeably apart from virtually all of its counterparts save that of the Bella Coola. Jenness wondered if this lone exception might point to the trait's northern derivation, the central feature of an ancient belief system brought southward by the region's founding Salishan population, as Franz Boas had first proposed over thirty years earlier. Far simpler, of course, was the likelihood that the Katzie high deity represented a recent accretion, one stemming from missionary teachings introduced in the second half of the nineteenth century and subsequently reworked into an "orderly mythology" built atop an "imported monotheistic base." While the weight of evidence Jenness gathered elsewhere on the Fraser and across the Strait, on Vancouver Island, indicated much the same conclusion, his Katzie teacher held firm in his convictions to the contrary, convinced in his own mind that "He Who Dwells Above" was in fact indigenous in origin, not the distillate of Christian doctrine assimilated in relatively recent times.[77]

On taking leave of Peter and Simon Pierre for the final time in early March, Jenness enthused about an early return to Coast Salish research, his Katzie experience convincing him that a second six months would prove as fruitful as the first. For the time being, however, he had reached the limit of his stamina, the daily commute between Vancouver and Katzie, a round trip of forty-plus miles, draining him of energy. "Don't be alarmed if I go to sleep every afternoon in my office during [my] first week" back in Ottawa, he kidded Ethel Kenney; "just tell visitors I am in conference!!!"[78]

In what, by now, was an all-too-familiar story, the hoped-for second season never came to pass, initially pushed aside, as the next chapter explains, by a host of new responsibilities and then, at decade's end, by the outbreak of world war and the museum's relapse into dormancy. Also shunted aside was the bulk of ethnographic material gathered during the autumn among the Saanich and their Vancouver Island neighbours. Originally drafted as two reports, some four hundred typescript pages in total, neither ever found its way into print.[79] Happily, Peter Pierre's masterful interpretation of Katzie thought met a different fate, though not until the mid-fifties. By then, a new generation of anthropologists, most trained at American universities, were hard at work reviving research on Salishans and other First Peoples of Canada's Pacific coast, another in a long list of projects left in abeyance since the division's founding. Introduced to Jenness, now retired, when he spent a term at the University of British Columbia in the autumn of 1951, two of those anthropologists, Wilson Duff and Wayne Suttles, received his permission to ready the manuscript for publication. *The Faith of a Coast Salish Indian* appeared four years later, issued under the provincial museum's imprint.[80]

CHAPTER THIRTEEN

Behind High Walls,
1936–1948

WOULD-BE REVOLUTIONARY

Being denied Duncan Campbell Scott's office at Indian Affairs in 1932 did little to dampen Jenness's interest in nudging federal policy off its present course. What he lacked was a sympathetic ear anywhere in the upper echelons of official Ottawa. That changed, at least in theory, not long after his return from Salish fieldwork, the outcome of an unlikely, if fortuitous, convergence of events. The stage was set when in 1936 the freshly elected Liberals, under William Lyon Mackenzie King, implemented a major internal reorganization of government, merging the Departments of Immigration, Interior, Mines (including the National Museum and Geological Survey), and Indian Affairs – a demotion from its former, free-standing departmental status – into a massive ministry called the Department of Mines and Resources. When the dust settled, geologist Charles Camsell emerged as the mega-department's deputy minister, the position he had held at Mines since 1920.[1] Recognizing in Camsell a well-placed and potentially open-minded ally, Jenness decided to test the waters by sending him a set of proposals he had drawn up for reforming state policy. Deeming them worthy of serious consideration, the deputy forwarded the recommendations to Scott's successor, Harold McGill, and requested that Jenness be given an opportunity to discuss his ideas with officials of the renamed Indian Affairs Bureau.[2]

Even with hope revived for bringing desperately needed changes to a sclerotic administrative system, Jenness was again contemplating leaving the museum, this time for something definite: the offer of the William Wyse chair in anthropology at Cambridge, due to be vacated shortly by its incumbent, Thomas C. Hodson. Having spent most of summer 1936 in England, where he had attended the British Association meetings at Blackpool and visited museums, including the Cambridge Museum of Archaeology and Ethnology, he certainly had had opportunity to sound out those directly involved about his chances. He was suitably qualified for the job, Cambridge then preferring to put career government men, not academics, in the Wyse chair. Family lore has it that the offer was turned down for financial reasons, Eilleen evidently convinced that the salary, £1,200 per year, didn't warrant uprooting her family from their long-time home. This roughly accords with what Jenness told Henry Skinner about the situation, mentioning to his New Zealand friend that looking after the education of three young sons took precedence over all else. Freed of that responsibility, he allowed, retirement, rather than relocating overseas, would be his preference.[3] The chair was eventually given to J.H. Hutton who, like his predecessor, had been a career officer in the Indian Civil Service.[4] Though hardly equivalent to the prestige attached to a Cambridge professorship, four years later British anthropology recognized Jenness's record of accomplishment in the field of arctic studies by awarding him the Rivers Memorial Medal of the Royal Anthropological Institute.

For his part, Camsell was none too keen on the prospect of losing Jenness, not least because he had recently agreed to return to his former position as division chief on the death of William Collins. With Harlan Smith's retirement that same year, moreover, Jenness's resignation would further diminish what was already a depleted staff just as improving economic conditions were slowly resuscitating a long-moribund research program. To forestall the possibility, Camsell announced in December that the department was appointing Jenness as its permanent special consultant on Indian affairs. Responsible to the deputy, not to McGill, his duties – to be taken up over and above his regular work load – involved providing advice, undertaking investigations of existing policy-related problems, and, where appropriate, developing proposals "that in your opinion will conduce to the welfare and advancement of the Indian population."[5] Minister T.A. Crerar approved the appointment. Even so, this didn't deter the Civil Service Commission's chief bureaucrat from raising objections, the long-serving William Foran insisting that the consultancy entailed work already within Jenness's existing job description, and therefore did not warrant the requested pay increase. Camsell resolved the dispute by assuring Foran that "What is now proposed ... has to do with the economic and sociological problems of the Indians," matters quite separate from "scientific research" on anthropological and ethnological problems which is "in no way connected with the administration of Indian Affairs." The minister "is very anxious indeed to retain Mr Jenness," he added for good measure, having authorized an additional $500 per year as compensation for the extra work involved and, more to the point, as inducement not to accept the Cambridge professorship.[6]

"I am not sure yet whether the new job is going to be a sinecure only," Jenness told a colleague. "Actually I'm trying to stir up a revolution in the administration, but may find it beyond my power."[7] Had he succeeded in changing policy along the lines spelled out in his proposals, the result, if not revolutionary, would certainly have marked a shift in Ottawa's troubled relations with the country's Aboriginal peoples. His timing was premature, however, coming years before settlement of federal-provincial wrangling over taxation and other jurisdictional issues opened the door to wide-ranging economic and social reforms, including some in Indian Affairs.[8] For the moment, the deck was stacked against any sort of rethinking of existing policies and practices. Instead, what was officially expected of him amounted to institutional research: compiling and analyzing vital statistics, preparing demographic profiles, gathering data on rates of intermarriage and population increase among people of "pure" and "mixed" descent. These were tasks Jenness considered necessary, if secondary, to policy development itself, initially suggesting they be undertaken "by a competent statistician," not by him. McGill was perfectly satisfied with the job's limited scope, determined as he was to stick to the same well-worn path Scott had followed, showing little more than polite interest in the road his new consultant was urging be explored. But he did see a fine opportunity to draw on the anthropologist's "wide knowledge of Indian sociology, capabilities and present attainments in primitive industries" in order to advance one of the bureau's main objectives: fostering economic self-sufficiency by encouraging artisans to produce and sell crafts. Beyond that, he expected that Jenness would continue to answer inquiries about Native peoples from government and the public at large, something he already had been doing for many years.[9]

Despite the evident disconnect between what was originally promised and what, in fact, was actually delivered, Jenness stayed on as consultant until 1940, when a war-time government needed his services to deal with more urgent matters. In the meantime, his ambivalence, and frustration, remained undiminished. This comes through loud and clear in a March 1939 memorandum addressed to T.R.L. MacInnes, secretary of Indian Affairs, concerning participation in an upcoming international conference dealing with contemporary conditions among Indians in the United States and Canada. "Government officials who take part ... enter with their hands tied," he wrote, in thinly disguised reference to himself. "For political reasons, if for no other, they are not free to express their own opinions," opinions that, in his own case, were largely at odds with the general drift of existing federal policy. He wound up at-

tending, but insisted on doing so in the capacity of silent observer.[10] The
two-week event, held in Toronto and co-organized by his friend Thomas
McIlwraith, began on 4 September. Little did the planners know how
unfortunate this scheduling would turn out to be, coming three days
after the German army swept into Poland. Naturally enough, this stroke
of terrible luck left the proceedings all but unnoticed by a public whose
attentions were understandably drawn elsewhere. Nevertheless, the
event did gain certain notoriety for being the first of its kind to include
Natives among its delegates. Equally noteworthy, those same delegates,
from both sides of the border, put organizers and participants on notice that, in a democratic society, Aboriginal peoples have a right to
"develop a wide measure of self-expression and self-determination" in
seeking appropriate solutions to the many problems of reserve life, and
to gather for the purpose in settings "free of political, anthropological,
missionary, administrative, or other domination."[11]

Harold McGill was among the speakers at the ill-timed Toronto conference, presenting an overview of current Canadian policy. Its goal, he
said, "is simply this: so to treat our native races that they may become
self-supporting and enjoy thereby some degree of economic security and
increase their welfare and happiness besides being a source of strength
to the nation." While the language may differ, an 1837 report to Whitehall issued by Lord Gosford, governor general of British North America, conveyed much the same intent: "inducing the Indians to change
their present ways for more civilized Habits of Life." Linking both statements across a full century is the widely held (and slow-to-fade) public
perception of Aboriginals as child-like, lacking the habits of mind and
temperament necessary to govern themselves and their lands, and therefore needing protection from debasement and exploitation, and careful guidance in becoming "industrious, sober, and useful" members of
society at large.[12] Soon after Confederation, the means to realize these
ends were enshrined in the Indian Act, an instrument that defined who,
in law, is an Indian; the benefits and rights associated with that status,
including their surrender – the process known as enfranchisement;[13]
and the responsibilities constitutionally vested in the federal government and administered by Indian Affairs. The resulting arrangement
gave Ottawa near-total control over a population effectively reduced
to a condition of wardship – "minors in the eye of the law," in Scott's
paternalistic turn of phrase – and consigned to reserves intended to be
incubators of Western civilization.[14] Solely authorized to exercise that
control, Indian Affairs effectively operated as a "quasi-colonial govern-

ment," one whose subjects shared little in common with its officials, or, indeed, with Canadians in general, and were "deprived of the opportunity to exercise open political influence of its shortcomings and drawbacks" because they were denied the ordinary rights of citizenship.[15]

When resistance to the system broke out, as it frequently did during Scott's long tenure, the most common response was to tighten the reins, amending the Indian Act to make school attendance mandatory, for instance, or banning the potlatch and other customary practices or prohibiting fund-raising for pursuing legal claims against the government.[16] Arguably the most egregious use of the legislation came in 1920 when Scott sought an amendment providing for compulsory enfranchisement of individuals, or entire bands, whose continuing status under the act was judged "no longer in the interest of the public or the Indians." Up until this point, only about 350 people had exercised this option voluntarily, a proceeding requiring them, among other things, to prove they were self-supporting and had "ceased to follow the Indian way of life." Of these, nearly three-quarters of the cases had occurred after 1918 when certain modifications to qualifications were implemented. Speaking publically in defence of the more radical step now being proposed, a measure eliciting near-universal condemnation from Aboriginal groups and skepticism from opposition Liberal MPs, Scott argued that it was simply unconscionable to expect the Dominion to "continuously protect a class of people who are able to stand alone." "Our objective," he asserted, "is to continue until there is not a single Indian in Canada that has not been absorbed into the body politic, and there is no Indian question, and no Indian Department." A Conservative-dominated Parliament enacted compulsory enfranchisement, but the provision was quickly repealed in 1921 on the election of a new Liberal government.[17] The right to relinquish status on a voluntary basis went unchanged. The option continued to be as unattractive in the post-war years as it had been before, few willing to swap what security there was in treaty and other entitlements – including health care and education, such as they were, and exemption from taxation – for the uncertain future awaiting them in the mainstream. Judging by the realities faced by those who, for various reasons, were never covered by the Indian Act – estimated to comprise well over half of the country's Aboriginal population – that future was almost certain to be grim, haunted by impoverishment, landlessness, and racial discrimination. Unlike their on-reserve kin, non-status Indians and Métis, citizens in theory, were truly forgotten peoples, their existence all but invisible on the national stage.

Looking back on what had been accomplished over the span of sixty years, the last twenty under his own watch, Scott frankly admitted that his department continued to be "confronted with serious problems in the slow process of weaning the Indian from his primitive state," some problems attributed, in his view, to their susceptibility to the common temptations of life beyond the reserve, some to their ill-conceived desire to retain a sense of peoplehood. Nonetheless, he assured his readers, significant advances already had been achieved, and "the Government will in time reach the end of its responsibility as the Indians progress into civilization and finally disappear as a separate and distinct people."[18] Where the bureaucrat claimed progress, however, the anthropologist found failure, symptomatic, Jenness believed, of an organization mired in contradictions between its stated policy objectives, many of them long out-dated, and the ability of its approach to deliver the desired ends. Immediate culpability lay with a penny-pinching institutional culture – fittingly, Scott was a bookkeeper by trade – prepared to work only with the status quo in order to contain costs. Ultimate responsibility for these failures belonged to an indifferent political class and a largely uninformed and unquestioning citizenry. In the twenties and thirties, the "head of administration disliked [Indians] as people," Jenness would later claim, writing from the relatively safe haven of retirement. Meanwhile, "Parliament ... contented itself with voting whatever amount of money seemed necessary to fulfill ... treaty obligations towards its aborigines and then promptly forgot them," an attitude somehow excused because, as a relatively small population, they "exercised no influence at the ballot box." As for the promised transition from wardship to citizenship, supposedly the primary objective of state policy, "No one ever asked how long the training should endure," least of all those delegated to carry out the mandate of Indian Affairs. "[I]ts job was simply to administer, and like many a custodian, it was so involved in the routine of its administration that it forgot the purpose of its custodianship, especially since the fulfilment of that purpose would sign its own death warrant."[19]

While still in harness, Jenness chose his words more guardedly, as he did in setting forth ideas for policy reform in his 1936 memorandum to Camsell. Originally conceived as a place of temporary isolation, he wrote, the reserve was where First Peoples were supposed to pass through a "purely probational period" before "tak[ing] their place as citizens of the Dominion." In fact, it had degenerated into a "system of permanent segregation," one whose inhabitants have been stripped of all but a token remnant of control over their own material and spiritual well being. Rather than bringing opportunity, choice, and self-sufficiency, reserves brought hardship, hopelessness, and dependency, "destroy[ing] their morale and their health," and making them outcasts in the wider society. To Jenness's mind, a policy meant to help had only harmed, leaving the overwhelming majority of status Indians a "dejected, prison-like population, despised by its white neighbours ... and a burden on the whole Dominion." Strong language for a civil servant. Two decades later he made it stronger still, likening the relationship of Aboriginals and non-Aboriginals to apartheid, the stringent legalities of Indian status its colour bar, the reserves and settlements scattered across the country its "bantustans," while the climate of opinion cast them as "half-regenerate savages," peoples believed to lack a "true cultural background" of their own.[20]

"Without doubt," the memo continued, "the most crying need today is to restore the reserve system to its original purpose, i.e., to make it a purely transitional phase of education and training leading to full citizenship."[21] With that, he went on to outline several remedial measures to achieve this seemingly forgotten purpose. Unlike Indian New Dealers who sought to scrap assimilation in favour of allowing the different tribes to determine how they would live and be governed, Jenness favoured New Zealand's approach, one that treated the indigenous Maori as full and equal citizens but also encouraged "Maoritanga," maintenance of their distinct cultural identity, values, and traditions. Combing through that country's recent legislation convinced him that self-determination could only be realized once legal and institutional impediments to social mobility in Canada had been dismantled, full political rights granted, and meaningful alternatives to the reserve made readily available. In practical terms, this meant re-ordering public policy priorities to provide the people with all means necessary to determine who, in the first place, is an Indian, to set their own goals, and to develop leadership at the local level to see them through.[22]

Needless to say, investment in education was all-important to accomplishing these laudable ends. The system Indian Affairs had put in place was counter-productive even to its own publically declared purposes, sacrificing those objectives to the high god of administrative expediency and, in the process, estranging successive generations of Aboriginals from their families and communities, and from any meaningful prospect of shaping their own futures, on or off the reserve. On the strength of their historical involvement in mission work, Ottawa had entrusted its responsibilities in this key area to various church organizations, an arrangement that eventually spawned a network of federally subsidized parochial day and residential schools. Toward the end of his career, Scott took special pride in remarking on steadily rising school enrolments, unmistakable evidence, in his estimation, of the "growing conviction on the part of our wards that their children must be better fitted for the future." In reality, rising numbers probably owed far more to strict (and coercive) enforcement of sections of the Indian Act that made school attendance compulsory, often until the age of eighteen.[23]

Typical of the times, the system itself was chronically starved of funds. This, in turn, left it perennially under-staffed, lacking in qualified teachers, and hobbled in its capacity to provide "satisfactory educational facilities" and instruction comparable to the academic and technical preparation offered in provincially run public schools. In practice, Jenness wrote, such schools accomplished little more than churning out youngsters who were "well indoctrinated in the Christian faith, but totally unfitted for life in an Indian community and, of course, not acceptable in any white one." Only later – much later – would Canadians learn of yet another, darker legacy born of that system: the widespread physical and emotional abuse children suffered at the hands of lay and clerical teachers alike.[24]

Excepting remote regions of the country, where doing so was infeasible, he recommended that separate schooling be phased out in a timely manner and students transferred to the public system. Along with improving curricular standards, the experience of studying in integrated classrooms was certain to be psychologically beneficial as well, helping to "break down their present inferiority complex, broaden their outlook and increase their confidence, thus rendering it much easier ... to obtain employment away from the reserve." To improve the chances of success, moreover, he proposed that Ottawa encourage provincial education authorities to increase public awareness of the problems the country's First Peoples faced, perhaps by introducing an annual day devoted to fostering understanding of Aboriginal cultures and history. Last but not least, it was imperative that scholarships be established for promising students to continue on to secondary and post-secondary studies, and with them a program to assist graduates with finding employment, a far better investment than allowing them to "drift back into a life of idleness on the reserves."[25]

As critical as educational reform was to their future, health care reform was even more so to their present. This was an area over which government had been painfully slow to assume responsibility and, all-too-predictably, reluctant to allocate sufficient resources thereafter. Early in the twentieth century, the steady downward spiral of population began tapering off, and by the early 1930s, numbers began inching upward. Despite gains, the official count of those who came under the authority of the Indian Act, estimated at some 110,000 people, constituted a bit more than one percent of the country's overall population, their lowest proportion since Confederation. In a bizarre bit of callous calculation, Ottawa's historic strategy for dealing with its wards was predicated, in part, on the expectation that they would not merely "disappear as a separate and distinct people," as Scott had written, but would disappear as a people. Period.[26] Now, with their numbers on the upswing,

In Twilight and in Dawn

the situation demanded a different calculation. As the Great Depression worked its own heavy demands on public finances, the continuing low priority accorded to all things Aboriginal, not least their health, did little to stem the spread of tuberculosis and other infectious diseases in communities increasingly plagued by poor diet, shoddy housing, lack of sanitation, over-crowded schools, and the federal government's penchant for what amounted to wilful neglect.

On occasion, Indian Affairs might be prodded to respond to local medical emergencies, as happened in 1920 when it sent one of its few Indian agent-physicians to the Sarcee reserve where an outbreak of tuberculosis was threatening to decimate a population already in steep decline. Just two years earlier, Scott's unwavering "economizing attitude" had left his department without the services of a supervising medical officer at the very moment Spanish influenza was reaping a horrific toll among Native peoples, accounting for some fifteen percent of all deaths in the Dominion attributed to the globe-spanning pandemic.[27] Indicative of its customary tight-fisted style, the department only hired its first general medical superintendent, Dr Peter Bryce, in 1904, and he then spent years squabbling with a recalcitrant Scott, and other ranking bureaucrats, over the need for more money and for a systematic, comprehensive approach to tackling endemic health problems. Of those problems, none struck Bryce as more calamitous than sky-high mortality rates resulting from the spread of tuberculosis in residential schools, a scourge he estimated was then carrying off as many as one in three children. He would eventually go public with *The Story of a National Crime*, his account of Ottawa's half-measures in dealing with a catastrophe largely of its own making.[28]

By 1935, E.L. Stone, Bryce's successor, was trumpeting the fact that "[free] medical services carried on for the benefit of the Indians is the only fully developed system of public medicine in operation in Canada." Eleven physicians, eight medically trained Indian agents, and eleven nurses were in the department's employ at the time, along with a roster of some 250 civilian doctors who attended cases on an on-call basis. It also operated 200 hospitals, although critics have been quick to point out that most "were quite small and not definable as 'hospitals' per se." Patients sent to mainstream facilities were subsidized at a daily rate of $2.50. "This might be considered low," Stone remarked, "but most hospitals find it fairly acceptable and appreciate the steady cash income from Indian sources[!]"[29]

It goes without saying that doing something was surely better than doing nothing, or next to nothing, as had once been the preferred practice. Still, the service Stone oversaw was clearly inadequate to meet the needs of over 100,000 people living in 800 communities, the majority in rural or hinterland regions, and especially not at an estimated per capita expenditure of under ten dollars, one-third of the amount then being spent on health care for the population at large. Seen against this backdrop, Jenness could hardly be accused of exaggeration when he characterized reserves as "breeding grounds of diseases." Nor was he unreasonable to advise that standards of care correspond to those for everyone else and that service be extended beyond the treatment of illness to include preventive medicine as well. Before the First World War, Bryce had tried, but failed, to convince the powers-that-be to shift responsibility in this crucial area from Indian Affairs to the federal Department of Health. Now Jenness was proposing a different tack, recommending close cooperation with provincial health authorities in supplying reserves with water and sanitation facilities comparable to those in place in neighbouring white communities and in conducting regular health-related "inspections" of school-age children, the group most at risk from tubercular and other infectious diseases. He also urged that special attention be given to the inhabitants of Canada's remote northern districts, a thinly dispersed population of Aboriginals and whites generally left to their own devices in health emergencies. Conditions there called for a mix of "medical outposts" connected to larger centres via radio and the deployment of air ambulances to evacuate cases of serious illness or injury. Aiming to appeal to the cost-conscious propensities of branch administrators, he helpfully suggested that Royal Canadian Air Force pilots could be assigned to do the flying, an arrangement that would yield an added dividend in providing them with "admirable training facilities."[30]

Two other issues, both of long-standing concern to anthropologists and both in need of urgent action, were also addressed in the memorandum. One involved Ottawa's relentless campaign to eradicate religious and ceremonial activities judged antithetic to its assimilation polices. The provisions of the Indian Act known as the Potlatch Law actually had applicability beyond the confines of the Pacific northwest, being used to root out any custom seen as offensive to Christian morality, including the prairie Sun Dance as well as communal distributions of gifts, so-called give-aways. Doubtful that the "needless oppression" that the effort spawned would ever result in more than persistent psychological suffering and defiant resistance in affected communities, Jenness counselled against the law's continued enforcement. Unlike his proposed reforms to health care and education, this one came without a price tag – or the need to enter into potentially delicate negotiations with nine provincial governments. Even then, Indian Affairs remained undeterred, holding firm until the early fifties when a different climate of opinion finally induced it to drop the much-despised provisions.[31]

As his parting shot, Jenness renewed Speck and Cooper's earlier call for federal-provincial cooperation in protecting hunting and fishing grounds from white trespass. This was "absolutely necessary for the maintenance of the Indians and their families" in some of the country's remotest precincts, he warned, places where there were few, if any, opportunities to gain a livelihood by alternative means, where game was becoming scarce even as enforcement of provincial game laws was playing havoc with age-old subsistence patterns, and where, in consequence, a significant portion of the population was permanently malnourished. Northern Indians "cannot ... pull up stakes and return south if the living becomes unprofitable," he later remarked, referring to the usual recourse of white trappers who intrude into Aboriginal home turf, sometimes "by threat of violence." In concert, these conditions leave them "ready victims of every sickness ... [which,] combined with the [ordinary] hardships of a hunting life, produces a very high mortality."[32] As was its well-honed practice, the Indian Affairs Branch opted to pass on finding long-term solutions in favour of employing stopgap measures – in this instance, relieving destitute cases. Nonetheless, Indian agents were carefully instructed to withhold "the actual necessaries of life" unless intended recipients, including the sick, the elderly, and orphans, were found to be truly bereft of alternative means of support. Doing otherwise, they were warned, constituted abrogation of a "first principle" of policy: that is, "to promote self support among the Indians and not to provide gratuitous assistance to those ... who can provide for themselves."[33] If Depression-era provincial spending on poor relief for mainstream Canadians, just over $60 per head, can be described as "mean-spirited and stingy," then its corresponding outlay of about $20 for Aboriginals is deservedly condemned as "miserly [and] inhumane."[34]

MAORI INDIANS

The summer of 1938 brought a chilling foretaste of the horrors soon to be visited on Europe and the rest of the world. In July of that year, Eilleen and Diamond headed overseas for a whirlwind tour of ethnological museums in eight different countries, combined with a stopover in Copenhagen for the inaugural meeting of the International Congress of Anthropological and Ethnological Sciences. The trip was exhausting, their itinerary taking them northward to Finland, Sweden, and Denmark, then eastward into Germany, Austria, and Hungary. One final destination, Czechoslovakia, was planned for early September, mere weeks before escalating political tensions reached their climax in Hitler's annexation of Sudetenland. Wisely heeding the advice of a British consular official in Budapest, the travellers skipped Prague for the rela-

Eilleen and Diamond Jenness, Ottawa, ca. 1940. Photo
courtesy of Stuart Jenness

tive calm of Brussels. Securing accommodation for the voyage back to Canada took some doing, virtually every liner being filled to capacity with tourists fleeing the gathering storm. Complicating the situation further, there were also new travel arrangements to be made for their twelve-year-old son Stuart, in Wiesbaden for a summer-long stay with a family friend from Toronto. Accompanied by his host, the youngster departed for home via Paris, his parents shortly thereafter from Rotterdam. The couple took comfort in knowing that the freighter on which they managed to book passage had Norwegian registry, and thus "[we] should be in no danger ... even if war should break out before we sail."[35]

When it finally came, the outbreak of fighting weighed heavily on Jenness's mind. "Personally I hope that the government will find useful war work for me to do," he wrote to Marius Barbeau, mere hours after the long-expected news from Europe first broke in Ottawa. "I do not feel I should 'cultivate the garden,' as it were, while the house is burning!" And to Frederica de Laguna, just months later: "we have so many friends in Europe ... that we perhaps feel this war more than many people on this side of the Atlantic ... I love Germany, and many of the German people; yet if it were possible, I would enlist tomorrow. Are we intelligent human beings?" He was especially apprehensive over the well-being of colleagues Kaj Birket-Smith and Therkel Mathiassen, having passed an enjoyable week with them in Copenhagen the previous summer, and offered Birket-Smith's son "temporary haven ... on this side," should the worst come to pass. "I am afraid that life will be rather miserable for them for some time to come," he told de Laguna; "My life is so filled with Denmark and Norway that life here seems unreal," she admitted in reply."[36] As the conflict entered its third gruesome year, concerns shifted from the safety of friends and associates to that of his first-born son, John, now in England with a reconnaissance unit. "It gives me a strange feeling ... to have him go and fight for me when it should be the other way around ... That is the tragedy of war," Jenness explained in a note to Henry Collins; "It takes all the fine young fellows who are the promise of their generation and leaves behind the old men like myself who should be put on the shelf anyway."[37]

In a repeat of previous experience, Canada's all-out mobilization forced the National Museum back into the doldrums and, for a brief time, threatened to shutter it entirely. The first full year of fighting saw its budget drop twenty-five percent below what it was in 1939–40, and by the time Japan surrendered, the decline was on the order of sixty-five percent.[38] Meanwhile, with William Wintemberg's death in 1941, only Barbeau, Jenness, and Douglas Leechman remained on the payroll. Unlike his colleagues, however, Jenness willingly left anthropology, and the realm of Native affairs, behind in order to do his bit with the

Department of National Defence, then poaching senior civil servants for various assignments in its profusion of branches. Along with Barbeau, a reluctant poachee, the department initially assigned him a clerical job with the Dependents Allowance Board, processing paperwork for the monthly cheques sent to the spouses, children, and widows of the country's soldiers and sailors.[39] Hardly the sort of job either considered worthy of their expertise, Barbeau lost no time in finding a way back to his beloved folklore studies. His erstwhile friend, true to form, stuck it out for a full year before landing a more challenging position with military intelligence. More in keeping with his idea of doing something useful, the switch also rescued him from a brewing controversy over the board's handling of benefits for Aboriginal dependents. The trouble originated with officials at the Indian Affairs Branch who believed "Indians could not wisely manage or save money," and certainly not sums whose upper limit neared $100 per month. By 1942, attempts to manage this and subsidiary issues had given rise to a separate division within the board to deal with upwards of a thousand claimants, in accordance with new polices and procedures designed solely for native recipients. Before long, it also led to reduced benefits for those unwilling to allow local Indian agents to manage their funds in trust. Taking umbrage at the discriminatory cast of these actions, one branch bureaucrat was moved to observe, without the slightest hint of irony, that penalizing reserve residents was "contrary to the principles for which this war is being fought."[40]

Secondment as a civilian Air Force employee came in 1941, the pay-off for Jenness's determined lobbying of higher-ups at defence. The position's qualifications called for "an almost encyclopaedic knowledge of world geography" and, in faint echoes of the Dependents Allowance Board, an "ability to maintain records." In recommending his appointment, the unit's commanding officer was especially impressed with the successful candidate's "comprehensive knowledge of the north," expertise that "might prove invaluable to us in connection with certain problems that may arise" in future, a prescient reading of strategic needs in the coming Cold War era and Jenness's eventual contributions to meeting them. For the time being, at least, his duties as deputy director of special intelligence, a title that "naturally means nothing," as he told a colleague, involved compiling photographs, maps, and other information relevant to the conduct of military operations in east Asia and preparing reports on a range of topics, including one on the feasibility of supplying air bases in Yukon Territory with oil from the fields at Norman Wells, in the Mackenzie valley.[41] After Pearl Harbour, Canada began sharing his research on Japan and neighbouring countries with military intelligence in the United States. In turn, Washington requested

Jenness's services for another, quite different purpose: the intriguingly named M Project, a highly classified initiative of the Roosevelt White House. Beginning in 1942, he joined a select group of analysts whose task was to identify areas of the world where environmental and social conditions were suitable for resettling millions of refugees once the war was over. Because of the highly sensitive nature of the project, he was never informed of the project's actual purpose, being told instead that his specific task – evaluating Canadian data – was connected to a non-governmental program.[42]

As the war entered its final months, in 1944, Jenness was reassigned to a newly created outfit, the Inter-Service Topographical Section. Made its chief, he was responsible for reporting to the Joint Intelligence Committee, a group consisting of the heads of intelligence for Canada's air force, army, and navy. The job was little different from the one he had been doing since 1941, building up reference collections of maps, photographs, and detailed area studies, but now with the assistance of a professional staff. In keeping with Ottawa's emerging strategy for post-war reconstruction, the work also entailed planning for the section's conversion to a peacetime role, one emphasizing technical studies of the military and economic potentials of Canada's vast northern hinterland. Moving up the ladder at defence effectively ended Jenness's long tenure with the Anthropological Division, where he had remained as nominal chief, drawing a salary from the Department of Mines, since signing on with the Dependents Allowance Board in 1940. Now the Air Force issued his pay, unchanged, at $5,000 annually since Camsell had raised it as inducement to accept the Indian Affairs consultancy in the mid-thirties. Offered a chance to return to the National Museum as acting curator in 1946, he declined, in no mood to grapple with the headaches of restarting an institution left to languish for lack of a wartime mission. "I dropped out of museum work long ago," he told an associate, perfectly content to stay on with military intelligence for the time being. "When the war ends," he added, in what, by now, was quite a familiar refrain, "I hope my employment will end too, [and] that the government will pension me off and let me become a gentleman of leisure."[43] That long-anticipated reprieve finally came in the autumn of 1948, three months shy of his sixty-third birthday. Before collecting his final pay cheque, however, there was one last job to tackle: organizing a Geographic Bureau in the Department of Mines. A spin-off of the joint intelligence operation at defence, the bureau's official mandate entailed gathering and disseminating topographic, climatic, and other information pertaining to the country's different regions, particularly its north, for civilian purposes.[44] Meantime, the museum was again showing signs of life, as was its Anthropological Division, the last due in no small measure to the industry and foresight of Douglas Leechman. Promoted to the rank of archaeologist in 1941, Leechman had spent the ensuing war years eliminating a backlog of research and annual reports meant for publication and authoring several studies recommending ways to revive the institution's fortunes after nearly a decade of neglect.[45]

❖

Grass-roots demand for societal change took hold in Depression-era Canada and continued unabated through the war years. The rising popularity of the socialist CCF, the Co-operative Commonwealth Federation, was perhaps its most potent expression. Founded on a platform promising social justice through universal welfare and state control of key industries, the party made inroads at the federal and provincial levels during the thirties and, in 1944, won power in Saskatchewan under the leadership of Tommy Douglas. Determined to prevent recurrence of the labour unrest that had come on the heels of the First World War, the governing Liberals in Ottawa succeeded in out-flanking their upstart rival by embracing a Keynesian approach to economic and social reform, a move that laid the groundwork for a national social security system even as fighting still raged overseas.[46] Unemployment insurance was its first component, implemented in 1940, followed by the family allowance five years later. The next decade witnessed the introduction of additional measures, including old-age pensions and a hospitalization insurance scheme, forerunner of today's universal system of Medicare. Glaringly absent from government plans for post-war reconstruction, however, were initiatives pertaining to Indian Affairs, a personal concern of many CCF politicians who regarded the continued ill-treatment of Indians, in Douglas's words, as "'one of the blackest pages' in Canadian history." Rhetorical differences aside, the party's staunchly pro-integration position corresponded in its details and its philosophical underpinnings in progressive liberalism with the one Jenness advanced in his 1936 memorandum, asserting, in line with its "Humanity First" motto, that there can be no justice in a democratic society as long as a portion of its populace is relegated to a state of permanent segregation.[47]

Having waged a long and costly war against a fascist regime whose ideology of racial superiority had condemned millions to systematic brutalization and murder, there was no escaping the paradox of the institutional racism that persisted on the home front. Compounding the contradiction, thousands of Aboriginals had served with Canada's armed forces overseas, as they had in the First World War, yet, unlike other veterans, they were returning to an inequitable, impoverished existence underpinned by a way of thinking akin to the one they had risked life and limb to defeat. Just weeks after V-J Day, the Indian Association of Alberta added its voice to a growing chorus of Aboriginal and non-aboriginal organizations, among them church and veterans groups, calling on Ottawa to redress injustices wrongly sustained for generations by openly discriminatory policies and laws. In its formal petition the association urged timely establishment of a royal commission to investigate every aspect of the so-called Indian problem with a view to overhauling the Indian Act. It was imperative, they urged further, that both the letter and spirit of the revision embody the lofty ideals of Franklin D. Roosevelt's Four Freedoms – of speech and religion, from want and fear – founding principles of a new moral and legal world order first articulated in 1941 and, seven years later, enshrined in the Universal Declaration of Human Rights.[48]

Backed by stirring public awareness of, and concern for, the plight of Native peoples, the nationwide campaign demanding government action came to fruition in May 1946 when a special joint Senate-Commons committee convened to begin investigating the Indian Act, treaty rights, and the administration of Indian affairs.[49] After sitting 128 times, hearing from 122 witnesses – mostly bureaucrats, although in a break with past practice, representatives of several Native organizations also appeared – and reviewing hundreds of briefs, the committee issued its final report to Parliament two years and one month later. Its message was mixed. On the one hand, it recommended thorough revision of the Indian Act to purge its most anachronistic provisions, curtail the considerable powers of Indian Affairs officials, and cede to bands an increased measure of control over their reserves. On the other, members were not prepared to renounce assimilation as the ultimate goal of national policy. However, they did think that a different strategy to achieve it was needed, counselling replacement of old-style coercive tactics with a more even-handed approach designed to encourage individuals to relinquish status by lowering – not eliminating – the institutional barriers impeding their access to the mainstream. Among their proposals was phasing out separate schooling in favour of integrated education under provincial authority, granting the federal franchise, and establishing a claims commission to adjudicate land and treaty-related grievances.[50]

An entire generation would pass before government was finally prepared to act on key pieces of the agenda Aboriginal leaders brought to the committee: treating their bands as self-governing First Nations and reserves as national territories and recognizing that retaining their birth right as First Peoples and enjoying the rights of Canadian citizenship were not mutually exclusive goals. Though modest, the rewritten Indian Act that emerged from the hearings was, nonetheless, a first step in that direction, not least in its revocation of compulsory enfranchisement and prohibition of the potlatch and other formerly proscribed practices and annulment of the largely ineffectual pass system that restricted the movement of residents off reserve. So, too, was the government's 1945 decision to turn over responsibility for health to the Department of National Health and Welfare and, in the fifties, its extension of child allowance and social security measures to native families and the dismantling of residential schools. Voting rights took longer to achieve, coming in 1960, followed fourteen years later by an office to deal with treaty and land claims. Apart from opening the door to these developments, moreover, the committee's well-publicized proceedings boosted the public profile of Native peoples and issues, signalled in the transfer of Indian Affairs from Mines and Resources to a newly created Department of Citizenship and Immigration in 1949. They also facilitated the introduction of new ideas to internal branch operations, endorsing involvement of anthropologists, economists, sociologists, and other researchers in studying problems in Aboriginal communities and using their findings to inform policy and administrative practice. The Canadian Social Science Research Council was the main player on the latter front. Following the lead of physician Frederick Tisdale's earlier work on the health and nutritional status of Cree in northern Manitoba, in 1947, the council organized a large-scale investigation of general conditions among Algonkians across the James Bay region under the leadership of G. Gordon Brown, an applied anthropologist newly appointed to the University of Toronto faculty. Interestingly enough, it was Jenness who had sowed the seeds for this type of research in the late thirties, proposing that the council, then in embryonic form, give priority to launching a multi-disciplinary project designed to gather baseline demographic, economic, and social information and to assess the effects of the reserve system at the community level.[51]

By the time the joint parliamentary committee called its first witness, Jenness had been ensconced in the country's intelligence establishment for six years and a dozen more had gone by since he was last in the field. Even so, personal commitment to righting the wrongs now receiving (long-overdue) public scrutiny remained strong enough that, as the senators and MPs were settling down to their work, he revised his original 1936 proposals for reforming state policy and forwarded them to Brooke Claxton, the minister of national health and welfare, and R.A. Hoey, McGill's successor at Indian Affairs. On the advice of Thomas Reid, a Liberal MP from British Columbia's lower mainland and one

In Twilight and in Dawn

of its members, the committee called Jenness – officially billed as "Dominion Anthropologist," an apt if non-existent title – to appear during its second round of hearings in late March 1947. Given all of three days' notice, he had little time to prepare a formal statement other than his updated set of recommendations, read into the record as a "Plan for Liquidating Canada's Indian Problem Within 25 Years." Unlike its predecessor, the reworked proposals singled out the need for action on three main fronts, two of which, ending separate schooling and granting full access to social security benefits, were in keeping with changes the committee advised be adopted. The third, dealing with the future of reserves and, by implication, with the future of Indian status itself, proved a far more contentious issue, pitting the state's assimilation agenda against Native aspirations to survive as culturally distinct peoples in their own homelands. Three-plus decades of politicking and negotiating were to pass before the latter vision prevailed, an amendment to Canada's constitution affirming the existence of Aboriginal and treaty rights, including rights of self-determination.[52]

More than a few recent writers have denounced Jenness as an apologist for the long-discredited policies espoused most forcefully, and notoriously, by Indian Affairs during the Duncan Campbell Scott era. They have interpreted his plan as ardently pro-assimilation, and thus anti-Native, criticising, above all else, its support for abolishing reserves and enfranchising status Indians. One writer suggested that the source of these convictions lay in his overly pessimistic estimation of the fate of indigenous groups in the modern world, citing passages from *The Indians of Canada* to argue that negativity ultimately blinded him "to any possibility of a cultural revival or a separate nationhood for Indian peoples."[53] In the estimation of another critic, its roots lay elsewhere, principally in a nineteenth-century mindset steeped in racism, paternalism, and patriarchy and in his fundamental sympathy for the state's ideologically hegemonic "project of ... national definition," a project that assigned central importance to the exclusion of Aboriginals as socially and politically distinct peoples.[54]

In fairness, Jenness was certainly a proponent of enfranchisement, albeit in the sense of recognizing all native peoples as full citizens, just as his outlook was tinged with a pessimism conditioned by the eye-opening experience of seeing at first-hand the often-wretched condition in which community after community had been left by the colonial juggernaut and its nation-building successors. But to conclude that he favoured Scott's conception of enfranchisement, a process offering the vote in return for outright rejection of Aboriginal values and identity, and forfeiture of special rights, is perhaps to misinterpret his thinking on the subject. So, too, is overlooking the depth of his pessimism about the blind indifference of politicians and public alike to the multitude of problems plaguing the whole of Indian country. In hindsight, his priorities probably do seem misplaced, at least in relation to the nativist consensus that has defined the main current of Aboriginal politics over the past forty years.[55] Yet given what he knew of the situation on the ground in the twenties and thirties, a period when key elements of the later consensus had yet to coalesce into anything resembling a nationalist front, putting cultural distinctiveness and other explicitly (ethno)-political ambitions second to alleviating material privation and ending the cycle of dependence and social isolation scarcely seems an unsupportable position. Indeed, the first priority his plan enumerated was timely amelioration of "the Indians' social and economic position," a morally indefensible state of affairs he described as "so depressed as to create 'leprous' spots in many parts of the country."[56]

A more reliable gauge of where he stood on these issues isn't found in the few roughly sketched points outlined in the plan itself but in what Jenness said in the committee room back in 1947, his comments and replies to questions informed in large part by core values instilled during his New Zealand upbringing and by personal admiration for that country's track-record in the field of Maori affairs. Reprising the perspective underlying his initial foray into policy reform ten years earlier, he argued that the "Indian Problem" writ large was not the manifestation of inherently inferior peoples, the "half-regenerate savages" of popular imagination and loathing. Rather, it was the creation of a political establishment that effectively ignored the obligations it pledged to fulfil. "We thought that, since they did not appear capable of taking care of themselves under modern conditions," he told the committee, "we would protect them, we would train them and educate them" to take their rightful place as citizens in the wider society. Having forsaken the promise to prepare them "for citizenship and the free life that was just around the corner," however, "we shut them up indefinitely [on reserves] where they would be out of the way of the white man." Treated as "pariahs and outcasts," their day-to-day lives in many parts of the country had come to resemble those of African Americans under the cruel dictates of "Jim Crow," the realities of segregation disadvantaging them economically and socially, and sapping their "dignity, their self-reliance and self-respect."[57] Ottawa "should cease to close her eyes" to the inequities its own policies and practices have spawned, he said, especially now, at a moment in history when concerns for human rights, and for the rights of peoples under various forms of trusteeship, were in the ascendant, both at home and internationally. To emphasize the point, he reminded politicians in the room of a recent speech by one of their own, Senator Wishart Robertson, pledging Canada's acceptance of the

United Nations–mandated "sacred trust" to safeguard "the well-being of the inhabitants of all non-self-governing territories." "How can our representatives abroad continue to champion the rights of small nations and subject peoples," he asked, "when here at home we continue to keep our Indians, generation after generation, in what have become, whether we like to call them so or not, confinement camps?"[58]

Jenness counter-balanced his unflattering assessment of the course Canada had doggedly pursued since Confederation with an upbeat estimation of New Zealand's handling of native affairs in the aftermath of inter-ethnic warfare in the 1860s. In his birthplace, he confidently asserted, with progressive liberal Pakeha conviction, "there is no Maori problem because they are citizens on an equal footing with whites." In fact, their standing as such pre-dated the wars, the foundational Treaty of Waitangi granting them "all the Rights and Privileges of British Subjects" back in 1840.[59] Subsequent law did not make exercise of those rights contingent on sacrificing tribal identity. Nor did it circumscribe that identity, or interfere with customary determination of tribal membership, unlike widely disparaged sections of the Indian Act. "A man is proud to call himself a Maori," the anthropologist remarked, cognizant of lingering public misconceptions about the supposedly inherent linkage of bloodlines and status ascription. "If he has quarter blood he can call himself a white man or a Maori, whichever he wishes." He admitted that, as in every settler society, racial prejudice was, and remained, an inevitable fact of life, much as it was for other ethnic minorities. Because they are "free citizens," however, Maori are neither segregated on reserves, nor subject to state-sanctioned institutional barriers limiting their participation in national life. On the contrary, voters in four Maori electoral districts began sending their own MPs to the House of Representatives in 1868, and before century's end office-holders were being drawn from an elite of university-educated professionals, among them James Carroll, the first Maori politician to hold the post of native minister, serving from 1899 to 1912. The period also saw local communities become largely self-governing, operating in accord with customary tribal authority and having access to a system of courts to settle disputes over land. At a time when Indian Affairs comprised little more than an administrative backwater, moreover, the Department of Native Affairs stood as a prominent feature on New Zealand's political landscape, evident in the fact that three sitting prime ministers had added the portfolio to their responsibilities in order to advance Maori interests. While official Ottawa contented itself with preserving the status quo, Wellington was implementing a range of programs that, by the end of the Second World War, had made notable progress toward narrowing the once-significant gap in health, education, and living standards between the country's indigenous population – still largely rural in character – and its Pakeha majority. Two British dominions, two divergent paths, two dissimilar outcomes: one verging on becoming what its Depression-era governor general optimistically portrayed as "two peoples, one nation," the other, a full decade later, still struggling with the pros and cons of wardship and Jim Crow.[60]

"[A] truth ... we often overlook," Jenness wrote before the war, "[is] that the strongest forces for the regeneration or upbuilding of peoples comes from within their own ranks, not from without." If there were any worth in this perspective, and the sharply differing situations of Maoris and Indians certainly suggested there was, then Canada might do well to follow New Zealand's lead. Doing so required sustained public investment in fostering, not impeding, the development of those regenerative forces, he noted, along with strategies to assist the work of grass-roots leaders able to "command the confidence of their people and guide them toward that goal."[61] At the same time, it was equally important to recognize the extent to which cultural change had already taken hold in different regions of the country, reason enough to rethink administrative practice and its underlying paternalism. In the post-war era, it was only proper that Canada's broadly based commitment to social reform include justice for a segment of its population long denied any appreciable measure of fair and equitable treatment. While his own proposals for furthering that end might have some merit, Jenness told the committee, there certainly were other approaches to be weighed, especially those originating with the peoples whose future hung in the balance. "Yes," the witness replied, when an MP asked whether "the Indians themselves should be asked what they think" of the changes he and others were contemplating, and yes again to respecting the scope of their interests and priorities in piecing together whatever package of legislative and policy reforms were to come from the present parliamentary proceedings.[62]

Jenness wasn't alone in advocating what he took to be New Zealand's more enlightened approach to the vexing problem of enfranchisement. It figured in briefs various civic and political organizations submitted to the Senate-Commons committee, including one representing Salish peoples from the Fraser Valley and interior portions of British Columbia. Withholding full political rights on the fallacious grounds of intellectual and moral inferiority must end, they urged, to be replaced by an unconditional grant of citizenship: that is, without need to renounce "all our traditions, aboriginal rights, interests and benefits." In effect, their goal was implementation of an arrangement "identical to that granted to the Maori Indians ... viz. representation in Parliament, and in the administration of the Native General Affairs." A month after Jenness's appearance, Peter Kelly, from the Haida Nation, proposed much the same solution. Speaking on behalf of the Native Brotherhood of British Columbia, he said that it was simply unacceptable for the country's laws to deny Indians "a voice in the formation of such laws" without first surrendering their "hereditary rights as Indians." In New Zealand, the Maori "retain their aboriginal rights, but at the same time have full representation in parliament ... Why cannot this be done in Canada?"[63]

Seemingly more interested in getting out from under the financial burdens those rights represented than in accepting the legal and moral obligation to honour them in full, Canadian politicians of the day were unprepared to embrace the major lessons of the New Zealand model and their successors would remain like-minded for years to come. As the hearings were entering their third and final year, however, what evidence had been presented on the subject, particularly with reference to policies and practices in the area of Maori schooling, proved sufficiently interesting to warrant commissioning a fact-finding trip to look into that system's nuts and bolts at first hand. Government recruited Jenness for the task, an obvious choice given his familiarity with legislative developments in Wellington and, more to the point, that he was already heading in that direction for an extended visit with family and friends, unseen in thirty years. The Geographic Bureau arranged what was effectively a four-month leave, offered as compensation for his agreeing to delay retirement temporarily until the fledgling agency was up and running. As part of the deal, the bureau asked that he make the junket a working holiday, looking into what New Zealand was doing by way of supporting geographic work. Now Indian Affairs wanted his services, too. Hopeful of a new beginning on that all-important front, Jenness flew off across the Pacific armed with a letter of introduction and instructions to learn whatever he could about the state's role in administering, and financing, primary through post-secondary schooling; community-level involvement in the operation of local schools; employment of Maori teachers; and the pros and cons of integrated classrooms.[64] With welcome assistance from the ministers of Maori Affairs and the Department of Education, provision was made for him to carry out a virtual "one-man royal commission" on Ottawa's behalf, visiting school after school, community after community, across rural districts of the North Island, home to the largest concentration of Maoris. The pace of the month-long investigation was strenuous, but at least it was undertaken in a modicum of style, a car and driver being put at his disposal courtesy of Alfred Rive, the Canadian high commissioner in Wellington. Jenness did foot the bill for his own personal expenses, thinking it improper to take undue advantage of his host's hospitality.[65]

What he learned during his North Island tour, and from interviews with government officials, did nothing to dampen his enthusiasm for New Zealand–style reforms or their applicability in the Canadian context. Filled with facts and figures covering a range of education and welfare-related matters, the brief report he submitted to Indian Affairs was deemed "invaluable in enabling our Canadian officials to compare such policies with the proposals now being considered as a basis for a new ... Indian Act." Branch officials were especially impressed with the "most progressive step" of employing local welfare officers to assist graduates in finding jobs or in moving on to advanced studies, and with the generally high standards and degree of integration already achieved in Maori schools. With respect to the bigger picture, the official response was more restrained, combining matter-of-fact interest in select details with wariness of an aggressive legislative strategy reminiscent of the one introduced by Indian New Dealers in the thirties.[66] As Parliament's work on revisions to the Indian Act neared completion, the branch adopted a more critical stance, predictably downplaying aspects of the New Zealand approach that ran counter to policies that the amended law had been re-designed to implement. A briefing paper prepared in late 1950 for the minister of citizenship and immigration, Indian Affairs' new departmental home, speaks to this shift unequivocally.

The internal document's opening section sets the tone by quoting from a recently published scholarly examination of native-white relations in four British-dominated settler societies. "New Zealanders claim that their treatment of the Maoris has been exceptionally satisfactory," writes A. Grenfell Price, an Oxford-trained, Australian-born, historian, "but the facts of history hardly support this contention. They demonstrate, for example, that the New Zealand record is certainly not as good as that of Canada." Presented as an authoritative defence of business as usual, the memo weighs each country's experience in various policy areas in accord with that judgment, offering little more than faint praise for certain features of Wellington's approach – the absence of wardship and reserves, for instance, and the participation of Maoris at the highest levels of national decision making – and levelling pointed comments at others, notably the evident lag between statutory protections and social reality in the sphere of race relations. "[W]hile there is legal equality," it observes, "there is still considerable antipathy to Maoris shown by Europeans," particularly in urban areas where prejudicial attitudes limit their opportunities to earn a decent living.[67]

While scarcely free of problems, New Zealand's experience nonetheless appears exceptional when compared to its Canadian counterpart, a country where Aboriginal peoples were, with precious few exceptions, still being denied social and political equality under the law. They also faced profound problems in securing livelihoods on reserve and, owing to deep-seated racist sentiment, even greater ones off reserve. On these grounds alone, the memorandum's claim that the approach to administering native affairs in both countries "has been much the same," though politically expedient, certainly begs credibility. True, the professed aim of policy in both has been "to assist the natives in adjusting themselves to a dominant foreign culture and way of life."[68] Yet only in one has that policy incorporated the right of self-determination and, with it, the right to participate in shaping laws and policies affecting the greater society. In the other, none of this was possible, at least not yet. Nor was it to come without a protracted struggle against exceedingly long odds.

CHAPTER FOURTEEN

A Brand New Day,
1948–1969

WHIRLING WITH IDEAS

As he was settling into retirement, the National Museum Jenness had pronounced "deader than a doornail" only a few years before was not merely stirring but bounding back to life.[1] Keeping with tradition, Frederick J. Alcock, its new chief curator, appointed in 1947, came from the ranks of the Geological Survey. Alcock, however, lacked his immediate predecessors managerial short-sightedness, instead overseeing timely restoration of the institution's funding and professional ranks, and initiating refurbishment of its exhibition halls in response to burgeoning public interest in the nation's heritage. Furthermore, in 1950, in what amounted to a truly decisive break with the past, he presided over the separation of the museum from the Geological Survey, the break-up coming in the wake of a government reorganization that bequeathed the museum quasi-independent status within the newly established Department of Resources and Development. Even then, ties between the museum and the survey were not completely severed as the two continued to live under the same roof in the cramped Victoria Memorial Museum building until the survey finally moved out nine years later. Within a year the National Gallery was gone, too, marking the first time since it opened half a century earlier that the grand old edifice on Metcalfe Street truly realized the purpose for which it was built.[2]

For the Anthropological Division, revival brought the first permanent hires in a quarter century, beginning with Marcel Rioux, appointed in late 1947, and its first female employees, among them Helen Creighton, Catherine McClellan, and Carmen Roy. Along with new blood came new priorities, mainly in ethnology where Rioux – Marius Barbeau's protégé and son-in-law – Creighton, Roy, and several others developed French and English folklore at the (temporary) expense of research on Aboriginal peoples. Douglas Leechman, the lone veteran of the interwar period, enjoyed similar good fortune in rebuilding the division's archaeological program, hiring Richard MacNeish and Thomas Lee to fill positions once held by Harlan Smith and William Wintemberg. Seemingly overnight, the rejuvenated section became a national archaeological survey in more than just name, mounting investigations in nearly every part of the country on its own or in collaboration with other institutions, both domestic and foreign.[3]

Given the time and energy Jenness had expended on defending anthropology from the ax-wielding proclivities of bureaucratic higher-ups, he took a certain satisfaction in the division's rejuvenation after years of depression and war-induced neglect. Among its early successes, the resuscitation of arctic archaeology in 1948 was the most personally gratifying, particularly since he had laid the groundwork for the first major project in the region before stepping down from his post at the Geographic Bureau. With Alcock's blessing, he had recruited Henry Collins, his long-time associate from the Smithsonian, to delve into the lingering conundrum of Dorset-Thule relations in the eastern Arctic, much the same project Therkel Mathiassen had turned down twenty years before. While Collins was working north of Hudson Strait, Jean Michea worked south of it, conducting a survey across Quebec's Ungava peninsula in conjunction with a multi-disciplinary expedition to the region under the leadership of botanist Jacques Rousseau. The next year MacNeish opened a new window on the indigenous past in the northwest, making the first in a series of expeditions that would eventually take him from the upper Mackenzie basin to Yukon's Beaufort Sea coast.[4] Although his own days as an active researcher on problems of Eskimoan prehistory were now behind him, Jenness never lost interest in the ongoing quest for new evidence and new interpretations. As he freely admitted, staying current with the latest developments in a rapidly expanding field was no mean feat; like nuclear science, he told delegates to the International Congress of Americanists in 1949, "each fresh discovery opens up new and alluring vistas, but only deepens the principal mystery."[5]

Jenness left the civil service full of aspirations for whatever years still lay ahead of him. Above all else, he wanted to travel and, until ill health finally interfered, that's precisely what he did, every year, for nearly twenty years, usually with Eilleen, sometimes alone, and always during the long, hard months of Canadian winter. Mediterranean Europe was the destination of choice, doubly alluring as the ancient world of his youthful imagination, a place no less enchanting in retirement than it had been when George von Zedlitz had introduced him to the intellectual satisfactions of classical scholarship a lifetime ago in Wellington. A winter on Cyprus in the mid-fifties was spent indulging that long-lasting fascination, collecting documentary evidence for what he initially conceived of as a geographic, rather than a economic history, of the island, focusing on key factors such as land use and settlement patterns since neolithic times. At present, however, his attentions were drawn to social and economic conditions in contemporary Europe, an outgrowth of his days with military intelligence and, before that, his brief foray into studying Canada's potential for population growth in the decades to come. Once the conflict ends, he told a friend at the time, he hoped to land a job in the post-war reconstruction effort somewhere on the Continent. No such opportunity materialized. In the winter of 1949–50, he did the next best thing, spending ten weeks motoring, solo, through war-torn Italy, to see for himself what progress had been made toward recovery.[6]

From a starting point on the country's Riviera where, a year earlier, he and Eilleen had taken a crash course in conversational Italian, Jenness headed down the Adriatic shore, continued southwest into Calabria, crossed over to Sicily, and then returned northward along an inland route via Naples, Rome, Florence, and Genoa. Hitchhikers and townspeople encountered along the way proved invaluable guides and interpreters of the passing scene, offering up a broad spectrum of opinion on the day's most pressing concerns and controversies. What he discovered was a nation whose personal and collective determination to move on from the devastation of war was inseparable from their determination to overcome a raft of structural problems rooted in the recent and more distant past, and in the nature of the land itself. Among these, arguably none had greater bearing on national life, and national prospects, than unrelenting population pressure on an inadequate resource base, pressures unrelieved despite massive out-migration – in the millions since Italian unification in 1861 – to the Americas and elsewhere. The weight of this and other economic and social problems had fallen disproportionately on Italy's under-developed countryside, especially on its largely rural and agrarian south, where endemic privation was the result of too many people, too little productive soil, and negligible capital investment. The outward signs of impoverishment were in evidence wherever he went, "visible in the miserable, over-crowded hovels, ragged clothes and pinched faces of many rural workers, the prevalence of child labour ... the chronic unemployment even in ... [the more] fertile areas." Pockets of joblessness and poverty marked the urban landscape as well. Nevertheless, the yawning gulf in living conditions that had separated north and south before the war, along with the divisive political and social frictions it had engendered, were scarcely lessened in its immediate aftermath, the inadvertent consequence of policies instituted under the European Recovery Program – the Marshall Plan – which was aimed at boosting industrial capacity and competitiveness, liberalizing foreign trade, and instilling a taste for American-style consumerism. Italy's agricultural sector was left to stagnate, disadvantaged as much by a lack of mechanization as by availability of plentiful, and relatively inexpensive, foods imported from abroad.[7]

Later, as the fifties were drawing to a close, Italy would find itself at the threshold of a period of sustained economic growth that would turn it into one of the world's leading industrial powers. From Jenness's vantage point, however, so speedy and substantial a turn-around – the so-called "economic miracle" – must have seemed little better than a distant hope, if that, as he toured the country at a time when nearly one in four Italians was living at or below subsistence level and farmers, almost half of the Italian labour force, accounted for less than a quarter of its economic output.[8] "There is a restlessness about the whole country," he observed, "a restlessness not only economic and political, but also psychological." His characterization – in many respects, equally applicable to Canada's Aboriginal population – speaks of a people scrambling to secure the essentials of a decent existence, all the while struggling with the powerful forces of modernity which the times had unleashed: with the deep contradictions between traditional values and identity on the one hand, and rising expectations on the other; with the competing visions of political rivals on the left and right; and with the question of their place in a world being transformed by liberal reform, de-colonization, and the new realities of Cold War polarization.[9] Though hardly a cure-all for the many ills brought on by a century of mistreatment, Jenness was confident that the way forward for Aboriginal peoples in Canada rested, first and foremost, with a political decision in Ottawa to dismantle the state-sanctioned system of segregation. Italy's future, by contrast, appeared much less certain, its ability to improve living standards across the board confounded by the tenacious lag between population growth and economic resources, even as historic levels of emigration continued unabated and major reforms of the ancient landholding system of latifundia or landed estates – one of Italy's "besetting weaknesses" – were being implemented. Short of a successful nationwide campaign to reduce fertility rates by contraceptive or other means, he reasoned, Italians were likely to remain a restless people for some time to come.[10]

◆

Along with the freedom to travel, Jenness relished the freedom retirement offered to explore new interests or return to old ones simply because they appealed to his intellectual curiosity. Putting even modest plans into action came with a price tag, though, one not always manageable on a superannuate's income. This became obvious in 1953 when he was struggling to finish *Dawn in Arctic Alaska*, a popular account of his post-*Karluk* experiences, intended as a (belated) companion volume to *People of the Twilight*. As the manuscript grew longer and emendations more numerous, engaging a typist seemed necessary if he had any reasonable hope of seeing the work through to completion. On a whim, he approached the Guggenheim Foundation in New York, an organization for whom he had vetted applications over the years, about his chances of obtaining a small subvention. He pitched the book to Henry Moe, the foundation's administrative head, noting that it was a timely portrayal of a people just now feeling the modernizing effects of militarization and of oil exploration in their remote homeland. A thousand dollars, he reckoned, would suffice to hire an assistant, have an accompanying map or two prepared, and commission an artist to produce a set of illustrative sketches based on his own Arctic Expedition photographs. The foundation's trustees had bigger things in mind, offering him a "drawing account" of $10,000 – more than two and a half times his annual pension – and with it, carte blanche to use the funds for whatever scholarly purposes he deemed fit. "For the present I shall go full steam ahead on the book," a delighted, if astounded, Jenness wrote to Moe in thanks, but in the meantime, "my mind is whirling with ideas and projects that I might take up when ... [it] is finished."[11]

When that time finally arrived, a bit more than a year later, he elected to work on the geographic history of Cyprus. But Cyprus was actually his second choice, as he had opted for another Mediterranean winter when the precariousness of East-West relations ruled out a summer-long visit to the Russian Republic and Siberia in search of new insight into the origins and development of Eskimoan cultures. During the Stalinist period just ended, Soviet archaeologists had been forbidden to cooperate, or even communicate, with foreign scientists and dissemination of their published findings abroad was largely restricted. Like most of his European and American colleagues, Jenness didn't read Russian. Still, he knew of Sergei Rudenko's 1945 excavations on the Chukotka peninsula, a pioneering expedition aimed at determining whether the earliest phases of Eskimoan development had occurred somewhere to the east of Bering Strait, as was now generally suspected. With his own work on the strait's opposite shore having garnered several citations in Rudenko's monograph, Jenness felt confident that Soviet authorities would deem him a worthy scholar and thus grant permission to study Rudenko's collections in Leningrad's State Museum of Ethnography during a visit planned for summer 1955. More ambitious (and optimistic) still, he also hoped to mount a small expedition down Siberia's Lena River for the purpose of assessing whether proto-Eskimos might have followed the valley northward from a hypothetical homeland somewhere in the central interior. Preferring, if possible, to reconnoitre the region in the company of a Soviet archaeologist, he proposed descending the river from Yakutsk to its outlet on the Laptev Sea, then taking passage aboard a sea-going vessel calling at Eskimo settlements along the coast from East Cape to the Gulf of Anadyr, before returning to Moscow by air.[12] Ambitious, but it was not to be.

After sitting on the necessary paperwork for six months, Ottawa effectively scuppered the project, judging it inadvisable to request visas and permissions "for reasons that need no explanation," not least of which, Jenness suspected, was fear of "a quid pro quo request which it might find embarrassing." Though hardly as adventurous, he agreed to spend July in Montreal instead, lecturing on arctic ethnology and archaeology in McGill's Geography Department.[13] McGill was to be his second (and last) taste of the professorial life, the first coming in 1951 when he had accepted an invitation from Harry Hawthorn to offer a seminar at the University of British Columbia. Appointed four years earlier, Hawthorn, originally from Wellington and trained in the discipline at the University of Hawaii and Yale, was then in the early stages of developing the school's anthropology program as a division of its Department of Economics, Political Science, and Sociology. Hoping to make good use of his compatriot's expansive knowledge and professional expertise, Hawthorn asked Jenness to remain in Vancouver for the entire academic year. He elected to stay for the fall term only, preferring to recuperate from his academic labours in the warm winter sunshine of southern Spain. His term was a busy one, spent sitting in on program-planning sessions by day and giving weekly, two-hour seminars by night, their topics encompassing virtually the whole of northwestern North American ethnology.[14]

Nine years after signing on to establish the discipline's presence on campus and in the province more generally, a task underwritten with a grant from the Carnegie Foundation, Hawthorn became the first chair of a separate Department of Anthropology, Sociology, and Criminology. Joining him on staff were his wife Audrey, appointed curator of the newly established Museum of Anthropology in 1949, and three other faculty members, all hired in the early fifties: archaeologist Carl Borden and ethnologists Wayne Suttles and Cyril Belshaw, the last another transplanted New Zealander. To mark the auspicious occasion, Hawthorn tried to lure Jenness back into the classroom for an encore. Still recuperating, this time from heart troubles that had interrupted his work in Cyprus the previous winter, Jenness thought it best to defer in favour of "some one more competent than myself."[15]

◆

The decision to make Cyprus the focus of his Guggenheim-funded study was strictly a matter of practicality. Initially, he had set his sights on Crete or Rhodes, fabled Aegean islands of classical antiquity that had enchanted him since his days as a Greats man at Balliol. With only limited ability to read modern Greek, however, at least for the present, much of the primary source material pertinent to researching patterns of land use and settlement would have been virtually inaccessible to him. From that perspective, Cyprus, a distant outlier of the Hellenic world since the first millennium BC, was the better bet, its archives containing a wealth of land surveys and technical reports in English dating back to 1878, the year Great Britain acquired administrative control of the island from the Ottomans in return for helping defend the sultan's deteriorating empire against tsarist Russia's territorial designs.[16] But as a place to pass a leisurely winter of sightseeing and study, as was Jenness's intention, it had one glaring drawback: on 1 April 1955, seven months before he and Eilleen disembarked at the port of Limassol to begin what was to be a six-month stay, members of the armed faction of EOKA – the National Organisation of Cypriot Fighters – launched a guerrilla campaign to drive out the British, marginalize the ethnic Turkish minority, and bring about enosis – political union with Greece, their presumptive motherland.[17]

Despite the discord, Jenness's health, not the ever-present threat of terrorist bombs, turned out to be the more serious impediment to his work. In February, a heart attack put him in bed for nearly two months, interrupting plans to visit some of the more environmentally and historically interesting parts of the island, particularly its mountainous terrain, and necessitating an earlier-than-anticipated departure. On the bright side, being confined to their rented cottage in the northern port town of Kyrenia – since 1983 part of a separatist Turkish Republic – allowed him ample opportunity to pore over a selection of published histories and archaeological accounts, some exceedingly rare, borrowed, courtesy of its director, from the well-stocked library of the Museum of Antiquities in nearby Nicosia. It also afforded the chance to practice using what modern Greek he had learned under the tutelage of a schoolteacher neighbour, making it a habit to read local newspapers and even peruse elementary level textbooks with an eye to ferreting out their use of nationalist rhetoric.[18] Returning home in April with a miscellany of facts and figures gleaned from census records and official reports on the state of agriculture, forestry, mining, and commerce, he spent his convalescence starting on the formidable task he had set for himself: depicting the long sequence of changes in patterns of land and resource use from the time of Cyprus's first Neolithic inhabitants – the hunter-farmers of the indigenous Khirokitia culture – a span then thought to be some five thousand years in duration and more recently reckoned to be upwards of twice as long.[19]

Properly done, the job required delving into the histories of the diverse peoples and polities that had fought for, held sway over, and settled Cyprus at various points in the past and, in the process, left their imprint on its landscape, economy, and population, and on the fabric of its social, cultural, and religious life. Sitting as it does astride sea lanes linking the whole of the Levantine world, the list of those who conquered the island, or sought to capitalize on its economic and military potential, is a lengthy one. The roster begins with Egyptian, Phoenician, and Greek traders and colonists of the Bronze and Iron ages, followed in the Middle Ages by the great powers of Rome, Byzantium, and the Islamic caliphates and the lesser ones of Lusignan France and Venice. Finally, and perhaps most fatefully for contemporary Cyprus, was the ascendancy of Ottoman rule in 1571, a three-hundred-year period when feudalism was abolished and the seeds of communal conflict the British later inherited in maturing form were first sown.[20] As Jenness had to concede, doing the subject justice turned out to be "more complicated and difficult than I had anticipated," largely owing to the tendency of the scholarly works on which he relied – including the most recent and comprehensive of them, classicist George Hill's monumental *A History of Cyprus*, the fourth and final volume of which appeared in 1952 – to concentrate on political and religious history while relegating economic developments, and their environmental consequences, to the background. The "fog that surrounded the island" was thickest throughout the long centuries preceding tenure of the Crusader states, Jenness noted, "but only about 1850 did it clear sufficiently to provide us with a few firm statistics." How well he managed to penetrate the mists is evident in the fact that the lone yield of his efforts – *The Economics of Cyprus: A Survey to 1914* – devotes 50 of its 200 pages to the first five millennia of the island's history, an equal number to its days as an imperial Ottoman province, and the remainder, divided into two chapters, to the first thirty-six years of Great Britain's abundantly documented administration, a stretch ending in 1914 with its formal annexation of Cyprus at the outbreak of the First World War.[21]

A project inspired by a "youthful vision" of the "mystic radiance" of Mediterranean antiquity became, in its final realization, a "sober economic study," to cite its author's judgment.[22] The book is certainly that, chronicling the various ventures undertaken by Cyprus's multiple foreign overlords to meet domestic needs and the needs of their overseas interests: opening up arable lands for cultivating carob, cotton, cereal grains, grapes, olives, pulses, and a host of other crops, and marginal areas for herding sheep and goats; mining asbestos, copper, and gypsum; harvesting the island's forests, mainly its stands of pine and cedar. Moreover, it examines the slow-to-change technological, social, and political conditions – systems of governance, inheritance, land tenure, and taxation – that affected economic production and shaped the everyday existence of those few who inhabited the island's towns and the masses who continued to people its rural districts well into the twentieth century. As history, however, it stands apart from comparable works in one important regard: instead of reducing environment to little more than backdrop to past happenings, a common historiographic convention at the time, Jenness treats the island's biotic, climatic, geologic, and topographical features as integral components of his narrative, taking into account the effects of factors such as its susceptibility to drought and earthquakes, and lack of perennial rivers, on the course of human activities, as well as some leading consequences of those activities: the introduction of new species of plants, animals, and pathogens, for instance, or environmental degradation in the form of wide-spread deforestation and soil erosion. In this respect, his approach resembles aspects of the American school of historical geography and its more recent anthropological offshoot cultural ecology, the one conceiving of regional landscapes as cultural landscapes – that is, as products of natural and cultural forces that modify them over time – the other focusing on the processes – technological, demographic, and social – by which inhabitants adapt to the potentials and constraints of their physical and natural surroundings.[23]

His debut as an economic historian barely registered in scholarly circles. In fact, he despaired of even finding a publisher, several academic houses, including Minnesota (which had brought out *Dawn in Arctic Alaska*) and Oxford, turning down the manuscript owing to its "limited appeal" before McGill University's newly established press accepted it in late 1960, two years after its completion.[24] There is reason to think that the contribution would have gotten more notice had he taken the

In Twilight and in Dawn

story forward to the present day, as Hill did in his 640-page fourth volume devoted to Cyprus under the Ottomans and British, and as a host of other writers were beginning to do because the island's escalating troubles were making headline news around the planet. Cloaking himself in the historian's guise, Jenness noted that he had deliberately refrained from doing that very thing, maintaining that the immediacy of some of the more contentious issues feeding the growing insurgency effectively precluded examining them with the measure of detachment that reputable scholarship demanded.[25] However, observations on the contemporary situation contained in a handful of his surviving letters – including a longish "back-grounder" written for his youngest son Robert, then a foreign service officer with External Affairs in Ottawa – suggest how he might have judged developments on Cyprus to mid-century had he been of a different mind about the propriety of commenting on unfinished events.

Before taking up his perception of the troubles, a synopsis of key happenings preliminary to the outbreak of bloodshed in 1955 is in order.

❖

Greek Cypriots had reason to believe that their dreams of enosis would be realized under the dominion of Great Britain, an empire that had demonstrated its liberality toward Hellenic national interests twice before in the nineteenth century: first, by assisting Greece to win independence from Constantinople, and then, three decades later, by relinquishing its protectorate in the Ionian archipelago. Over the next fifty years that liberality was manifest in its campaign to modernize what was merely a backwater when the imperial colours were hoisted over Cyprus for the first time, with investments made in the construction of schools, hospitals, and roads; sanitation and public health; experimental farms and re-forestation and soil conservation projects; and reforms to the civil service and banking systems.[26] On the all-important question of union with Greece, by contrast, the British failed to live up to native expectations. Instead they implemented several unpopular measures whose unintended outcome was to reignite nationalist, anti-colonial passions dormant since the end of Ottoman rule. The first of these entailed matters of finance and taxation. More decisive were actions taken in the aftermath of an uprising sparked by proposed tax increases, a short-lived affair that claimed several lives and led to the torching of Government House in Nicosia. Clamping down hard on the simmering insurrection, Governor Ronald Storrs, wielding near-dictatorial powers, dissolved the island's tri-ethnic legislative council, suspended civil liberties, banned political parties, and curtailed the press. Of most consequence, however, was his government's attempted interference in the internal workings of the Church of Cyprus, the historical bastion of both religious and secular authority in the Greek Cypriot community and of late an increasingly forceful voice espousing the cause of political union. A brief period of detente followed the 1940 Nazi invasion of Greece, but tensions quickly revived in the post-war era. On one side, the NATO-allied British, now determined to retain the colony because of its strategic position close to Suez and other eastern Mediterranean hot-spots, proposed the restoration of constitutional governance in exchange for political stability. On the other, the opposition, under its young, well-educated new leader Archbishop Makarios III, adopted a two-pronged approach, using diplomacy on the floor of the United Nations to win backing for their demands for self-determination and, in 1950, engaging the Greek Cypriot majority in a plebiscite whose result – ninety-six percent in favour of enosis – was widely heralded as an outright repudiation of Great Britain's revised colonial ambitions. In response, another crackdown was threatened as EOKA, along with a cast of supporters and detractors – Cyprus's communist party and allied trade unions, Greece and Turkey, and Volkan, an upstart Turkish Cypriot resistance movement – pressed their respective factional interests.[27] And with that, the stage was set for the eruption of murder and mayhem on the streets of Nicosia, Famagusta, and elsewhere, the opening act of a protracted struggle that was to play itself out to an inconclusive end on local and international stages.

When the Jennesses arrived in late November, the island had just been placed under a state of emergency, security entrusted to hundreds of young men drawn from the ranks of Britain's National Service, the population subject to harsh laws that prohibited public gatherings and strikes, and made possession of weapons a capital crime. Despite these measures, bombings and shootings, most directed toward government facilities and personnel, occurred with some regularity throughout their stay, as did strikes, mass demonstrations, and other acts of resistance. In March, Governor John Harding aggravated the situation further by arresting Makarios and banishing him to the Seychelles, a move that effectively handed control of EOKA to George Grivas, the militant leader of the organization's armed wing.[28] Yet with all that was unfolding, it was the underlying dynamic fuelling the crisis that drew Jenness's attention. What he saw, heard, and read convinced him that a seemingly unstoppable "tide of unreasoning nationalism" was blinding Greek Cypriot partisans to the potential dangers of pursuing self-determination and political union with the motherland as inseparable goals.[29]

Though hardly negligible, the least of the dangers he foresaw was the likelihood that severing ties with the Commonwealth and its preferential market arrangements, and merging with Greece – a country then grappling with high levels of debt and unemployment, and with the residue of a long and bitter civil war – would spell "economic suicide" for Cyprus. As things stood, the economic effects of mounting tensions were already evident in steep rises to the cost of living and the near death of foreign tourism. Moreover, the prospect of prolonged political instability cast a long shadow over foreign investment, particularly in mining, a sector employing thousands. "There can be no doubt that economically, the island will be ruined if the English and NATO ... let it join with Greece politically, but what are economics when nationalism with a capital letter is at stake."[30]

Far more ominous, he believed, was an aspect of the problem that was fast becoming all too real on the ground in Cyprus but so far had garnered scant mention in the international press: the rapid breakdown of what was once a relationship of mutual toleration and accommodation between Greek and Turkish Cypriots. During the uprising's early stages, British troopers bore the brunt of insurgent attacks. Mixed in, however, were outbreaks of communal violence, including a "nasty riot" that engulfed a small village on the outskirts of Kyrenia and sent thirteen people to hospital. For days afterward, Jenness noted, "every Greek shop in our little town was shuttered for fear the Turks would attack and sack them."[31] Over the ensuing months, disturbances of this kind were to become increasingly common, and, as they did, many Turkish Cypriots felt compelled to leave the sidelines of a struggle that had begun as a Greek fight for enosis and, under the banner of Volkan, take direct action to advance their own anti-enosis cause: taksim, partition of Cyprus into separate ethnic enclaves. There is no mistaking the "extremely bitter feeling of the Turkish Cypriots for the Greek Cypriots and vice versa," a situation, he feared, that was almost certain to spiral into "civil strife ... if the British leave the island, and the danger is then of [its becoming] a situation as explosive as that between Israel and the Arab states." More dire still, he imagined the possibility of the involvement of Greece and Turkey escalating beyond the role they were already playing in supplying the main factions with arms, an escalation that might well result in an invasion from the Turkish mainland, "even at the risk of a war with Greece."[32]

The analogy proved correct, as did his prediction of the internecine struggle that followed in the wake of independence in 1960 and the eventual intervention from abroad. The "fanaticism of modern nationalism" is a powerful force all but immune to compromise and destined to ebb only once it has "run its course," he wrote, reason enough to warrant Great Britain's early (and, he believed, likely) exit from a place growing ever more expensive to maintain, and whose military value, especially in an age of nuclear weaponry, was dubious at best. And yet "England cannot wash her hands of the island without further concern," not least for the sake of the vulnerable Turkish minority, who risked losing their homes and livelihoods, and possibly their lives, should the aspirations of their Greek neighbours ever come to pass.[33]

"I felt some sympathy for the movement" before heading off to Cyprus, Jenness told Stefansson, having thought of enosis, like liberation movements underway elsewhere, as a cause justifiably pressed against an unprincipled colonizer bent on exploiting its overseas possession for economic and military advantage. Findings from his own researches changed that opinion, convincing him that over the span of their occupation, the British had succeeded in "raising the island from a state of pure barbarism to the position of being probably the most prosperous area in the E. Mediterranean." Confirming his reading of the evidence were the misgivings and anxieties expressed to him by ordinary Cypriots about the very real prospect of seeing those gains evaporate, their fortunes held hostage to the unknowable outcome of protracted strife. Their worries were equally apparent in their inquiries about immigration to Canada, to Australia, or to other stable, prosperous havens. Tellingly, virtually none counted Greece or Turkey as an acceptable destination.[34]

With respect to other aspects of colonial policy, however, the anthropologist's judgment was less sanguine, especially in terms of Britain's handling – or, as he sized up the situation, mishandling – of what was surely the most bedevilling legacy of Constantinople's three hundred year rule: the millet system. Adopted from traditional Islamic practice in governing ethnically heterogeneous provinces, this system delegated responsibility for various state functions, including tax collection, to millets, semi-autonomous religious communities.[35] On Cyprus, the institution had served to transform the Orthodox Church, already the focus of Greek Cypriot life and identity since the fifth century AD, into a "political church" and its head, the archbishop, into an ethnarch empowered "to speak on *all* matters in the name of the Greek Cypriot people." In hindsight, the decision to preserve this arrangement after 1878, for whatever reasons, could only be seen as a grave miscalculation, he believed, one that left virtually undisturbed a wellspring of intensely parochial sentiment and a well-oiled organization capable of rousing some three-quarters of the island's population to action in defence of communal interests. This is precisely what happened in the concluding chapters of the Ottoman era, a time when crushing taxes, and a stagnating economy, symptoms of a declining empire, sparked a rebellious spirit among an impoverished, inward-looking, medieval-like peasantry.[36] Now, seventy years later, it was happening again, the church using its considerable power to mobilize the masses (and silence dissenters) from the pulpit and, to even greater effect, in Jenness's estimation, through its absolute control over the "education of Greek Cypriot children from the cradle to the grave."[37] It was with respect to this last, he thought, that the colonial administration had committed the "most serious mistake" in implementing its program of reforms, failing to introduce sweeping educational changes that would liberalize and standardize instruction for children on both sides of Cyprus's ethnic divide. Instead, curricular content remained in the hands of partisan functionaries who, with support from Athens and Istanbul, used the classroom to instil sharply ethnocentric points of view. "Archbishop Makarias [sic] and his coadjutors are heroes in a region where truth is merely expediency and the end justifies whatever means are necessary to attain it," he told his Oxford friend Beatrice Blackwood; "and if you peruse the [Greek] school readers, as we have done, you can understand why this is so – and also why 90% of all crimes committed in Cyprus are committed by youths between the ages of 15 and 22."[38]

Not a pretty picture. His prognosis for what lay ahead was no cheerier.

SWAN SONG

There were to be several more Mediterranean trips over the coming years, including a solo excursion through the French Pyrenees in 1960 in search of "my beloved Romanesque [and Gothic] churches," one more vestige of his Oxonian intellectual coming-of-age. Meantime, the study of Cyprus had exhausted Jenness's enthusiasm for taking on new European researches and, with it, his Guggenheim drawing account. But he was not yet ready to set aside his typewriter for good. As the book manuscript was being shopped around in search of a publisher, he began formulating quite a different project, one that would allow him to remain close to home: writing a narrative history of the pioneering investigations of some of the Geological Survey's most accomplished explorers. He was thinking of figures such as A.P. Low and J.B. Tyrell, men whose "remarkable journeys in what was then unknown territory" yielded a vast wealth of knowledge about the country's northern hinterlands. Assuming survey management would grant his request for access to their unpublished field notes, he told Henry Moe, "I shall have enough work to keep me out of mischief for the rest of my life."[39] Before the proposal's fate was decided, however, the Department of Northern Affairs and Natural Resources proffered an opportunity to take on something altogether different, a project tailor-made for someone of his professional expertise and personal inclinations: a critical retrospective of Inuit administration in Alaska, Canada, and Greenland.

Despite having been retired for a full decade, Jenness was no stranger around the corridors of Northern Affairs, having been recruited in the late fifties as an "unofficial consultant" by sons John and Robert, both now in senior-level positions with the ministry.[40] Some long-time associates were there, too, including Graham Rowley, who had worked on Dorset archaeology in the eastern Arctic. The idea that he should put his many years of experience to more purposeful use came from anthropologist Victor Valentine, director of the department's social sciences research arm, the Northern Research Coordination Centre. With John's assurances that his father, now seventy-four, was up to the task, Valentine offered him a $5,000 grant-in-aid to tackle the project as an independent researcher. In seeking approval for the expenditure from Treasury Board, Deputy Minister R.G. Robertson explained that the study's goal was to "appraise the degrees of success with which the United States, Canada, and Denmark have managed to bring about the integration of their Eskimo populations into the economy and society of western civilization," the means – chiefly educational and economic – employed to that end, and the potential lessons for Canadian policy-makers to be taken from the experiences of their counterparts elsewhere. Such "a critique of the policies and programmes of the Government of Canada would be valuable," he added, "especially as these originate with a person with no connection with the government, hence [he] is able to be objective."[41]

"It is rather a tough assignment for a man of my age," Jenness admitted to Blackwood at the time, his heart attack on Cyprus, followed a year later by a near-fatal car crash in which he "'sputniked' over a 40' bank in my Volkswagen one dark foggy night," doubtless taking a bounce or two out of his step. "But I did not wish to turn down the job," he told his friend; "Well done, it might be very useful and timely; badly done, it should damn the writer to – oblivion." In any event, the very real possibility of the effort serving the greater good, made the opportunity all but irresistible. "I believe that Canada has much to learn from her neighbours on either side and that a careful study of all three regions may strengthen the hands of the new administration here, which has already done much to redeem Canada's shameful neglect of her Eskimos in past years. It will be my swan-song."[42] It was just that, a final reflection on the fate of a people whose future remained as uncertain in the 1960s as it had been when he breathed polar air for the first time a half-century ago.

Setting qualms aside, Jenness committed himself to the project whole-heartedly, his keen sense of purpose driving him to jump the gun in the spring of 1960, months before receiving official notice of the grant's approval.[43] Northern Affairs allotted two years to complete the work and assumed that a mix of published sources, government records, and consultations with public officials directly involved in each country's northern administration would provide sufficient grist for the mill. Their expectations seemed reasonable enough in the initial stages, a complete draft of the study's first part, on Alaska, landing on Valentine's desk in October that same year, followed nine months later by the first portion (the years to 1940) of his examination of Canada. Early submission of the Alaska manuscript gave rise to several weeks' worth of memo writing to determine whether all three case studies should be published as a single volume or in separate parts, as was eventually decided, and, more importantly, whether the coordination centre should issue the report(s) in its own series or solicit the services of an outside press. Jenness recommended the latter option, pointing out to Valentine that what he had written about Alaska "contains criticisms of a foreign government's policies with which the Canadian government may be loth to associate itself." His reasoning prevailed. On the further assumption that a domestic outlet was preferable to one in the United States – the University of Chicago had already expressed interest – an agreement was brokered with the Montreal-based Arctic Institute of North America to take on this and subsequent volumes.[44]

With that hurdle behind him, a second quickly cropped up: the unevenness of information in department files pertaining to contemporary conditions in Canada's eastern Arctic, especially in Arctic Quebec. Compounding the problem, Jenness's lack of personal experience of the area limited his ability to appreciate the full effect of changes local Inuit had been confronted with in recent decades. As a result, arrangements were made for him to board the government patrol vessel *C.D. Howe* at Frobisher Bay (now Igaluit) in mid-September 1961 for her homeward voyage, a fortnight's cruise that allowed him to visit half a dozen villages situated on the Quebec side of Hudson Strait and around the shores of Ungava Bay to Port Burwell, off the northern tip of the Labrador peninsula.[45] Oddly enough, Labrador itself, a region whose administrative history had unfolded almost entirely under British and Newfoundland authority, had somehow been omitted from the project's original scope.[46] The inadvertent oversight was belatedly corrected, bringing with it funding to extend the research into a third year and to make possible Jenness's second foray into a part of Inuit territory as unfamiliar to him as Arctic Quebec had been: the coastline stretching northward from Goose Bay to the village of Nain. Finally, supplementary backing from the Danish National Museum allowed one last excursion, in 1964, a trip that began with a stopover in Copenhagen to consult government officials and records and concluded with a month-long voyage to Greenland's southwestern shores, the island's most densely populated region.[47] Missing entirely from the picture was Siberia, an area still closed to westerners and for which precious few English-language sources were then available. What scant comment Jenness offered on contemporary conditions there drew on the *Soviet News Bulletin* and a handful of scholarly papers, among them a recently published piece on culture change under four flags, including the Hammer and Sickle.[48]

In all, the project lasted twice as long as intended and cost more than double the official estimates. Nevertheless, the additional investment made possible a first-of-its-kind contribution to the literature: a comparative historical and analytical study of national policies – chiefly in the areas of health, education, and economic development – and their cumulative effects on the ground. Reported in five volumes, some 600 pages in total, the first part, on Alaska, appeared in the Arctic Institute's technical papers series in 1962, the last, an extended essay reflecting on lessons learned and future prospects, in 1968, the year its author turned eighty-two and a year before his weakened heart finally gave out. Although it didn't always keep him close to home, as the Geological Survey project was meant to do, the research and writing certainly kept him busy for the remainder of his days. But, as a hefty stack of letters and memoranda amply attests, the work turned out to be less successful in keeping him out of mischief, his wide-ranging and often strongly worded criticisms of Ottawa's role in the Arctic following the Second World War ruffling more than a few feathers within the Northern Affairs establishment. Through it all, his resolve never flagged, sticking with the project and defending the central tenets of his argument to the end. "This work is my last crusade on ... behalf [of Canada's Inuit]," he told Deputy Minister Robertson at the time, "and despite the many errors it doubtless contains, I cherish the hope that it will contribute a little to their future welfare."[49]

Readers need look no further than the first few chapter headings in the second volume of *Eskimo Administration* – "Wards of the Police," "A Shackled Administration," "Bureaucracy in Inaction" – to get the gist of their author's take on Ottawa's handling of Inuit affairs to mid-century. Unlike Greenland and Labrador, regions whose history of state involvement dates back to the eighteenth century, or Alaska, where it began with "Seward's Folly" in 1867, Canada's version of the story begins only in 1903 with the planting of a trio of police posts atop the permafrost. Meant to check the activities of foreign whalers frequenting its distant arctic shores, the decision to dispatch a few Mounties marked the country's first public demonstration of its authority in territories over which it had held de jure sovereignty for a generation.[50] Slow as it was to show the flag in its northern hinterlands, the Dominion was even slower to accept responsibility for protecting, let alone advancing, the material and social well-being of the few thousand Inuit who lived there, "shamefully evading [doing so] when it shuffled off those tasks on the traders and missionaries, neither of whom possessed the means to carry them out." The government's position began to shift in the early twenties, if only slightly and only as an afterthought, spurred by the discovery of oil in the vicinity of Norman Wells, along the mid-course of the Mackenzie. This led to formation of a Northwest Territories and Yukon Branch within the Department of Interior, a section of the bureaucracy charged with overseeing orderly development of the frontier's non-renewable resources. To his credit, branch director O.S. Finnie recognized that any meaningful exercise of national sovereignty must also entail "the duty ... to civilize the Eskimos and to safeguard their health and welfare," something the Americans had been doing in Alaska since the 1880s and the Danes in Greenland for far longer.[51] As subsequent events were to make painfully apparent, though, a duty recognized is hardly guarantee of a duty fulfilled. This unfortunate reality resulted from years of squabbling over questions bearing on the legal status of Inuit – were they effectively "Indians" and thus a constitutionally mandated federal responsibility, a view Quebec advanced and the Supreme Court eventually upheld in a 1939 ruling – and vacillation over whether their administration belonged to Indian Affairs (as it did for a brief time when they were included under the Indian Act) or to the Northwest Territories Branch, its principal home to mid-century.[52] While Ottawa dithered, the Arctic "stagnated," the federal government, "overly jealous of its sovereignty in the region," exhibiting an unwillingness – or incapacity – to decide "what it should do with it, or with the Eskimos who inhabited it." In the meantime, it operated in the north by "remote control," ceding de facto responsibility for education, health care, and the relief of destitute cases to missionaries and Hudson's Bay Company factors who did what they could but always in accord with their respective religious beliefs or business practices and at whatever level their own resources allowed.[53]

Back in 1921, when he was with the Fifth Thule Expedition on Hudson Bay, explorer Knud Rasmussen was shocked to discover the deplorable state of health and general welfare prevailing among the Inuit he encountered in that remote precinct. The contrast with conditions in his native Greenland could not have been more stark. There, the Danes had implemented a "radically new theory of colonial rule" in the second half of the nineteenth century, one with the overriding objective of preparing the Inuit "to lead their people up civilization's steep path." It was "only the requirements of international courtesy and his appreciation of the hospitality and assistance he had received from Canadian officials, [that] restrained [Rasmussen] from publishing his judgement," Jenness would later explain in a letter addressed to the Council of the Northwest Territories, hoping that the veiled threat of negative international publicity, like periodic fears of foreign disregard for its sovereignty, might finally stir Ottawa to action.[54] Indeed, he hoped to accomplish something similar in writing *People of the Twilight*, at one point telling Anglican bishop Archibald Fleming that the 1928 memoir was conceived with a "definite purpose ... to enlist the sympathy of Canadians in the people whom we have too long neglected. I think you will agree with me that the Eskimo can render valuable service in any development of our Arctic and should be protected and assisted on that account, no less than for humanitarian reasons." Yet as "you doubtless know," he continued, on a note of obvious resignation, "the outlook for them at present is very cheerless," made so by politicians and bureaucrats seemingly content to do as little as possible in order to "limit the expense of administering the north country," all the while claiming that they were allowing the Inuit to live their lives in their own way.[55] "Inactivity," Jenness later wrote of the pre-war situation, "brings its own nemesis. While the government idly drifted, the fur trade collapsed, dragging in its fall the only pillars that were holding up the Eskimo economy. Destitution and hunger stalked the Arctic, and Ottawa could see no remedy except unending relief."[56]

The Second World War would come and go before the first concrete measures were introduced to begin undoing the myriad problems that had accumulated over the preceding half century or more. Even then, it was not merely the winds of progressive social reform blowing across the country that finally roused the government to action; it was also concern for the nation's reputation should pan-Arctic DEW-Line construction and other Cold War continental defence projects shine a very public light on the "degradation of her Eskimos," a people "dragged out of their isolation and caught up in the turmoil" spawned by unchecked disease, recurrent economic upheavals, rapid culture change, and a traditional way of life teetering on the brink.[57] The first signs of a new era dawned in 1945 when the Department of National Health and Welfare assumed direct responsibility for Inuit health care, giving priority to diagnosing and treating tuberculosis, the region's most widespread and devastating scourge, and to lowering infant mortality rates. Establishment of the Department of Northern Affairs and Natural Resources followed eight years later. Heralding the country's change of course were key public pronouncements from Prime Minister Louis St-Laurent and his Northern Affairs minister, Jean Lesage, the leader acknowledging that past governments had administered the north "in an almost continuing state of absence of mind," his minister committing the country to affording "the Eskimos the same rights, privileges, opportunities, and responsibilities as all other Canadians ... to enable them to share fully the national life of Canada."[58] With that, the treasury's taps opened and a torrent of money and personnel – doctors and nurses, teachers, settlement managers, social scientists, economic development specialists – began flowing northward in a concerted effort to resettle the population in year-round communities and to modernize every facet of their existence, seemingly at any price. As the Danes had already done to admirable effect, moreover, their aim was to "place the direction of local affairs" squarely in Inuit hands. Having refrained from making any but the most paltry public investments before 1950, two years into the new regime Ottawa's expenditures on electrification, education, health and sanitation, housing, welfare, and other social programs in the Northwest Territories alone ran to twelve million dollars, hit sixty million by decade's end, and continued on an upward trajectory thereafter. Whatever else this barrage of money and good intentions might eventually achieve, virtually overnight it turned a people who had been all but invisible for generations into "one of the most heavily assisted, administered and studied groups on earth."[59]

Given his negative opinion of the government's pre-war track record, or lack thereof, Jenness took some comfort in the prospect that Ottawa's newfound determination (and hefty commitment of resources) could repair the considerable harm its prolonged neglect had worked on Inuit society. But what he had observed to this point filled him with doubts about where that new resolve might ultimately be leading, especially when compared with the exemplary progress already achieved in Greenland, then verging on becoming a self-governing province of Denmark. Canada's modus operandi, he wrote, put him in mind of a builder "trying to erect a skyscraper ... without drafting an architectural plan or locating a firm foundation," working to achieve an array of laudable and necessary objectives – eradicating disease, improving educational standards, promoting economic opportunities – but failing to link its efforts to accomplishing an overarching, long-term goal, or even to fully orchestrate its activities so that attempts to solve one problem didn't create, or aggravate, others. Sadly, the unintended consequences born of policy-makers seemingly "steering without a compass" – among them rising levels of poverty and dependency on state assistance, alcohol abuse and domestic violence, and a deepening social malaise, particularly among the young – were making themselves evident in virtually every locality across the Arctic.[60]

Nothing spoke more forcefully to the shortcomings of government policy, Jenness believed, than its failure to plan adequately for the ramifications of what was certainly its greatest post-war success: arresting, and then reversing, the population's precipitous downward slide. The turn-around had been stunning, numbers rebounding by nearly sixty-five percent in a single generation and showing little sign of retreating from an annual rate of increase bordering on four percent. As that crisis eased, however, another emerged in its place: the widening disparity between demographic growth and growth of opportunities for families to earn incomes sufficient to "provide security, the necessities of life and a few of its comforts," without need to depend on "heavy doles."[61] By his count, approximately one-fifth of the Arctic's 2,500 Inuit families in 1962 had achieved that measure of independence, earning steady incomes from employment, typically unskilled jobs, mainly at government-run facilities. This left the remainder to cobble together livelihoods from various sources, most scraping by on a mix of land-based activities and casual labour, augmented with welfare and other social benefits. Development of the region's non-renewable resources held unquestionable potential to create large numbers of jobs sufficient to boost living standards to southern, or near-southern, levels. Early indication of that promise came in the late fifties when a nickel mine opened at Rankin Inlet with eighty Inuit on its payroll. That momentous occasion was not long in setting off a frenzy of mineral-prospecting and claim-staking across a vast area encompassing Hudson Bay and Baffin Island. The mine's closure after only five years pointed to the considerable risks entailed in operating on a frontier as remote, and as environmentally challenging, as Canada's Arctic. Such risks, and their attendant costs, Jenness believed, were likely to discourage private investment on a scale "capable of absorbing [the Arctic's] fast-growing labour force," at least in the short term. Nor was it certain that those who might decide to invest in capital-intensive projects would actually hire Inuit workers in appreciable numbers, especially when government-run schools were slow to provide students with the marketable skills – perhaps most importantly, a reasonable command of English (or French) – needed to compete for better-paying jobs, and when lingering racial bias against Aboriginal peoples all across the country regularly translated into whites-only hiring practices.[62]

Notwithstanding Ottawa's vaunted vision of an Arctic soon to be dotted with oil wells and mines, there were some less optimistic planners who pinned their hopes for the region's revived fortunes on an intermediate form of development: a mixed economy based on labour-intensive commercial schemes for harvesting renewable resources, including animal husbandry, combined with the production of artwork and crafts, tourism, and other cottage industries. Robert Jenness counted himself among those at Northern Affairs who saw the possibilities of such an approach, explaining to a co-worker that of the 2,000 families his father had identified as being dependent on assistance in some degree, a good 400 were actually maintaining self-supporting households from the proceeds of hunting and fishing alone and another 500 "might gain an equally satisfactory livelihood" from engaging in both the old and new sectors of the economy. Although he was certain that utilization of wildlife would continue indefinitely for cultural and domestic purposes, Jenness senior didn't share his son's enthusiasm for the potentials of new industries predicated on the Arctic's renewable resources, especially when both stocks, and their markets, were prone to fluctuate, sometimes wildly, or might dry up entirely. Of course, even if such schemes were able to operate under optimal conditions, Robert noted, for the present this would still leave "the equivalent of 800 Eskimo families with no future but sub-marginal living standards and/or Government relief." While he was convinced that the current situation "was not as critical as suggested by Dr. Jenness," his fellow planners could ill-afford to downplay the economic consequences of adding 800 or more families to the people-resource equation over the next ten years, as was certain to happen.[63]

This was precisely his father's point: government estimates of the timing, and likely benefits, of non-renewable resource development were too rosy, the impact of its economic (and educational) policies and programs too little and, he feared, too late to contain, let alone reverse, the widening gap between local aspirations for a decent standard of living and the necessary means to satisfy them. Without a drastic decrease of population or a fortuitous demand for Inuit labour sufficient to guarantee stable employment and adequate wages across the board – something equivalent to the modest prosperity that commercial cod fisheries and ancillary industries were bringing to Greenland at the time – the coming years were certain to find politicians and bureaucrats "called upon to feed and clothe not 13,000 only, but 25,000." From his perspective, neither of those prospects seemed likely, at least not for the foreseeable future. Combined with what appeared to be policies and spending practices favourable to retaining most of the population in the north – effectively a palliative approach to development – what he feared loomed on the near horizon were the "shadows of a welfare society," the very condition least conducive to realizing the state's lofty (and long overdue) ambition of empowering Inuit to determine their own futures from a range of possible alternatives.[64] By the mid-seventies, other observers were echoing that same bleak forecast: the government's chosen path was the "path to welfare colonialism," one destined to "'shut out' the local community and the native people from the processes directed toward their own modernity."[65]

◆

In wrapping up his assessment of Canada's record, Jenness was given to remark that, for the present, "it is the optimists who are steering our arctic vessel; and whoever has the welfare of the Eskimos at heart will pray that their hopes and predictions will come true."[66] For someone who had spent the best part of fifty years keeping tabs on where that ship was heading, hoping against hope probably comes closer to describing his state of mind. Asked by Northern Affairs to render an opinion on whether the country's policies had succeeded in integrating Inuit into the mainstream of national social and economic life, the preponderance of evidence led him to conclude they had not. Nor was that lofty goal likely to be achieved anytime soon, convinced as he was that time for decisive action was fleeting and that sitting politicians were unlikely to write a blank cheque to create thousands of permanent jobs. As both anthropologist and citizen, however, he was unprepared to leave it at that. Hoping to shine new light on the dilemma, Jenness used the occasion of a federally sponsored conference in Montreal – "Resources for Tomorrow" – to advocate speedy adoption of an alternative approach, one he believed would help to ease the Arctic's mounting economic crisis at reasonable cost while simultaneously opening the door to de facto integration. Achieving those goals, he argued from the podium on that mid-autumn day in 1961, hinged on revamping a system of state-run schooling presently ill-equipped to prepare youngsters for much of anything, let alone for making hard choices about their own futures in a rapidly changing world. "Education and work. Those two keys, and those alone, can unlock the door of Canada's baffling Eskimo problem. Neither by itself can be effective, for education cannot supply work where there is none, and work, steady work, is scarcely attainable today without education."[67]

Central to his strategy was implementation of a federally run and financed program specially tailored to provide promising teenagers and young adults – females and males, from sixteen to twenty-one years of age – with the technical skills and language proficiency needed to participate in the national workforce. Falling somewhere between the "time-honoured method of emigration" and Depression-era labour mobilization schemes in the United States, he envisioned formation of a "special youth corps" whose recruits would receive funding, and other assistance, in relocating to urban areas outside the Arctic where they would train as teachers and nurses, pilots and weather observers, police officers and administrators – a range of possible fields for which no instruction was then available through the lone vocational school in the north, in Yellowknife. On completing their courses, a government bureau set up for the purpose would place graduates with employers, mostly in the large and vibrant job markets of the country's major towns and cities but, whenever feasible, also in the north "so that they can speed up that region's development."[68] The broader significance of this last could hardly be underestimated. Grooming an elite to take positions long reserved for qallunaat outsiders would lay the groundwork for restoring Inuit autonomy over their own affairs. Yet for the moment it was the first outcome that interested Jenness more. Seeing in their example great promise to persuade others to follow suit, he anticipated the scheme setting in motion a process of chain migration that, if sustained, would serve to lessen the Malthusian-like predicament facing those whose preference was to remain in their ancestral territory. Equally important, it would help to break down the social and cultural barriers preventing Inuit – and other Aboriginal peoples, for whom similar programs, he believed, were needed – from availing themselves of the same range of opportunities and choices open to all other Canadians.

Although crucial to its purpose, requiring students to forego the familiar surroundings of home for "a strange and perhaps unfriendly world" in southern Canada loomed large as the leading obstacle to getting such an initiative off the ground, let alone to achieving any appreciable measure of success. Even so, "young Eskimos *will* volunteer," he asserted, but only "if we carefully work out a suitable plan and sell it to them with the same fervor as we sell our television sets and our automobiles." Unlike ordinary pitchmen, however, we "must never fail to live up to our obligations, and never promise what we cannot or will not fulfill." Towering above all other considerations in this regard was the need to guard against participants being cut off from the moral support of their families and communities, among the most grievous of individual and collective harms inflicted under the Indian Affairs system of residential schools, by then nearly defunct. "Human beings are not automata," he wrote elsewhere on the issue, "and it violates our conception of human needs and rights, it disorganizes the family and the society, arbitrarily to separate parents and children more than seems absolutely necessary." The remedy he contemplated was both enlightened and straightforward: making provision for recruits entering the program to relocate with family members, to lodge together in subsidized housing, and to receive financial assistance to help defray day-today expenses for themselves and their kin. "These are not hard conditions," he told conference delegates; aside from the state subsidy, "they hardly differ from the conditions an Italian immigrant expects to find when he disembarks at Montreal or Toronto."[69] And they were certainly far better than the conditions faced by status Indians, whose inability to find work on over-crowded reserves had begun to push them into towns and cities following the end of the last war. Within twenty years, close to one in five had moved, some 40,000 people, most possessing little education or training, virtually all without benefit of subsidies or special facilities to ease their adjustment to urban life. In reporting findings from the first nationwide survey of conditions in contemporary Aboriginal communities, Harry Hawthorn would observe "it is a basic tenet of economics that greater mobility of the labour force contributes to the increased efficiency and higher per capita income over the economy as a whole. Logically, it should apply to individual Indians bands as well." Previously on the record (as discussant) in support of the means and ends of Jenness's Montreal proposal, Hawthorn now urged Ottawa to invest heavily in training programs specifically geared to encourage off-reserve migration as a viable and effective strategy for economic development.[70]

Jenness's unflinching criticism of Canada's pre-war role in the Arctic elicited sparse comment from the few Northern Affairs staffers who read the manuscript's opening section. But when the chapters examining recent developments were circulated more widely midway through 1962, Jenness had a good idea of what was coming. Above all else, their pages amplified core arguments – namely, the uncertainty of renewable and non-renewable resource potentials, and the impermanence of national interests in the Arctic – that a pair of department officials had vociferously challenged as unfounded when he first aired them at the "Resources for Tomorrow" conference.[71] As expected, the majority of bureaucrats who reviewed the draft were similarly critical, most taking strong exception to a publically funded study that impugned the value of educational and economic policies they were responsible for formulating, and implementing, and did so on grounds they found factually deficient, analytically suspect, and, in the main, exceedingly bleak. Shortly before the months' long back-and-forth debating of these issues began – a strenuous patch he later admitted felt like being "under heavy machine-gun fire from several quarters" at once – Jenness reminded Deputy Minister Robertson that the department's grant-in-aid had been offered with no strings attached and that his decision to accept had been rooted in the understanding that with the money came "complete freedom to state my own convictions and pass my own untrammeled judgement on past events and policies." Without that independence, he reasoned, neither the government, nor especially the Inuit, were likely to derive any benefit from his years of experience and reflection.[72] Despite having consulted various people inside Northern Affairs over the preceding months, that he chose to make the draft available for their review at all was thus a professional courtesy only, not a contractual obligation to obtain official endorsement for his ideas. Even so, with the thoroughly scrutinized (and partly revised) manuscript finally in the Arctic Institute editor's hands in late November, its author was still left to wonder if the "final shots" over the matter had yet to be fired. What troubled him, he confessed to Hawthorn, was not knowing whether the press "will be allowed to publish it – as is," or if the government might decide to withhold its subvention rather than be seen as authorizing a study that advanced positions at odds with its own.[73] As it happened, his suspicions on that score were not entirely without foundation.

His harshest critic was B.G. Sivertz, director of the Northern Administration Branch and the official who had led the charge against what he believed to be the "thoroughly untenable premises" of the Montreal presentation. To his mind, the most galling of Jenness's statements that day was the allegedly erroneous assertion that government interest in the Arctic was solely contingent on the region's continuing military importance, a claim since published, to Sivertz's chagrin, "with no correction," in the conference proceedings. In a bluntly worded memorandum meant for Robertson's eyes alone, he went on to characterize the study as deeply and variously flawed, and construed its main conclusion – in his words, that "Canada's northland is worthless and Canadians should withdraw from it" – as both unwarranted and inimical to the purposes for which the project was originally authorized. What he expected to find in the monograph's pages was a work of science, he told the deputy, a fair and balanced assessment of the documentary record bearing on the state's involvement in the Arctic over the past six decades, and especially since the founding of Northern Affairs in 1954. What he discovered instead was polemic thinly disguised as history, a treatise whose tone was unaccountably gloomy and whose central arguments reflected a highly subjective and simplistic interpretation of a deficient and selective body of evidence. "I think the impact of [Canadian writer Farley] Mowat and Jenness are remarkably similar," he allowed, "a feeling of being disturbed, – of something seriously wrong, – that government people from Ministers down have (perhaps unconsciously) unworthy motivations, – a national policy is questionable, – judgement of administrators is poor."[74] Ironically, this was in good part the point of

Jenness's self-proclaimed "last crusade," an effort not undertaken with the purpose of condemning the motives and competence of politicians and bureaucrats but of calling public attention to glaring inconsistencies between the country's declared goals in the sphere of contemporary Inuit affairs, and its capacity – and perhaps its commitment – to deliver in a timely fashion, if ever. In the circumstances, being lumped together with the author of two acclaimed and persuasive best-sellers, *People of the Deer* and *The Desperate People*, was actually a compliment, Mowat's unsettling depictions of unimaginable hardship among Inuit in the barren grounds west of Hudson Bay having focused international attention on a remote group of people seemingly ignored by Ottawa's reinvented, post-war northern strategy. Being an insider, of course, Sivertz's words were scarcely meant to flatter, Jenness's monograph, at least in its present form, striking him as a baseless condemnation of policies and initiatives alleged to be ineffectual despite what he – Sivertz – took to be ample indications to the contrary.[75]

"I think it would be a catastrophe if this were published under the imprimatur of the [Northern Research Coordination Centre], or the Arctic Institute as the 'findings' of the well-known Canadian scientist, Dr. Diamond Jenness," Sivertz admitted, barely concealing his frustration – and irritation – with the situation. That said, he continued, "I hesitate to suggest that the department decline to print it," assured as he was that some other outlet would eventually take on the job. All things considered, it was probably best to "place our entire comment right into Dr. Jenness' hands," a straightforward tactic that just might encourage him to dampen the most troublesome of his contentions, or better still, convince him to withdraw the work altogether. Sivertz, for one, seemed to be keen on the latter possibility, sensing from previous conversations with the man "that he does not intend to finish his task of making the studies of Eskimo administration in Greenland and the Soviet Union, – that he has little enthusiasm for the Canadian study and realizes he does not know much about it."[76] And why not: after all, Jenness was closing in on his seventy-seventh birthday, was not in the best of health, and for over two years now had been keeping up a steady pace of research and writing and northern travel, enough to sap the energies of someone very much his junior. If Jenness were indeed ready to back down, however, his spirited exchanges with Sivertz and Robertson on the substance of their criticisms revealed no trace of it. Instead, they signalled determination to let honestly given opinions be proven right, or wrong, through the test of time. Prepared for the possibility that his interpretation of the record might well "prejudice my claim to Olympian impartiality, I took the risk with open eyes," he told Robertson, "because, as you know, I have been deeply concerned with the welfare of the Eskimos throughout most of my life." For now, he wryly added, the wisest course is to remember "quot homines, tot sententiae" – many people, many minds.[77]

◆

The comparative study of northern administration completed after six arduous and sometimes tumultuous years, Jenness settled into a second retirement of sorts, this one a retreat into quiet contemplation. Spending the coldest months in rented digs in Ottawa, and the warmer ones at the family's country home overlooking the picturesque Gatineau River, north of town, he kept busy by trying his hand – apparently with some reluctance, at least at first - as memoirist.[78] Given his life-long avoidance of pretense, it is scarcely surprising that he elected to overlook practically the whole of his professional career in the resulting manuscript, preferring to recount his adventurous skirting of Soviet authority in the Diomedes, for instance, and his tension-ridden travels in a Europe verging on war rather than to set the record straight about formative intellectual influences, his falling-out with Barbeau, or negotiating the tricky byways of a life as citizen, anthropologist, and government employee. In large part, these conspicuous silences reveal a great deal about the man. Ever inclined to take his work, but never himself, seriously, he must have been content in the knowledge that his sizeable scholarly bibliography stood as statement enough on the things that mattered to him most.

His adoption of a playfully self-deprecating subtitle – "Some Memories of a Taugenichts" – a good-for-nothing – was equally in character. However, the motivation and intent behind his main title – "Through Darkening Spectacles" – are less evident.[79] It may well be that "darkening spectacles" simply referred to the vantage point from which the senior Jenness was writing – that of an octogenarian conjuring images of people, places, and events from the near and more distant reaches of his past. Either that or perhaps it was an expression of his darkening mood, a deepening disillusionment not with himself but with the general drift of post-war developments in his adoptive homeland. As dubious about Canada's political culture in the sixties as he had been before shipping out for the battlefield in 1917, what troubled him for the present was the uncertainty, and evident disorganization, gripping official Ottawa, a situation that persisted through the decade's middle years owing to a succession of minority governments and extensive "reshuffling" of ministries of state, including the merger of Indian and Northern Affairs into a single department. In a letter to Harry Hawthorn, he vented his frustration with the state of affairs in uncharacteristically cynical terms, telling his friend that "If there is an election this coming year I'm going to vote for Mao-Tse-tung or Fidel Castro." "Meanwhile," the rant continued, "Canada will puff out its chest at the U.N., tell the world what it should be doing, point to its own magnificent achievements in the spheres of education and welfare, and continue to breed slums, turn out illiterate graduates, and fill the air with radio and television puerilities."[80]

In view of the work that had engaged him so thoroughly during the preceding half-dozen years, surely it was the unrelenting problems plaguing the country's First Peoples that weighed most heavily on Jenness's mind, problems, he feared, "the Canadian government ... will doubtless close its eyes to unless they are brought to its attention from abroad." Weeks earlier, he had told geographer Trevor Lloyd, only partly in jest, that the Arctic Institute should nominate *Eskimo Administration* for a Nobel Prize. If nothing else, he mused, the ensuing publicity just might "force the Canadian government to initiate action and positive measures to redeem the plight of its Eskimos, and with them, the Indians."[81] As it happened, events in the early to mid-sixties hinted that those long-awaited steps finally might be in the offing. More importantly, those years also witnessed the renewal of public awareness of the crisis confronting the country's Aboriginal population and of calls for government to take ameliorative action. A trend stirred back to life by a confluence of emergent domestic forces analogous to developments unfolding in the United States and elsewhere across the globe, two factors proved particularly consequential in shaping popular perceptions of the issue: the challenge to Canadian unity posed by a new brand of Quebec nationalism and its demands for special status within confederation and growing consciousness of the grave injustices worked by the Indian Act, a law sanctioning race-based discrimination against a minority group. Sensitive to the shifting climate of opinion, and to its own negligible record of success, Indian Affairs took various steps aimed at accelerating the removal of barriers still standing between Aboriginals and society's mainstream, and, in what amounted to a departure from long-standing practice, explored ways to systematize, and streamline, the resolution of mounting grievances and claims pertaining to treaty and land issues. With few exceptions, however, these initiatives fell well short of the mark, undone by squabbles internal to the branch and, on the national stage, to contentious matters of inter-governmental relations affecting Ottawa's plans to devolve education, health, and welfare service for Indians to the provinces and to the remarkably low priority accorded Aboriginal issues on the day's political agenda. Indicative of the last, six different ministers held the Indian Affairs portfolio through six uninterrupted years of minority government, hardly conditions conducive to mustering the political capital necessary for implementing substantial policy reforms.[82]

Meanwhile, the 1967 general release of volume one of *A Survey of the Contemporary Indians of Canada*, a first-of-its-kind, government-funded study conducted under Hawthorn's direction, captured media attention and further galvanized public sentiment, offering readers a detailed account of the unpardonable extent of poverty, ill-health, and other disparities from national norms, along with trenchant analyses of institutional factors – chiefly legal, fiduciary, and administrative – deterring improvement on virtually every front. However, the report's greatest impact, especially for Aboriginal leaders, and its principal legacy derived from its assertion that realization of justice ultimately depended on every person's right to choose freely how and where to live. To that end, the authors urged adoption of a principle they dubbed "citizens plus," their refinement of a "vaguely worded recommendation" that had emerged from parliamentary hearings into the internal workings of the Indian Affairs Branch held between 1959 and 1961. At the time, the investigative committee's members concluded that First Peoples' exercise of the full rights of citizenship "must be without prejudice to the retention of cultural, historical, and other economic benefits which they have inherited." Articulated more precisely in what came to be known as the Hawthorn Report, the concept of "citizens plus" hinged on recognition that, along with "the normal rights and duties of citizenship," Indians "also possess certain rights simply by virtue of being Indians" – that is, rights emanating from historic statutory and treaty arrangements, and from their status as descendants of the first occupants of territories that have since come to comprise Canada.[83] For a growing segment of the Aboriginal population, the way forward was evident: it hinged on formal recognition, and protection, of those special rights. Within government, by contrast, satisfying that demand effectively posed much the same predicament as it did when Ottawa instituted the means and ends of its administration at the time of Confederation, a full century earlier: "how to protect Indian interests while at the same time integrating Indians into the mainstream of Canadian society on an equal basis with other citizens."[84]

Prospects for reaching an equitable resolution of these complex problems appeared to brighten midway through 1968 when voters ended the string of minority federal governments by handing the Liberals, and the party's newly chosen leader, Pierre Elliott Trudeau, a majority at the polls. Soon thereafter, Indian Affairs embarked on a series of open consultations across the country with the stated purpose of engaging Aboriginal peoples as partners in revising the Indian Act. In his opening remarks, Minister Jean Chrétien set the tone by characterizing the discussions as an exercise in "consultative democracy" meant to provide Indians with "a sense of participation" in determining their own future. But his words also included a crucial caveat: in essence, whatever positions the proceedings eventually produced would not necessarily translate into policy, or legislative action, on the part of government.[85]

The implications of this frank admonition became abundantly clear on 25 June 1969 when Chrétien rose in the House of Commons to outline the government's plans for reforming the entire sphere of Indian affairs. The outgrowth of a year-long parallel process of closed-door, sub rosa deliberations among cabinet members and upper-echelon bureaucrats, the new policy directive embodied Liberal principles of individual equality, freedom of choice, and responsibility. It also espoused the idea that preserving special rights for cultural collectivities such as those spelled out in the Indian Act – or in the case of Quebec, acceding to nationalist demands for special status – was incompatible with advancing universal equality and the guarantee of every individual's right to "full, free, and non-discriminatory participation" in the many dimensions of Canadian life.[86] Consistent with Liberal values, no less with the prime minister's personal vision of a just society, the government's otherwise lofty ambitions proved blind to a growing conviction among Aboriginals in favour of retaining, even expanding, their special rights. Instead, the (aptly named) white paper the minister tabled in the House prescribed a set of sweeping changes – including repeal of the Act and transfer to native hands of lands held by the Crown in trust – whose inevitable effect constituted wholesale denial of their historical identity as First Peoples. Combined with sparking a deep sense of betrayal among leaders who had entered into the concurrent round of consultations with the branch in good faith, the immediate consequence of the Liberal initiative was to harden Indian resolve – and with it, the resolve of all peoples of Aboriginal descent in Canada – to push for a different deal, one that did not force them to jettison their heritage and historic rights as the price of realizing the long-denied promise of equality.[87] Their first victory, official withdrawal of the white paper, was two years in the making. Other successes, none easily achieved, were to follow in due course, among them entrenchment of Aboriginal rights in the Constitution Act of 1982, a suite of landmark court decisions clarifying those rights, and a new generation of comprehensive treaties, including settlement of an Inuit claim that resulted in creation of the territory of Nunavut in 1999. Yet despite these monumental gains, glaring inequalities persist to this day, most noticeably in the disproportionately low levels of health and economic well being that are the unpardonable lot of the country's First Peoples, rural and urban. These were much the same disparities that first spurred Jenness's commitment to policy reform back in the thirties and to which he spoke most force-fully during his appearance before the joint parliamentary committee a decade later. Clearly, the struggle to right innumerable historical wrongs is still a long way from completion.

While these separate and unequal processes were inching toward their fateful collision, the fates also held Jenness in their ever-tightening grip. Mind and wit as sharp as ever, it was his body that was rapidly fail-ing him, his frailty the cumulative result of periodic heart attacks, the first suffered soon after the war. Now permanently ensconced at their winterized bungalow on the Gatineau, he relied on the media, and the occasional visitor, to stay reasonably up-to-date with the day's happen-ings, foreign and domestic. But as he quipped in a belated Christmas note to Harry Hawthorn in January 1969, three weeks shy of his eighty-third birthday, "I have thrown away my pen, having done more than enough mischief in my lifetime." Three months later he was in hospital, recuperating from yet another bout of heart trouble. In typical form, he told Beatrice Blackwood that ever since then he had "been tagged a semi-invalid, of no further use to myself or to society. My reason tells me that after 83 years of misdoings it is time I abandoned the planet for 'parts unknown.'"[88] On 29 November 1969 he did just that, carried off by a heart too weak to do its job any longer. "He was sitting up in bed reading the Manchester Guardian. Sunshine streaming in on him ... an exquisite Beethoven program" playing on the radio, Eilleen eloquently recalled of the last day of their fifty years of married life together. "Sud-denly, so quietly Death came – an utterly peaceful, mystic transition from the fine life he had led on earth. How could I ask for more, for him, for me, or for his dear sons and friends."[89]

Almost a year before his death, Jenness was named a Companion of the Order of Canada, an award recognizing exceptional contributions to the life of the country. Illness prevented him from accepting the hon-our in person. Fittingly, in a letter acknowledging its receipt, he allowed himself one final statement for the public record, writing to Governor General Roland Michener of his fervent wish "that the honour accorded to me would arouse more public interest in Canada's Eskimos and In-dians, and for ever banish the slumber of our languid bureaucracy."[90]

EPILOGUE

The Afterlife of Diamond Jenness

Today, makes yesterday mean.
Emily Dickinson

When I began digging into Diamond Jenness's life over two decades ago, I didn't expect to uncover many references to him in the general literature on disciplinary history, but his near-invisibility in the handful of publications that deal with Canadian anthropology up to the mid-twentieth century was unforeseen.[1] While happy to do my bit to make up for the apparent oversight, it occurred to me at the time that several facts fundamental to the man's professional biography probably accounted for his being of little more than passing interest to subsequent generations. For one, the entirety of his career with the National Museum was played out in the long shadow of Edward Sapir, his mentor and friend but also the founder, chief architect, and driving force behind the Anthropological Division's nationwide research program and a theorist and linguist of uncommon accomplishment and influence, especially after he decamped from Ottawa for the University of Chicago. Although Jenness was determined to build on what his colleague had started when he succeeded him as division chief, the mix of bureaucratic indifference and fiscal restraint he repeatedly ran up against throughout the remainder of the interwar era frustrated his efforts to do more than maintain the status quo, and then only barely. In combination with strict government intolerance of "meddling" – that is, unauthorized research – in matters bearing on its administration of Indian affairs, these same stringent conditions also held him back from transcending the dictates of an institutional mandate increasingly out of step with emerging disciplinary trends, or from publishing findings, let alone opinions, without ministerial approval. Finally, at a moment when universities, except those in Canada, were supplanting museums as anthropology's centres of gravity and creativity, he remained far from the action in Ottawa, nearly bereft of the stimulation that comes of ready exchanges of ideas with colleagues and students.[2]

These various constraints, and the contradictions inherent in his status as a scientist in the public's employ, left their mark on the form and substance of Jenness's many contributions to knowledge, confining them, by and large, to works of description and, with particular reference to *Indians of Canada*, of synthesis. His writings, both about his initial fieldwork experience in British New Guinea and the better-known investigations in the western Arctic that followed, were also greatly affected by the belief, held by most anthropologists at the time he joined the field, that anthropology's most important task was salvaging information about indigenous ways of life imperilled by the relentless tide of colonial expansion. Virtually absent from the body of his scholarship, particularly work that predates his retirement from government service, are the sorts of innovative explorations of theoretical, methodological, and applied problems that have long been of singular interest to those who study the discipline's recent and more distant past. Rightly or wrongly, this, probably more than any other factor, has determined Jenness's near-invisibility in the ever-lengthening bibliography of their researches. Robert Hancock has recently argued that, having "founded no formal school of Canadian anthropological thought," he left nothing of value to be mined for "new perspectives on and into the challenges currently facing the discipline" in this, or indeed, any other country.[3]

That said, it is erroneous to conclude that the content of his own sizable bibliography is entirely free of theoretical undertones, or ramifications. On the contrary, the material he reported, and the research that produced it, fit easily within the context of developments and priorities prevalent at successive stages in his career. Now and then, they anticipate new directions. There is no mistaking the lineage of his Athapaskan ethnographies of the 1920s as works of Americanist historical ethnology, for instance. Each study is premised on the school's focal conception of cultures as outgrowths of historical forces operating at regional and local levels (as were his pioneering reconstructions of arctic culture history, for that matter) and each draws heavily on oral tradition to impart a sense of how the people themselves understood their customary ways of being in the world. The same can be said of the research that followed over the ensuing decade, though now, at Sapir's prompting, he shifted attention to culture's influence on individual character and world view. Jenness initially pursued this theme in relation to Wet'suwet'en and Parry Island Ojibwa conceptions of nature, causation, and personal well being and later elaborated on it through the medium of Simon Pierre's masterful narration of the origins, transformations, and workings of the Katzie universe. These works comprise significant early contributions to the offshoot culture-and-personality school that was ascendant through the 1940s and a precursor of latter-day psychological anthropology.

Not all of his scholarship in these years fits neatly within this frame. His claims for the post-contact origins of family-based land tenure systems among the Ojibwa (and Sekani) is certainly a case in point, as his position is diametrically opposed to the mainline view presented most forcefully in the writings of Frank Speck and his students and later used as key evidence supporting Eleanor Leacock's definitive resolution of what came to be called the Algonkian hunting territory debate. A second example is contained in an extended essay, *The Indian Background of Canadian History*, published by the museum in 1937. The opening section of this largely forgotten (and previously unmentioned) work tackles an explicitly theoretical problem: explaining why the general trajectory of technological and political development in the Americas diverged so markedly from its Eurasian analogue, a divergence with fateful consequences once Europeans established a foothold in the New World half a millennium ago. In other words, why did complex, agrarian societies in the Old World develop earlier, grow larger, and spread their influence farther than did those in the New? Jenness begins his analysis by reviewing, and dismissing, a number of hoary viewpoints accounting for this conspicuous "backwardness," everything from the usual hard-wired causes – "pure vs. hybridized" races, biologically based or climatically induced disparities in intelligence and temperament – to random ones, notably the chance appearance of "supermen" and "momentous discoveries." Taking a different tack, he argues for a broadened historical perspective that acknowledges the central importance of diffusionary processes on the one hand, and on the other, assumes that environmental factors – the nexus of physiographic features and natural and biotic resources – limit the range of possible subsistence strategies and their productive capacities in any given region and facilitate, or hinder, their spread, along with much else of cultural value, from one region to the next.[4] Reduced to its essentials, Jenness's position has a good deal in common with what Julian Steward later christened cultural ecology, a highly influential approach in post-war North American anthropology founded on the idea that patterns of social and cultural life comprise adaptations to prevailing environmental conditions. Still novel in the thirties, it was anything but sixty years later when Jared Diamond examined the same problem as the lesser-known Diamond and reached similar conclusions, on similar grounds, in his popularly acclaimed, Pulitzer-winning, *Guns, Germs, and Steel.*

The American field's transformation under Franz Boas's extraordinary sway was effectively complete before Jenness took up permanent duties with the Anthropological Division, itself a major centre of historically oriented research from its founding. But the comparable shift in Britain was still unfolding when he entered the fledgling diploma program at Oxford, passing through a flirtation with variants of diffusionism during the century's first two decades, then turning away from historical and evolutionary concerns and embracing structural functionalism, the discipline's pre-eminent school into the 1960s. As a result, his formal introduction to anthropological thought drew from the old and the new, as he learned about Morgan's evolutionism and Durkheim's comparative sociology from Robert Marett, the roles of independent invention and diffusion from Henry Balfour, and the latest in research techniques from Alfred Haddon and William Rivers, late of the landmark Cambridge Torres Strait Expedition.[5] Marett himself, writing in 1910, argued that with richer ethnographic evidence acquired by "exacter [read empirical] methods" casting doubt on long-standing conceptions of "primitive" society, a "clean sweep ... of the greater part of the standard anthropological authorities" was necessarily in the offing. "This is not to abandon the hope of discovering universal tendencies amid the bewildering variety of man's efforts after culture." Rather, "it is simply to defer that hope until we are in a better position to appreciate each piece of evidence in relation to that organic context whence most of its significance is derived."[6]

Seen in the light of a discipline in transition, it is hardly surprising that the complexion of the fieldwork that launched Jenness's career the very next year mirrors the betwixt and between state of British anthropological thought at the time; that is, "the hiatus ... between the collapsing evolutionary paradigm and the evolving sociological approach."[7] Like the work of the Torres Strait veterans who encouraged it, the D'Entrecasteaux study is probably notable more for his (faltering) attempts to employ techniques Rivers and company pioneered than for what actually came of the effort. Even so, when it appeared in print, the general ethnography he co-authored with Andrew Ballantyne, his missionary brother-in-law, garnered recognition as a worthy addition to anthropological "knowledge of a practically unknown region," precisely what the discipline then required and what Jenness had set out to achieve.[8] Nowadays, the book, and the research on which it was based, appear to be more than that. Unquestionably, it is a work of description, a systematic survey of the archipelago as habitat and socio-economic milieu, and of the organization and dimensions of ordinary life. It is also a stodgy read, an account whose objectivity is (intermittently) compromised by some of the day's commonplace ethnocentric assumptions, lacks even a pretence of analytical insight, and overall, bears a heavier stamp of the fading evolutionist perspective than of emerging theoretical trends.[9] One is left to speculate how the research – an effort Jenness himself pronounced wanting in numerous ways – might have unfolded otherwise had the thoroughly revised fourth edition of *Notes and Queries* been available when he departed England for his apprenticeship in the Pacific; or if the island hadn't been in the grips of famine when he arrived; or if the conditions under which he drafted *The Northern D'Entrecasteaux* had been more conducive to scholarly reflection than they turned out to be. Yet for all the work's shortcomings, the photographs Jenness took and the oral traditions he and Ballantyne transcribed have weathered the test of time, coming to serve another (higher) purpose than either originally intended: helping Goodenough islanders to re-engage with their own past. Elizabeth Edwards put it best, writing that the pictures – and by implication, the texts – "are not only what they were but what they have become. They are the stuff of history."[10]

The D'Entrecasteaux began Jenness's career, but Coronation Gulf defined it. Of the several reasons why this is so, one stands out above all others: if fieldwork inevitably reduces to a sink or swim proposition, as many anthropologists candidly admit, then the Arctic he encountered on stepping ashore into the gathering Alaskan winter of 1913 must have impressed him as a place where sinking really wasn't an option. What the circumstances called for, and what he did, to remarkable advantage for the best part of the next three years, was to follow the prescription Bronislaw Malinowski was to outline nearly a decade later in the opening chapter of *Argonauts of the Western Pacific*. The "proper conditions" for ethnographic work, Malinowski wrote, hinge on "remaining in as close contact with the natives as possible, which really can only be achieved by camping right in their villages." This allows the researcher to "learn to know [the native], to become familiar with his customs and beliefs far better than when he is a paid, and often bored, informant" answering questions on the mission-house veranda. Little used at this early stage in the discipline's modernization, the strategy he was describing has since become the most valued of tools in the ethnographer's toolkit: participant observation, a means to build rapport and, with it, understanding of the makeup and rhythms of everyday life, the modes of thinking and feeling that guide it, and ultimately, a sense of the reality that is the native's world.[11]

Life of the Copper Eskimo is no *Argonauts*, a work widely credited with having "forever changed" the British discipline and perhaps other national anthropological traditions as well.[12] Even so, Jenness's competence in Inuktitut, determination to observe at first hand the annual cycle of Inuit existence on land and sea, and struggle to overcome the "Oxford skepticism" that so frustrated him in New Guinea combined to make the first of his eight expedition reports a work of appreciable accomplishment. Owing to Henri Beuchat's miserable fate, moreover, it was also a work of theoretical note, comprising the first empirical test of Marcel Mauss's hypothesis that the intensity of the social and religious bonds on which communal life is founded waxes and wanes with the seasons. On its publication in 1922 – coincidentally, the very year *Argonauts* debuted – Clark Wissler wrote admiringly of its author's evident "genius for gathering a large body of data in a short time" and of the book itself as a foundational contribution to the emerging field of arctic ethnology, a "primary source" of descriptive detail on a people, and a way of life, verging on profound change. Half a century on, at a moment of disciplinary preoccupation with the business of writing, rather than doing, ethnography, David Riches singled out Jenness's account "as the first recognisably modern anthropological production on the Eskimo, its format of closely researched socio-cultural matter, snippets of local colour and personal experience anticipating such later landmarks as [New Zealand-born, Malinowski protégé, Raymond Firth's] *We the Tikopia*."[13]

The scientific results of the Canadian Arctic Expedition filled fifteen volumes. One-third of them contained the product of Jenness's investigations. A fitting testimonial to his presumed "genius" for industry, the scope of their content is truly remarkable, augmenting his ethnographic observations in Copper Inuit country with compilations of folk traditions and music, a detailed description of material culture, and data on language and physical characteristics. Added to his published output are sizeable collections acquired on behalf of the museum in Ottawa, including 2,500 ethnographic specimens, some 90 sound recordings, over 200 photographs, and scores of botanical and zoological specimens. Plans for a sixth volume, his analysis of 3,000 artifacts unearthed on Barter Island, in northeast Alaska, probably the very first systematic excavation in the far north, never came to fruition. But his experiences there eventually proved to be as influential in the development of his career as were his ethnographic accomplishments, nurturing an abiding interest in the problem of Eskimoan origins that, a decade later, eventuated in a pair of discoveries of crucial importance to piecing together the full picture of human occupation across the American Arctic: Dorset culture in the east and in the west, Old Bering Sea. Steadfastly refusing to describe himself as an archaeologist, in his day (and since) he was certainly recognized as one, his reputation resting as much on twenty-plus years of promoting international cooperation in studying the region's ancient past and in encouraging up-and-coming generations of aspiring specialists – among them Henry Collins, Frederica de Laguna, George Quimby, Graham Rowley, and William Taylor – as on the value of his research findings. For good measure, members of the recently formed American Archaeological Society elected him their president in 1936, two years before the American Anthropological Society did the same. "Actually I feel a little embarrassed," he explained on receiving the news, "for I have never considered myself an archaeologist, though I have been forced (quite willingly) to dabble in the subject in the course of my ethnological work." [14]

In her presidential address to the American Anthropological Association in 1967, Frederica de Laguna remarked that "It is not given to us, or at least most of us, to be a Boas or a Kroeber who can work at first hand in all branches of our discipline."[15] All things considered, Jenness came pretty close, and certainly much closer than did any of his Canadian contemporaries. Not only did his scholarship span the traditional four fields – ethnology, linguistics, archaeology, and physical (biological) anthropology – it also encompassed applied anthropology, now widely accorded status as a bona fide fifth field. Opinions on this vary, but there is good reason to credit him as being this country's first practitioner of what Harry Hawthorn later dubbed "useful anthropology" – research relevant to policy-making. Indeed, Jenness's engagement with practical matters played out over half of his lifetime, beginning in the thirties with his efforts to persuade Ottawa to reform its approach to Aboriginal affairs and ending two years before his death when he completed the fifth and final volume of what may well stand as the true high point of his professional career: *Eskimo Administration*, his history and analysis of Inuit-state relations under four flags.[16]

No facet of Jenness's career has garnered more attention of late, or more pointed criticism, than what he thought and wrote about the federal government's deplorable treatment of the country's Aboriginal minority and the changes needed to begin setting right the terrible wrongs of the past. That this should be so seems entirely reasonable. After all, the policy reforms he outlined during the post-war Senate-Commons hearings into the Indian Act, his most accessible, and most quoted, statement on the issue, all but deny the aspirations of the very people whose interests he sought to champion, while anticipating, at least in spirit, Jean Chretien's ill-fated white paper of 1969, the catalyst behind the major shift in direction that soon followed. What he failed to do on that most public of occasions was to urge political and legal recognition of the right of the first peoples of Canada to govern their own territories, now regarded as the preconditon to determining their own futures.

Instead, the position he advocated, one seeking social and economic justice for people denied both for generations, has been interpreted as differing little in its objectives from those that had formed the bedrock of state policy since the time of Confederation. At best, then, Jenness has been seen as a well-intentioned, if misguided (and unduly pessimistic), supporter of assimilation, his thinking very much in line with popular sentiment regarding the inevitability – and necessity – of the complete absorption of First Peoples into the social and cultural mainstream. At worst, in the words of Peter Kulchyski, his severest critic, he was a "ruthless" assimilationist, an ardent imperialist ideologue "whose intellectual project [that is, the whole of his life's work as scientist and citizen] was not unrelated to a project of Canadian national definition that excluded Native peoples." More resolute in his convictions than were the politicians and administrators he often criticized, Kulchyski's reasoning continues, what Jenness proposed that day was "not a plan of half-measures: abolish separate schools, abolish reserves, and eventually the 'Indian problem' would be solved, because the Indian would have disappeared."[17]

Over the years, I have given much thought to what others have written about this highly politicized, highly public, and unavoidably controversial side of Jenness's career. Eventually, it occurred to me that my focus was misdirected. While their conclusions matter, the grounds on which they rest surely matter too. It is one thing to impute motive and mindset from a close reading of one or two published sources, *The Indians of Canada*, for instance, or *Arctic Odyssey*. But it is quite another to understand them – as the preceding fourteen chapters make clear they were – as distillates of myriad influences and experiences absorbed over a lifetime; or to presume that intellectual freedom is a pre-condition of the scholarly life, including for scholars on government payrolls; or to overlook the realpolitik in the business of making and advocating policy; and so on. With apologies to Clifford Geertz, late éminence grise of American anthropology, it seems to me that what comes of such rigorous, albeit lightly contextualized, analysis, is thin history, if it is history at all, good for making a point about how things look to us now, perhaps, but not for furthering our understanding of the past, that proverbial foreign country where people think and act differently, and occasionally change their minds.[18] The product of this approach, whatever else it may accomplish, offers an object lesson in the potential pitfalls of presentism. There is an "undoubted truth" in Dickinson's lovely double entendre that heads this concluding section: it is that "perspectives of the present invariably colour the meanings we ascribe to the past."[19] Today really does have a way of making yesterday mean.

In his own day, Diamond Jenness earned wide recognition as an anthropologist of considerable accomplishment, someone whose often-pioneering contributions to knowledge and commitment to the betterment of public life, especially for Canada's First Peoples, made him not merely an interesting figure but an important one. I, for one, am certain that for those reasons his legacy still matters today. Needless to say, there are those who disagree, some having put their dissenting views on the record already, others bound to do so in future. Such is the nature of the scholarly life, as it is the political one. As Jenness himself would surely remind us, "quot homines, tot sententiae" – many people, many minds.

Notes

JCC Father John Cooper Correspondence. Washington: Catholic University of America Archives

MBC C. Marius Barbeau Correspondence. Gatineau, QC: Canadian Museum of Civilization Archives

MRC Department of Mines and Resources Correspondence. Ottawa: Library and Archives Canada

NCC Northern Coordination and Research Centre Correspondence. Ottawa: Library and Archives Canada

OSC E.O.S. Scholefield Correspondence. Victoria: Archives of British Columbia

PSC Records of the Public Service Commission. Ottawa: Library and Archives Canada

RAC Rudolph Anderson Correspondence [re: Canadian Arctic Expedition]. Ottawa: Library and Archives Canada

RBC R.B. Bennett Papers. Ottawa: Library and Archives Canada

RMC Robert R. Marett Correspondence. Oxford: University of Oxford Archives

RMP Royal Northwest Mounted Police Correspondence. Ottawa: Library and Archives Canada

TMC Thomas F. McIlwraith Correspondence. Toronto: University of Toronto Archives

VSC Vilhjalmur Stefansson Correspondence. Hanover, NH: Dartmouth College Archives

WNC W.A. Newcombe Correspondence. Victoria: Archives of British Columbia

PREFACE

1 De Laguna, "Diamond Jenness," 250; see also Lotz and Lotz, eds., *Pilot Not Commander.*

2 Among these works, the following are cited elsewhere in this text: Edwards, "Jenness and Malinowski" and "Visualizing History"; Hancock, "Diamond Jenness's Arctic Anthropology"; S. Jenness, "Diamond Jenness's Archaeological Investigations"; Kulchyski, "Anthropology in the Service of the State"; Morrison, *Diamond Jenness Collections* and "Diamond Jenness"; Riches, "Forces of Tradition"; Wright, "Fieldwork Photographs of Jenness and Malinowski." A reasonably complete list of relevant works, including obituaries and reviews, is found in Appendix 3 of Jenness and Jenness, *Through Darkening Spectacles*, 375–7.

3 Wilson, "Thomas Jefferson," 57; Stocking, "History of Anthropology: Whence/Whither," 6. cf. Hancock, "Toward a Historiography of Canadian Anthropology," 39.

4 Stocking, "On the Limits of 'Presentism' and 'Historicism,'" 5.

5 Ibid., 3; Wilson, "Thomas Jefferson," 62; cf. Stocking, "History of Anthropology: Whence/Whither," 3–4.

6 Swayze, *Canadian Portraits.*

7 S. Jenness, in Jenness and Jenness, *Through Darkening* Spectacles, xxii.

8 S. Jenness, personal correspondence, 1 July 1986.

9 S. Jenness, in Jenness, *Arctic Odyssey*, ixx; in Jenness and Jenness, *Through Darkening Spectacles*, xviii–ix.

10 HMC: D.J. to H.A. Moe, 18 April 1958.

CHAPTER ONE

1 Gardner, "Colonial Economy," 85.

2 Gibbons, "Climate of Opinion," 305–7; see also Hatch, *Respectable Lives*.

3 Howe, *Singer*, 75; Oliver, "Social Policy," 25.

4 Butterworth and Young, *Maori Affairs*, ch. 5; Walker, *Ka Whawhai Tonu Matou*, ch. 9.

5 Vowles, "Liberal Democracy," 219.

6 Graham, "Settler Society," 114.

7 Kawharu, ed., *Waitangi*; Orange, *Treaty of Waitangi*.

8 Hodgson, *Colonial Capital*, 17. Previously, Auckland served as the seat of government.

9 The children are Violet Hannah (1873–1952), May (1875–1953), George Arthur (1876–1927), Amy (1878–1936), Eva (died in infancy, 1879), William Lewis (1880–1952), Celia (1881–1883), Frederick (1883–1944), Grace (1884–?), Diamond (1886–1969), Ruby (died in infancy, 1888), Leonard (1889–?), Pearl (1891–1960), and Lewis (1893–1894).

10 A transplanted friendly society – the Independent Order of Rechabites – was founded in England in the 1830s.

11 Anon., "Anthropological Expedition," 530–1.

12 Anon., "Battle of the Sites," 9.

13 James Urry, personal communication, 8 July 1987.

14 Jenness, Excerpt of letter (2 September 1933), 20.

15 Jenness, Appendix B, in von Zedlitz, *Search*, 165.

16 GZC: D.J. to G. von Zedlitz, 21 December 1917.

17 GZC: D.J. to G. von Zedlitz, 17 January 1917.

18 J.C. Beaglehole, *Victoria University*, 298–302; Gibbons, "Climate of Opinion," 313; von Zedlitz, *Search*, 15–16. Von Zedlitz resumed academic life soon after the war, founding the University Tutorial School in downtown Wellington, where he taught for many years. In 1936, at age sixty-five, he returned to Victoria College, having been granted an appointment as professor emeritus.

19 GZC: D.J. to G. von Zedlitz, 11 January 1916.

20 Hawthorn, "Diamond Jenness," 83; cf. Swayze, *Canadian Portraits*, 40.

21 RMC: D.J. to R.R. Marett, 2 August 1914.

22 Graham, "Settler Society," 130–1.

23 Craig, *Man of the Mist*, 138; Freeman, "Henry Devenish Skinner," 20–1.

24 Graham, "Settler Society," 118, 133.

25 Sorrenson, *Maori Origins*, ch. 1.

26 Sorrenson, *Manifest Duty*, 24.

27 Butterworth, "Rural Maori Renaissance," 160.

28 Ibid., 168; cf. Sorrenson, "Polynesian Corpuscles," 9; Sorrenson, *Manifest Duty*, 32, 34.

29 For example, Kuklick, *Savage Within*, ch. 2.

30 King, *Maori*, 73–5, 195.

31 For example, Butterworth and Young, *Maori Affairs*.

32 Metge, *Maoris*, 43, 303; Sutherland, "Introduction," in *Maori People Today*, 27; cf. O'Connor, "Keeping New Zealand White," 41–65.

33 Bellich, *Victorian Interpretation*, 299–300; Lorimer, "Theoretical Racism," 428, 430.

34 Fleras and Elliott, *Nations Within*, 181–2; Metge, *Maoris*, 303–4; cf. Sorrenson, "Maori and Pakeha," 189.

35 Hanson, "Making of the Maori," 892–3.

36 For example, Te Rangi Hiroa, *Coming of the Maori*; S.P. Smith, *History and Traditions*.

37 James Urry, personal communication, 4 December 1991; see also Urry, "Compromising Correspondence," 77.

38 Sorrenson, *Maori Origins*, 30.

39 Howe, *Singer*, 39.

40 Tregear cited in Belich, *Victorian Interpretation*, 300.

41 Ibid.

42 Vowles, "Liberal Democracy," 220.

43 King, *Maori*, 160; Parsonson, "Pursuit of Mana," 154.

44 Ngata, "Anthropology and Government of Native Races;" Sorrenson, "Polynesian Corpuscles," 19–20.

45 Ngata cited in Butterworth, "Politics of Adaptation," 35, 76; Hanson, "Making of the Maori," 893; Walker, *Ka Whawhai Tonu Matou*, 173.

46 Ngata to Buck, 1 August 1928, in Sorrenson, ed., *Na To Hoa Aroha*, vol. 1, 123.

47 Oliver, "Social Policy," 31.

CHAPTER TWO

1 Trollope, *Australia and New Zealand*, vol. 2, 457.

2 Gibbons, "Climate of Opinion," 308; DJC: D.J. to R.U. Sayce, 27 October 1936.

3 Gibbons, "Climate of Opinion," 317. The situation was especially grim for aspiring anthropologists. Following Henry Skinner's 1919 appointment to the faculty at Otago, the first such position in the country, an entire generation would pass before Ralph Piddington became the second, taking up duties in a newly established department at the University of Auckland in 1950. Meantime, New Zealanders aiming for a life in the emerging profession had little recourse but to look elsewhere, going abroad to study and to pursue careers in the field.

4 D.J. to V.J. Whitehead, 10 November 1908. Copies of this letter and a second to brother Frederick, dated 16 June 1909, were provided by Mrs Kelly Jones of Lake Rotoma, New Zealand, Diamond Jenness's grand-niece.

5 Leach, "Glimpses," 3.

6 Ibid., 13.

7 J. Harris, *Private Lives*, 36, 255.

8 Davis, *History of Balliol*, 254–5; L. Stone, "Size and Composition," 67.

9 Elliott, ed., *Balliol Register*. In the thirties, Jenness had a brief correspondence with another Balliol classmate, the eminent historian Arnold Toynbee.

10 Howarth, "Science Education," 353; Kuklick, *Savage Within*, 28.
11 D.J. to V.J. Whitehead, 10 November 1908.
12 Davis, *History of Balliol*, 232.
13 Wallis, "Anthropology in England," 787.
14 D.J. to F. Jenness, 16 June 1909; RMC: D.J. to R.R. Marett, 2 August 1914.
15 RMC: D.J. to R.R. Marett, 17 August 1911. The university bestowed an MA four years after the BLitt, a formality for those who, following completion of the baccalaureate, "kept their names on the book"; Wallis, "Anthropology in England," 785.
16 Besnard, "'Année Sociologique' Team," 11–39.
17 Cardin, "Bio-Biographie," 23; de Laguna, "Diamond Jenness," 248; Nowry, *Man of Mana*, 67–86; Swayze, *Canadian Portraits*, 40–1.
18 Wallis alone continued his formal education on leaving Oxford, earning a doctorate at the University of Pennsylvania with a dissertation on Australian Aborigine social organization; Spencer and Colson, "Wilson D. Wallis," 257.
19 Stocking, *Victorian Anthropology*, 47.
20 Ridgeway, "Relation of Anthropology," 11.
21 Frazer, *New Golden Bough*, xxv; cf. Ackerman, *Frazer*, 35–52.
22 Marett, "Preface," in *Anthropology and Classics*, 2.
23 Kluckhohn, *Anthropology and Classics*, 6. The title is no accident: a Rhodes Scholar, Kluckhohn studied under Marett and Gilbert Murray in the 1930s.
24 Swayze, *Canadian Portraits*, 40.
25 HMC: D.J. to H.A. Moe, 14 October 1955.
26 Kuklick, *Savage Within*, 28; cf. Reining, "Lost Period," 598.
27 Ibid., 49, 196, 199.
28 RMC: D.J. to R.R. Marett, 17 August 1911.
29 Skinner, Review of *Northern D'Entrecasteaux*, 61.
30 Huxley, *Man's Place in Nature*, 6.
31 Kluckhohn, *Anthropology and Classics*, 24; cf. Kuklick, *Savage Within*, 6.
32 Darnell, "Professionalization," 91–9.
33 Bernstein, "First Recipients," 560–3.
34 Kuklick, *Savage Within*, 28.
35 Howarth, "Science Education," 334, 351; Kuklick, *Savage Within*, 28.
36 Cited in Mulvaney and Calaby, *"So Much That Is New,"* 40.
37 E.B. Tylor cited in Fortes, "Social Anthropology," 428; Langham, *Building British Social Anthropology*, 18–19; Leach, "Glimpses," 4–5.
38 Hays, *From Ape to Angel*, 31.
39 Mulvaney and Calaby, *"So Much That Is New,"* 41; Howarth, "Science Education," 335.
40 Balfour, "Presidential Address," 690; Stocking, *Victorian Anthropology*, 245, 263–4.
41 Avrith, "Science at the Margins," ch. 5.
42 Howarth, "Science Education," 339, 369; Chapman, "Arranging Ethnology," 34–9.
43 Marett, *Jerseyman*, 167; Stocking, "Tylor," 170–7.
44 E.B. Tylor to Professor H. Acland, 27 June 1895, cited in Howarth, "Science Education," 352.

45 Haddon, "Anthropology," 11, 22.
46 Duckworth et al., "Anthropology at the Universities," 85; Read, "Anthropology at the Universities," 56.
47 Frazer, "Anthropology as University Subject," 260.
48 Kuklick, *Savage Within*, 203; Ruel, "Marett," 567.
49 Marett, "Anthropology as University Subject," 263; Temple, "Presidential Address (Section H)," 620.
50 E. Beaglehole, "New Zealand Anthropology," 158–9; Stocking, "Radcliffe-Brown," 158; Temple, et al., "Suggestions for a School," 185–92.
51 Marett, *Jerseyman*, 167.
52 Ibid., 164; see also Ruel, "Marett," 565–6.
53 Leach, "Glimpses," 5.
54 Wallis, "Anthropology in England," 788.
55 Marett, *Jerseyman*, 168–9.
56 Wallis, "Anthropology in England," 785–7.
57 Jenness, "Magic Mirror," 233–4.
58 Marett, *Jerseyman*, 173; Wallis, "Anthropology in England," 787.
59 Stocking, "Ethnographer's Magic," 76–7.
60 Temple, "Presidential Address," 616.
61 Rivers cited in Stocking, "Ethnographer's Magic," 87; Rivers, "General Account of Method," 108–27.
62 Stocking, "Ethnographer's Magic," 70, 82.
63 Fortes, "Social Anthropology," 432; Marett, "Present State of Anthropology," 299.
64 Wallis, "Methods of English Ethnologists," 178, 181; cf. Balfour, "Presidential Address – Section H," 697; Marett, "Anthropology as University Subject," 8.
65 Marett in Wallis, "Methods of English Ethnologists," 183.
66 Rivers, "Report on Anthropological Research," 18.
67 Ibid., 5.

CHAPTER THREE

1 See RMC; see also Marett's preface in Jenness and Ballantyne, *Northern D'Entrecasteaux*, 5–6.
2 RMC: D.J. to R.R. Marett, 11 July 1911; G. L. Jenness to R.R. Marett, 7 November 1911.
3 RMC: D.J. to R.R. Marett, 28 June 1911; 2 August 1914.
4 RMC: D.J. to R.R. Marett, 6 December 1911.
5 West, *Hubert Murray*, 210; West, ed., *Letters of Hubert Murray*, x; RMC: D.J. to R.R. Marett, 6 January 1917; see also Healy, "Papua," 884.
6 RMC: D.J. to R.R. Marett, 27 July [August?], 1911.
7 Rivers, "Genealogical Method," 1–12.
8 Urry, *"Notes and Queries,"* 48.
9 RMC: Mrs Frazer to R.R. Marett, n.d. [1911]; Mrs Frazer to D.J., 2 July 1911; "The Phonograph for Ethnological Purposes," n.d.; Ackerman, *J.G. Fraser*, 126.
10 RMC: D.J. to R.R. Marett, 15 June, 1911; 28 June, 1911; see also "Preface" in Jenness and Ballantyne, *Northern D'Entrecasteaux*, 11–13.

11 RMC: D.J. to R.R. Marett, 27 July [August] 1911; Jenness and Jenness, *Through Darkening Spectacles*, 23.

12 RMC: D.J. to R.R. Marett, 27 July [August] 1911.

13 RMC: D.J. to R.R. Marett, 7 November 1911 (underlined in original).

14 AHC: D.J. to A. Hamilton, 1 December 1912. On returning home the following year, Jenness donated several Papuan artifacts and lantern slides to the Dominion Museum. A second collection went to Dunedin's Otago Museum, a gift from May Jenness Ballantyne shortly before her death in 1953.

15 Craig, *Man of the Mist*, 177–8.

16 GZC: D.J. to G. von Zedlitz, 16 October 1913.

17 RMC: D.J. to R.R. Marett, 6 December 1911.

18 Ibid. By coincidence, among the passengers aboard the vessel carrying Jenness to England to begin studies at Oxford were three French priests returning home from the same Yule Island mission; Jenness and Jenness, *Darkening Spectacles*, 6.

19 M. Young, "Intensive Study," 5, fn. 7.

20 Wallis, "Anthropology in England," 787.

21 RMC: D.J. to R.R. Marett, 6 December 1911.

22 Dunmore, *French Explorers*, vol. 1, 320–1.

23 M. Young, "Doctor Bromilow," 149–50.

24 Jenness and Ballantyne, *Northern D'Entrecasteaux*, 45–6.

25 RMC: D.J. to R.R. Marett, 27 May 1911.

26 Seligman, "Classification of Natives," 253, 268–9; M. Young, "Massim," 4.

27 Jenness and Ballantyne, *Northern D'Entrecasteaux*, 27; Malinowski, *Argonauts*, 39.

28 Haddon, cited in Stocking, "Ethnographer's Magic," 81; cf. Rivers, "Report on Anthropological Research," 7; cf. Wallis, "Methods of English Ethnologists," 185.

29 RMC: D.J. to R.R. Marett, 27 May 1911; 6 December 1911.

30 RMC: D.J. to R.R. Marett, 2 August 1914; DJC: A.L. Kroeber to D.J., 4 January 1932; D.J. to Kroeber, 11 January 1932.

31 Jenness and Ballantyne, *Northern D'Entrecasteaux*, 70; D. Jenness, "Ascent of Mount Madawana," 108; M. Young, *Fighting with Food*, 5.

32 Jenness and Ballantyne, *Northern D'Entrecasteaux*, 30, 82; M. Young, "Doctor Bromilow," 131.

33 M. Young, *Fighting with Food*, 3.

34 Jenness and Ballantyne, *Northern D'Entrecasteaux*, 32.

35 RMC: D.J. to R.R. Marett, 11 April 1912.

36 RMC: D.J. to R.R. Marett, 4 May 1912.

37 RMC: D.J. to R.R. Marett, 26 July 1912.

38 Michael Young, personal correspondence, 9 October 1990.

39 M. Young, *Fighting with Food*, 177, 185.

40 Jenness and Ballantyne, *Northern D'Entrecasteaux*, 203.

41 Ibid.

42 M. Young, *Fighting with Food*, 174.

43 Jenness and Ballantyne, *Northern D'Entrecasteaux*, 11, 32.

44 RMC: D.J. to R.R. Marett, 20 January 1912.

45 Jenness and Ballantyne, *Northern D'Entrecasteaux*, 17, 51; cf. Jenness, "Ex-Cannibals," 33.

46 MBC: D.J. to C.M. Barbeau, 4 June 1912; RMC: D.J. to R.R. Marett, 11 April 1912; Ward and Lea, *Papua and New Guinea*, 28.

47 RMC: A. Ballantyne to R.R. Marett, 26 March 1915.

48 RMC: D.J. to R.R. Marett, 20 January 1912.

49 MBC: D.J. to C.M. Barbeau, 4 June 1912.

50 Jenness and Ballantyne, "Language," 290; Jenness and Ballantyne, *Northern D'Entrecasteaux*, 53.

51 Rivers, "Geneological Method," 108; MBC: D.J. to C.M. Barbeau, 4 June 1912.

52 RMC: D.J. to R.R. Marett, 20 January 1912.

53 RMC: D.J. to R.R. Marett, 9 March 1913; DJC: D.J. to H.D. Skinner, 18 March 1929; Jenness and Ballantyne, "Language, Mythology, and Songs of the Bwaidoga." The reissue, under the same title, appeared as Memoir 8 of the Polynesian Society in 1928.

54 RMC: D.J. to R.R. Marett, 11 April 1912.

55 Ibid.

56 Jenness, "Singing People," 197.

57 Stocking, "Before the Falling Out," 3.

58 Malinowski, *Argonauts*, 466; Stocking, "Ethnographer's Magic," 74; M. Young, "Intensive Study," 8.

59 DJC: D.J. to A.L. Kroeber, 11 January 1932.

60 Malinowski, *Argonauts*, 467; the episodes in question appear on pages 110 and 129–31 in *Northern D'Entrecasteaux*.

61 Malinowski, *Argonauts*, 500, fn.; Wayne, *Story of a Marriage*, vol. 1, 105; cf. M. Young, "Intensive Study," 17–18.

62 RMC: D.J. to R.R. Marett, 11 April 1912.

63 RMC: D.J. to R.R. Marett, 26 July 1912.

64 RMC: D.J. to R.R. Marett, 11 April 1912; 9 March 1913.

65 Rivers, "Genealogical Method," 11.

66 RMC: D.J. to R.R. Marett, 26 July 1912.

67 RMC: D.J. to R.R. Marett, 11 April 1912.

68 Langham, *Building of British Social Anthropology*, 68.

69 Jenness, "Papuan Cat's Cradles," 300–1; "Ascent of Mount Madawana," 106; K. Haddon, cited in Langham, *Building of British Social Anthropology*, 68; Rivers and Haddon, "Method of Recording String Figures."

70 RMC: D.J. to R.R. Marett, 26 July 1912.

71 Malinowski, *Argonauts*, 25.

72 RMC: D.J. to R.R. Marett, 26 July 1912.

73 Jenness, "Cannibal Trails," 37.

74 RMC: D.J. to R.R. Marett, 26 July 1912.

75 Marett in Jenness and Ballantyne, *Northern D'Entrecasteaux*, 7.

76 Malinowski, *Argonauts*, 17; cf. Stocking, "Ethnographer's Magic," 105; Urry, "History of Field Methods," 51.

77 Malinowski, *Argonauts*, 20; RMC: D.J. to R.R. Marett, 26 July 1912.

78 Jenness, "Ascent of Mount Madawana," 106.

79 Ibid., 108.

1 "Freight & insurance (£50) were payable at Oxford," Jenness informed Marett, "so it will not be quite a total loss"; RMC: D.J. to R.R. Marett, 9 March 1913; 2 August 1914; cf. Edwards, "Visualizing History," 14, fn. 5.

2 Jenness, *Dawn*, 3; ESC: E. Sapir to D.J., 28 February 1913 (telegram).

3 R.R. Marett to C.M. Barbeau, 26 January 1913, and W. Wallis to Barbeau, 31 January 1913, cited in Nowry, *Man of Mana*, 135.

4 Swayze, *Canadian Portraits*, 47.

5 ESC: D.J. to E. Sapir, 1 May 1913; Sapir to D.J., 8 May 1913.

6 MBC: D.J. to C.M. Barbeau, 7 July 1913.

7 Cole and Müller-Wille, "Franz Boas' Expedition," 42; Levere, *Science and the Canadian Arctic*, 336.

8 F. Boas to A. Bastien, 5 January 1886, cited in Stocking, "Introduction" to *Shaping of American Anthropology*, 87.

9 R. Bell to F. Boas, 15 May 1886, cited in Avrith, "Science at the Margins," 136.

10 Dyck, "Founding the Anthropology Division," 16–20; Hale, "Third Report of the Committee," 174.

11 Avrith, "Science at the Margins," 227.

12 Hale, "Remarks on North American Ethnology," 801.

13 Zaslow, *Reading the Rocks*, ch. 8; see also Levere, *Science and the Canadian Arctic*, ch.9; cf. Dyck, "Founding the Anthropology Division," 22–33.

14 Zaslow, *Reading the Rocks*, 241, 257.

15 *Summary Report, Geological Survey of Canada for 1908*, 9.

16 *SR/GSC 1909*, 8.

17 *SR/GSC 1910*, 7; Avrith, "Science at the Margins," 268–9.

18 Stefansson, *My Life With the Eskimo*, 11–12. Other sources attribute the name "Copper Eskimo" to explorer Frederick Schwatka: see Damas, "Copper Eskimo," 413.

19 Diubaldo, *Stefansson*, 49; Jenness, "'Blond' Eskimos," 257; Stefansson, *My Life With the Eskimo*, 201–2.

20 Diubaldo, *Stefansson*, 66–8; Levere, *Science and the Canadian Arctic*, ch. 10.

21 HBC: D.J. to H. Balfour, 3 July 1913; ESC: H. Beuchat to E. Sapir, 15 July 1913; R.R. Marett to Sapir, 17 April 1913; Sapir to Marett, 2 May 1913.

22 ESC: W.H. Mechling to E. Sapir, 10 February 1913.

23 ESC: E. Sapir to W. Thalbitzer, 13 March 1913; Thalbitzer to Sapir, 29 March 1913.

24 ESC: E. Sapir to F. Boas, 2 December 1911.

25 ESC: E. Sapir to V. Stefansson, 26 February 1913; Stefansson to Sapir, 28 February 1913.

26 RAC: Rudolph M. Anderson, [Re: Death of H. Beuchat] and [Canadian Arctic Expedition Investigation, Memorandum of 29 March 1922]; McKinlay, *Karluk*, 148–51.

27 Anon., "Soldiers of Science," 6.

28 RAC: Anderson, [Canadian Arctic Expedition], 9; McKinlay, *Karluk*, 117; Stefansson, *Friendly Arctic*, 717–18.

29 Diubaldo, *Stefansson*, 91.

30 RMC: D.J. to R.R. Marett, 7 July 1913; HBC: D.J. to H. Balfour, 3 July 1913.
31 Balikci, "Ethnography and Theory," 105; Barbeau, "Henri Beuchat," 107; Fox, Translator's Forward, in Mauss, *Seasonal Variations*, 6–7; Saladin d'Anglure, "Mauss et l'anthropologie," 102–4.
32 Barbeau, "Henri Beuchat," 106, 109; Bender, "French Anthropology," 145–6; Parkin, "French-Speaking Countries," 158–9.
33 ESC: E. Sapir to D.J., 7 May 1913; Thalbitzer, "Phonetical Study."
34 MBC: D.J. to C.M. Barbeau, 7 July 1913.
35 HBC: D.J. to H. Balfour, 3 July 1913; Stefansson to J.D. Hazen, 1 June 1913, cited in Levere, *Science and the Arctic*, 400–1.
36 Jenness, *Dawn*, 5; MBC: H. Beuchat to C.M. Barbeau, 15 July 1913.
37 McKinlay, *Karluk*, 17.
38 Stefansson, *Friendly Arctic*, 27; McKinlay, *Karluk*, 18.
39 S. Jenness, in Jenness, *Arctic Odyssey*, xli; McKinlay, *Karluk*, 26–7. Some time after his death, Eilleen Bleakney Jenness donated her husband's three-volume expedition diary to the National Archives of Canada, now Library and Archives Canada. Their son Stuart typed and edited the diary for publication and it appeared under the title *Arctic Odyssey*. References to the diary in this and the following chapters refer to the published version.
40 S. Jenness, in Jenness, *Arctic Odyssey*, xlii; McKinlay, *Karluk*, 28.
41 Bartlett and Hale, *Last Voyage;* McKinlay, *Karluk*, ch. 23; Niven, *Ice Master*.
42 ESC: D.J. to E. Sapir, 26 October 1913.
43 Diary, 8 October 1913, 17.
44 Diary, 12 November 1913, 55. Within a decade, cash would all but replace barter transactions in the north Alaskan economy.
45 GZC: D.J. to G. von Zedlitz, 16 October 1913.
46 D.G. Smith, "Mackenzie Delta Eskimo," 348; Spencer, "North Alaska Coast Eskimo," 335–6.
47 Gruber, "Ethnographic Salvage," 1289–99; Stocking, *Victorian Anthropology*, 243.
48 RMC: D.J. to R.R. Marett, 17 October 1913.
49 Diary, 5 October 1913, 14; 4 November 1913, 42–3.
50 Diary, 25 July 1915, 487; Jenness, "Eskimos of Northern Alaska"; "Cultural Transformation."
51 Jenness, *People of the Twilight*, 248.
52 Stefansson, *My Life With the Eskimo*, 11.
53 ESC: D.J. to E. Sapir, 30 July 1914 (emphasis added).
54 OSC: D.J. to E.O.S. Scholefield, 14 December 1913.
55 RMC: D.J. to R.R. Marett, 17 October 1913.
56 Jenness, *Dawn*, 101.
57 Diary, 6 February 1914, 744, fn. 5.
58 GZC: D.J. to G. von Zedlitz, 29 June 1914.
59 Diary, 20 January 1914, 122; 5 February 1914, 135.
60 ESC: D.J. to E. Sapir, 2 December 1913.
61 For example, see ESC: D.J. to E. Sapir, 30 May 1914.
62 GZC: D.J. to G. von Zedlitz, 29 June 1914.
63 Diary, 14 December 1913, 85; GZC: D.J. to G. von Zedlitz, 29 June 1914.

64 Diary, 27 September 1913, 7–8.
65 Diary, 28 November 1913, 67; 1 December 1913, 70.
66 Jenness, *Dawn*, 41, 100.
67 Ibid., 51–3, 100, 131.
68 ESC: Jenness to E. Sapir, 2 December 1913.
69 Diary, 10 December 1913, 79; 6 January 1914,108–9.
70 ESC: E. Sapir to D.J., 7 May 1913; cf. Darnell, "Text Tradition," 43.
71 Diary, 27 January 1914, 127; 15 February 1914, 144.
72 Jenness, *Myths and Traditions*; RMC: D.J. to R.R. Marett, 2 August 1914.
73 Ibid.
74 Diary, 20 March 1914, 166.
75 Diary, 22 March 1914, 169.
76 Diubaldo, *Stefansson*, 90–1; Jenness, "Review of 'Friendly Arctic,'" 11; Stefansson, *Friendly Arctic*, ch. 12.
77 Kleinschmidt, *Grammatik*.
78 Diary, 14 March 1914, 158; cf. Stefansson, *My Life With the Eskimo*, 172–6.
79 Diary, 3 May 1914, 194–6; RMC: D.J. to R.R. Marett, 2 August 1914.
80 Diary, 21 and 26 May 1914, 207, 211; Jenness, *Arctic Odyssey*, 757, fn. 1.
81 Diary, 22 May 1914, 207; 14 June 1914, 221; S. Jenness, "Archaeological Investigations," 93.
82 Diary, 30 June 1914, 231–2.
83 Diary, 15 June 1914, 222; 18 June 1914, 225.
84 D.J. to Edwin S. Hall, Jr, 9 April 1967, cited in Hall, Jr, *'Land Full of People,'* 18.
85 de Laguna, "Therkel Mathiassen," 10–33; cf. Morrison, "Diamond Jenness," 61.
86 RMC: D.J. to R.R. Marett, 2 August 1914.
87 GZC: D.J. to G. von Zedlitz, 29 June 1914; ESC: D.J. to E. Sapir, 30 July 1914.
88 S. Jenness, "Archaeological Investigations," 93–4.
89 Diary, 6 June 1914, 217–18.
90 RMC: D.J. to R.R. Marett, 2 August 1914; Diary, 17 July 1914, 240–1.
91 GZC: D.J. to G. von Zedlitz, 29 June 1914; Jenness, *Dawn*, 187–8.
92 Diary, 12 June 1914, 220.
93 MBC: D.J. to C.M. Barbeau, 10 August 1914.
94 Diary, 22 July 1914, 243–4; Hall, *'Land Full of People,'* 15.
95 Ibid., 240–1; S. Jenness, "Archaeological Investigations," 100–1.
96 Jenness, "Archaeological Notes on Eskimo Ruins" (unpublished).
97 Hall, *"Land Full of People."*
98 McKinlay, *Karluk*, 24; Bartlett and Hale, *Last Voyage*, 91.
99 ESC: E. Sapir to D.J., 22 June 1914; MBC: D.J. to C.M. Barbeau, 10 August 1914.
100 Niven, *Ice Master*, 158, 164.
101 ESC: E. Sapir to R.G. McConnell, 17 November 1914; H. Beuchat to Sapir, 15 July 1913.
102 RMC: D.J. to R.R. Marett, 2 August 1914.
103 GZC: D.J. to G. von Zedlitz, 29 June 1914.
104 RMC: D.J. to R.R. Marett, 2 August 1914; ESC: D.J. to E. Sapir ["Summary Report ... Sept. 1913 – July 1914," (undated)].
105 RMC: D.J. to R.R. Marett, 2 August 1914.

1 Archdeacon Stuck, cited in Jenness, *Eskimo Administration Canada*, 14, fn. 1.
2 G.J. Desbarats to V. Stefansson, 30 April 1914, cited in Jenness, *Arctic Odyssey*, 765 fn. 34.
3 Diary, 15 and 16 August 1914, 266–7.
4 Diary, 27 August 1914, 281.
5 Jenness, *People of the Twilight*, 10.
6 S. Jenness in Jenness, *Arctic Odyssey*, 765, fn. 30.
7 Diary, 17 September 1914, 298.
8 Hickey, "Examination of Processes of Cultural Change," 16–17; Stefansson, "Work Among the Arctic Eskimos," 389.
9 ESC: D.J. to E. Sapir, 30 July 1914.
10 Condon et al., *Northern Copper Inuit*, 35–45; Jenness, "Cultural Transformation," 544; Jenness, *Copper Eskimos*, 31.
11 Oswalt, *Eskimos and Explorers*, 51.
12 Hearne, *Journey*; Neatby, "Exploration and History," 379.
13 Diary, 14 February 1915, 387; R. Anderson, "Canadian Arctic Expedition," 225.
14 Mountfield, *History of Polar Exploration*, 95–107; Wallace, "Geographical Exploration," 22–7.
15 Hickey, "Examination of Processes of Cultural Change," 24–7; Jenness, *Material Culture*, 116; McGhee, *Copper Eskimo Prehistory*, 126–7; Stefansson, *Prehistoric and Present Commerce*.
16 McGhee, *Copper Eskimo Prehistory*, 129.
17 Jenness, *People of the Twilight*, 248; Vanast, "Death of Jennie Kanajuq," 75–104.
18 Flaherty, *Nanook;* cf. Jenness, *Copper Eskimos*, 186.
19 Diary, 27 September 1914, 305; 28 September 1914, 306–7; 25 November 1914, 335.
20 Diary, 19 November 1914, 330; Jenness, *People of the Twilight*, 46; see also S. Leacock, "Ethnological Theory of Marcel Mauss," 69.
21 ESC: R.M Anderson to E. Sapir, 29 July 1915; Diary, 30 September 1914, 309–10.
22 Fox, Translator's Foreword in Mauss, *Seasonal Variations*, 7; S. Leacock, "Ethnological Theory of Marcel Mauss," 65; cf. Bravo, "Against Determinism," 45–6.
23 Lukes, "Mauss," 79.
24 Damas, "Copper Eskimo," 413–14.
25 Jenness, *Copper Eskimos*, 143; Mauss cited in Lukes, "Mauss," 79.
26 Jenness, *Copper Eskimos*, 143–4, 195.
27 D.J. to M. Mauss, 7 July 1925, cited in Saladin d'Anglure, "Mauss et l'anthropologie," 95. Bernard Saladin d'Anglure unearthed Jenness's revealing letter in the Collège de France archives in the 1990s.
28 Diary, 28 November 1914, 338.
29 Diary, 11 December 1914, 351.
30 Diary, 20 December 1914, 358–9.
31 Diary, 8 December 1914, 348; Jenness, *Twilight*, 37–8.
32 Diary, 4 March 1915, 400; cf. Jenness, *Twilight*, 85–9.

33 Diary, 11 December 1914, 350.
34 Diary, 2 January 1915, 366; 10 January 1915, 370; Jenness, *Copper Eskimos*, 158; Jenness, *Arctic Odyssey*, 787, fn. 22.
35 Diary, 11 December 1914, 350. Norem, a cook-cum-steward aboard *Mary Sachs*, shot himself on 16 April 1914. Jenness heard the gun's report. A casket was built and a funeral held three days later; Diary, 16 and 19 April 1914, 183, 185.
36 Diary, 19 December 1914, 357; cf. Jenness, *Twilight*, 53.
37 Appendices 3 through 6 in *Arctic Odyssey* contain inventories of the artifacts, and biological specimens Jenness collected during the expedition, along with the photographs and sound recordings he made.
38 Jenness, *Physical Characteristics*, 6.
39 Jenness, *Copper Eskimos*, 65–77.
40 Jenness, *Physical Characteristics*, 5.
41 Ibid.
42 Jenness, "Ethnological Results," 614.
43 Jenness, *Copper Eskimos*, 10–11; Diary, 14 December 1914, 354; ESC: D.J. to E. Sapir, 26 December 1915.
44 Diary, 23 February 1915, 393.
45 Stefansson, *My Life with the Eskimo*, 218.
46 Diary, 24 and 25 February 1915, 393–5.
47 Jenness, *People of the Twilight*, 77–80; Moyles, *British Law*, 5–9; *Royal Northwest Mounted Police, Annual Report for 1918–19*, cited in Zaslow, *Northward Expansion*, 12; Diary, 16 and 17 May 1916, 597–8.
48 Jenness, *Copper Eskimos*, 119.
49 Malinowski, *Argonauts*, 25.
50 Diary, 13 March 1915, 404; 19 June 1915, 462–3; Jenness, *People of the Twilight*, 90.
51 Diary, 15 April 1915, 416.
52 Diary, 28 April 1915, 423.
53 Diary, 23 April 1915, 420; Jenness, *People of the Twilight*, 97.
54 Jenness, *People of the Twilight*, 108–9; GZC: D.J. to G. von Zedlitz, 11 January 1916. Now known as the Wollaston Peninsula, the name bestowed by explorer Sir John Richardson in 1826 in honour of the eminent English chemist William Hyde Wollaston.
55 Diary, 8 and 9 May 1915, 428–9.
56 Diary, 5 May 1915, 427.
57 Diary, 31 May 1915, 446–7.
58 Diary, 24 May 1915, 440; 28 May 1915, 445.
59 Diary, 2 June 1915, 448.
60 Diary, 4 June 1915, 450.
61 Diary, 14 August 1915, 501–2; Jenness, *People of the Twilight*, 126.
62 Diary, 2 October 1915, 528.
63 Diary, 5 April 1916, 582.
64 Diary, 5 June 1915, 451.
65 Diary, 12 July 1915, 478; 16 July 1915, 481.
66 Diary, 29 June 1915, 470.
67 Diary, 16 July 1915, 481–2; Jenness, *People of the Twilight*, 149.
68 Diary, 20 July 1915, 485.

69 Diary, 21 and 22 July 1915, 485–6; GZC: D.J. to G. von Zedlitz, 11 January 1916.

70 Diary, 25 July 1915, 487.

71 Diary, 14 August 1915, 501.

72 Diary, 21 August 1915, 506.

73 Jenness, *People of the Twilight*, 187.

74 Diary, 28 April 1915, 422; 15 July 1915, 481.

75 Diary, 17 May 1916, 597; RMP: D.J. to Commissioner, R.N.W.M. Police, 18 July 1916.

76 Jenness, "Cultural Transformation," 541.

77 GZC: D.J. to George von Zedlitz, 11 January 1916.

78 Diary, 27 and 28 February 1916, 570–3; 1 March 1916, 573.

79 Diary, 19–21 January 1916, 560; 23 January 1916, 560; Jenness, *Copper Eskimos*, 166.

80 Jenness, *People of the Twilight*, 214.

81 Ibid., 220.

82 Diary, 15 March 1916, 579.

83 Diary, 5 April 1916, 582; Jenness, *Copper Eskimos*, 216.

CHAPTER SIX

1 RMC: D.J. to R.R. Marett, 22 November 1916.

2 Diary, 8 November 1915, 545.

3 GZC: D.J. to G. von Zedlitz, 11 January 1916.

4 MBC: D.J. to C.M. Barbeau, 9 October 1917.

5 Darnell, *Edward Sapir*, 167–8.

6 ESC: E. Sapir to W. McInness, 14 October 1916.

7 GMC: R.G. McConnell to M.F. Gallagher, 12 May 1917 (emphasis in the original).

8 RMC: D.J. to R.R. Marett, 22 November 1916.

9 GZC: D.J. to G. Von Zedlitz, 7 January 1917.

10 RMC: D.J. to R.R. Marett, 6 January 1917.

11 Ibid.

12 ESC: F. Boas to E. Sapir, 2 January 1914.

13 For example, ESC: E. Sapir to R.G. McConnell, 18 November 1916.

14 RMC: D.J. to R.R. Marett, 6 January 1917.

15 Dyck, "Founding the Anthropology Division," 22–5; Haddon, "Anthropological Survey," 597.

16 *Geological Survey of Canada, Summary Report for 1909*, 9; Avrith, "Science at the Margins," 271.

17 For example, Gruber, "Horatio Hale," 5–37.

18 Avrith, "Science at the Margins," 271–2; F. Boas to R.W. Brock, 9 May 1910, cited in ibid., 271.

19 R.W. Brock to E. Sapir, 3 June 1910, cited in Darnell, *Edward Sapir*, 41–2.

20 *GSC/SR 1909*, 8; Gruber, "Ethnographic Salvage," 1296–8.

21 Richling, "Archaeology, Ethnology," 110–11.

22 Fenton, "Sapir as Museologist," 218–24.

23 Darnell, *Edward Sapir*, 52–3; cf. Avrith, "Science at the Margins," 283–4.

24 Barker, "T.F. McIlwraith," 253; Levin et al., "Historical Sketch," 1–5.

25 Cole, "Origins," 43–4; Bunzel, "Franz Boas," 17–18.
26 Boas, "Growth of Indian Mythologies," 5; "Methods of Ethnology," 286; Goldenweiser, "Diffusionism," 20, 38; Stocking, "Introduction: Basic Assumptions," 5–7, 12.
27 Boas, "Limitations of the Comparative Method," 280; F. Boas to R.S. Woodward, 13 January 1905, cited in Cole and Long, "Boasian Anthropological Survey," 235.
28 Boas, "Ethnological Problems," 530–1, 539; Anon., "Anthropology at the British Association," 477.
29 Sapir, "Work of the Division," 62.
30 R.W. Brock to E. Sapir, 3 June 1910, cited in Darnell, *Edward Sapir*, 42.
31 Sapir, "Work of the Division," 63, and "Anthropological Survey of Canada," 793.
32 H. Smith, "Work of Museums," 362–78, 417–30.
33 *GSC/SR 1915*, 265–8; *GSC/SR 1916*, 387–90.
34 Zaslow, *Reading the Rocks*, 328–9.
35 Ibid., 264; ESC: E. Sapir to F. Boas, 19 October 1916.
36 GMC: R.G. McConnell to M.F. Gallagher, 12 May 1917.
37 Alcock, *Century in the History of the Geological Survey*, 73; Woods, *Ottawa*, 224, 232–5; Zaslow, *Reading the Rocks*, 310.
38 Russell, *National Museum*, 25.
39 GZC: D.J. to G. von Zedlitz, 12 June 1917.
40 Ibid.
41 RMC: D.J. to R.R. Marett, 6 January 1917.
42 S. Jenness, "First World War," in Jenness and Jenness, *Through Darkening Spectacles*, 70–1.
43 RMC: D.J. to R.R. Marett, 22 November 1916.
44 VSC: D.J. to V. Stefansson, 20 February 1919.
45 GZC: D.J. to G. von Zedlitz, 21 December 1917.
46 MBC: D.J. to C.M. Barbeau, 9 October 1917.
47 GZC: D.J. to G. von Zedlitz, 21 December 1917.
48 MBC: D.J. to C.M. Barbeau, 25 February 1918.
49 MBC: D.J. to C.M. Barbeau, 25 November 1917.
50 RMC: D.J. to R.R. Marett, 18 December 1918.
51 MBC: D.J. to C.M. Barbeau, 4 December 1918.
52 RMC: D.J. to R.R. Marett, 29 April 1918.
53 VSC: D.J. to V. Stefansson, 20 February 1919.

CHAPTER SEVEN

1 MBC: D.J. to C.M. Barbeau, 9 January 1918.
2 S. Jenness, "First World War and Its Aftermath," in Jenness and Jenness, *Through Darkening Spectacles*, 76–7.
3 MBC: D.J. to C.M. Barbeau, 6 October 1920.
4 ESC: E. Sapir to W. Foran, 10 July 1919.
5 PSC: Personnel Records – Diamond Jenness; MBC: D.J. to C.M. Barbeau, 13 September 1920.

6 Canada. Parliament, "Auditor General's Report, 1911–12," P6–10; "Auditor General's Report, 1920–21," Q12–16.

7 MBC: D.J. to C.M. Barbeau, 17 August 1920.

8 Anon., "Maori Studies," 257. As he had done eight years before while en route to the D'Entrecasteaux, Jenness visited the director of Wellington's Dominion Museum during his honeymoon. Given the unsettled state of his employment situation in Canada, he may have been testing the waters for a job at home. What came of the meeting instead was a set of proposals for instituting a nationwide anthropological survey akin to the one based in Ottawa. He drew them up at the director's request; "Proposals," 213–16.

9 VSC: D.J. to V. Stefansson, 20 February 1919.

10 MBC: D.J. to C.M. Barbeau, 17 August 1920.

11 MBC: D.J. to C.M. Barbeau, 13 September 1920.

12 MBC: D.J. to C.M. Barbeau, 24 August 1920.

13 MBC: D.J. to C.M. Barbeau, 6 October 1920.

14 Lacking a physical anthropologist on staff, Dalhousie University anatomist John Cameron agreed to write up a collection of skeletal remains obtained by various expedition members, including specimens Beuchat and Jenness had acquired during their final days together on the west coast of Alaska. Appended to Cameron's paper is a special report on dentition, prepared by two other Dalhousie professors, S.G. Ritchie and J.S. Bagnall; Cameron and Ritchie, *Osteology and Dentition*.

15 *Geological Survey of Canada, Summary Report for 1921*, 20; *for 1922*, 23.

16 Diubaldo, *Stefansson*, 188. Diubaldo's book provides a detailed account of this entire affair. A more Stefansson-friendly perspective appears in Hunt, *Stefansson*, 172–94.

17 VSC: D.J. to V. Stefansson, 20 February 1919; Stefansson to D.J., 16 February 1920.

18 VSC: V. Stefansson to D.J., 22 June 1920; D.J. to Stefansson, 26 June 1920.

19 Diubaldo, *Stefansson*, 195–6, 198.

20 Anderson's cutting remark appeared in a story published in the 14 January 1922 issue of the *Montreal Gazette*; see Diubaldo, *Stefansson*, 197. On the same day the *Toronto Star* ran Jenness's views on the Collinson Point mutiny under the headline "Declares Stefansson Acted Aggressively."

21 Diubaldo, *Stefansson*, 198–9; Stefansson, "Letter to the Editor," 666.

22 Jenness, Review of *Friendly Arctic*, 8–12. The earlier review, by Raymond Pearl, appeared in the 24 March 1922 issue of *Science* (320–1).

23 CSC: R.M. Anderson et al. to The Honourable Charles Stewart, 25 February 1922.

24 Diubaldo, *Stefansson*, 199–200.

25 VSC: D.J. to V. Stefansson, 30 January 1922; Stefansson to D.J., 28 February 1922.

26 ESC: D.J. to E. Sapir, 30 March 1922.

27 Mae Belle Anderson raised the matter in a September 1922 letter to William McKinlay. McKinlay, a Scottish magnetician, was among those rescued from Wrangel Island in the aftermath of the *Karluk* fiasco; Diubaldo, *Stefansson*, 200, 251, fn. 58.

28 It was the publication of Raymond Pearl's review (see note 22) that moved Jenness and company to seek official permission to offer their own comments on the book; ESC: D.J. to E. Sapir, 30 March 1922.

29 McConnell and Noice, "Friendly Arctic," 369–73; the text of Desbarat's letter to Stefansson, dated 1 August 1922, with its original emphasis, appears in the review at page 372.

30 VSC: V. Stefansson to D.J., 22 June 1920; Diubaldo, *Stefansson*, 201.

31 FBC: D.J. to F. Boas, 23 March 1920; Boas to D.J., 5 April 1920.

32 CCC: Re: Call from V. Stefansson and Dr Prince [to Charles Camsell], 7 April 1923; Memorandum, Rudolph Anderson to Charles Camsell, 24 April 1923.

33 CCC: E.E. Prince to C. Camsell, 19 April 1923; Camsell to Prince, 20 April 1923.

34 Camsell, "Friendly Arctic," 666.

35 Darnell, *Edward Sapir*, 133–5, 189–90.

36 DJC: L.L. Bolton to D.J., 24 September 1925.

37 MBC: D.J. to C.M. Barbeau, 7 October 1925; Nowry, *Man of Mana*, 265.

38 C. Stewart to R. Lemieux, 18 December 1925, cited in Nowry, *Man of Mana*, 265.

39 MBC: D.J. to C.M. Barbeau, 15 September 1925.

40 MBC: D.J. to C.M. Barbeau, 7 October 1925.

41 Ibid.

42 MBC: D.J. to C.M. Barbeau, 8 October 1925.

43 ESC: E. Sapir to H.I. Smith, 21 June 1925; Smith to Sapir, 29 June 1925.

44 Fenton, "Sapir as Museologist," 223.

45 ESC: H.I. Smith to E. Sapir, 25 July 1925.

46 ESC: E. Sapir to C.M. Barbeau, 7 October 1918.

47 E. Sapir to F. Boas, 22 December 1923, cited in Preston, "Barbeau," 130; ESC: Boas to Sapir, 15 October 1912.

48 E. Sapir to R.H. Lowie, 12 August 1916, cited in Preston, "Barbeau," 128.

49 Nowry, *Man of Mana*, 169, 273.

50 Darnell, *Edward Sapir*, 67; Preston, "Reflections," 191.

51 Darnell, *Edward Sapir*, 68.

52 DJC: D.J. to E. Sapir, 22 December 1926.

53 Preston, "Social Structure," 288.

54 DJC: D.J. to L.L. Bolton, 21 December 1925.

55 PSC: Personnel Records – Diamond Jenness; DJC: L.L. Bolton to D.J., 1 February 1926.

56 DJC: D.J. to E. Sapir, 2 February 1926; D.J. to F.S.H. Knowles, 28 February 1927.

57 DJC: D.J. to E. Sapir, 16 March 1927; to A. Hrdlička, 19 October 1926.

58 DJC: D.J. to L.L. Bolton, 21 December 1925.

59 Author's interviews with Frederica de Laguna, 28–29 September 1987; with William E. Taylor, 22 October 1987; with Richard Slobodin, 4 November 1987.

60 Duff, [notes of interview with Marius Barbeau], 4.

61 Nowry, *Man of Mana*, 273.

62 MBC: C.M. Barbeau to D.J., 5 October 1925; D.J. to Barbeau, 8 October 1925.

63 DJC: D.J. to W.H. Collins, 31 May 1927; D.J. to F.C.C. Lynch, 12 November 1936; PSC: Personnel Records – Diamond Jenness.

64 Canada. Department of Mines, *Report of the Department of Mines ... 1921*, 23–6.
65 HHC: D.J. to H.B. Hawthorn, 3 December 1966.
66 Miers and Markham, *Museums of Canada*, 25; see also Falconer, "Royal Ontario," 174.
67 W. Collins, "National Museum," 50.
68 Zaslow, *Reading the Rocks*, 337–40.
69 W. Collins, "National Museum," 47.
70 DJC: D.J. to W.H. Collins, 2 February 1928 (emphasis in original).
71 DJC: D.J. to W.H. Collins, 15 September 1930.
72 DJC: D.J. to W.H. Collins, 9 December 1930.
73 Waugh was en route to Ottawa from fieldwork in southern Labrador at the time of his disappearance. He was last seen on the Mohawk reserve at Kahnawake. Sent to investigate, Jenness theorized that his colleague died accidentally while attempting to walk across the Lachine railway bridge linking Kahnawake to Montreal; ESC: "Report of D. Jenness on His Investigation at Caughnawaga Reserve Re: Disappearance of Mr. F.W. Waugh, 1921."
74 Hodgetts et al., *Biography*, 53–4.
75 Barker, "McIlwraith," 253; TMC: T.F. McIlwraith to D.J., 13 December 1932.
76 DJC: D.J. to T.F. McIlwraith, 6 February 1926; McIlwraith to D.J., 8 February 1926; Barker, "McIlwraith," 257–8.
77 DJC: D.J. to E. Sapir, 22 February 1927; 29 November 1927; to F. Boas, 21 November 1927.
78 DJC: E. Sapir to D.J., 13 March 1927; Sapir to D.J., 15 June 1928; D.J. to Sapir (telegram), 15 June 1928.
79 ADC: L.L. Bolton to W. Foran, 31 May 1930.
80 Ibid.; DJC: C.D. Forde to D.J., 31 May 1930.
81 DJC: D.J. to C.D. Forde, 21 June 1930.
82 Robinson, *Grant*, 117–18.
83 J.C.B. Grant, "Progress," 2715–21.
84 DJC: D.J. to J.C.B. Grant, 29 April 1931; JCC: D.J. to J.M. Cooper, 13 November 1933.
85 DJC: D.J. to J.C.B. Grant, 30 October 1933; D.J. to E.A. Hooton, 22 October 1928; 11 December 1928.
86 A fourth report, Knowles' analysis of skeletal materials recovered at the Lawson site in the teens, appeared in print in 1937. By comparison, the museum issued only one monograph on physical anthropology while Sapir was chief, Knowles' *Glenoid Fossa*.
87 For example, see Armitage, *Comparing the Policy of Aboriginal Assimilation*, 221–2.
88 DJC: D.J. to O.S. Finnie, 17 April 1928; D.J. to R.R. Gates, 14 May 1928; Fogelson, "Interpretations of the American Indian Psyche," 15.
89 DJC: D.J. to F.C.C. Lynch, 3 April 1937.
90 Bloomfield, *Sacred Stories*.
91 ESC: E. Sapir to R.G. McConnell, 18 November 1916.
92 TMC: D.J. to T.F. McIlwraith 8 March 1927; H.I. Smith, "Materia Medica," 47–68.
93 DJC: D.J. to T.F. McIlwraith, 21 March 1927; McIlwraith to D.J., 28 March 1927; ADC: Memorandum re: Conference of 29 January 1930.

94 Barker, "Publication of *The Bella Coola Indians*," 9. An unexpurgated version of the two-volume ethnography appeared under the University of Toronto imprint in 1947; that press reissued it in 1992.

95 DJC: D.J. to C. Osgood, 16 November 1929.

96 DJC: D.J. to I.A. Lopatin, 7 May 1930.

97 TMC: D.J. to T.F. McIlwraith, 29 November 1930.

98 Zaslow, *Reading the Rocks*, 353–4, 357, 379.

99 DJC: D.J. to C. Camsell, 27 December 1930; to W.H. Collins, 5 December 1930.

100 DJC: D.J. to K. Birket-Smith, 3 April 1936; 6 June 1936.

CHAPTER EIGHT

1 Gruber, "Ethnographic Salvage," 1294.

2 Cole and Long, "Anthropological Survey Tradition," 227, 244; Boas, "Growth of Indian Mythologies," 4, 11.

3 Sapir, "Work of the Division," 62–3; cf. Jenness, "Fifty Years of Archaeology," 71; Rivers, "Report on Anthropological Research," 13.

4 ESC: J.A. Mason to E. Sapir, 7 July 1913; Goddard, "Beaver Indians," 203.

5 Lowie, "Native Languages," 84.

6 Boas, cited in Codere, "Introduction," in Boas, *Kwakiutl Ethnography*, xi; Boas cited in Hatch, *Theories of Man and Culture*, 45; Berman, "Culture as It Appears to the Indian," 217–19.

7 Ibid, 219; ESC: E. Sapir to W.D. Wallis, 10 June 1913; Darnell, "Boasian Text Tradition," 42–4.

8 DJC: D.J. to W.H. Collins, 9 July 1928; Bloomfield, *Sacred Stories*.

9 ESC: D.J. to E. Sapir [Summary Report ... Sept. 1913–July 1914] (undated); Sapir to D.J., 7 May 1913; DJC: Sapir to D.J., 5 August 1930.

10 Lowie, "Native Languages," 87, 89.

11 Boas, "Limitations of the Comparative Method," 276–7.

12 Sapir designed a corresponding alpha-numeric coding system for cataloguing accessions according to the area and group from which they had come; *Geological Survey of Canada, Summary Report for 1911*, 379.

13 Jenness, *Indians of Canada*, Part II.

14 Fenton, "Problems," 162; Tuck, "Northern Iroquoian Prehistory," 322.

15 ESC: E. Sapir to R.W. Brock, 7 May 1912; Sapir to Brock, 18 May 1912.

16 ESC: E. Sapir to F. Boas, 23 September 1912; 18 October 1912.

17 Sapir, "Anthropological Survey," 792.

18 ESC: E. Sapir to J.A. Teit, 4 June 1913; Goddard and Swanton, "Athapascan Family," 50.

19 Boas, "Ethnological Problems," 533–4.

20 Vanstone, *Athapaskan Adaptations*, 125; cf. Bennett, *Northern Plainsmen*, 14.

21 Lowie, *Robert H. Lowie*, 32; ESC: J.A. Mason to Edward Sapir, 25 October 1913; J.A. Teit to Sapir, 7 July 1912.

22 *GSC/SR 1912*, 452; *GSC/SR 1913*, 374; ESC: E. Sapir to J.A. Teit, 12 November 1912.

23 ESC: E. Sapir to J.A. Mason, 26 October 1914.

24 Sapir, "Work of the Division of Anthropology," 173–4.

25 Goddard, "Dancing Societies," 461–74; "Notes on the Sun Dance," 271–82.

26 E. Sapir to A.L. Kroeber, cited in Darnell, *Edward Sapir*, 134, 238.

27 Dempsey, "Sarcee," 629; Jenness, *Sarcee*, 3; Krauss and Golla, "Northern Athapascan Languages," 84.

28 Dempsey, "Sarcee," 635; Jenness, *Sarcee*, 8.

29 ESC: D.J. to E. Sapir, 3 July 1921; 18 July 1921.

30 Jenness, *Indians of Canada*, 261.

31 Ibid., 261, 263.

32 ESC: E. Sapir to T.F. Murray, 4 May 1921; Murray to Sapir, 10 May 1921.

33 ESC: D.J. to E. Sapir, 3 July 1921; 18 July 1921.

34 ESC: E. Sapir to F.W. Waugh, 3 October 1911.

35 ADC: D.J. to W. McInness, 6 July 1921.

36 ESC: D.J. to E. Sapir, 3 July 1921; Jenness, *Sarcee*, 83, 88.

37 Sapir, "Note on Sarcee Pottery," 247–9. Ceramics are now reasonably well documented in many pre-contact plains cultures but at the time Clark Wissler and other authorities considered their distribution to be far more limited.

38 Cited in Dempsey, "Sarcee," 635.

39 MBC: D.J. to C.M. Barbeau, 2 July 1922; ESC: D.J. to E. Sapir, 19 July 1922; Darnell, *Edward Sapir*, 240; Sapir, "Pitch·Accent," 185–205.

40 ESC: D.J. to E. Sapir, 18 July 1921; Darnell, *Edward Sapir*, 85, 240.

41 ESC: E. Sapir to R.H. Lowie, 15 February 1921; Sapir to A.L. Kroeber, 1 October 1921; Foster, "Language and Culture History," 76–7; Sapir, "Na-Dene Languages," 534–58.

42 Ruhlen, "Origin of the Na-Dene," 13, 994–6; "Dene-Yeniseian Languages."

43 Jenness, "List of Sarcee Songs" (unpublished). A second collection of Sarcee material also went unpublished: "Sarcee Myths and Traditions."

44 ESC: E. Sapir to C.M. Barbeau, 16 July 1920; Nowry, *Man of Mana*, 196.

45 MBC: D.J. to C.M. Barbeau, 8 July 1922. In the preface to his Carrier monograph, Jenness mistakenly dated his research to the winter of 1924–25; Jenness, "Carrier Indians of the Bulkley," 473.

46 Jenness unearthed two unpublished accounts of early contact period Chipewyan, one of which, attributed to Alexander Mackenzie's contemporary John Macdonell, he later edited for publication; MBC: D.J. to C.M. Barbeau, 24 August 1923; Jenness, "Chipewyan," 15–33.

47 Boas, "Ethnological Problems," 533; ESC: D.J. to E. Sapir, 23 June 1923; 12 July 1923; 13 August 1923; MBC: D.J. to C.M. Barbeau, 24 August 1923.

CHAPTER NINE

1 Furniss, "Carrier," 516; Jenness, "Carrier Indians of the Bulkley," 475; Tobey, "Carrier," 430.

2 Jenness, "Myths of the Carrier," 240–1.

3 MBC: D.J. to C.M. Barbeau, 10 February 1924.

4 Once systematic archaeological research in this portion of the province's western interior began in earnest after the Second World War, it revealed a record of human occupation millennia deep. Just how far down Athapaskan roots may run has yet to be firmly ascertained, although their presence is certainly of some longevity. Nor, it should be said, have findings been reached as to the

nature and extent of settlement at Dizkle. Nonetheless, the legendary village remains, to this day, a potent symbol of the enduring spiritual connection of the Wet'suwet'en to the life-sustaining river, and to its natural surroundings; Daly, *Our Box Was Full*, 126–7; Mills, *Eagle Down Is Our Law*, 87–9.

5 Campbell, *American Indian Languages*, 110.

6 Jenness, "Carrier Indians of the Bulkley," 475, 553.

7 Jenness, "Ancient Education," 22; Jenness, *Sekani*, 8; cf. Tobey, "Carrier," 415.

8 Jenness, "Carrier Indians of the Bulkley," 495.

9 Fisher, *Contact and Conflict*, 25.

10 Ridington, "Beaver," 359; Duff, *Indian History*, 63–9. Changes in its practice have come slowly, but the province's historic approach to the contentious land rights issue accounts for the fact there are now some 1,600 reserves in British Columbia, nearly 70% of the Canadian total.

11 Jenness, "Carrier Indians of the Bulkley," 475; Muckle, *First Nations*, 69–71; Tobey, "Carrier," 425–6. The early contact estimate approximates the population of the two principal West'suwet'en reserves today, places that were once major summer fishing villages, but have since become year-round communities: Moricetown (Kya Wiget), the larger of them, and Tse'khene-kya, usually known by its original Gitskan name, Hagwilget.

12 MBC: D.J. to C.M. Barbeau, 29 October 1923.

13 MBC: D.J. to C.M. Barbeau, 5 July 1923; 24 August 1923; 29 October 1923.

14 ESC: D.J. to E. Sapir, 21 October 1923; MBC: D.J. to C.M. Barbeau, 23 October 1923.

15 ESC: D.J. to E. Sapir, 21 October 1923; 13 November 1923.

16 ESC: D.J. to E. Sapir, 23 November 1923; Sapir to D.J., 13 January 1924.

17 ESC: E. Sapir to C.M. Barbeau, 16 July 1920.

18 Mulhall, *Will to Power*, 95–9; Darnell, *Edward Sapir*, 73.

19 While church duties had taken Morice to the Hazelton area on several occasions over the years, and he was certainly familiar with conditions there, he was prone to drawing inferences about the various sub-tribes on the basis of the one he knew best, the people of Stuart Lake, well to the east of the Bulkley Basin. This accounts for his assumption that the "exotic" (i.e., foreign-derived), rather than "indigenous," character of society and culture was no more pronounced in western precincts than elsewhere in Carrier territory; Morice, "Carrier Sociology and Mythology," 114–15.

20 ESC: D.J. to E. Sapir, 15 May 1924; Jenness, "Carrier Indians of the Bulkley," 541, 543, 559–61; Mills, *Eagle Down Is Our Law*, 40.

21 J.W. Grant, *Moon of Wintertime*, 122; Jenness, "Carrier Indians of the Bulkley," 557.

22 Ibid., 513; Mulhall, *Will to Power*, 159.

23 Jenness, "Ancient Education," 27.

24 Jenness, "Carrier Indians of the Bulkley," 541, 543, 559–61.

25 Jenness, "Indian Method," 13–14, 18–20; D.J.C: D.J. to F.G. Banting, 30 November 1929; Banting to D.J., 9 December 1929.

26 MBC: D.J. to C.M. Barbeau, 25 November 1923; Tobey, "Carrier," 430.

27 ESC: D.J. to E. Sapir, 10 February 1924; Cole, *Captured Heritage*, 268.

28 MBC: D.J. to C.M. Barbeau, 25 November 1923; 25 February 1924; Cole, *Captured Heritage*, 272.

29   MBC: D.J. to C.M. Barbeau, 25 November 1923.

30   MBC: D.J. to C.M. Barbeau, 10 December 1923; Cole, *Captured Heritage*, 271–2.

31   ESC: E. Sapir to D.J., 16 January 1924; D.J. to Sapir, 4 February 1924.

32   ESC: D.J. to E. Sapir, 3 March 1924; Jenness, "Yukon Telegraph Line," 695, 705.

33   MBC: D.J. to C.M. Barbeau, 25 February; Barbeau, *Totem Poles*, 126–7.

34   ESC: D.J. to E. Sapir, 3 March 1924.

35   ESC: D.J. to E. Sapir, 10 March addendum to letter of 3 March 1924.

36   ESC: D.J. to E. Sapir, 25 November 1923; 6 January 1924.

37   ESC: D.J. to E. Sapir, 20 January 1924; 3 March 1924.

38   ESC: D.J. to E. Sapir, 10 March addendum to letter of 3 March 1924; 28 March 1924.

39   Ibid., 13 March 1924; ESC: D.J. to E. Sapir, n.d. (March) 1924.

40   ESC: D.J. to E. Sapir, 28 March 1924.

41   ESC: D.J. to E. Sapir, 6/7 April 1924; Jenness, *Eskimo Language and Technology*, 3; A. Woodbury, "Eskimo and Aleut Languages," 56.

42   MBC: D.J. to C.M. Barbeau, 3 May 1924.

43   ESC: D.J. to E. Sapir, 15 May 1924.

44   ESC: D.J. to E. Sapir, 13 January 1924; 2 June 1924; MBC: D.J. to C.M. Barbeau, 15 December 1923; J.C. Grant, *Anthropometry*, 9, 11.

45   Sullivan, "'Blond' Eskimo," 225–8; MBC: D.J. to C.M. Barbeau, 25 November 1923. Stefansson's Northern Party associate, Harold Noice, also took occasion to criticize Jenness's "Blond Eskimo" findings, though his arguments had more to do with personal loyalties than with questions of anthropometric method; Noice, "Further Discussion," 228–32.

46   MBC: D.J. to C.M. Barbeau, 3 May 1924; ESC: D.J. to E. Sapir, 15 May 1924; University of Alberta, *Who's Who*, 125.

47   ESC: D.J. to E. Sapir, 15 May 1924.

48   Jenness, *Sekani*, 5; Harmon, *Journal of Voyages and Travels*.

49   Pritzker, *Native North American Encyclopedia*, 510; Jenness, *Sekani*, 13.

50   Denniston, "Sekani," 433–4, 438; Ridington, "Beaver," 350–2.

51   ESC: D.J. to E. Sapir, 24 June 1924; Jenness, *Sekani*, 8.

52   ESC: D.J. to E. Sapir, 12 June 1924; Jenness, *Sekani*, 28–43.

53   Ridington, "Beaver Dreaming," 115. The collection of Sekani folklore went unpublished. The original material is in the Canadian Museum of Civilization archives: see "Mythology of the Sekani."

54   ESC: D.J. to E. Sapir, 2 June 1924.

55   Jenness, *Sekani*, 12–13.

56   Jenness, "Sekani Indians," 31–2.

57   Ibid., 47.

58   ESC: D.J. to E. Sapir, 12 June 1924.

59   Jenness, "Sekani Indians," 32–3; *Sekani*, 64.

60   Jenness, *Sekani*, 12–13.

61   MBC: D.J. to C.M. Barbeau, 25 November 1923; Jenness, *Sekani*, 13.

62   MBC: D.J. to C.M. Barbeau, 20 January 1924; ESC: D.J. to E. Sapir, 4 February 1924; Teit, "Field Notes," 40–171.

63   Jenness, *Sekani*, 14–15; "Sekani Indians," 29.

64 Swayze, *Canadian Portraits*, 89–91.

CHAPTER TEN

1 DJC: D.J. to L.L. Bolton, 21 December 1925.
2 Kleivan and Burch, "Work of Knud Rasmussen," 6–7; Mathiassen, *Report of the Fifth Thule Expedition*, 9–13.
3 Rasmussen in ibid., 103; see also Rasmussen, *Across Arctic America*.
4 Steensby, "Anthropogeographical Study," 204–5, 210–12.
5 Rasmussen, cited in Burch, "Knud Rasmussen," 81; Birket-Smith in Rasmussen et al., "Danish Ethnographic Expedition," 542–3; Birket-Smith, *Caribou Eskimos*, 219–26.
6 Mathiassen in Rasmussen et al., "Danish Ethnographic Expedition," 547.
7 Ibid., 547–8; Mathiassen, *Archaeology*, vol. 1, 6–11; see also Giddings, *Ancient Men*, 77; de Laguna, "Therkel Mathiassen," 20.
8 Mathiassen, *Archaeology*, vol. 2, 184.
9 Ibid., 198–201; Mathiassen, "Question of the Origin," 606–7; McGhee, *Ancient People*, 20–4.
10 ESC: D.J. to E. Sapir, 1 November 1923; 13 November 1923; Sapir, "Anthropological Division … 1924," 38–9.
11 Jenness, "New Eskimo Culture," 430–1; Sapir, "Anthropological Division … 1925," 39.
12 Birket-Smith, "Foreløbig om Femte Thule-Ekspedition," 191–208.
13 Jenness, "New Eskimo Culture," 430.
14 Ibid., 431–5, 437.
15 Jenness, "Origin of Copper Eskimos," 541, 544; Jenness, *Copper Eskimos*, 23, 45–6.
16 Jenness, "Origin of Copper Eskimos," 544–5.
17 Ibid., 549–51; Jenness, "Canada's Eskimo Problem," 318; cf. Birket-Smith in Rasmussen et al., "Danish Expedition," 544.
18 DJC: D.J. to K. Birket-Smith, 23 April 1923.
19 Jenness, "Origin of Copper Eskimos," 551.
20 DJC: T. Mathiassen to D.J., 9 October 1925; 5 January 1926; D.J. to Mathiassen, 21 January 1926; 3 April 1926; see also Mathiassen, *Archaeology*, vol. 1, 206–12; *Archaeological Collections*, 72.
21 Years later, archaeologists established that the Dorset abandoned use of the drill, though why remains a mystery; e.g., McGhee, *Ancient People*, 142–4.
22 DJC: T. Mathiassen to D.J., 9 October 1925; Jenness, Review of *Archaeology of Central Eskimos*, 697; Mathiassen, *Archaeology*, vol. 2, 164–5.
23 DJC: K. Birket-Smith to D.J., 6 August 1925.
24 Jenness and Jenness, *Through Darkening Spectacles*, 126–7.
25 ESC: F.W. Waugh to E. Sapir, 17 January 1922.
26 Canada, "Auditor General's Report, 1922–23 Q-16; "Auditor General's Report, 1926–27," vol. 1, P-11; DJC: D.J. to L.L. Bolton, 21 December 1925; to K. Birket-Smith, 23 December 1926; to E. Sapir, 23 November 1925; W.H. Collins to D.J., 21 May 1926.
27 Sapir, "Anthropological Survey," 790.

28 DJC: D.J. to E. Sapir, 26 April 1926.

29 DJC: D.J. to K. Birket-Smith, 7 May 1926; to T. Mathiassen, 21 January 1926.

30 DJC: D.J. to O.W. Geist, 23 August 1934.

31 DJC: D.J. to J.W. Fewkes, 30 April 1926; Hrdlička, "Origin and Antiquity," 481–94; *Alaska Diary*, 3; Wiley and Sabloff, *History of American Archaeology*, 50.

32 DJC: D.J. to A. Hrdlička, 12 May 1926; Jenness, "Little Diomede," 78.

33 DJC: D.J. to A. Hrdlička, 12 May 1926; Hrdlička to D.J., 11 October 1926; Hrdlička, *Alaska Diary*, 102.

34 DJC: L.L. Bolton to undersecretary of state, external affairs, 31 May 1926; Jenness, "Archaeological Investigations in Bering Strait, 71; Jenness and Jenness, *Through Darkening Spectacles*, 131. On the Wrangel Island affair, see Diubaldo, *Stefansson*, 161–86.

35 Jenness, "Eskimos of Northern Alaska," 89–93; Spencer, "North Alaska Coast Eskimo," 326. Remembered as the "Big Sickness," nearly all the deaths at Wales occurred within the outbreak's first week, an experience repeated at nearby Teller, where almost as many succumbed; Arctic Circle, "Big Sickness."

36 DJC: D.J. to C.M. Garber, 18 May 1927.

37 Jenness, "Archaeological Investigations in Bering Strait," 72–3, 77–9; Morrison, *Diamond Jenness Collections*, 3.

38 ESC: D.J. to E. Sapir, 28 March 1924.

39 Jenness and Jenness, *Through Darkening Spectacles*, 136.

40 Ibid., 137; DJC: D.J. to A. Hrdlička, 6 October 1926; to T. Mathiassen, 6 November 1926; to A.E. Porsild, 26 November 1926.

41 DJC: A. Hrdlička to D.J., 4 October 1926; D.J. to Hrdlička, 6 October 1926; Jenness, "Archaeological Investigations in Bering Strait," 78.

42 Jenness and Jenness, *Through Darkening Spectacles*, 133–4.

43 Ibid., 75, Jenness, "Little Diomede," 79, 81.

44 Jenness, "Archaeological Investigations in Bering Strait," 75–6; "Little Diomede," 81, 84.

45 Forsyth, *History of the Peoples of Siberia*, 242–3; Hughes, "Siberian Eskimo," 248. From the late twenties onward, Moscow's strategic interests in the Bering Strait intensified, reaching a climax of sorts in 1948 when Big Diomede was cleared of its few remaining inhabitants in order to exploit its critical location on the doorstep of North America. By the time evacuation was implemented, most of its people were already gone, the majority furtively crossing the strait's Cold War "iron curtain" to find homes among Ingaliqmuit with whom they shared close cultural, linguistic, and social ties. The rest were resettled at East Cape; Krupnik "'Siberians' in Alaska," 63–9.

46 Jenness and Jenness, *Through Darkening Spectacles*, 135.

47 Jenness, "Archaeological Investigations in Bering Strait," 76; "Little Diomede," 78.

48 Ibid., 85; Jenness, "Archaeological Investigations in Bering Strait," 73.

49 Carl Heinrich Merck, cited in Gurvich, "Ethnic Connections," 20; Nelson, *Eskimo About Bering Strait*, 330.

50 DJC: W.H. Collins to D.J., 21 May 1926.

51 Jenness, "Archaeological Investigations in Bering Strait," 78.

52 Hrdlička, *Alaska Diary*, 96, 104; Anon., "Alaska Yields Secrets."

53 S. Young, "Beringia: An Ice Age View," 106; cf. Jenness, "Ethnological Problems," 172–3; Johnston, "Quarternary Geology," 28–32.

54 DJC: D.J. to E. Sapir, 19 October 1926; Jenness, "Archaeological Investigations in Bering Strait ," 72.

55 Jenness, "Division of Anthropology ... 1926," 11; Jenness, "Archaeological Investigations in Bering Strait," 76; cf. Morrison, *Diamond Jenness Collections*, 102.

56 Jenness, "Archaeological Investigations in Bering Strait," 75; "Little Diomede," 84.

57 Giddings, *Ancient Men*, 112–13.

58 DJC: D.J. to E. Sapir, 19 October 1926; Jenness, "Archaeological Investigations in Bering Strait," 77; "Eskimo Art," 161.

59 DJC: D.J. to A. Hrdlička, 6 October 1926; Hrdlička, *Arctic Diary*, 86, 90; Jenness, "Archaeological Investigations in Bering Strait," 77–8.

60 DJC: T. Mathiassen to D.J., 22 March 1927; Mathiassen, "Some Specimens," 33–56.

61 DJC: D.J. to E. Sapir, 19 October 1926; Jenness, "Little Diomede," 86.

62 Seemingly more certain than its employee, the museum issued a press release pegging the materials' age at 1,000 to 1,500 years old; see Anon., "Early Eskimo Culture," 710; cf. Anon., "Eskimo Relics."

63 H. Collins, "Prehistoric Eskimo Culture," 108–9; Jenness, "Archaeological Investigations in Bering Strait," 78; "Ethnological Problems," 170; see also H. Collins, *Archaeology of St. Lawrence Island;* cf. R.E. Ackerman, "Prehistory," 106–15; Dumond, *Eskimos and Aleuts*, 118–25.

64 DJC: D.J. to K. Birket-Smith, 23 December 1926; to E. Sapir, 22 December 1926; Jenness, *Eskimo Language and Technology*, Part A: *Comparative Vocabulary*, 3; "Notes on the Phonology of the Eskimo Dialect," 168; Jenness and Jenness, *Through Darkening Spectacles*, 138.

65 Jenness, "Archaeological Investigations in Bering Strait," 79.

66 Foster, "Language and the Culture History," 72–3; Jenness, "Archaeological Investigations in Bering Strait," 78; Krauss, "Eskimo-Aleut," 189–90; Woodbury, "Eskimo and Aleut," 60–1.

67 Jenness, "Archaeological Investigations in Bering Strait," 79; Burch, "Kotzebue Sound Es-kimo," 314; Ray, "Bering Strait Eskimo," 287.

68 Jenness, *Eskimo Language*, 3; Lantis, "Nunivak Eskimo," 209.

69 DJC: D.J. to E. Sapir, 22 December 1926; Dorais, *Language of the Inuit*, 9.

70 Jenness, "Archaeological Investigations in Bering Strait," 79; DJC: D.J. to E. Sapir, 19 October 1926; 22 December 1926.

71 For example, Foster, "Language and Culture History," 71; A. Woodbury, "Eskimo and Aleut," 61–2.

72 Jenness, "Ethnological Problems," 174; see also H. Collins, "History of Research," 14; Foster, "Language and Culture History," 71; Woodbury, "Eskimo and Aleut," 56.

73 Jenness, "Ethnological Problems," 174; "Problem of the Eskimo," 380. The assumption to which Jenness referred is sometimes called the geographical centre of gravity principle, presumably after Sapir's early discussion of the idea; see Sapir, *Time Perspective*, 79.

74 Jenness, "Problem of the Eskimo," 380.

1 DJC: T. Mathiassen to D.J., 6 October 1926; D.J. to Mathiassen, 6 November 1926.

2 DJC: A.V. Kidder to D.J., 27 October 1926; 11 November 1926; A. Hrdlička to D.J., 11 October 1926.

3 DJC: D.J. to A. Hrdlička, 19 October 1926; to A.V. Kidder, 5 November 1926. Taking a leap of faith, in 1934 organizers of the International Congress of Anthropological and Ethnological Sciences created under its banner the very sort of select group that Boas had contemplated, called the Committee for Systematic Research on Circumpolar Peoples. Jenness joined Kaj Birket-Smith, Boas, Waldemar Bogoras, and several other specialists from both sides of the Atlantic as one of its founding members; DJC: A.H. Brodrick to D.J., 31 August 1934; K. Birket-Smith to D.J., May 1936.

4 DJC: D.J. to K. Birket-Smith, 23 December 1926. The *Times* pieces appeared on 27 September and 26 December 1926, the second with the headline "Alaska Yields Secrets of First Americans."

5 VSC: D.J. to V. Stefansson, 1 October 1926 (with press release dated October 1926 attached); Stefansson to D.J., 3 October 1926 (with undated draft story attached); Anon., "Eskimo Relics."

6 DJC: D.J. to K. Birket-Smith, 23 December 1926.

7 DJC: A.V. Kidder to D.J., 1 March 1927.

8 DJC: D.J. to A.V. Kidder, 4 March 1927.

9 Over the span of several hundred years, people equipped with this arctic-adapted, mainly land-hunting technology spread eastward, eventually reaching northern Greenland where Danish explorer Eigil Knuth first uncovered their traces – dubbed Independence culture – in 1948, the same year as the Denbigh discovery. Clearly a banner year for northern archaeology, 1948 also found Henry Collins initiating a series of investigations in Canada's eastern arctic archipelago, work that soon turned up remains of a related culture: Pre-Dorset. It, in turn, gave rise to Dorset, a way of life geared to both land and sea that emerged around 1,000 BC. Following Steensby's lead, all these ancient pioneers of the Arctic are known collectively as Paleo-Eskimos nowadays, and their Thule successors as Neo-Eskimos; Dekin, "The Arctic," 22; Giddings, *Ancient Men*, 246–76; McGhee, *Ancient People*, 25–31.

10 DJC: A.V. Kidder to D.J., 21 March 1927.

11 DJC: D.J. to A.V. Kidder, 24 March 1927; to E Sapir, 16 March 1927.

12 DJC: H.B. Collins to D.J., 17 Feb. 1931; H. Collins, "Prehistoric Eskimo Culture," 109, 116; *Archaeology of St. Lawrence Island;* Giddings, *Ancient Men*, 154–60.

13 Boas, "Ethnological Problems," 538; Holly, "Ahistory of Hunter-Gatherers," 3.

14 Ironically, Alfred Kidder brought this collection to light, purchasing it while exploring for Viking remains in 1910; see Howley, *Beothuks*, 330, 339, and plate 24 [figs 29–32]; Wintemberg, "Eskimo Sites" [Part I], 86, fn. 112; R. Woodbury, *Kidder*, 21.

15 DJC: D.J. to A.J. Bayly, 26 April 1926; to K. Birket-Smith, 30 May 1927; W.H. Collins to D.J., 2 June 1927.

16 DJC: D.J. to T. Mathiassen, 21 January 1926; cf. D.J. to A.C. Haddon, 17 February 1926, cited in Jenness and Jenness, *Through Darkening Spectacles*, 123.

17 DJC: K. Birket-Smith to D.J., 28 November 1926; T. Mathiassen to D.J., 5 January 1926; D.J. to A. Bayly, 26 April 1926.

18 Marshall, *History and Ethnography*, 242–3; Pastore, "Beothuks," 260; see also Maunder, "Newfoundland Museum."

19 Marshall, *History and Ethnography*, 272, 283–4; Pastore, "Archaeology, History, and the Beothuks," 269; cf. Holly, "Beothuk."

20 Marshall, *History and Ethnography*, 217–21.

21 Speck, *Beothuk and Micmac*, 9–20.

22 Jenness, "Red Indians," 29; DJC: D.J. to J.M. Swaine, 23 August 1927.

23 Speck, *Beothuk and Micmac*, 20.

24 Jenness, "Vanished Red Indians," 29; Mannion, "Introduction," in Mannion, ed., *Peopling of Newfoundland*, 5; Marshall, *History and Ethnography*, 275–6.

25 DJC: D.J. to J.M. Swaine, 23 August 1927.

26 Ibid.; Marshall, *History and Ethnography*, 414.

27 Howley, *Beothuk*, 288–91; Marshall, *History and Ethnography*, 404, 413. At Jenness's request, Hrdlička prepared a brief report on the Long Island burials. The recovered skeletal material consisted of the calvarium of an elderly female, the fragmented skull of a three- to four-year-old child, and the mandible and several post-cranial fragments of a second adult, presumably male and seemingly of mixed (Indian-white) ancestry; DJC: A. Hrdlička to D.J., 30 November 1929.

28 DJC: D.J. to J.M Swaine, 23 August 1927; Jenness, "Vanished Red Indians," 31; Marshall, *History and Ethnography*, 568, fn. 40.

29 DJC: A.J. Bayly to D.J., 26 June 1927. Newfoundland's Secretary of Agriculture at the time, Bayly assisted the expedition in various ways, including facilitating the export of artifacts and skeletal material to Canada once the work was complete.

30 Howley, *Beothuk*, 341 and plate XXXII; Jenness, *Indians of Canada*, 265, fn. 3; cf. "Red Indians," 29.

31 Jenness, "Vanished Beothuk," 37; Wintemberg, "Eskimo Sites" [Part I], 89, 102; [Part II], 311, 332, fn. 466.

32 Fitzhugh, "Review of Paleo-Eskimo Culture History," 22.

33 DJC: D.J. to W.D. Strong, 17 September 1927; to J.M. Swaine, 23 August 1927; cf. Jenness, "Vanished Beothuk," 38.

34 DJC: F. Johansen to D.J., 28 October 1927; D.J. to A.C. Haddon, 17 February 1926, cited in Jenness and Jenness, *Through Darkening Spectacles*, 123. Elsewhere, Jenness refers to the "tornrin" as possible builders of unusual structures in the vicinity of Coronation Gulf. Local opinion had it that there were "dwarf people ... driven underground by the Copper Eskimos long ago"; see Jenness, *Material Culture*, 58; cf. Hawkes, *Labrador Eskimo*, 143.

35 DJC: D.J. to F. Johansen, 31 October 1927.

36 E. Leacock and Rothschild, eds, *Labrador Winter*.

37 DJC: W.D. Strong to D.J., 30 March 1927; D.J. to Strong, 5 April 1927.

38 DJC: W.D. Strong to D.J., 21 October 1927; 28 November 1928; Strong, "Stone Culture," 140–2; cf. Harp, *Cultural Affinities*, 8–9.

39 DJC: D.J. to E. Sapir, 9 May 1927; to K. Birket-Smith, 13 January 1928; Jenness, "Indians of Canada," 79–91. *The Indians of Canada*, whose working title had been the more inclusive "Aborigines of Canada," appeared in six subsequent editions, the last published by the University of Toronto Press in 1977.

40 DJC: D.J. to T. Mathiassen, 21 October 1927; Mathiassen to D.J., 30 November 1927; D.J. to Mathiassen, 27 March 1928.

41 DJC: D.J. to T. Mathiassen, 27 December 1928.

42 DJC: D.J. to W. Wintemberg, 20 September 1927; Wintemberg to D.J., 26 September 1927; Wintemberg, "Preliminary Report," 40–1; "Artifacts from Ancient Workshop," 13–40.

43 DJC: W. Wintemberg to D.J., 1 August 1928; Marshall, *History and Ethnography*, 396, 400.

44 DJC: W. Wintemberg to D.J., 21 August 1929; Jenness, "Division of Anthropology ... 1929," 7; D.J. to T. Mathiassen, 2 June 1930.

45 DJC: D.J. to T. Mathiassen, 8 April 1930; to F. Boas, 16 April 1931; to C.E. Guthe, 31 October 1931; to F. Hunter, 27 April 1931.

46 DJC: D.J. to R. Dixon, 20 March 1930.

47 Although information about them was not published for a full decade, Junius Bird's 1934 excavations near Hopedale, on the Labrador coast, produced indication of both Thule and Dorset remains; Bird, "Archaeology of Hopedale Area," 180.

48 Jenness, "Problem of the Eskimo," 390–1, 394–5; Harp, "Cultural Affinities," 9.

49 Jenness, "Problem of the Eskimo," 388, 395.

50 DJC: H.B. Collins to D.J., 4 March 1931; author's interview with Frederica de Laguna, 28–29 September 1987; de Laguna, "Therkel Mathiassen," 22; Harp, *Cultural Affinities*, 9. While Mathiassen's flirtation with it was short-lived, the theory itself had staying power – its advocates included Birket-Smith and, more recently, their compatriot Jørgen Meldgaard, the latter famously remarking, in the 1960s, that the evidence of early Dorset culture "smells of forest"; McGhee, *Ancient People*, 188.

51 Jenness, "Problem of the Eskimo," 395–6; DJC: H.B. Collins to D.J., 22 April 1931.

52 DJC: W.H. Collins to D.J., 17 April 1934; D.J. to Collins, 19 April 1934; Anon., "Division of Anthropology ... 1934," 6. As a cost-cutting measure in the thirties, Ottawa began renting space on Hudson's Bay Company ships for its annual arctic patrol; Zaslow, *Northward Expansion*, 198–9.

53 Anon., "Anthropological Division ... 1935–36," 5.

54 Jenness, "Anthropological Division ... 1936–37," 6; Leechman, "Two New Cape Dorset Sites," 365–6; Harp, *Cultural Affinities*, 11; W. Taylor, *Arnapik*, 3.

55 Dyck, "Toward a History of Archaeology," 127–9.

56 Bentham and Jenness, "Eskimo Remains," 41; Jenness, "Archaeological Collection," 189; Quimby, "Manitunik Eskimo Culture," 148; Rowley, "Dorset Culture," 490.

57 DJC: O.S. Finnie to D.J., 9 April 1929; D.J. to D.L. McKeand, 6 March 1930; Canada, Department of Interior, "Ordinance Respecting the Protection and Care of Eskimo Ruins"; "Regulations for the Protection of Eskimo Ruins in the North West Territories."

58 DJC: O.S. Finnie to D.J., 14 September 1927; Canada, Department of Interior, "Ordinance Respecting Scientists and Explorers."

59 Quimby, "Manitunik Eskimo Culture," 165; cf. Taylor, *Arnapik*, 2; DJC: D.J. to G. Quimby, 22 April 1940.

60 Rowley, "Dorset Culture," 496; DJC: D.J. to H.B. Collins, 9 November 1939.

61 Quimby, "Brief History," 111, 119–20; Stocking, "Ideas and Institutions," 30.

62 DJC: O.W. Geist to D.J., 7 June 1934.

63 DJC: F. Rainey to D.J., 19 January 1940; 4 August 1940; 2 January 1941.

64 D. Anderson, "Prehistory of North Alaska," 88–90; Newton, "Ipiutak," 1023–4.

65 DJC: K. Birket-Smith to D.J., 1 February 1935; D.J. to Birket-Smith, 23 February 1935.

66 DJC: D.J. to W. Thalbitzer, 18 October 1929; to A. Kroeber 17 January 1939.

67 Drawing on his valuable expertise, the National Museum commissioned Jenness to comment on Robert McGhee's *Copper Eskimo Prehistory* mere months before his death in late November 1969. Fittingly, that review would bring his professional work full circle, the final word in a career launched at Coronation Gulf half a century before; Jenness, "Notes on Copper Eskimo Prehistory" (unpub.).

68 Jenness, "Prehistoric Culture Waves," 383, 389–90; Taylor, *Arnapik*, 2; author's interview with William E. Taylor, 22 October 1987.

69 Shalett, "'Lebensraum' Wars."

CHAPTER TWELVE

1 DJC: D.J. to J.M. Cooper, 13 March 1926.

2 The work eventually passed to the very capable hands of Irving Goldman, then a doctoral candidate at Columbia University. With guidance from Jenness and Harlan Smith, Goldman spent the winter of 1935–36 with the Ulkatcho Carriers in the vicinity of Anahim Lake, studying, among other things, their absorption of coastal elements: in this case, derived chiefly from the adjacent Bella Coola. "The culture is disintegrating rapidly," the result of a collapsing fur-based economy, he later reported to Smith from New York. "But shamans still flourish and potlatches celebrating cessation of mourning are still regarded as proper form"; DJC: I. Goldman to D.J., 25 June 1935; Goldman to H.I. Smith, 27 June 1936.

3 DJC: E. Sapir to D.J., 4 May 1927; D.J. to C. Osgood, 15 January 1928.

4 DJC: E. Sapir to D.J., 5 August 1930; C. Osgood to D.J., 1 July 1929; Osgood, *Winter*, xvii.

5 ESC: E. Sapir to R.G. Brock, 5 December 1911; P. Radin to E. Sapir, 2 November 1911.

6 Radin, "On Ojibwa Work in Southeastern Ontario," 482–3; Sapir, "Anthropological Division," 473–4.

7 ESC: P. Radin to E. Sapir, 16 October 1913; 8 February 1914; Steinbring, "Saulteaux," 244, 251–2.

8 ESC: F.W. Waugh to E. Sapir, 20 July 1916; 27 June 1919; Hallowell, "Passing of the Midewiwin," 32. In 1920, Waugh sent to Ottawa for a phonograph in hopes of recording the ceremony, but the machine failed to reach him in time; ESC: to Sapir, 29 August 1920.

9 DJC: D.J. to J.M. Cooper, 5 October 1928; Cooper, *Notes on the Ethnology of the Otchipwe*, 1.

10 Jenness, "Java," 112–27; DJC: D.J. to J.M. Cooper, 24 September 1929. Fortunately, the Saulteaux were not neglected for long: in 1930, A.I. Hallowell, of the University of Pennsylvania, initiated decade-long fieldwork in the Berens

River region, on the eastern side of Lake Winnipeg, and two years later, on Jenness's recommendation, Ruth Landes took up doctoral research for Columbia on the Rainy River, south of Lake of the Woods; DJC: J.M. Cooper to D.J., 1 October 1929; Hallowell, *Ojibwa of Berens Rivers*, ch. 1; DJC: D.J. to R. Benedict, 4 June 1932.

11 Jenness, *Ojibwa Indians*, 1.

12 Clifton, "Potawatomi," 725, 728; Jenness, *Indians of Canada*, 277; Pritzker, *Native American Encyclopedia*, 406–7.

13 Clifton, "Potawatomi," 739; Rogers, "Algonkian Farmers of Southern Ontario," 122–4; Jenness, *Ojibwa Indians*, 6. Nowadays, these resentments are largely forgotten, intermarriages across the bounds of formerly separate enclaves, each with its own village, helping to foster a communal spirit given form in shared Anishinabe identity; Wasuaksing First Nation.

14 Rogers, "Southeastern Ojibwa," 764–5; "Algonkian Farmers," 128.

15 Brownlie, *A Fatherly Eye*, 8, 19, 172, fn. 26.

16 DJC: D.J. to J.M. Cooper, 24 September 1929.

17 Johnson, "Notes on the Ojibwa and Potawatomi," 207, 215; Norcini, "Frederick Johnson's Canadian Ethnology," 123–4.

18 Jenness, *Ojibwa Indians*, v, 69–78.

19 Ibid., v; Steckley and Cummins, "Pegahmagabow of Parry Island," 37, 39.

20 DJC: D.J. to E. Sapir, 17 October 1929.

21 Stocking, "Ideas and Institutions," 15–16.

22 Barnouw, *Culture and Personality*, 139.

23 Jenness, "Ancient Education," 24–6.

24 Boas, "The Mind of Primitive Man," 11; Benedict, *Patterns of Culture*, 254.

25 Stocking, "Ideas and Institutions," 16; Darnell, *Edward Sapir*, 140–1.

26 DJC: E. Sapir to D.J., 7 June 1927.

27 Boas, "The Methods of Ethnology," 284–5; cf. Stocking, Jr, "Essays on Culture and Personality," 9.

28 Jenness, "Indian's Interpretation," 57.

29 For example, Hallowell, "Ojibwa Ontology," 19–20; Redfield, *Primitive World*, 86; Barnouw, *Culture and Personality*, 24.

30 Jenness, *Ojibwa Indians*, 29; cf. Redfield, *Primitive World*, 106.

31 Jenness, *Ojibwa Indians*, 79.

32 Ibid., 88.

33 Ibid., 68, 87–8; cf. Hallowell, "Ojibwa Ontology," 40; Landes, "Personality of the Ojibwa," 53–5.

34 Hallowell, "Aggression in Saulteaux Society," 261.

35 Landes, cited in Barnouw, *Culture and Personality*, 147.

36 Ibid., 147–50; Landes, "Personality of Ojibwa," 57.

37 Ibid., 54.

38 Jenness, *Ojibwa Indians*, 47, 53–4; Hallowell, "Ojibwa Ontology," 46.

39 Speck, "Family Hunting Band," 289–90; Feit, "Construction of Algonquian Hunting Territories," 114, 125; Lowie, *Primitive Society*, 211–12.

40 Jenness, *Indians of Canada*, 124; Speck and Eisley, "Significance of Hunting Territory Systems," 269–71; Tanner, "New Hunting Territory Debate," 20–1.

41 DJC: D.J. to C. Osgood, 26 May 1928.

42 Jenness, *Ojibwa Indians*, 4; *Sekani Indians*, 44; "Carrier Indians of the Bulkley River," 483.

43 Speck, *Family Hunting Territories*, 12–17; Jenness, *Ojibwa Indians*, 5–6. Change followed a similar course in the eastern Cordillera where "the fur trade induced the Indian to return year after year to the same trapping district and to conserve its supply of beaver": Jenness, *Sekani Indians*, 44.

44 Jenness, *Ojibwa Indians*, 6–7.

45 Bailey, *Conflict*, 87–8; DJC: D.J. to F. Speck, 20 February 1928; Speck to D.J., 1 March 1928.

46 Leacock, *Montagnais Hunting Territory*, 12–17.

47 Speck, "Family Hunting Band," 289, 305; Feit, "Construction of Algonquian Hunting Territories," 115–17, 120–2.

48 JCC: John Cooper, "Aboriginal Land Holding Systems." Memorandum to Dr Harold W. McGill, deputy superintendent general for Indian affairs, 11 October 1933.

49 Canada, Department of Indians Affairs, *Annual Report for 1919–20*, 7; Cole and Chaikin, *Iron Hand Upon the People*, 101–3.

50 Titley, *Narrow Vision*, 52–6; Scott, *Administration of Indian Affairs*, 13.

51 Scott, cited in J. Taylor, *Canadian Indian Policy*, 5.

52 ESC: E. Sapir to C.M. Barbeau, 16 July 1920.

53 DJC: D.C. Scott to D.J., 11 January 1927; D.J. to Scott, 12 January 1927.

54 DJC: D.J. to J. Arverkieva, 5 February 1932; to S. Lesage, 5 April 1935.

55 ESC: J. Teit to E. Sapir, 5 January 1914; Darnell, *Edward Sapir*, 58.

56 RBC: D.J. to R.B. Bennett, 15 September 1932.

57 Kelly, "Why Applied Anthropology Developed When It Did," 123; Shore, *Science of Social Redemption*, 85–6.

58 Jenness, [Diary of Trip to Pacific Science Congress, Batavia, 1929] (unpub.).

59 Meriam, *Problem of Indian Administration*; Hawthorn et al., *Survey of the Contemporary Indians*.

60 Jenness, "Population Possibilities"; "Canada's Fishery and Fishery Population"; DJC: D.J. to F.C.C. Lynch, 27 February 1932.

61 DJC: D.J. to T.F. McIlwraith 29 November 1930.

62 DJC: J. Cooper to D.J., 23 November 1932; D.J. to Cooper, 3 December 1932.

63 McNickle, "Anthropology and the Indian Reorganization Act," 51–3.

64 Anon., "Anthropologists and the Federal Indian Program," 170; Kelly, "United States Indian Policies," 73; DJC: D.J. to H.W. McGill, 1 March 1935.

65 WNC: D.J. to W.A. Newcombe, 11 January 1934; DJC: W. Malcolm to D.J., 25 September 1935.

66 DJC: D.J. to E. Kenny, 9 November 1935; 26 November 1935; 4 February 1936.

67 Suttles, "Recent Emergence of the Coast Salish," 256; B.G. Miller, "Salish," 238–9, 242; Jenness, "Saanich Indians," 52–3 (unpub.).

68 Maud, ed., *The Salish People*; Sapir, "Anthropological Survey of Canada," 792.

69 ESC: T.F. McIlwraith to E. Sapir, 21 September 1921; Sapir to P. Radin, 5 October 1920.

70 DJC: W.A. Newcombe to D.J., 20 January 1934.

71 Jenness, "Saanich Indians," 6; DJC: D.J. to E. Kenney, 15 October 1935.

72 DJC: D.J. to E. Kenney, 15 October 1935.

73 Fisher, *Contact and Conflict*, 66–7; Jenness, "Saanich Indians," 2–3, 19, 31–2.

74 DJC: D.J. to E. Kenney, 9 November 1935.

75 Duff, *Upper Stalo Indians*, 11; Suttles, "Central Coast Salish," 453–6.

76 DJC: D.J. to E. Kenney, 23 January 1936; 4 February 1936; WNC: D.J. to W.A. Newcombe, 13 March 1936; Jenness and Jenness, *Through Darkening Spectacles*, 155.

77 Jenness, *Faith of a Coast Salish Indian*, 35, 88; cf. Suttles, *Katzie Ethnographic Notes*, 6.

78 DJC: D.J. to E. Kenney, 6 March 1936.

79 The companion to his general report on Saanich ethnography is Jenness's "Saanich and Other Coast Salish Notes and Myths" (unpub.).

80 Suttles, *Katzie Ethnographic Notes*, 5.

CHAPTER THIRTEEN

1 Zaslow, *Reading the Rocks*, 379.

2 DJC: D.J. to C. Camsell, 25 August 1936; H. McGill to C. Camsell, 15 December 1936.

3 DJC: D.J. to H.D. Skinner, 7 August 1937; Jenness and Jenness, *Through Darkening Spectacles*, 172–3.

4 Stocking, *After Tylor*, 430.

5 DJC: C. Camsell to D.J., 10 December 1936.

6 PSC: C. Camsell to W. Foran, 8 February 1937; C. Camsell to C.H. Bland, 12 February 1937.

7 DJC: D.J. to C. Guthe, 8 June 1937.

8 Bumstead, *Peoples of Canada*, vol. 2, 200, 206.

9 PSC: Civil Service Commission to Indian Affairs Branch, n.d.; H. McGill to C. Camsell, 5 October 1937; DJC: D.J. to C. Camsell, 26 November 1936.

10 DJC: D.J. to T.R.L. MacInnes, 15 March 1939.

11 Loram and McIlwraith, eds, *North American Indian Today*, 349; D.B. Smith, "Now We Talk," 52.

12 McGill, "Policies and Problems," 132–3; Gosford cited in Armitage, *Comparing the Policy of Aboriginal Assimilation*, 75–6.

13 Historically, the question of rights for Aboriginal peoples in Canada was an all-or-nothing proposition, one in which they would be required to forfeit special rights granted to them under the Indian Act – including retention of their native status, living on reserves, and exemption from taxation – in order to be entitled to vote. First introduced into pre-confederation law in the 1857 Act to Encourage the Gradual Civilization of the Indians Tribes of Canada, the enfranchisement process entailed strict requirements that probably would have disqualified "a good portion of the Euro-Canadian community," notably being of "good moral character and free from debt"; Dickason, *Canada's First Nations*, 229.

14 Scott, *Administration*, 5.

15 Hawthorn, ed., *Survey of the Contemporary Indians of Canada*, pt. 1, 368.

16 Tobias, "Protection, Civilization, Assimilation," 127, 137–8.

17 Scott in Titley, *Narrow Vision*, 48–50; J.L. Taylor, *Canadian Indian Policy*, 143–6.

18 Scott, *Administration*, 25, 27.

19 Jenness, "Canada's Indians Yesterday," 98; Hawthorn, ed., *Contemporary Indians of Canada*, pt. 1, 369.

20 DJC: D.J. to C. Camsell, 25 August 1936; Jenness, "Canada's Indians Yesterday," 96.
21 DJC: D.J. to C. Camsell, 25 August 1936.
22 DJC: D.J. to W. Nash, 19 April 1938; King, "Between Two Worlds," 301; Jenness, "Canada's Indian Problems," 372.
23 Scott cited in Titley, *Narrow Vision*, 92.
24 DJC: D.J. to C. Camsell, 25 August 1936; Jenness, "Canada's Indians Yesterday," 99; for a comprehensive history of the residential school experience, see J.R. Miller, *Shingwauk's Vision*.
25 Ibid., DJC: D.J. to R.A. Hoey, 17 December 1937.
26 J.R. Miller, *Skyscrapers*, 212–13.
27 Jenness, "Canada's Indians Yesterday," 99; Titley, *Narrow Vision*, 57.
28 Waldram et al., *Aboriginal Health*, 156–7.
29 E.L. Stone, "Canadian Indian Medical Services," 160.
30 DJC: D.J. to C. Camsell, 25 August 1936.
31 Ibid.; Pettipas, *Severing the Ties*, 107; Cole and Chaikin, *Iron Hand*, 167–8.
32 DJC: D.J. to C. Camsell, 25 August 1936; Jenness, "Canada's Indian Problems," 376.
33 Cited in J.L. Taylor, *Canadian Indian Policy*, 99.
34 Shewell, "What Makes the Indian Tick?," 145.
35 DJC: D.J. to E. Kenny, 19 August 1938; 14 September 1932; Jenness and Jenness, *Through Darkening Spectacles*, 175–91.
36 DJC: D.J. to C.M. Barbeau, 2 September 1939; to F. de Laguna, 24 January 1940; de Laguna to D.J., 18 April 1940.
37 DJC: D.J. to H.B. Collins, 16 November 1942.
38 Zaslow, *Reading the Rocks*, 390.
39 Nowry, *Man of Mana*, 313; DJC: D.J. to A.G. Bailey, 20 September 1943.
40 Sheffield, "Search for Equity," 22–4, 27.
41 DDC: Memorandum from F.V. Heakes, 12 May 1941; Jenness and Jenness, *Through Darkening Spectacles*, 195.
42 After years of effort and the generation of enormous quantities of data, M Project was scrapped in 1945. Fifteen years on, its commissioned reports, over 650 of them, were declassified and published in summary form; D.H. Price, *Anthropological Intelligence*, 122–7.
43 DJC: D.J. to A.G. Bailey, 20 September 1943.
44 Canada, Department of Mines and Resources, "Geographic Bureau," 132–3.
45 Jenness and Jenness, *Through Darkening Spectacles*, 197–9; Dyck, "Toward a History of Archaeology," 127–8.
46 Bumstead, *Peoples of Canada*, vol. 2, 206–7.
47 Pitsula, "Saskatchewan CCF," 26.
48 Dickason, *Canada's First Nations*, 310; Indian Association of Alberta, "Memorial on Indian Affairs."
49 Canada, Department of Indian and Northern Affairs, *Historical Development*, 133.
50 Tobias, "Protection, Civilization, Assimilation," 51–2; Zaslow, *Northward Expansion*, 298.
51 Shewell, "What Makes the Indian Tick?," 146–7; DJC: D.J. to J.E. Robbins, 1 November 1938.

52 Canada, Parliament, *Special Joint Committee*, 305, 310–11; Dickason, *Canada's First Nations*, chs. 26, 27.

53 Cairnes, *Citizens Plus*, 17, 54–5; see also Sluman and Goodwill, *John Tootoosis*, 195; Weaver, *Making Canadian Indian Policy*, 4.

54 Kulchyski, "Anthropology in the Service of the State," 24, 32; cf. Hancock, "Diamond Jenness's Arctic Ethnography," 204.

55 Weaver, *Making Canadian Indian Policy*, 171.

56 Canada, Parliament, *Special Joint Committee*, 310; in summarizing the plan, Jenness's most strident modern-day critic ignores this crucial point altogether: Kulchyski, "Anthropology in the Service of the State," 29.

57 Canada, Parliament, *Special Joint Committee*, 307–8; Jenness, "Canada's Indians Yesterday," 96.

58 See also United Nations Charter, ch. 11, Articles 73–7, Declaration Regarding Non-Self-Governing Territories.

59 Canada, Parliament, *Special Joint Committee*, 309; Orange, *Treaty of Waitangi*, 258.

60 Canada, Parliament, *Special Joint Committee*, 312; Dalziel, "Politics of Settlement," 102; King, "Between Two Worlds," 283–7, 300.

61 Jenness, "Canada's Indian Problems," 372.

62 Canada, Parliament, *Special Joint Committee*, 316–17.

63 Ibid., 52, 766; Patterson, *Canadian Indian*, 12–13.

64 MRC: T. Lloyd to H.L. Keenleyside, 26 November 1947; Keenleyside to deputy minister, Department of Native Affairs, 4 December 1947.

65 BBC: D.J. to B. Blackwood, 6 July 1948; MRC: D.J. to H.L. Keenleyside, 25 May 1948.

66 MRC: D.J. to H.L. Keenleyside, 25 May 1948; L. Jackson to D.J., 5 August 1948.

67 A.G. Price, *White Settlers*, 150; MRC: Memorandum to the Deputy Minister, 20 November 1950; cf. Sinclair, "Why are Race Relations in New Zealand Better," 121.

68 Jenness, "Canada's Indians Yesterday," 97; MRC: Memorandum to the Deputy Minister, 20 November 1950.

CHAPTER FOURTEEN

1 DJC: D.J. to C. Osgood, 20 January 1943.

2 Russell, *National Museum*, 8–9, 12.

3 Ibid., 21–2; Canada, Department of Mines and Resources, *Annual Report … 1948–1949*, 5–8; Canada, Department of Resources and Development, *Annual Report of the National Museum … 1949–50*, 8–13.

4 Canada, Department of Mines and Resources, *Annual Report … 1948–1949*, 5–6, 18; Canada, Department of Resources and Development, *Annual Report … 1949–50*, 9. In the winter months, MacNeish shifted his attentions to the Mexican highlands, where his excavations uncovered evidence of early plant domestication.

5 Jenness, "Discussion," 30.

6 DJC: D.J. to C. Osgood, 20 January 1943; Jenness and Jenness, *Through Darkening Spectacles*, ch. 17.

7 Jenness, "Some Impressions of Post-War Italy," 344, 348; "Italy's Demographic Crisis," 272.

8 Zamagni, *Economic History*, 323, 333.

9 Jenness, "Impressions of Post-War Italy," 344, 347.

10 Ibid., 344; "Italy's Demographic Crisis," 277, 279–80.

11 HMC: D.J. to H.A. Moe, 13 April 1953; Moe to D.J., 23 June 1954; D.J. to Moe, 24 June 1954.

12 HMC: D.J. to H.A. Moe, 29 July 1954; Rudenko, *Ancient Culture*, 3; Trigger, *History of Archaeological Thought*, 216–17.

13 HMC: D.J. to H.A. Moe, 17 February 1955; 14 October 1955.

14 BBC: D.J. to B. Blackwood, 3 August 1951; Wayne Suttles, personal communication, 12 May 1987.

15 Whittaker and Ames, "Anthropology and Sociology," 159, 161; HHC: D.J. to H.B. Hawthorn, 19 September 1956.

16 HMC: D.J. to H.A. Moe, 14 October 1955. When the two allies wound up on opposing sides in the First World War, Great Britain annexed Cyprus and in 1925, made it a crown colony; Keefe and Solsten, "Historical Setting," ch. 1.

17 For Great Britain, the resulting state of emergency effectively ended in 1960 when Whitehall granted the island independence, reserving for itself a pair of military bases vital to its geo-political interests in the eastern Mediterranean. Sadly, the aftermath of statehood played out differently for the Cypriots themselves, the ensuing decades witnessing communal violence despite UN-sponsored intervention, a Greek coup d'état followed by armed invasion from the Turkish mainland, major population displacements instigated by partition into antagonistic ethnic enclaves, and finally, in 1983, declaration of an independent Turkish Republic of Northern Cyprus whose status is recognized only in Istanbul. Rapprochement has been slow in coming ever since; Holland, *Britain and the Revolt*.

18 BBC: D.J. to B. Blackwood, 5 June 1956; HMC: D.J. to H.A. Moe, 15 July 1956; D.J. to R. Jenness, February 1956.

19 Since the 1980s, archaeological investigations have pushed back the time horizon to as much as 11,000 years before the present; see Swinz, ed., *Earliest Prehistory of Cyprus*.

20 Keefe and Solsten, "Historical Setting," ch. 1.

21 Jenness, *Economics of Cyprus*, v–vi.

22 Ibid., v.

23 M. Harris, *Rise of Anthropological Theory*, 662.

24 HMC: D.J. to H.A. Moe, 5 January 1959; D.J. to G.N. Ray, 4 November 1960.

25 Hill, *History of Cyprus*; Jenness, *Economics of Cyprus*, vi.

26 Holland, *Britain and the Revolt*, 5; Jenness, *Economics of Cyprus*, 132; HMC: D.J. to R. Jenness, February 1956.

27 Keefe and Solsten, "Historical Setting," ch. 1; Royal Institute of International Affairs, *Cyprus*, 10–11.

28 Ibid., 17–19.

29 HMC: D.J. to R. Jenness, February 1956.

30 Ibid.; D.J. to H.A. Moe, 29 December 1955.

31 BBC: D.J. to B. Blackwood, 5 June 1956; VSC: D.J. to V. Stefansson, 15 July 1957; Meleagrou and Yesilada, "Society and Its Environment," ch. 2.

32 BBC: D.J. to B. Blackwood, 5 June 1956; HMC: D.J. to R. Jenness, February 1956; VSC: D.J. to V. Stefansson, 15 July 1957.

33 HMC: D.J. to R. Jenness, February 1956.

34 VSC: D.J. to V. Stefansson, 15 July 1957; HMC: to R. Jenness, February 1956.

35 Keefe and Solsten, "Historical Setting," ch. 1.

36 Jenness, *Economics of Cyprus*, 114.

37 VSC: D.J. to V. Stefansson, 15 July 1957.

38 HMC: D.J. to H.A. Moe, 26 February 1956; BBC: D.J. to B. Blackwood, 5 June 1956.

39 BBC: D.J. to B. Blackwood, 23 July 1960; Jenness and Jenness, *Through Darkening Spectacles*, 293–99; HMC: D.J. to H.A. Moe, 5 January 1959.

40 BBC: D.J. to B. Blackwood, 12 August 1959.

41 NCC: J.L. Jenness to V. Valentine, 20 October 1959; R.G. Robertson to Treasury Board, 28 April 1960.

42 BBC: D.J. to B. Blackwood, 23 July 1960; HHC: D.J. to H. Hawthorn, 4 June 1958; HMC: D.J. to G.N. Ray, 4 November 1960.

43 NCC: D.J. to F. Ross, 7 July 1960.

44 NCC: D.J. to V. Valentine, nd; G.W. Rowley to R.G. Robertson 23 November 1960; Jenness, *Eskimo Administration: Alaska*.

45 NCC: C.M. Bolger to V. Valentine, 31 May 1961.

46 Under the 1949 terms of Newfoundland's confederation with Canada, the Labrador Inuit (along with the region's Montagnais and Naskapi population) were recognized as citizens of the new province and, as such, were not regarded as a federal responsibility, as were Inuit elsewhere in the country; Jenness, *Eskimo Administration: Labrador*, 73–4. Their status has since changed.

47 NCC: Northern Affairs to Treasury Board, 15 May 1962; Jenness, *Eskimo Administration: Greenland*.

48 Hughes, "Under Four Flags," 15–17.

49 NCC: D.J. to R.G. Robertson, 22 June 1962.

50 Jenness, *Eskimo Administration: Canada*, 18–19. In 1870, Canada annexed Rupert's Land, the Hudson's Bay Company's immense land grant, and, ten years later, Great Britain ceded its rights in the arctic islands.

51 Jenness, *Eskimo Administration: Canada*, 30.

52 Ibid., 40, 49; Diubaldo, "Absurd Little Mouse," 34. Oddly enough, Ottawa extended the federal franchise to Inuit in 1949, a full decade before Indians were granted that same right.

53 Jenness, *Eskimo Administration: Analysis*, 25; *Eskimo Administration: Canada*, 91.

54 DJC: D.J. to Council of the NWT, 5 November 1934; Jenness, *Eskimo Administration: Analysis*, 14–15.

55 DJC: D.J. to A.L. Fleming, 2 December 1932; to K. Rasmussen, 7 October 1928.

56 Jenness, *Eskimo Administration: Analysis*, 25.

57 Ibid.; Paine, "Path to Welfare Colonialism," 12.

58 By 1956, one in six Inuit (out of a population of some 7,000) had been evacuated to sanatoria in the south; Jenness, *Eskimo Administration: Canada*, 96; St. Laurent and Lesage, cited in Diubaldo, *Government of Canada and the Inuit*, 113.

59 Paine, "Path to Welfare Colonialism," 15–19; Zaslow, *Northward Expansion*, 301.

60 Jenness, *Arctic Administration: Canada*, 90.

61 Ibid., 105–6; Jenness, "Administration of Northern Peoples, 123; Jenness, *Eskimo Administration: Analysis*, 26–7.

62 Jenness, *Eskimo Administration: Canada*, 134–5, 161, 172–4; Zaslow, *Northward Expansion*, 322.

63 DPC: R.A. Jenness to D. Snowden, 30 October 1962.

64 Ibid., 29; Jenness, *Eskimo Administration: Canada*, 161. The penultimate chapter of the volume on Canada was originally entitled "Shadows of a Welfare Society." An exchange of correspondence with Walter Rudnicki, head of the Welfare Division of Northern Affairs, led Jenness to rename it "Shadows of an Uprooted Society"; NCC: W. Rudnicki to D.J., 5 July 1962.

65 Jenness, *Arctic Administration: Canada*, 161; Paine, "Welfare Colonialism," 22; Brody, *People's Land*, 231.

66 Jenness, *Eskimo Administration: Canada*, 173.

67 Jenness, *Eskimo Administration: Analysis*, 56. In the words of one observer, education for Inuit and Indian children alike "has been an expensive failure," its goals "never clearly defined," its curricula "inappropriate," its overall impact "harmful to the psychological and social well-being of the natives"; NCC: A. Cooke to J. Lotz, 22 October 1962.

68 Jenness, "Human Resources," 370–1; Jenness, *Eskimo Administration: Analysis*, 44.

69 Jenness, "Human Resources," 370; *Eskimo Administration: Canada*, 126.

70 Frideres and Gadacz, *Aboriginal Peoples*, 144–5; cf. Hawthorn, ed., *Contemporary Indians of Canada*, vol. 1, 13, 109; Hawthorn in Jenness, "Human Resources," 371.

71 NCC: B.G. Sivertz to R.G. Robertson, 15 October 1962.

72 HHC: D.J. to H.B. Hawthorn, 21 January 1961; NCC: D.J. to R.G. Robertson, 22 June 1962.

73 NCC: D.J. to D. Rowley, 29 November 1962; HHC: D.J. to H.B. Hawthorn, 21 January 1961. The Institute's editor, Diana Rowley, was Graham Rowley's wife.

74 NCC: B.G. Sivertz to R.G. Robertson, 15 October 1962; cf. Jenness, "Human Resources," 367.

75 Zaslow, *Northward Expansion*, 272; Mowat, *People of the Deer*; *Desperate People*.

76 NCC: B.G. Sivertz to R.G. Robertson, 15 October 1962.

77 DPC: D.J. to R.G. Robertson, 4 November 1962; 5 January 1963; D.J. to B.G. Sivertz, 15 January 1963.

78 Jenness and Jenness, *Through Darkening Spectacles*, xviii.

79 In prefatory notes to the much-enhanced, posthumously published version of the memoir, Stuart Jenness described his father's choice of title as a "curious but meaningful" one. That said, he then inexplicably confines his few clarifying remarks to the inappropriateness of the Taugenichts label; ibid., xxii.

80 HHC: D.J. to H. Hawthorn, 3 December 1966.

81 Ibid.; DPC: D.J. to T. Lloyd, 7 September 1968.

82 Bumstead, *Peoples of Canada*, vol. 2, 335; Weaver, *Making Canadian Indian Policy*, 13, 20, 23, 45.

83 Ibid., 20–2; Hawthorn, ed., *Contemporary Indians of Canada*, vol. 1, 396–7.

84 Weaver, *Making Canadian Indian Policy*, 47.

85 Ibid., 62.
86 Ibid., 53–4; Canada, Department of Indian Affairs and Northern Development, *Statement of the Government of Canada on Indian Policy*, 5.
87 Cardinal, *Unjust Society*, ch. 13.
88 HHC: D.J. to H.B. Hawthorn, 25 September 1969; BBC: D.J. to B. Blackwood, 25 September 1969.
89 BBC: E. Jenness to B. Blackwood, 14 December 1969.
90 Anon., "Diamond Jenness Is Awarded the Order of Canada," 77.

EPILOGUE

1 For example, Epp and Sponsel, "Major Personalities and Developments;" Freedman, ed., *The History of Canadian Anthropology*; McFeat, *Three Hundred Years of Anthropology*; Trigger, "Giants and Pygmies."
2 Richling, "An Anthropologist's Apprenticeship," 71–2.
3 Lotz and Lotz, *Pilot Not Commander*, 18; Hancock, "Toward a Historiography of Canadian Anthropology," 40.
4 Jenness, *Indian Background of Canadian History*, 2–24.
5 Stocking, "Ethnographer's Magic," 83–4; Wallis, "Anthropology in England," 786.
6 Marett, "Present State of Anthropology," 299; Marett cited in Wallis, "Methods of English Ethnologists," 183.
7 Edwards, "Jenness and Malinowski," 89.
8 Lowie, Review of *Northern D'Entrecasteaux*, 226; cf. Barton, Review of *Northern D'Entrecasteaux*, 187; Skinner, Review of *Northern D'Entrecasteaux*, 61–2.
9 Hancock, "Diamond Jenness's Arctic Ethnography," 167–9; Wright, "Fieldwork Photographs," 43–8.
10 Edwards, "Visualizing History," 14; Michael Young, personal communication, 8 November 1990.
11 Malinowski, *Argonauts*, 6–8, 25.
12 Barth, "Britain and the Commonwealth," 20.
13 Wissler, Review of *Life of the Copper Eskimos*, 72–3; Riches, "Force of Tradition in Eskimology," 81.
14 DJC: D.J. to W.C. McKern, 26 January 1936.
15 de Laguna, "Presidential Address," 475–6.
16 Weaver, "Role of Social Science," 86; Richling, "Applied Anthropology," 52–8.
17 Kulchyski, "Anthropology in the Service of the State," 24, 29–30; cf. Ervin and Holyoak, "Applied Anthropology in Canada," 135.
18 Geertz, *The Interpretation of Cultures*, ch. 1.
19 Wilson, "Thomas Jefferson," 57.

References

ARCHIVAL MATERIALS

Canada
Canadian Museum of Civilization Archives
  C. Marius Barbeau Correspondence, B206
  Diamond Jenness Correspondence, 1921–1946. B 639–61 [microfilms 82-117-82-124].
  Diamond Jenness Correspondence, 1947–1968. Box 253.f 6
  Edward Sapir Correspondence, 1910–1925. B620–38 [microfilms 82-124-82-131]
Library and Archives Canada
  Charles Camsell Correspondence, Department of Mines, RG 45, vol. 67, file 45078C
  Charles Stewart Correspondence, Department of Mines, RG 45, vol. 67, file 4078C
  Department of Mines and Resources Correspondence, RG 10 B3e(ix) vol. 8587, file 1/1-10-2
  George von Zedlitz Correspondence, MG 30-B89
  Northern Coordination and Research Centre Correspondence, RG 85 vol. 1656, file NR 2/3-34
  Papers Relating to the Anthropological Division, National Museum of Canada. RG 45, vol. 49, file 3109A
  R.B. Bennett Papers, M1075, vol. 374
  Records of the Department of Defence, Directorate of Intelligence. Ottawa: Library and Archives Canada, RG 24, 83–84/216, Box 2968, vol. 1
  Records of the Public Service Commission, RG 32, vol. 563
  R.G. McConnell Correspondence, Department of Mines, RG 45, vol. 49, file 3109A
  Royal Northwest Mounted Police Correspondence, RG 84, vol. 571, file 244
  Rudolph Anderson Correspondence [re: Canadian Arctic Expedition], MG 30 B40 vol. 10

Archives of British Columbia
    E.O.S. Scholefield Correspondence
    W.A. Newcombe Correspondence
University of British Columbia Archives
    Harry B. Hawthorn Correspondence
University of Toronto Archives
    Thomas F. McIlwraith Correspondence, B79-0011, Box 2

New Zealand
New Zealand National Art Gallery and Museum Archives
    Augustus Hamilton Correspondence

United Kingdom
Pitt Rivers Museum Archives
    Beatrice Blackwood Correspondence
    Henry Balfour Correspondence
University of Oxford Archives
    Robert R. Marett Correspondence, UDC/2/4

United States
American Philosophical Society Archives
    Franz Boas Correspondence
Catholic University of America Archives
    Father John Cooper Correspondence
Dartmouth College Archives
    Vilhjalmur Stefansson Correspondence
John Simon Guggenheim Foundation
    Henry Moe Correspondence

UNPUBLISHED MANUSCRIPTS

Barker, John. "The Publication of The Bella Coola Indians: T.F. McIlwraith and the National Museum." Unpub. ms. Canadian Museum of Civilization, n.d.

Duff, Wilson. [Notes of interview with Marius Barbeau], typescript in possession of author, n.d.

Jenness, Diamond. "Diary of D. Jenness, 1913–16." Ottawa: Library and Archives Canada, MG30, B89 1913–16

– "Archaeological Notes on Eskimo Ruins at Barter Island, on the Arctic Coast of Alaska, Excavated by D. Jenness, 1914." Unpub. ms. Gatineau, QC: Canadian Museum of Civilization, Archaeological Survey of Canada, MS. 85 1914

– "List of Sarcee Songs, and a Memorandum regarding the report on 'The Sarcee of Alberta.'" Unpub. ms. Gatineau, QC: Canadian Museum of Civilization, B38 F1 1921

– "Sarcee Myths and Traditions." Unpub. ms. Gatineau, QC: Canadian Museum of Civilization, B38 f1 1921

– "Mythology of the Sekani Indians. Fort McLeod and Fort Grahame." Unpub. ms. Gatineau, QC: Canadian Museum of Civilization MS. B38 f8 1924

– [Diary of Trip to Pacific Science Congress, Batavia, 1929], in possession of Stuart Jenness 1929
– "The Saanich Indians of Vancouver Island." Unpub. ms. Gatineau, QC: Canadian Museum of Civilization, MS. B38 f6 1934–5
– "Saanich and Other Coast Salish Notes and Myths." Unpub. ms. Gatineau, QC: Canadian Museum of Civilization, MS B39 f1 1935–6
– "Notes on Copper Eskimo Prehistory." Gatineau, QC: Canadian Museum of Civilization, Box 420, folder 4 (typescript) n.d.

PUBLISHED SOURCES AND THESES

Ackerman, Robert. *J.G. Frazer: His Life and Work*. Cambridge: Cambridge University Press 1987
Ackerman, Robert E. "Prehistory of the Asian Eskimo Zone." In *Handbook of North American Indians*, vol. 5, *Arctic*, edited by David Damas, 106–18. Washington: Smithsonian Institution 1984
Alcock, F.J. *A Century in the History of the Geological Survey of Canada*. Ottawa: King's Printer 1947
Anderson, Douglas D. "Prehistory of North Alaska." In *Handbook of North American Indians*, vol. 5, *Arctic*, edited by David Damas, 80–93. Washington: Smithsonian Institution 1984
Anderson, Rudolph. "Canadian Arctic Expedition 1915." *Geological Survey of Canada, Summary Report for 1915*, 220–36. Ottawa: King's Printer 1916
Anon. "The Battle of the Sites." *Victoria College Review* 1, no. 1 (1902): 8–12
– "Anthropology at the British Association." *Science* 81, no. 2085 (1909): 477–8
– "Anthropological Expedition to New Guinea." *Nature* 86, no. 2172 (11 June 1911): 530–1
– "Maori Studies and Ethnology in Education." *New Zealand Journal of Science and Technology* 1, no. 5 (1918): 257–8
– "Soldiers of Science." *The Ottawa Journal*, 29 April 1926
– "An Early Eskimo Culture." *Nature* 118, no. 2976 (13 November 1926): 710–12
– "Eskimo Relics Lay Basis for History." *The New York Times*, 3 October 1926
– "Alaska Yields Secrets of First Americans." *The New York Times*, 26 December 1926
– "Division of Anthropology." In *National Museum of Canada, Annual Report for 1934, Bull. 76*, 6–9. Ottawa: King's Printer 1935
– "Anthropologists and the Federal Indian Program." *Science* 81, no. 2094 (15 February 1935): 170–1
– "Diamond Jenness Is Awarded The Order of Canada." *Arctic* 22, no. 1 (March 1969): 77
Arctic Circle. "The 'Big Sickness' in Arctic Alaska – 1918." Accessed 3 May 2006: http://www.arcticcircle.uconn.edu/History/Culture/Sickness.html
Armitage, Andrew. *Comparing the Policy of Aboriginal Assimilation: Australia, Canada and New Zealand*. Vancouver: UBC Press 1995
Avrith, Gale. "Science at the Margins: The British Association for the Advancement of Science and the Foundations of Canadian Anthropology, 1884–1910." PhD diss. University of Pennsylvania. Ann Arbor: University Microfilms 1986

Bailey, Alfred G. *The Conflict of European and Eastern Algonkian Cultures, 1504–1700*. Toronto: University of Toronto Press 1976 [orig. 1937]

Balfour, Henry. "Presidential Address, Section H." *British Association for the Advancement of Science, Report of the 74th Meeting, Cambridge, 1904*. London (1905): 689–700

Balikci, Asen. "Ethnography and Theory in the Canadian Arctic." *Études/Inuit/Studies* 13, no. 2 (1989): 103–11

Barbeau, C. Marius. "Henri Beuchat." *American Anthropologist* 18, no. 1 (1916): 105–10

– *Totem Poles of the Gitksan, Upper Skeena River, British Columbia*. National Museum of Canada Bull. 61, Anthro. Series 12. Ottawa: King's Printer 1929

Barker, John. "T.F. McIlwraith and Anthropology at the University of Toronto 1925–63." *Canadian Review of Sociology and Anthropology* 24, no. 2 (1987): 252–68

Barnouw, Victor. *Culture and Personality*. Homewood, IL: Dorsey 1963

Barth, Fredrik. "Britain and the Commonwealth." In Fredrik Barth et al., *One Discipline, Four Ways: British, German, French, and American Anthropology*, 3–57. Chicago: University of Chicago Press 2005

Bartlett, Robert A., and R.T Hale. *The Last Voyage of the Karluk*. Boston: Small, Maynard 1916

Barton, F.R. Review of *The Northern D'Entrecasteaux*. *Man* 21 (December 1921): 187–9

Beaglehole, Ernest. "New Zealand Anthropology To-Day." *Journal of the Polynesian Society* 46, no. 183 (1937): 154–72

Beaglehole, J.C. *Victoria University College: An Essay Towards a History*. Wellington: New Zealand University Press 1949

Bellich, James. *The Victorian Interpretation of Racial Conflict: The Maori, The British, and the New Zealand Wars*. Montreal: McGill-Queen's University Press 1986

Bennett, John W. *Northern Plainsmen: Adaptive Strategy and Agrarian Life*. Chicago: Aldine 1969

Bentham, Robert, and Diamond Jenness. "Eskimo Remains in S.E. Ellesmere Island." *Transactions of the Royal Society of Canada*, Section II (1941): 41–55

Bender, Donald. "The Development of French Anthropology." *Journal of the History of the Behavioral Sciences* 1, no. 2 (1965): 139–51

Benedict, Ruth. *Patterns of Culture*. Boston: Houghton Mifflin 1959 [orig. 1934]

Berman, Judith. "The Culture as It Appears to the Indian Himself: Boas, George Hunt, and the Methods of Ethnography." In *Volksgeist as Method and Ethic: Essays on Boasian Ethnography and the German Anthropological Tradition*, edited by George W. Stocking, Jr, 215–56. Madison: University of Wisconsin Press 1996

Bernstein, Jay H. "First Recipients of Anthropological Doctorates in the United States, 1891–1930." *American Anthropologist* 104, no. 2 (2002): 551–64

Besnard, Philippe. "The 'Année Sociologique' Team." In *The Sociological Domain: The Durkheimians and the Founding of French Sociology*, edited by P. Besnard, 11–39. Cambridge: Cambridge University Press 1983

Bird, Junius. "Archaeology of the Hopedale Area, Labrador." *Anthropological Papers of the American Museum of Natural History* 39, pt. 2 (1945): 117–88

Birket-Smith, Kaj. "Foreløbig om Femte Thule-Ekspedition far Grønland til Stillehavet." [Forecast for the Fifth Thule Expedition from Greenland to the Pacific.] *Geografisk Tidskrift* 27 (1924): 191–208

– *The Caribou Eskimos: Material and Social Life and Their Cultural Position*. Report of the Fifth Thule Expedition, 1921–24, vol. 5. Copenhagen: Gyldendal 1929

Bloomfield, Leonard. *Sacred Stories of the Sweet Grass Cree*. National Museum of Canada Bull. 60, Anthro. Series 11. Ottawa: King's Printer 1930

Boas, Franz. "The Growth of Indian Mythologies: A Study Based Upon the Growth of the Mythologies of the North Pacific Coast." *The Journal of American Folklore* 9, no. 32 (1896): 1–11

– "The Mind of Primitive Man." *The Journal of American Folklore* 14, no. 52 (1901): 1–11

– "Ethnological Problems in Canada." *Journal of the Royal Anthropological Institute* 40 (1910): 529–39

– "The Limitations of the Comparative Method of Anthropology." In Boas, *Race, Language and Culture*, 270–80. [orig. 1896]

– "The Methods of Ethnology." In Boas, *Race, Language, and Culture*, 281–9. [orig. 1920]

– *Race, Language and Culture*. New York: Free Press 1940

Bravo, Michael T. "Against Determinism: A Reassessment of Marcel Mauss's Essay on Seasonal Variation." *Études/Inuit/Studies* 30, no. 2 (2006): 33–49

Brody, Hugh. *The People's Land: Eskimos and Whites in the Eastern Arctic*. Markham, ON: Penguin 1975

Brownlie, Robin M. *A Fatherly Eye: Indian Agents, Government Power, and Aboriginal Resistance in Ontario, 1918–1939*. Oxford: Oxford University Press 2003

Bumstead, J.M. *The Peoples of Canada*, vol. 2, *A Post-Confederation History*. Toronto: Oxford University Press 1992

Bunzel, Matti. "Franz Boas and the Humboldtian Tradition: From Volksgeist and Nationalcharakter to an Anthropological Concept of Culture." In *Volksgeist as Method and Theory: Essays on Boasian Ethnography and the German Anthropological Tradition*, edited by George W. Stocking, Jr, 17–78. Madison: University of Wisconsin Press 1996

Burch, Ernest S., Jr. "Kotzebue Sound Eskimo." In *Handbook of North American Indians*, vol. 5, *Arctic*, edited by David Damas, 303–19. Washington: Smithsonian Institution 1984

– "Knud Rasmussen and the 'Original' Inland Eskimos of Southern Keewatin." *Études/Inuit/Studies* 12, nos. 1–2 (1988): 81–100

Butterworth, G.V. "The Politics of Adaptation: The Career of Sir Apirana Ngata, 1874–1928." MA thesis, Victoria University of Wellington 1969

– "A Rural Maori Renaissance? Maori Society and Politics 1920 to 1951." *Journal of the Polynesian Society* 81, no. 2 (1972): 160–95

Butterworth, G.V., and H.R. Young. *Maori Affairs/Nga Take Maori*. Wellington: Iwi Transition Agency 1990

Cairnes, Alan C. *Citizens Plus: Aboriginal Peoples and the Canadian State*. Vancouver: UBC Press 2000

Cameron, John, and Stephen G. Ritchie, *The Copper Eskimos*. Part C: *Osteology and Dentition of the Western and Central Eskimos*. Reports of the Canadian Arctic Expedition, 1913–18, vol. 12. Ottawa: King's Printer 1923

Campbell, Lyle. *American Indian Languages: The Historical Linguistics of Native America*. New York: Oxford University Press 1997

Camsell, Charles. "The Friendly Arctic." *Science* 57, no. 1484 (8 June 1923): 665–6

Canada, Department of Indians Affairs. *Annual Report for 1919–20*. Ottawa: King's Printer 1921

Canada, Department of Indian and Northern Affairs. *The Historical Development of the Indian Act*, 2nd ed. Ottawa: Indian and Northern Affairs 1978

Canada, Department of Indian Affairs and Northern Development. *Statement of the Government of Canada on Indian Policy*. Ottawa: Queen's Printer 1969

Canada, Department of Interior. "An Ordinance Respecting Scientists and Explorers." (Assented to 23 June 1926)

– "Ordinance Respecting the Protection and Care of Eskimo Ruins." (Assented to 5 February 1930)

– "Regulations for the Protection of Eskimo Ruins in the North West." (Approved by Commissioner in Council 18 May 1931)

Canada, Department of Mines. *Report of the Department of Mines for the Fiscal Year Ending March 31, 1921*. Ottawa: King's Printer 1922

Canada, Department of Mines and Resources. "Geographic Bureau." In *Report of the Department of Mines and Resources for 1948*, 132–4. Ottawa: King's Printer 1949

– *Annual Report of the National Museum for the Fiscal Year 1948–1949*. National Museum of Canada, Bulletin 118. Ottawa: NMC 1950

Canada, Department of Resources and Development. *Annual Report of the National Museum for the Fiscal Year 1949–50*. National Museum of Canada, Bulletin 123. Ottawa: NMC 1951

Canada, Parliament. "Auditor General's Report, 1911–12, Department of Mines." *Sessional Papers*, 2nd Session, 12th Parliament. Ottawa: King's Printer 1913

– "Auditor General's Report, 1920–21, Department of Mines." *Sessional Papers*, 5th Session, 13th Parliament. Ottawa: King's Printer 1922

– "Auditor General's Report, 1922–23, Department of Mines." *Sessional Papers*, vol. 1. Ottawa: King's Printer 1924

– "Auditor General's Report, 1926–27, Department of Mines." *Sessional Papers*, vol. 1. Ottawa: King's Printer 1928

– *Special Joint Committee of the Senate and House of Commons Appointed to Continue and Complete the Examination of the Indian Act*, vol. 1. Ottawa: King's Printer 1947

Cardin, C. "Bio-Bibliographie de Marius Barbeau." *Les Archives de Folklore* 11, *Hommage à Marius Barbeau*, 17–96. Quebec: Université Laval 1947

Cardinal, Harold. *The Unjust Society: The Tragedy of Canada's Indians*. Edmonton: M.G. Hurtig Publishers 1969

Chapman, William R. "Arranging Ethnology: A.H.L. Pitt Rivers and the Typological Tradition." In *Objects and Others: Essays on Museums and Material Culture*, edited by George W. Stocking, Jr, 15–48. Madison: University of Wisconsin Press 1985

Clifton, James A. "Potawatomi," in *Handbook of North American Indians*, vol. 15, *Northeast*, edited by Bruce G. Trigger, 725–42. Washington: Smithsonian Institution 1978

Codere, Helen. Introduction to Boas, *Kwakiutl Ethnography*, xi–xxxii. Chicago: University of Chicago Press 1966

Cole, Douglas. "The Origins of Canadian Anthropology, 1850–1910." *Journal of Canadian Studies* 8, no. 1 (1973): 33–45

– *Captured Heritage: The Scramble for Northwest Coast Artifacts*. Vancouver: UBC Press 1985

Cole, Douglas, and Ira Chaikin. *An Iron Hand Upon the People: The Law Against the Potlatch on the Northwest Coast*. Vancouver: Douglas & McIntyre 1990

Cole, Douglas, and Alex Long. "The Boasian Anthropological Survey Tradition: The Role of Franz Boas in North American Anthropological Surveys." In *Surveying the Record: North American Scientific Exploration to 1930*, edited by E.C. Carter II, 225–49. Philadelphia: American Philosophical Society 1999

Cole, Douglas, and Ludger Müller-Wille. "Franz Boas' Expedition to Baffin Island." *Études/Inuit/Studies* 8, no. 1 (1984): 37–63

Collins, Henry B. "Prehistoric Eskimo Culture on St. Lawrence Island." *Geographical Review* 22, no. 1 (1932): 107–19

– *Archaeology of St. Lawrence Island, Alaska*. Smithsonian Miscellaneous Collections 96, no. 1. Washington: Smithsonian Institution 1937

– "History of Research Before 1945." In *Handbook of North American Indians*, vol. 5, *Arctic*, edited by David Damas, 8–16. Washington: Smithsonian Institution 1984

Collins, William H. "The National Museum of Canada." In *Canada, Department of Mines, Annual Report for 1926*, 32–70. Ottawa: King's Printer 1928

Condon, Richard G., et al. *The Northern Copper Inuit: A History*. Toronto: University of Toronto Press 1996

Cooper, John M. *Notes on the Ethnology of the Otchipwe of Lake of the Woods and Rainy Lake*. Catholic University of America, Anthropological Series 3. Washington 1936

Craig, W.E.G. *Man of the Mist: A Biography of Elsdon Best*. Wellington: Reed 1964

Daly, Richard. *Our Box Was Full: An Ethnography for the Delgamuukw Plaintiffs*. Vancouver: UBC Press 2005

Dalziel, Raewyn. "The Politics of Settlement." In *Oxford History of New Zealand*, edited by H.W. Oliver, 87–111. Auckland: Oxford University Press 1981

Damas, David. "Copper Eskimo." In *Handbook of North American Indians*, vol. 5, *Arctic*, edited by David Damas, 397–414. Washington: Smithsonian Institution 1984

Darnell, Regna. "The Professionalization of American Anthropology: A Case Study in the Sociology of Knowledge." *Social Science Information* 10, no. 2 (1971): 91–9

– *Edward Sapir: Linguist, Anthropologist, Humanist*. Berkeley: University of California Press 1990

– "The Boasian Text Tradition and the History of Anthropology." *Culture* 12, no. 1 (1992): 39–48

Davidson, Janet M. "The Polynesian Foundation." In *Oxford History of New Zealand*, edited by W.H. Oliver, 3–27. Auckland: Oxford University Press 1981

Davis, W.H.C. *A History of Balliol College*. Oxford: Oxford University Press 1963

Dekin, Albert A., Jr. "The Arctic." In *The Development of North American Archaeology*, edited by J.A. Fitting, 14–48. Garden City: Anchor Press/Doubleday 1973

de Laguna, Frederica. "Presidential Address – 1967." *American Anthropologist* 70 (1968): 469–76

– "Diamond Jenness, C.C., 1886–1969." *American Anthropologist* 73, no. 1 (1971): 248–53

– "Therkel Mathiassen and the Beginnings of Eskimo Archaeology." In *Thule Eskimo Culture: An Anthropological Retrospective*, edited by A.P. McCartney, 10–33. National Museum of Man, Archaeological Survey of Canada Paper 88. Ottawa 1979

Dempsey, Hugh. "Sarcee." In *Handbook of North American Indians*, vol. 13, pt. 1, *Plains*, edited by Raymond J. De Mallie, 629–37. Washington: Smithsonian Institution 2001

Denniston, Glenda. "Sekani." In *Handbook of North American Indians*, vol. 6, *Subarctic*, edited by June Helm, 433–41. Washington: Smithsonian Institution 1981

Dickason, Olive. *Canada's First Nations: A History of Founding Peoples from Earliest Times*. 3rd ed. Don Mills, ON: Oxford University Press 2002

Diubaldo, Richard J. *Stefansson and the Canadian Arctic*. Montreal: McGill-Queen's University Press 1978

– "The Absurd Little Mouse: When Eskimos Became Indians." *Journal of Canadian Studies* 16, no. 2 (1981): 34–40

– *The Government of Canada and the Inuit, 1900–1967*. Ottawa: Indian and Northern Affairs Canada 1985

Dorais, Louis-Jacques. *The Language of the Inuit: Syntax, Semantics, and Society in the Arctic*. Montreal: McGill-Queen's University Press 2010

Duckworth, W.L.H., et al., "Anthropology at the Universities." *Man* 6, no. 56–7 (1906): 85

Duff, Wilson. *The Upper Stalo Indians of the Fraser River of B.C.* Anthropology in British Columbia, Memoir No. 1. Victoria: Provincial Museum of British Columbia 1952

– *The Indian History of British Columbia*, vol. 1, *The Impact of the White Man*. Anthropology in British Columbia Memoirs 5. Victoria: Provincial Museum of British Columbia 1964

Dumond, Don E. *The Eskimos and Aleuts*, rev. ed. London: Thames and Hudson 1987

Dunmore, John. *French Explorers in the Pacific*. 2 vols. Oxford: The Clarendon Press 1965

Dyck, Ian. "Toward a History of Archaeology in the National Museum of Canada: The Contributions of Harlan I. Smith and Douglas Leechman, 1911–1950." In *Bringing Back the Past: Historical Perspectives on Canadian Archaeology*, edited by Pamela J. Smith and Donald Mitchell, 115–33. Archaeological Survey of Canada Paper 158. Hull, QC: Canadian Museum of Civilization 1998

– "Founding the Anthropology Division at the National Museum of Canada: An Intertwining of Science, Religion and Politics." In *Revelations: Bi-Millenial Papers for the Canadian Museum of Civilization*, edited by Robert B. Klymasz and John Wills, 3–41. Canadian Centre for Folk Culture Studies Paper 75. Gatineau, QC: Canadian Museum of Civilization 2001

Edwards, Elizabeth. "Jenness and Malinowski: Fieldwork and Photographs." *Journal of the Anthropological Society of Oxford* 23, no. 1 (1992): 89–91

– "Visualizing History: Diamond Jenness's Photographs of D'Entrecasteaux Islands, Massim, 1911–1912 – A Case Study in Re-Engagement." *Canberra Anthropology* 17, no. 2 (1994): 1–25

Elliott, I., ed. *Balliol College Register*. 2nd ed. Oxford: Oxford University Press 1934

Falconer, Sir Robert. "The Royal Ontario and Other Museums in Canada." *University of Toronto Quarterly* 2 (1932–33): 168–85

Epp, Henry T., and Leslie E. Sponsel. "Major Personalities and Developments in Canadian Anthropology, 1860–1940." *Na'Pao* 10, no. 1–2 (September 1980): 7–13

Ervin, Alexander M., and Lorne Holyoak. "Applied Anthropology in Canada: Historical Foundations, Contemporary Practice, and Policy Potentials." *NAPA Bulletin* 25 (2006): 134–55

Feit, Harvey A. "The Construction of Algonquian Hunting Territories: Private Property as Moral Lesson, Policy Advocacy, and Ethnographic Error." In *Colonial Situations: Essays on the Contextualization of Ethnographic Knowledge*, edited by George W. Stocking, Jr, 109–34. Madison: University of Wisconsin Press 1991

Fenton, William N. "Problems Arising from the Historic Northeastern Position of the Iroquois." In *Essays in Historical Anthropology in North America*, 159–252. Smithsonian Miscellaneous Collections 100. Washington: Smithsonian Institution 1940

– "Sapir as Museologist and Research Director, 1910–1925." In *New Perspectives in Language, Culture and Personality: Proceedings of the Edward Sapir Centenary Conference*, edited by W. Cowan, 215–40. Amsterdam: John Benjamins 1986

Fisher, Robin. *Contact and Conflict: Indian-European Relations in British Columbia, 1774–1890*. Vancouver: UBC Press 1977

Fitzhugh, William W. "A Review of Paleo-Eskimo Culture History in Southern Québec, Labrador and Newfoundland." *Études/Inuit/Studies* 4, no. 1–2 (1980): 21–31

Flaherty, Robert. *Nanook of the North*. Film produced by Revillon Frères 1922

Fleras, Augie, and Jean L. Elliott. *The Nations Within: Aboriginal-State Relations in Canada, the United States, and New Zealand*. Toronto: Oxford University Press 1992

Fogelson, Raymond D. "Interpretations of the American Indian Psyche: Some Historical Notes." In *Social Contexts of American Ethnology, 1840–1984*, edited by June Helm, 4–27. Washington: American Ethnological Society 1985

Forsyth, James. *A History of the Peoples of Siberia: Russia's North Asian Colony 1581–1990*. Cambridge: Cambridge University Press 1992

Fortes, Meyer. "Social Anthropology at Cambridge Since 1900." In *Readings in the History of Anthropology*, edited by Regna Darnell, 426–39. New York: Harper and Row 1974

Foster, Michael K. "Language and the Culture History of North America." In *Handbook of North American Indians*, vol. 17, *Languages*, edited by Ives Goddard, 64–76. Washington: Smithsonian Institution 1996

Fox, James J. Translator's Introduction to Mauss, *Seasonal Variations of the Eskimo: A Study in Social Morphology*. London: Routledge and Kegan Paul 1979 [orig. 1904]

Frazer, James G. "Anthropology as a University Subject." *New Zealand Journal of Science and Technology* 1, no. 5 (1918): 262–3

– *The New Golden Bough*, abridged ed. New York: Criterion Books 1959 [orig. 1890]

Freedman, Jim, ed. *The History of Canadian Anthropology*. Proceedings No. 3, Canadian Ethnology Society. Ottawa: National Museum of Man 1976

Freeman, J.D. "Henry Devenish Skinner: A Memoir." In *Anthropology in the South Seas: Essays Presented to H.D. Skinner*, edited by J.D. Freeman and W.R. Geddes. New Plymouth: Thomas Avery & Sons 1959

Frideres, James S., and Rene R. Gadacz. *Aboriginal Peoples in Canada: Contemporary Conflicts*. 6th ed. Toronto: Prentice Hall 2001

Furniss, Elizabeth. "The Carrier Indians and the Politics of History." In *Native Peoples: The Canadian Experience*, edited by R. Bruce Morrison and C. Roderick Wilson, 508–46. 2nd ed. Toronto: McClelland and Stewart 1995

Gardner, W.J. "A Colonial Economy." In *Oxford History of New Zealand*, edited by W.H. Oliver, 57–86. Auckland: Oxford University Press 1981

Geological Survey of Canada. *Summary Report of the Geological Survey of Canada for the Calendar Year 1908*. Ottawa: King's Printer 1909

– *GSC/SR for 1909*. Ottawa: King's Printer 1910

– *GSC/SR for 1910*. Ottawa: King's Printer 1911

– *GSC/SR for 1912*. Ottawa: King's Printer 1914

– *GSC/SR for 1913*. Ottawa: King's Printer 1915

– *GSC/SR for 1915*. Ottawa: King's Printer 1916

– *GSC/SR for 1916*. Ottawa: King's Printer 1917

– *GSC/SR for 1921*. Ottawa: King's Printer 1922

– *GSC/SR for 1922*. Ottawa: King's Printer 1923

Geertz, Clifford. *The Interpretation of Cultures*. New York: Basic Books 1973

– *Works and Lives: The Anthropologist as Author*. Stanford: Stanford University Press 1988

– *Available Light*: *Anthropological Reflections on Philosophical Topics*. Princeton: Princeton University Press 2000

Gibbons, P.J. "The Climate of Opinion." In *Oxford History of New Zealand*, edited by W.H. Oliver, 303–32. Auckland: Oxford University Press 1981

Giddings, J. Louis. *Ancient Men of the Arctic*. Seattle: University of Washington Press 1967

Goddard, Pliny E. "Dancing Societies of the Sarsi Indians." *Anthropological Papers of the American Museum of Natural History* 11 (1914): 461–74

– "The Beaver Indians." *Anthropological Papers of the American Museum of Natural History* 10, pt. 4 (1916): 201–93

– "Notes on the Sun Dance of the Sarsi." *Anthropological Papers of the American Museum of Natural History* 16 (1919): 271–81

Goddard, Pliny E., and John R. Swanton, "Athapascan Family." In *Handbook of Indians of Canada*, edited by F.W. Hodge, 48–51. New York: Kraus Reprint 1969 [orig. 1913]

Goldenweiser, Alexander. "Diffusionism and the American School of Historical Ethnology." *The American Journal of Sociology* 31, no. 1 (1925): 19–38

Graham, Jeanine. "Settler Society." In *Oxford History of New Zealand*, edited by W.H. Oliver, 112–39. Auckland: Oxford University Press 1981

Grant, J.C. Boileau. *Anthropometry of the Beaver, Sekani, and Carrier Indians*. National Museum of Canada Bull. 81, Anthro. Series 18. Ottawa: King's Printer 1936

Grant, John W. *Moon of Wintertime: Missionaries and the Indians of Canada in Encounter Since 1534*. Toronto: University of Toronto Press 1984

Gruber, Jacob. "Horatio Hale and the Development of American Anthropology." *Proceedings of the American Philosophical Society* 111, no. 1 (1967): 5–37

– "Ethnographic Salvage and the Shaping of Anthropology." *American Anthropologist* 72, no. 6 (1970): 1289–99

Gurvich, I.S. "Ethnic Connections Across Bering Strait." In *Crossroads of Continents: Cultures of Siberia and Alaska*, edited by William W. Fitzhugh and Aron Crowell, 17–21. Washington: Smithsonian Institution 1988

Haddon, A.C. "Anthropology, Its Position and Needs." *Journal of the Anthropological Institute* 33 (1903): 11–23

– "The Anthropological Survey of Canada." *Nature* 88, no. 2209 (1912): 597–8

Hale, Horatio. "Third Report of the Committee to Investigate the Northwestern Tribes of the Dominion of Canada." In *British Association for the Advancement of Science, Report of the 57th Meeting, 1887*, 173–83. London 1888

– "Remarks on North American Ethnology: Introductory to the Report on the Indians of British Columbia." In *British Association for the Advancement of Science, Report of the 59th Meeting, 1889*, 797–801. London 1890

Hall, Edwin S., Jr. *'Land Full of People, a Long Time Ago': An Analysis of Three Archaeological Sites in the Vicinity of Kaktovik, Northern Alaska*. Brockport, NY: Edwin Hall and Associates 1987

Hallowell, A. Irving. "The Passing of the Midewiwin in the Lake Winnipeg Region." *American Anthropologist* 38, no. 1 (1936): 32–51

– "Ojibwa Ontology, Behavior, and World View." In *Culture in History: Essays in Honor of Paul Radin*, edited by Stanley Diamond, 19–52. New York: Columbia University Press 1960

– "Aggression in Saulteaux Society." In *Personality in Nature, Society and Culture*, edited by Clyde Kluckhohn and Henry A. Murray, 260–75. 2nd ed. New York: Alfred A. Knopf 1961

– *The Ojibwa of Berens River, Manitoba: Ethnography into History*, edited by Jennifer S.H. Brown. Forth Worth: Harcourt Brace Jovanovich 1992

Hancock, Robert L.A. "Diamond Jenness's Arctic Ethnography and the Potential for a Canadian Anthropology." In *Histories of Anthropology Annual* 2, edited by Regna Darnell and Frederic Gleach, 155–211. Lincoln: University of Nebraska Press 2006

– "Toward a Historiography of Canadian Anthropology." In *Historicizing Canadian Anthropology*, edited by Julia Harrison and Regna Darnell, 30–40. Vancouver: UBC Press 2006

Hanson, Allan. "The Making of the Maori: Culture Invention and Its Logic." *American Anthropologist* 91, no. 4 (1989): 890–902

Harmon, Daniel. *A Journal of Voyages and Travels in the Interior of America*. New York: A.S. Barnes 1903

Harp, Elmer, Jr. *The Cultural Affinities of the Newfoundland Dorset Eskimo*. National Museum of Canada, Bull. 200, Anthro. Series 67. Ottawa: Queen's Printer 1964

Harris, Jose. *Private Lives, Public Spirit: Britain 1870–1914*. London: Penguin 1993

Harris, Marvin. *The Rise of Anthropological Theory*. New York: Thomas Crowell 1968

Hatch, Elvin. *Theories of Man and Culture*. New York: Columbia University Press 1973

– *Respectable Lives: Social Standing in Rural New Zealand*. Berkeley: University of California Press 1992

Hawkes, E.W. *The Labrador Eskimo*. Geological Survey of Canada Memoir 91, Anthro. Series 14. Ottawa: King's Printer 1916

Hawthorn, H.B. "Diamond Jenness (1886–1969)." *Canadian Review of Sociology and Anthropology* 7, no. 1 (1970): 83–4

Hawthorn, H.B., ed. *A Survey of the Contemporary Indians of Canada: Economic, Political, and Educational Needs and Policies*. 2 vols. Ottawa: Canada, Department of Indian Affairs and Northern Development 1967

Hays, H.R. *From Ape to Angel: An Informal History of Social Anthropology*. New York: Alfred Knopf 1971

Healy, A.M. "Papua – Native Administration to 1942." In *Encyclopedia of Papua and New Guinea*, edited by Peter Ryan, 883–5. Melbourne: University of Melbourne Press 1972

Hearne, Samuel. *A Journey to the Northern Ocean*. Toronto: Macmillan 1958

Hickey, Clifford G. "An Examination of Processes of Cultural Change Among Nineteenth Century Copper Inuit." *Études/Inuit/Studies* 8, no. 1 (1984): 13–36

Hill, George. *A History of Cyprus*, vol. 4, *The Ottoman Province, the British Colony, 1571–1948*. Cambridge: Cambridge University Press 1952

Hodgetts, J.E. et al. *The Biography of an Institution: The Civil Service Commission of Canada, 1908–1967*. Montreal: McGill-Queen's University Press 1972

Hodgson, Terence. *Colonial Capital: Wellington 1865–1910*. Auckland: Random Century 1990

Holland, R.F. *Britain and the Revolt in Cyprus, 1954–1959*. Oxford: Oxford University Press 1998

Holly, Donald H., Jr. "An Ahistory of Hunter-Gatherers: The Beothuk Indians of Newfoundland and the Anthropological Imagination." Accessed 26 February 2000: http://www.brown.edu/Departments/ Anthropology/ HollyAAApaper.htm

– "The Beothuk on the Eve of Their Extinction." *Arctic Anthropology* 37, no. 1 (2000): 79–95

Howarth, Janet. "Science Education in Late-Victorian Oxford: A Curious Case of Failure?" *The English Historical Review* 102, no. 403 (1987): 334–69

Howe, K.R. *Singer in a Songless Land: A Life of Edward Tregear, 1846–1931*. Auckland: Auckland University Press 1991

Howley, James P. *The Beothuks or Red Indians: The Aboriginal Inhabitants of Newfoundland*. Cambridge: Cambridge University Press 1915

Hrdlička, Aleš. "The Origin and Antiquity of the American Indians." In *Annual Report of the Smithsonian Institution for 1923*, 481–94. Washington: Smithsonian Institution 1925

− *Alaska Diary, 1926–1931*. Lancaster: Jacques Cattell Press 1943

Hughes, Charles C. "Under Four Flags: Recent Culture Change Among the Eskimos." *Current Anthropology* 6, no. 1 (1965): 3–69

− "Siberian Eskimo." In *Handbook of North American Indians*, vol. 5, *Arctic*, edited by David Damas, 247–61. Washington: Smithsonian Institution 1984

Hunt, William R. *Stef: A Biography of Vilhjalmur Stefansson*. Vancouver: UBC Press 1986

Huxley, Thomas. *Man's Place in Nature and Other Anthropological Essays*. New York: D. Appleton 1898

Indian Association of Alberta. "Memorial on Indian Affairs Presented by the Indian Association of Alberta, September 1945." Glenbow Museum Archives. Accessed 18 March 2010: http://www.glenbow.org/collections/search/finding aids/archhtm/Ind.AssocAlta ina.cfm.

Jenness, Diamond. "The Magic Mirror: A Fijian Folk-Tale." *Folk-Lore* 24, no. 1 (1913): 233–4

− "The Ethnological Results of the Canadian Arctic Expedition, 1913–1916." *American Anthropologist* 18, no. 4 (1916): 612–15

− "The Eskimos of Northern Alaska: A Study in the Effect of Civilization." *Geographical Review* 5, no. 2 (1918): 89–101

− "The Ex-Cannibals of Goodenough Island." *Travel* 30 (1918): 32–6, 40

− "Papuan Cat's Cradles." *Journal of the Royal Anthropological Institute* 50 (1920): 299–326

− "Proposals for Ethnological Research in New Zealand." *New Zealand Journal of Science and Technology* 3, no. 4 (1920): 213–16

− "The 'Blond' Eskimos." *American Anthropologist* 23, no. 3 (1921): 257–67

− "The Cultural Transformation of the Copper Eskimo." *Geographical Review* 11, no. 4 (1921): 541–50

− *The Copper Eskimos*, Part A: *Life of the Copper Eskimo*. Reports of the Canadian Arctic Expedition, 1913–18, vol. 12. Ottawa: King's Printer 1922

− "Eskimo Art." *Geographical Review* 12, no. 2 (1922): 161–74

− Review of *The Friendly Arctic*. *Science* 56, no. 1436 (1922): 8–12

− *The Copper Eskimos*, Part B: *Physical Characteristics of the Copper Eskimos*. Reports of the Canadian Arctic Expedition, 1913–18, vol. 11. Ottawa: King's Printer 1923

− "Origin of the Copper Eskimos and Their Copper Culture." *Geographical Review* 13, no. 4 (1923): 540–51

− *Eskimo Folk-Lore*, Part A: *Myths and Traditions from Northern Alaska, The Mackenzie Delta and Coronation Gulf*. Reports of the Canadian Arctic Expedition, 1913–18, vol. 13. Ottawa: King's Printer 1924

− "The Singing People of the South Seas." In *The Outline of Knowledge*, edited by J.A. Richards, vol. 15, 192–202. New York: J.A. Richards 1924

− "A New Eskimo Culture in Hudson Bay." *Geographical Review* 15, no. 3 (1925): 28–37

− "Canada's Eskimo Problem." *Queen's Quarterly* 32, no. 4 (1925): 17–29

- "Notes on the Phonology of the Eskimo Dialect of Cape Prince of Wales, Alaska." *International Journal of American Linguistics* 4, nos. 2–4 (1927): 168–80
- "Archaeological Investigations in Bering Strait, 1926." In *National Museum of Canada, Annual Report for 1926*, Bull. 50, 71–80. Ottawa: King's Printer 1928
- "Division of Anthropology." In *National Museum of Canada, Annual Report for 1926*, Bull. 50, 5–13. Ottawa: King's Printer 1928
- *Eskimo Language and Technology*, Part A: *Comparative Vocabulary of the Western Eskimo Dialects*. Reports of the Canadian Arctic Expedition, 1913–18, vol. 15. Ottawa: King's Printer 1928
- "Ethnological Problems of Arctic America." In *Problems of Polar Research*, edited by W.L.G. Joerg, 167–75. American Geographical Society, Special Publication 7, 1928
- Review of *Archaeology of the Central Eskimos*. *Geographical Review* 18, no. 4 (1928): 696–8
- "The Ancient Education of a Carrier Indian." In *National Museum of Canada, Annual Report for 1928*, Bull. 62, 22–7. Ottawa: King's Printer 1929
- "Little Diomede Island, Bering Strait." *Geographical Review* 19, no. 1 (1929): 78–86
- "The Indians of Canada." In *Cambridge History of the British Empire*, vol. 6, *Canada and Newfoundland*, edited by J.H. Rose, et al., 79–91. Cambridge: Cambridge University Press 1930
- "The Indian's Interpretation of Man and Nature." *Proceedings and Transactions of the Royal Society of Canada* 3rd series, vol. 24, section II (1930): 57–62
- "The Yukon Telegraph Line." *Canadian Geographical Journal* 1, no. 8 (1930): 695–705
- "Division of Anthropology." In *National Museum of Canada, Annual Report for 1929*, 6–12. Ottawa: King's Printer 1931
- "Sekani Indians of British Columbia." *Proceedings and Transactions of the Royal Society of Canada*, Section II (1931): 21–35
- "Fifty Years of Archaeology in Canada." In *The Royal Society of Canada, Fifty Year Retrospect, 1882–1932*, 71–6. Ottawa: Royal Society of Canada 1932
- *The Indians of Canada*. National Museum of Canada Bull. 65, Anthro. Series 15. Ottawa: King's Printer 1932
- "Java, Land of Mystery." *Canadian Geographical Journal* 5 (1932): 112–27
- "The Population Possibilities of Canada." *University of Toronto Quarterly* 1 (1932): 387–423
- "An Indian Method of Treating Hysteria." *Primitive Man* 6, no. 1 (1933): 13–20
- "Canada's Fishery and Fishery Population." *Transactions of the Royal Society of Canada* 27 (1933): 41–6
- "The Problem of the Eskimo." In *The American Aborigines: Their Origin and Antiquity*, edited by Diamond Jenness, 373–96. Toronto: University of Toronto Press 1933
- Excerpt of Letter from D. Jenness (2 September 1933). In "Memories From Abroad," *Victoria College Review* (1934): 20
- "The Vanished Red Indians of Newfoundland." *Canadian Geographical Journal* 8, no. 1 (1934): 27–32
- "Myths of the Carrier Indians of British Columbia." *The Journal of American Folklore* 47, nos. 184–5 (1934): 97–257

- *The Ojibwa Indians of Parry Island, Their Social and Religious Life*. National Museum of Canada Bull. 78, Anthro. Series 17. Ottawa: King's Printer 1935
- "Anthropological Division." *National Museum of Canada Annual Report for 1936–37*, Bull. 89, 6–10. Ottawa: King's Printer 1937
- *The Indian Background of Canadian History*. National Museum of Canada Bull. 86, Anthro. Series 21. Ottawa: King's Printer 1937
- *The Sekani Indians of British Columbia*. National Museum of Canada Bull. 84, Anthro. Series 20. Ottawa: King's Printer 1937
- *The Sarcee Indians of Alberta*. National Museum of Canada Bull. 90, Anthro. Series 23. Ottawa: King's Printer 1938
- "An Archaeological Collection from the Belcher Islands in Hudson Bay." *Annals of the Carnegie Museum* 28 (1941): 189–206
- "Prehistoric Culture Waves from Asia to America." In *Annual Report of the Board of Regents of the Smithsonian Institution, 1940*, 383–96. Washington: Smithsonian Institution 1941
- "Canada's Indian Problems." In *Annual Report of the Board of Regents of the Smithsonian Institution 1942*, 367–80. Washington: Smithsonian Institution 1943
- "The Carrier Indians of the Bulkley River: Their Social and Religious Life." *Bureau of American Ethnology Bulletin* 133, Anthro. Papers 25, 469–586. Washington: Smithsonian Institution 1943
- *Material Culture of the Copper Eskimo*. Reports of the Canadian Arctic Expedition, 1913–18, vol. 16. Ottawa: King's Printer 1946
- "Some Impressions of Post-War Italy." *International Journal* 4, no. 4 (1949): 342–50
- "Italy's Demographic Crisis." *Queen's Quarterly* 57, no. 3 (1950): 269–80
- [Discussion of H. Larsen, 'The Ipiutak Culture: Its Origin and Relationships']. In *Indian Tribes of Aboriginal America: Selected Papers of the 24th International Congress of Americanists*, edited by Sol Tax, 30–4. Chicago: ICA 1952
- "Canada's Indians Yesterday. What of Today?" *Canadian Journal of Economics and Political Science* 20, no. 1 (1954): 95–100
- *The Faith of a Coast Salish Indian*. Anthropology in British Columbia, Memoir No. 3. Victoria: Provincial Museum of British Columbia 1955
- "The Chipewyan: An Account by an Early Explorer." *Anthropologica* 3 (1956): 15–33
- *People of the Twilight*. Chicago: University of Chicago Press 1959 [orig. 1928]
- *The Economics of Cyprus: A Survey to 1914*. Montreal: McGill University Press 1962
- *Eskimo Administration* I: *Alaska*. Arctic Institute of North America, Technical Paper 10. Montreal: AINA 1962
- "Human Resources of Canada's Northlands." In *Resources for Tomorrow: Proceedings of the Conference*, vol. 3, 365–71. Ottawa: Ministry of Northern Affairs and National Resources 1962
- Appendix B. In George W. von Zedlitz, *The Search for a Country: The Autobiography of G.W. von Zedlitz*, 165–6. Plymouth: Latimer Trend & Co. 1963
- *Eskimo Administration* II: *Canada*. Arctic Institute of North America, Technical Paper 14. Montreal: AINA 1964
- *Eskimo Administration* III: *Labrador*. Arctic Institute of North America, Technical Paper 16. Montreal: AINA 1965

- "The Administration of Northern Peoples: America's Eskimos – Pawns of History." In *The Arctic Frontier*, edited by R.St.J. Macdonald, 120–9. Toronto: University of Toronto Press 1966
- "The Ascent of Mount Madawana, Goodenough Island." *Canadian Geographical Journal* 74, no. 3 (1967): 100–8
- *Eskimo Administration* IV: *Greenland*. Arctic Institute of North America, Technical Paper 19. Montreal: AINA 1967
- *Eskimo Administration* V: *Analysis and Reflections*. Arctic Institute of North America, Technical Paper 21. Montreal: AINA 1968
- *Dawn in Arctic Alaska*. Chicago: University of Chicago Press 1985 [orig. 1957]
- *Arctic Odyssey: The Diary of Diamond Jenness, 1913–1916*, edited by Stuart E. Jenness. Hull, QC: Canadian Museum of Civilization 1991
Jenness, D., and Rev. A. Ballantyne. *The Northern D'Entrecasteaux*. Oxford: The Clarendon Press 1920
- "Language, Mythology and Songs of Bwaidoga, Goodenough Island, S.E. Papua." *Journal of the Polynesian Society* 35, no. 4 (1926): 290–314; 36, no. 2 (1927): 71; 36, no. 3 (1927): 207–38, 303–29; 37, no. 1 (1927): 30–56; 37, no. 2 (1928): 139–64; 37, no. 3 (1928): 271–99; 37, no. 4 (1928): 377–402; 38, no. 1 (1929): 29–47
Jenness, Diamond, and Stuart E. Jenness. *Through Darkening Spectacles: Memoirs of Diamond Jenness*. Mercury Series, History Paper 55. Gatineau, QC: Canadian Museum of Civilization 2008
Jenness, Stuart E. "Diamond Jenness's Archaeological Investigations on Barter Island, Alaska." *Polar Record* 26, no. 157 (1990): 91–102
Johnson, Frederick. "Notes on the Ojibwa and Potawatomi of the Parry Island Reservation, Ontario." *Museum of the American Indian, Heye Foundation, Indian Notes* 6, no. 3 (1929): 193–216
Johnston, W.A. "Quarternary Geology of North America in Relation to the Migration of Man." In *The American Aborigines: Their Origin and Antiquity*, edited by Diamond Jenness, 9–45. Toronto: University of Toronto Press 1933
Kawharu, I.H., ed. *Waitangi: Maori and Pakeha Perspectives of the Treaty of Waitangi*. Auckland: Oxford University Press 1989
Keefe, Eugene, and Eric Solsten. "Historical Setting." In *Cyprus: A Country Study*, edited by Eric Solsten, ch. 1. Washington: Library of Congress 1993: http://www.memory.loc.gov/fed/cs/cytoc.html#cy0000
Kelly, Lawrence C. "Why Applied Anthropology Developed When It Did: A Commentary on People, Money, and Changing Times." In *Social Contexts of American Ethnology, 1840–1984*, edited by June Helm, 122–38. Washington: American Ethnological Society 1985
- "United States Indian Policies, 1900–1980." In *Handbook of North American Indians*, vol. 4, *History of Indian-White Relations*, edited by Wilcomb E. Washburn, 66–80. Washington: Smithsonian Institution 1988
King, Michael. "Between Two Worlds." In *Oxford History of New Zealand*, edited by W.H. Oliver, 279–301. Auckland: Oxford University Press 1981
- *Maori: A Photographic and Social History*. Auckland: Heinnemann Reed, 1983
Kleinschmidt, Samuel. *Grammatik der grönländischen Sprache, mit theilweisem Einschluss des Labradordialekts* [Grammar of Greenlandic Speech, with a Sketch of the Labrador Dialect]. Berlin: G. Reimer 1851

Kleivan, Inge, and Ernest S. Burch, Jr. "The Work of Knud Rasmussen Among the Inuit: An Introduction." *Études/Inuit/Studies* 12, no. 1–2 (1988): 5–10

Kluckhohn, Clyde. *Anthropology and the Classics*. Providence: Brown University Press 1961

Knowles, Francis S.H. *The Glenoid Fossa in the Skull of the Eskimo*. Geological Survey, Museum Bull. 9, Anthro. Series 4. Ottawa: King's Printer 1915

Krauss, Michael E. "Eskimo-Aleut." In *Native Languages of the Americas*, vol. 1, edited by Thomas A. Sebeok, 175–281. New York: Plenum Press 1976

Krauss, Michael E., and Victor Golla. "Northern Athapascan Languages." In *Handbook of North American Indians*, vol. 6, *Subarctic*, edited by June Helm, 67–85. Washington: Smithsonian Institution 1981

Krupnik, Igor. "'Siberians' in Alaska: The Siberian Eskimo Contribution to Alaskan Population Recoveries, 1880–1940." *Études/Inuit/Studies* 18, no. 1–2 (1994): 49–80

Kuklick, Henrika. *The Savage Within: The Social History of British Anthropology, 1885–1945*. New York: Cambridge University Press 1991

Kulchyski, Peter. "Anthropology in the Service of the State: Diamond Jenness and Canadian Indian Policy." *Journal of Canadian Studies* 28, no. 2 (1993): 21–50

Landes, Ruth. "The Personality of the Ojibwa." *Journal of Personality* 6, no. 1 (1937): 51–60

Langham, Ian. *The Building of British Social Anthropology: W.H.R. Rivers and His Cambridge Disciples in the Development of Kinship Studies, 1898–1931*. Boston: D. Reidel 1981

Lantis, Margaret. "Nunivak Eskimo." In *Handbook of North American Indians*, vol. 5, *Arctic*, edited by David Damas, 209–23. Washington: Smithsonian Institution 1984

Leach, Edmund. "Glimpses of the Unmentionable in the History of British Social Anthropology." *Annual Review of Anthropology* 13 (1984): 1–23

Leacock, Eleanor B. *The Montagnais Hunting Territory and the Fur Trade*. American Anthropological Association, Memoir 78. Menasha, WI: American Anthropological Association 1954

Leacock, Eleanor B., and Nan A. Rothschild, eds. *Labrador Winter: The Ethnographic Journals of William Duncan Strong, 1927–1928*. Washington: Smithsonian Institution 1994

Leacock, Seth. "The Ethnological Theory of Marcel Mauss." *American Anthropologist* 56, no. 1 (1954): 58–73

Leechman, Douglas. "Two New Cape Dorset Sites." *American Antiquity* 8, no. 4 (1943): 363–75

Levere, Trevor H. *Science and the Canadian Arctic: A Century of Exploration 1818–1918*. Cambridge: Cambridge University Press 1993

Levin, Michael, et al. *An Historical Sketch Showing the Contribution of Sir Daniel Wilson and Many Others to the Teaching of Anthropology at the University of Toronto*. Toronto: University of Toronto, Department of Anthropology 1984

Loram, C.T., and T.F. McIlwraith, eds. *The North American Indian Today*. Toronto: University of Toronto Press 1943

Lorimer, Douglas. "Theoretical Racism in Late-Victorian Anthropology, 1870–1900." *Victorian Studies* 31 (1988): 405–30

Lotz, Pat, and Jim Lotz, eds. *Pilot Not Commander: Essays in Memory of Diamond Jenness*. Ottawa: St. Paul's University 1971

Lowie, Robert H. *Primitive Society*. New York: Horace Liveright 1920

– Review of *The Northern D'Entrecasteaux. American Anthropologist* 23 (1921): 226–7

– "Native Languages as Ethnographic Tools." *American Anthropologist* 42, no. 1 (1940): 81–9

– *Robert H. Lowie, Ethnologist: A Personal Record*. Berkeley: University of California Press 1959

Lukes, Steven. "Mauss, Marcel." In *International Encyclopedia of the Social Sciences*, vol. 9, edited by David L. Sills, 78–82. New York: Macmillan 1968

McConnell, Burt M., and Harold Noice. "The Friendly Arctic." *Science* 57 (30 March 1923): 368–73

McFeat, Tom. *Three Hundred Years of Anthropology in Canada*. Occasional Papers in Anthropology No. 7. Halifax: Department of Anthropology, St Mary's University 1980

McGhee, Robert. *Copper Eskimo Prehistory*. National Museum of Man, Publications in Archaeology 2. Ottawa: National Museum of Canada 1972

– *Ancient People of the Arctic*. Vancouver: UBC Press 1996

McGill, Harold W. "Policies and Problems in Canada." In *The North American Indian Today*, edited by C.T. Loram and T.F. McIlwraith, 132–9. Toronto: University of Toronto Press 1943

McKinlay, William L. *Karluk: The Great Untold Story of Arctic Exploration*. New York: St. Martin's Press 1976

McNickle, Darcy. "Anthropology and the Indian Reorganization Act." In *The Uses of Anthropology*, edited by Walter Goldschmidt, 51–60. Washington: American Anthropological Association 1979

Malinowski, Bronislaw. *Argonauts of the Western Pacific*. London: Routledge and Kegan Paul 1978 [orig. 1922]

Mannion, J.J. Introduction to *The Peopling of Newfoundland: Essays in Historical Geography*, edited by J.J. Mannion, 1–13. Social and Economic Papers No. 8. St John's: Memorial University, Institute of Social and Economic Research 1977

Marett, R.R. Preface to *Anthropology and the Classics*, edited by R.R. Marett. Oxford: The Clarendon Press 1908

– "The Present State of Anthropology." *The Athenaeum* 4298 (1910): 299–300

– *Anthropology*. New York: Holt 1912

– "Anthropology as a University Subject." *New Zealand Journal of Science and Technology* 1, no. 5 (1918): 263–4

– *A Jerseyman at Oxford*. Oxford: Oxford University Press 1941

Marshall, Ingeborg. *A History and Ethnography of the Beothuk*. Montreal: McGill-Queen's University Press 1996

Mathiassen, Therkel. *Archaeology of the Central Eskimo*. 2 vols. Report of the Fifth Thule Expedition 1921–24, vol. 4. Copenhagen: Gyldendal 1927

– "Some Specimens from the Bering Sea Culture." *Indian Notes* 6 (1929): 33–56

– *Archaeological Collections from the Western Eskimos*. Report of the Fifth Thule Expedition 1921–24, vol. 10. Copenhagen: Gyldendal 1930

– "The Question of the Origin of Eskimo Culture." *American Anthropologist* 32, no. 4 (1930): 591–607

– *Report of the Fifth Thule Expedition 1921–24, Report on the Expedition*, vol. 1, no. 1. Copenhagen: Gyldendal, 1945

Maud, Ralph, ed. *The Salish People: The Local Contribution of Charles Hill-Tout*, vol. 3, *The Mainland Halkomelem*; vol. 4, *The Sechelt and South-Eastern Tribes of Vancouver Island*. Vancouver: Talonbooks 1978

Maunder, John E. "The Newfoundland Museum: Origins and Development." Accessed 3 May 2006: http://www.nfmuseum.com/ studies2.htm

Mauss, Marcel. *Seasonal Variations of the Eskimo: A Study in Social Morphology*. Translated by James J. Fox. London: Routledge and Kegan Paul 1979 [orig. 1904]

Meleagrou, Elani, and Birol Yesilada. "The Society and Its Environment." In *Cyprus: A Country Study*, edited by E. Solsten, ch. 2. Washington: Library of Congress 1993: http://www.memory.loc.gov/fed/cs/cytoc.html#cy0000

Meriam, Lewis. *The Problem of Indian Administration*. Baltimore: Johns Hopkins Press 1928

Metge, Joan. *The Maoris of New Zealand*. 2nd ed. London: Routledge and Kegan Paul 1976

Miers, Sir H.A., and S.F. Markham. *A Report on the Museums of Canada*. Edinburgh: T. and A. Constable 1932

Miller, Bruce G. "Salish." In *Aboriginal Peoples of Canada: A Short Introduction*, edited by Paul Robert Magosci, 237–50. Toronto: University of Toronto Press 2002

Miller, J.R. *Skyscrapers Hide the Heavens: A History of Indian-White Relations in Canada*. Toronto: University of Toronto Press 1988

– *Shingwauk's Vision: A History of Native Residential Schools*. Toronto: University of Toronto Press 1997

Mills, Antonia. *Eagle Down Is Our Law: Witsuwit'en Law, Feasts, and Land Claims*. Vancouver: UBC Press 1994

Morice, Father A.G., OMI. "Are the Carrier Sociology and Mythology Indigenous or Exotic?" *Transactions and Proceedings of the Royal Society of Canada* vol. 10, Section II (1892): 109–126

Morrison, David. *The Diamond Jenness Collections from Bering Strait*. Archaeological Survey of Canada no. 44. Hull, QC: Canadian Museum of Civilization 1991

– "Diamond Jenness: The First Canadian Arctic Archaeologist." In *Honoring Our Elders: A History of Eastern Arctic Archaeology*, edited by William W. Fitzhugh et al., 61–5. Contributions to Circumpolar Anthropology 2. Washington: Smithsonian Institution 2002

Mountfield, David. *A History of Polar Exploration*. New York: Dial Press 1974

Mowat, Farley. *People of the Deer*. Boston: Little Brown 1952

– *The Desperate People*. Boston: Little Brown 1959

Moyles, R.G. *British Law and Arctic Men*. Saskatoon: Western Producer Prairie Books 1979

Muckle, Robert J. *The First Nations of British Columbia*. Vancouver: UBC Press 1998

Mulhall, David. *Will to Power: The Missionary Career of Father Morice*. Vancouver: UBC Press 1986

Mulvaney, D.J., and J.H. Calaby. *"So Much That Is New": Baldwin Spencer, 1860–1929, A Biography*. Melbourne: University of Melbourne Press 1985

Neatby, L.H. "Exploration and History of the Canadian Arctic." In *Handbook of North American Indians*, vol. 5, *Arctic*, edited by David Damas, 377–90. Washington: Smithsonian Institution 1984

Nelson, E.W. *The Eskimo About Bering Strait*. Washington: Smithsonian Institution 1983 [orig. 1899]

Newton, Jennifer I.M. "Ipiutak." In *Encyclopedia of the Arctic*, vol. 2, edited by Mark Nuttal, 1023–4. New York: Routledge 2005

Ngata, Apirana. "Anthropology and the Government of Native Races in the Pacific." *New Zealand Affairs* 1 (1929): 22–44

Niven, Jennifer. *The Ice Master: The Doomed 1913 Voyage of the Karluk*. New York: Hyperion 2000

Noice, H.H. "Further Discussion of the 'Blond' Eskimo." *American Anthropologist* 24 (1922): 228–32

Norcini, Marilyn. "Frederick Johnson's Canadian Ethnology in the Americanist Tradition." *Histories of Anthropology Annual* 4 (2008): 106–34

Nowry, Laurence. *Man of Mana: Marius Barbeau*. Toronto: NC Press 1995

O'Connor, P.S. "Keeping New Zealand White, 1908–1920." *New Zealand Journal of History* 2, no. 1 (1968): 41–65

Oliver, W.H. "Social Policy in the Liberal Period." *New Zealand Journal of History* 13, no. 1 (1979): 25–33

Orange, Claudia. *The Treaty of Waitangi*. Wellington: Allen and Unwin 1987

Osgood, Cornelius. *Winter: The Strange and Haunting Record of One Man's Experiences in the Far North*. Lincoln: University of Nebraska Press 1953

Oswalt, Wendell H. *Alaskan Eskimos*. San Francisco: Chandler 1967

– *Eskimos and Explorers*. Novato: Chandler and Sharp 1979

Paine, Robert. "The Path to Welfare Colonialism." In *The White Arctic: Anthropological Essays on Tutelage and Ethnicity*, edited by Robert Paine, 7–28. Newfoundland Social and Economic Papers 7. St John's: Memorial University of Newfoundland 1977

Parkin, Robert. "The French-Speaking Countries." In *One Discipline, Four Ways: British, German, French, and American Anthropology*, edited by Fredrik Barth, et al., 157–253. Chicago: University of Chicago Press 2005

Parsonson, Ann. "The Pursuit of Mana." In *Oxford History of New Zealand*, edited by W.H. Oliver, 140–67. Auckland: Oxford University Press 1981

Pastore, Ralph T. "Archaeology, History, and the Beothuks." *Newfoundland Studies* 9, no. 2 (1993): 260–78

Patterson, E. Palmer. *The Canadian Indian: A History Since 1500*. Toronto: Collier Macmillan Canada 1965

Pettipas, Katherine. *Severing the Ties That Bind: Government Repression of Indigenous Religious Ceremonies on the Prairies*. Winnipeg: University of Manitoba Press 1994

Pitsula, James M. "The Saskatchewan CCF Government and Treaty Indians, 1944–64." *Canadian Historical Review* 75, no. 1 (1994): 21–52

Preston, Richard. "C. Marius Barbeau and the History of Canadian Anthropology." In *The History of Canadian Anthropology: Proceedings of the Canadian*

Ethnology Society, edited by J. Freedman, 123–35. Hamilton: Canadian Ethnology Society 1976

– "The Social Structure of an Unorganized Society: Beyond Intentions and Peripheral Boasians." In *Consciousness and Inquiry: Ethnology and Canadian Realities*, edited by Frank Manning, 286–305. National Museum of Man, Canadian Ethnology Service Paper No. 89E. Ottawa: National Museums of Canada 1983

– "Reflections on Sapir's Anthropology." In *Edward Sapir: Appraisals of His Life and Work*, edited by K. Koerner, 179–94. Amsterdam: J. Benjamins 1984

Price, A. Grenfell. *White Settlers and Native Peoples: An Historical Study of Racial Contacts between English-speaking Whites and Aboriginal Peoples in the United States, Canada, Australia and New Zealand*. Westport: Greenwood Press 1972 [orig. 1950]

Price, David H. *Anthropological Intelligence: The Deployment and Neglect of American Anthropology in the Second World War*. Durham: Duke University Press 2008

Pritzker, Barry M. *A Native North American Encyclopedia: History, Culture, and Peoples*. Oxford: Oxford University Press 2000

Quimby, George I. "The Manitunik Eskimo Culture of East Hudson's Bay." *American Antiquity* 6, no. 2 (1940): 148–65

– "A Brief History of WPA Archaeology." In *The Uses of Anthropology*, edited by Walter Goldschmidt, 110–23. Washington: American Ethnological Society 1979

Radin, Paul. "On Ojibwa Work in Southeastern Ontario." In *Geological Survey of Canada, Summary Report for 1912*, 482–3. Ottawa: King's Printer 1914

Rasmussen, Knud. *Across Arctic America: Narrative of the Fifth Thule Expedition*. New York: G.P. Putnam's Sons 1927

Rasmussen, Knud, et al. "The Danish Ethnographic and Geographic Expedition to Arctic America: Preliminary Report of the Fifth Thule Expedition." *Geographical Review* 15, no. 4 (1925): 521–92

Ray, Dorothy Jean. "Bering Strait Eskimo." In *Handbook of North American Indians*, vol. 5, *Arctic*, edited by David Damas, 285–302. Washington: Smithsonian Institution 1984

Read, C.H. "Anthropology at the Universities." *Man* 6, no. 37–8 (1906): 56–9

Redfield, Robert. *The Primitive World and Its Transformations*. Ithaca: Cornell University Press 1953

Reining, Conrad. "A Lost Period of Applied Anthropology." *American Anthropologist* 64, no. 3 (1962): 593–600

Riches, David. "The Forces of Tradition in Eskimology." In *Localizing Strategies: Regional Traditions in Ethnographic Writing*, edited by Richard Fardon, 71–89. Washington: Smithsonian Institution Press 1990

Richling, Barnett. "An Anthropologist's Apprenticeship: Diamond Jenness' Papuan and Arctic Fieldwork." *Culture* 9, no. 1 (1989): 71–85

– "Applied Anthropology and Aboriginal Peoples in Canada, 1910–1939." *Australian-Canadian Studies* 13, no. 1 (1995): 49–62

– "Archaeology, Ethnology, and Canada's Public Purse, 1910–1921." In *Bringing Back the Past: Historical Perspectives on Canadian Archaeology*, edited by Pamela J. Smith and Donald Mitchell, 103–14. Archaeological Survey of Canada Paper 158. Hull, QC: Canadian Museum of Civilization 1998

Ridgeway, William. "The Relation of Anthropology to Classical Studies." *Journal of the Royal Anthropological Institute* 34 (1909): 10–25

Ridington, Robin. "Beaver Dreaming and Singing." In *Pilot Not Commander: Essays in Memory of Diamond Jenness*, edited by Pat Lotz and Jim Lotz, 115–28. Ottawa: St. Paul's University 1971

– "Beaver." In *Handbook of North American Indians*, vol. 6, *Subarctic*, edited by June Helm, 350–60. Washington: Smithsonian Institution 1981

Rivers, W.H.R. "The Genealogical Method of Anthropological Inquiry." *The Sociological Review* 3, no. 1 (1910): 1–12

– "A General Account of Method." In *Notes and Queries on Anthropology*, 4th ed., edited by Barbara Freire-Marreco and J.L. Myres, 108–127. London: British Association for the Advancement of Science 1912

– "Report on Anthropological Research Outside America." In *Reports on the Present Condition and Future Needs of the Science of Anthropology*, 5–28. Washington: Carnegie Institution 1913

Rivers, W.H.R., and A.C. Haddon. "A Method of Recording String Figures and Tricks." *Man* 2 (1902): 146–53

Robinson, Clayton L.N. *J.C. Boileau Grant: Anatomist Extraordinary*. Markham, ON: Dundurn Press 1993

Rogers, Edward S. "Southeastern Ojibwa." In *Handbook of North American Indians*, vol. 15, *Northeast*, edited by Bruce G. Trigger, 760–71. Washington: Smithsonian Institution 1978

– "The Algonkian Farmers of Southern Ontario, 1830–1945." In *Aboriginal Ontario: Historical Perspectives on the First Nations*, edited by Edward S. Rogers and Donald B. Smith, 122–66. Toronto: Dundurn Press 1994

Rowley, Graham. "The Dorset Culture of the Eastern Arctic." *American Anthropologist* 42, no. 3 (1940): 490–9

Royal Institute of International Affairs. *Cyprus: Background to Enosis*. London: RIIA 1957

Rudenko, Sergei I. *The Ancient Culture of the Bering Sea and the Eskimo Problem*. Translated by Paul Tolstoy. Toronto: University of Toronto Press 1961 [orig. 1948]

Ruel, M.J. "Marett, Robert Ranulph." In *International Encyclopedia of the Social Sciences*, vol. 9, edited by David L. Sills, 565–7. New York: Macmillan 1968

Ruhlen, Merritt. "The Origin of the Na-Dene." *Proceedings of the National Academy of Sciences of the United States of America* 95 (1998): 13,994–6

– "Dene-Yeniseian Languages." Alaskan Native Languages Center. Accessed 18 June 2009: http://www.uaf.edu/anlc/dy-html

Russell, Loris S. *The National Museum of Canada, 1910 to 1960*. Ottawa: Department of Northern Affairs and National Resources 1961

Saladin d'Anglure, Bernard. "Mauss et l'anthropologie des Inuit." *Sociologie et Sociétés* 36, no. 2 (2004): 91–130

Sapir, Edward. "An Anthropological Survey of Canada." *Science* 34 (1911): 789–93

– "The Work of the Division of Anthropology of the Dominion Government." *Queen's Quarterly* 20, no. 1 (1912): 60–9

– "Anthropological Division." In *Geological Survey of Canada, Summary Report for … 1913*, 448–53. Ottawa: King's Printer 1914

- "Division of Anthropology: Ethnology and Linguistics." In *Geological Survey of Canada, Summary Report for ... 1914*, 168–77. Ottawa: King's Printer 1915
- "The Na-Dene Languages: A Preliminary Report." *American Anthropologist* 17 (1915): 534–58
- *Time Perspective in Aboriginal American Culture: A Study in Method*. Geological Survey, Memoir 90, Anthro. Series 13. Ottawa: King's Printer 1916
- "A Note on Sarcee Pottery." *American Anthropologist* 25, no. 2 (1923): 247–53
- "Anthropological Division: Ethnology and Linguistics." In *Report of the Department of Mines for ... 1924*, 36–40. Ottawa: King's Printer 1925
- "Pitch Accent in Sarcee, an Athabaskan Language." *Journal, Société des Américanistes de Paris* 17 (1925): 185–205
- "Anthropological Division: Ethnology and Linguistics." *Report of the Department of Mines for ... 1925*, 37–41. Ottawa: King's Printer 1926
Scott, Duncan Campbell. *The Administration of Indian Affairs in Canada*. Toronto: Canadian Institute of International Affairs 1931
Seligman, Charles G. "A Classification of the Natives of British New Guinea." *Journal of the Royal Anthropological Institute* 39, no. 1 (1904): 246–74, 314–33
Shalett, Sidney. "'Lebensraum' Wars Old American Tale." *The New York Times*, 30 December 1939
Sheffield, R. Scott. "A Search for Equity: A Study of the Treatment Accorded to First Nations Veterans and Dependents of the Second World War and the Korean Conflict." *Final Report of the National Roundtable on First Nations Veterans Issues*. Ottawa: Assembly of First Nations 2001
Shewell, Hugh. "'What Makes the Indian Tick?' The Influence of Social Sciences on Canada's Indian Policy, 1947–1964." *Social History/Histoire Sociale* 34, no. 67 (2001): 133–67
Shore, Marlene. *The Science of Social Redemption: McGill, the Chicago School, and the Origins of Social Science Research in Canada*. Toronto: University of Toronto Press 1987
Sinclair, Keith. "Why Are Race Relations in New Zealand Better than in South Africa, South Australia, or South Dakota?" *New Zealand Journal of History* 5, no. 2 (1971): 121–7
Skinner, H.D. Review of *The Northern D'Entrecasteaux*. *The Victoria University College Review* 21, no. 1 (1922): 61–4
Sluman, Norma, and Jean Goodwill. *John Tootoosis: Biography of a Cree Leader*. Toronto: University of Toronto Press 1982
Smith, Derek G. "Mackenzie Delta Eskimo." In *Handbook of North American Indians*, vol. 5, *Arctic*, edited by David Damas, 347–58. Washington: Smithsonian Institution 1984
Smith, Donald B. "Now We Talk – You Listen." *Rotunda* (Fall 1990), 48–52
Smith, Harlan I. "The Work of Museums in War Time." *The Scientific Monthly* 6 (1917): 362–78, 417–30
- "Materia Medica of the Bella Coola and Neighbouring Tribes of British Columbia." In *National Museum of Canada, Annual Report for 1927*, Bull. 56, 47–68. Ottawa: King's Printer 1929
Smith, James G.E. "Chipewyan." In *Handbook of North American Indians*, vol. 6, *Subarctic*, edited by June Helm, 271–84. Washington: Smithsonian Institution 1981

Smith, S. Percy. *History and Traditions of the Maoris of the West Coast, North Island, New Zealand*. Memoirs of the Polynesian Society no. 1. New Plymouth: The Polynesian Society 1910

Sorrenson, M.P.K. *Maori Origins and Migrations*. Auckland: Auckland University Press 1979

– "Maori and Pakeha." In *Oxford History of New Zealand*, edited by W.H. Oliver, 68–96. Auckland: Oxford University Press 1981

– "Polynesian Corpuscles and Pacific Anthropology: The Home-Made Anthropology of Sir Apirana Ngata and Sir Peter Buck." *Journal of the Polynesian Society* 91, no. 1 (1982): 7–27

– *Manifest Duty: The Polynesian Society Over 100 Years*. Auckland: The Polynesian Society 1992

Sorrenson, M.P.K., ed. *Na To Hoa Aroha: From Your Dear Friend. The Correspondence Between Sir Apirana Ngata and Sir Peter Buck, 1925–50*. 3 vols. Auckland: Auckland University Press 1986

Speck, Frank G. "The Family Hunting Band as the Basis of Algonkian Social Organization." *American Anthropologist* 17 (1915): 289–305

– *Family Hunting Territories and Social Life of Various Algonkian Bands of the Ottawa Valley*. Geological Survey of Canada, Memoir 70. Ottawa: King's Printer 1915

– "Beothuk and Micmac." *Indian Notes and Monographs*. New York: Museum of the American Indian 1922

Speck, Frank G., and Loren C. Eisley. "Significance of Hunting Territory Systems of the Algonkian in Social Theory." *American Anthropologist* 41, no. 2 (1939): 269–80

Spencer, Robert F. "North Alaska Coast Eskimo: Introduction." In *Handbook of North American Indians*, vol. 5, *Arctic*, edited by David Damas, 278–84. Washington: Smithsonian Institution 1984

Spencer, Robert F., and Elizabeth Colson. "Wilson D. Wallis, 1886–1970." *American Anthropologist* 73, no. 2 (1971): 257–66

Steckley, John, and Brian Cummins. "Pegahmagabow of Parry Island: From Jenness Informant to Individual." *Canadian Journal of Native Studies* 25 (2005): 35–50

Steensby, H.P. "An Anthropogeographical Study of the Origin of Eskimo Culture." *Meddeleser om Grønland* 53 (1917): 39–288

Stefansson, Vilhjalmur. "Work Among the Arctic Eskimos." In *Geological Survey of Canada, Summary Report for 1911*, 389–90. Ottawa: King's Printer 1912

– *Prehistoric and Present Commerce Among the Arctic Coast Eskimo*. Geological Survey Museum Bull. 6. Ottawa: King's Printer 1914

– *The Friendly Arctic: The Story of Five Years in Polar Regions*. New York: MacMillan and Company 1921

– Letter to the Editor. *Science* 57, no. 1484 (8 June 1923): 666

– *My Life With the Eskimo*. New York: Collier Books 1962 [orig. 1913]

Steinbring, Jack. "Saulteaux of Lake Winnipeg." In *Handbook of North American Indians*, vol. 6, *Subarctic*, edited by June Helm, 244–55. Washington: Smithsonian Institution 1981

Stocking, George W., Jr. "On the Limits of 'Presentism' and 'Historicism.'" In Stocking, *Race, Culture, and Evolution: Essays in the History of Anthropology*, 1–12. New York: The Free Press 1968

- "Tylor, Edward Burnett." In *International Encyclopedia of the Social Sciences*, vol. 16, edited by David L. Sills, 170–7. New York: Macmillan 1968
- "Introduction: The Basic Assumptions of Boasian Anthropology." In Stocking, *The Shaping of American Anthropology, 1883–1911: A Franz Boas Reader*, 1–20. New York: Basic Books 1974
- "Ideas and Institutions in American Anthropology: Thoughts Toward a History of the Interwar Years." In *Selected Papers from the American Anthropologist, 1921–1945*, edited by George W. Stocking, Jr, 1–53. Washington: American Anthropological Association 1976
- "History of Anthropology: Whence/Wither." In *Observers Observed: Essays on Ethnographic Fieldwork*, edited by George W. Stocking, Jr, 3–11. Madison: University of Wisconsin Press 1983
- "The Ethnographer's Magic: Fieldwork in British Anthropology from Tylor to Malinowski." In *Observers Observed: Essays on Ethnographic Fieldwork*, edited by George W. Stocking, Jr, 70–120. Madison: University of Wisconsin Press 1983
- "Radcliffe-Brown and British Social Anthropology." In *Functionalism Historicized: Essays on British Social Anthropology*, edited by George W. Stocking, Jr, 106–30. Madison: University of Wisconsin Press 1984
- "Essays on Culture and Personality." In *Malinowski, Rivers, Benedict and Others: Essays in Culture and Personality*, edited by George W. Stocking, Jr, 3–12. Madison: University of Wisconsin Press 1986
- *Victorian Anthropology*. New York: Free Press 1987
- "Before the Falling Out: W.H.R. Rivers on the Relation Between Anthropology and Mission Work." *History of Anthropology Newsletter* 15, no. 2 (1988): 3–8
- *After Tylor: British Social Anthropology, 1881–1951*. Madison: University of Wisconsin Press 1995
Stone, E.L. "Canadian Indian Medical Services." *The Canadian Medical Association Journal* (July 1935): 82–5
Stone, Lawrence. "The Size and Composition of the Oxford Student Body, 1580–1910." In *The University in Society*, vol. 1, edited by Lawrence Stone, 3–110. Princeton: Princeton University Press 1974
Strong, William Duncan. "A Stone Culture From Northern Labrador and Its Relation to the Eskimo-Like Cultures of the Northeast." *American Anthropologist* 32, no. 1 (1930): 126–44
Sullivan, Louis R. "The 'Blond' Eskimo – A Question of Method." *American Anthropologist* 24, no. 2 (1922): 225–8
Sutherland, I.L.G. Introduction to *The Maori People Today: A General Survey*, edited by I.L.G. Sutherland, 1–36. Wellington: New Zealand Institute of International Affairs 1940
Suttles, Wayne. *Katzie Ethnographic Notes*. Anthropology in British Columbia, Memoir no. 2. Victoria: Provincial Museum of British Columbia 1955
- "The Recent Emergence of the Coast Salish – The Function of an Anthropological Myth." In Suttles, *Coast Salish Essays*, 256–64. Seattle: University of Washington Press 1987
- "Central Coast Salish." *Handbook of North American Indians*, vol. 7, *Northwest Coast*, edited by Wayne Suttles, 453–75. Washington: Smithsonian Institution 1990

Swayze, Nansi. *Canadian Portraits: Jenness, Barbeau, Wintemberg, The Man Hunters*. Toronto: Clarke Irwin 1960

Swinz, Stuart, ed. *Earliest Prehistory of Cyprus: From Colonization to Exploitation*. Boston: Cyprus American Archaeological Research Institute 2001

Tanner, Adrian. "The New Hunting Territory Debate: An Introduction to Some Unresolved Issues." *Anthropologica* 28 (1986): 19–36

Taylor, John L. *Canadian Indian Policy During the Inter-war Years, 1918–1939*. Ottawa: Department of Indian Affairs and Northern Development 1984

Taylor, William E. *The Arnapik and Tyara Sites: An Archaeological Study of Dorset Culture Origins*. Memoirs of the Society for American Archaeology no. 22. Salt Lake City: SAA 1968

Teit, James. "Field Notes on the Tahltan and Kaska Indians: 1912–15." Edited by June Helm MacNeish. *Anthropologica* 3 (1956): 40–171

Temple, Richard. "Presidential Address (Section H): Administrative Value of Anthropology." In *British Association for the Advancement of Science, Reports for 1913*, 613–23. London: BAAS 1913

Temple, Richard, et al. "Suggestions for a School of Applied Anthropology." *Man* 13, no. 102 (1913): 185–92

Te Rangi Hiroa (Peter Buck). *The Coming of the Maori*. 2nd ed. Wellington: Maori Purposes Fund Board 1950

Thalbitzer, William. "A Phonetical Study of the Eskimo Language Based on Observations Made on a Journey in North Greenland, 1900–1901." *Meddelelser om Grønland* 31 (1904): 1–405

Titley, E. Brian. *A Narrow Vision: Duncan Campbell Scott and the Administration of Indian Affairs in Canada*. Vancouver: UBC Press 1986

Tobey, Margaret L. "Carrier." In *Handbook of North American Indians*, vol. 6, *Subarctic*, edited by June Helm, 413–32. Washington: Smithsonian Institution 1981

Tobias, John L. "Protection, Civilization, Assimilation: An Outline History of Canada's Indian Policy." In *Sweet Promises: A Reader on Indian-White Relations in Canada*, edited by J.R. Miller, 127–44. Toronto: University of Toronto Press 1991 [orig. 1976]

Trigger, Bruce G. "Giants and Pygmies: The Professionalization of Canadian Archaeology." In *Towards a History of Archaeology*, edited by Glyn Daniel, 69–84. London: Thames and Hudson 1981

– *A History of Archaeological Thought*. Cambridge: Cambridge University Press 1989

Trollope, Anthony. *Australia and New Zealand*. 2 vols. London: Chapman and Hall 1873

University of Alberta. *Who's Who at the University of Alberta, 1919–1939*. Edmonton: University of Alberta 1993

Tuck, James. "Northern Iroquoian Prehistory." In *Handbook of North American Indians*, vol. 15, *Northeast*, edited by Bruce G. Trigger, 322–33. Washington: Smithsonian Institution 1978

Urry, James. "*Notes and Queries on Anthropology* and the Development of Field Methods in British Anthropology, 1870–1920." In *Proceedings of the Royal Anthropological Institute of Great Britain and Ireland for 1972*, 45–57. London: RAI 1972

– "A History of Field Methods." In *Ethnographic Research: A Guide to General Conduct*, edited by R.F. Ellen, 35–61. New York: Basic Books 1984

– "Compromising Correspondence. Review of *Na To Hoa Aroha: From Your Dear Friend. The Correspondence Between Sir Apirana Ngata and Sir Peter Buck 1925–1950.*" *Pacific Viewpoint* 28, no. 1 (1987): 76–9

Vanast, Walter J. "The Death of Jennie Kanajuq: Tuberculosis, Religious Competition and Cultural Conflict in Coppermine, 1929–31." *Études/Inuit/Studies* 15, no. 1 (1991): 75–104

VanStone, James W. *Athapaskan Adaptations: Hunters and Fishermen of the Subarctic Forests*. Arlington Heights, IL: AHM Publishing 1974

Von Zedlitz, George W. *The Search for a Country: The Autobiography of G.W. von Zedlitz*. Plymouth: Latimer Trend & Co. 1963

Vowles, Jack. "Liberal Democracy: Pakeha Political Ideology." *New Zealand Journal of History* 21, no. 2 (1987): 215–27

Waldram, James B. et al. *Aboriginal Health in Canada: Historical, Cultural, and Epidemiological Perspectives*. Toronto: University of Toronto Press 1995

Walker, Ranginui. *Ka Whawhai Tonu Matou, Struggle Without End*. Auckland: Penguin 1990

Wallace, Hugh. "Geographical Exploration to 1880." In *A Century of Canada's Arctic Islands*, edited by Morris Zaslow, 15–32. Ottawa: Royal Society of Canada 1981

Wallis, Wilson D. "The Methods of English Ethnologists." *American Anthropologist* 14 (1912): 178–86

– "Anthropology in England Early in the Present Century." *American Anthropologist* 59, no. 5 (1957): 781–90

Ward, R.G., and D.A.M. Lea, eds. *An Atlas of Papua and New Guinea*. Port Moresby: University of Papua and New Guinea 1970

Wasuaksing First Nation. Accessed 8 October 2009: angelfire.com/band/Wasuaksing FN/WFN.html

Wayne, Helena, ed. *The Story of a Marriage: The Letters of Bronislaw Malinowski and Elsie Masson*. 2 vols. London: Routledge 1995

Weaver, Sally. "The Role of Social Science in Formulating Canadian Indian Policy: A Preliminary History of the Hawthorn-Tremblay Report." In *Proceedings of the Canadian Ethnology Society*, edited by James Freedman, 51–97. Hamilton: Canadian Ethnology Society 1976

– *Making Canadian Indian Policy: The Hidden Agenda, 1968–1970*. Toronto: University of Toronto Press 1981

West, Francis. *Hubert Murray: The Australian Proconsul*. Melbourne: Melbourne University Press 1968

West, Francis, ed. *Selected Letters of Hubert Murray*. Melbourne: Oxford University Press 1970

Whittaker, Elvie, and Michael M. Ames. "Anthropology and Sociology at the University of British Columbia from 1947 to 1980." In *Historicizing Canadian Anthropology*, edited by Julia Harrison and Regna Darnell, 157–72. Vancouver: UBC Press 2006

Wiley, Gordon R., and Jeremy A. Sabloff. *A History of American Archaeology*. 2nd ed. San Francisco: Freeman 1980

Wilson, Douglas L. "Thomas Jefferson and the Character Issue." *The Atlantic Monthly* 270, no. 5 (1992): 57–74

Wintemberg, William J. "Preliminary Report on Field Work in 1927." In *National Museum of Canada, Annual Report for 1927*, Bull. 56, 40–1. Ottawa: King's Printer 1929

– "Eskimo Sites of the Dorset Culture in Newfoundland." *American Antiquity* [Part I] 5, no. 2 (1939): 83–102; [Part II] 5, no. 4 (1940): 309–33

– "Artifacts from Ancient Workshop Sites Near Tadoussac, Saguenay County, Québec." *American Antiquity* 8, no. 4 (1943): 13–40

Wissler, Clark. Review of *The Life of the Copper Eskimos*. *Canadian Historical Review* 4, no. 1 (March 1923): 70–4

Woodbury, Anthony C. "Eskimo and Aleut Languages." In *Handbook of North American Indians*, vol. 5, *Arctic*, edited by David Damas, 49–63. Washington: Smithsonian Institution 1984

Woodbury, Richard B. *Alfred V. Kidder*. New York: Columbia University Press 1973

Woods, Shirley E., Jr. *Ottawa: The Capital of Canada*. Toronto: Doubleday 1980

Wright, Terrence. "The Fieldwork Photographs of Jenness and Malinowski and the Beginnings of Modern Anthropology." *Journal of the Anthropological Society of Oxford* 22, no. 1 (1991): 41–58

Young, Michael W. *Fighting With Food: Leadership, Values and Social Control in a Massim Society*. Cambridge: Cambridge University Press 1971

– "Doctor Bromilow and the Bwaidoka Wars." *The Journal of Pacific History* 12, no. 1–2 (1977): 130–53

– "The Massim: An Introduction." *The Journal of Pacific History* 18, no. 1–2 (1983): 1–7

– "The Intensive Study of a Restricted Area, Or, Why Did Malinowski Go to the Trobriand Islands?" *Oceania* 55, no. 1 (1984): 1–26

Young, Steven B. "Beringia: An Ice Age View." In *Crossroads of Continents: Cultures of Siberia and Alaska*, edited by W.W. Fitzhugh and A. Crowell, 106–10. Washington: Smithsonian Institution 1988

Zamagni, Vera N. *The Economic History of Italy, 1860–1990*. Oxford: Oxford University Press 1993

Zaslow, Morris. *Reading the Rocks: The Story of the Geological Survey of Canada 1842–1972*. Toronto: Macmillan Canada 1975

– *The Northward Expansion of Canada, 1914–1967*. Toronto: McClelland and Stewart 1988

Index

Chipman, Kenneth, 61; and CAE controversy, 133
Chrétien, Jean, 327–8
citizens plus, 327
Coast Salish, 267–9; of the lower Fraser valley, 270–1; relationship to Interior Salish, 267; on Vancouver Island, 269–70
Collier, John, 265
Collins, Henry B., 226, 242
Collins, William H., 144–5, 152–3
Committee to Investigate the Northwest Tribes of the Dominion of Canada, 29. *See also* British Association for the Advancement of Science
Cooper, John M., 245, 248; Aboriginal property rights, 260–1
Co-operative Commonwealth Federation (CCF), 288
Copper Inuit, 81; at Bernard Harbour, 91–2; contact with explorers, 90; health of, 90–1; origins of, 202; relative isolation of, 88–91; shamanism among, 95; spouse exchange among, 96–7. *See also* Jenness, Diamond, Copper Inuit fieldwork of
Cosgrove, F.P., 146
Cox, Constance, 192
Cox, John, 61, 112, 123, 125
Creighton, Helen, 298–9
culture and personality, 252–3
culture areas, 42, 158

Davidson, D.S., 258, 262
Dawson, George M., 116
D'Entrecasteaux archipelago, 41. *See also* Goodenough Island; Jenness, Diamond, D'Entrecasteaux research of
de Laguna, Frederica, 238, 243, 285, 336
Desbarats, G.J., 60; and CAE controversy, 135–6
Diomede Islands. *See* Big Diomede Island; Little Diomede Island

Dorset Culture, 199–201, 226–7, 235–5; origin of, 203–4. *See also* Jenness, Diamond, discovery of Dorset Culture
Duff, Wilson, 272

education, Aboriginal (Canada), 279–80
Edwards, Elizabeth, 334
ethnographic research methods. *See* Boas, Franz; Haddon, Alfred Cort; Malinowski, Bronislaw; Rivers, William, H.R; Sapir, Edward
Ethnological and Archaeological Survey of California, 154
Evans, Arthur, 25, 36

Fifth Thule Expedition (1921–24), 195–6
Firth, Raymond, 21, 335
folk culture studies. *See* Anthropological Division
Forde, C. Daryll, 147
Frazer, Elizabeth (Lilly): advises D.J. on use of phonograph, 38
Frazer, James G., 24–5, 30; advises D.J. on D'Entrecasteaux fieldwork, 37–8; *Questions on the Customs, Beliefs, and Languages of Savages*, 38, 51
Freire-Marreco, Barbara, 31

Garber, Clark, 209
Gates, R. Ruggles, 149
Geist, Otto, 242
Geological Survey of Canada, 57–9, 111–13, 311; Brock as director, 115–20; Collins as director, 144–6; McConnell as director, 115; status of anthropology within, 113–14. *See also* Anthropological Division (Geological Survey of Canada)
George, Felix: assists D.J. in Wet'suwet'en fieldwork, 174–5
Giddings, J. Louis: discovery of Denbigh Flint Complex, 225; discovery of Ipiutak Culture, 242

312–25; Copper Inuit fieldwork of, 92, 94–110; Cypriot crisis, observations on 307–11; Cyprus fieldwork of, 304–7; death of, 329; D'Entrecasteaux fieldwork of, 42–3, 45–54; discovery of Dorset Culture, 198–201; discovery of Old Bering Sea Culture, 216–18; early education and interests, 8–12, 18; Eskimo-Aleut linguistics research, 184, 218–21; "Eskimo Ruins Ordinance, 1930," 240–1; estrangement from Barbeau, 142–3; family background, 4–8; Guggenheim fellowship awarded, 302; *Indian Background of Canadian History*, 332; "Indian Method of Treating Hysteria," 178; *Indians of Canada*, 234, 246; on international cooperation in arctic archaeology, 222–3; Iñupiat fieldwork, 74–9; *Life of the Copper Eskimo*, 334–5; marriage to Eileen Bleakney, 27; and Mauss's theory of dual social morphology, 93–4; *Northern D'Entrecasteaux*, 333–4; Ojibwa fieldwork, 249–52, 254–7; Oxford years, 20, 22–4; and Pacific Science Congress (Third, Java), 248; and Pacific Science Congress (Fourth, Vancouver), 236; permanent appointment with Anthropological Division, 128–9; *Physical Characteristics of the Copper Eskimos*, 135; policy-related research and advocacy, 108, 263–5, 273–5, 280, 282–3 290–3; and psychological anthropology, 252–4; publication of arctic diaries (*Arctic Odyssey*), 48n9; purchase of Gitksan totem poles by, 178–82; resignation as Anthropological Division chief, 144, 152–3; retirement, 299; Sarcee fieldwork, 163, 165–9; Sekani fieldwork of, 187–93; special consultant on Indian affairs, 274–5; study of Maori education, 294–7; study of post-war conditions in Italy,

300–2; theoretical orientation of research, 331–5; *Through Darkening Spectacles*, 325; university teaching, 303–4; views on Canadian political culture, 122, 325–6; wartime service, 122–6, 285–7; Wet'suwet'en fieldwork of, 174–8; and William Wyse chair in anthropology (Cambridge), 273–4

Jenness, Eilleen (nee Bleakney), 122–3, 127

Jenness, John Lewis, 127–8, 312

Jenness, May (Mrs Andrew Ballantyne), 7–8, 12, 42; deaths of her children, 47

Jenness, Robert Allan, 127–8, 312, 319

Jenness, Stuart Edward, 127–8

Jesup North Pacific Expedition (1897–1902), 154, 267

Johansen, Fritz, 61, 232–3

Johnson, Frederick, 251

Kaiyutak: interprets for D.J.'s with Iñupiat, 71, 74, 76, 79

Karluk, 64, 66–70, 85

Kaska, 141, 162, 188, 192

Katzie. *See* Coast Salish

Kelly, Peter, 295

Kidder, Alfred V., 222–3, 224–5

King, Jonas: consults with D.J. on Ojibwa, 251

Klengenberg, Patsy: assists D.J. with Copper Inuit fieldwork, 99, 109

Knowles, Francis H.S., 31, 117, 128, 160

Knuth, Eigel: discovers Independence Culture, 364n9

Kotahitanga mo Te Aute (Young Maori Party), 4, 17

Kroeber, Alfred, 154, 336

Kulchyski, Peter, 337

Kwakiutl, 267–8, 270

Landes, Ruth, 252, 255, 256–7, 367n10

Larocque, Marie (Mme Barbeau): on First World War conscription, 112

Larsen, Helge, 242

Old Sam, Wet'suwet'en elder, 177–8
Old Sam, Mrs, Wet'suwet'en elder, 177–8
O'Neill, John, 136
Osgood, Cornelius, 151, 157, 245–6
Otoyuk, 74–5, 78
Oxford, University of: conservatism of, 20–8 passim; denies academic degrees to women, 31; Huxley-Wilberforce debate on *Origin of the Species*, 28–9
Oxford committee for anthropology: and D.J.'s D'Entrecasteaux fieldwork, 36–7; founded, 32; members, 32–3

Palaiyak, Silas, 99
Pegahmagabow, Francis: assists D.J. in Ojibwa fieldwork, 251
Perry, Aylesworth B., 108
Phillips, W.G., 108
Pierre, Peter: consults with D.J. on Katzie (Coast Salish), 271–2
Pierre, Simon: interprets for D.J. at Katzie, 271–2
Pitt Rivers, Augustus H. (Land Fox), 29
Pitt Rivers Museum, 29–30
Polynesian Society, 13
Porsild, Alf and Robert, 210
Potawatomi, 249, 251, 256
Potlatch. *See under* Carrier; Wet'suwet'en
Prophet Dance movement, 176, 191–2

Qanajuk ("Jennie"), D.J.'s adoptive Copper Inuit sister, 101–2
Quimby, George, 240–1, 336

Radcliffe-Brown, Alfred R.: and applied anthropology, 263
Radin, Paul, 117, 160, 247, 268
Rasmussen, Knud, 195–6, 198, 205, 315
Rawson-MacMillan Subarctic Expedition, Second (1927–28), 233
Read, Hercules, 32

reserves, Canadian: health, morale, and culture on, 163–5
Ridgeway, William, 24
Rioux, Marcel, 298
Rivers, William H.R., 32; advises D.J. on D'Entrecasteaux fieldwork, 37; on cat's cradles, 52; on concrete (genealogical) method, 34, 51; on use of native languages in fieldwork, 48
Roberts, Helen, 130
Robertson, R.G., 312, 323–4
Robinson Huron Treaty (1850), 250
Rouvière, Jean-Baptiste, 100
Rowley, Graham, 240, 312, 336; excavates Dorset Culture site at Foxe Basin, 241–2
Royal Ontario Museum, 117, 146, 153
Royal Society of Canada: promotes state-supported anthropological research in Canada, 59
Rudnicki, Walter, 375n64

Saanich (Coast Salish), 269–70. *See also* Jenness, Diamond, Coast Salish fieldwork of
Salter, Frederick, 186
salvage ethnology, 73, 154, 155–6
Sapir, Edward: Anthropological Division research program, 118–19, 158–62, 206; appointed Anthropological Division chief, 116; Athapaskan linguistics, 163, 168; and Barbeau, 138–9; and Beuchat, 85; chief of Anthropological Division, 120, 150; coaches D.J. in linguistic methods, 139, 157, 175; on collecting "genuine" Aboriginal artifacts, 166; defense of potlatch, 262–3; and D.J.'s appointment to Anthropological Division, 111–13, 128; and Harlan Smith, 137–8; Na-Dene hypothesis, 168; opinion of Stefansson's anthropology, 62; pacifism, 112–13; promotion of academic anthropology in Canada, 117; on psychological anthropology, 253; recommends

Victoria College (Victoria University of Wellington), 8–9
Victoria Memorial Museum, 58–9, 121–2; and National Gallery of Canada, 298

Wallis, Wilson D., 11, 23–4, 117, 160, 163
Wasauksing First Nation (Parry Island reserve), 249
Waugh, Frederick, 117, 130, 160, 205, 233, 246–8; D.J. investigates disappearance of, 356n73
Wet'suwet'en (Bulkley River Carrier), 171–2; Babine-Witsuwit'en language, 173; diffusion of beliefs and practices, 176; kyan (medicine-dream illness), 177–8; origin myth, 171; potlatch, 173, 176–7

white paper (*Statement of the Government of Canada on Indian Policy*), 328, 336
Whitney, John: assists D.J. in Sarcee fieldwork, 165
Windle, Sir Bertram, 117
Wintemberg, William, 117, 160, 205; identifies Dorset culture in Newfoundland, 235–6
Wissler, Clark, 163, 335
Wrinch, Dr H.C., 177

Young, Michael, 45–6
Young Maori Party. *See* Kotahitanga mo Te Aute (Young Maori Party)

Zedlitz, George von, 9–11, 266, 300, 341n18